ARIS EN 1615

P. S. Bernard

W9-CPG-506

Notre Dame
Eglise nostre Dame

La Pont   Place Maubert

le vieux Marché

La Chapelle

Dauphine

Le pont neuf

LA SEINE

S. Nicolas

S. Thomas

Porte de Nesle

Copyright 2001 by The Palancar Company Limited
All rights reserved
Printed by EBS, Verona, Italy

Publishers Cataloguing in Publication
Patricia Twohill Lown & David Amory Lown
All Paris: The Source Guide by Patricia Twohill Lown and David
Amory Lown: illustrated by Megan Green
P.cm.
Includes index

ISBN: 0-9643256-6-7

Decorative Arts – France – Paris -
Directories. 3. Artisans – France - Paris
Interior Decoration – France – Paris - Directories

Library of Congress Catalogue Card Number 99-093374

The Palancar Company Limited
111 East 80th Street, New York, NY 10021
E-mail: TwoLowns@aol.com

ALL PARIS

Tout Paris Source Guide

by

Patricia Twohill Lown

and

David Amory Lown

Illustrated by Megan Green

The Palancar Company Limited
New York • United Kingdom

👑 After diligent search, the authors have selected dealers, galleries and craftsmen representing the best in their fields. The outstanding ones are marked with a crown.

The authors' selections are based on their subjective opinions of the subject concerned. Their standards include reliability, authenticity, quality, value and courtesy.

TOUT PARIS is a registered trade mark in the USA
TOUT PARIS is a marque déposée in France

THE HAND OF MAN

Paris: The dream and the reality. The dream is still alive and well, but it is important for the visitor to have a sense of the reality as well.

Paris is still one of the most beautiful cities in the world, but in recent years has become cluttered with some dreadful architecture of the last half of the 20th century. Automobile traffic can be as congested as anywhere in the western world. Many restaurants have become second rate, the cafés are often over-priced and service is quite often less than professional. But you can close your eyes to all that and still drink in the joys of the city along with the good food and the excellent wines still available. Now, however, one needs to be more careful in choosing and shopping for anything from a *croissant* to an XVIII century desk or chandelier.

The very good thing about Paris is that it is so well laid out for the pedestrian shopper. Antique and Art Dealers are concentrated in several areas organized, it seems, to fit the pocketbooks of the guests in the hotels in the different quarters of the city.

On the Left Bank, across the Seine from the Louvre, there is a dense concentration of art and antique dealers as well as another on the Right Bank, flanking the other side of the Louvre Museum, on the rue de Rivoli. The Marais also houses a number of excellent dealers and is one of the most delightful areas of old Paris. Finally, there is the "Golden Triangle", close by the Elysée Palace, where one finds the heavy hitters who deal in the masterpieces and the priceless antiques, all of which carry very heavy price-tags.

Thankfully, France, and the city of Paris, can still boast of a population of splendid craftsmen skilled at restoring and creating everything from antique treasures to fine reproductions, exquisite porcelain and table linens. As the years pass and the world becomes more crowded, the appetite for beautiful things has exploded. Prices have soared to unbelievable heights and competition for the traveller's money has become intense. Keep well in mind the fact that the prices of fine art, rare antiques and precious collectibles have been elevated to astronomic levels by the large auctioneers. Some of these great auction firms have tarnished their own reputations a bit in recent years.

Many art and antique dealers in Paris, as well as other cities, have taken their pricing cues from the exaggerated prices paid at highly publicized auctions. So, be careful. Never buy in haste and remember, any reputable dealer will share his love of a good transaction with you.

There are plenty of Street Fairs and Salons throughout the year. You will find them listed in the airline magazines, as well as special sections appearing every week in the daily papers, including very good listings in the Herald Tribune. "Art & Auction" Magazine has an especially fine calendar of events in every issue. When it comes to getting your treasures back home, be certain to ask for an estimate for the packing and shipping and then make certain you ask for a copy of the shipping waybill and the tracking number. Please remember that you should require the shipper to prepare all the documentation in English for any shipments to America. This can prevent delays in customs and even save additional costs.

The authors wish to thank Judy Easton, Aude Aguilera, Michelle Solal-Kapnist, Christian de Tailly, and Marcia Torrey for their invaluable help. We earnestly hope that you, dear reader, will have as much inspiration, revelation and fun as we have had in preparing this guide. Bon voyage and welcome to Paris!

CATEGORY INDEX

ANTIQUE DEALERS

Antiquaires

The city of light, love and magic. Paris has it all, including one of the world's greatest concentrations of beautiful antiques and fascinating collectibles. And Paris is manageable, especially when you are on foot. Antique dealers are, to a large extent, concentrated in particular areas of town and in special buildings in convenient sections of the city. The authors of ALL PARIS have covered most of Paris, on foot, and have made their selections based on their well-established standards of quality, dependability, convenience and courtesy.

One of the best concentrations of dependable dealers in excellent quality antiques and collectibles is the LOUVRE DES ANTIQUAIRES. This beautiful building contains 200 of the best dealers in France. Another very convenient location is the area called the CARRÉ RIVE GAUCHE. Four blocks square, it is the home of some of the best dealers in the world: 120 of them. Not quite so large a group, but excellent quality is the group of dealers organized as the QUARTIER DROUOT, located in the streets close by the famous auction rooms, The Hotel des Ventes Drouot.

Paris, as always, offers plenty of attractive cafés and restaurants where one can sit down to rest tired feet, enjoy a delicious coffee or indulge in a sumptuous lunch. There, it might be a good idea to mull over your discovery and decide if, how and when you will buy that special treasure you can't live without.

One word of caution. If you are being sold an antique of a particular period, make certain you ask for a certificate of authenticity, showing *provenance*. Reputable dealers will never hesitate to offer one.

So, dear reader, sally forth, have a marvellous time and don't forget to check and double-check your bill. Good luck. Remember you are a stranger in town and ripe for the plucking!

Antique Dealers
by Arrondissement

---------- I ----------

GALERIE DU PASSAGE
20-22 Galerie Véro-Dodat, 10 rue Croix-des-Petits-Champs, 75001 Paris ■ Tel: 01 42 36 01 13 ■ Fax: 01 40 41 98 86 ■ E-mail: gpassage@club-internet.fr ■ Tue-Sat 11:00-19:00 ■ Pierre Passebon ■ English spoken ■ Prices medium to high ■ Professional discount

XX century decorative arts. From entire rooms to unique pieces such as the wedding chests of the late Duke and Duchess of Windsor. An eclectic mix of furniture, decorative objects and, sometimes, wonderful Giacometti lamps.

---------- II ----------

JEAN VINCHON
77 rue de Richelieu, 75002 Paris ■ Tel: 01 42 97 50 00 ■ Fax: 01 42 86 06 03 ■ E-mail: vinchon@wanadoo.fr ■ Web: www.vinchon.com ■ Mon-Fri 9:00-18:00 ■ Jean and Françoise Berthelot-Vinchon speak English and Spanish

Coins from Croesus to the end of the Third Republic (1940).

---------- III ----------

BALMÈS RICHELIEU
21 place des Vosges, 75003 Paris ■ Tel: 01 48 87 20 45 ■ Mon 14:00-18:30, Tue-Sat 9:00-11:30/14:00-18:30 ■ Mr. Balmès speaks some English and has been at this location for fifty years

Superb quality furniture of the Haute Epoque. XVII to XIX century clocks, marine and astronomical instruments and scientific objects of curiosity. Expert to the Court of Appeals of Paris.

LES DEUX ORPHELINES
21 place des Vosges, 75003 Paris ■ Telfax: 01 42 72 63 97 ■ E-mail: edovar1b@worknet.fr ■ Mon-Fri 11:30-19:00 ■ Thérèse Bernadac ■ English spoken ■ Prices medium ■ 10% professional discount ■ Major credit cards

Late XVIII and early XIX century French Popular Art, regional furniture, objects of curiosity, lamps. XIX century linen and china.

ATELIER GUIGUE

37 bd de Marché, 75003 Paris ■ Tel: 01 48 04 04 95 ■ Mon-Fri 10:00-18:00/Sat by appointment ■ Prices medium to high ■ 15% professional discount

Painted antique furniture. Custom furniture painted on order. Also gives intensive classes in painting on wood and screens.

ALDO PELLAS

15 rue Payenne, 75003 Paris ■ Tel: 01 42 78 15 69 ■ Mon-Sat 11:00-12:30/14:00-18:00 ■ Some English and Spanish spoken ■ Prices reasonable ■ Professional discount

Furniture, paintings and decorative accessories from the XVIII century to 1940.

———————————— **IV** ————————————

MARTIN BOLTON

48 rue des Archives, 75004 Paris ■ Tel: 01 42 72 27 19 ■ Fax: 01 44 21 38 11 ■ Tue-Thu-Fri-Sat 11:00-14:00/15:00-19:00 ■ Martin & Mercedes Bolton speak English ■ Prices medium

XIX century English furniture, silver plate, porcelain.

CATH ART

13 rue Ste-Croix-de-la-Bretonnerie, 75004 Paris ■ Tel: 01 48 04 80 10 ■ Fax: 01 48 04 02 08 ■ Mon-Sat 11:30-19:30/Sun 15:00-19:00 ■ Pascal Le Gouet speaks English ■ Prices medium to high ■ 10% professional discount

Humorous pieces: furniture, art objects, lamps, frames, clocks, glass, ceramics in limited editions.

ALEXIS RENARD

5 rue des Deux-Ponts, Ile Saint-Louis, 75004 Paris ■ Telfax: 01 44 07 33 02 ■ E-mail: courier@alexis.renard.com ■ Web: www.alexisrenard.com ■ Tue-Sat 14:00-19:00 ■ Alexis Renard ■ English, Spanish and Portuguese spoken ■ Prices medium to high ■ Professional discount ■ Major credit cards

Fascinating and aesthetic mix of furniture from mediaeval times to the early XX century. Arts of the Orient, sculptures from the X century to the XVII and early XX centuries, and curiosities.

MARIE-TOURNELLE ANTIQUITES

5 rue des Deux-Ponts, Ile Saint-Louis, 75004 Paris ■ Telfax : 01 56 24 07 70 ■ E-mail : mtournel@club-internet.fr ■ Tue-Sat 11:00-19:00 and by appointment ■ Valerie and Patrice Maillett ■ Some English spoken ■ Prices medium ■ Professional discount ■ Amex and Visa

Furniture and decorative accessories of the Haute Epoch, from the Renaissance to the XVI and XVII centuries. Some very nice glassware of the XVIII and XIX centuries and candlesticks of the XVIII century.

VI

♕ G. BAC

35-37 rue Bonaparte, 75006 Paris ■ Tel: 01 43 26 82 67 ■ Fax: 01 46 34 51 58 ■ E-mail: gbac@cybercable.fr ■ Mon-Fri 9:00-12:00/14:00-19:00 ■ Georges Gross ■ English, German and Italian spoken ■ Professional discount ■ Major credit cards

Gilded wood frames from France, Spain, Holland and Italy. French mirrors and consoles. Some of the XVI century and mainly XVII and XVIII century. Wonderful collection.

BAROQUES ANTIQUITÉS

67 rue du Cherche-Midi, 75006 Paris ■ Tel: 01 45 49 31 14 ■ Tue-Sat 14:30-19:00 ■ Christiane Delrieu speaks English ■ Prices medium ■ Professional discount

Period of Napoleon III: furniture, silver, art objects, paintings.

♕ J.M. BEALU & FILS

169 bd Saint-Germain, 75006 Paris ■ Tel: 01 45 48 46 53 ■ Fax: 01 42 84 09 80 ■ Mon 14:00-18:30,Tue-Sat 10:00-12:30/14:00-18:30 ■ Christian Bealu speaks English ■ Prices high to very high ■ 10% professional discount ■ Major credit cards

XVI to XVIII century faience and porcelain. Furniture and objets d'art of the XVII and XVIII centuries. Expert C.N.E.S. and C.E.D.E.A.

MADELEINE CASTAING

30 rue Jacob, 75006 Paris ■ Tel: 01 43 54 91 71 ■ Tue-Fri 10:00-13:00/15:00-19:00 ■ Some English spoken ■ Prices medium to high ■ Professional discount

Very good and unusual collection of XIX century French, English, Austrian and Russian furniture, decorative objects and some very nice lamps. They also have their own line of fabrics.

COURTEAUX-ENAULT
41 rue Saint-André-des-Arts, 75006 Paris ■ Tel: 01 43 26 99 61
■ Mon-Sat 14:15-19:00 ■ English spoken ■ Prices medium

Superb XVIII century painted panels, screens and sculptured wood. Frames and lamps.

LA GALERIE DES LAQUES
74 rue du Cherche-Midi, 75006 Paris ■ Tel: 01 45 48 88 82 ■ Fax: 01 45 44 31 81 ■ Mon-Sat 10:30-12:30/14:00-19:00 ■ J.C. Hureau speaks English, Italian and Portuguese ■ Prices high ■ Professional discount

Furniture and objects of the XVIII century: Lacquer of China, Japan and Europe. XVII, XVIII, XIX century furniture, objects, gilded wood (*bois doré*) and Oriental and European lacquered furniture and screens.

GALERIE JONAS
12 rue de Seine, 75006 Paris ■ Tel: 01 43 26 50 28 ■ Fax: 01 43 29 65 66 ■ Tue-Sat 10:00-12:30/14:30-18:30 ■ Martine Thomas speaks some English ■ Prices medium to high ■ Professional discount

Specialist in the Barbizon School and pre-Impressionist painters of the XIX century. Expert.

GALERIE YVONNE MOREAU-GOBARD
5 rue des Saints-Pères, 75006 Paris ■ Tel: 01 42 60 88 25 ■ Fax: 01 42 60 08 55 ■ E-mail: yvonne.moreau@wanadoo.fr ■ Mon-Fri 10:00-12:30/14:00-19:00, Sat 10:00-12:30/14:30-19:00 ■ Yvonne Moreau-Gobard speaks English and Dutch ■ Professional discount

Asian art, especially the Himalayas, India and Southeast Asia: sculptures and bronzes.

♛ GALERIE NAVARRO – MIRROIRS ANCIENS
15 rue Saint-Sulpice, 75006 Paris ■ Telfax: 01 46 33 61 51 ■ Tue-Sat 15:00-19:00 ■ Mme Colette Navarro ■ Spanish and Italian spoken ■ Prices high ■ Professional discount ■ Major credit cards

XVII, XVIII and XIX century mirrors in sculptured gilded wood and decorative objects. Barometers, putti and decorative freizes.

GALERIE 9
9 rue Jacob, 75006 Paris ■ Tel: 01 26 83 83 ■ Fax: 01 43 26 40 39 ■ Mon 14:30-19:00, Tue-Sat 11:00-13:30/14:30-19:00 ■ Professional discount

Antique furniture, boiseries (wood panelling), decorative objects, paintings and limited editions of furniture.

GALERIE ORIENT-OCCIDENT

5 rue des Saints-Pères, 75006 Paris ■ Tel: 01 42 60 77 65 ■ Fax: 01 42 60 08 55 ■ Mon-Fri 10:30-12:30/14:00-19:00, Sat 10:00-12:30/14:30-19:00 ■ Colette Semin speaks English and Dutch ■ Some professional discounts

Art of Egypt, Greece and Rome, specializing in sculpture.

GALERIE VIRGINIE PITCHAL

40 rue Jacob, 75006 Paris ■ Tel: 01 42 61 16 33 ■ Fax: 01 42 61 16 79 ■ E-mail: vpitchal@club-internet.fr ■ Web: www.galleryvpitchal.com ■ Tue-Sat 11:00-19:00 ■ Virginie Pitchal speaks English ■ Prices high ■ Professional discount

Old Master paintings.

GALERIE PAUL PROUTÉ

74 rue de Seine, 75006 Paris ■ Tel: 01 43 26 89 80 ■ Fax: 01 43 25 83 41 ■ Tue-Sat 9:30-12:00/14:00-19:00 ■ Sylvie Tocci Prouté and Annie Martinez Prouté speak English, German and Italian ■ Prices medium to high ■ 10% professional discount ■ Visa, MC

Drawings and prints of the XV to the XX century. Publication of three catalogues a year, two of which can be sent free-of-charge upon request.

GALERIE SAMARCANDE

13 rue des Saints-Pères, 75006 Paris ■ Tel: 01 42 60 83 17 ■ Fax: 01 42 61 41 64 ■ E-mail: gal.samarcande@wanadoo.fr ■ Joseph Uzan speaks English and Italian ■ Prices medium to high ■ Professional discount ■ Major credit cards

Antique art and objects: Greek, Roman, Egyptian, Sumerian and some Islamic art. Also some Old Master paintings.

VÉRONIQUE GIRARD

7 rue des Saints-Pères, 75006 Paris ■ Tel: 01 42 60 74 00 ■ Fax: 01 47 03 41 54 ■ Tue-Sat 10:30-12:30/14:30-19:00 ■ Véronique Girard speaks English and Spanish ■ Prices medium to high ■ Professional discount ■ Amex

XVIII century French silver. Member of the Chambre Nationale des Experts. Repair and expertise.

LE DOUZE

12 rue Jacob, 75006 Paris ■ Tel: 01 46 33 73 14 ■ Telfax: 01 43 29 42 44 ■ Mon-Sat 11:00-13:00/14:00-19:00 ■ English spoken ■ Professional discount ■ Major credit cards

Furniture, lighting and decorative objects of the XVIII century through to the 1940s.

LE ONZE
11 rue Jacob, 75006 Paris ■ Telfax: 01 43 29 42 44 ■ Cell: 06 0727 0554 ■ Mon-Sat 11:00-13:00/14:00-19:00 ■ Nicolas Sergeeff speaks English ■ Prices modest ■ Professional discount ■ Major credit cards

Decorative objects from the XVIII century to 1940, lighting, chandeliers, sconces.

L'IMPRÉVU
21 rue Guénégaud, 75006 Paris ■ Tel: 01 43 54 65 09 ■ Tue-Sat 14:30-19:00 ■ Jean Rosen speaks English ■ Prices high ■ 10% professional discount

French decorative objects, English majolica, ceramics in the Palissy style, trompe l'oeil on faience. All from the second half of the XIX century.

CHRISTIAN LEPRINCE
48 rue Jacob, 75006 Paris ■ Tel: 01 42 60 07 66 ■ Fax: 01 46 62 63 23 ■ By appointment ■ English and Spanish spoken ■ Major credit cards

French bronzes, lighting, sconces and furniture of the XVII to the XIX century.

SEBASTIEN MIOCHE
42 rue Bonaparte, 75006 Paris ■ Tel: 01 43 54 33 37 ■ Mon-Sat 10:30-13:00/14:30-18:30 ■ Tatiana Mioche speaks a bit of English ■ Prices medium ■ Professional discount ■ Amex and Visa

Louis XIII tables, chairs and fabrics.

ALAIN MOATTI
77 rue des Saints-Pères, 75006 Paris ■ Tel: 01 42 22 91 04 ■ Fax: 01 45 44 86 17 ■ Mon-Fri 10:00-13:00, 14:00-19:00 ■ Alain Moatti and Dr. Gall speak English, Spanish, Italian and German ■ Professional discount

Specialist in fine bronzes, sculpture and objects of the Middle Ages, the Renaissance to the XVIII century. Expertise.

MUNÉ
29 rue des Saints-Pères, 75006 Paris ■ Telfax: 01 42 60 82 95 ■ Jean-Philippe Muné ■ English spoken ■ Prices medium to high ■ Professional discount

XVIII century furniture and XVIII and early XIX century gilded bronzes; also First Empire.

PASCAL SARFATI

220 bd Saint-Germain, 75006 Paris ■ Tel: 01 45 49 32 09 ■ Mon-Fri 14:30-19:00 and by appointment ■ Prices high ■ Professional discount

XVIII century Italian furniture, mirrors, chandeliers, consoles, sculptures, grisaille and Venetian glass. Grandiose.

MICHEL SOUILLAC

6 rue Antoine-Dubois, 75006 Paris ■ Tel: 01 43 29 43 04 ■ Tue-Sat 10:00-18:00 ■ Professional discount

XIX century antiques and decorative objects. Also Art Nouveau and Art Deco through the 1940s and 1950s. Antique jewellery.

♛ OLIVIER WATELET

11 rue Bonaparte, 75006 Paris ■ Tel: 01 43 26 07 87 ■ Fax: 01 43 25 99 33 ■ E-mail: watelet@club-internet.fr ■ Tue-Sat 10:30-13:00/14:30-19:00 ■ Matthieu de Prémont, Directeur/Decorator/Author ■ English spoken ■ Prices high ■ 10% professional discount ■ Visa and MC

Decorative arts of the 1930s, 1940s and 1950s and specially the greats of the 40s: Jacques Quinet, Arbus, Poillerat, Royère.

YVELINE

4 rue de Furstemberg, 75006 Paris ■ Telfax: 01 43 26 56 91 ■ Mon-Fri 11:00-18:30, Sat morning ■ English spoken ■ Prices medium ■ Visa

Objects of charm, mannequins in wood, lamps, furniture of the XVIII and XIX century and paintings. Lovely place.

VII

♛ AKKO VAN ACKER

3 rue de l'Université, 75007 Paris ■ Tel: 01 42 60 22 03 ■ Fax: 01 42 60 46 87 ■ Mon 14:30-19:00, Tue-Sat 10:30-12:30/14:30-19:00 ■ English, German and Dutch spoken ■ Prices high ■ Professional discount

XVII, XVIII and XIX century art objects and objects of high curiosity. Worth a visit.

ANTIQUITÉS PHILIPPE DELPIERRE

3 rue du Bac, 75007 Paris ■ Tel: 01 47 03 32 25 ■ Fax: 01 49 27 98 28 ■ Tue-Fri 10:00-12:30/14:00-19:00/Sat 11:00-12:30/14:00-19:00 ■ Arnaud Tonder speaks English ■ Prices medium ■ Professional discount

XVIII, XIX century furniture, chandeliers and art objects.

♛ ARCHÉOLOGIE

40 rue du Bac, 75007 Paris ■ Tel: 01 45 48 61 60 ■ Fax: 01 45 48 75 25 ■ Mon 14:00-19:00/Tue-Sat 11:00-12:30/14:00-19:00 ■ English spoken ■ Prices high ■ 10% professional discount

Greek terracotta, Etruscan and Roman bronze, antique marbles, antique jewellery.

CATHERINE ARIGONI

14 rue de Beaune, 75007 Paris ■ Tel: 01 42 60 50 99 ■ Fax: 01 42 60 24 97 ■ Mon-Sat 14:00-19:00 ■ English spoken ■ Prices high ■ 20% professional discount

XVIII, XIX, XX century furniture, chandeliers, sconces, lamps, art objects. Some Art Deco of 1925 to 1930, jewellery, gifts, collectible buttons, cigarette boxes.

♛ ARTS ET BOISERIES

16 rue des Saints-Pères, 75007 Paris ■ Tel: 01 42 60 23 13 ■ Mon-Sat 14:00-19:00 ■ Guy Leclerc speaks English ■ Prices medium ■ 10% professional discount

XVIII century French furniture and decorative objects. XVIII century bois doré mirrors, consoles and wall motifs.

♛ ATELIER A. BRUGIER

74 rue de Sèvres, 75007 Paris ■ Tel: 01 47 34 83 27 ■ Fax: 01 40 56 91 40 ■ Mon-Fri 08:30-18:30 ■ Nicole Judet-Brugier speaks English ■ 10% professional discount

Important collection of lacquer screens, armoires, boxes, trays, chests, panels from which they can make to measure low tables, consoles and bookshelves. Restoration of Chinese, Japanese and European lacquer; Martin varnish and Art Deco lacquer. Museum quality work.

AU DIRECTOIRE

12 bd Raspail, 75007 Paris ■ Tel: 01 42 22 67 09 ■ Mon 14:30-19:00/Tue-Sat 10:30-12:00/14:30-19:00 ■ Thierry Winsall speaks English ■ Prices medium ■ Professional discount

French furniture, art objects: Empire, Directoire, Consulat.

L'AUTRE JOUR

26 av de la Bourdonnais, 75007 Paris ■ Tel: 01 47 05 36 60 ■ Mon-Fri 14:30-19:00 ■ Dorothée d'Orgéval speaks English ■ Prices medium

Antiques, curiosities, fabrics.

BASTIEN ET ASSOCIÉS

13 rue de Lille 75007 Paris ■ Tel: 01 42 60 76 27 ■ Fax: 01 42 66 07 93 ■ Mon-Sat 8:00-18:00 ■ English spoken ■ Prices medium ■ 5% professional discount

XVIII, XIX century French furniture. Restoration.

GUY BENETON

36 rue de Varenne, 75007 Paris ■ Tel: 01 42 22 78 02 ■ Mon-Fri 15:00-19:00

XVIII century ceramics, faiences and porcelain. Superb.

JEAN-FRANCOIS DE BLANCHETTI

2 rue des Saints-Pères, 75007 Paris ■ Tel: 01 42 60 22 43 ■ Fax: 01 42 96 23 47 ■ E-mail: blanchetti@wanadoo.fr ■ Mon 14:00-19:00, Tue-Fri 10:00-13:00/14:00-19:00/Sat 14:00-19:00 ■ Jean-François de Blanchetti speaks English and Spanish ■ Prices medium to high ■ Professional discount

Furniture and decoration of the XIX and the first half of the XX century.

BRESSET

197 bd Saint-Germain, 75007 Paris ■ Tel: 01 45 48 18 24 ■ Fax: 01 412 60 59 38 ■ Mon-Sat 10:30-12:30/14:30-19:00 ■ Gilles and Stèphane Bresset speak English and Italian ■ Prices high ■ Professional discount

Art of the Haute Epoch, the Middle Ages, Louis XIII and the Renaissance: furniture, sculptures and art objects.

BOIS DORÉ - CAPANGELA

15 quai Voltaire, 75007 Paris ■ Tel: 01 42 61 02 01 ■ Fax: 01 42 61 25 63 ■ E-mail: boisdore@netcourrier.com ■ Web: www.art-face.com/bois_dore ■ Tue-Sat 10:00-18:30 ■ Madame Cécile Perrier-Lecompte ■ English spoken ■ Prices medium to high ■ Professional discount ■ Major credit cards

Bois doré and boiseries. Gilded wood furniture, consoles, panelling, furniture, decorative objects and frames. Custom work. Clients include the Louvre Museum.

CHEZ SWANN

5 rue de Beaune, 75007 Paris ■ Telfax: 01 42 61 27 22 ■ Mon-Sat 14:30-19:00 ■ Jean-Francois Caisse ■ Prices high

XVIII century furniture and chairs. Specialist in gilded wood (bois doré). Expert of the C.N.E.

CONIL

1 rue de Varenne, 75007 Paris ■ Tel: 01 45 49 19 85 ■ Fax: 01 45 49 19 92 ■ Tue-Sat 11:00-13:00/14:00-19:30 ■ Mme Monique Conil ■ Prices high ■ Professional discount ■ Amex, Visa

XVII to early XX century furniture, paintings and interesting decorative objects. Leather furniture by Adnet and Dupré Lafon. Restoration of furniture and leather. Upholstery.

DU CÔTÉ DE CHEZ VIANE

11 rue de Luynes, 75007 Paris ■ Tel: 01 45 48 57 26 ■ Mon-Sat 11:00-12:45/14:00-19:00 ■ Mme Dyer speaks English ■ Prices medium ■ 10% professional discount

XIX century furniture, art objects, paintings.

♛ ANTONY EMBDEN

15 quai Voltaire, 75007 Paris ■ Tel: 01 42 61 04 06 ■ Fax: 01 42 61 40 89 ■ Mon-Sat 10:30-12:30/14:30-18:30 ■ Antony Embden speaks English

Art objects of the XVI, XVII centuries. Specialist in European sculpture.

GALERIE AGAMÈDE

12 rue de l'Université, 75007 Paris ■ Tel: 01 40 15 93 12 ■ Fax: 40 15 62 69 ■ Tue-Sat 11:00-12:30/15:00-19:00 ■ Mr. Bilheux speaks English ■ Professional discount ■ Major credit cards

Furniture, paintings and objets d'art of the XIX and the XX century. Oriental art objects from Japan and China.

♛ GALERIE BAILLY

25 quai Voltaire, 75007 Paris ■ Tel: 01 42 60 36 47 ■ Fax: 01 42 60 54 92 ■ E-mail: bailly@imaginet.fr ■ Web: www.galeriebailly.com ■ Mon-Fri 10:00-13:00/14:00-19:00 ■ Charles, André and Patricia Bailly ■ English and Spanish spoken ■ Prices high ■ Professional discount possible ■ Major credit cards

Old Masters, Modern and contemporary paintings, drawings, watercolours and sculptures. High quality, wide range.

GALERIE B.J.F.

27 rue de Verneuil, 75007 Paris ■ Tel: 01 42 61 36 46 ■ Fax: 01 42 61 22 00 ■ Tue-Sat 14:00-19:00 ■ José Alcantara ■ Italian, Spanish and English spoken ■ Prices medium to high ■ Professional discount ■ Major credit cards

XVIII and XIX century furniture, art objects and paintings.

GALERIE DE BEAUNE
7 rue de Beaune, 75007 Paris ■ Tel: 01 42 86 05 72 ■ Fax: 01 40 15 96 81 ■ E-mail: galerie.beaune@wanadoo.fr ■ Mon-Sat 10:00-19:15 ■ Rosine and Marc Richer ■ English spoken ■ Prices medium to high ■ Professional discount ■ Amex, Visa

Furniture and objets d'art of the XVII, XVIII and early XIX centuries.

GALERIE DE VERNEUIL
45 rue de Verneuil, 75007 Paris ■ Telfax: 01 40 15 01 15 ■ Mon-Sat 14:30-19:30 ■ Bernard Sève ■ English spoken ■ Prices medium ■ 5 to 10% professional discount ■ Major credit cards

XVIII and early XIX century furniture, art objects, silver, paintings and engravings, faience. Sculptured wood statues of the XII to XVI centuries. Sculptures in bronze and terra-cotta of the XIX and XX century.

GALERIE DES LAMPES
9 rue de Beaune, 75007 Paris ■ Tel: 01 40 20 14 14 ■ Mon 14:00-19:00/Tue-Sat 11:00-19:00 ■ Antoine Pialoux speaks English ■ Prices medium to high ■ Professional discount

Beautiful selection of antique lamps.

GALERIE JEAN-FRANÇOIS DUBOIS
15 rue de Lille, 75007 Paris ■ Tel: 01 42 60 40 17 ■ Fax: 01 42 96 04 24 ■ Mon-Sat 14:00-19:00 ■ Jean-François Dubois ■ English spoken ■ Prices medium ■ Professional discount ■ Visa and Amex

Decorative arts of the XX century.

GALERIE EPOCA
60 rue de Verneuil, 75007 Paris ■ Tel: 01 45 48 48 66 ■ Fax: 01 45 44 85 82 ■ E-mail: Einstein@epoca.fr ■ Web: www.epoca.fr ■ Mon-Fri 11:00-19:00, Sat 14:30-19:00 ■ Mony Linz-Einstein speaks English, German and Italian ■ Professional discount ■ Major credit cards

Extraordinary collection of furniture and objects of great curiosity from the II century B.C. to the period of Modern art. Paintings and sculpture. Worth a detour.

GALERIE GILGAMESH
9 rue de Verneuil, 75007 Paris ■ Telfax: 01 42 61 37 66 ■ Tue-Sat 12:30-19:15, mornings by appointment ■ Daniel Lebeurrier ■ English and Spanish spoken ■ Professional discount

Archaeology: Mediterranean and Oriental, some Iranian. Mr. Lebeurrier is preparing his doctoral thesis on the funerary customs of the Iranian Iron Age. The place is fascinating, especially if you love the history of the ancients. Expertise for auctions; qualified expert in archaeology.

GALERIE MONGIN-POMMOIS
16 rue de Beaune, 75007 Paris ■ Tel: 01 40 20 06 35 ■ Cell: 06 13 43 64 61 ■ Mon-Sat 14:30-19:30 ■ Isabelle Pommois ■ English spoken ■ Prices high ■ Professional discount

Furniture and glass objects of the XVIII century.

GALERIE RENONCOURT
7 quai Voltaire, 75007 Paris ■ Tel: 01 42 60 15 63 ■ Fax: 01 42 60 15 14 ■ Mon-Sat 10:30-12:45/14:15-19:00 ■ Mme Diacre speaks English ■ Prices high ■ Professional discount

Early XIX century French furniture and art objects: Charles X and Restoration.

GALERIE RENONCOURT
1 rue des Saints-Pères, 75007 Paris ■ Tel: 01 42 60 75 87 ■ Fax: 01 42 60 15 14 ■ Mon-Sat 10:30-12:45/14:00-19:00 ■ Mr. Renoncourt speaks English and German ■ Prices high ■ Professional discount

Beautiful early XIX century French furniture and art objects: Charles X.

👑 FRANÇOIS HAYEM
13 rue du Bac, 75007 Paris ■ Tel: 01 42 61 25 60 ■ Fax: 01 42 61 59 02 ■ Mon-Sat 10:00-19:00 ■ François Hayem ■ English spoken ■ Prices high ■ Professional discount ■ Amex, Visa

A great collection of XVII, XVIII and XIX century furniture, art objects and decorative items. Expert of the C.N.E. and C.N.E.S.

👑 ANDRÉE HIGGINS
52-54 rue de l'Université, 75007 Paris ■ Tel: 01 45 48 75 28 ■ Fax: 01 45 48 07 98 ■ Tue-Sat 9:30-12:30/14:00-19:00 ■ Mme Andrée Higgins speaks English and Spanish ■ Prices medium to high

Superb collection of XVIII and XIX century English and French furniture and decorative objects.

MARIE HAOUR
3 rue de Luynes, 75007 Paris ■ Tel: 01 45 44 79 85 ■ Tue-Sat 14:00-19:00 ■ Prices medium to high ■ Professional discount

XVIII and XIX century furniture and decorative accessories.

ILSE B
56 rue de l'Université, 75007 Paris ■ Tel: 01 45 48 98 96 ■ Fax : 01 42 84 00 17 Mon-Sat 14:00-19:00 ■ Ilse B speaks English, Spanish and German ■ Prices medium

XVIII century painted furniture from Italy, Sweden, France and Germany and unusual objects.

BERNARD JULLIEN

26 rue Surcouf, 75007 Paris ■ Telfax: 01 45 51 00 07 ■ Mon-Sat 11:30-19:15 ■ Bernard Jullien ■ English spoken ■ Prices medium ■ 7 to 10% professional discount

XVIII and XIX century furniture and art objects. Repair of paintings.

KIN LIOU

81 rue du Bac, 75007 Paris ■ Tel: 01 45 48 80 85 ■ Fax: 01 42 84 32 78 ■ Tue-Sat 10:30-19:00, Mon 14:00-19:00 ■ English spoken ■ Prices medium ■ Professional discount ■ Amex, Visa

Wonderful XIX century objects of curiosity: inkwells; tobacco jars; unique art objects; unusual lamps made of bronze candlesticks, representing men and women from all over the world, with an Orientalist influence and specially created lampshades. Small format furniture.

ETIENNE LÉVY

42 rue de Varenne, 75007 Paris ■ Tel: 01 45 44 65 50 ■ Fax: 01 45 49 05 38 ■ E-mail : info@lévy-antiques.com ■ Web: www.lévy-antiques.com ■ Mon-Sat 10:00-19:00 ■ Pierre Lévy ■ English and Spanish spoken ■ Professional discount

XVIII and XIX century mahogany furniture and objets d'art. Restoration services by S.E.R.O.D. at the same address.

L.V.S. ANTIQUITÉS

10 rue de Beaune, 75007 Paris ■ Tel: 01 42 96 90 90 ■ Fax: 01 42 96 90 92 ■ E-mail: LVSantiqites@wanadoo.fr ■ Web: www.artface.com/LVS_antiquites ■ Mon-Sat 10:00-13:00/14:00-19:00 ■ Stèphane and Virginie Baquet ■ English spoken ■ Professional discount ■ Major credit cards

Great XVII, XVIII and XIX century fireplace accessories; fireplaces, furniture, art objects, paintings, drawings.

EDOUARD DE LA MARQUE

2 rue des Saints-Pères, 75007 Paris ■ Telfax: 0142 60 71 62 ■ E-mail: de.la.marque@wanadoo.fr ■ Web: www.artface.com/delamarque ■ Mon 14:00-19:00, Tue-Fri 10:30-12:30/14:00-19:00 ■ Edouard de la Marque speaks English ■ Prices medium ■ Professional discount

XIX and XX century furniture and decorative items.

CLAUDE NICOLET

24 rue de Bourgogne, 75007 Paris ■ Tel: 01 45 51 30 40 ■ Mon-Fri 9:00-20:00/Sat 14:00-20:00 ■ Claude Nicolet ■ English spoken ■ Prices medium ■ 10 to 15% professional discount ■ Amex

French furniture, art objects, chandeliers and clocks of the early XIX century (1790 to 1830). Especially Parisian furniture in mahogany.

NOIR D'IVOIRE

22 & 27 rue de Verneuil, 75007 Paris ■ Tel: 01 42 86 99 11 ■ Fax: 01 42 61 44 33 ■ Mon-Fri 9:30-18:30, Sat 14:00-18:30 ■ Chantal Bernard ■ English and Spanish spoken ■ Prices high ■ Professional discount

Interior decoration, ceramics, decorative objects, mosaics, murals, washbasins and taps. Constant surprises.

♛ MICHEL OTTIN

33 quai Voltaire, 75007 Paris ■ Tel: 01 47 03 45 13 ■ Fax: 01 42 61 32 41 ■ E-mail: Mcompain@aol.com ■ Mon-Sat 10:00-19:00 ■ Michel and Sandrine Ottin speak English ■ Prices medium to high ■ Professional discount ■ Amex

XVIII century French regional furniture in natural wood. Italian XVIII century furniture, objets d'art.

REFLETS D'ÉPOQUE

17 bd Raspail, 75007 Paris ■ Telfax: 01 45 48 42 07 ■ E-mail: Epoque@cybercable.fr. ■ Mon-Fri 11:00-19:00, Sat 14:00-19:00 ■ Sylvère Schmitt ■ Prices medium ■ Professional discount

XVIII, XIX century furniture, clocks and objects of curiosity.

MAROUN H. SALLOUM

17bis quai Voltaire, 75007 Paris ■ Tel: 01 40 15 95 01 ■ Fax: 01 49 27 09 84 ■ E-mail: mhsalloum@cybercable.fr ■ Mon 14:30-19:00, Tue-Sat 10:30-13:00/14:30-19:00 ■ Maroun H. Salloum ■ English spoken ■ Prices high ■ Professional discount

XIX and early XX century furniture and objects of the Secession period from Vienna and Berlin.

TRF ANTIQUITÉS

16 rue de Beaune, 75007 Paris ■ Tel: 01 42 61 11 33 ■ Fax: 01 42 61 11 51 ■ E-mail: trfantik@club-internet.fr ■ Web: www.art-face.com ■ Mon-Sat 10:30-19:30 ■ Yves Cherest ■ English and Spanish spoken ■ Prices medium ■ Professional discount ■ MC and Visa

Cynegetic art - everything to do with the hunt: paintings, objets d'art and furniture.

♔ VANDERMEERSCH

21 quai Voltaire, 75007 Paris ■ Tel: 01 42 61 23 10 ■ Fax: 01 49 27 98 49 ■ Tue-Sat 10:00-12:30/14:00-18:30 ■ Michel Vandermeersch speaks English ■ Prices high ■ Amex

XVI to XVIII century ceramics, faience and porcelain. Expert advice and estimates.

LE VIEUX MANOIR (GINTZBURGER)

8 rue de Beaune, 75007 Paris ■ Tel: 01 42 61 17 50 ■ Fax : 01 42 86 02 46 ■ Tue-Sat 11:00-19:00 ■ Nicole Gintzburger ■ English spoken ■ Prices medium ■ Professional discount ■ Amex and Visa

XVIII century furniture, faience, porcelain and objets d'art.

MARTINE DE POLIGNAC

199bis bd Saint Germain, 75007 Paris ■ Tel : 01 45 48 97 71 ■ Fax : 01 42 84 11 39 ■ Mon-Sat 14:30-19:00 ■ English and Spanish spoken ■ Prices medium to high ■ Professional discount

XIX century paintings. XVIII century furniture in fruit woods and XVIII century painted furniture.

VIA VARENNE

38 rue de Varenne, 75007 Paris ■ Tel: 01 40 49 06 49 ■ Fax: 01 40 49 00 16 ■ Tue-Sat 14:30-19:30 ■ Christine Mireux speaks English, Italian and German ■ Prices medium ■ 10% professional discount ■ Visa

XIX century paintings and Old Masters. Silverware and decorative objects.

ANNE VINCENT

31 bd Raspail, 75007 Paris ■ Tel: 01 40 49 02 21 ■ Tue-Sat 11:00-13:00/14:30-19:00 ■ Anne de l'Harpe speaks English ■ Prices medium ■ Professional discount

Antique furniture and objects of curiosity of the XIX century to 1950.

———————————— VIII ————————————

♔ DIDIER AARON & CIE

118 rue du Faubourg-Saint-Honoré, 75008 Paris ■ Tel: 01 47 42 47 34 ■ Fax: 01 42 66 24 17 ■ E-mail: contact@didieraaron-cie.com ■ Web: www.didieraaron-cie.com ■ Mon-Fri 10:00-12:30/14:30-18:30, Sat 11:00-12:30/14:30-18:00 ■ English and Spanish spoken ■ Prices very high ■ Professional discounts ■ Major credit cards

Didier and Hervé are among the very best, not only in Paris but in the entire world. Superb XVIII century French furniture, paintings and objets d'art. Also a collection of some wonderful Chinese objects. Furniture specialists: Lise Guénot and Véronique de Croisilles. Painting specialists: Laure Pouzol and Françoise Risso. They have galleries in London and New York.

♔ JEAN-FRANÇOIS ANNE
174 rue du Faubourg-Saint-Honoré, 75008 Paris ■ Tel: 01 45 61 15 61 ■ Fax: 01 53 75 04 83 ■ Mon-Sat 10:00-19:00 ■ Jean-François Anne ■ English and German spoken ■ Prices high ■ Professional discount ■ Amex

Furniture and objets d'art of the XVII, XVIII and early XIX centuries. Old Master and Modern paintings. Expert.

ANTIQUITÉS FOUQUET
157 rue du Faubourg-Saint-Honoré, 75008 Paris ■ Tel: 01 42 89 62 82 ■ Fax: 01 42 89 62 66 ■ Web: www.parisantiques.com ■ Mon-Sat 10:00-19:00 ■ English, Greek, Spanish, Italian and German spoken ■ 10% professional discount

French furniture and objets d'art of the XVIII and XIX century.

♔ AVELINE - JEAN-MARIE ROSSI
94 rue du Faubourg-Saint-Honoré, Place Beauvau, 75008 Paris ■ Tel: 01 42 66 60 29 ■ Fax: 01 42 66 45 91 ■ Web: www.aveline.com ■ Mon-Sat 9:30-19:00 ■ Jean-Marie Rossi, Barbara Hottinguer ■ English, Spanish and Portuguese spoken ■ Prices high to very high ■ Possible professional discount

Superb quality XVII, XVIII and XIX furniture and objets d'art.

EUGÈNE BECKER ANTIQUITES
136 rue du Faubourg-Saint-Honoré, 75008 Paris ■ Tel: 01 42 89 44 90 ■ Fax: 01 42 89 44 91 ■ Tue-Fri 14:00-19:00/Mornings by appointment ■ Eugène Becker ■ English and German spoken ■ Prices high to very high ■ 10% professional discount

French furniture, sculpture, drawings and art objects of the XVIII century.

♔ PATRICE BELLANGER
136 rue du Faubourg-Saint-Honoré, 75008 Paris ■ Tel: 01 42 56 14 50 ■ Fax: 01 42 25 95 11 ■ E-mail: gbellang@worldnet.fr ■ Mon-Sat 10:00-12 :30/14:00-19:00 ■ Patrice Bellanger speaks English ■ Prices medium to high ■ 10% professional discount

Superb European sculpture of the XVII, XVIII and XIX century. One of the best. Expert to the Court of Appeals and French Customs.

COATALEM
93 rue Faubourg-Saint-Honoré, 75008 Paris ■ Tel: 01 42 66 17 17 ■ Fax: 01 42 66 03 50 ■ E-mail: coatalem@freesurf.fr ■ Mon-Fri 10:00-19:00 and by appointment ■ Eric Coatalem ■ English spoken ■ Prices high

Old Master paintings and drawings.

♛ COMPAGNIE DE LA CHINE ET DES INDES
39 av Friedland, 75008 Paris ■ Tel: 01 42 89 05 45 ■ Fax: 01 42 89 11 07 ■ E-mail: chineinde@compuserve.com ■ Mon-Sat 10:00-12:00/14:00-18:30 ■ Mike Winter-Rousset ■ English spoken ■ Prices medium to very high ■ Professional discount

Antiques of the Far East: China, Japan, Tibet, Nepal, India, Khmer, Cambodia. Furniture, art objects, porcelain, sculpture, paintings, Japanese and Chinese screens, bronzes of China, Nepal and Tibet. Pottery Han to Tong. Chinese porcelain. 5,000 B.C. to XVIII century.

♛ ARIANE DANDOIS
92 rue du Faubourg-Saint-Honoré, Place Beauvau, 75008 Paris ■ Tel: 01 43 12 39 39 ■ Fax: 01 43 12 39 29 ■ E-mail: ariane.dandois@wanadoo.fr ■ Web: www.arianedandois.com ■ Mon-Sat 10:00-19:00 ■ Ariane Dandois ■ English spoken ■ Prices high ■ Professional discount

European neoclassical furniture and works of art from the XVIII and XIX century.

♛ FABIUS FRÈRES ANTIQUAIRES
152 bd Haussmann, 75008 Paris ■ Tel: 01 45 62 39 18 ■ Fax: 01 45 62 53 07 ■ E-mail: fabiusfreres@neumail.net ■ Mon-Fri 9:30-12:30/14:00-18:00 ■ François Fabius ■ English spoken ■ Prices high

XVII to XIX century paintings, sculpture, furniture and art objects.

FABRE & FILS
19 rue Balzac, 75008 Paris ■ Tel: 01 45 61 17 52 ■ Fax: 01 43 59 03 97 ■ E-mail: fabre.antiquites@wanadoo.fr ■ Mon-Fri 10:00-12:30/14:30-19:00 ■ Jean-Paul Fabre and Michel Fabre ■ English and German spoken ■ Prices high ■ Major credit cards

Art objects and French XVIII century furniture.

GALERIE D'ART SAINT-HONORÉ
69 rue du Faubourg-Saint-Honoré, 75008 Paris ■ Tel: 01 42 66 36 63 ■ Fax: 01 42 66 92 65 ■ Mon-Fri 10:30-13:00/14:30-18:30 ■ Monika Kruch, France-Michèle Eibl ■ English and German spoken ■ Prices high

Old Master and XVII century Flemish paintings.

👑 GALERIE DE JONCKHEERE
100 rue du Faubourg-Saint-Honoré, 75008 Paris ■ Tel: 01 42 66 69 49 ■ Fax: 01 42 66 13 42 ■ E-mail: art.gallery@dejonckheere.fr ■ Mon-Sat 10:30-19:00/ closed Mon 13:00-14:30 ■ Georges de Jonckheere ■ English spoken ■ Prices high ■ Professional discount

Old Master paintings and drawings.

👑 GALERIE JEAN-LUC MÉCHICHE
182 rue du Faubourg-Saint-Honoré, 75008 Paris ■ Tel: 01 45 63 20 11 ■ Fax: 01 42 25 91 34 ■ Mon 14:30-19:00, Tue-Sat 10:30-13:00/14:30-19:00 ■ Jean-Luc Méchiche and Claire Larroquette ■ English spoken ■ Prices high ■ Professional discount

Archaeological objects from China, Egypt and Greece. Primitive art of Africa and Indonesia. XVII, XVIII and XIX century furniture, mainly French. Modern and contemporary paintings and sculptures. Contemporary furniture in limited edition, on order. 2000 BC to 2000 AD. Expert to the C.N.E.

GALERIE MERMOZ
6 rue du Cirque, 75008 Paris ■ Tel: 01 42 25 84 80 ■ Fax: 01 40 75 03 90 ■ Mon-Sat 10:00-12:30/14:00-19:30 ■ Santo Micali ■ Spanish and English spoken ■ Prices medium to high

Pre-Columbian art from Mexico and Central America. Objects in jadeite, stone, serpentine and terracotta. From 1500 B.C. to 1500 A.D.

👑 GALERIE PATRICK PERRIN
178 rue du Faubourg-Saint-Honoré, 75008 Paris ■ Tel: 01 40 76 07 76 ■ Fax: 01 40 76 09 37 ■ E-mail: galerie.perrin@liberty-surf.fr ■ Mon-Sat 10:00-13:00/14:00-19:00 ■ Patrick Perrin speaks English ■ Prices high

XVIII century furniture, chandeliers, mirrors and objets d'art. French drawings 1600 to 1920 and some Old Master paintings.

👑 GALERIE SEGOURA
14 place François 1er, 75008, Paris ■ Tel: 01 42 89 20 20 ■ Fax: 01 42 89 64 13 ■ Mon-Sat 9:00-19:00 ■ Maurice, Marc and Pierre Segoura speak English and some German ■ Prices high to very high ■ Professional discount possible

Very good French furniture and objets d'art of the XVIII century. Old Master paintings.

GALERIE GAUBERT
80 rue de Miromesnil, 75008 Paris ■ Telfax: 01 43 87 09 88 ■ Mon-Sat 14:30-19:30 ■ Pierre Gaubert ■ Prices medium to high ■ Professional discount ■ Major credit cards

Drawings and paintings of the XVII to XIX century.

☗ GISMONDI

20 rue Royale, 75008 Paris ■ Tel: 01 42 60 73 89 ■ Fax: 01 42 60 98 94 ■ Tue-Fri 10:00-19:00/Sat 10:00-18:00 ■ English spoken ■ Prices high ■ Professional discount

High quality Italian furniture and objects from the XVII century. French furniture and art objects from the XVIII century and paintings from the XVII, XVIII and XIX century. Some very good old drawings.

☗ PASCAL IZARN

126 rue du Faubourg-Saint-Honoré, 75008 Paris ■ Tel: 01 42 25 04 84 ■ Fax: 01 42 25 04 80 ■ Mon-Sat 14:30-19:00 ■ Dr. Pascal Izarn speaks English ■ Professional discount

XVIII to early XIX century clocks, candelabra, sconces and objets d'art. Superb.

☗ KRAEMER

43 rue de Monceau, 75008 Paris ■ Tel: 01 45 63 31 23 ■ Fax: 01 45 63 54 36 ■ Mon-Sat 9:30-19:00 ■ The Kraemer family speak English, German and Spanish ■ Prices very high

Top quality and museum quality French furniture, chairs and objets d'art of the XVII and XVIII century: Louis XIV, XV and XVI periods. All displayed in a private air-conditioned house near the Camondo Museum.

☗ KUGEL

279 rue Saint-Honoré, 75008 Paris ■ Tel: 01 42 60 19 45/01 42 60 86 23 ■ Fax: 01 42 61 06 72 ■ E-mail: kugel@francenet.fr ■ Mon 14:30-18:30/Tue-Sat 10:00-13:00/14:30-18:30 ■ Nicholas and Alexis Kugel ■ English spoken ■ Prices high ■ Major credit cards

Superb furniture, sculpture, objets d'art and paintings from the end of the XV to the middle of the XIX century. An extraordinary collection of silver. Noted for highly unusual and very rare antiques.

☗ L'AIGLE IMPÉRIAL (GALERIES DE SOUZY)

3 rue de Miromesnil, 75008 Paris ■ Tel: 01 42 65 27 33 ■ Fax: 01 42 65 90 97 ■ E-mail: info@desouzy.com ■ Web: www.desouzy.com ■ Mon-Sat 10:30-13:00/14:30-19:00 ■ Pierre de Souzy speaks English and Latin ■ Prices high ■ 10% professional discount

Antique arms, armour. Military and Napoleonic memorabilia, paintings and sculpture. Great collection.

👑 LA PENDULERIE

134 rue du Faubourg-Saint-Honoré, 75008 Paris ■ Tel: 01 45 61 44 55 ■ Fax: 01 45 61 44 54 ■ Mon 14:30-19:00, Tue-Sat 9:30-12:00/14:00-19:00 ■ Stèphane Gagnon ■ English spoken ■ Prices high ■ Professional discount ■ Major credit cards

Superb museum quality XVIII and XIX century clocks and decorative objects. Museum quality restoration. Mr. Gagnon will travel to the clock when necessary.

👑 FRANÇOIS LÉAGE

178 rue du Faubourg-Saint-Honoré, 75008 Paris ■ Tel: 01 45 63 43 46 ■ Fax: 01 42 56 46 30 ■ Mon-Fri 9:00-19:00, Sat 10:00-12:45/14:00-18:00 ■ François Léage speaks English and Spanish ■ Prices high ■ Professional discount

French furniture and art objects of the XVIII century, of great quality. Specialist in Louis XIV, Louis XV and Louis XVI.

👑 LOUIS XV

3 rue du Faubourg-Saint-Honoré, 75008 Paris ■ Tel: 01 42 66 39 68 ■ Fax: 01 42 66 20 52 ■ Mon 14:00-19:00/Tue-Fri 10:00-12:00/14:00-19:00/Sat 14:00-19:00 ■ English spoken ■ Competitive prices ■ 10% professional discount

Furniture, paintings and art objects of the XVII, XVIII centuries.

👑 CLAUDE DE LUPIA

137 rue du Faubourg-Saint-Honoré, 75008 Paris ■ Tel: 01 43 59 56 56 ■ Fax: 01 42 67 90 28 ■ Tue-Sat 10:00-13:00/14:00-18:30 ■ English spoken ■ Prices medium to high ■ 10% Professional discount

Sumptuous low tables, antique mirrors, decorative objects, paintings, pastels.

👑 JEAN LUPU

43 rue du Faubourg-Saint-Honoré, 75008 Paris ■ Tel: 01 42 65 93 19 ■ Fax: 01 42 65 49 16 ■ E-mail: jlupu43@aol.com ■ Mon-Fri 10 :00-13 :00/14 :00-18 :30 ■ English spoken ■ Prices very high ■ Professional discount

XVII and XVIII century furniture and paintings.

👑 ANDRÉE MACE

266 rue du Faubourg-Saint-Honoré, 75008 Paris ■ Tel: 01 42 27 43 03 ■ Fax: 01 44 40 09 63 ■ E-mail: andree.mace@wanadoo.fr ■ Mon-Sat 9:00-12:30/14:00-18:30 ■ English spoken ■ Prices medium to very high ■ Professional discount

XVI to XIX century objects in stone and marble. Specialty: fireplaces of the XVIII century. Large selection of cast-iron fireplace backplates.

A. COLIN MAILLARD
11 rue de Miromesnil, 75008 Paris ■ Telfax: 01 42 65 43 62 ■ Mon 14:00-18:30, Tue-Fri 10:30-12:30/14:00-18:30, Sat 14:00-18:30 ■ Pierre-Jacques Chauveau ■ English spoken ■ Prices high ■ Professional discount

Antique lamps; lampshades made to order.

JEAN-PIERRE MANTION
59 rue du Faubourg-Saint-Honoré, 75008 Paris ■ Tel: 01 47 66 41 37 ■ Fax: 01 42 66 96 63 ■ Mon-Sat 15:00-18:30 ■ Jean-Pierre Mantion speaks English ■ Prices medium ■ 10% professional discount

First Empire, French, Russian, Swedish lighting. Reproductions of period lighting on special order. Furniture of the XVII century to the end of the XIX century.

👑 MICHEL MEYER
24 av Matignon, 75008 Paris ■ Tel: 01 42 66 62 95 ■ Fax: 01 49 24 07 88 ■ E-mail: galerie.m.meyer@wanadoo.fr ■ Mon-Sat 10:00-13:00/14:00-19:00 ■ English spoken ■ Prices high

High quality French furniture and objets d'art of the XVII and XVIII century.

👑 YVES MIKAELOFF
10 rue Royale, 75008 Paris ■ Tel: 01 42 61 64 42 ■ Fax: 01 49 27 07 32 ■ E-mail: yvesmikaeloff@wanadoo.fr ■ Mon-Fri 10:00-18:00 ■ English and Spanish spoken ■ Prices very high ■ 10% professional discount

Antique furniture of the XVIII, XIX and XX century. Paintings and drawings from the XVI to the XIX century. XVIII century decorations. XV to XX century textiles. Contemporary art. Creation of decoration projects. Restoration of furniture, textiles and drawings. Re-creation with living artisans using the techniques of the XVIII century of painting, sculpture, panelling, architectural decorations, tapestries and upholstery.

👑 GÉRALD DE MONTLEAU
236 rue du Faubourg-Saint-Honoré, 75008 Paris ■ Tel: 01 42 25 40 45 ■ Fax: 01 42 25 49 60 ■ E-mail: gdm@antiquaire-montleau.com ■ Web: www.antiquaire-montleau.com ■ Mon-Fri 11:00-19:00, Sat 11:00-19:00 ■ English and Spanish spoken ■ Prices high ■ Professional discount

XVII and XVIII century French furniture and decorative objects. Paintings and sculptures up to the XIX century. The website is a virtual gallery and you can see the sculptures in three dimensions.

♛ GÉRARD ORTS

164 rue du Faubourg-Saint-Honoré, 75008 Paris ■ Tel: 01 42 89 44 48 ■ Fax: 01 45 63 46 66 ■ E-mail: orts_gvo@club-internet.fr ■ Mon-Sat 10:00-19:00 ■ Jean Alliaume speaks English ■ 10% professional discount ■ Amex accepted

Furniture, paintings and objets d'art of the XVII, XVIII and early XIX centuries.

♛ JACQUES PERRIN

98 rue du Faubourg-Saint-Honoré, 75008 Paris ■ Tel: 01 42 65 01 38 ■ Fax: 01 49 24 04 08 ■ Mon-Sat 10:00-19:00 ■ English spoken ■ Prices high ■ Professional discount

Very high quality XVIII century furniture and art objects, paintings and drawings. Worth the trip.

ROLLAND

7 rue de Miromesnil, 75008 Paris ■ Tel: 01 42 66 58 92 ■ Fax: 01 42 66 59 07 ■ E-mail: ergastere@wanadoo.fr ■ Mon-Sat 10:00-19:00 ■ English spoken ■ Prices high

XIX and early XX century paintings.

REINOLD FILS

233 rue du Faubourg-Saint-Honoré, 75008 Paris ■ Telfax: 01 47 63 47 19 ■ Mon-Fri 8:00-12:00/13:00-18:00, Sat 13:00-18:00 ■ André Sloth ■ English spoken ■ Prices medium to high ■ Professional discount

XVIII century marquetry furniture. Fine restoration of furniture and chairs.

♛ JEAN RENONCOURT

77 rue du Faubourg-Saint-Honoré, 75008 Paris ■ Tel: 01 44 51 11 60 ■ Fax: 01 42 66 25 89 ■ Mon-Sat 10:00-19:00 ⌐ English spoken ■ Prices high ■ 10% professional discount

Furniture and art objects, late XVIII century to Charles X.

♛ MARC RÉVILLON D'APREVAL

28 rue Washington, 75008 Paris ■ Tel: 01 42 61 27 36 ■ Fax: 01 42 61 43 70 ■ Mon-Sat 10:00-12:30/14:30-19:00 ■ English spoken ■ Prices medium ■ 10% professional discount

French furniture and objects of the XVII, XVIII, XIX centuries. Expertise and repair.

♛ G. SARTI

137 rue du Faubourg-Saint-Honoré, 75008 Paris ■ Tel: 01 42 89 33 66 ■ Fax: 01 42 89 33 77 ■ Tue-Sat 10:00-13:00/14:00-19:00 ■ Giovanni Sarti, Director ■ English, Italian and German spoken ■ Prices medium to very high

XIV to XIX century Italian furniture. Their specialty is the XIV and XV century.

LE SPHINX (GALERIES DE SOUZY)

104 rue du Faubourg-Saint-Honoré, 75008 Paris ■ Tel: 01 42 65 90 96 ■ Fax: 01 42 65 90 97 ■ E-mail:■ info@desouzy.com ■ Web: www.desouzy.com ■ Mon-Sat 10:30-13:00/14:00-19:00 ■ Pierre-Edouard de Souzy speaks English ■ Prices high ■ 10% professional discount ■ Major credit cards

Paintings of the XIX and early XX century. Sculptures and objets d'art.

♛ BERNARD STEINITZ

9 rue du Cirque, 75008 Paris ■ Tel: 01 42 89 40 50 ■ Fax: 01 42 89 40 60 ■ E-mail: info@steinitzantiques.com ■ Web: www.steinitzantiques.com ■ Mon-Fri 9:00-18:00, Sat by appointment ■ Bernard, Simone and Benjamin Steinitz speak English ■ Prices high to very high ■ Professional discount

An extraordinarily large collection: furniture, objects and boiseries of the XVII, XVIII and XIX century. This is one of the great collections in Paris.

TALABARDON & GAUTIER

134 rue du Faubourg-Saint-Honoré, 75008 Paris ■ Tel: 01 43 59 13 57 ■ Fax: 01 43 59 10 29 ■ Bertrand Gautier and Bertrand Talabardon ■ English spoken ■ Prices quite high ■ Professional discount

Old Master and XIX century paintings, drawings and sculptures.

VILLA ANTICA

34 rue de Penthièvre, 75008 Paris ■ Telfax: 01 42 56 59 56 ■ Mon-Fri 14:00-19:00 ■ Christine Mireux ■ English, Italian and German spoken ■ Prices medium to high ■ Professional discount ■ Amex and visa

Old Masters and XIX century paintings. Small precious furniture and cabinets.

VIVALDI ANTIQUITÉS

39 rue de Rome, 75008 Paris ■ Tel: 01 43 87 68 39 ■ Mon-Fri 10:00-19:00 ■ Prices medium ■ Professional discount

XVIII, XIX century furniture, paintings, art objects, clocks, lamps.

IX

In the ninth arondissement, there is an imposing list of dealers and specialists, organized in what is called Antiquaires et Galeries d'Art du Quartier Drouot. Please see the section Quartier Drouot.

LUDION
175 av du Maine, 75014 Paris ■ Tel: 01 45 39 56 02 ■ Tue-Sat 11:00-12:30/14:30-19:00 ■ Françoise Besson speaks English ■ Prices medium ■ 20% professional discount

Furniture and art objects of the XIX and early XX centuries.

―――――――――――――――― **XV** ――――――――――――――――

ARMAND GODARD DESMAREST
1 bis rue de la Cavalerie, 75015 Paris ■ Tel: 01 45 66 97 46 ■ Fax: 01 43 06 03 32 ■ By appointment only ■ Armand Godard Desmarest speaks English and Spanish ■ Prices medium ■ Professional discount

French furniture, clocks and art objects of the XVIII century.

MONIQUE MARTEL
9 rue François Mouthon, 75015 Paris ■ Tel: 01 56 08 10 65 ■ Fax: 01 56 08 10 45 ■ E-mail: karine.martel@wanadoo.fr ■ Mon-Fri 11:00-19:00 ■ Pascal Martel speaks English ■ Prices reasonable ■ 25% professional discount ■ Visa and Amex

XVI to XVIII century drawings, XVIII to XIX century sculpture and XVIII century furniture.

MICHEL SCHMITT
84 av de Breteuil, 75015 Paris ■ Tel: 01 43 06 28 90 ■ Mon-Fri 15:00-19:00 and by appointment ■ English and some Spanish spoken ■ Prices medium to high

Furniture, objects, sculptures and paintings of the XVII to the XIX century. Third generation dealer who works mainly with professionals and will search for special items upon request. Expert to the C.N.E.

―――――――――――――――― **XVI** ――――――――――――――――

GALERIE BEAUSÉJOUR - R.R. SOUDIT
35 bd Beauséjour, 75116 Paris ■ Tel: 01 45 27 97 06 ■ By appointment ■ R.R. Soudit

XIX century silver, paintings, bronzes, porcelain.

COMPTOIR DES OBJETS D'ART
13 av Théophile-Gautier, 75116 Paris ■ Tel: 01 40 50 60 92 ■ Fax: 01 40 50 66 22 ■ Mon-Sat 11:00-19:00/Sun 15:00-19:00 ■ Farid Zamouri speaks English ■ Prices medium ■ 20 to 35% professional discount

Furniture of all the XIX century, especially Empire. Old paintings, engravings and drawings, decorative objects, table arts.

EUGENIE-VICTORIA
1 rue Lekain, 75116 Paris ■ Tel: 01 45 25 79 10 ■ Tue-Sat 10:30-12:30/15:30-19:00, Sun 10:30-14:00/15:00-19:00 ■ Marie-France Theullier speaks English ■ Prices medium ■ 10% professional discount
XIX century French furniture and decorative objects. Bridal registry.

GALERIE JOSEPH KARAM
61 av Raymond-Poincaré, 75116 Paris ■ Tel: 01 44 05 06 06 ■ Fax: 01 44 05 09 20 ■ Mon-Sat 10:00-19:00 ■ English spoken ■ Prices medium to high ■ Professional discount
Eclectic mix of XVIII, XIX century French, Italian, Spanish furniture, art objects, archaeological objects. Interior design services.

GILDAS GUEDEL
101 rue de la Tour, 75116 Paris ■ Telfax: 01 45 03 39 53 ■ 7 rue Franklin, 75116 Paris ■ Tel : 01 45 20 63 00 ■ Tue-Sat 14:30-19:00 ■ English spoken ■ Professional discount
XVIII and XIX century French furniture and decorative objects.

JEAN-CLAUDE LANTELME
15 av du Président Wilson, 75016 Paris ■ Tel: 01 47 20 23 92 ■ Fax: 01 47 20 73 18 ■ Mon-Fri by appointment ■ English spoken ■ Prices high
XVII and XVIII century furniture and objets d'art.

MINOT ANTIQUITÉS
9 rue de la Tour, 75116 Paris ■ Tel: 01 45 20 71 27 ■ Fax: 01 45 20 47 22 ■ Mon-Sat 11:00-19:30 ■ Guy Minot ■ English spoken ■ Prices medium ■ 10 to 20% professional discount
Furniture of the late XIX century to 1950, decorative objects, lighting, tableware.

JACQUES PELLEGRIN
19 rue de l'Annonciation, 75016 Paris ■ Tel: 01 42 88 64 73 ■ Fax: 01 42 30 94 36 ■ Tue-Sat 10:00-12:30/14:00-19:00 ■ Some English spoken ■ Prices medium to high ■ Professional discount ■ Major credit cards
XVIII century French furniture, decorative objects, silver, paintings, tapestries and chandeliers. Everything for an interior.

CAROLLE THIBAUT-POMERANTZ

75116 Paris ■ Tel: 01 45 04 54 68 ■ Fax: 01 45 04 11 53 ■ By appointment ■ New York City ■ Tel: (212)759-6048 ■ Fax: (212)308-3486 ■ By appointment

Superb collection of hand-painted scenic wallpapers and decorative arts.

──────────── XVII ────────────

PHILIPPE DE BEAUVAIS

112 bd de Courcelles, 75017 Paris ■ Tel: 01 47 63 20 72 ■ Mon-Sat 10:00-12:30/14:00-19:00 ■ Philippe de Beauvais speaks English ■ Prices medium ■ 10% professional discount

Furniture and art objects of the XVIII and XIX centuries.

BLEU PASSÉ

24bis bd de Courcelles, 75017 Paris ■ Tel: 01 42 67 57 40 ■ Mon-Sat 11:00-19:00 ■ English spoken ■ Prices medium ■ 10 to 20% professional discount

XIX century furniture, curiosities, paintings, silver, porcelain, embroidered linen.

SERGE MALAUSSENA

10 place de la Porte-de-Champerret, 75017 Paris ■ Tel: 01 43 80 17 29 ■ Tue-Sat 11:00-19:00 ■ Prices medium ■ Professional discount

XVIII, XIX century furniture and decorative objects. Sculpture, clocks, chandeliers, ceramics, glass.

JEAN RIGAL

12 av MacMahon, 75017 Paris ■ Tel: 01 44 09 02 34 ■ Mon-Sat 11:00-19:00 ■ Jean Rigal speaks English ■ Prices high ■ 20% professional discount

Furniture, art objects and paintings of the XIX and XX centuries.

MARIA SANDORFI

90 rue Jouffroy, 75017 Paris ■ Tel: 01 47 63 97 57 ■ Mon-Fri 11:00-19:00, Sat 15:00-18:00 ■ Maria Sandorfi speaks English ■ Prices medium ■ 10 to 20% professional discount

XVIII and XIX century decorative objects, small furniture, paintings, porcelain, silver.

AU TEMPS QUI PASSE
11 rue Pierre-Demours, 75017 Paris ■ Telfax : 01 45 74 09 36 ■ Tue-Sat 11:00-19:00, Sun 11:00-13:00 ■ Chantal Bartent speaks English ■ Prices medium ■ Professional discount ■ Major credit cards

XVIII and XIX century furniture, decorative objects, silver and jewellery.

---------------- XVIII ----------------

ALAIN ATLAN
56 rue Caulaincourt, 75018 Paris ■ Tel: 01 42 55 25 97 ■ Fax: 01 42 52 65 16 ■ Mon-Sat 14:00-20:00 ■ English and German spoken ■ Prices medium to high ■ Professional discount

Furniture and objets d'art of the XVII and XVIII century and the First Empire.

SOPHIE DUPONT
49 rue Ramey, 75018 Paris ■ Tel: 01 42 54 69 30 ■ Mon-Sat 14:00-19:00 ■ Sophie Dupont speaks English ■ Prices medium ■ Professional discounts

XVIII and XIX century furniture and decorative objects. Lots of antique linen.

---------------- NEUILLY ----------------

LYDIA BICAL
31 rue de Chartres, 92200 Neuilly ■ Telfax: 01 46 24 14 30 ■ Tue-Sat 15:00-19:30 ■ German and English spoken ■ Prices medium to high ■ Professional discount

Beautiful collection of canes, Napoleonic souvenirs and lead soldiers (Luçotte, CBG, Mignot, Vertuni, MIM). Figurines: Heinrichsen, all finely painted. Some decorative boxes and snuffboxes.

CHARTRES ANTIQUITÉS
35 rue de Chartres, 92200 Neuilly ■ Telfax: 01 47 22 39 91 ■ Mon-Sat 8:30-12:30/14:30-18:30 ■ Christian Doddoli ■ English, Spanish and Italian spoken ■ Professional discount

XVII, XVIII and XIX century French furniture for town and country, mirrors, paintings, miniatures, chairs, clocks and decorative accessories.

♔ Le Carré Rive Gauche

Some of the world's best antique and art dealers are located in a compact, manageable area on the Left Bank of Paris. Located just across the river from the Louvre Museum, the Carré Rive Gauche is an association of art and antiques dealers working to serve their clients more effectively and efficiently. It is truly a convenient area for the serious buyer of fine art, collectibles and antiques. The Carré Rive Gauche is bounded by the Rue du Bac, the Quai Voltaire, the Rue des Saints-Pères and the Rue de l'Université.

A wide variety of specialties is available, from Old Masters to contemporary paintings. You will also find some of the best examples of museum quality antique furniture, along with some of the more eclectic disciplines such as old engravings, archaeological artifacts, porcelain, ethnic art, tapestries and carpets. Just about everyone in the area is expert in the decorative arts and will willingly share their knowledge.

Every year, in the late spring, the Carré Rive Gauche invites the public to a week-long open house. The pavements are literally carpeted in red and traffic is barred from late afternoon to evening's end. Most establishments will welcome you with a smile and a glass of champagne. It's the real start of the Paris season for treasure hunting.

Opening hours are generally the same throughout the Carré Rive Gauche: Mon-Sat 10:00-13:00/14:00-19:00 although some close in the mornings. There is ample parking in the area and excellent bus and metro service. For information call Céline Letessier at the Press Service ■ Tel: 01 42 60 70 10 ■ Fax: 01 42 60 70 07 ■ E-mail: colonnes@worldnet.fr ■ Web: www.carrerivegauche.com

A very good launching pad for your exploration of the Carré Rive Gauche is the brace of hotels on the rue du Bac, the Hotel Pont Royal and the Hotel Montelambert; long-time favourites with the decorating and literary sets.

ALL PARIS has organized the CARRÉ RIVE GAUCHE street-by-street so that you can find your heart's desire much more easily.

H.P. ANTIQUITÉS – LE STUDIO
1 rue Allent, 75007 Paris, between 15 and 17 rue de Lille ■ Tel: 01 40 20 00 56 ■ Fax: 01 45 35 44 54 ■ Elizabeth Hervé and Marc-Antoine Patissier

Furniture and decorative arts of the XIX and XX century.

👑 D. MILANO BACSTREET
1 rue du Bac, 75007 Paris ■ Tel: 01 42 61 24 20 ■ Fax: 01 49 27 90 85 ■ Mon 14:00-19:00/Tue-Sat 11:00-19:00 ■ Daniel Milano speaks English ■ Prices medium to high ■ 15 to 20% professional discount ■ Major credit cards

Far Eastern furniture, art objects, archaeology, porcelain, bronze, ivory from China, Japan, India, Burma and Siam. Antique and modern jewellery. Expert to CECOA and expert in gemology.

👑 GALERIE JEAN-GABRIEL PEYRE – JEAN-CLAUDE SIEBERTH
17 rue du Bac, 75007 Paris ■ Tel: 01 42 61 18 77 ■ Fax: 01 42 61 14 99 ■ Mon-Sat 10:00-20:00 ■ Jean-Claude Sieberth speaks English and Spanish ■ Prices high ■ 10% professional discount ■ Amex, Visa

XVII and XVIII century ceramics and French porcelain and faience.

👑 JOSY ARMENGAUD
19 rue du Bac, 75007 Paris ■ Tel: 01 47 03 99 07 ■ Fax: 01 47 03 99 37 ■ Mon-Sat 10:30-13:00/14:30-19:00 ■ Josy Armengaud speaks English ■ Prices medium ■ Professional discount

XVIII century French furniture, decorative objects. Restoration of furniture. Expert and guaranteed attribution.

👑 CHRISTIAN DEYDIER - ORIENTAL BRONZES LTD
21 rue du Bac, 75007 Paris ■ Tel: 01 40 20 97 34 ■ Fax: 01 40 20 97 39 ■ E-mail: stbonnet@imaginet.fr ■ Web: www.franceantiq.fr/sna/deydier ■ Tue-Sat 10:00-12:30/14:00-18:30 ■ Eulalie Steens speaks English, Chinese and German

Art of the Far East and Chinese archaeology from 1500B.C. to the XIV century: bronzes, terracotta, sculpture, gold and silver. Catalogues of exhibitions.

GALERIE BAC-ST GERMAIN
23 rue du Bac, 75007 Paris ■ Tel: 01 40 20 44 80 ■ Fax: 01 40 20 44 81 ■ Alexis Brasilier ■ Tue-Sat 10:00-12:30/14:30-19:00

Modern and Contemporary paintings.

GALERIE FLORENCE MARTIN
23 rue du Bac, 75007 Paris ■ Telfax: 01 42 61 52 88 ■ Mon-Sat
10:30-19:00 ■ Florence Martin speaks English and Italian ■
Prices medium to high ■ Professional discount ■ Amex, Diners

XVII and XVIII century furniture, objects and paintings; objects of curiosity. Stone and marble fireplaces, consoles, tables, garden ornaments and fountains. French and Italian bois doré, Roman sculpture.

♔ LEFÈBVRE & FILS
24 rue du Bac, 75007 Paris ■ Tel: 01 42 61 18 40 ■ Fax: 01 42
86 91 58 ■ E-mail: lefebvrelouis@netscape.net ■ Mon-Sat
10:00-12:30/14:00-19:00 ■ Louis Lefèbvre speaks English ■
Prices high to very high ■ Professional discount

Extraordinary European ceramics of the XVI to the XIX century. Porcelain of the Compagnie des Indes: important and rare pieces. Expert to the Cour d'Appel, Paris.

───────── RUE DE BEAUNE ─────────

PHILIPPE MURAT-DAVID
3 rue de Beaune, 75007 Paris ■ Telfax: 01 42 61 64 53 ■ Tue-Sat
11:00-13:00/15:00-19:00 ■ Philippe Murat-David speaks English and
Spanish ■ Prices medium to high ■ 10 to 20% professional discount

Furniture, art objects and decoration of the XVII to the XX century.

ERIC ALLART
5 rue de Beaune, 75007 Paris ■ Tel: 01 42 61 31 44 ■ Mon-Sat
11:00-13:00/14:00-19:00

Objects of art and decoration.

GOSSELIN – DUBREUIL
6 rue de Beaune, 75007 Paris ■ Tel: 01 42 61 35 88 ■ Fax: 01 34
86 94 25 ■ J.F. Gosselin and Marc Dubreuil

Furniture and objets d'art of the XVIII to the XX century.

FLORE
6 rue de Beaune, 75007 Paris ■ Tel: 01 42 61 42 22 ■ Fax: 01 42
61 42 32 ■ E-mail: flore@antland.net ■ Web: www.antique-expo.com/flore ■ Flore de Brantes speaks English and Spanish ■
Professional discount ■ Major credit cards

French furniture and objets d'art of the XVIII and XIX centuries.

ALAIN ET GÉRARD
7 rue de Beaune, 75007 Paris ■ Tel: 01 42 61 23 95 ■ Fax: 01 40
20 01 92 ■ Mon-Sat 10:00-12:00/14:00-19:00 ■ Alain Finard ■
English spoken ■ Prices medium ■ Professional discount

Art objects, collectibles.

GALERIE DE BEAUNE
7 rue de Beaune, 75007 Paris ■ Tel: 01 42 86 05 72 ■ Fax: 01 40 15 96 81 ■ Marc Richer
XVII, XVIII and XIX century furniture, objets d'art and decoration.

LE VIEUX MANOIR (GINTZBURGER)
8 rue de Beaune, 75007 Paris ■ Tel: 01 42 61 17 50 ■ Fax : 01 42 86 02 46 ■ Tue-Sat 11:00-19:00 ■ Nicole Gintzburger ■ English spoken ■ Prices medium ■ Professional discount ■ Amex and Visa
XVIII century furniture, faience, porcelain and objets d'art.

♕ **ANTOINE LEBEL**
8 rue de Beaune, 75007 Paris ■ Tel: 01 40 20 02 14 ■ Fax: 01 40 20 16 88 ■ Tue-Sat 14:00-19:00 ■ English spoken ■ Professional discount ■ Visa, Amex
XVII to XIX century Chinese Porcelain and Compagnie des Indes.

♕ **GALERIE BERNARD CAPTIER**
10 rue de Beaune, 75007 Paris ■ Tel: 01 42 61 81 41 ■ Fax: 01 47 49 04 25 ■ Mon 14:30-19:00/Tue-Sat 10:30-19:00 ■ Bernard and Sylvie Captier ■ English spoken ■ Prices medium ■ Professional discount ■ Amex, Visa
XVIII and XIX century furniture, paintings, screens and decorative objects from China and Japan.

MYRNA MYERS
11 rue de Beaune, 75007 Paris ■ Tel: 01 42 61 11 08 ■ Fax: 01 30 82 49 17 ■ Tue-Sat 14:30-18:30 ■ English spoken ■ Prices medium
Far Eastern art, ceramics and textiles.

♕ **GABRIELLE LAROCHE**
12 rue de Beaune, 75007 Paris ■ Tel: 01 42 97 59 18 ■ Fax: 01 49 27 07 31 ■ Mon-Sat 11:00-19:00 and by appointment ■ Gabrielle Laroche speaks English ■ Professional discount
Furniture and objets d'art of the Haute Epoque and the Renaissance.

LENGLET
12 rue de Beaune, 75007 Paris ■ Tel: 01 40 20 02 28 ■ Christine Lenglet ■ Mon-Sat 10:30-12:00/14:00-19:00
XVI to XVIII century faience and porcelain.

♛ DRAGESCO-CRAMOISAN

13 rue de Beaune, 75007 Paris ■ Tel: 01 42 61 18 20 ■ Fax: 01 42 85 40 37 ■ Mon-Sat 10:30-13:00/13:30-19:00 ■ Bernard Dragesco and Didier Cramoisan speak English and German ■ 10% professional discount ■ Major credit cards

XVI to XIX century porcelain and glass. Expertise and rental for cinema and television. Suppliers to the great museums of the world: Louvre, Versailles, Sèvres, British Museum, Getty, Chicago Museum.

GALERIE SYLVAIN LÉVY-ALBAN

14 rue de Beaune, 75007 Paris ■ Tel: 01 42 61 25 42 ■ Fax: 01 42 61 24 44 ■ E-mail: artparis@club-internet.fr ■ Mon-Sat 10:30-19:00 ■ Sylvain Lévy-Alban speaks English, Italian and German ■ Prices high ■ Professional discount ■ Major credit cards

XVII and XVIII century French and Italian decorative items, furniture, giltwood and painted furniture.

GALERIE DELVAILLE

15 rue de Beaune, 75007 Paris ■ Tel: 01 42 61 23 88 ■ Fax: 01 40 15 98 33 ■ Mon 14:30-19:00, Tue-Sat 10:00-13:00/14:30-19:00 ■ Josette and Olivier Delvaille speak English and Spanish ■ Prices high ■ Amex, MC

Paintings of the XVII, XVIII century and especially XVIII century and XIX century furniture.

TRF ANTIQUITÉS

16 rue de Beaune, 75007 Paris ■ Tel: 01 42 61 11 33 ■ Fax: 01 42 61 11 51 ■ E-mail: trfantik@club-internet.fr ■ Web: www.antiqueexpo.com/yvescherest ■ Yves Cherest speaks English ■ Professional discount ■ Visa

Paintings, objets d'art and furniture of the XVII, XVIII and XIX centuries. The hunt, curiosities, decoration and sculpture.

GÉRARD LÉVY

17 rue de Beaune, 75007 Paris ■ Tel: 01 42 61 26 55 ■ Fax: 01 42 96 03 91 ■ Mon-Sat 10:00-13:00/14:00-19:00 ■ Gérard Lévy speaks English and Spanish ■ Prices high ■ 10% professional discount ■ Amex and Visa

Antique photography and Asian art (not porcelain). Expert to the French Customs.

PETROUCHKA

18 rue de Beaune, 75007 Paris ■ Tel: 01 42 61 66 65 ■ Fax: 01 42 61 06 53 ■ Mon-Sat 10:30-13:00/15:00-19:00 ■ Mr. de Fabrest ■ English spoken

The art of Russia: early XX century.

BIANCARELLI
19 rue de Beaune, 75007 Paris ■ Tel: 01 42 61 23 05 ■ Fax: 01 42 61 24 55 ■ Mon-Sat 10:30-13:00/14:30-19:30 ■ Mr. Dominique Biancarelli speaks English ■ Prices high

Objects of art and decoration, sculpture, gold and silver.

GALERIE GOLOVANOFF
21 rue de Beaune, 75007 Paris ■ Tel: 01 42 61 03 75 ■ Fax: 01 42 61 12 99 ■ E-mail: galgol@cybercable.fr ■ F. and André Golovanoff ■ Mon 15:00-19:00, Tue-Sat 11:00-19:00 ■ English, Spanish and Russian spoken ■ Professional discount ■ Major credit cards

Furniture and objets d'art of the Neoclassical period, especially Russian and northern European.

JEAN-MICHEL GUENEAU
22 rue de Beaune, 75007 Paris ■ Telfax: 01 42 61 49 94 ■ Mon-Sat 14:00-19:00 ■ Jean-Michel Guenau speaks English ■ Professional discount

Objects of curiosity and antique European and Islamic arms and armour.

LE CABINET DE CURIOSITÉS
23 rue de Beaune, 75007 Paris ■ Telfax: 01 42 61 09 57 ■ Claudine Guérin

Objects of art and decoration.

MONSEIGNEUR L'ANCIEN
24 rue de Beaune, 75007 Paris ■ Tel: 01 42 61 29 92 ■ Mon-Fri 10:30-19:00 ■ Mme Estelle Bitton speaks English, Spanish and Italian

XIX century Oriental carpets from Persia, the Caucasus, Turkey and China. Restoration and cleaning.

DENIS DERVIEUX
25 rue de Beaune, 75007 Paris ■ Telfax: 01 40 15 99 20 ■ Mon-Sat 14:00-19:00 ■ English spoken ■ Prices medium to high ■ Professional discount

XVIII and XIX century furniture, paintings and bibelots.

RENÉ-FRANCOIS TEISSEDRE
25 rue de Beaune, 75007 Paris ■ Tel: 06 07 63 35 61

Old Master paintings.

ANDRÉ METROT
31 rue de Beaune, 75007 Paris ■ Tel: 01 42 61 09 06 ■ Fax: 01 42 61 04 47 ■ Tue-Sat 10:00-12:30/14:30-19:00

XVII and XVIII century furniture.

LUC DEBRUILLE
3 rue de Lille, 75007 Paris ■ Tel: 01 42 61 78 72
XX century furniture and objects of art and decoration.

ALB ANTIQUITÉS
3 rue de Lille, 75007 Paris ■ Tel: 01 47 03 45 48
XX century furniture and art objects.

♔ GALERIE BLONDEEL-DEROYAN
11 rue de Lille, 75007 Paris ■ Tel: 01 49 27 96 22 ■ Fax: 01 49 27 96 18 ■ E-mail: galerie@galerie-blondeel-deroyan.fr ■ Web: www.galerie-blondeel-deroyan.fr ■ Mon 14:30-18:30, Tue-Sat 10:30-13:00/14:30-18:30 ■ English spoken ■ Amex
XVI to XVIII century tapestries and carpets. Some archaeological objects.

JEAN-PIERRE ORINEL
12 rue de Lille, 75007 Paris ■ Tel: 01 42 97 58 66 ■ Fax: 01 42 97 58 67
Curiosities and objets d'art.

GALERIE JEAN-FRANCOIS DUBOIS
15 rue de Lille, 75007 Paris ■ Tel: 01 42 60 40 17 ■ Fax: 01 42 96 04 24 ■ Mon-Sat 14:00-19:00 ■ Jean-Francois Dubois speaks English ■ Professional discount ■ Visa
XX century decorative arts. Restoration and transformation.

GALERIE JACQUES LACOSTE
22 rue de Lille, 75007 Paris ■ Tel: 01 40 20 41 82 ■ Fax: 01 40 53 85 19 ■ E-mail: Lacoste-jacques@wanadoo.fr ■ Tue-Sat 14:00-18:30 ■ English and Spanish spoken ■ Professional discount
Furniture and objets d'art of the 1930s, 1940s and 1950s. Expert C.N.E.

GALERIE RADJABI
23 rue de Lille, 75007 Paris ■ Telfax: 06 07 72 13 55 ■ Tue-Sat 14:00-19:00 ■ Visa, Amex
Old carpets and tapestries.

GALERIE DANBON-POKORNY
25 rue de Lille, 75007 Paris ■ Tel: 01 40 20 01 79 ■ Fax: 01 49 27 07 94 ■ Tue-Sat 11:00-13:00/14:30-19:00 ■ Mme Danbon-Pokorny ■ English spoken ■ Visa
XIX and XX century objets d'art and furniture.

♛ GABRIELLE LAROCHE
25 rue de Lille, 75007 Paris ■ Tel: 01 42 60 37 08 ■ Fax: 01 49 27 07 31 ■ Mon-Sat 11:00-19:00 ■ Gabrielle Laroche speaks English ■ Professional discount

Furniture and decorative objects of the Middle Ages, the Renaissance and the XVII century. Sculpture, objets d'art and chandeliers.

GALERIE MOUGIN
30 rue de Lille, 75006 Paris ■ Tel: 01 40 20 08 33

Contemporary furniture.

JEAN-MICHEL DE DION
35 rue de Lille, 75007 Paris ■ Tel: 01 42 60 13 80 ■ Fax: 01 49 27 02 80 ■ E-mail: jmdedion@club-internet.fr ■ Web: www.carrerivegauche.com ■ Mon-Sat 10:00-13:00/14:00-19:00 ■ English spoken

XVIII century French furniture, objets d'art, drawings and paintings.

PHILIPPE VICHOT
37 rue de Lille, 75007 Paris ■ Tel: 01 40 15 00 81 ■ Fax: 01 42 61 07 52 ■ E-mail: philippe@vichot.com ■ Web: www.vichot.com ■ Mon-Fri 10:00-19:00, Sat 10:30-13:00/15:00-19:00 ■ English spoken ■ Professional discount ■ Visa, Amex

XVIII and early XIX century French furniture, paintings, carpets and art objects in marble, wrought iron and stone. Some European and Asian objects. Restoration and estimates.

DIDIER-JEAN NENERT
38 rue de Lille, 75007 Paris ■ Telfax: 01 42 61 55 79 ■ 01 42 61 49 77 ■ Mon-Sat 10:00-19:00 ■ English spoken ■ Professional discount ■ Major credit cards

Furniture: Neoclassical and Empire. Paintings, objets d'art and decorative arts of the XX century. Decoration and installation.

XAVIER CHOLLET – RENAUD VUAILLAT
44 rue de Lille, 75007 Paris ■ Tel: 01 42 61 28 08 ■ Fax: 01 47 57 40 14 ■ Mon-Sat 10:00-19:00 ■ English spoken ■ Prices high ■ Professional discount

XVIII and XIX century furniture and objets d'art.

GALERIE DE LILLE

50 rue de Lille, 75007 Paris ■ Telfax: 01 49 27 04 40 ■ E-mail: jbesson@cybercable.fr ■ Mon-Sat 11:00-19:00 ■ Jean and Magali Besson speak English, Spanish and some Italian ■ Professional discount

XVII, XVIII and XIX century furniture; XVIII century faience; XVIII century glass. Decoration.

────────────── **RUE DES SAINTS-PÈRES** ──────────────

EDOUARD DE LA MARQUE

2 rue des Saints-Pères, 75007 Paris ■ Telfax: 0142 60 71 62 ■ E-mail: de.la.marque@wanadoo.fr ■ Web: www.artface.com/delamarque ■ Mon 14:00-19:00, Tue-Fri 10:30-12:30/14:00-19:00 ■ Edouard de la Marque speaks English ■ Prices medium ■ Professional discount

Antique furniture, objets d'art and decoration.

LE CABINET D'AMATEUR

2 rue des Saints-Pères, 75006 Paris ■ Telfax: 01 42 60 60 00 ■ France Courtaud-Tessier ■ Mon-Sat 14:00-19:00

Faience, porcelain and furniture of the XVIII century. Paintings of the XIX century.

JEAN-FRANCOIS DE BLANCHETTI

2 rue des Saints-Pères, 75007 Paris ■ Tel: 01 42 60 22 43 ■ Fax: 01 42 96 23 47 ■ E-mail: Blanchetti@wanadoo.fr ■ Mon 14:00-19:00, Tue-Fri 10:00-13:00/14:00-19:00/Sat 14:00-19:00 ■ Jean-Francois de Blanchetti speaks English and Spanish ■ Prices medium to high ■ Professional discount

Furniture and decoration of the XIX and the first half of the XX century.

VALERIE LEVESQUE

3 rue des Saints-Pères, 75006 Paris ■ Tel: 01 42 60 56 57 ■ Fax: 01 45 48 29 30 ■ Mon-Sat 14:30-19:00 ■ Valerie Levesque speaks English ■ Professional discount ■ Visa, MC

XVIII century furniture and art objects from China and Japan.

♕ VERONIQUE GIRARD

7 rue des Saints-Pères, 75006 Paris ■ Tel: 01 42 60 74 00 ■ Fax: 01 47 03 41 54 ■ Tue-Sat 10:30-12:30/14:30-19:00 ■ Véronique Girard speaks English and Spanish ■ Prices medium to high ■ Professional discount ■ Amex

Silversmith and objects in silver and gold.

GALERIE GUY BELLOU
7bis rue des Saints-Pères, 75006 Paris ■ Tel: 01 42 60 81 33 ■ Fax: 01 42 60 81 33 ■ Tue-Fri 10:30-12:30/14:30-19:00/Sat 10:30-13:00/14:30-19:00 ■ Guy Bellou speaks some English ■ Prices medium ■ Professional discount

XVIII century furniture and art objects.

P. MINARET – J. L. KARSENTY
8 rue des Saints-Pères, 75007 Paris ■ Tel: 01 40 20 45 44

Furniture and art objects of the XVIII and XIX century.

♔ **ROBERT FOUR**
8 rue des Saints-Pères, 75007 Paris ■ Tel: 01 40 20 44 96 ■ Fax: 01 40 20 44 97 ■ E-mail: rfour@club-internet.fr ■ Web: www.franceantiq.fr/sna/four ■ Mon 14:00-19:00, Tue-Sat 10:00-19:00 ■ Monique Claude-Lanier speaks English ■ Professional discount ■ Major credit cards

XVIII to XIX century tapestries and contemporary artists: Sonia Delaunay, Magritte, Klee, Picasso, Douanier Rousseau, Folon, Miotte, Lurçat, Toffoli, made in their workshops at Aubusson. Carpets woven in their workshops and in Tunisia. Restoration of carpets and tapestries in the Aubusson ateliers. Beautiful exhibition.

GALERIE DES SAINTS-PÈRES
11 rue des Saints-Pères, 75006 Paris ■ Tel: 01 42 60 25 94 ■ Fax: 01 49 27 95 83 ■ Mon 14:00-19:00, Tue-Sat 10:30-19:00 ■ Anne-Marie Farnier speaks English ■ Prices high ■ Amex

Portraits to order by any one of the gallery's 13 painters and sculptors. You choose the artist according to style, technique, price and work method (photos or sittings).

GALERIE SAINT MARTIN
11 rue des Saints-Pères, 75006 Paris ■ Tel: 01 42 60 83 65 ■ Fax: 01 42 60 44 19 ■ Mon 14:00-19:00, Tue-Sat 10:30-13:00/14:00-19:00 ■ Eric Chapoulart speaks English ■ Professional discount ■ Major credit cards

French furniture and objets d'art of the XVIII century. French paintings of the XIX and XX centuries.

♔ **JEAN WANECQ**
12 rue des Saints-Pères, 75006 Paris ■ Tel: 01 42 60 83 64 Fax: 01 42 60 41 48 ■ E-mail: jean.wanecq@wanadoo.fr ■ Mon-Fri 10:00-13:00/14:30-18:30 ■ Mme Gertrude Wanecq speaks German, English, Italian and Spanish ■ Professional discount

XVIII century French furniture and art objects.

FAIVRE-REUILLE
13 rue des Saints-Pères, 75006 Paris ■ Telfax: 01 42 60 13 60 ■
Bruno Faivre-Reuille ■ Mon-Sat 11:15-12:30/14:15-19:00
XVIII and XIX century furniture.

GALERIE VERNEUIL SAINTS-PÈRES
JOELLE MORTIER-VALAT
13 rue des Saints-Pères, 75006 Paris ■ Tel: 01 42 60 28 30 ■
Fax: 01 42 60 28 16 ■ Tue-Sat, 15:00-19:00 ■ Joelle Mortier-
Valat speaks English ■ Prices high ■ Professional discount
Painting and sculpture of the XIX and XX century.

GALERIE HOPILLIART-LEROUX
14 rue des Saints-Pères, 75007 Paris ■ Telfax: 01 47 03 41 07 ■
Francoise Leroux
XVIII century furniture, art objects and curiosities.

LA DUCHESSE BRISÉE
14 rue des Saint-Pères, 75007 Paris ■ Tel: 01 40 15 91 37
Crafts.

ANNE LAJOIX
16 rue des Saints-Pères, 75007 Paris ■ Tel: 01 42 86 90 94
Arts du feu. Decorative objects for the fireplace. Excellent choice.

HELENE FOURNIER-GUERIN
18 rue des Saints-Pères, 75007 Paris ■ Telfax: 01 42 60 21 81 ■
Mon 15:00-19:00/Tue-Sat 11:00-13:00/15:00-19:00 ■ Hélène
Fournier-Guerin speaks English and Spanish ■ Prices medium ■
Professional discount ■ Amex
XVI to XVIII century French and Chinese porcelain and faience

HERVÉ LORGÈRE
25 rue des Saints-Pères, 75006 Paris ■ Tel: 01 42 86 02 02 ■ Fax: 01
42 86 02 14 ■ Mon-Sat 11:00-19:00 ■ Hervé Lorgère speaks English,
Italian and Spanish ■ Professional discount ■ Major credit cards
XVIII century to the 1940s: furniture, objets d'art and decoration.

——————————— **RUE DE L'UNIVERSITÉ** ———————————

GALERIE NICOLE MUGLER
2 rue de l'Université, 75007 Paris ■ Telfax: 01 42 96 36 45 ■
Nicole Mugler ■ Mon-Sat 10:30-19:30
Art objects.

CÔTÉ GALERIE
5 rue de l'Université, 75007 Paris ■ Tel: 01 42 96 40 58 ■ Fax: 01 42 86 09 42 ■ Mr. Mauduy

XVIII century furniture and paintings by contemporary artists.

ML ANTIQUITÉS
6 rue de l'Université, 75007 Paris ■ Telfax: 01 42 86 93 64 ■ Martine Calmels

Furniture, paintings and objets d'art of the XVIII and XIX century.

MONLUC
7 rue de l'Université, 75007 Paris ■ Tel: 01 42 96 18 19 ■ Fax: 01 42 60 20 51 ■ English spoken ■ Prices high

XIX century Louis Philippe, Napoleon III and Romantic period antiques.

JEANNINE DE BRITO
12 rue de l'Université, 75007 Paris ■ Tel: 01 42 60 26 27

XVIII century furniture.

HUMEURS
14 rue de l'Université, 75007 Paris ■ Tel: 01 42 86 89 11 ■ Fax: 01 42 86 89 31 ■ Mr. Dubrana

Curiosities, objets d'art and furniture of the XVIII and XIX century.

♔ GALERIE MARIE-CHRISTINE DE LA ROCHEFOUCAULD
16 rue de l'Université, 75007 Paris ■ Tel: 01 42 86 02 40 ■ Fax: 01 42 60 21 17 ■ Mon-Sat 11:00-19:00 ■ Countess de la Rochefoucauld speaks English and Spanish ■ 10% professional discount ■ Major credit cards

Creation of special editions of furniture made from old books. Fabrics, painted toiles, articulated lighting and an excellent selection of unusual decorative objects. Worth the trip.

♔ PHILIPPE COUQUE
36 rue de l'Université ■ Telfax: 01 42 96 40 08

Faience and porcelain of the XVI to the XVIII century.

GALERIE FK
38 rue de l'Université, 75007 Paris ■ Tel: 01 42 86 92 25 ■ Georges François

Antique garden furniture and statuary.

♔ GALERIE PIERRE M. DUMONTEIL
38 rue de l'Université, 75007 Paris ■ Tel: 01 42 61 23 38 ■ Fax: 01 42 61 14 61 ■ E-mail: Pierredo@aol.com ■ Pierre Dumonteil speaks English ■ Tue-Sat 11:00-19:00 ■ Professional discount ■ Amex, Visa

Figurative sculpture of the XX century, paintings and drawings.

GALERIE MERCIER
40 rue de l'Université, 75007 Paris ■ Tel: 01 42 86 00 40 ■ Fax: 01 42 86 03 02 ■ Mon-Fri 10:00-12:30/14:00-19:00, Sat 14:00-19:00 ■ Mr. Mercier speaks English and Spanish ■ Prices high ■ CB and Amex

Old Master paintings of the XVI to the XIX century, drawings, sculpture.

♔ REYNAL HERVOUËT
40 rue de l'Université, 75006 Paris ■ Tel: 01 42 61 24 18 ■ Fax: 01 42 61 25 19 ■ Tue-Sat 11:00-12:30/14:00-19:00

Exceptional antique frames, chairs and gilded furniture. Mainly XVIII century.

──────────── **RUE DE VERNEUIL** ────────────

GHP BAYAT
7 rue de Verneuil, 75007 Paris ■ Tel: 01 42 86 80 94 ■ Fax: 01 42 86 90 33 ■ Mon-Sat 11:00-19:30 ■ English spoken ■ Professional discount

XVI to XX century carpets; large sizes, Indian, Persian and French Savonnerie. Aubusson tapestries. Restoration. Expert.

♔ BERNARD CAPTIER
25 rue de Verneuil, 75007 Paris ■ Tel: 01 42 61 00 57 ■ Fax: 01 47 49 04 25 ■ Mon 14:30-19:00/Tue-Sat 10:30-19:00 ■ Bernard and Sylvie Captier ■ English spoken ■ Prices medium ■ Professional discount ■ Amex, Visa

XVIII and XIX century furniture, paintings, screens and objects from China and Japan.

GALERIE A.L.
31 rue de Verneuil, 75007 Paris ■ Tel: 01 42 86 95 53 ■ Fax: 01 42 86 95 34 ■ Tue-Sat 14:00-19:00 ■ Anne Lacombe speaks English and Spanish

Modern and contemporary paintings.

♕ JACQUELINE BOCCADOR & FILS

1 quai Voltaire, 75007 Paris ■ Tel: 01 42 60 75 79 ■ Fax: 01 42 60 31 27 ■ English spoken ■ Prices medium to high ■ Professional discount ■ Major credit cards

Middle Ages, Renaissance and XVII century furniture, sculpture, tapestries and objets d'art. Jacqueline Boccador is an Expert to the Court of Appeals, Paris.

GALERIE GHISLAINE DAVID

1 quai Voltaire, 75007 Paris ■ Tel: 01 42 60 73 10 ■ Fax: 01 42 96 02 69 ■ Mon-Sat 10:00-13:00/14:00-19:00 ■ Ghislaine David speaks English ■ Prices medium to high ■ 10% professional discount

XVIII century French furniture, sculpture, art objects. Will research and find special items for professional clients.

♕ PHILIPPE PERRIN

3 quai Voltaire, 75007 Paris ■ Tel: 01 42 60 27 20 ■ Fax: 01 42 61 32 61 ■ Mon-Wed 10:00-13:00/14:00-19:00, Tue-Thu-Sat 10:00-19:00 ■ English spoken ■ Prices high

Excellent quality antiques of the XVII and XVIII century.

♕ BRESSET

5 quai Voltaire, 75007 Paris ■ Tel: 01 42 60 78 13 ■ Fax: 01 42 60 59 38 ■ Mon-Sat 10:30-12:30/14:30-19:00 ■ Gilles and Stèphane Bresset speak English and Italian ■ Prices high ■ Professional discount

Furniture, sculptures and art objects of the Middle Ages, Renaissance and the XVII century.

♕ FREMONTIER ANTIQUAIRES

5 quai Voltaire, 75007 Paris ■ Tel: 01 42 61 64 90 ■ Fax: 01 42 61 04 96 ■ E-mail: fremontierantic@post.club-internet.fr ■ Mon-Sat 9:00-19:00 ■ Patrick Fremontier speaks English and Italian ■ Prices high ■ Professional discount

Highly decorative objects and furniture of the XVII to the late XIX century. Restoration of furniture.

♕ BRIMO DE LAROUSSILHE

7 quai Voltaire ■ Tel: 01 42 60 74 76 ■ Fax: 01 42 60 74 76 ■ E-mail: brimodl@aol.com ■ Philippe Carlier ■ English spoken

Furniture and decorative objects of the Middle Ages and the Renaissance.

LUC BOUVERET

7 Quai Voltaire, 75006 Paris ■ Tel : 01 40 20 91 21

Furniture, art objects and paintings of the XVIII century.

♔ GALERIE CAMOIN DEMACHY

9 quai Voltaire, 75007 Paris ■ Tel: 01 42 61 82 06 ■ Fax: 01 42 61 24 09 ■ Mon-Sat 10:00-13:00/14:30-19:00 ■ Jocelyne Le Brenn and Alain Demachy speak English, Spanish and Italian ■ Professional discount

XVIII, XIX and XX century French and European furniture, objets d'art, carpets, chandeliers.

♔ GALERIE RATTON-LADRIÈRE

11 quai Voltaire, 75007 Paris ■ Tel: 01 42 61 29 79 ■ Fax: 01 42 61 13 79 ■ E-mail: galerie.ratton-ladrière@wanadoo.fr ■ Web: www.franceantiq.fr/sna/ladrière■ Mon-Fri 10:00-13:00/14:30-19:30/Sat 15:00-18:00 ■ Guy Ladrière speaks English and Italian ■ Prices high ■ Amex,Visa

Superb sculptures from classical antiquity to the XIX century. Ivories and decorative objects of the Middle Ages. Paintings and drawings of the XVI to the XVIII century.

♔ GALERIE JACQUES OLLIER

11 quai Voltaire, 75007 Paris ■ Tel: 01 42 61 50 02 ■ Fax: 01 42 61 50 04 ■ Mon-Sat 10:30-12:30/14:00-18:30 ■ Jacques Ollier speaks English, Italian and German ■ Professional discount ■ Major credit cards

Old Master paintings and marquetry furniture of the XVII and XVIII century.

♔ GALERIE CHEVALIER

17 quai Voltaire, 75007 Paris ■ Tel: 01 42 60 72 68 ■ Fax: 01 42 86 99 06 ■ E-mail: chevalier@francenet.fr ■ Web: www.galerie-chevalier.com ■ Mon 14:00-19:00/Tue-Fri 10:00-13:00/14:00-19:00/Sat 11:00-19:00 ■ Dominique Chevalier and Nicole de Pazzis Chevalier speak English ■ Prices high ■ Amex

Incredible collection of tapestries dating from the XV to the XX century. Oriental carpets from the XVI to the XIX century and European carpets from the XVI to the XX century. Qualified expert. Clients include: The Musée du Louvre, The Paul Getty Museum, The Boston Museum of Fine Arts, The Los Angeles Museum.

♔ GALERIE ALTERO

21 quai Voltaire, 75007 Paris ■ Tel: 01 42 61 19 90 ■ Fax: 01 40 20 03 30 ■ Mon 14:30-19:00, Tue-Sat 10:30-12:30/14:30-19:00 ■ Nicole Altero and Nicole Houtebeyrie speak English ■ 5 to 10% professional discount ■ Visa, Amex

XVII and XVIII century furniture, objects and glass.

♔ VANDERMEERSCH

21 quai Voltaire, 75007 Paris ■ Tel: 01 42 61 23 10 ■ Fax: 01 49 27 98 49 ■ Tue-Sat 10:00-12:00/14:00-18:30 ■ Michel Vandermeersch speaks English ■ Prices high ■ Professional discount ■ Amex

XVI to XVIII century ceramics, faience and porcelain. Expert.

♔ MARC ET LUC REVILLON D'APREVAL

23 quai Voltaire, 75007 Paris ■ Tel: 01 42 61 27 36 ■ Fax: 01 42 61 43 70 ■ Mon-Sat 10:00-12:30/14:30-19:00 ■ English spoken ■ Prices high ■ 10% professional discount ■ Visa

Excellent collection of XVII, XVIII, XIX century furniture and art objects. Paintings of the XVIII and XIX century. Both are experts and members of the C.N.E. Restorations.

♔ GALERIE J. O. LEEGENHOEK

23 quai Voltaire, 75007 Paris ■ Tel: 01 42 96 36 08 ■ Fax: 01 40 20 03 97 ■ Tue-Sat 14:30-18:30 and by appointment ■ Italian and English spoken ■ Prices high to very high

Flemish paintings of the XVI and XVII century.

♔ GALERIE BAILLY

25 quai Voltaire, 75007 Paris ■ Tel: 01 42 60 36 47 ■ Fax: 01 42 60 54 92 ■ E-mail: bailly@imaginet.fr ■ Web: www.galeriebailly.com ■ Mon-Fri 10:00-13:00/14:00-19:00 ■ Charles, André and Patricia Bailly ■ English Spanish spoken ■ Prices high ■ Professional discount possible ■ Major credit cards

Old masters, Modern and contemporary paintings, drawings, watercolours and sculptures. High quality, wide range.

♔ GALERIE BERÈS

25 quai Voltaire, 75007 Paris ■ Tel: 01 42 61 27 01 ■ Fax: 01 49 27 95 88 ■ E-mail: beres@easynet.fr ■ English spoken ■ Prices high

Paintings of the XIX and early XX century.

♔ GALERIE CUETO-MONIN

27 quai Voltaire, 75007 Paris ■ Tel: 01 49 26 90 40 ■ Fax: 01 49 26 90 44 ■ E-mail: galmonin@club-internet.fr ■ Mon-Sat 10:00-13:00/14:00-19:00 ■ Anne-Marie Monin speaks English

Furniture and objets d'art of the XVIII and XIX century. Paintings, drawings and sculpture of the XVIII to the XX century.

GALERIE LUCCHINI-MORON

33 quai Voltaire, 75006 Paris ■ Tel: 01 42 61 81 34

Furniture, art objects and paintings from the XVIII to the XX century

♛ Le Louvre des Antiquaires

2 Place du Palais Royal, 75001 Paris ■ Tel: 01 42 97 27 00/
01 42 97 27 20 ■ Fax: 01 42 97 00 14 ■ Web: www.louvre-
antiquaires.com ■ Administrative Office hours: Mon-Fri
9:00-19:00 ■ Gallery hours: Tue-Sun 11:00-19:00 ■
Catherine Delachaux, Director of Communications ■ During July and August, the Centre is closed on Sundays.

**The Louvre des Antiquaires is one of the world's most
extraordinary concentrations of top-quality antique
dealers. It is comprised of three floors of galleries, the
basement, ground floor and first floor, all connected by
broad staircases and escalators.**

**The authors have visited every one of the galleries in
the building and have made their selections based on
their opinions of quality, dependability and courtesy.
Most dealers will give you a warm welcome, but you
will encounter an arrogant and rude "dragon" here and
there. Hopefully, none of them is included here.**

**There is a bar, a restaurant and a tea room as well as a
currency exchange, a shipping company and a car park.
You may find these telephone numbers useful: Expertise: 01 42 97 27 00 ■ Restaurant: 01 42 92 04 04 ■ Bar:
01 42 97 27 23 ■ Bureau de Change: 01 42 97 27 28/29 ■
Shipper: 01 42 97 29 76. Web: www.louvre-
antiquaires.com.**

**We have listed the 200 galleries according to category
or product so that you might more easily target exactly
what you need. Organize your search by subject and
then go directly to the merchants who specialize in the
treasures you seek. Browsing is pleasant, educational
and rewarding, but be prepared, prices can be high to
very, very high.**

GALERIE LA BILLEBAUDE, 4 Allée Jacob ■ Tel: 01 40 20 42 70 ■ Fax: 01 42 97 40 85 ■ Thierry Taravel ■ English and Spanish spoken ■ Professional discount ■ Amex, Visa
Paintings and bronzes of the XIX century, especially of animals and the hunt.

INTERIEUR DE CHASSE, 13 Allée Jacob ■ Telfax: 01 42 61 32 44 ■ English spoken ■ Professional discount ■ Major credit cards
Black Forest and Swiss furniture. Specialist in furniture of the hunt.

GALERIE MIGUET FRÈRES, 4 Allée Guimard ■ Tel: 01 42 61 58 25
Art of the hunt.

L'HERMINETTE, 6 Allée Germain ■ Tel: 01 42 61 57 81 ■ Christine Leblic ■ English spoken ■ Professional discount ■ Amex and Visa
Popular art and antique tools.

ARKA, 3 Allée Bellange ■ Tel: 01 42 97 53 68
Antique jewellery.

BALIAN, 2-4 Allée Odiot ■ Tel: 01 42 60 17 05 ■ Fax: 01 42 60 22 31 ■ Herve Balian ■ English spoken ■ Professional discount ■ Major credit cards
Antique jewellery.

B.G.C. BOSCHER, 17 Allée Boulle ■ Tel: 01 40 20 40 70
Antique jewellery.

J.P. BLANC-ANSELME, 5-7 Allée Bellange ■ Tel: 01 42 60 18 43 ■ Italian and English spoken ■ Professional discount ■ Visa and Amex
Antique silver and jewellery.

CASTIGLIONE, 4 Allée Bellange ■ Tel: 01 42 60 18 41 ■ Fax: 01 48 78 08 54 ■ Mme Castiglione ■ English spoken ■ Professional discount ■ Major credit cards
Antique jewellery.

CAROLINE CHOQUET, 13 Allée Odiot ■ Telfax: 01 42 60 27 11 ■ English and Spanish spoken ■ Major credit cards

Pearls from Japan, Tahiti and Australia. Antique and second-hand watches. XIX century jewellery. Restringing of pearls.

CHRISDAY, 7 Allée Odiot ■ Tel: 01 42 60 17 39

Antique jewellery.

ELIZABETH DANENBERG, 2 Allée Boulle ■ Tel: 01 42 61 57 18

Antique jewellery.

VALERIE DANENBERG, 3 Allée Boulle ■ Telfax: 01 42 60 19 59 ■ E-mail: danenberg@aol.com danenberg@aol.com ■ English spoken ■ 10% professional discount ■ Major credit cards

Antique jewellery. Expert gemologist.

DE MAYO BIJOUX, 14 Allée Odiot ■ Tel: 01 42 60 17 59 ■ Corinne Yoel ■ English and Spanish spoken ■ 10 to 15% professional discount ■ Major credit cards

Antique jewellery and watches, some signed. Precious stones. Sell, buy exchange and deal on consignment. Their atelier will create and restore and restring pearls.

DUBOIS, 4 Allée Boulle ■ Tel: 06 10 86 73

Antique jewellery.

FAIVRE-ANDRIEUX-VERDILLON, 9-11 Allée Odiot ■ Tel: 01 42 60 17 97

Antique jewellery.

GALERIE AR'THEM, 9 Allée Bellange ■ Telfax: 01 42 60 54 22 ■ E-mail: arthem@wanadoo.fr ■ Gilles Zalulyan ■ English and Russian spoken ■ Major credit cards

Russian art, Fabergé, silver and gold, antique jewellery.

GALERIE D.S., 5 Allée Odiot ■ Tel: 01 42 61 83 83

Antique jewellery.

GALERIE RENÉ DUPONT, 10-12 Allée Odiot ■ Tel: 01 42 60 17 19

Antique jewellery.

GALERIE JESSICA DE RY, 7 Allée Roentgen ■ Tel: 01 42 60 00 85 ■ Fax: 01 42 60 00 90 ■ English, German and Italian spoken ■ 10% professional discount ■ Major credit cards

Jewellery of the 1960s and the 1970s; antique cuff-links.

GALERIE MARDJAN, 8 Allée Odiot ■ Tel: 01 42 60 75 78 ■ Fax: 01 42 97 55 98 ■ Mardjan Handjani speaks English and Persian ■ Professional discount ■ Major credit cards

Precious stones, antique and contemporary jewellery. Expertise.

MELVILLE ANTIQUITÉS, 1 Allée Bellange ■ Tel: 01 40 20 04 08 ■ M. & Mme Melville ■ English, Spanish and Italian spoken ■ Major credit cards

Antique jewellery and art objects. Antique watches.

GALERIE MIBEDO, 6 Allée Boulle ■ Tel: 01 42 60 05 56

Antique jewellery.

GALERIE ORELYA, 1 Allée Roentgen ■ Tel: 01 42 61 16 55

Antique jewellery.

GALERIE SAINTE-IRENÉE, 6 Allée Majorelle ■ Tel: 01 42 60 19 64 ■ 9-11 Allee Odiot ■ Tel: 01 42 60 17 97 ■ English spoken ■ 10 to 15% professional discount ■ Major credit cards

Antique jewellery, precious stones, gold and silver and objects of collection.

GALERIE SAPHIR ART, 3 Allée Odiot ■ Tel: 01 42 60 17 07 ■ Fax: 42 60 24 19 ■ Saul Tordjman ■ English, Arabic, Hebrew and Italian spoken ■ Professional discount ■ Major credit cards

Jewellery, both antique and new, precious stones and engagement rings; Australian pearls. Pearl stringing and mounting of precious stones.

GORKY ANTIQUITÉS, 6 Allée Odiot ■ Telfax: 01 42 60 22 76 ■ E-mail: vkrisyan@wanadoo.fr ■ Web: www.louvre-antiquaires.com ■ M. Krisyan ■ English, Armenian and Turkish spoken ■ 20% professional discount ■ Major credit cards

Russian and Ottoman art and antique jewellery.

MIREILLE JACQUEY, 13 Allée Bellange ■ Tel: 01 42 60 18 16

Antique jewellery.

DANIÈLE KOBRINE, 1 Allée Odiot ■ Tel: 01 42 60 16 95 ■ Fax: 01 42 96 08 02 ■ English spoken ■ Professional discount ■ Visa, MC, Amex

Jewellery from the XVIII century to the present; religious jewellery. Repairs and restringing of necklaces.

LA FAUCILLE D'OR, 3 Allée Marjorelle ■ Tel: 01 47 03 07 21
Antique jewellery.

LE CLIPS, 19 Allée Boulle ■ Tel: 01 42 86 87 07 ■ Mr. Kaspanian ■ English spoken ■ Professional discount ■ Major credit cards
Antique jewellery and bijoux de charme.

LEFRAN-WUILLOT, 15 Allée Bellange ■ Tel: 01 42 60 18 82
Antique jewellery.

MOUGIN-BERTHET, 15-17-19-21 Allée Odiot ■ Tel: 01 42 60 21 11 ■ Fax: 01 42 60 21 44 ■ Martine and Camille Berthet ■ English and German spoken ■ Professional discount ■ Major credit cards
Antique jewellery, most of it signed by the grand masters: Cartier, VC.A., Boucheron, Chaumet, Wiese, Froment Meurice, Lalique and others. Specialty: collectible pocket watches.

OSPREY, 2 Allée Bellange ■ Tel: 01 42 60 64 28 ■ E-mail: info@osprey.org ■ Web: www.osprey.org. ■ Mme Delarue ■ English and Cambodian spoken ■ Professional discount ■ Major credit cards
Antique and estate jewellery, silverware, archaeology, coins, medals and ivories. Repair, expertise and consignments.

BRUNO PEPIN, 23-25-27 Allée Odiot ■ Tel: 01 42 60 20 97 ■ Fax: 01 42 60 58 69 ■ Mme Schwarz-Bart ■ Also at 26 rue Daniel Casanova, 75002 Paris ■ Tel: 01 42 86 96 30 ■ English and Spanish spoken ■ Major credit cards
Antique and second-hand jewellery, much of it signed. Silver.

RIMBAUD, JEAN-JACQUES, 2 Allée Thomire ■ Tel: 01 42 61 57 70
Antique jewellery.

THIERRY B., 19 Allée Marjorelle ■ Tel : 01 42 86 95 31
Antique jewellery.

─────────── **ANTIQUE PRINTS - ESTAMPES** ───────────

GALERIE TAMIN, 22 Allée Desmalter ■ Tel: 01 40 20 92 53
Antique prints.

B.G.C. BOSCHER, 17 Allée Boulle ■ Tel: 01 40 20 40 70
Antique jewellery and silver.

J.P. BLANC-ANSELME, 5-7 Allée Bellange ■ Tel: 01 42 60 18
43 ■ English and Italian spoken ■ 30% professional discount ■
Amex and Visa
Antique jewellery and silver.

BALIAN, 2-4 Allée Odiot ■ Tel: 01 42 60 17 05 ■ Fax: 01 42 60
22 31 ■ Hervé Balian ■ English spoken ■ Professional discount
■ Major credit cards
Antique jewellery.

DE MAYO, 14 Allée Odiot, Tel: 01 42 60 17 59
Antique silver.

GALERIE AR'THEM, 9 Allée Bellange ■ Telfax: 01 42 60 54 22
■ E-mail: arthem@wanadoo.fr ■ Gilles Zalulyan ■ English and
Russian spoken ■ Major credit cards
Russian art, Fabergé, silver and gold, antique jewellery.

GALERIE D.S., 5 Allée Odiot ■ Tel: 01 42 61 83 83
Antique jewellery and silver.

GORKY ANTIQUITÉS, 6 Allée Odiot ■ Telfax: 01 42 60 22 76 ■ E-
mail : vkrisyan@wanadoo.fr ■ Mr. Krisyan ■ English, Armenian and
Turkish spoken ■ 20% professional discount ■ Major credit cards
Russian and Ottoman art and antique jewellery.

LA FAUCILLE D'OR, 3 Allée Marjorelle ■ Tel: 01 47 03 07 21
Antique silver and jewellery.

MELVILLE ANTIQUITÉS, 1 Allée Bellange ■ Tel: 01 40 20 04 08
■ M. & Mme Melville ■ English, Spanish and Italian spoken ■ Ma-
jor credit cards
Antique jewellery and art objects. Antique watches and silver.

MOUGIN-BERTHET, 15-17-19-21 Allée Odiot ■ Tel: 01 42 60 21
11 ■ Fax: 01 42 60 21 44 ■ Martine and Camille Berthet ■ English
and German spoken ■ Professional discount ■ Major credit cards
Antique jewellery, most of it signed by the grand masters: Cartier, VC.A., Boucheron, Chaumet, Wiese, Froment Meurice, Lalique and others. Specialty: collectible pocket watches. Antique silver.

OSPREY, 2 Allée Bellange ■ Tel: 01 42 60 64 28 ■ E-mail: info@osprey.org ■ Web: www.osprey.org ■ Mme. Delarue ■ English and Cambodian spoken ■ Professional discount ■ Major credit cards

Antique and estate jewellery, silverware, archaeology, coins, medals and ivories. Repair, expertise and consignments.

GALERIE SAPHIR ART, 3 Allée Odiot ■ Tel: 01 42 60 17 07 ■ Fax: 42 60 24 19 ■ Saul Tordjman ■ English, Arabic, Hebrew and Italian spoken ■ Professional discount ■ Major credit cards

Jewellery, both antique and new, precious stones and engagement rings, Australian pearls. Pearl stringing and mounting of precious stones. Antique silver.

DESEVIN, EDOUARD, 9 Allée Desmalter ■ Tel: 01 42 61 57 99 ■ Fax: 01 47 03 32 07

Antique silver.

SUGER, 6-8 Allée Cressent ■ Tel: 01 42 61 57 72 ■ Fax: 01 42 61 57 73 ■ Mr. Suger ■ English, Spanish, German, Portugese and Italian spoken ■ Professional discount ■ Major credit cards

Art of the table: antique Baccarat and silver by J.E. Puiforcat.

────────── ARCHAEOLOGY ──────────

ALAIN ELEB, 22 Allée Riesener ■ Tel: 01 42 61 57 04 ■ Fax: 01 42 96 08 02 ■ Some English, Spanish, Japanese and German spoken ■ Visa accepted

Antique coins and bank notes, medals, archaeological and prehistoric items. Post cards.

GALERIE ANANDA, 1-3 Allée Jacob ■ Tel: 01 42 97 48 88

Archaeological items.

JACQUES BARRÈRE
36 rue Mazarine, 75006 Paris ■ Tel: 01 43 26 57 61 ■ Fax: 01 46 34 02 83 ■ English spoken ■ Prices high

Archaeological artifacts and art objects.

GALERIE BASSALI – L'ART ET LES HOMMES, 2 Allée Saunier ■ Tel: 01 42 60 21 25 ■ E-mail: jbassali@yahoo.fr ■ Mr. & Mrs Bassali ■ English and Spanish spoken ■ Visa and Diners

Haute Epoque textiles, archaeology, carpets and icons.

GALERIE PYTHEAS, 4 Allée Molitor ■ Telfax: 01 40 15 93 28 ■ Regine and F. Reboul ■ English spoken ■ Major credit cards

Archaeological antiquities from Egypt, Greece, Gandhara, Rome and China.

HAN FONG GALERIE, 1 Allée Thomire ■ Tel: 01 42 60 72 52 ■ Fax: 01 42 60 72 55 ■ Tian Li ■ Chinese and English spoken ■ Professional discount ■ Amex, Visa and CB

Chinese antiquities: furniture, terracotta, ceramics, jade, bronzes, diverse objects.

MOUSEION (ANTONOVICH), 4 Allée Desmalter ■ Tel: 01 42 61 57 93

Objects of antiquity.

NOUJAIM, JULIETTE, 3 Allée Roentgen ■ Tel: 01 42 60 18 92

Archaeological objects and antiquities.

OSPREY, 2 Allée Bellange ■ Tel: 01 42 60 64 28 ■ E-mail: info@osprey.org ■ Web: www.osprey.org ■ Mme. Delarue ■ English and Cambodian spoken ■ Professional discount ■ Major credit cards

Antique and estate jewellery, silverware, archaeology, coins, medals and ivories. Repair, expertise and consignments.

—— **ARMS, MILITARY & HISTORIC COLLECTIBLES** ——

A.C. HAGONDOKOFF, 15 Allée Desmalter ■ Tel: 01 42 61 58 08 ■ English spoken ■ Professional discount ■ Major credit cards

Military curiosities, lead soldiers and historic memorabilia.

ALAIN BAUDOT-VISSER - GALERIE L'ESPADON, 6 Allée Weisweiler ■ Telfax: 01 42 61 56 44 ■ English spoken ■ Amex and Diners

High quality collection of antique arms, military objects and historic souvenirs. Official expert.

JAPON ANTIQUE, 7 Allée Riesener ■ Telfax: 01 42 61 56 88 ■ Professional discount ■ Amex

Japanese art objects, antique arms and armour.

LAVERGNE, 25 Allée Riesener ■ Tel: 01 42 60 21 63 ■ Fax: 01 39 55 97 88

Ceramics, faience and porcelain.

♛ **PATRICE REBOUL - ART ET CHEVALERIE**, 3&6 Allée Riesener, 9 Allée Carlin ■ Tel: 01 42 60 80 80/01 42 97 57 16 ■ Fax: 01 42 61 90 90 ■ English, Russian and Spanish spoken ■ Major credit cards

Antique arms, orders of chivalry, lead soldiers, historic souvenirs. Qualified expert UFE. Supplier to the National Museums.

ART BOOKS

LA LIBRAIRIE DES ANTIQUAIRES, 9 Allée Canabas ■ Tel: 01 42 61 56 79
A splendid collection of books on art and antiques.

ART OF THE FAR EAST

GALERIE ANANDA, 1-3 Allée Jacob ■ Tel : 01 42 97 48 88
Archaeological items.

GALERIE BUTTER, 3 Allée Desmalter ■ Tel: 01 40 15 61 61
Art of the Extreme Orient.

GALERIE KURITA, 4 Allée Majorelle ■ Tel: 01 42 60 21 06
The arts of Japan.

GALERIE PYTHEAS, 4 Allée Molitor ■ Telfax: 01 40 15 93 28 ■ Regine and F. Reboul ■ English spoken ■ Major credit cards
Archaeological antiquities from Egypt, Greece, Gandhara, Rome and China.

HAN FONG GALERIE, 1 Allée Thomire ■ Tel: 01 42 60 72 52 ■ Fax: 01 42 60 72 55 ■ Tian Li ■ Chinese and English spoken ■ Professional discount ■ Amex, Visa and CB
Chinese antiquities: furniture, terracotta, ceramics, jade, bronzes, diverse objects.

JAPON ANTIQUE, 7 Allée Riesener ■ Telfax: 01 42 61 56 88 ■ Professional discount ■ Amex
Japanese art objects, antique arms and armour.

BERTRAND DE LAVERGNE, 1 Allée Saunier ■ Tel: 01 42 60 21 63 ■ Fax: 01 39 55 97 88 ■ English and German spoken ■ Professional discount ■ Major credit cards
XVII & XVIII century Chinese and Japanese porcelain, Compagnie des Indes and tobacco bottles.

GALERIE THÉORÈME, 18-19 Allée Jacob ■ Telfax: 01 40 15 93 23 ■ Vincent l'Herrou ■ English, Spanish and Portuguese spoken ■ Professional discount ■ Major credit cards
XVI to XVIII century faience and porcelain from Europe, China and Japan. Certificates of authenticity. Armorial research. Expertise and advice on building collections. Clients include French and international museums as well as the British Royal Family.

GALERIE PARIS-ISPAHAN, 3 Allée Guimard ■ Tel: 01 42 96 16 57
Art of India and Tibet.

■ **GALERIE SLIM BOUCHOUCHA,** 8 Allée Boulle ■ Tel: 01 42 61
57 25 ■ Fax: 01 42 61 37 70 ■ E-mail: info@slimgallery.com ■
Web: www.slimgallery.com ■ Jean Lostalem ■ English spoken ■
15% professional discount ■ Major credit cards
Antiquities of Tibet, Islam and India.

NOUJAIM, JULIETTE, 3 Allée Roentgen ■ Tel: 01 42 60 18 92
Archaeological and antiquities.

BORLETTA-MORCOS, 9 Allée Saunier ■ Tel: 01 42 61 01 92
Art Nouveau and Art Deco.

CENTO ANNI, 26 Allée Boulle ■ Tel: 01 42 60 48 77
Art Deco and Art Nouveau.

ELIZABETH DANENBERG, 2 Allée Boulle ■ Tel: 01 42 61 57 18
Antique jewellery as well as Art Deco and Art Nouveau objects.

GALERIE DES ARTS-OUAISS ANTIQUITÉS, 15-17 Allée
Riesener ■ Tel: 01 42 60 22 66 ■ Fax: 01 42 97 45 41 ■ Antoine
and Nada Ouaiss ■ Arabic, English, German, Spanish, and Italian spoken ■ Professional discount ■ Major credit cards
**Pâte de verre 1900 to 1930: Gallé, Daum, Walter, Lalique.
Gilded bronze lighting of the XVIII and XIX centuries.**

GALERIE BOOMRANG, 13 Allée Riesener ■ Tel: 01 49 26 05 81
Art Nouveau and Art Deco.

GALERIE FORET VERTE, 35 Allée Boulle ■ Telfax: 01 40 20 95
52 ■ Francine Grunwald speaks English ■ Amex
Art of the XX century.

GALERIE FERRE-LEFORT LESTRIGANT, 39 Allée Boulle ■
Telfax: 01 42 61 57 65 ■ English spoken
Arts of the XX century. Picasso ceramics.

GALERIE FOURNIER, 27 Allée Riesener ■ Tel: 01 42 61 23 65
Art Nouveau and Art Deco.

GALERIE LESIEUTRE, 22 Allée Boulle ■ Tel: 01 42 61 57 13
Art Nouveau and Art Deco.

GALERIE J. POINT, 9-11 Allée Riesener ■ Tel: 01 42 61 56 98
■ Fax: 01 49 52 07 21 ■ English and Japanese spoken ■ Major
credit cards
**Art Nouveau and Art Deco glass by Gallé, Daum and
Lalique. Furniture by Majorelle. Bronzes.**

GALERIE SPICILEGE, 24 Allée Boulle ■ Tel: 01 42 61 77 56
Art Nouveau and Art Deco.

GALERIE TOURBILLON, 1&4 Allée Riesener ■ Tel: 01 42 61 56
58 ■ Fax: 01 47 43 32 60 ■ Jean-François Bourriaud speaks
English ■ Professional discount ■ Major credit cards
**Art Nouveau, Art Deco: bronzes, engravings and prints, ce-
ramics, glass. Gallé, Daum, Argy Rousseau, R. Lalique.**

GIRAUD, MICHEL ■ 53 Allée Boulle ■ Tel: 01 47 03 07 55
Art Nouveau and Art Deco.

GUELFUCCI, L.A., 2-4 Allée Germain ■ Tel: 01 40 15 00 57
Art Nouveau and Art Deco.

IMPULSION B, 26 Allée Riesener ■ Tel: 01 42 61 57 09
Art Nouveau and Art Deco.

LACAR MONTERDE, 2-4 Allée Weisweiler ■ Tel: 01 40 15 02 89
Art Nouveau and Art Deco.

L'OR VERRE, 12-14 Allée Riesener ■ Tel: 01 42 61 56 94
Art Nouveau and Art Deco.

♛ **MAKASSAR FRANCE,** 4-6 Allée Thomire ■ 11/13 Allée Boulle ■
Tel: 01 42 61 57 79
Beautiful Art Nouveau and Art Deco.

MEDICIS, 57 Allée Boulle ■ Tel: 01 42 61 14 25
Art Nouveau and Art Deco.

MOON STONE GALLERY, 21 Allée boulle ■ Tel: 01 40 20 42 44
Art Nouveau and Art Deco.

MONIQUE PHILIPPE, 10 Allée Boulle, ■ Tel: 01 42 61 57 26
Art Nouveau and Art Deco.

YELLOW GALLERY, 19 Allée Riesener ■ Tel : 01 47 03 49 45
Art Nouveau and Art Deco.

────────── **ART OBJECTS & CURIOSITIES** ──────────

BORLETTA-MORCOS, 9 Allée Saunier ■ Tel: 01 42 61 01 92
Art Nouveau and Art Deco.

♔ **GALERIE COLOMBELLE,** 14 Allée Boulle ■ Telfax: 01 42 61 57
34 ■ Agnès Chabanier ■ English and Spanish spoken ■ Professional discount ■ Visa
Dolls and their environment. Objects of charm, collectibles and miniatures. Expertise.

DOMINIQUE DELALANDE, 1-2-3 Allée Majorelle ■ Telfax: 01 42
60 19 35 ■ English and Spanish spoken ■ Professional discount
■ Major credit cards
Marine and scientific objects, tobacco and opium items and erotica. Catalogues in French and English.

GALERIE COLANNE-ANTIQUITÉ, 3 Allée Topino ■ Tel: 01 42 60 16
72 ■ Fax: 01 42 61 15 27 ■ Web: www.antiques.tm.fr/colanne ■ Martin Colas ■ 15% professional discount ■ Visa and Amex
Furniture and decorative objects of the XVII to the early XX century. Expertise.

♔ **GALERIE LA BILLEBAUDE,** 4 Allée Jacob ■ Tel: 01 40 20 42 70
■ Fax: 01 42 97 40 85 ■ Thierry Taravel ■ English and Italian spoken ■ Professional discount
Paintings and bronzes of the XIX century, especially of animals and the hunt.

MELVILLE ANTIQUITÉS, 1 Allée Bellange ■ Tel: 01.40 20 04 08
■ M. & Mme Melville ■ English, Spanish and Italian spoken ■ Major credit cards
Antique jewellery and art objects. Antique watches.

GALERIE NOTRE-DAME, 3 Allée Boulle ■ Telfax: 01 42 61 19
44 ■ E-mail: dlibert@masonic-antiques.com ■ Web: www.masonic-antiques.com ■ Mr. Dominique Libert ■ English spoken ■ Professional discount ■ Major credit cards
Porcelain: Sèvres, Meissen. Decorative items including Masonic and esoteric objects.

GALERIE SAINTE-IRENÉE, 6 Allée Majorelle ■ Tel: 01 42 60 19 64 ■ 9-11 Allee Odiot ■ Tel: 01 42 60 17 97 ■ English spoken ■ 10 to 15% professional discount ■ Major credit cards

Antique jewellery, precious stones, gold and silver and objects of collection.

♛ **LAURENCE JANTZEN,** 11 Allée Desmalter ■ Tel: 01 42 61 58 05 ■ Fax: 01 47 09 35 55 ■ E-mail: ijantzen@club-internet.fr ■ Web: www.antique-expo.com/jantzen ■ English and Italian spoken ■ Professional discount ■ Visa and Amex

XVII to XX century canes, both decorative and with special mechanisms. Objects of curiosity. Delivery to any part of the world in 24 to 48 hours.

♛ **LA FILLE DU PIRATE,** 1-3 Allée Weisweiler ■ Tel: 01 42 60 20 30 ■ Fax: 01 42 60 20 31 ■ Marie-Noëlle and Jean-Pierre Dieutegard ■ English spoken ■ Professional discount ■ Major credit cards

XVIII to XX century marine, science, topography, medicine, astronomy. Expert to the Customs. Great!

LAURENT OÏFFER, 8 Allée Jacob ■ Tel: 01 40 20 90 95 ■ Fax: 01 40 20 90 97 ■ E-mail: Loiffer@aol.com ■ Laurent Oiffer speaks English and Spanish ■ Professional discount possible ■ Visa, Amex, Diners

Antique corkscrews and other collectible objects.

OUAISS-GALERIE DES ARTS, 18-20 Allée Riesener ■ Tel: 01 42 61 56 99 ■ English, German, Arabic, Spanish and Italian spoken ■ 15% professional discount ■ Major credit cards

Objects of vertu, cameos, enamel boxes, opaline, miniatures, Bohemian glass.

———————————— **ART OF RUSSIA** ————————————

GALERIE AR'THEM, 9 Allée Bellange ■ Telfax: 01 42 60 54 22 ■ E-mail: arthem@wanadoo.fr ■ Gilles Zalulyan ■ English and Russian spoken ■ Major credit cards

Russian art, Fabergé, silver and gold, antique jewellery.

BALIAN, 2-4 Allée Odiot ■ Tel: 01 42 60 17 05 ■ Fax: 01 42 60 22 31 ■ Hervé Balian ■ English spoken ■ Professional discount ■ Major credit cards

Antique jewellery.

GORKY ANTIQUITÉS, 6 Allée Odiot ■ Telfax: 01 42 60 22 76 ■ E-mail: vkrisyan@wanadoo.fr ■ Mr. Krisyan ■ English, Armenian and Turkish spoken ■ 20% professional discount ■ Major credit cards
Russian and Ottoman art and antique jewellery.

─────────── ARTS OF THE TABLE ───────────

B.G.C. BOSCHER, 17 Allée Boulle ■ Tel: 01 40 20 40 70
Antique jewellery, silver.

MME CUBY, 2 Allée Molitor ■ Tel: 01 42 61 57 97 ■ Fax: 01 42 96 08 02 ■ Mme Jeanine Cuby ■ Major credit cards
XVIII and XIX century porcelain for collectors. XVIII and XIX century furniture and decorative objects.

ELIZABETH DANENBERG, 2 Allée Boulle ■ Tel: 01 42 61 57 18
Antique jewellery and table arts.

GALERIE GIOVANNI, 1 Allée Carlin ■ Tel: 01 42 61 56 73
Art Deco and Art Nouveau as well as some table arts.

GALERIE PASSIFLORA, 12 Allée Boulle ■ Telfax: 01 42 61 15 11 ■ Mme M. Naman-Ghez ■ English and Spanish spoken ■ Major credit cards
Antique porcelain and glass. Arts of the table. Collectible and utilitarian glasses and cups. Complete services.

GALERIE PITTORESQUE, 13 Allée Desmalter ■ Tel: 01 42 61 58 06 ■ Dominique and Michel Martin ■ English spoken ■ Professional discount ■ Amex
Antique objects of cuisine and gastronomy. Specialists in copper and terrines in animal forms. Porcelain terrines and copper cake moulds.

LA FAUÇILLE D'OR, 3 Allée Marjorelle ■ Tel: 01 47 03 07 21
Antique jewellery and tableware.

GALERIE THÉORÈME, 18-19 Allée Jacob ■ Telfax: 01 40 15 93 23 ■ Vincent l'Herrou ■ English, Spanish and Portuguese spoken ■ Professional discount ■ Major credit cards
XVI to XVIII century faience and porcelain from Europe, China and Japan. Certificates of authenticity. Armorial research. Expertise and advice on building collections. Clients include French and international museums as well as the British Royal Family.

CELINE SERRANO, 4 Allée Roentgen ■ Tel: 01 42 60 97 20 ■ E-mail: CelineSerrano@hotmail.com ■ English spoken ■ Major credit cards

English porcelain of the XIX and early XX century. Table arts and tea services.

SUGER, 6-8 Allée Cressent ■ Tel: 01 42 61 57 72 ■ Fax: 01 42 61 57 73 ■ Mr. Suger ■ English, Spanish, German, Portuguese and Italian spoken ■ Professional discount ■ Major credit cards

Art of the table: antique Baccarat exclusively, silver of J.E. Puiforcat.

GALERIE H. TRUONG, 2 Allée Roentgen ■ Tel: 01 42 60 18 95

Arts of the table.

BOOKS, OLD AND RARE

♛ **PAUL-LOUIS COUAILHAC**, 10 Allée Riesener ■ Tel: 01 42 61 56 91 ■ Fax: 01 42 61 10 70 ■ English, Spanish and Chinese spoken ■ Professional discounts ■ Amex and Visa

Rare old books and manuscripts. Expertise.

CANES

♛ **LAURENCE JANTZEN**, 11 Allée Desmalter ■ Tel: 01 42 61 58 05 ■ Fax: 01 47 09 35 55 ■ E-mail: ljantzen@club-internet.fr ■ Web: www.antique-expo.com/jantzen ■ English and Italian spoken ■ Professional discount ■ Visa and Amex

XVII to XX century canes, both decorative and with special mechanisms. Objects of curiosity. Delivery to any part of the world in 24 to 48 hours.

CARPETS, TAPESTRIES & TEXTILES

AVEDIS-BAHADOURIAN, 8 Allée Riesener ■ Tel: 01 42 61 56 89 ■ Fax: 01 42 61 52 67 ■ Website: www.gigaweb.net/avedis. ■ English spoken ■ Professional discount ■ Major credit cards

Carpets and tapestries of the XVI to the XIX century.

GALERIE BASSALI – L'ART ET LES HOMMES, 2 Allée Saunier ■ Tel: 01 42 60 21 25 ■ E-mail: jbassali@yahoo.fr ■ Mr. & Mrs Bassali ■ English and Spanish spoken ■ Visa and Diners accepted

Haute Epoque textiles, archaeological items, carpets and icons.

GALERIE DARIO BOCCARA, 1 Allée Topino ■ Tel: 01 40 20 07 70
Carpets and tapestries.

─────────────── CLOCKS ───────────────

♔ **ANTIC-TAC,** 1 Allée Boulle ■ Tel: 01 42 61 57 16 ■ Fax: 01 42
61 75 86 ■ E-mail : tomvicai@easynet.fr ■ By appointment ■
Thomas Vicai ■ English, German and Hungarian spoken ■ Major credit cards
**One of the best collections of all types of antique clocks of
the XVIII and XIX century. Restoration and expertise.**

ARKA, 3 Allée Bellange ■ Tel: 01 42 97 53 68
Antique clocks and jewellery.

GALERIE RENÉ DUPONT, 10-12 Allée Odiot ■ Tel: 01 42 60 17 19
Antique clocks as well as jewellery.

MOUGIN-BERTHET, 15-17-19-21 Allée Odiot ■ Tel: 01 42 60 21
11 ■ Fax: 01 42 60 21 44 ■ Martine and Camille Berthet ■ English
and German spoken ■ Professional discount ■ Major credit cards
**Antique jewellery, most of it signed by the grand masters:
Cartier, VC.A., Boucheron, Chaumet, Wiese, Froment
Meurice, Lalique and others. Specialty: collectible pocket
watches and antique clocks.**

HADY OUAISS, 5 Allée Majorelle ■ Telfax: 01 42 60 66 61 ■ E-
mail : Houaiss@teaser.fr ■ English and Spanish spoken ■ 20%
professional discount ■ Visa, Amex
Antique wrist watches. Repair and restoration.

─────────────── COINS & STAMPS ───────────────

ALAIN ELEB, 22 Allée Riesener ■ Tel: 01 42 61 57 04 ■ Fax: 01
42 96 08 02 ■ Some English, Spanish, Japanese and German
spoken ■ Visa accepted
**Antique coins and bank notes, medals, archaeological and
prehistoric items. Post cards.**

LA VIE AU CHATEAU - OSPREY, 2 Allée Bellange ■ Tel: 01 42
60 64 28 ■ E-mail: info@osprey.org ■ Web: www.osprey.org ■
Mme Delarue ■ English and Cambodian spoken ■ Professional
discount ■ Major credit cards
**Antique and estate jewellery, silverware, archaeology, coins,
medals and ivories. Repair, expertise and consignments.**

CRYSTAL, OPALINE, GLASS

AURELIO BIS, 8 Allée Desmalter ■ Tel: 01 42 61 57 98
Antique crystal and glass.

CENTO ANNI, 26 Allée Boulle ■ Tel: 01 42 60 48 77
Art Deco and Art Nouveau; especially glass.

DUBOIS, 4 Allée Boulle ■ Tel: 06 10 86 73
Antique jewellery and glass.

GALERIE GIOVANNI, 1 Allée Carlin ■ Tel: 01 42 61 56 73
Art Deco and Art Nouveau as well as some table arts and glass.

♛ **GALERIE PASSIFLORA,** 12 Allée Boulle ■ Telfax: 01 42 61 15 11 ■ Mme M. Naman-Ghez ■ English and Spanish spoken ■ Major credit cards
Antique porcelain and glass. Arts of the table. Collectible and utilitarian glasses and cups. Complete services.

RIMBAUD, JEAN-JACQUES, 2 Allée Thomire ■ Tel: 01 42 61 57 70
Antique jewellery and glass.

♛ **SUGER,** 6-8 Allée Cressent ■ Tel: 01 42 61 57 72 ■ Fax: 01 42 61 57 73 ■ Mr. Suger ■ English, Spanish, German, Portuguese and Italian spoken ■ Professional discount ■ Major credit cards
Art of the table: antique Baccarat and silver by J.E. Puiforcat.

GALERIE H. TRUONG, 2 Allée Roentgen ■ Tel: 01 42 60 18 95
Arts of the table.

DECORATIVE OBJECTS IN BRONZE

COLETTE AUBINIÈRE, 30 Allée Boulle ■ Tel: 01 42 61 57 59
Bronze objects.

GALERIE THÉORÈME, 18-19 Allée Jacob ■ Telfax: 01 40 15 93 23 ■ Vincent L'Herrou ■ English, Spanish and Portuguese spoken ■ Professional discount ■ Major credit cards
XVI to XVIII century faience and porcelain from Europe, China and Japan. Certificates of authenticity. Armorial research. Expertise and advice on building collections. Clients include French and international museums as well as the British Royal Family.

L'HERROU, 20 Allée Jacob ■ English, Spanish and Portuguese spoken ■ Professional discount ■ Major credit cards

XVI to XVIII century faience and porcelain from Europe, China and Japan. Certificates of authenticity. Armorial research. Expertise and advice on building collections. Clients include French and international museums as well as the British Royal Family.

OUAISS-GALERIE DES ARTS, 18-20, Allée Riesener ■ Tel: 01 42 61 56 99 ■ Fax: 01 42 97 45 41 ■ English, German, Arabic, Spanish and Italian spoken ■ 15% professional discount ■ Major credit cards

Objets de vertu, enamel boxes, cameos, opalines, miniatures, Bohemian glass: XVIII and XIX century.

───── **DECORATIONS AND ORDERS OF CHIVALRY** ─────

A.C. HAGONDOKOFF, 15 Allée Desmalter ■ Tel: 01 42 61 58 08
Military antiques and lead soldiers.

PATRICE REBOUL – ART ET CHEVALERIE, 3-6 Allée Riesener, 9 Allée Carlin ■ Tel: 01 42 60 80 80/01 42 97 57 16 ■ Fax: 01 42 61 90 90 ■ Patrice Reboul speaks English, Russian and Spanish ■ Major credit cards

Antique arms, orders of chivalry, lead soldiers, historic souvenirs. Expert UFE, supplier to the National Museums.

───────────── **DOLLS** ─────────────

GALERIE COLOMBELLE, 14 Allée Boulle ■ Telfax: 01 42 61 57 34 ■ Agnès Chabanier ■ English and Spanish spoken ■ Professional discount ■ Visa

Dolls and their environment. Objects of charm, collectibles and miniatures. Expertise.

───────────── **ESOTERIC COLLECTIBLES** ─────────────

GALERIE NOTRE-DAME, 3 Allée Boulle ■ Telfax: 01 42 61 19 44 ■ E-mail: Dlibert@masonic-antiques.com ■ Web: www.masonic-antiques.com ■ Mr. Dominique Libert ■ English spoken ■ Professional discount ■ Major credit cards

Porcelain: Sèvres, Meissen. Decorative objects, antiquities. Masonic and esoteric objects.

A.V.O.A. - BERNARDINO GOMES, 6-8 Allée Molitor ■ Tel: 01 49 27 96 65 ■ English, Portuguese and Spanish spoken ■ Major credit cards

Faience, porcelain and furniture of the XVII and XVIII century.

GALERIE 7 - MME CUBY, 2 Allée Molitor ■ Tel: 01 42 61 57 97 ■ Fax: 01 42 96 08 02 ■ Mme Jeanine Cuby ■ Major credit cards

XVIII and XIX century porcelain. XVIII and XIX century furniture and decorative objects.

GALERIE J. NATUR, 18 Allée Jacob ■ Tel: 01 42 86 92 84

Porcelain and faience.

GALERIE PASSIFLORA, 12 Allée Boulle ■ Telfax: 01 42 61 15 11 ■ Mme M. Naman-Ghez ■ English and Spanish spoken ■ Major credit cards

Antique porcelain and glass. Arts of the table. Collectible and utilitarian glasses and cups. Complete services.

GALERIE THÉORÈME, 18-19 Allée Jacob ■ Telfax: 01 40 15 93 23 ■ Vincent l'Herrou ■ English, Spanish and Portuguese spoken ■ Professional discount ■ Major credit cards

XVI to XVIII century faience and porcelain from Europe, China and Japan. Certificates of authenticity. Armorial research. Expertise and advice on building collections. Clients include French and international museums as well as the British Royal Family.

BERTRAND DE LAVERGNE, 1 Allée Saunier ■ Tel: 01 42 60 21 63 ■ Fax: 01 39 55 97 88 ■ English and German spoken ■ Professional discount ■ Major credit cards

XVII & XVIII century Chinese and Japanese porcelain, Compagnie des Indes and tobacco bottles.

MOON STONE GALLERY, 21 Allée boulle ■ Tel: 01 40 20 42 44

Art Nouveau and Art Deco, porcelain and faience.

CELINE SERRANO, 4 Allée Roentgen ■ Tel: 01 42 60 97 20 ■ E-mail: CelineSerrano@hotmail.fr ■ English spoken ■ Major credit cards

English porcelain of the XIX and early XX century. Table arts and tea services.

FANS

LUCIE SABOUDJIAN, Cour Palais-Royal ■ Telfax: 01 42 61 57 85 ■ English, Armenian and Spanish spoken ■ Professional discount ■ Major credit cards
Antique fans and collectibles. Very special.

MARIE-MAXIME, 19 Allée Boulle ■ Tel: 01 42 86 87 07 ■ Mme Der Manoukian-Stefani ■ English spoken ■ Professional discount ■ Major credit cards
Fans, objets de vitrine and objets de vertu.

FIREPLACES

TOBOGAN ANTIQUES, 18-20&25 Allée Boulle ■ Tel: 01 42 86 89 99 ■ Fax: 01 40 12 33 90 ■ E-mail: pz10@calva.net ■ Website: www.philippe-antic.com ■ Philippe Zoi ■ English, Italian and German spoken ■ Professional discount ■ Major credit cards
French furniture, objets d'art, fireplaces, sculptures and paintings of the XIX century.

FURNITURE & ART OBJECTS, HAUTE EPOQUE

GALERIE BASSALI –L'ART ET LES HOMMES, 2 Allée Saunier ■ Tel: 01 42 60 21 25 ■ E-mail: jbassali@yahoo.fr ■ Mr. & Mrs Bassali ■ English and Spanish spoken ■ Visa and Diners accepted
Haute Epoque textiles, archaeological items, carpets and icons.

FURNITURE - ART OBJECTS - XVII, XVIII CENTURIES

ABBAYE ANTIQUITÉS (Galerie Rive-Droite), 9 Allée Jacob ■ Tel: 01 40 15 97 87 ■ Fax: 01 42 60 46 05 ■ Jean-Denis Dubois ■ English and Spanish spoken ■ Professional discount ■ Major credit cards
Furniture of the XVIII and XIX century in mahogany, marquetry and gilded wood (bois doré).

PHILIPPE ANTONI, 7 Allée Desmalter ■ Tel: 01 40 20 91 90 ■ English spoken ■ Visa and Amex
Paintings of the XIX century. Furniture and art objects of the XVIII and XIX century.

A.V.O.A. - BERNARDINO GOMES, 6-8 Allée Molitor ■ Tel: 01 49 27 96 65 ■ English, Portuguese and Spanish spoken ■ Major credit cards

XVII and XVIII century faience, porcelain and furniture.

BLEU-VERT ANTIQUITÉS, 25 Allée Riesener ■ Tel: 01 42 61 57 02 ■ Fax: 01 42 61 57 03 ■ Mme Forêt ■ English spoken ■ Professional discount ■ Visa

Flemish paintings of the XVII century. Marquetry furniture of the XVIII and XIX century.

GÉRARD CONTE, 16 Allée Desmalter ■ Tel: 01 42 60 18 62

Furniture and objects of the XVII and XVIII century.

DEPIEDS, 24 Allée Desmalter ■ Tel: 01 42 61 18 53 ■ Fax: 01 42 60 44 07 ■ English and Spanish spoken ■ Major credit cards

Furniture, paintings and drawings of the XVIII and early XIX century.

BERNARD & DANIELLE DEVILLE, 3/5 Allée Cressent ■ Tel: 01 40 20 95 37

Objects and furniture of the XVII and XVIII century.

GALERIE DAYAN, 2/4 Allée Carlin ■ Tel: 01 42 60 59 49

Furniture and art objects of the XVII and XVIII century.

GALERIE DOMENICO CASCIELLO, 12 Allée Saunier ■ Telfax: 01 42 61 13 73 ■ English and Italian spoken ■ 20% professional discount ■ Major credit cards

Furniture, paintings and art objects of the XVII, XVIII and XIX century. Restoration, expertise.

♛ **GALERIE JACQUES OLLIER,** 7-9 Allée Guimard ■ Tel: 01 42 61 58 30 ■ Fax: 01 42 61 58 32 ■ Mon-Sat 10:00-19:00 ■ Jacques Ollier speaks English, Italian and German ■ Professional discount ■ Major credit cards

Old Master paintings. Furniture in marquetry from the XVII and XVIII century.

GALERIE CHARLES SAKR, 12bis-14 Allée Desmalter ■ Tel: 01 42 61 58 61 ■ Fax: 01 42 61 39 40 ■ English spoken ■ Professional discount ■ Major credit cards

Italian furniture, paintings and art objects of the XVIII and XIX century. An exceptional collection of gilded wood items (bois doré).

GALERIE 7 - MME CUBY, 2 Allée Molitor ■ Tel: 01 42 61 57 97 ■ Fax: 01 42 96 08 02 ■ Mme Jeanine Cuby ■ Major credit cards
XVIII and XIX century porcelain. XVIII and XIX century furniture and decorative objects.

GALERIE DES ARTS-OUAISS ANTIQUITÉS, 15-17 Allée Riesener ■ Tel: 01 42 60 22 66 ■ Fax: 01 42 97 45 41 ■ Antoine and Nada Ouaiss ■ Arabic, English, German, Spanish, and Italian spoken ■ Professional discount ■ Major credit cards
Pâte de verre 1900 to 1930: Gallé, Daum, Walter, Lalique. Gilded bronze lighting of the XVIII and XIX centuries.

ADRIENNE LEBRUN, 7/9 Allée Molitor ■ Tel: 01 42 96 05 27
Furniture and art objects.

ANDRÉ PANDIRIS, 8-10 Allée Saunier ■ Tel: 01 42 60 59 96 ■ Fax: 01 42 60 59 98 ■ André Pandiris ■ English and Greek spoken ■ Amex accepted
XVII and XVIII century furniture and decorative objects.

LES ARMES DU CHEVALIER (JEAN-ROBERT DE LAVERGNE), 25 Allée Riesener ■ Tel: 01 40 15 03 10
Militaria and arms and art objects of the XVII and XVIII century.

REY, 2 place du Palais Royal, 75001 Paris ■ Tel: 01 42 61 56 62 ■ Fax: 01 42 61 56 63 ■ E-mail: jeanery@club-internet.fr ■ Some English spoken ■ Prices quite high
XVII and XVIII century antique furniture and objects of decoration.

GALERIE TAMIN, 22 Allée Desmalter ■ Tel: 01 40 20 92 53
Antique prints and objects.

GALERIE THÉORÈME, 18-19 Allée Jacob ■ Telfax: 01 40 15 93 23 ■ Vincent l'Herrou ■ English, Spanish and Portuguese spoken ■ Professional discount ■ Major credit cards
XVI to XVIII century faience and porcelain from Europe, China and Japan. Certificates of authenticity. Armorial research. Expertise and advice on building collections. Clients include French and international museums as well as the British Royal Family.

GERALDINE ANTIQUITÉS, 6 Allée Jacob ■ Telfax: 01 42 60 42 42 ■ Géraldine Tumson ■ English spoken ■ Major credit cards
Furniture of the Haute Epoque and the XVI and XVII century. Chests, chairs, armchairs, tables. Faience from Delft. Glass and statuary.

GILLES LINOSSIER, 10bis Allée Riesener ■ Tel: 01 53 29 00 18
Furniture and art objects.

LA TOUR CAMOUFLE, 3/5/7 Allée Saunier ■ Tel: 01 42 60 22 32
Art objects and furniture of the XVII and XVIII century.

MACHERET, 4bis Allée Desmalter ■ Tel: 01 42 61 57 94
Art objects and furniture.

POSTE D'ANTAN, 23 Allée Boulle ■ Tel: 01 42 61 57 49
Objects and furniture.

JEAN REY ET CIE, 1/3/5 Allée Canabas ■ Tel: 01 42 61 56 62
Furniture and art objects.

SCÈNE ANTIQUE GALERIE, 29 Allée Boulle ■ Tel: 01 42 97 44 66
Furniture and decorative objects.

--------- **FURNITURE - ART OBJECTS - XIX CENTURY** ---------

ABBAYE ANTIQUITÉS (Galerie Rive-Droite), 9 Allée Jacob ■
Tel: 01 40 15 97 87 ■ Fax: 01 42 60 46 05 ■ Jean-Denis Dubois
■ English spoken ■ Professional discount ■ Major credit cards
Furniture of the XVIII and XIX century in mahogany, marquetry and gilded wood (bois doré).

PHILIPPE ANTONI, 7 Allée Desmalter ■ Tel: 01 40 20 91 90 ■
English spoken ■ Visa, Amex
Paintings of the XIX century; sculpture, furniture and art objects of the XVIII and XIX century. Expert in art history.

COLETTE AUBINIÈRE, 30 Allée Boulle ■ Tel: 01 42 61 57 59
Bronze objects of the XVIII and XIX century.

GALERIE 7 - MME CUBY, 2 Allée Molitor ■ Tel: 01 42 61 57 97
■ Fax: 01 42 96 08 02 ■ Mme Jeanine Cuby ■ Major credit cards
XVIII and XIX century porcelain. XVIII and XIX century furniture and decorative objects.

GÉRARD CONTE, 16 Allée Desmalter ■ Tel: 01 42 60 18 62
Furniture and objects of the XVII, XVIII and XIX century.

DEPIEDS-PARIENTE, 24 Allée Desmalter ■ Tel: 01 42 61 18 53 ■ Fax: 01 42 60 44 07 ■ English and Spanish spoken ■ Major credit cards

Furniture, paintings and drawings of the XVIII and early XIX century.

ELISE DEUTSCH - ANTOINE SALSEDO, 10-12 Allée Desmalter ■ Tel: 01 42 61 58 02/03 ■ Fax: 01 42 62 47 76 ■ English spoken and some Italian and Spanish ■ Professional discount ■ Major credit cards

XVIII and early XIX century furniture, paintings and objets d'art.

GALERIE BLEU DE FRANCE, 28 Allée Boulle ■ Tel: 01 42 61 57 55

Furniture and objects.

GALERIE BUTTER, 3 Allée Desmalter ■ Tel: 01 40 15 61 61

Furniture and decorations.

GALERIE DAYAN, 2-4 Allée Carlin ■ Tel: 01 42 60 59 49

Furniture and art objects of the XVII, XVIII and XIX century.

GALERIE DES ARTS-OUAISS ANTIQUITÉS, 15-17 Allée Riesener ■ Tel: 01 42 60 22 66 ■ Fax: 01 42 97 45 41 ■ Antoine and Nada Ouaiss ■ Arabic, English, German, Spanish, and Italian spoken ■ Professional discount ■ Major credit cards

Pâte de verre 1900 to 1930: Gallé, Daum, Walter, Lalique. Gilded bronze lighting of the XVIII and XIX centuries.

GALERIE DOMENICO CASCIELLO, 12 Allée Saunier ■ Telfax: 01 42 61 13 73 ■ English and Italian spoken ■ Professional discount ■ Major credit cards

Furniture, paintings and art objects of the XVIII and XIX century. Restoration, expertise and shipping.

GALERIE COLANNE-ANTIQUITÉ, 3 Allée Topino ■ Tel: 01 42 60 16 72 ■ Fax: 01 42 61 15 27 ■ Website: www.antiques.tm.fr/colanne ■ M. Martin Colas ■ English and Italian spoken ■ 20% professional discount ■ Major credit cards

Furniture and unusual objects of the XVII to the early XX century. Expertise and documentation for export.

THIERRY GITTON, 20 Allée Desmalter ■ Tel: 01 42 60 78 23 ■ Fax: 01 42 86 08 20 ■ English spoken ■ Professional discount ■ Visa, Amex

Paperweights, Neapolitan gouaches, objets de vitrine, opaline and Mauchline ware: all of the mid-XIX century.

GALERIE ROGER HASSAN, 2 Allée Desmalter ■ Tel: 01 42 60 21 10
Objects of the XIX century.

GALERIE SABBAN, 31 Allée Boulle ■ Tel: 01 42 61 57 62
Furniture and art objects.

GUY KALFON, 13/15/17/19 Allée Jacob ■ Tel: 01 40 15 08 67
Furniture and objects.

LANDRIEUX, 2/4 Allée Cressent ■ Tel: 01 42 61 56 48
Art objects and furniture.

MONIQUE PHILIPPE, 10 Allée Boulle, ■ Tel: 01 42 61 57 26
Art Nouveau of the late XIX century and Art Deco.

TOBOGAN ANTIQUES, 18-20&25 Allée Boulle ■ Tel: 01 42 86
89 99 ■ Fax: 01 40 12 33 90 ■ E-mail: pz10@calva.net ■ Web:
www.philippezoi-antic.com ■ Philippe Zoi ■ English, Italian and
German spoken ■ Professional discount ■ Major credit cards
French furniture, objets d'art, sculptures and paintings of
the XIX century.

—————— **FURNITURE AND OBJECTS** ——————
FROM SWITZERLAND & GERMANY

INTERIEUR DE CHASSE, 13 Allée Jacob ■ Telfax: 01 42 61 32
44 ■ English spoken ■ Professional discount ■ Major credit cards
Black Forest and Swiss furniture. Specialist in furniture of
the hunt.

—————— **FURNITURE AND OBJECTS OF NAPOLEON III** ——————

JEAN PHILIPPE HUSSARD, 3 Allée Saunier ■ Tel: 01 42 97 55 14
Napoleon III furniture and objects.

—————— **FURNITURE AND OBJECTS OF THE XX CENTURY** ——————

BORLETTA-MORCOS, 9 Allée Saunier ■ Tel: 01 42 61 01 92
Art Nouveau and Art Deco.

FORÊT VERTE, 35 Allée Boulle ■ Telfax: 01 40 20 95 52 ■
Françine Grunwald speaks English ■ Amex
Art of the XX century.

GALERIE AFTA, 21 Allée Riesener ■ Tel: 01 49 27 08 02
Furniture of the XX century.

GALERIE FERRE-LEFORT LESTRIGANT, 39 Allée Boulle ■
Telfax: 01 42 61 57 65 ■ English spoken
Arts of the XX century. Specialist in Picasso ceramics.

GALERIE 4, 14 Allée Jacob ■ Tel: 01 42 61 56 55
Furniture and objects of the XX century.

GALERIE GIOVANNI, 1 Allée Carlin ■ Tel: 01 42 61 56 73
Art Deco and Art Nouveau.

GALERIE L'ÉCLAT DU VERRE, Tel: 01 47 03 37 19 ■ Fax: 01
49 27 00 86 ■ Elodie Bernard-Schubnel ■ English and German
spoken ■ 10% professional discount ■ Major credit cards
**Contemporary glass sculpture and decorative objects. All
unique pieces.**

GUELFUCCI, L.A., 2/4 Allée Germain ■ Tel: 01 40 15 00 57
Art Nouveau and Art Deco.

MEDICIS, 57 Allée Boulle ■ Tel: 01 42 61 14 25
Art Nouveau and Art Deco.

─────────── **FURNITURE – ENGLISH** ───────────

BRITISH GALLERY, 11 Allée Bellange ■ Tel: 01 42 60 19 12
English furniture and decorative objects.

GALERIE HÉRITAGES, 8 Allée Weisweiller ■ Tel: 01 42 97 55 12
English furniture and objects for decoration.

───── **GOUACHES NAPOLITAINES – WATERCOLOURS** ─────

THIERRY GITTON, 20 Allée Desmalter ■ Tel: 01 42 60 78 23 ■
Fax: 01 42 86 08 20 ■ English spoken ■ Professional discount ■
Visa, Amex
**Paperweights, Neapolitan gouaches, objets de vitrine, opa-
line, Mauchline ware: all mid-XIX century.**

HISTORIC FIGURINES AND LEAD SOLDIERS

A.C. HAGONDOKOFF, 15 Allée Desmalter ■ Tel: 01 42 61 58 08 ■ English spoken ■ Professional discount ■ Major credit cards
Military curiosities, lead soldiers and historic memorabilia.

PATRICE REBOUL - ART ET CHEVALERIE, 3-6 Allée Riesener, 9 Allée Carlin ■ Tel: 01 42 60 80 80 ■ Fax: 01 42 61 90 90 ■ English, Russian and Spanish spoken ■ Major credit cards
Ancient arms, orders of chivalry, lead soldiers, historic souvenirs. Qualified expert UFE. Supplier to National Museums.

ICONS

GALERIE BASSALI – L'ART ET LES HOMMES, 2 Allée Saunier ■ Tel: 01 42 60 21 25 ■ E-mail: jbassali@yahoo.fr ■ Mr. & Mrs Bassali ■ English and Spanish spoken ■ Visa and Diners
Haute Epoque textiles, archaeology, carpets and icons.

GALERIE MANIC, 18 Allée Desmalter ■ Telfax: 01 42 61 58 12 ■ Liliane Manic ■ German, English, Italian and Spanish spoken as well as a bit of Russian and Greek ■ Major credit cards
Icons and statuary of the XV to XIX century; XVII to XIX century jewellery; art objects of the XVI to XIX century. Expertise and restoration.

ILLUMINATIONS - MANUSCRIPTS

LES ENLUMINURES, 34 Allée Riesener ■ Tel: 01 42 60 15 58 ■ Fax: 01 40 15 00 25 ■ E-mail: lesenluminures@compuserve.com ■ Web: www.louvre-antiquaires.com ■ Dr. Sandra Hindeman ■ English, Italian and German spoken ■ Professional discount ■ Visa and Amex
Illuminations and illuminated manuscripts of the Middle Ages and Renaissance. This is the only gallery in the world devoted to this specialty. Objects and sculpture of the Haute Epoque.

MARINE & SCIENCE

PATRICK ADAM, 11 Allée Bellange ■ Tel: 01 42 60 17 77 ■ Fax: 01 42 60 17 76 ■ Some English, Italian and Spanish spoken ■ Professional discount ■ Major credit cards
XVII to XIX century scientific and marine instruments, paintings and arms and a beautiful collection of marine furniture and objects.

DOMINIQUE DELALANDE, 1/2/3 Allée Majorelle ■ Tel: 01 42 60 19 35 ■ English and Spanish spoken ■ Professional discount ■ Credit cards

Marine and scientific instruments, tobacco and opium items and erotica. Catalogues in English and French.

LA FILLE DU PIRATE, 1-3 Allée Weisweiler ■ Tel: 01 42 60 20 30 ■ Fax: 01 42 60 20 31 ■ Marie-Noëlle and Jean-Pierre Dieutegard ■ English spoken ■ Professional discount ■ Major credit cards

Marine and scientific instruments, topography, medicine, astronomy. Expert and assessor.

— OBJECTS OF THE RENAISSANCE AND HAUTE EPOQUE —

GALERIE MANIC, 20 Allée Desmalter ■ Telfax: 01 42 61 58 12 ■ Liliana Manic ■ German, English, Italian, Spanish, Russian and Greek spoken ■ Major credit cards

Icons and statuary of the XV to the XIX century; XVII to XIX century jewellery; art objects of of the XVI to the XIX century. Expertise and restoration.

GALERIE BASSALI – L'ART ET LES HOMMES, 2 Allée Saunier ■ Tel: 01 42 60 21 25 ■ E-mail: jbassali@yahoo.fr ■ Mr. & Mrs Bassali ■ English and Spanish spoken ■ Visa and Diners accepted

Haute Epoque textiles, archaeological items, carpets and icons.

MOUSEION (ANTONOVICH), 4 Allée Desmalter ■ Tel: 01 42 61 57 93

Objects of antiquity; the Renaissance and Haute Epoch

MATHIEU SISMAN, 10 Allée Jacob ■ Tel: 01 42 97 47 71

Objects of decoration of the Renaissance and the Haute Epoch

————— ORIENTAL ART AND ANTIQUES —————

BERTRAND DE LAVERGNE, 1 Allée Saunier ■ Tel: 01 42 60 21 63 ■ Fax: 01 39 55 97 88 ■ English and German spoken ■ Professional discount ■ Major credit cards

XVII & XVIII century Chinese and Japanese porcelain, Compagnie des Indes and tobacco bottles.

GALERIE KURITA, 2 Allée Bellange ■ Tel: 01 42 60 21 06
Oriental art and antiques.

MAGNIER - JAPON ANTIQUE, 7 Allée Riesener ■ Telfax: 01 42
61 56 88 ■ Professional discount ■ Amex
Japanese art objects, arms and armour.

─────── **PAINTINGS & DRAWINGS BEFORE 1830** ───────

PHILIPPE ANTONI, 7 Allée Desmalter ■ Tel: 01 40 20 91 90 ■
English spoken ■ Visa, Amex
Paintings of the XIX century; sculpture, furniture and art objects of the XVIII and XIX century. Expert in art history.

DEPIEDS-PARIENTE, 24 Allée Desmalter ■ Tel: 01 42 61 18 53
■ Fax: 01 42 60 44 07 ■ English and Spanish spoken ■ Major
credit cards
Furniture, paintings and drawings of the XVIII and early XIX century.

GALERIE JACQUES OLLIER, 7-9 Allée Guimard ■ Tel: 01 42
61 50 02 ■ Fax: 01 42 61 50 04 ■ Mon-Sat 10:00-19:00 ■
Jacques Ollier speaks English, Italian and German ■ Professional discount ■ Major credit cards
Old Master paintings; furniture in marquetry from the XVII and XVIII century.

GALERIE LAURY-BAILLY, 32 Allée Riesener ■ Tel: 01 42 61 56 86
Paintings and drawings of the period prior to 1830.

LA TOUR CAMOUFLE, 3/5/7 Allée Saunier ■ Tel: 01 42 60 22 32
Paintings and drawings of the XVII and XVIII century.

ADRIENNE LEBRUN, 7/9 Allée Molitoe ■ Tel: 01 42 96 05 27
Furniture and art objects.

ANDRÉ PANDERIS, 8-10 Allée Saunier ■ Tel: 01 42 60 59 96 ■
Fax: 01 42 60 59 98 ■ André Panderis ■ English and Greek spoken ■ Amex accepted
XVII and XVIII century furniture and paintings.

GALERIE FLORENCE DE VOLDÈRE, 2 Allée Molitor ■ Tel: 01
40 15 93 26 ■ Fax: 01 40 20 07 14 ■ E-mail: fvoldere@club-internet.fr ■ English spoken ■ Prices high
Old Master paintings from the Renaissance to the XVIII century from northern Europe.

PHILIPPE ANTONI, 7 Allée Desmalter ■ Tel: 01 40 20 91 90 ■ English spoken ■ Visa, Amex

Paintings of the XIX century; sculpture, furniture and art objects of the XVIII and XIX century. Expert in art history.

A TEMPERA, 28 Allée Riesener ■ Tel: 01 49 27 94 95 ■ Fax: 01 49 27 94 79 ■ Christine Gros ■ English spoken ■ 10 to 20% professional discount ■ Major credit cards

French paintings and drawings of the XIX and XX century. Impressionists, Post-Impressionists, fauvists, cubists.

ARTBRIDGE, 7 Allée Weisweiler ■ Telfax: 01 42 61 34 01 ■ Marie-Beatrice Lavau ■ English spoken ■ Professional discount ■ Major credit cards

XIX and XX century paintings, sculpture and chefs d'oeuvre. Brokerage for important paintings.

♛ **BERKO FINE PAINTING,** 9 Allée Boulle ■ Tel: 01 42 60 19 40 ■ Fax: 01 42 60 19 41 ■ Patrick Berko ■ English, Russian, German and Italian spoken ■ 20% professional discount ■ Major credit cards

XIX century European paintings.

GALERIE BERT, 5-7 Allée Jacob ■ Tel: 01 42 61 58 50 ■ Fax: 01 42 61 58 49 ■ Dominique Bert ■ English spoken ■ Professional discount ■ Major credit cards

Original drawings, lithographs and ceramics of Jean Cocteau and paintings of the XIX and XX century masters.

♛ **GALERIE LA BILLEBAUDE,** 4 Allée Jacob ■ Tel: 01 40 20 42 70 ■ Fax: 01 42 97 40 85 ■ Thierry Taravel ■ English and Italian spoken ■ Professional discount

Paintings and bronzes of the XIX century, especially of animals and the hunt.

GALERIE LAURY-BAILLY, 32 Allée Riesener ■ Tel: 01 42 61 56 86

Paintings and drawings of the period prior to 1830.

B.G.C. BERNARD GRASSIN CHAMPERNAUD, 11 Allée Guimard ■ Tel: 01 42 61 35 10

Paintings and drawings of the XIX century.

BOUTERSKY, 6 Allée Desmalter ■ Telfax: 01 42 61 57 96 ■ Jacques Boutersky speaks English ■ 10% professional discount ■ Major credit cards

Paintings of the XIX century and specialist in the works of the painter Toshio Bando 1895-1974.

CENTO ANNI, 26 Allée Boulle ■ Tel: 01 42 60 48 77
Art Deco, Art Nouveau and XIX century art.

GALERIE DES PEINTRES VOYAGEURS - RACHEL LIBER-MAN, 12 Allée Jacob ■ Tel: 01 47 61 66 78 ■ Fax: 01 42 96 26 29 ■ English and German spoken ■ 15% professional discount ■ Major credit cards
Orientalist paintings.

GALERIE GIOVANNI, 1 Allée Carlin ■ Tel: 01 42 61 56 73
Art Deco and Art Nouveau furniture, objects and paintings as well as some table arts.

GALERIE R. MANCHERON, 5 Allée Mackintosh ■ Tel: 01 42 60 20 26
Paintings and drawings of the XIX century.

GALERIE MIGUET FRÈRES, 4 Allée Guimard ■ Tel: 01 42 61 58 25/26 ■ Fax : 01 42 60 23 79 ■ English spoken ■ Professional discount ■ Major credit cards
XIX and XX century sculpture in bronze and marble. Animal subjects.

GALERIE DES MODERNES, 8 Allée Guimard ■ Tel: 01 40 15 00 15 ■ Fax: 01 40 15 00 48 ■ E-mail: galerie.desmodernes@wanadoo.fr ■ Philippe Bismuth and Vincent Amiaux ■ English spoken ■ Visa and Amex
Modern paintings, drawings and sculpture.

GALERIE GLADYS SANI, 7 Allée Canabas ■ Telfax: 01 42 61 56 92 ■ English spoken ■ Professional discount ■ Major credit cards
XIX and XX century paintings and jewellery. Animal objects in wood. Collection of XIX and XX century cuff-links in gold, silver, gold plate and enamel. Sculptured wooden dog bookends and objects of charm. Restoration of paintings. Restringing of necklaces and transformation of jewellery.

GALERIE SPICILÈGE, 24 Allée Boulle ■ Tel: 01 42 61 77 56
Art Nouveau and Art Deco furniture and paintings.

GALERIE THOMIRE, 13bis-15 Allée Thomire ■ Tel: 01 42 61 57 78
Paintings and drawings of the XIX century.

GALERIE FLORENCE DE VOLDÈRE, 2 Allée Molitor ■ Tel: 01 40 15 93 26 ■ Fax: 01 40 20 07 14 ■ English spoken
Old Master paintings from the Renaissance to the XVIII century from northern Europe. Some XIX century art.

LEFÈVRE, 16 Allée Boulle ■ Tel: 01 42 61 57 36
XIX century art.

RACHEL LIBERMAN, 12 Allée Jacob ■ Tel: 01 42 61 66 78
Paintings and drawings of the XIX century.

—— PAINTINGS AND DRAWINGS OF THE XX CENTURY ——

ARTBRIDGE, 7 Allée Weisweiler ■ Telfax: 01 42 61 34 01 ■
Marie-Beatrice Lavau ■ English spoken ■ Professional discount
■ Major credit cards
**XIX and XX century paintings, sculpture and chefs d'oeuvre.
Brokerage for important paintings.**

A TEMPERA, 28 Allée Riesener ■ Tel: 01 49 27 94 95 ■ Fax: 01
49 27 94 79 ■ M. C. Gros ■ English spoken ■ 10 to 20% professional discount ■ Major credit cards
**Drawings, paintings and sculpture of the French Schools of
XIX and XX century, Pont Aven and Rouen. Impressionism
and Post-impressionism, Nabis,
Fauvism, Cubism.**

B.G.C. BERNARD GRASSIN CHAMPERNAUD, 11 Allée Guimard
■ Tel: 01 42 61 35 10
Paintings and drawings of the XIX century.

BOUTERSKY, 6 Allée Desmalter ■ Telfax: 01 42 61 57 96 ■
Jacques Boutersky speaks English ■ 10% professional discount
■ Major credit cards
**Paintings of the XIX and XX century and specialist in the
works of the painter Toshio Bando 1895-1974.**

BROOMHEAD JUNKER & CIE, 5 Allée Desmalter ■ Tel: 01 42 96 35
95 ■ Fax: 01 45 23 41 93 ■ E-mail: broomhead.junker@wanadoo.fr ■
Michel Broomhead and Bruno Junker speak English ■ 10 to 20% professional discount ■ Amex, Visa
**Modern Art. Paintings of the XX century: Jean Cocteau, Erté.
Sculpture in bronze and ceramic of the 1920s to 1950s. Expertise, creation of collections and decoration.**

GALERIE BERT, 5-7 Allée Jacob ■ Tel: 01 42 61 58 50 ■ Fax: 01
42 61 58 49 ■ Dominique Bert ■ English spoken ■ Professional
discount ■ Major credit cards
**Original drawings, lithographs and ceramics of Jean
Cocteau and paintings of the XX century masters.**

GALERIE DES MODERNES, 8 Allée Guimard ■ Tel: 01 40 15 00 15 ■ Fax: 01 40 15 00 48 ■ E-mail: galeriedesmodernes@wanadoo.fr ■ Philippe Bismuth and Vincent Amiaux ■ English spoken ■ Visa and Amex

Modern paintings, drawings and sculpture.

GALERIE GIOVANNI, 1 Allée Carlin ■ Tel: 01 42 61 56 73

Art Deco and Art Nouveau furniture, objects and paintings as well as some table arts.

GALERIE SABBAN, 31 Allée Boulle ■ Tel: 01 42 61 57 62

Furniture and art objects.

GALERIE INTEMPOREL, 1 Allée Desmalter ■ Tel: 01 42 60 22 65

XX century art.

GALERIE GLADYS SANI, 7 Allée Canabas ■ Telfax: 01 42 61 56 92 ■ English spoken ■ Professional discount ■ Major credit cards

XIX and XX century paintings and jewellery. Animal objects in wood. Collection of XIX and XX century cuff-links in gold, silver, gold plate and enamel. Sculptured wooden dog book-ends. Restoration of paintings. Restringing of necklaces and transformation of jewellery.

GALERIE SPICILÈGE, 24 Allée Boulle ■ Tel: 01 42 61 77 56

Art Nouveau and Art Deco furniture and paintings.

GALERIE THOMIRE, 13bis-15 Allée Thomire ■ Tel: 01 42 61 57 78

Paintings and drawings of the XIX century.

GALERIE VARENNE, 10 Allée Guimard ■ Tel: 01 42 60 06 57 ■ 01 34 51 75 ■ Alexandre and Catherine Varenne ■ English, Portuguese and Spanish spoken ■ 20% professional discount ■ Major credit cards

Paintings and sculpture 1910 to 1950. Masters of the School of Paris, the Schools of Montmartre and Montparnasse.

LEFÈVRE, 16 Allée Boulle ■ Tel: 01 42 61 57 36

XIX century art.

───────── **PAINTINGS - PRIMITIVE** ─────────

CLAUDE VITTET, 36 Allée Riesener ■ Tel: 01 42 60 11 39

Painters of the North and of the XVII century.

GALERIE FLORENCE DE VOLDÈRE, 2 Allée Molitor ■ Tel: 01 40 15 93 26 ■ Fax: 01 40 20 07 14 ■ English spoken
Old Master paintings from the Renaissance to the XVIII century from northern Europe.

─────────── **POPULAR ART** ───────────

L'HERMINETTE, 6 Allée Germain ■ Tel: 01 42 61 57 81 ■ Christine Leblic ■ English spoken ■ Professional discount ■ Amex and Visa
Popular art and antique tools.

GALERIE PITTORESQUE, 13 Allée Desmalter ■ Tel: 01 42 61 58 06 ■ Dominique and Michel Martin ■ English spoken ■ Professional discount ■ Major credit cards
Antique gastronomy and kitchen objects specializing in brass, terrines in animal forms and moulds.

─────────── **RENAISSANCE - ITALIAN** ───────────

VISCA ANTIQUAIRE, 13-15 Allée Guimard ■ Tel: 01 40 15 05 45
Italian Renaissance art.

─────────── **SACRED ART** ───────────

GALERIE MANIC, 18 Allée Desmalter ■ Telfax: 01 42 61 58 12 ■ Liliane Manic ■ German, English, Italian and Spanish spoken as well as a bit of Russian and Greek ■ Major credit cards
Icons and statuary of the XV to XIX century; XVII to XIX century jewellery; art objects of the XVI to the XIX century. Expertise and restoration.

─────────── **SCULPTURE** ───────────

A TEMPERA, 28 Allée Riesener ■ Tel: 01 49 27 94 95 ■ Fax: 01 49 27 94 79 ■ M. C. Gros ■ English spoken ■ 10 to 20% professional discount ■ Major credit cards
French paintings, drawings and sculpture of the XIX and XX century. French Schools of Pont Aven and Rouen. Impressionists and Post-Impressionists, Nabis, Fauvists and Cubists.

PHILIPPE ANTONI, 7 Allée Desmalter ■ Tel: 01 40 20 91 90 ■ English spoken ■ Major credit cards
Sculpture of the XVIII and XIX century. Paintings of the XIX century. Furniture and art objects of the XVIII and XIX century. Expert in art history.

BROOMHEAD JUNKER & CIE, 5 Allée Desmalter ■ Tel: 01 42 96 35 95 ■ Fax: 01 45 23 41 93 ■ E-mail: broomhead.junker@wanadoo.fr ■ Michel Broomhead and Bruno Junker speak English ■ 10 to 20% professional discount ■ Amex, Visa
Modern art: paintings of the XX century, Jean Cocteau, Erté; sculpture in bronze and ceramic of the 1920s to the 1950s. Expertise, decoration and creation of collections.

CENTO ANNI, 26 Allée Boulle ■ Tel: 01 42 60 48 77
Art Deco and Art Nouveau and XIX century art.

GALERIE LA BILLEBAUDE, 4 Allée Jacob ■ Tel: 01 40 20 42 70 ■ Fax: 01 42 97 40 85 ■ Thierry Taravel ■ English and Italian spoken ■ Professional discount
Paintings and bronzes of the XIX century, especially of animals and the hunt.

GALERIE ROGER HASSAN, 2 Allée Desmalter ■ Tel: 01 42 60 21 10
Objects of the XIX century.

GALERIE LESIEUTRE, 22 Allée Boulle ■ Tel: 01 42 61 57 13
Art Nouveau and Art Deco.

GALERIE MIGUET FRÈRES, 4 Allée Guimard ■ Tel: 01 42 61 58 25/26 ■ Fax: 01 42 60 23 79 ■ English spoken ■ Professional discount ■ Major credit cards
XIX and XX century sculpture in bronze and marble. Animal subjects.

GALERIE DES MODERNES, 8 Allée Guimard ■ Tel: 01 40 15 00 15 ■ Fax: 01 40 15 00 48 ■ E-mail: galeriedesmodernes@wanadoo.fr ■ English spoken ■ Major credit cards
Modern paintings, drawings and sculpture.

GALERIE SPICILÈGE, 24 Allée Boulle ■ Tel: 01 42 61 77 56
Art Nouveau and Art Deco furniture and paintings.

GALERIE TOURBILLON, 1&4 Allée Riesener ■ Tel: 01 42 61 56 58 ■ Fax: 01 47 43 32 60 ■ Jean-François Bourriaud speaks English ■ Professional discount ■ Major credit cards
Art Nouveau, Art Deco: bronzes, engravings and prints, ceramics, glass. Gallé, Daum, Argy Rousseau, Lalique.

GALERIE VARENNE, 10 Allée Guimard ■ Tel: 01 42 60 06 57 ■ Fax: 01 34 51 75 ■ Alexandre and Catherine Varenne ■ English, Portuguese and Spanish spoken ■ 20% professional discount ■ Major credit cards

Paintings and sculpture 1910 to 1950. Masters of the School of Paris, the Schools of Montmartre and Montparnasse.

LANDRIEUX, 2/4 Allée Cressent ■ Tel: 01 42 61 56 48

Art objects and furniture.

TOBOGAN ANTIQUES, 18-20&25 Allée Boulle ■ Tel: 01 42 86 89 99 ■ Fax: 01 40 12 33 90 ■ E-mail: pz10@calva.net ■ Web: www.philippezoi-antic.com ■ Philippe Zoi ■ English, Italian and German spoken ■ Professional discount ■ Major credit cards

French furniture, objets d'art, fireplaces, sculptures and paintings of the XIX century.

───────────── SMOKERS' COLLECTIBLES ─────────────

DOMINIQUE DELALANDE, 1-3 Allée Majorelle ■ Telfax: 01 42 60 19 35 ■ English and Spanish spoken ■ Professional discount ■ Major credit cards

Marine and scientific collectibles, tobacco and opium objects; erotica. Catalogues in French and English.

───────────────────── TOYS ─────────────────────

PATRICE REBOUL - ART ET CHEVALERIE, 3-6 Allée Riesener, 9 Allée Carlin ■ Tel: 01 42 60 80 80 ■ Fax: 01 42 61 90 90 ■ English, Russian and Spanish spoken ■ Major credit cards

Ancient arms, orders of chivalry, lead soldiers, historic souvenirs. Qualified expert UFE.

───────── WINE CELLARS, BOXES AND COFFRETS ─────────

HELENE D'HELMERSEN, 17-19 Allée Desmalter ■ Tel: 01 42 97 43 33 ■ Fax: 01 49 28 98 89 ■ E-mail: helmerse@club-internet.fr ■ English spoken ■ Possible professional discount ■ Visa, Amex

Superb collection of liqueur caddies and boxes of the XIX century. Portraits of the XVII, XVIII, and XIX century.

GALERIE HÉRITAGES, 8 Allée Weisweiller ■ Tel: 01 42 97 55 12
English furniture and objects for decoration, wine cellar objects.

M.J. SENEMAUD, 8 Allée Majorelle ■ Tel: 01 42 60 19 09
Collectibles for the wine cellar.

Quartier Drouot

In the ninth arondissement, you will find an imposing list of dealers and specialists, organized in what is called Les Antiquaires et Galeries d'Art du Quartier Drouot. This is a new association of antique and art galleries formed by the dealers who surround the well-known auction house, Hotel des Ventes Drouot. This section has been organized so one can browse as one walks along the pleasant streets and alleys.

SABINE BOURGEY
7 rue Drouot, 75009 Paris ■ Tel: 01 47 70 35 18 ■ Fax: 01 42 46 58 48 ■ Mon-Fri 9:30-12:00-13:00-18:00 ■ Prices medium to high
Stamps and old coins.

FRANÇOIS FELDMAN
10 rue Drouot, 75009 Paris ■ Tel: 01 45 23 10 22 ■ Fax: 01 48 01 03 45 ■ Mon-Fri 9:00-12:30/14:00-18:30 ■ English spoken ■ Prices medium to high ■ Dealers welcome ■ Visa
Stamps for collectors.

TEMPLIER & FILS
10 rue Drouot, 75009 Paris ■ Tel: 01 42 47 00 23 ■ Fax: 01 42 47 00 15 ■ Mon-Fri 10:00-18:00
Signed jewellery, precious stones and silver.

GALERIE FRÉDÉRICK CHANOIT
12 rue Drouot, 75009 Paris ■ Tel: 01 47 70 22 33 ■ Fax: 01 47 70 22 44 ■ Mon-Fri 9:00-13:00/14:00-18:00 ■ English spoken ■ Prices medium to high ■ Professional discount
XIX century French paintings.

ARMAND DEROYAN
13 rue Drouot, 75009 Paris ■ Tel: 01 48 00 07 85 ■ Fax: 01 48 00 06 34 ■ E-mail: deroyan@aol.com ■ Mon-Fri 10:00-18:00 ■ Prices high
XV to XVIII century tapestries and carpets of Europe and the Orient. Rare, old fabrics.

PATRICK MARÉCHAL
15 rue Drouot, 75009 Paris ■ Tel: 01 47 70 61 09 ■ Mon-Fri 10:00-18:00 ■ Prices medium

Stamps and postal history of all countries.

ANTIQUAIRES DROUOT
21 rue Drouot, 75009 Paris ■ Tel: 01 47 70 20 18 ■ Fax : 01 47 70 32 50 ■ E-mail: info@antiquaires-drouot.com ■ Web: www.antiquaires_drouot.com ■ Mon-Fri 11:00-18:30 ■ Jacques Larochas ■ English spoken ■ Prices medium ■ Visa

Antique collectibles and jewellery.

GALERIE JACQUES ANCELY
34 rue Drouot, 75009 Paris ■ Telfax: 01 45 23 20 25 ■ E-mail: jancely@online.fr ■ Mon-Fri 10:00-18:00 ■ Jacotte Briens, Jacques Ancely ■ Prices medium to high ■ Professional discount

Paintings of the French School and others of 1900 to 1940.

EURO ART & COLLECTION
5 rue de la Grange Batelière, 75009 Paris ■ Tel: 01 47 70 96 66 ■ Fax: 01 48 01 07 99 ■ Mon-Fri 10:00-18:00 ■ Prices medium to high

Watches, antique and contemporary jewellery.

GALERIE DOMINIQUE WEITZ
6 rue de la Grange Batelière, 75009 Paris ■ Tel: 01 42 46 35 95 ■ Fax: 01 43 78 95 04 ■ E-mail: weitdom@aol.com ■ Mon-Fri 10:00-19:00 and by appointment ■ English spoken ■ Prices medium to high ■ Professional discount ■ Major credit cards

Original photography of the XIX and XX century on themes of travel and ethnography. Old Master and Modern paintings. Some watercolours and sculpture.

GALERIE AITTOUARES
10 rue de la Grange Batelière, 75009 Paris ■ Tel: 01 45 23 41 13 ■ Fax: 01 42 47 03 90 ■ Mon-Fri 10:00-13:00/14:00-18:00 ■ Prices medium ■ Professional discount

Impressionist paintings and drawings. Abstract, Cubist and Surrealist art of the early XX century. Sculpture in bronze by César, Rodin, Daumier. Watercolours and works on paper. Drawings of Rodin and Carpeaux.

GALERIE SABATIER
10 rue de la Grange Batelière, 75009 Paris ■ Tel: 01 47 70 07 11 ■ Fax: 01 47 70 07 47 ■ Cell: 06 12 11 07 49 ■ E-mail: galeriesabatier@hotmail.com ■ Mon-Fri 10:00-18:00 ■ Michel and Nicole Sabatier

Old paintings. Faience and restoration of faience.

ANDRÉ GOMBERT
10 rue de la Grange Batelière, 75009 Paris ■ Tel: 01 42 46 94 97
■ Fax : 01 42 46 06 64 ■ Mon-Fri 9:30-18:30 ■ English spoken

Old Master and XIX century paintings.

BOULE MONACO COLLECTIONS
10 rue de la Grange Batelière, 75009 Paris ■ Tel: 01 4 0 22 60
04 ■ Fax: 01 40 22 60 05 ■ E-mail : steph.boule@worldnet.fr ■
Web : www.boule-monaco-collections.mc ■ Jason and Stèphane
Boule ■ English, Italian and Spanish spoken ■ Prices low to high
■ Professional discount ■ Visa, MC

Stamps and the histories of the postal services. Autographs, books, posters and archives.

VINCENT LÉCUYER
12 rue de la Grange Batelière, 75009 Paris ■ Tel: 01 42 46 05 74
■ Fax: 01 42 46 10 16 ■ E-mail: lecuyer@worldnet.fr ■ Mon-Sat
10:00-18:00 ■ English spoken ■ Prices medium ■ Professional
discount

Paintings of all periods.

♕ LESAGE PARIS
13 rue de la Grange Batelière, 75009 Paris ■ Tel: 01 48 24 14 20
■ Fax: 01 48 00 02 26 ■ Mon-Fri 9:00-12:30/13:00-18:00 ■
François Lesage

Perhaps the best establishment for embroidery and embroidery accessories. Mr. Lesage also conducts an excellent training school for embroidery. This is an artisan of the first rank. His atelier produces some of the most beautiful embroidery for the Haute Couture Houses of Paris.

L'ESPRIT CULTUREL - GROUPE EAC
13 rue de la Grange Batelière and 24 rue Buffault, 75009 Paris
■ Tel: 01 52 21 05 48/01 47 70 23 83 ■ Fax: 01 47 70 17 83 ■
Mon-Fri ■ 8:30-18:00 ■ Céline Petiot, Secretary-General ■ English and German spoken ■

The Associations of the Métiers d'Art and the experts of the Quartier Drouot. Membership includes visits to museums, shows, wine tastings, children's entertainment.

GALERIE DUMOUSSAUD
13 rue de la Grange Batelière ■ Telfax: 01 4246 68 55 ■ E-mail:
vincent.dumoussaud@worldnet.fr ■ Mon-Fri 10:00-18:00 ■ Vincent Dumoussaud ■ Prices medium to high

Italian and French paintings of the XVII and XVIII century.

GALERIE AB
14 rue de la Grange Batelière, 75009 Paris ■ Tel: 01 45 23 41 16
■ Fax: 01 42 47 03 90 ■ E-mail: galerie.ab@wanadoo.fr ■ Mon-Fri
10:00-18:00 ■ Agnès Aittouares and Nicolas Brient ■ English and
Italian spoken ■ Prices medium to very high ■ Major credit cards
XIX and XX century drawings, 1830-1950. French Impressionist and Post-Impressionist paintings.

COUR 14
14 rue de la Grange Batelière, 75009 Paris ■ Tel: 01 48 00 07 13 ■
Mon-Fri 9:30-13:00/14:30-18:00 ■ Jacques Bertrand, Christophe
Longin, Michel Souchon, Chantal Jollot ■ English and Spanish
spoken ■ Prices medium to high ■ Professional discount
Furniture, objets d'art, curiosities, paintings, and sculptures of the XX century.

TRANSITAIRE FRANCE EXPORT
14 rue de la Grange Batelière, 75009 Paris ■ Tel: 01 44 79 00 69
■ Fax: 01 44 79 03 56 ■ E-mail: franceexport@wanadoo.fr ■
Mon-Fri 9:00-18:00 ■ Dominique speaks English
Packing and shipping of works of art, paintings and furniture anywhere in the world.

ROBERT BINNENWEG
15 rue de la Grange Batelière, 75009 Paris ■ Fax: 01 43 42 31
75 ■ Cell: 06 86 48 43 05 ■ Mon-Fri 10:00-13:00/15:00-18:30 ■
English, German and Dutch spoken ■ Professional discount
Furniture, faience and curiosities of the XIV to the XIX century.

IMPRIMERIE RAPIDE MODERNE
15-17 rue de la Grange Batelière, 75009 Paris ■ Tel: 01 47 70 80 65
■ Fax: 01 47 70 17 01 ■ E-mail: irm.blaimont@wanadoo.fr ■ Mon-
Fri 9:00-19:00 ■ Jean-Pierre Blaimont ■ Some English spoken
A printing service in the Quartier which specializes in art printing. They offer everything from pre-press through flashing and high quality printing.

J.C. CAZENAVE
16 rue de la Grange Batelière, 75009 Paris ■ Tel: 01 45 23 19
42 ■ Fax: 01 42 47 02 97 ■ Mon-Fri 10:00-13:00/15:00-18:00
■ Appointment preferred
Specialist in dolls, automates and toys.

GÉRARD ETIENBLED
16 rue de la Grange Batelière, 75009 Paris ■ Tel: 01 48 01 67
84 ■ Fax: 01 48 01 67 85 ■ Mon-Fri 10:00-13:00/15:00-18:00
■ Appointment preferred
Automates, toys and dolls.

GALERIE DROUART

16 rue de la Grange Batelière, 75009 Paris ■ Tel: 01 47 70 52 90 ■ Fax: 01 48 00 93 72 ■ E-mail: galerie.drouart@fnac.fr ■ Web: www.la-galeriedrouart.fnac.fr ■ Mon-Fri 10:30-13:00-14:30-18:30 ■ English, Italian and Spanish spoken ■ Professional discount ■ Amex, Visa

Paintings of the Belle Epoque and the beginning of the XX century.

VINCENT GUERRE

16 rue de la Grange Batelière, 75009 Paris ■ Tel: 01 42 46 48 50 ■ Fax: 01 47 70 02 42 ■ Mon-Fri 10:00-13:00/14:30-18:00 ■ Prices medium to high

Antiques, decorative objects of the XIX and XX century. Old frames and mercury mirrors.

ALAIN MARCUS

16 rue de la Grange Batelière, 75009 Paris ■ Tel: 01 45 23 25 58 ■ Mon-Fri 10:00-13:00/15:00-19:00 by appointment ■ English spoken ■ Prices medium to high

Furniture and decorative objects of the XVIII and XIX century. Expert of the C.N.E. in furniture of the second half of the XIX century.

NEW-LIST

16 rue de la Grange Batelière, 75009 Paris ■ Tel: 01 42 46 30 38 ■ Fax: 01 42 46 30 28 ■ Mon-Fri 10:00-13:00/14:30-18:00 ■ Véronique Legaret ■ English and Italian spoken ■ Prices medium ■ Professional discount

Silver and everything for the table, as well as furniture. Bridal registry.

GALERIE LAURA PECHEUR

16 rue de la Grange Batelière, 75009 Paris ■ Tel: 01 47 70 04 38 ■ Fax: 01 48 74 64 91 ■ Mon-Fri 12:00-18:30 ■ English and Italian spoken ■ Professional discount

Drawings of the XVI to the XIX and early XX century.

ROSSINI-BATELIÈRE

17 rue de la Grange Batelière, 75009 Paris ■ Tel: 01 40 22 07 08 ■ Fax: 01 42 46 99 67 ■ François Piet, France de Forceville ■ Mon-Fri 10:18:00

Antique furniture and objets d'art of all periods.

CABINET D'EXPERTISES CAMARD

18 rue de la Grange Batelière, 75009 Paris ■ Tel: 01 42 46 35 74 ■ Fax: 01 40 22 05 70 ■ E-mail: infoanad@camard-expertises.fr ■ Web: www.camard-expertises.fr ■ Mon-Fri 9:30-13:00/14:30-18:30 ■ English, Spanish and Italian spoken

Experts in works of art and public auctions.

MARION CHAUVY
18 rue de la Grange Batelière, 75009 Paris ■ Tel: 01 47 70 18 08
■ Fax: 01 47 70 44 04 ■ E-mail: mchauvy@aol.com ■ Web : www.galerie.france.com ■ Mon-Sat 11:00-19:30 ■ Marc and Marion Chauvy ■ English spoken ■ Prices medium to high ■ Professional discount ■ Amex, Visa

XIX century paintings by well-known and lesser-known masters. Decorative and Modern paintings. Impressionist and Post-Impressionist.

CALVET
10 rue Chauchat, 75009 Paris ■ Tel: 01 47 70 87 03 ■ Fax: 01 42 46 12 36 ■ Mon-Fri 10:00-13:00-14:00-18:30 ■ Gérard Calvet ■ English and Spanish spoken ■ Prices high to very high ■ Professional discount

XIX century furniture and objets d'art in the taste of the XVIII century.

RENAUD RINALDI
11 rue Chauchat, 75009 Paris ■ Telfax: 01 42 46 35 88 ■ Mon-Fri 10:00-13:00-15:00-18:00 ■ English, Spanish and Italian spoken ■ Prices medium ■ Professional discount

XIX century paintings of the French and other Schools. Restoration of paintings and frames.

GALERIE MARCUS
20 rue Chauchat, 75009 Paris ■ Tel: 01 47 70 91 23 ■ Fax: 01 45 23 20 41 ■ Mon-Fri 10:00-18:00

Marvellous paintings of the XVIII and XIX century.

♛ **GALERIE 34 – MGW SEGAS EXPERT**
34 Passage Jouffroy, 75009 Paris ■ Tel: 01 47 70 89 65 ■ Fax: 01 48 00 08 24 ■ E-mail: mgwsegas@club-internet.fr ■ Web: www.canesegas.com ■ Mon-Sat 11:00-18:30 ■ Miguel and Gilbert Segas ■ English spoken ■ Professional discount ■ Major credit cards

An extraordinary collection of antique canes, mostly from the XIX century. One of the best collections anywhere. Expert.

THOMAS BOOG
36 Passage Jouffroy, 75009 Paris ■ Telfax: 01 47 70 98 10 ■ Web: www.thomasboog.com ■ Mon-Sat 10:00-13:00/14:00-19:00 ■ English spoken ■ Professional discount ■ Major credit cards

An extraordinary artisan who creates lamps in unusual shapes, chinoiserie, silk lanterns and objects of shells and stone.

♛ LIBRAIRIE DU PASSAGE
48-62 Passage Jouffroy, 75009 Paris ■ Tel: 01 48 24 54 14 ■ Fax: 01 45 23 08 83 ■ Mon-Sat 12:00-19:00 ■ Karine Langlande ■ English spoken ■ Prices medium ■ Major credit cards

Old, rare and contemporary books on the decorative arts.

OLIVIER
63 Passage Jouffroy, 75009 Paris ■ Tel: 01 45 23 26 23 ■ E-mail : olivier.orfevrerie@wanadoo.fr ■ Mon-Fri 10:00-13:00/14:00-19:00 ■ Olivier Pomez ■ English and Spanish spoken ■ Prices medium to high ■ Professional discount

XVIII and XIX century silver, mainly French. Some early XX century.

GALERIE JOUFFROY
64 Passage Jouffroy, 75009 Paris ■ Tel: 01 45 23 02 57 ■ Mon-Fri 10:30-13:00/14:00-18:00 ■ Philippe Michel ■ Italian and Spanish spoken ■ Professional discount

XIX and XX century paintings and drawings. Expert to the Tribunal of Commerce.

GARY ROCHE
18 rue Le Pelletier ■ Tel: 01 47 70 32 16 ■ Fax: 01 42 46 82 91 ■ Mon-Fri 10:00-18:30

Expert. Paintings by the masters of the XIX and early XX century.

PHILIPPE DELARUE
3 rue de Provence, 75009 Paris ■ Tel: 01 40 22 02 93 ■ Fax: 01 48 00 96 46 ■ Mon-Fri 10:00-18:00

Paintings of all periods.

J.C. POULIQUEN
3 rue de Provence, 75009 Paris ■ Telfax: 01 48 24 02 20 ■ Mon-Fri 10:00-13:00/14:00-19:00 ■ Jean-Christophe Pouliquen ■ English spoken ■ Prices medium to high ■ Professional discount

Furniture and art objects of the XVIII, XIX and XX century.

MIRON ANTIQUITÉS
5 rue de Provence, 75009 Paris ■ Tel: 01 47 70 54 17 ■ Fax: 01 48 00 08 71 ■ Mon-Fri 9:00-13:00/14:00-19:30 ■ Mr.Miron ■ English, Italian and German spoken ■ Prices medium ■ Professional discount

XVIII and XIX century mahogany and gilded furniture.

BERNARD SELLEM
5 rue de Provence, 75009 Paris ■ Tel: 01 45 23 20 73 ■ Fax: 01 47 70 11 70 ■ Mon-Fri 10:00-18:00

Furniture, objects and antiques, especially Napoleon III.

👑 **ATELIER BRIGITTE MALAVOY**
5 rue de Provence, 75009 Paris ■ Tel: 01 42 46 15 25 ■ Fax: 01 40 22 61 90 ■ E-mail : atelier.malavoy@free.fr ■ Mon-Fri by appointment ■ English and Italian spoken ■ Prices medium to high

Restoration of paintings and ceramics for museums, dealers and collectors. She has established a school with courses in the restoration of paintings and works on paper, ceramics and gilding.

ANDRÉ GUEVENOUX
7 rue de Provence, 75009 Paris ■ Tel: 01 47 70 46 97 ■ Fax: 01 40 22 91 75 ■ Mon-Fri 10:00-18:00

Furniture of the XVIII century.

C. BLANC - G. PELLERIN
9 rue de Provence, 75009 Paris ■ Tel: 01 39 60 53 16 ■ Fax: 01 39 95 61 34 ■ Mon-Fri 10:00-19:00 by appointment ■ Cyril Blanc and Gérard Pellerin ■ Spanish and English spoken ■ Prices medium to high ■ Professional discount

XVIII and XIX century furniture and objects of decoration.

GALERIE ANNE
13 rue de Provence, 75009 Paris ■ Tel: 01 45 61 15 61 ■ Fax : 01 53 75 04 83 ■ Mon-Fri 10:00-18:00

XVIII and XIX century furniture and objets d'art.

ROXANNE RODRIGUEZ
16 rue de Provence, 75009 Paris ■ Telfax: 01 45 23 53 39 ■ E-mail: roxanne.rodriguez@wanadoo.fr ■ Mon-Fri 10:00-13:00/14:00-18:00 ■ English and Spanish spoken ■ Prices medium

Furniture and objets d'art of the second half of the XIX century.

JML ANTIQUITÉS
17 rue de Provence, 75009 Paris ■ Telfax: 01 44 79 05 61 ■ Mon-Fri 10:00-18:00

Paintings of various periods.

SOPHIE MARCELLIN
18 rue de Provence, 75009 Paris ■ Tel: 01 48 01 02 37 ■ Fax: 01 48 01 06 29 ■ Denis Ozanne ■ Mon-Fri 10:00-18:00 by appointment

XIX century drawings, paintings and curiosities.

JEAN-FRANÇOIS CHABOLLE

18 rue de Provence, 75009 Paris ■ Telfax: 01 42 47 18 95 ■ E-mail: gchabolle@club-internet.fr ■ Mon-Fri 10:00-18:30 ■ Marie-Christine Gaussen ■ English spoken ■ Prices medium to high ■ Professional discount

Furniture, objets d'art and paintings of the XVII, XVIII and XIX century.

ROSSINI ANTIQUITÉS

1 rue Rossini, 75009 Paris ■ Tel: 01 48 24 23 09 ■ Fax : 01 47 70 06 82 ■ Mon-Fri 9:30-17:00 ■ Patrick Choucroun ■ English spoken

Furniture and objets d'art.

J. F. COLLIN – J. DELBOS

3 rue Rossini, 75009 Paris ■ Tel: 01 47 70 28 57 ■ Fax: 01 42 46 57 92 ■ E-mail : collin.delbos@ifrance.com ■ Mon-Sat 9:30-18:30 ■ English spoken ■ Prices medium ■ Professional discount

Antique furniture, objets d'art and paintings.

CHRISTIAN PEINTRE

3 rue Rossini, 75009 Paris ■ Telfax: 01 47 70 69 35 ■ Mon-Fri 9:00-17:00 ■ English spoken ■ Prices medium ■ Professional discount

All periods of furniture, paintings, drawings and decorative objects.

👑 CAMILLE BURGI

3 rue Rossini, 75009 Paris ■ Tel: 01 48 24 22 53 ■ Fax: 01 47 70 25 99 ■ E-mail: camille.burgi@wanadoo.fr ■ Web: www.camille-burgi.com ■ Mon-Fri 10:00-18:00 ■ Camille Burgi speaks English ■ Prices very high ■ 10% professional discount ■ Amex

French objets d'art and furniture of the XVII and XVIII century and First Empire. One of the best. Expertise and long-term maintenance.

👑 GALERIE CANESSO

8 rue Rossini, 75009 Paris ■ Tel: 01 40 22 61 71 ■ Fax: 01 40 22 61 81 ■ E mail: mcanesso@canesso.com ■ Web: www.canesso.com ■ Mon-Fri by appointment ■ Maurizio Canesso ■ Italian and English spoken

Italian paintings from the Renaissance to the XVIII century.

LIBRAIRIE BURET

6 Passage Verdeau, 75009 Paris ■ Tel: 01 47 70 62 99 ■ Fax: 01 42 46 00 75 ■ Tue-Sat 12:30-18:30 ■ Roland Buret ■ English and Italian spoken ■ Prices medium to very high ■ Visa

Specialists in comic strips, original drawings and books, especially TinTin. Experts to Drouot.

GÉRARD GANET

10 Passage Verdeau, 75009 Paris ■ Tel: 01 42 46 31 15 ■ Fax: 01 40 22 97 63 ■ Cell: 06 08 51 38 67 ■ Mon-Sat 10:00-11:00/15:00-19:00 ■ English and Japanese spoken ■ Prices medium ■ Professional discount ■ Major credit cards

Old and rare books. Decorative engravings of the hunt, flowers, birds and marine. Old postcards, maps and city views.

JULIE MAILLARD

11 Passage Verdeau, 75009 Paris ■ Tel: 01 42 46 53 20 ■ Fax: 01 45 23 40 22 ■ Mon-Fri 13:00-19:00 ■ Some English spoken ■ Prices medium to high ■ Professional discount

Antique engravings from the late XV century to the late XIX century.

RUBY-CABINETS DES CURIEUX

12 Passage Verdeau, 75009 Paris ■ Tel: 01 44 83 09 57 ■ Mon-Fri 11:00-19:00, Sat 14:00-17:30 ■ Thierry Ruby, Samuel Vezinat ■ English spoken ■ Professional discount

Antique books from the XVI to XVIII century. European arms from the XVI to XIX century. Religious sculpture, especially heads of the Virgin and bishops. Archaeological objects from Egypt, 600 B.C. to 200 A.D.

GALERIE AMICORUM

19 Passage Verdeau, 75009 Paris ■ Tel: 01 48 01 02 41 ■ Mon-Fri 10:30-18:30, Sat 14:30-18:30 ■ Riva Rasimi, Fabrice Riva, Olivier Rasimi, André-Marie Ricoux ■ Some English spoken ■ Professional discount ■ Major credit cards

Old drawings and watercolours from the XVI to the early XX century.

LA FRANCE ANCIENNE

26 Passage Verdeau, 75009 Paris ■ Tel: 01 45 23 09 54 ■ Mon-Fri 11:00-19:00 ■ Some English spoken ■ Prices medium

Collectible early XX century postal cards.

ATELIER 29 DENISE BECHOUCHE

29 Passage Verdeau, 75009 Paris ■ Tel: 01 42 46 60 76 ■ Mon-Fri 10:00-19:00, Sat by appointment ■ English spoken ■ Professional discount ■ Major credit cards

Antique, antique style, 1930s and contemporary frames and framing.

Antique Collectibles

────── **ANTIQUE ARMS & MILITARY** ──────

♛ **AU PLAT D'ETAIN**
16 rue Guisarde, 75006 Paris ■ Tel: 01 43 54 32 06 ■ Fax: 01 43
26 84 92 ■ E-mail: platdetain.lucotte@wanadoo.fr ■ Tue-Sat
10:30-12:30/13:30-19:00 ■ Lynda Franceschi, Owner and Denise
Rochard ■ English spoken ■ Prices medium ■ Amex and Visa
**Specialty: "Soldier Lucotte" for whom they have founded a
collectors' club. Antique lead soldiers as well as modern fabrication. CBG, Mignot, Lucotte, Tradition and Marlborough.**

♛ **AUX ARMES D'ANTAN**
Village Suisse - 1 av Paul-Déroulède, 54 av de La Motte-Picquet,
75015 Paris ■ Tel: 01 47 83 71 42 ■ Fax: 01 47 34 40 99 ■ Thu-
Mon 10:30-13:00/14:30-19:00 ■ Maryse Raso ■ English spoken ■
Prices medium to high ■ Professional discount ■ Major credit cards
**Antique arms and military souvenirs of the XVII, XVIII and
XIX century. Qualified expert.**

♛ **AUX SOLDATS D'ANTAN**
32 bd Saint-Germain, 75005 Paris ■ Tel: 0146 33 61 60 ■ Fax:
0144 07 33 45 ■ E-mail: auxsoldats@noos.fr ■ Mon-Sat 14:30-
19:00 ■ Jean-Pierre Stella ■ English and Italian spoken ■ Prices
medium to high ■ Major credit cards
**Military decorations and arms of the XVI to the early XX cen-
tury. Large military paintings, orders of chivalry and historical souvenirs. Mr. Stella is a counsellor for public auctions.**

♛ **AUX SOLDATS D'ANTAN**
67 quai de la Tournelle, 75005 Paris ■ Tel: 01 46 33 40 50 ■ Fax:
01 44 07 33 45 ■ E-mail : auxsoldats@noos.fr ■ Mon-Sat 10:30-
12:00/14:00-19:00 ■ Jean-Pierre Stella ■ Prices medium to high
■ Major credit cards
**Wonderful collection of lead soldiers. Small military paint-
ings and decorations. Restoration and maintenance of collections.**

CHARLES BOUCHE - GLOIRES DU PASSE
41 rue de Richelieu, 75001 Paris ■ Tel: 01 42 96 49 79 ■ Fax: 01
42 96 49 79 ■ E-mail: cbouche@club-internet.fr ■ Web:
www.franceantiq.fr/sna/bouche ■ Mon-Fri 10:30-12:30/14:30-
18:00 ■ German and some English spoken ■ Prices medium to
high ■ Professional discount
**Specialist in arms, armour and military collectibles of the
First Empire.**

BERNARD CROISSY

193 rue Armand Silvestre, 92400 Courbevoie ■ Tel: 01 47 88 46 09 ■ Fax: 01 47 88 60 40 ■ By appointment only ■ Some English spoken ■ Prices medium

XVIII and XIX century arms, elements of armour and military souvenirs.

♚ JEAN-CLAUDE DEY

8bis rue Schlumberger, 92430 Marnes-la-Coquette ■ Tel: 01 47 41 65 31 ■ Fax: 01 47 41 17 67 ■ E-mail: Jean-Claude.DEY @wanadoo.fr ■ Tue-Fri 14:00-19:30/Sat-Sun 11:00-12:00/14:00-19:00 and by appointment ■ Delphine Dey speaks English ■ 10% professional discount ■ Major credit cards

Exceptional collection, from all countries, from the XII to XX century: Antique arms, rifles, carbines, pistols, revolvers, cannons, daggers, sabers, swords, armour, uniforms, helmets, equipment. Historical memorabilia and objects, documents, paintings. Orders and decorations. Lead soldiers. Also restoration in their own atelier. Catalogues on request for the 50 auctions they hold anually all over France. Qualified expert.

GALERIE ROBERT BURAWOY

12 rue Le Regrattier, 75004 Paris ■ Tel: 01 43 54 67 36 ■ Fax: 01 40 46 92 29 ■ E-mail: rburawoy@club-internet.fr ■ Wed-Sat 14:00-19:00 ■ English spoken ■ Prices medium ■ Visa and Amex

Ancient Japanese arms and armour.

♚ L'AIGLE IMPÉRIAL (GALERIES DE SOUZY)

3 rue de Miromesnil, 75008 Paris ■ Tel: 01 42 65 27 33 ■ Fax: 01 42 65 90 97 ■ E-mail: info@desouzy.com ■ Web: www.desouzy.com ■ Mon-Sat 10:30-13:00/14:30-19:00 ■ Pierre de Souzy speaks English and Latin ■ Prices high ■ 10% professional discount

Antique arms, armour. Military and Napoleonic memorabilia, paintings and sculpture. Great collection.

LE CIMIER

38 rue Ginoux, 75015 Paris ■ Tel: 01 45 78 94 28 ■ Fax: 01 45 75 70 11 ■ E-mail: lecimier@aol.com ■ Web: www.lecimier.com ■ Tue-Sat 10:00-13:00/14:00-19:00 ■ Jacques Vuyet ■ English and Italian spoken ■ Prices high ■ Visa and MC

Historic military figurines from ancient times to 1918. Documentation on military uniforms. Figurines, unpainted and painted by artists.

LE POILU

18 rue Emile Duclaux, 75015 Paris ■ Tel: 01 43 06 77 32 ■ Mon-Sat 9:00-12:00/14:00-19:00 ■ Patrice Bouchery and Pierre Besnard ■ English and some Spanish spoken ■ Prices medium ■ Professional discount ■ Major credit cards

Military articles from 1870 to 1950: uniforms, insignia, decorations, wigs, equipment, documents. Catalogues available upon request.

POUSSIÈRES D'EMPIRES
33 rue Brezin, 75014 ■ Telfax: 01 45 42 42 06 ■ Tue-Sat 11:00-19:00 ■ Didier Bauland speaks some English ■ Prices medium ■ Professional discount ■ Visa

Historical military memorabilia, especially the French colonies and particularly French Indo-China. Regimental insignia, decorations and orders.

--- AUTOGRAPHS ---

TOMY ANKA
27 rue du Faubourg Montmartre, 75009 Paris ■ Tel: 01 47 70 45 72 ■ Fax: 01 47 70 18 71 ■ Mon-Fri 10:00-18:00 ■ English spoken

Old documents, autographs, coins, stamps and paintings.

ANTIQUAIRES DROUOT
21 rue Drouot, 75009 Paris ■ Tel: 01 47 70 20 18 ■ Fax: 01 47 70 32 50 ■ E-mail: infor@antiquaires-drouot.com

Specialists in old manuscripts, autographs, books and stamps. Experts in antique furniture, paintings and objets d'art.

♚ GALERIE FRÉDÉRIC CASTAING
13 rue Chapon, 75003 Paris ■ Tel: 01 42 74 69 09 ■ Fax: 01 42 74 00 89 ■ Tues-Fri 10:00-12:00/14:30-18:00 ■ Frédéric Castaing speaks English ■ Prices high ■ 10% professional discount

Letters, manuscripts, musical scores, historic documents, from Francois I to Francois Mitterrand, including Chopin, Marie-Antoinette, Voltaire, Monet, Freud, Victor Hugo, etc. Well worth a visit. Mr. Castaing is an expert and member of SNCAO and SLAM.

--- AUTOMOBILES ---

L'ORANGERIE MODERNE
33 rue de l'Orangerie, 78000 Versailles ■ Tel: 01 39 50 28 74 ■ Fax: 01 33 02 15 02 ■ Tue, Fri, Sat 14:30-19:30 and by appointment ■ English spoken ■ Prices high to very high ■ 10% professional discount

Miniature automobiles 1/43 scale. Specialist in Bugatti and Ferrari. Antique toys.

🗳 LYDIA BICAL

31 rue de Chartres, 92200 Neuilly ■ Telfax: 01 46 24 14 30 ■ Tue-Sat 15:00-19:30 ■ German and English spoken ■ Prices medium to high ■ Professional discount

Beautiful collection of canes, Napoleonic souvenirs and lead soldiers (Luçotte, CBG, Mignot, Vertuni, MIM). Figurines: Heinrichsen, all finely painted. Some decorative boxes and snuffboxes.

🗳 LAURENCE JANTZEN

Louvre des Antiquaires, 11 Allée Desmalter ■ Tel: 01 42 61 58 05 ■ Fax: 01 47 09 35 55 ■ E-mail: ijantzen@club-internet.fr ■ Web: www.antique-expo.com/jantzen ■ English and Italian spoken ■ Professional discount ■ Visa and Amex

XVII to XX century canes, both decorative and with special mechanisms. Objects of curiosity. Delivery to any part of the world in 24 to 48 hours.

🗳 GALERIE 34 – MGW SEGAS EXPERT

34 Passage Jouffroy, 75009 Paris ■ Tel: 01 47 70 89 65 ■ Fax: 01 48 00 08 24 ■ E-mail: mgwsegas@club-internet.fr ■ Web: www.canesegas.com ■ Mon-Sat 11:00-18:30 ■ Miguel and Gilbert Segas ■ English spoken ■ Professional discount ■ Major credit cards

An extraordinary collection of antique canes, mostly from the XIX century. One of the best collections anywhere. Expert.

———————— CLOCKS ————————

🗳 ANTIC-TAC

Louvre des Antiquaires, 1 Allée Boulle ■ Tel: 01 42 61 57 16 ■ Fax: 01 42 61 75 86 ■ E-mail : tomvicai@easynet.fr ■ By appointment ■ Thomas Vicai ■ English, German and Hungarian spoken ■ Major credit cards

One of the best collections of all types of antique clocks of the XVIII and XIX century. Restoration and expertise.

🗳 LA PENDULERIE

134 rue du Faubourg-Saint-Honoré, 75008 Paris ■ Tel: 01 45 61 44 55 ■ Fax: 01 45 61 44 54 ■ Mon 14:30-19:00, Tue-Sat 9:30-12:00/14:00-19:00 ■ Stèphane Gagnon ■ English spoken ■ Prices high ■ Professional discount ■ Major credit cards

Superb museum quality XVIII and XIX century clocks and decorative objects. Museum quality restoration. Mr. Gagnon will travel to the clock when necessary.

RAMPAL

11 rue Portalis, 75008 Paris ■ Tel: 01 45 22 17 25 ■ Fax: 01 45 22 09 72 ■ English spoken ■ Prices medium to high

One of the best-known dealers in antique clocks and timepieces.

COINS

JEAN VINCHON

77 rue de Richelieu, 75002 Paris ■ Tel: 01 42 97 50 00 ■ Fax: 01 42 86 06 03 ■ E-mail: vinchon@wanadoo.fr ■ Web: www.vinchon.com ■ Mon-Fri 9:00-18:00 ■ Jean and Françoise Berthelot-Vinchon speak English and Spanish

Coins from Croesus to the end of the Third Republic (1940).

ANNETTE VINCHON-GUYONNET

3 rue de la Bourse, 75002 Paris ■ Tel: 01 42 97 53 53 ■ Fax: 01 42 97 44 56 ■ E-mail: avinchon@club-internet.fr ■ Web: www.franceantiq.fr/ncp ■ Mon-Fri 9:00-18:00, Sat by appointment ■ Annette Vinchon-Guyonnet ■ English an Spanish spoken ■ Prices medium to high ■ Professional discount ■ Major credit cards

Collectible coins: gold coins from Louis XVI to the present. Books on coins and supplies for collectors. International reputation.

CROWNS AND DIADEMS

PRIVILÈGE

10 rue Demarquay, 75010 Paris ■ Tel: 01 40 05 12 43 ■ Fax: 01 40 35 03 76 ■ Mon-Sun: call ■ Stèphane Marant speaks English ■ Prices high ■ Professional discount

Producer, creator of crowns, tiaras and diadems in gold plated metal and 24 carat gold, crystal and jewels for collectors, museums, special events, beauty contests, weddings, special collection of Fabergé type eggs.

DOLLS AND DOLL HOUSES

♛ GALERIE COLOMBELLE

Louvre des Antiquaires, 14 Allée Boulle ■ Telfax: 01 42 61 57 34 ■ Agnès Chabanier ■ English and Spanish spoken ■ Professional discount ■ Visa

Dolls and their environment. Objects of charm, collectibles and miniatures. Expertise.

LA MAISON DE POUPÉE
40 rue de Vaugirard, 75006 Paris ■ Tel: 01 46 33 74 05 ■ Tue-Sat 14:30-19:00 and by appointment ■ Prices medium ■ Professional discount

Beautiful dolls for the collector. Restoration and expertise.

PAINS D'EPICES
23, 31, 33 Passage Jouffroy, 75009 Paris ■ Tel: 01 47 70 08 68 ■ Fax: 01 42 46 40 33 ■ Mon 10:00-19:00/Tue-Sat 12:30-19:00 ■ Francoise Bundermann, Dominique Chevry ■ English, Spanish and Portuguese spoken ■ Visa, MC

House of dolls and miniature vitrines. Accessories, toys and traditional games.

LES POUPÉES RETROUVÉES
16 rue Bremontier, 75017 Paris ■ Tel: 01 48 88 98 77 ■ Fax: 01 42 27 55 61 ■ Mon-Fri 14:00-19:00 ■ Arielle Ged speaks English ■ Prices reasonable ■ Professional discount

Antique dolls and toys of the XIX and early XX centuries, documents, books, small furniture. Restoration.

―――――――――――― **GAMES** ――――――――――――

AU COLLECTIONNEUR
15 rue Brey, 75017 Paris ■ Tel: 01 42 27 64 50 ■ Mon-Sat 11:00-14:30/16:00-19:00 ■ English spoken ■ Prices modest

Collectibles of all kinds: Stamps, money, bank notes, etc.

♛ LA TORTUE ELECTRIQUE
5 rue Frédéric-Sauton, 75005 Paris ■ Tel: 01 43 29 37 08 ■ Tue-Sat 14:00-19:00 ■ Georges Monnier speaks English ■ 20% professional discount

Antique games: chess, cards, magic, circus, mechanical banks.

GALERIE 13 - RUE JACOB
13 rue Jacob, 75006 Paris ■ Tel: 43 26 99 89 ■ Mon-Sat 14:30-19:00 ■ English spoken ■ Prices medium ■ Professional discount

Antique games: Chess, Backgammon, Mah Jong, others. Objects of curiosity.

MAGASIN LEDUC
9 rue Constance, 75018 Paris ■ Tel: 01 46 06 81 81 ■ Tue-Fri 16:00-19:30/Sat 11:00-13:00/16:00-19:30/Sun 11:00-13:00 ■ English spoken ■ Prices medium ■ 15% professional discount

Games and antique toys.

GALERIE MICHEL CACHOUX
16 rue Guénégaud, 75006 Paris ■ Tel: 01 43 54 52 15 ■ Fax: 01 46 33 48 69 ■ Tue-Sat 11:00-19:30 ■ Nicole Ruff speaks English ■ Prices medium ■ 10 to 20% professional discount

Minerals, fossils, spheres.

JEWELLERY AND SILVER

I

JEAN-LUC MARTIN DU DAFFOY
334 rue Saint-Honoré, 75001 Paris ■ Tel: 01 42 60 44 75/01 42 60 45 36 ■ Fax: 01 40 15 08 83 ■ Mon-Sat 10:00-18:30 ■ English spoken ■ Professional discount ■ Major credit cards

Antique silver and antique jewellery.

AU VIEUX PARIS
4 rue de la Paix 75002 Paris ■ Tel: 01 42 61 00 89 ■ Fax: 01 42 61 38 65 ■ Mon 14 :00-18 :00, Tue-Sat 10 :15-18 :00 ■ English spoken ■ Visa

Antique silver and jewellery.

(SEE ALSO: LE LOUVRE DES ANTIQUAIRES)

LUGGAGE

LE MONDE DU VOYAGE
Marché aux Puces, Marché Serpette, Allée 2, Stand 15 ■ Tel: 01 40 12 64 03 ■ Fax: 01 49 41 93 19 ■ E-mail: hzisul@club-inter-net.fr ■ Mme Helen Zisul ■ English spoken ■ Professional discount ■ Major credit cards

Antique vintage luggage. Excellent collection of Louis Vuitton and Hermès. Pocketbooks by Hermès and Chanel jewellery. Restoration miracles. They will repair what Vuitton will not.

MARINE & SCIENCE

ETS DIEUTEGARD
1 rue Furstemberg, 75006 Paris ■ Tel: 01 43 29 79 51 ■ Fax: 01 43 87 56 30 ■ Mon-Sun 11:00-13:00/14:00-19:00 ■ Jean-Pierre Dieutegard ■ Professional discount ■ Major credit cards

Marine and scientific curiosities.

LA ROSE DES VENTS
25 rue de Beaune, 75007 Paris ■ Tel: 01 42 60 11 17 ■ Fax: 01 42 60 34 17 ■ Messrs. B. and J.Y. Petitcollot ■ Tue-Sat 10:00-19:00

Marine curiosities and art objects.

♕ MARINE D'AUTREFOIS
80 av des Ternes, 75017 Paris ■ Tel: 01 45 74 23 97 ■ Fax: 01 45 74 61 70 ■ Tue-Sat 10:00-13:00/14:00-19:00 ■ Gildas de Kerdrel speaks English ■ Prices medium to high

Models of famous sailing yachts. America's cup yachts of the 1930s to the 1980s. Antique models of yachts and steam vessels. Antique navigational instruments. Antique marine equipment and ship fittings. Marine paintings and old marine photographs. Ship builders' models. Models of ships and yachts on order. Marvellous.

BERTRAND THIEBAUT
4 av de Villiers, 75017 Paris ■ Tel: 01 42 94 25 71 ■ Fax: 01 40 10 13 08 ■ Every day 9:00-18:00 ■ English spoken

Old scientific instruments, marine curiosities, special furniture, very unusual objects. Specialty: history of sciences.

♕ PHILIPPE WILMART
37 av de la Grande-Armée, 75116 Paris ■ Tel: 01 45 00 65 16 ■ Fax: 01 46 04 22 41 ■ Mon-Fri 10:00-18:00 ■ English spoken ■ Prices medium to high ■ Professional discount

Marine objects, ship models, books, boat pictures, navigational instruments, XVIII, XIX century French naval arms, curiosities, physical sciences. Qualified expert.

MINIATURES

ZÉRO FIGURE
38 rue de Seine, 75006 Paris ■ Tel: 01 43 26 85 91 ■ Mon-Sat: afternoons ■ English spoken ■ Prices medium

1900-1930 art objects, Chinese porcelain, Bohemian crystal, Opaline: all in miniature. Expert in antique miniatures.

MUSICAL INSTRUMENTS

ANDRÉ BISSONET
6 rue du Pas-de-la-Mule, 75003 Paris ■ Tel: 01 48 87 20 15 ■ Mon-Sat 14:00-19:00

Antique European musical instruments.

ORPHÉE

8 rue du Pont-Louis-Philippe, 75004 Paris ■ Telfax: 01 42 72 68 42 ■ Mon-Sat 13:30-19:30 ■ English spoken ■ Prices medium ■ 20% professional discount

Antique musical instruments.

PERFUME AND SCENT BOTTLES

BEAUTÉ DIVINE

40 rue Saint-Sulpice, 75006 Paris ■ Tel: 01 43 26 25 31 ■ Mon 14:00-19:99/Tue-Sat 10:00-13:00/14:00-19:00 ■ English spoken ■ Prices medium high ■ 10% professional discount

Specialty: perfume flacons, art deco objects, small furniture in the spirit of 1900 to 1930. Old bathroom accessories.

TOYS AND TRAINS

AU PETIT MAYET

10 rue Mayet, 75006 Paris ■ Tel: 01 45 67 68 29 ■ Mon-Sat 14:00-19:00 ■ Philippe Lepage speaks English ■ Prices medium to high

Antique toys, automated toys.

FREDERIC MARCHAND

6 rue de Montfaucon, 75006 Paris ■ Tel: 01 43 54 32 82 ■ Fax: 01 44 07 04 82 ■ Tue-Sat 14:00-19:00 ■ English spoken ■ Prices medium ■ Professional discount

Antique toys and other collectibles, including Art Deco and Art Nouveau bisquit, perfume flacons.

PAIN D'ÉPICES

29-31-33 passage Jouffroy, 75009 Paris ■ Tel: 01 47 70 08 68 ■ Fax: 01 42 46 40 33 ■ Mon 12:30-19:00, Tue-Sat 10:00-19:00 ■ Françoise Bundermann, Dominique Chevry ■ English, Spanish and Portuguese spoken ■ Prices medium ■ Visa, MC

Dolls' houses and glass cabinets; miniature furniture, accessories, tools and kits. Traditional games and toys. Catalogue for sale by correspondence.

TOILE D'ARAIGNÉE

8 rue Mandar, 75002 Paris ■ Tel: 01 40 28 47 48 ■ Mon-Sat 11:00-19:30 ■ Prices medium ■ 10 to 15% professional discount

Antique toys in tôle, old publicity items, enamel signs, presentation cases, items of curiosity 1950-1960.

DAVID ET SES FILLES
27 rue Bonaparte, 75006 Paris ■ Tel: 01 43 26 81 40 ■ Tue-Sat 10:30-18:30 ■ Prices medium ■ 10% professional discount

Antique silver, boxes and art objects.

NOSTALGIE BROCANTE
21 rue des Carmes, 75005 Paris ■ Tel: 01 46 34 59 03 ■ Tue-Fri 13:00-19:00 ■ English spoken ■ Prices medium ■ 20% professional discount

Old phonographs, cameras and stereoscopes, dolls, celluloids and restoration of these objects.

Antiquities
Antiquités

♔ ARCHÉOLOGIE
40 rue du Bac, 75007 Paris ■ Tel: 01 45 48 61 60 ■ Fax: 01 45 48 75 25 ■ Mon 14:00-19:00, Tue-Sat 11:00-12:30/14:00-19:00 ■ English spoken ■ Prices high ■ 10% professional discount

Greek terracotta, Etruscan and Roman bronze, antique marbles, antique jewellery.

BL ANTIQUITÉS
8 rue des Saints-Pères, 75007 Paris ■ Tel: 06 84 78 86 43 ■ Fax: 01 42 96 60 60 ■ E-mail: kingdanieli@cybercable.fr ■ Mon 14:00-19:30, Tue-Sun 9:30-19:30 ■ Dan Danieli speaks English, Russian, Italian, German and Spanish ■ Professional discount

Objects of art, old paintings along with some modern paintings.

♔ GALERIE BLONDEEL-DEROYAN
11 rue de Lille, 75007 Paris ■ Tel: 01 49 27 96 22 ■ Fax: 01 49 27 96 18 ■ E-mail galerie@galerie-blondeel-deroyan.fr ■ Web: www.galerie-blondeel-deroyan.fr ■ Mon 14:30-18:30, Tue-Sat 10:30-13:00/14:30-18:30 ■ English spoken ■ Amex

XVI to XVIII century tapestries and carpets. Archaeology.

♛ CHRISTIAN DEYDIER - ORIENTAL BRONZES LTD

21 rue du Bac, 75007 Paris ■ Tel: 01 40 20 97 34 ■ Fax: 01 40 20 97 39 ■ E-mail: stbonnet@imaginet.fr ■ Web: www.www.francean-tiq.fr/ana/deydier ■ Tue-Sat 10:00-12:30/14:00-18:30 ■ Eulalie Steens ■ English, Chinese and German spoken

Art of the Far East and Chinese archaeology from 1500 B.C. to the XIV century: bronzes, terracotta, sculpture, gold and silver. Catalogues of exhibitions. Catalogues of exhibitions available.

GALERIE L'ÉTOILE-D'ISHTAR

11 rue des Beaux-Arts, 75006 Paris ■ Tel: 01 46 33 83 55 ■ Fax: 01 43 29 86 25 ■ E-mail: letoile@club-internet.fr ■ Tue-Sat 11:00-13:00/14:30-19:15 ■ Didier Wormser speaks English ■ Visa accepted

Ancient Egyptian and Near Eastern Art.

GALERIE GILGAMESH

9 rue de Verneuil, 75007 Paris ■ Telfax: 01 42 61 37 66 ■ Tue-Sat 12:30-19:15, mornings by appointment ■ Daniel Lebeurrier ■ English and Spanish spoken ■ Professional discount

Archaeology: Mediterranean and Oriental, some Iranian. Mr. Lebeurrier is preparing his doctoral thesis on the funerary customs of the Iranian Iron Age. The place is fascinating, especially if you love the history of the ancients. Expertise for auctions; qualified expert in archaeology.

♛ GALERIE JEAN-LUC MÉCHICHE

182 rue du Faubourg-Saint-Honoré, 75008 Paris ■ Tel: 01 45 63 20 11 ■ Fax: 01 42 25 91 34 ■ Tue-Sat 10:00-13:00/14:30-19:00 ■ Claire Laroquette speaks English ■ Prices high ■ Professional discount

XVIII and XIX century French furniture, contemporary paintings, archaeological objects from China. Contemporary furniture in limited edition on order.

GALERIE SAMARCANDE

13 rue des Saints-Pères, 75006 Paris ■ Tel: 01 42 60 83 17 ■ Fax: 01 42 61 41 64 ■ E- mail: gal.samarcande@wanadoo.fr ■ Joseph Uzan ■ English, Italian and Arabic spoken ■ Prices medium to high ■ Professional discount ■ Amex, Visa

Archaeological art and objects from Rome, Greece, Egypt and Mesopotamia. Expert.

GALERIE URAEUS

24 rue de Seine, 75006 Paris ■ Tel: 01 43 26 91 31 ■ Tue-Sat 10:00-19:00 ■ A. Matheos

Archaeological objects.

GUDEA GALLERY
22 rue Bonaparte, 75006 Paris ■ Tel: 01 46 33 78 62 ■ Fax: 01 46 33 42 30 ■ Tue-Sat 11:00-12:30/13:30-19:00 ■ Marie-Ange Barbet speaks English ■ Prices medium to high ■ 20% professional discount

Objects of antiquity, archaeology: Sumerian, Egyptian, Greek, Roman. Expert in the archaeology of the Mediterranean Basin.

Asian Antiques and Art
Antiquités et Art d'Asie

♛ ASIE ANTIQUE
232 bd Saint Germain, 75007 Paris ■ Tel: 01 45 48 68 88 ■ Fax: 01 45 48 76 77 ■ Tue-Sat 15:00-19:00 ■ Lee Thanapoomikul speaks English ■ Prices medium ■ Professional discount

Wonderful sculpture and furniture of China and Japan. Statuary, bas reliefs, sculptured heads of Khmer, Thailand and Burma.

AU VIEUX CHINOIS
1 rue d'Anjou, 75008 Paris ■ Tel: 01 42 65 23 83 ■ Fax: 01 42 68 09 63 ■ E-mail: auvieuxchinois@aol.com ■ Mon-Sat 10:30-13:00/13:30-18:30 ■ Marc Higonnet ■ English spoken ■ Prices medium to high ■ Professional discount ■ Visa, Amex

XVIII and XIX century porcelain, bronzes, ivory and jade mainly from China and Japan.

D. MILANO BACSTREET
1 rue du Bac, 75007 Paris ■ Tel: 01 42 61 24 20 ■ Fax: 01 49 27 90 85 ■ Mon 14:00-19:00/Tue-Sat 11:00-19:00 ■ Daniel Milano speaks English ■ Prices medium to high ■ 15 to 20% professional discount ■ Major credit cards

Far Eastern furniture, art objects, archaeology, porcelain, bronze, ivory from China, Japan, India, Burma and Siam. Antique and Modern jewellery. Expert CECOA and expert in gemology.

♛ JACQUES BARRÈRE
36 rue Mazarine, 75006 Paris ■ Tel: 01 43 26 57 61 ■ Fax: 01 46 34 02 83 ■ E-mail: Barrere@aol.com ■ Tue-Sat 14:00-19:30, mornings and Saturday by appointment ■ Jacques and Marie Barrère ■ English and Spanish spoken ■ Prices high to very high ■ Professional discount

Asian art, especially from China. Archaeological objects, sculpture and decorative art. Excellent quality and charming people.

☗ COMPAGNIE DE LA CHINE ET DES INDES

39 av Friedland, 75008 Paris ■ Tel: 01 42 89 05 45 ■ Fax: 01 42 89 11 07 ■ E-mail: chineinde@compuserve.com ■ Mon-Sat 10:00-12:00/14:00-18:30 ■ Mike Winter-Rousset ■ English spoken ■ Prices medium to very high ■ Professional discount

Antiques of the Far East: China, Japan, Tibet, Nepal, India, Khmer, Cambodia. Furniture, art objects, porcelain, sculpture, paintings, Japanese and Chinese screens, bronzes of China, Nepal and Tibet. Pottery: Han to Tong. Chinese porcelain. 5,000 B.C. to XVIII century.

☗ CHRISTIAN DEYDIER - ORIENTAL BRONZES LTD

21 rue du Bac, 75007 Paris ■ Tel: 01 40 20 97 34 ■ Fax: 01 40 20 97 39 ■ E-mail: stbonnet@imaginet.fr ■ Web: www.www.franceantiq.fr/ana/deydier ■ Tue-Sat 10:00-12:30/14:00-18:30 ■ Eulalie Steens ■ English, Chinese and German spoken

Extraordinary collection of art of the Far East and Chinese archaeology from 1500 B.C. to the XIV century: bronzes, terracotta, sculpture, gold and silver. Catalogues of exhibitions available.

☗ GALERIE BERNARD CAPTIER

10 rue de Beaune, 75007 Paris ■ Tel: 01 42 61 81 41 ■ Fax: 01 47 49 04 25 ■ and 25 rue de Verneuil, 75007 Paris ■ Tel: 01 42 61 0057 ■ same Fax ■ Mon 14:30-19:00/Tue-Sat 10:30-19:00 ■ Bernard and Sylvie Captier ■ English spoken ■ Prices medium ■ Professional discount ■ Amex, Visa

XVIII and XIX furniture, paintings, screens and decorative objects from China and Japan.

☗ GALERIE DES LAQUES

74 rue du Cherche-Midi, 75006 Paris ■ Tel: 01 45 48 88 82 ■ Fax: 01 45 44 31 81 ■ Mon-Sat 10:30-12:30/14:00-19:00 and by appointment ■ J.C. Hureau ■ English and Italian spoken ■ Prices high ■ Professional discount

XVIII century furniture and objects. Chinese and Japanese lacquer and European lacquered furniture.

GALERIE ROGER DUCHANGE

12 rue des Saints-Pères, 75007 Paris ■ Tel: 01 42 60 89 55 ■ Fax : 01 49 27 91 27 ■ Mon 14:00-18:30/Tue-Sat 10:00-12:00/14:00-18:30 ■ English spoken

Chinese and Japanese art objects, porcelain, bronze, semi-precious stones, paintings, furniture, ivories.

GALERIE KERVORKIAN

21 quai Malaquais, 75006 Paris ■ Tel: 01 42 60 72 91 ■ Fax: 01 42 61 01 52 ■ Mon-Sat 10:30-12:30/14:30-19:00 ■ English and Spanish spoken ■ Prices medium

Antiques of the Near and Middle East, archaeological objects, Islamic Art, Persian and Indian miniatures.

GALERIE J. & H. LUHL

19 quai Malaquais, 75006 Paris ■ Tel: 01 42 60 76 97 ■ Fax: 01 42 60 20 19 ■ E-mail: galerieluhl@yahoo.fr ■ Web: www.antique-expo ■ Tue-Sat 14:00-19:00 ■ English, German, Dutch, Italian and Spanish spoken ■ Prices medium to high ■ Professional discount ■ Major credit cards

Japanese estampes, paintings and books.

♛ GALERIE JEAN SOUSTIEL

146 bd Haussmann, 75008 Paris ■ Tel: 01 45 62 27 76 ■ Fax: 01 45 63 44 63 ■ Mon-Fri 10:00-12:00/14:00-18:00 ■ E-mail: galerie@soustiel.com ■ English spoken ■ Prices medium to high ■ Professional discount

Islamic art from North Africa, Egypt, Syria, Turkey, Iran, India. Ceramics, miniatures, textiles.

GENJI L'ART D'EXTREME ORIENT

68 rue Mademoiselle, 75015 Paris ■ Telfax: 01 44 49 99 84 ■ By appointment only ■ Annette Landau ■ English and German spoken

Japanese and Chinese art.

JEAN-MICHEL GUENEAU

22 rue de Beaune, 75007 Paris ■ Telfax: 01 42 61 49 94 ■ Mon-Fri 10:30-12:30/14:00-19:00 ■ English spoken ■ Prices medium ■ 10% professional discount

Specialist in Islamic Arms. Antiques, objects, French XVII and XVIII century paintings and paintings from the Middle East.

BERNARD LE DAUPHIN

87 av de Villiers, 75017 Paris ■ Tel: 01 40 54 80 91 ■ Fax: 01 42 27 14 93 ■ Cell: 06 07 51 15 30 ■ By appointment ■ English spoken ■ Prices high ■ Professional discount

Japanese art objects, especially arms and armour.

C. T. LOO & CIE

48 rue de Courcelles, 75008 Paris ■ Tel: 01 45 62 53 15 ■ Fax: 01 45 62 07 02 ■ E-mail: c.t.loo.et.cie@wanadoo.fr ■ Tue-Fri 10:30-12:30/14:30-18:30 and by appointment ■ Michel Dubosc ■ English spoken ■ Prices high ■ Professional discount

High-quality Oriental furniture, art objects and screens from China. Objects from Korea, India and Japan. All in the beautiful Chinese House built by C.T. Loo.

PHILIPPE AND CLAUDE MAGLOIRE
13 place des Vosges, 75004 Paris ■ Telfax: 01 42 74 40 67 ■ Tue-Sat 13:00-18:00 ■ English spoken ■ Prices high ■ 20% professional discount
Specialty: archaeology and art of the Orient.

YVONNE MOREAU-GOBARD
5 rue des Saints-Pères, 75006 Paris ■ Tel: 01 42 60 88 25 ■ Fax 01 42 60 08 55 ■ E-mail: yvonne.moreau@wanadoo.fr ■ Mon-Sat 10:00-12:30/14:00-19:00 ■ English spoken ■ Prices high ■ 10% professional discount
Asian archaeological objects in stone, bronze, wood, especially Southeast Asia and the Himalayas.

MYRNA MYERS
11 rue de Beaune, 75007 Paris ■ Tel: 01 42 61 11 08 ■ Fax: 01 30 82 49 17 ■ Tue-Sat 14:30-18:30 ■ English spoken ■ Prices medium
Far Eastern art, ceramics and textiles.

BERNARD ROUSSEAU
2 rue de Provence, 75009 Paris ■ Tel: 01 45 23 52 65 ■ By appointment ■ English spoken ■ Prices medium
Specialty: graphic arts of Japan from the XVI to the XIX century. Estampes, paintings, illustrated books.

TANAKAYA ARTS DU JAPON
4 rue Saint-Sulpice, 75006 Paris ■ Telfax: 01 43 25 72 91 ■ E-mail : tanakaya@aol.com ■ website : www.tanakaya.fr ■ Tue-Sat 13:00-19:00 ■ Prices medium ■ Professional discount
Japanese original estampes and antiques. Paintings, bronzes, lacquer, porcelain, stoneware.

VALÉRIE LEVESQUE
3 rue des Saint-Pères, 75006 Paris ■ Tel: 01 42 60 56 57 ■ Fax: 01 45 48 29 30 ■ Mon-Sat 14:30-19:00 ■ English spoken ■ Prices high ■ Professional discount ■ Visa, MC
Art of China and Japan.

ARCHITECTURAL ELEMENTS

When you want the "real thing", whether it is an entire panelled room from a XVII century chateau, a fireplace from an elegant XVIII century Paris townhouse or splendid garden ornaments from a royal garden, these are the places to visit. We suggest you call, fax or e-mail in advance and give them an idea of what you are looking for. There are lots of choices, but remember, patience is always rewarded.

♛ ORIGINES
14 Porte d'Epernon/Maulette, 78550 Houdan ■ Tel: 01 30 88 15 15 ■ Fax: 01 30 88 11 80 ■ E-mail: info@origines-fr ■ Web: www.origines-fr ■ Mon-Fri 9:00-12:00/14:00-18:00/Sat 10:00-12:00/15:00-18:00/Sun 15:00-18:00 ■ English spoken by Samuel Roger ■ Prices medium to high ■ Major credit cards

A remarkable collection of architectural items including fireplaces of all styles and periods in stone, marble, wood. Flooring in tile, terracotta, stone, parquet. Wood panelling, doors, windows, grilles, garden ornaments. All architectural elements interior and exterior of all styles and periods. Catalogues available. Also transport services and installations.

ETS. TOURY
171 rue de Bezons, 78420 Carrières-sur-Seine ■ Tel: 01 39 14 09 00 ■ Fax: 01 39 14 57 57 ■ Every day by appointment ■ Philippe Toury speaks English ■ Prices medium to high ■ Professional discount

Large choice of wood panelling, doors, parquet, beams, wrought iron grilles and balconies, fireplaces, paving stones, tiles, staircases, ornamental stone, garden furniture and more from demolitions.

♛ MARC MAISON
■ 15 rue Jules-Vallès ■ Tel: 01 40 12 52 28■ Fax: 01 40 12 26 47 ■ E-mail: marcmaison@easynet.fr ■ Web: www.marcmaison.com ■ English spoken ■ Prices medium to high ■ Professional discount

A large selection of architectural elements for the exterior and interior: all in stock. Fountains, grilles and gates in wrought iron, flooring, paneling, doors, gates, marble, lead statuary, fireplaces and elements for the garden. Also restorations.

Cork
Liège

VII

AU LIEGEUR (J. PONTNEAU)
17 av de la Motte-Piquet, 75007 Paris ■ Tel: 01 47 05 53 10 ■
Fax: 01 47 53 79 29 ■ Tue-Fri 9:00-12:30/14:00-19:00 ■ English
spoken ■ Prices medium ■ Professional discount

Cork materials for walls, floors, ceilings as well as gift items in cork.

XIV

AU CHÊNE LIEGE
74 bd du Montparnasse, 75014 Paris ■ Tel: 01 43 22 02 15 ■
Fax: 01 42 79 81 23 ■ Tue-Sat 9:30-12:30/13:45-18:30 ■ Prices
medium ■ Professional discount

The cork source in Paris. Cork fabric for wall upholstery and fashion (sold by the yard). Cork tiles for walls, floors and ceilings. Corks for wine, floor mats, table mats.

XV

PORPHYRE
39 rue Santos Dumont, 75015 Paris ■ Tel: 01 45 31 13 36 ■ Fax:
01 45 31 35 12

Raw cork, cork for artists and cork for decoration.

Doors and Windows
Fenêtres at porte-fenêtres

ANJOU VITRERIE MIROITERIE
57 rue d'Anjou, 75008 Paris ■ Tel: 01 42 65 59 29 ■ Fax: 01 42
65 21 43 ■ Mon-Fri 8:30-12:30/13:30-18:30 ■ Robert Touzard ■
Professional discount

Double-glazed windows and French doors in PVC. Glass and mirror for all uses.

IRIS FENÊTRES

41 rue Douy Delcupe, 93100 Montreuil ■ Tel: 01 41 72 06 20 ■ Fax: 01 41 72 06 29 ■ Web: www.iris-fenetres.com ■ Louis Sandzer and Americo Soares ■ English, Spanish and Portuguese spoken ■ Professional discount ■ Major credit cards

Double-glazed windows and French doors in PVC, wood and aluminium; rolling metal shutters and doors.

ISO FRANCE FENÊTRES

111 rue La Fayette, 75010 Paris ■ Tel: 01 42 85 03 16 ■ Fax: 01 48 78 14 01 ■ 158 av du Maine, 75014 Paris ■ Tel: 01 40 64 00 01 ■ Fax: 01 43 27 11 74 ■ Mon-Fri 9:30-12:00/14:00-19:30, Sat by appointment ■ Xavier Lecomte ■ Professional discount ■ Major credit cards

Specialists in the replacement of windows and doors with double-glazed and sound-proofed models, in PVC, wood or aluminium. High-security entry doors, pocket doors; exterior shutters and blinds.

ROUSSEL

177 bd Haussmann, 75008 Paris ■ Tel: 01 43 59 33 14 ■ Fax: 01 42 89 33 15 ■ Web: www.roussel-stores.fr ■ Mon-Fri 9:00-18:00, Sat 10:00-13:00/14:00-18:30 ■ Gilles Roussel ■ English spoken ■ Professional discount ■ Visa

Renovation specialists. Replacement of existing windows and doors with double glazing, thermal and sound insulation. Rolling metal shutters, grilles and regular shutters. Exterior blinds and interior blinds made in a variety of fabrics; Venetian blinds in wood. Residential work as well as restaurants and hotels.

Marble and Stone
Marbre et pierre

JEAN DARTIGUES

20 rue de la Félicité, 75017 Paris ■ Tel: 01 42 27 52 36 ■ Fax: 01 47 64 10 64 ■ E-mail: Dartigues.marbres@wanadoo.fr ■ Mon-Fri 9:30-12:00/14:30-18:30/ Sat by appointment ■ Jean Dartigues (Artisan) speaks English ■ Prices high ■ 15% professional discount

Tiling, installations, restoration, construction and original creations in marble, stone, onyx and granite. Mosaics, bathrooms, furniture and decorative objects.

BONNEL INTERNATIONAL
3 rue de l'Arrivée, 75015 Paris ■ Tel: 01 43 35 01 22 ■ Fax: 01 40
47 61 10 ■ E-mail: bonnel@club-internet.fr ■ Mon-Fri 9:00-17:00 ■
English spoken ■ Prices medium to high ■ Professional discount

Suppliers of limestone, marble and granite for construction, facings and paving. Specialists in restoration of historical monuments. (Qualification #15).

MADR
22 av Franklin-Roosevelt, 94300 Vincennes ■ Tel: 01 43 98 03 00
■ Fax: 01 43 08 16 62 ■ Mon-Fri 8:00-12:00/13:00-17:30 ■ English spoken ■ Prices medium ■ Professional discount

Specialist in marble. Restoration of marble and sculptures in marble and other stone. Mounting of bronzes on marble bases. Installation of bathrooms.

MARCO POLO CREATION
21 rue de Belfort, 92400 Courbevoie-Paris La Défense ■ Tel: 01
47 89 16 25 ■ Fax: 01 46 67 74 83 ■ Mon-Fri 10:00-13:00/14:30-
18:30/Closed Wednesday ■ English spoken ■ Prices high to very
high ■ 15% professional discount

High-quality custom installation of marble, horizontal and vertical, natural stone and granite.

NHT-CGPM
CARRELAGE-GRANIT-PIERRE-MARBRE
9 bis rue de la Gare, 92130 Issy-les-Moulineaux ■ Tel: 01 46 42
83 45 ■ Mon-Fri 7:30-19:30 ■ Luigi Sanna speaks English ■
Prices medium ■ Professional discount

Supply and installation of natural stone, granite and marble. High-quality tiles.

J. POULAIN ET FILS
7-11 bd Ménilmontant, 75011 Paris ■ Tel: 01 43 79 04 32 ■ Fax:
01 43 79 22 32 ■ Mon-Fri 8:30-12:30/13:30-17:30 ■ Prices medium to high ■ Professional discount

Installation and renovation of marble, stone and granite.Vertical and horizontal interior installations. Bathrooms, stairs and all decorative applications. Flagstones.

SERVICE PARISIEN DE PONÇAGE
121 rue Véron, 94149 Alfortville ■ Tel: 01 43 75 13 14 ■ Fax: 01
49 77 04 14 ■ E-mail: jean.pierre.goden@wanadoo.fr ■ Mon-Fri

8:00-12:00/13:30-19:00 ■ English spoken ■ Prices medium ■ 10% professional discount

Sanding and crystallization of marble, stone and granite. Maintenance and sale of products for maintenance.

SOLS MAJEURS
12 rue Jacques-Coeur, 75004 Paris ■ Tel: 01 42 71 74 28 ■ Fax: 01 42 71 74 29 ■ Mon-Fri 9:30-18:30/Sat 14:00-17:30 ■ Elizabeth Bascher ■ Spanish and English spoken ■ Prices medium ■ Professional discount

Marble and mosaics. Burgundy stone floors. Paving in aged marble and limestone, slate, terracotta. Wrought iron.

TECHNIQUE ET MATERIAUX DE BATIMENT
81 rue Victor-Hugo, 92400 Courbevoie ■ Tel: 01 47 88 71 91 ■ Mon-Fri 9:00-19:00 ■ Elias Chammas speaks English ■ Prices medium to high ■ Professional discount

Marble, stone and granite for construction.

UNIVERS DU MARBRE
15 Passage Anne Popincourt, 75011 Paris ■ Tel: 01 43 57 08 70 ■ Fax: 01 43 57 07 19 ■ Tue-Sat 09:00-20:00 ■ Frank Neyraud ■ Italian spoken

Supply and installation of marble, stone and granite. Plans for kitchens, bathrooms, staircases, façades.

Parquet

👑 D. FILE
230 rue de Faubourg-Saint-Honoré, 75008 Paris ■ Tel: 01 53 96 95 95 ■ Fax: 01 53 96 95 91 ■ E-mail: ldfile@club-internet.fr ■ Mon-Sat 08:00-19:00 ■ François Goudard, Laurent Herpin ■ English, Spanish and German spoken ■ Professional discount ■ Major credit cards

Carpet, rug and wood floor supplier. Custom product development, installation and maintenance. Guide provided on request. Clients include: Bellagio Hotel, Las Vegas, Salle Pleyel, Euro-Disney, Holiday Inns and The Elysée Palace in Paris.

EURO-PARQUET

217 rue Béranger, 92700 Colombes ■ Tel: 01 47 85 73 97 ■ Fax: 01 47 85 66 92 ■ Mon-Fri 9:00-12:00/14:00-18:00 ■ Prices medium ■ Professional discount

Specialist in flooring. All types of parquet, new and renovated. Marble, stone and granite flooring as well as flagstones and tiles.

GEROCLAIR

21 rue Henri Duvernois, 75020 Paris ■ Tel: 01 40 30 21 46 ■ Fax: 01 40 30 23 74 ■ E-mail: contact@geroclair.fr ■ Web: www.geroclair.fr ■ Mon-Fri 09:00-12:00/14:00-19:00 ■ Bertrand Géraud speaks English and German ■ Prices medium ■ Professional discount ■ Visa, MC

Wood flooring, Versailles style, in oak, maple, ash, teak, and other. Laminated pre-finished floors, acrylic impregnated floors, solid hardwood floors, supplies of teak, portable floors. Technical assistance and world-wide delivery.

PARQUETS GAILLARD

57 bld Martial-Valin, 75015 Paris ■ Tel: 01 40 60 07 60 ■ Fax: 01 40 60 09 72 ■ E-mail: IG@parquets-gaillard.com ■ Web: www.parquets-gaillard.com ■ Mon-Sat 08:30-12:00/13:00-19:00 ■ Ivan Gaillard ■ English spoken ■ Major credit cards

Supply and installation of floating parquet floors. Traditional glued floors. Renovation.

ROCS

26 rue Paul-Vaillant-Couturier, 92000 Nanterre ■ Tel: 01 47 29 01 20 ■ Fax: 01 47 21 84 30 ■ Mon-Fri 8:30-12:30/14:00-19:00/Sat 10:00-13:00/14:00-18:00 ■ Prices medium ■ Professional discount

Supply and installation of all types of parquet.

ROWI SOL FRANCE

32 bd de Ménilmontant 75020 Paris ■ Tel: 01 47 97 95 06 ■ Fax: 01 47 97 93 33 ■ Tue-Sat 9:00-12:00/14:00-18:00 ■ Gérald Karsenty speaks some English ■ Prices medium ■ 10 to 25% professional discount

Floating parquet 8 mm thick. Stratified flooring 8 mm thick. Manufacture and installation.

TRADELI SOLS

1 rue Mouillon, 92500 Rueil-Malmaison ■ Tel: 01 47 49 73 50/01 47 14 08 14 ■ Mon-Fri 9:00-18:00 ■ Prices medium ■ 10 to 20% professional discount

Installation of all types of parquet.

(SEE ALSO WOOD CARVERS)

Shutters, Blinds, Awnings
Volets, stores interieurs et exterieurs

ARC EN CIEL
46 rue St-Antoine, 75004 Paris ■ Tel: 01 42 74 25 23 ■ Fax: 01 42 74 25 21

Large establishment servicing restaurants, industry and homes with blinds, awnings, grilles and curtains. Installations.

HERGÉ
73 rue Faubourg Poissonière, 75009 Paris ■ Tel: 01 47 70 44 79 ■ Fax: 01 47 70 97 32 ■ Mon-Fri 9:00-18:00/Sat 9:00-14:00 ■ Jeanine Barrasa speaks English ■ Prices medium ■ Professional discount

Fabrication, installation and maintenance of exterior awnings, interior and exterior blinds, security blinds, rolling shutters. Construction and counsel in window decoration: sheers and curtains, wall upholstery, bed covers.

MODO FRANCE
11 rue Forest, 75018 Paris ■ Tel: 01 42 93 56 93 ■ Fax: 01 45 22 57 63 ■ Mon-Fri 9:00-13:00/14:00-19:00 ■ English spoken ■ Prices medium ■ 10% professional discount

The most complete selection of wood venetian blinds.

NVS
8 rue Gustave-Flaubert, 75017 Paris ■ Tel: 01 46 22 88 27 ■ Fax: 01 47 63 09 16 ■ E-mail: sitic@wanadoo.fr ■ Mon-Fri 9:00-18:00 ■ Sylvie Lafitan and Emanuel Guillard speak English ■ Prices low ■ 10 to 35% professional discount

Interior and exterior blinds. Venetians, horizontal and vertical, in wood and metal, awnings, canopies. All window decoration.

STORES BELZACQ
23 bd Garibaldi, 75015 Paris ■ Tel: 01 042 70 43 43 ■ Fax: 01 42 70 91 57 ■ E-mail: store_belzacq@tecinostor.fr ■ Prices medium ■ 25% professional discount ■ Display room ■ Tel: 01 47 34 55 76

Interior and exterior blinds, awnings, tents. All custom made. Excellent quality.

STORES EURODRAP
3 impasse Bon-Secours, 75011 Paris ■ Tel: 01 43 70 97 60 ■
Fax: 01 43 70 26 99 ■ Mon-Fri 9:00-18:00/Sat 14:00-18:00 ■
Prices high
Custom-made interior blinds, in all fabrics. High quality.

Tile and Flagstone
Carrelage et dallage

---- VII ----

EMAUX DE BRIARE
7 rue du Bac, 75007 Paris ■ Tel: 01 42 61 16 41 ■ Fax: 01 42 61
53 31 ■ Mon-Sat 10:00-13:00/14:00-18:00 ■ English spoken ■
Prices medium ■ Professional discount
Manufacturer of ceramics. Tiles, lots of tiles, exterior or interior, for floors or walls. In all sizes. Stock or custom. 30 cm square slabs ready to install. They will make tile carpets or ceramic frescoes and friezes to your design or theirs. A very good place.

DIAGONALE
9 rue Verneuil, 75007 Paris ■ Tel: 01 40 20 99 59 ■ Fax: 01 40 20
44 71 ■ Mon-Sat 10:00-19:00 ■ M. Luso ■ Italian spoken ■ Prices
medium to high ■ Professional discount ■ Major credit cards

DIAGONALE
4bis rue St Sabin, 75011 Paris ■ Tel: 01 47 00 80 33 ■ Fax: 01
47 00 23 92 ■ Mon-Sat 9:30-19:00
Mosaics, tiles, terra-cotta, lave emaille (enamelled volcanic stone), pâte de verre, marble and aged marble. They work closely with decorators and architects for the installation of bathrooms and floors.

LES EMAUX DE LA FONTAINE
10 rue de Verneuil, 75007 Paris ■ Tel: 01 47 03 33 43 ■ Fax: 01 47
03 33 44 ■ Tue-Sat 10:00-13:00/14:15-19:00 ■ English spoken ■
Professional discount ■ Major credit cards ■ Warehouse: 21 rue
des Abbesses, Zone Industrielle77580 Crecy la Chapelle ■ Tel: 01
64 63 03 03 ■ Fax: 01 64 63 05 89 (manufacture and delivery)
Specialists in enamel for the bath. Beautiful enamel wash-basins

MARAZZI FRANCE

32 rue Bosquet, 75007 Paris ■ Tel: 01 47 53 92 72 ■ Fax: 01 47 53 77 04 ■ Tue-Fri 10:00-13:00/14:00-19:00 ■ English spoken ■ Prices medium to high ■ Professional discount

The showroom of the world's leading tile manufacturer. Tiles are principally from Italy, but they have some Spanish tiles.

NOIR D'IVOIRE

22 rue Verneuil ■ Tel: 42 86 99 11■ Fax: 01 42 66 44 33 ■ Mon-Wed 9:30-18:30/Sat 14:00-18:30 ■ English spoken ■ Professional discount ■ Major credit cards

Terracotta, stone, marble and cement tiles. Painted tiles and custom tiles made to your design.

PALATINO

40 rue Varenne, 75007 Paris ■ Tel: 01 45 49 46 01 ■ Fax: 01 42 22 46 03 ■ Tue-Fri 10:00-19:00 ■ English spoken ■ Professional discount ■ Major credit cards

Tiles from all over the world, Algeria, Morocco, Spain, Italy, Mexico, Tunisia, Turkey.

X

OPIOCOLOR MOSAIQUES

84 rue Cité de Hauteville, 75008 Paris ■ Tel: 01 40 22 60 13 ■ Fax: 01 40 22 60 26 ■ Web: www.opiocolor.com ■ Mon-Fri 9:30-12:30/13:30-18;30, Sat 9:30-12:30/13:30-17:30 ■ Prices medium to high ■ Professional discount

They specialize in the tiles and pâte de verre of Opio in the south of France.

XII

TERRES CUITES DES RAIRIES

Viaduc des Arts, 113 ave Daumesnil, 75012 Paris ■ Tel: 01 53 02 49 00 ■ Fax: 01 53 02 49 01 ■ E-mail: terres.cuites.des.rairies.@wanadoo.fr ■ Web: www.rairies.com ■ Web: www.terres.cuites.rairies.com ■ Mon-Fri 10:00-19:00 ■ Sat 10:00-18:00 ■ Rémy Montrieux speaks English ■ Prices quite high ■ 15% professional discount ■ Visa, CB and Eurocard accepted

Creator and manufacturer of both natural and enamelled tiles. They will make special tiles to your measure. Excellent collection.

LES CHOSES DE LA MAISON
2ter rue Alasseur, 75015 Paris ■ Tel: 01 42 73 24 35 ■ Fax: 01 47 34 51 97 ■ E-mail: promoceram@aol.com ■ Mon-Fri 10:00-19:00/Sat10:00-14:00 ■ Prices medium to high ■ Professional discount ■ Major credit cards

Tiles from Italy, Spain, Portugal and France. Tiles of all types.

TERRE ANDALOUSE
51 rue Entrepeneurs, 75015 Paris ■ Tel: 01 45 77 60 70 ■ E-mail: terreandalouse@online.fr ■ Tue-Sat 10:00-19:30/Mon 13:00-19-30 ■ Prices medium to high ■ Professional discount ■ Visa and CB

Tiles of Andalusia in Spain. Mosaic table tops and tables to your design. Also colorful painted furniture.

XVI

CERAMIS
130 av Versailles, 75016 Paris ■ Tel: 01 30 24 34 41 ■ Fax: 01 30 24 57 04 ■ Tue-Sat 10:00-19:00 ■ English spoken ■ Professional discount

Specialist in tiles (Azulejos) made by hand in their own workshop, of terracotta, stone, marble or cement.

PARIS SUBURBS

PIERRE CHALVIGNAC
6 rue de Baillage, 78000 Versailles ■ Tel: 01 30 42 52 20 ■ Prices medium ■ By appointment ■ Professional discount

Antique flagstones and tiling.

SOCIÉTÉ VERSAILLAISE DE CARRELAGE
26 rue du Pont-Colbert, 78000 Versailles ■ Tel: 01 39 02 01 32 ■ Fax: 01 39 50 35 46 ■ Mon-Fri 8:00-19:30 ■ Prices medium ■ 10% professional discount

Supply and installation of all types of tiles and marble.

Wall Panelling
Boiseries

👑 **BREDY**
63 rue Albert Dhalenne 93407 Saint-Ouen ■ Tel: 01 43 75 47 87 ■ Fax: 01 40 12 60 05 ■ Mon-Fri 7:30-12:00/13:30-17:30/Fri closing 17:00 ■ Jean-Pierre Fancelli speaks English ■ Prices high
One of the best in France. Fine wood carving of panelling.

👑 **JOËL FÉAU BOISERIES**
9 rue Laugier, 75017 Paris ■ Tel: 01 47 63 60 60 ■ Fax: 01 42 67 58 91 ■ E-mail: feaubois@aol.com ■ Mon-Fri 9:30-12:30/14:00-19:00 ■ Guillaume Féau ■ English and German spoken ■ Prices high to very high
Antique wood panelling specially of the XVIII century. Custom reproduction of panelling in wood, resin and plaster. Superb quality.

👑 **BERNARD STEINITZ**
9 rue du Cirque, 75008 Paris ■ Tel: 01 42 89 40 50 ■ Fax: 01 42 89 40 60 ■ E-mail: info@steinitzantiques.com ■ Web: www.steinitzantiques.com ■ Mon-Fri 9:00-18:00, Sat by appointment ■ Bernard, Simone and Benjamin Steinitz speak English ■ Prices high to very high ■ Professional discount
Large collection of boiseries of the XVII, XVIII and XIX century.

Walls and Ceilings
Murs et plafonds

G S HABITAT ISOLATION
350 rue des Pyrénées, 75020 Paris ■ Tel: 01 46 36 82 46 ■ Fax: 01 47 97 17 86 ■ Mon-Fri 9:15-12:30/14:00-18:30 ■ Prices medium to high ■ Up to 20% professional discount
Supply and installation of stretched PVC ceilings.

ORION INTERNATIONAL
39 bd Victor-Hugo, 92110 Clichy ■ Tel: 01 47 31 66 95 ■ Fax: 01 47 56 99 82 ■ Mon-Fri 9:00-18:00 ■ Prices medium to high ■ 10% professional discount
Fabrication and installation of office modular units. Choice of four different types.

SPID
63 rue Victor-Hugo, 94700 Maisons-Alfort ■ Tel: 01 43 75 16 08 ■ Fax: 01 43 96 58 66 ■ Mon-Fri 8:00-18:00 ■ Prices medium
Dropped ceilings, thermal and acoustic insulation. Technical flooring for computer rooms, movable office partitions.

ART AUCTION HOUSES
Salles des ventes

Auction procedures in France are very different from auctions elsewhere. A special group of highly-trained auctioneer/experts called "Commissaires-priseurs" have long held a monopoly on public auctions in France. With the new millenium, things are about to change. The highly visible international auction houses are entering the fray. Heretofore, the French system of Commissaires-Priseurs made auctions available to all economic levels of society. Now, with the entry of Sotheby's and Christie's onto the French marketplace, the auction action might become more the exclusive domain of the financially privileged. The trend might cause even more extreme price aberrations for antiques and fine art. Time will tell.

ALICE
2 av Montaigne, 75008 Paris ■ Tel: 01 53 67 52 85 ■ Fax: 01 53 67 52 80 ■ E-mail: info@alice-auction.com ■ Web: www.alice-auction.com ■ Office open Mon-Fri by appointment ■ Francis Simon ■ English, German, Italian and Spanish spoken ■ Prices will very likely be high

The new "kid on the block": A French boutique-style auction company with a new idea in marketing. At the time of this edition, they have announced just four sales per year. Two in New York and two in Paris from the year 2001 and beyond. They specialize in paintings, sculpture and works on paper of the XIX and XX century, particularly the Impressionists. We suggest you subscribe to their information service through the Website. In today's unsettled atmosphere, they will be giving the big boys a good run for their money.
Alice is also located in New York City at 630 Fifth Avenue, New York, NY 10011 ■ Tel: 212 332 3488 ■ Fax: 212 332 3489. By the way: Alice is an acronym for "Authenticity, Legality, Integrity, Credibility and Excellence". The best of luck to them.

CHRISTIE'S FRANCE
6 Avenue Matignon, 75008 Paris ■ Tel: 01 40 76 85 85 ■ Fax: 01 42 56 26 01 ■ Web: www.christies.com ■ Mon-Fri 9:00-18:00 ■ English spoken ■ Christie's Education, 11 rue Berryer, 75008 Paris

Organization and sale of art, antiques and objets d'art as well as free estimates of art and objects of art. Consultation and preparation and production of catalogues.

COMPAGNIE DES COMMISSAIRES-PRISEURS DE PARIS

9 rue Drouot, 75009 Paris ■ Tel: 01 42 46 17 11

The number to call for information on the auctions held by the various Commissaires-Priseurs.

DEPOT-VENTE DE PARIS

81 rue Laguy, 75020 Paris ■ Tel: 01 43 72 13 91 ■ Fax: 01 43 71 45 43 ■ Mon-Sat 9:30-19:30 ■ Prices low ■ 5% professional discount

Over 25,000 square feet of furniture and antique objects. Much of the offering is second-hand and of lower price and quality.

HOTEL DES VENTES DROUOT

9 rue Drouot, 75009 Paris ■ Tel: 01 48 00 20 20 ■ Fax: 01 48 00 20 33 ■ Mon-Sat 11:00-18:00 plus five Sundays per year ■ Web: www.gazette-drouot.com ■ Prices are high, low and medium.

Wonderful place to visit and one hopes it will retain its unique character. As you might expect, there are public auctions of everything from Old Master paintings to vintage wines. They have several locations in Paris and the suburbs. Be sure to pick up the Gazette de Drouot from any good news-stand. It contains complete details and schedules of their auctions. There is a wealth of information on estimates, prices and provenence with illustrations. A real man-on-the-street publication. One word of advice. The best time to attend any auction is when most of the dealers are at one of the expositions, or when they are off to the beach or the country.

HOTEL DES VENTES DE NEUILLY

164 bis Avenue Charles-de-Gaulle, 92200 Neuilly-sur-Seine ■ Tel: 01 47 45 55 53 ■ Fax: 01 47 45 54 31 ■ Public expositions Mondays 11:00-18:00, Tuesdays 7:00-11:00 ■ E-mail: aguttes@aguttes.com ■ Web: www.aguttes.com ■ Claude Aguttes, Commissaire-priseur ■ English spoken ■ Prices low to very high

A very comfortable small gallery where you will find a wide range of auction offerings. Since it is located in an affluent neighbourhood, you will quite often discover high quality treasures such as furniture, collectibles, porcelain and objets d'art.

POULAIN & LE FUR
HOTEL DES VENTES DU PALAIS
Palais des Congrès. 2 place de la Porte Maillot CIP 48 75853
Paris Cedex 17 ■ Tel : 01 58 05 06 07 ■ Fax : 01 45 72 07 77 ■
English spoken
New Auction House in the great Palais des Congrès: antiques, Old Master and Modern paintings, furniture and art objects, primitive art, Art Deco, rare books and collectible automobiles.

SOTHEBY'S FRANCE
76 rue du Faubourg-Saint-Honoré, 75008 Paris ■ Tel: 01 53 05
53 05 ■ Fax: 01 47 42 22 32 ■ Web: www.sothebys.com ■ Mon-Fri 10:00-18:00 ■ Presidente PDG Europe – Princess de Beauvau Craon ■ English spoken ■ Fees are high
Soon to be in operation.

OUTSIDE PARIS

SALLE DES VENTES
33 rue Général-Colin, 78400 Châtou ■ Tel: 01 39 52 10 40/01 39
52 48 06 ■ Fax: 01 39 52 05 14 ■ Every day except Tue 9:30-12:30/14:30-18:30 ■ Maître Rieffel
Auctions of furniture, art objects, tapestries, paintings, collectibles, chandeliers, glass.

ART NOUVEAU - ART DECO

People with a passion for Art Nouveau or Art Deco furniture, lighting and objets d'art will find the answer to their dreams in Paris. Some of the world's best dealers offering the works of the great artists of the Art Nouveau and Art Deco styles can be found in The Louvre des Antiquaires, The Carré Rive Gauche, The Village Suisse and the Marché aux Puces at Saint-Ouen. The following represents our difficult choices of those we consider among the best.

ALB ANTIQUITÉS
3 rue de Lille, 75007 Paris ■ Tel: 01 47 03 45 58 ■ Fax: 01 47 03 07 37 ■ Tue-Sat 14:30-19:00 ■ Antoine Broccardo ■ Prices medium to high ■ Major credit cards
Applied arts of the XX century.

ANTILOPE
17 rue Paul Bert, 93400 Saint-Ouen ■ Tel: 01 40 11 39 41 ■ Fri-Mon 09:00-18:00 ■ English and Spanish spoken ■ Prices high ■ Professional discount ■ Major credit cards
Art Deco lighting, chandeliers, lamps, sconces, mirrors, consoles and objets d'art.

ART DEPOT
3 rue du Pont-Louis-Philippe, 75004 Paris ■ Tel: 01 47 77 99 02 ■ English spoken ■ Prices medium ■ Professional discount ■ Major credit cards
Art Deco, aeronautic and industrial designs.

CENTO ANNI GALLERY
Louvre des Antiquaires, 26 Allée Boulle, 2 place du Palais Royal, 75001 Paris ■ Tel: 01 42 60 48 77 ■ Fax: 01 42 60 48 77 ■ Tue-Sun 11:00-19:00 ■ Rodrigo Diaz ■ Spanish, English and Italian spoken ■ Amex, Visa
Art Deco and Art Nouveau furniture, glass, sculptures.

DANENBERG
Louvre des Antiquaires, 2 Allée Boulle, 2 place du Palais Royal, 75001 Paris ■ Tel: 01 42 61 57 19 ■ Fax: 01 42 61 75 33 ■ English, Spanish and Italian spoken ■ 20% professional discount ■ Major credit cards
Art Nouveau glass: Gallé, Lalique, Daum. Jewellery of the 1930s and 1940s.

LUC DEBRUILLE

3 rue de Lille, 75007 Paris ■ Telfax: 01 42 61 78 72 ■ Cell: 06 09 04 95 07 ■ E-mail: luc.dubruille@wanadoo.fr ■ Mon 14:00-19:00, Tue-Sat 10:30-13:00/14:00-19:00 ■ English spoken ■ Professional discount■ Major credit cards

Decorative arts of the XX century, especially 1930s to 1950s: furniture, lighting, ceramics, carpets and objects. Furniture of architects: Prouvé, Perriand, Alva Alto, Adnet, Arbus.

♕ DUO 1900-1930

15 rue de Lille, 75007 Paris ■ Tel: 01 47 03 92 63 ■ Fax: 01 42 61 67 90 ■ Wed-Sat 14:00-19:00 and by appointment ■ Mr. Claude A. Cardinale ■ English spoken ■ Prices medium ■ 10% professional discount ■ Amex

Art Nouveau (1900s) furniture, objects, paintings, lighting, of European (non-French) origin. Art Deco (1930s) French furniture, objects, paintings, lighting, and some silver.

ANNE-SOPHIE DUVAL

5 quai Malaquais, 75006 Paris ■ Tel: 01 43 54 51 16 ■ Fax: 01 40 46 95 12 ■ Tue-Sat 10:00-18:00

Art Nouveau and Art Deco furniture and objects of the 1940s and 50s.

OLWEN FOREST

Marché Serpette, Allée 3, Stand 7, 110 rue des Rosiers, 93400 Saint-Ouen ■ Tel: 01 40 11 96 38 ■ Fax: 01 47 63 24 69 ■ English spoken ■ Professional discount ■ Major credit cards

Art Deco crystal, plated silver cocktail sets, bathing beauties. Costume and designer jewellery from the 1920s to 1960s. Hollywood jewellery worn by the stars. Very special.

♕ GALERIE L'ARC EN SEINE

27-31 rue de Seine, 75006 Paris ■ Tel: 01 43 29 11 02 ■ Fax: 01 43 29 97 66 ■ E-mail: ARCSEINE@artinternet.fr ■ Mon-Sat 11:00-13:00/14:00-19:00 ■ Christian and Catherine Boutonnet, Rafael Otiz ■ English and Spanish spoken ■ Prices high ■ Professional discount ■ Visa, MC

Art Deco furniture, paintings and art objects. Specialist in Eileen Gray and other great artists of the period including Legrain, Frank, Alberto Giacometti.

GALERIE JEAN-LOUIS DANANT

36 av Matignon, 75008 Paris ■ Tel: 01 42 89 40 15 ■ Fax: 01 42 89 40 10 ■ Mon-Fri 10:30-13:00/14:00-19:00 ■ English spoken

Art Deco to the 1950s.

GALERIE JACQUES DE VOS

34 rue de Seine, 75006 Paris ■ Tel: 01 43 26 29 26 ■ 7 rue Bonaparte ■ Tel: 01 43 29 88 94 ■ Fax: 01 40 46 95 45 ■ Mon-Sat 10:30-13:00/14:00-19:00 ■ English spoken ■ Prices high ■ 10% professional discount

The two galleries specialize in Art Deco furniture and art objects of 1920-1940. Furniture of Ruhlmann, Frank, Chareau, Printz. Sculptures of Lambert-Rucki and Csaky.

GALERIE DORIA

16 rue de Seine, 75006 Paris ■ Tel: 01 43 54 73 49 ■ Fax: 01 43 25 68 72 ■ Tue-Sat 11:00-13:00/14:30-19:00 ■ Denis Doria ■ English spoken ■ Prices medium ■ Professional discount

Objets d'art, furniture and lighting of the great Art Deco masters.

♕ GALERIE JEAN-JACQUES DUTKO

13 rue Bonaparte, 75006 Paris ■ Tel: 01 43 26 96 13 ■ Fax: 01 43 29 21 91 ■ Mon 14:30-19:00, Tue-Sat 10:30-19:00 ■ Jean-Jacques and Agnès Dutko ■ English spoken ■ Prices high ■ Professional discount ■ Major credit cards

One of the great collections Art Deco furniture, sculptures and paintings. Primitive art.

♕ GALERIE YVES GASTOU

12 rue Bonaparte, 75006 Paris ■ Tel: 01 53 73 00 10 ■ Fax: 01 53 73 00 12 ■ Tue-Sat 11:00-13:00/14:00-19:00 ■ English spoken ■ Prices medium ■ 10% professional discount ■ Amex

Furniture, sculpture, neo-classic painting 1935 to 1950 by Arbus, Poillerat, du Plantier, Gio Ponti, Adnet, Hermès, Jansen.

GALERIE JACQUES LACOSTE

22 rue de Lille, 75007 Paris ■ Tel: 01 40 20 41 82 ■ Fax: 01 40 53 85 19 ■ E-mail: Lacoste-jacques@wanadoo.fr ■ Tue-Sat 14:00-18:30 ■ English and Spanish spoken ■ Professional discount

Furniture and objets d'art of the 1930s, 1940s and 1950s. Expert C.N.E.

GALERIE LANDROT

5 rue Jacques-Callot, 75006 Paris ■ Tel: 01 43 26 71 13 ■ Mon-Sat 14:30-19:00 ■ Gérard and Dominique Landrot speak English ■ 10 to 15% professional discount

Art Deco ceramics of Chagall, Matisse, Maillol. Early XX century sculpture and paintings.

GALERIE FELIX MARCILHAC

8 rue Bonaparte, 75006 Paris ■ Tel: 01 43 26 47 36 ■ Fax: 01 46 05 01 58 ■ Mon-Sat 10:00-19:00 ■ English spoken ■ Prices high ■ Professional discount

Art Nouveau, Art Deco furniture, objects. Symbolist and Orientalist paintings, glass and ceramics of 1900 to 1925.

GALERIE ERIC PHILIPPE

25 Galerie Vero-Dodat, 10 rue Croix-des-Petits-Champs, 75001 Paris ■ Tel: 01 42 33 28 26 ■ Fax: 01 42 21 17 93 ■ Tue-Sat 14:00-19:00 ■ English spoken ■ Prices medium ■ Professional discount

European decorative arts of 1900-1950, furniture, lighting, carpets, photography.

♕ MAKASSAR-FRANCE

19 av Matignon, 75008 Paris ■ Tel: 01 53 96 95 85 ■ Fax: 01 53 96 95 94 ■ Mon-Sat 10:00-19:00 ■ Mme Magnan ■ English spoken ■ 10% professional discount ■ Visa, Amex

Superb Art Deco furniture, sculpture, objects, paintings and lighting from 1920 to 1940.

MARTINE MATHOUET

91 rue des Rosiers, 93400 Saint-Ouen ■ Telfax: 01 49 45 16 13 ■ E-mail: mem.antiques@wanadoo.fr ■ Sat-Mon 10:00-18:00 ■ English spoken ■ Prices high ■ Major credit cards

Art Deco, 1930-1940, lighting, furniture, decorative objects and crystal by Daum and Baccarat.

1900 MONCEAU ANTIQUITÉS

62 bd Malesherbes, 75008 Paris ■ Tel: 01 43 87 92 80 ■ Mon-Fri 10:00-18:30 ■ Patrick Kalfen ■ English spoken ■ Prices medium ■ Professional discount

Art Deco furniture and objects. Larger choice in their shop in the Marché aux Puces, 120 rue des Rosiers, Saint-Ouen.

NOIR EBÈNE

5 rue Bréa, 75006 Paris ■ Tel: 01 46 34 72 93 ■ Mon 15:00-19:00, Tue-Sat 11:00-13:00/15:00-19:00 ■ English spoken ■ Prices medium ■ 10% professional discount

Art Deco furniture (1930-1940) bars, chairs, desks, glass, enamels, lamps, objects.

LE ROI FOU

182 rue du Faubourg-Saint-Honoré, 75008 Paris ■ Tel: 01 45 63 82 59 ■ Fax: 45 63 40 57 ■ Tue-Sat 10:30-18:30 ■ English spoken ■ Prices medium to high ■ 10% professional discount

A great choice of Art Deco lighting, lamps, chandeliers, sconces, bronzes. Some furniture.

STUDIO SAINT-SULPICE
3 rue Saint-Sulpice, 75006 Paris ■ Tel: 01 40 51 06 33 ■ Mon-Sat 13:00-19:00 and by appointment ■ English spoken ■ Prices medium ■ Professional discount

Art Deco furniture, mirrors, lamps, objects.

♔ GALERIE VALLOIS
41 rue de Seine, 75006 Paris ■ Tel: 01 43 29 50 84 ■ Fax: 01 43 29 90 73 ■ E-mail: vallois@club-internet.fr ■ Web: www.vallois@vallois.com ■ Mon 14:00-19:00, Tue-Fri 10:00-19:00, Sat: 10:00-13:00/14:00-19:00 ■ English and Spanish spoken

A fine collection of Art Deco furniture and objects: Chareau, Cheuret, Dunand, Frank, Giacometti, Eileen Gray, Groult, Iribe, Legrain, Printz, Rateau, Ruhlmann, Sue et Mare. One of the very best.

JACQUES VERDIER ANTIQUES AND FINE ART
41 rue Saint-Sabin, 75011 Paris ■ Tel: 01 48 06 55 23 ■ Fax: 01 40 21 67 67 ■ By appointment ■ English spoken

Art Deco and Art Nouveau furniture, lighting and objects.

ART GALLERIES
Galeries d'Art

One should really never go shopping for a painting or a work of art. One should always just let it happen. When you encounter a work of art that should be yours something quite remarkable will occur. Something you won't be able to describe will pass between you and the work you encounter. It will be an emotional contact experience much like making eye contact across a crowded room. But, as with many experiences, an infatuation can never be compared to a real long-lasting love. The best advice we can give is: don't rush into things. Let the magic take time to happen. If it should be, it will be.

There is no shortage of art in Paris. Good, bad or indifferent, there are Art Galleries in nearly every part of the city. There is a wide range in quality as well as price levels. Except in the case of well-known painters and historic pieces, the prices asked often have little to do with the quality of the work. There are pictures galore, whether they are oil paintings, watercolours, lithographs, engravings or sculpture. If you are new at the game, as most of us are, there are a couple of things you might keep in mind when searching for the perfect work of art to set off a room, an office or a public building.

First, decide whether you are looking for a work of art, with either a current or future investment value, or a picture or sculpture that you like and that will fit the atmosphere of your home or office. If it is the former, you'd best consult an expert. There will very likely be quite a bit of money at stake. If it is the latter, your choice is almost limitless. Whatever your motive, we suggest you begin in one of the four different gallery concentrations in Paris.

For works by young unknown artists, as well as established names, you might try the galleries on the Left Bank, especially the 6th and 7th Arrondissements. Some of the better-known international dealers, dealing in prices that are often stratospheric, have galleries in the area of the Rue du Faubourg-Saint-Honoré, the Avenue Matignon and the Rue de Miromesnil. The area is known, for very good reason, as "The Golden Triangle".

The more daring buyer can explore the area of the Bastille, the Marais or one of the organized markets of Paris: "Le Village Suisse" and "Le Marché aux Puces" at the Porte de Clignancourt.

If you are looking for Old Master drawings, paintings or sculpture from the Haute Epoque, pre-dating 1850, you will need to visit the "Antique Dealers". Paintings and sculpture pre-dating the Modern and Contemporary periods are almost always found there rather than in the "Art Galleries".

I

GALERIE MARWAN HOSS
12 rue d'Alger, 75001 Paris ■ Tel: 01 42 96 37 96 ■ Fax: 01 49 27 04 99 ■ Mon-Fri 9:30-12:30/14:00-18:30, Sat 10:00-12:30/14:00-18:00 ■ Marwan Hoss, Owner, Brigitte Berna, Director ■ English, Italian and Spanish spoken ■ Prices high

Modern and contemporary art: painting, sculpture and drawings. Catalogues of past exhibitions: Pablo Gargallo, Music, Helion, Vagues, Torres-Garcia, Buraglio, Michaux and more. They also have a gallery in Brussels.

GALERIE RÉGIS LANGLOYS
169 rue Saint-Honoré, 75001 Paris ■ Telfax: 01 42 60 56 94 ■ Tue-Sat 11:00-12:30/13:30-18:30 and by appointment ■ Régis Langloys speaks English and Italian ■ Prices medium to high ■ Professional discount ■ Major credit cards

High-quality figurative paintings, Expressionist and primitive works, estampes. Reproductions of Impressionist Masters.

GALERIE CLAUDE MARUMO
243 rue Saint-Honoré, 75001 Paris ■ Tel: 01 42 60 08 66 ■ Fax: 01 40 15 96 04 ■ Web: www.franceantiq.fr ■ Mon-Fri 9:30-19:00 ■ Claude Marumo speaks English ■ Prices medium to very high ■ Professional discount ■ Amex

Paintings of the XIX and XX century. Specialists in the Barbizon school. Expert to the Court of Appeals, Paris.

👑 **GALERIE SCHMIT**
396 rue Saint-Honoré, 75001 Paris ■ Tel: 01 42 60 36 36 ■ Fax: 01 49 27 97 16 ■ Mon-Fri 10:00-12:30/14:00-18:30 ■ Robert and Manuel Schmit ■ English spoken ■ Prices high
Paintings by the Masters of Impressionism.

LES MUSARDS
JEAN-CLAUDE D'OZOUVILLE
91 rue Saint-Honoré, 75001 Paris ■ Tel: 01 42 33 96 39 ■ Mon-Sat 12:00-19:30 ■ Jean-Claude d'Ozouville speaks English ■ Prices medium ■ 20% professional discount
Primitive art, drawings, paintings, art objects.

II

GALERIE J. HAHN
10 rue de Louvois, 75002 Paris ■ Tel: 01 47 03 42 55 ■ Fax: 01 47 03 42 34 ■ Mon-Sat 10:00-19:00 ■ Emeric Hahn speaks English ■ Prices high
XVII and XVIII century French and Italian paintings, XIX century French school, sculpture of the XVIII and XIX centuries.

GALERIE ANTOINE LAURENTIN
65 rue Sainte-Anne, 75002 Paris ■ Tel: 01 42 97 43 42 ■ Fax: 01 42 97 58 85 ■ E-mail: alaurentin@aol.com ■ Mon-Fri 14:00-19:00 ■ English, Spanish and Russian spoken ■ Amex
Paintings, drawings and sculpture of the XIX and XX centuries. Limited editions of art books. Re-edition of the Dictionary "Artists of The French School" by Bellier de la Chavignerie and Auvray. Catalogue Raisonné of Ferdinand du Puigaudeau.

👑 **GALERIE DE BAYSER**
69 rue Sainte-Anne, 75002 Paris ■ Tel: 01 47 03 49 87 ■ Fax: 01 42 97 51 03 ■ E-mail: galerie@debayser.com ■ Web: www.de-bayser.com ■ Mon-Fri 9:30-19:00, Sat 11:00-17:00 ■ Bruno de Bayser ■ English spoken
Excellent drawings of the XVI to XIX century especially from France, Italy, Holland and Belgium.

GALERIE FRANÇOISE PAVIOT
57 rue Sainte-Anne, 75002 Paris ■ Tel: 01 42 60 10 01 ■ Fax: 01 42 60 44 77 ■ E-mail: paviofoto@wanadoo.fr ■ Tue-Sat 14:30-19:00 ■ Françoise Paviot speaks English ■ Professional discount on large purchases
Photography: XIX century, Modern and contemporary. Will advise on acquisition and maintenance of collections.

RYAUX
67 rue Sainte-Anne, 75002 Paris ■ Tel: 01 42 60 37 47 ■ Fax: 01
42 60 31 41 ■ Mon-Fri 9:30-13:00/16:00-18:30 ■ Jean-Luc and
Selma Ryaux speak English ■ Prices high

**Old paintings, drawings and sculptures. Expert to the Court
of Cassation.**

— III —

AREA
10 rue de Picardie, 75003 Paris ■ Tel: 01 42 72 68 66 ■ Fax: 01
42 72 12 75 ■ E-mail: area@wanadoo.fr ■ Wed-Sat 14:00-19:00,
Sun 15:00-19:00 ■ Francis Sichot ■ English spoken ■ Prices
medium ■ Professional discount

**Contemporary art, limited print editions, books for An-
glophiles.**

ASKEO
19 rue Debelleyme, 75003 Paris ■ Tel: 01 42 77 17 77 ■ Fax: 01
42 77 27 77 ■ Tue-Sat 14:30-19:00 ■ Christian Forestier ■ English spoken■ Prices medium to high ■ 10 to 15% professional
discount

**Contemporary painting, sculpture. They also have some
frames.**

PASCAL GABERT
11bis rue du Perche, 75003 Paris ■ Tel: 01 44 54 09 44 ■ Fax:
01 44 54 09 45 ■ Mon-Sat 11-12:30/14:00-19:00 ■ English and
Spanish spoken ■ Professional discount

Contemporary paintings, sculpture and photos.

GALERIE LISETTE ALIBERT
26 Place des Vosges, 75003 Paris ■ Tel: 01 48 87 45 50 ■ Fax:
01 48 87 75 78 ■ E-mail: alibertis@easynet.fr ■ Web: www.od-
arts.com/alibert ■ Every day 10:00-19:00 ■ Lisette Alibert ■ English spoken ■ Prices medium to high ■ Visa, Amex

**Contemporary sculpture and paintings in primitive style.
Artists' catalogues and their Website updated every month.**

GALERIE BERNARD BOUCHE
123 rue Vieille-du-Temple, 75003 Paris ■ Tel: 01 42 72 60 03 ■
Fax: 01 42 72 60 51 ■ Tue-Sat 14:00-19:00 ■ English spoken ■
Prices high

Modern and contemporary masters.

GALERIE FARIDEH CADOT

77 rue des Archives, 75003 Paris ■ Tel: 01 42 78 08 36 ■ Fax: 01 42 78 63 61 ■ Tue-Sat 10:00-19:00 ■ Farideh Cadot speaks English ■ Prices medium to very high

Contemporary paintings and sculpture.

GALERIE CASINI

13 rue Chapon, 75003 Paris ■ Tel: 01 48 04 00 34 ■ Fax: 01 48 04 06 08 ■ E-mail : galerie casini@lemel.fr ■ Tue-Sat 14:00-19:00 ■ Philippe Casini and Bénédicte Demeulenaere ■ English, German and Swedish spoken ■ 10% professional discount

Works by international living artists: François Bouillon, Helmut Dorner, François Righi, Osman, Horst Munch, Jean Zuber, Suzan Frecon, Katsuhito Nishikawa, Ruobing Chen, Byong-Juin Koh.

GALERIE VALERIE CUETO

10-12 rue des Coutures Saint-Gervais, 75003 Paris ■ Tel: 01 42 71 91 89 ■ Fax: 01 42 71 94 13 ■ E-mail: valerie.cueto@cybercable.fr ■ Tue-Sat 10:00-13:00/14:00-19:00 ■ English spoken ■ Prices medium to high ■ Professional discount ■ Major credit cards

Contemporary art, sculptures and photography.

GALERIE DU MUSÉE

16 rue du Parc Royal, 75003 Paris ■ Tel: 01 48 87 60 90 ■ Fax: 01 48 87 54 53 ■ Wed-Mon 11:30-18:30 ■ Monique Danner ■ English spoken ■ Major credit cards

Lithographs, engravings, sculpture, by Picasso, Dali, Miro.

GALERIE ERIC DUPONT

13 rue Chapon, 75003 Paris ■ Tel: 01 44 54 04 14 ■ Fax: 01 44 54 04 24 ■ Web: www.od-arts.com/dupont ■ Tue-Sat 14:00-19:00 and by appointment ■ Eric Dupont speaks English and Italian ■ Prices medium ■ Professional discount

Contemporary art: painting, sculpture, photography, by young artists from all over the world, such as Damien Cabanes, Hyun Soo Choi, Sylvie Fajfrowska, Carlos Kusnir, Siobhan Liddell, Didier Menceboni, François Mendras, Paul Pagk, Eric Poitevin, Philippe Poupet, Corinne Sentou.

GALERIE EFTE – FLORENCE TOUBER

117 rue Vieille-du-Temple, 75003 Paris ■ Telfax: 01 42 77 43 29 ■ Tue-Fri 14:00-19:00, Sat 11:00-19:00 ■ English spoken ■ Prices medium ■ Major credit cards

Contemporary paintings and sculpture.

GALERIE KARSTEN GREVE
5 rue Debelleyme, 75003 Paris ■ Tel: 01 42 77 19 37 ■ Fax: 01 42 77 05 58 ■ Tue-Sat 11:00-19:00 ■ English and German spoken ■ Prices high ■ Professional discount

Contemporary paintings.

GALERIE THESSA HEROLD
7 rue de Thorigny, 75003 Paris ■ Tel: 01 42 78 78 68 ■ Fax: 01 42 78 78 69 ■ Tue-Sat 14:00-18:30, Sat 11:00-18:30 ■ Thessa Herold speaks Spanish and English ■ Prices medium to high

Modern and contemporary art: painting and sculpture.

GALERIE LAHUMIÈRE
17 rue du Parc Royal, 75003 Paris ■ Tel: 01 42 77 27 74 ■ Fax: 01 42 77 27 78 ■ Tue-Fri 10:00-13:00/14:00-18:30, Sat 11:00-13:00/14:00-18:00 ■ Anne Lahumière ■ English and German spoken ■ Prices medium ■ Possible professional discount

Modern and contemporary paintings, drawings, watercolours, sculpture, estampes.

GALERIE LES FILLES DU CALVAIRE
17 rue des Filles-du-Calvaire, 75003 Paris ■ Tel: 01 42 74 47 05 ■ Fax: 01 42 74 47 06 ■ Tue-Sat 11:00-18:30 ■ Christine Ollier speaks English and Italian ■ Prices medium

Contemporary art: painting, photography and sculpture installation. Video installation. Works by Cho and Yun, François Daireaux, Gilles Pennaneac, Dominique Gauthier, James Hyde, Philippe Tourriol, Mireille Loup, Corinne Mercadier, Paul Pouvreau. Books on contemporary art.

GALERIE VÉRONIQUE MAXE - ALBERT BENAMOU
7 rue Froissart, 75003 Paris ■ Telfax: 01 47 74 20 53 ■ E-mail: bobbienamou@hotmail.com ■ By appointment ■ English, Russian and Italian spoken ■ Professional discount ■ Major credit cards

Contemporary art: paintings, sculpture, photographs, installations. Some of the artists are: Fabrice Langlade, Olivier Urman and Steve Miller.

GALERIE MODUS
23 Place des Vosges, 75003 Paris ■ Tel: 01 42 78 10 10 ■ Fax: 01 42 78 14 00 ■ E-mail: modus@galerie-modus.com ■ Web: www.galerie-modus.com ■ Everyday 10:30-20:00 ■ Karl Yeya, Director ■ English and Spanish spoken ■ Prices medium to high ■ Professional discount ■ Major credit cards

Contemporary paintings and sculptures.

GALERIE NATHALIE OBADIA
5 rue du Grenier Saint-Lazare, 75003 Paris ■ Tel: 01 42 74 67 68 ■ Fax: 01 42 74 68 66 ■ E-mail: gal.obadia@claranet.fr ■ Mon-Sat 11:00-19:00 ■ Nathalie Obadia, Florence Sinoni ■ English, Spanish and Italian spoken ■ Prices medium

Contemporary art: paintings, sculptures, installations, photographs.

GALERIE POLARIS – BERNARD UTUDJIAN
8 rue Saint-Claude, 75003 Paris ■ Tel: 01 42 72 21 27 ■ Fax: 01 42 76 06 29 ■ E-mail: polaris@easynet.fr ■ Web: www.od-arts.com ■ Tue-Sat 13:00-19:30 ■ English spoken ■ Prices medium

Contemporary art: photographs, paintings and drawings.

GALERIE SABINE PUGET
108 rue Vieille du Temple, 75003Paris ■ Tel: 01 42 71 24 20 ■ Fax: 01 42 79 06 20 ■ E-mail: galleries.Puget@worldnet.fr ■ Web: www.od-arts.com/spuget ■ Tue-Sat 14:00-19:00 ■ English spoken ■ 10% professional discount to galleries

Contemporary paintings, drawings and sculpture.

GALERIE DENISE RENÉ
Espace Marais, 22 rue Charlot, 75003 Paris ■ Tel: 01 48 87 73 94 ■ Fax: 01 48 87 73 95 ■ Tue-Sat 14:00-19:00 ■ English spoken ■ Prices medium to high

Modern and contemporary art: construction art and kinetic art.

GALERIE VÉRONIQUE SMAGGHE – SIMONE KERVERN
24 rue Charlot, 75003 Paris ■ Telfax: 01 42 72 83 40 ■ Web: www.shamaweb.fr/k-art ■ Tue-Sat 14:00-19:00 ■ English and Spanish spoken ■ Prices medium ■ 20% professional discount

New Realist painters of the 1960s. Support Surfaces of the 1970s. Expertise and restoration.

GALERIE THUILLIER
13 rue de Thorigny, 75003 Paris ■ Telfax: 01 42 77 33 24 ■ Mon-Sat 11:00-18:30 ■ Denis Cornet ■ English spoken ■ Prices modest ■ Professional discount ■ Visa, MC

Living artists, modern, classic, figurative and abstract. Each year new exhibitions of paintings and sculptures.

GALERIE TROISIÈME OEIL
98 rue Vieille-du-Temple, 75003 Paris ■ Tel: 01 48 04 30 25 ■ Fax: 01 48 04 09 98 ■ Tue 14:00-19:00, Wed-Sat 10:30-12:30/14:00-19:00 ■ Anne-Marie Marquette and Fausto Mata speak English ■ Prices medium

Contemporary paintings, drawings, sculptures and engravings, from 1950s to the present.

GALERIE UDM MARKETING

16 rue de Poitou, 75003 Paris ■ Tel: 01 42 77 63 22 ■ Tue-Sat 14:00-19:00 ■ English spoken ■ Prices reasonable

Contemporary French and international paintings and some sculptures. Promising young unknowns.

GALERIE ANTON WELLER

57 rue de Bretagne, 75003 Paris ■ Tel: 01 42 72 05 62 ■ Fax: 01 42 72 05 63 ■ E-mail: antonweller@starnet.fr ■ Tue-Sat 14:00-18:00 ■ Isabelle Suret ■ English and German spoken

Contemporary art by young artists. As they say, "Organized around a double structure since 1994, a fixed place, in this gallery and promoted in the traditional way, artists on exhibition are invited to choose individual and temporary spaces which will become an integral part of their work".

GALERIE XIPPAS

108 rue Vieille-du-Temple, 75003 Paris ■ Tel: 01 40 27 05 55 ■ Fax: 01 40 27 07 16 ■ E-mail: xippas@club-internet.fr ■ Tue-Fri 10:00-13:00/14:00-19:00, Sat 10:00-19:00 ■ Renos Xippas ■ English, Spanish Italian, Swedish and Greek spoken ■ Prices medium

Modern and contemporary paintings and sculpture, photography, video installations and catalogues of expositions.

GALERIE ZURCHER

56 rue Chapon, 75003 Paris ■ Tel: 01 42 72 82 20 ■ Fax: 01 42 72 58 07 ■ E-mail: zurchergal@easynet.fr ■ Tue-Sat 11:00-19:00 ■ Bernard and Gwenolee Zurcher ■ English spoken ■ Prices medium to high ■ Professional discount

Contemporary paintings, photos and sculptures by young artists.

MARION GOODMAN

7 rue Debelleyme , 75003 Paris ■ Tel: 01 48 04 70 52 ■ E-mail: mgood@magic.fr ■ Tue-Sat 10:00-18:00 and by appointment ■ Agnes Fierobe speaks English ■ Prices medium

Contemporary works.

LAHUMIÈRE

17 rue du Parc Royal, 75003 Paris ■ Tel: 01 42 77 27 74 ■ Fax: 01 42 77 27 78 ■ Tue-Sat 10:00-18:00 ■ Anne and Jean-Claude Lahumière ■ English spoken

Works of contemporary artists.

BERTHE LAURSEN
56-58 rue Vieille du Temple, 75003 Paris ■ Telfax: 01 44 54 04 07
■ Mon-Sat 10:00-18:00 ■ English spoken ■ Prices medium
Young contemporary Scandinavian painters, sculptors and photographers. Some installations.

ALAIN MARGARON
5 rue du Perche, 75003 Paris ■ Tel: 01 42 74 2052 ■ Fax: 01 42 74 20 89 ■ Tue-Sat 10:00-18:00 ■ English spoken ■ Prices medium
Works of contemporary artists.

MONTENAY-GIROUX
8 rue Charlot 75003 Paris ■ Tel: 01 40 29 00 44 ■ Fax: 01 43 29 42 21 ■ Tue-Sat 11:00-13:00/14:30-19:00 ■ Frédéric Giroux and Anne Mabin speak English ■ Prices medium to high
Contemporary art, especially the new young artists.

MOUSSION-RABUAN
121 rue Vieille du Temple 75003 Paris ■ Tel: 01 48 87 75 91 ■ Fax: 01 42 71 42 81 ■ Mon-Sat 10:00-12:30/ 2:00-18:00 ■ Jacqueline Moussion speaks English
Videos, installations and photographs.

NATHALIE PARIENTE
14-16 rue de Thorigny, 75003 Paris ■ Tel: 01 40 27 08 82 ■ Fax: 01 40 27 08 87 ■ Tue-Sat 10:00-17:30 ■ English spoken
Young emerging artists. Paintings, sculptures, photographs, videos and installations.

ROMAGNY
119 rue Vieille du Temple 75003 Paris ■ Tel: 01 42 77 38 10 ■ Fax: 01 42 77 35 80 ■ Mon-Fri 10:00-17:30/Sat 10:00-16:00
Contemporary artists.

THADDAEUS ROPAC
7 rue Debelleyme, 75003 Paris ■ Tel: 01 42 72 99 00 ■ Fax: 01 42 72 61 66 ■ Tue-Sat 10:00-18:00 ■ English spoken fluently ■ Prices medium
Contemporary art including photographs, installations, sculptures.

DANIEL TEMPLON
30 rue Beaubourg, 75003 Paris ■ Tel: 01 42 72 14 10 ■ Fax: 01 42 77 45 36 ■ Web: www.artnet.com/dtemplon.html ■ Mon-Sat 10:00-19:00 ■ Daniel Templon ■ English spoken ■ Prices medium
Contemporary paintings and sculptures.

TENDANCES

105 rue Quincampoix, 75003 Paris ■ Tel: 01 42 78 61 79 ■ Fax: 01 42 78 12 75 ■ Mon-Fri 10:00-18:00/Sat 10:00-17:00 ■ Michèle Heyraud speaks English ■ Prices medium

Contemporary works.

———————————— **IV** ————————————

A L'IMAGE DU GRENIER SUR L'EAU

45 rue des Francs-Bourgeois, 75004 Paris ■ Tel: 01 42 71 02 31 ■ Fax: 01 42 78 66 77 ■ E-mail: image.di-maria@wanadoo.fr ■ Web: www.image-di-maria.com ■ Mon-Sat 10:00-19:00, Sun 14:00-19:00 ■ Sylvain and Yves di Maria ■ English spoken ■ Prices medium ■ Professional discount ■ Major credit cards

Posters, estampes, postcards, books, photos, old original documents of the XIX to XX centuries classified by theme and country of origin. Specialty: Art Nouveau and Art Deco.

ART FORMEL

9 rue Saint-Paul, 75004 Paris ■ Telfax: 01 48 04 93 33 ■ Thu-Mon 14:00-19:30, Sun 15:00-19:30 ■ English spoken ■ Prices medium ■ Visa and Amex

Paintings, bronzes, ceramics and glass of 1890 to 1960.

CHANTAL CROUSEL

40 rue Quincampoix, 75004 Paris ■ Tel: 01 42 77 38 87 ■ Fax: 01 42 77 59 00 ■ E-mail: galerie.Chantal.crousel@wanadoo.fr ■ Web: http://www.crousel-svennung.com ■ Tue-Sat 10:00-19:00 ■ Prices medium

Contemporary artists' work.

CHOURLET

2 and 4 Place des Vosges, 75004 Paris ■ Tel: 01 42 76 04 09 ■ Fax: 01 42 77 40 26 ■ E-mail: Chourlet@wanadoo.fr ■ Web: www.perso.wanadoo.fr/chourlet/ ■ Mon-Sun 10:00-20:00 ■ Jean-François Ducos ■ English spoken ■ Prices high ■ Amex, Visa

Artist's own paintings. Nice gallery and others in Vence and Luxembourg.

GALERIE AMYOT

60 rue Saint-Louis-en-l'Ile, 75004 Paris ■ Tel: 01 44 07 23 41 ■ Fax: 01 44 07 23 48 ■ Tue-Sun 11:00-12:30/14:30-19:30 ■ English spoken ■ Prices medium

Figurative paintings, watercolours, pastels.

GALERIE BELLINT

28bis bd de Sébastopol, 75004 Paris ■ Tel: 01 42 78 01 91 ■ Fax: 01 42 76 00 69 ■ E-mail: Fagniez@easynet.fr ■ Web: www.od-arts.com/bellint ■ Tue-Sat 14:00-19:00 and by appointment ■ Annie-José Lemant speaks English and Spanish ■ Prices medium ■ Professional discount

Contemporary art: paintings, sculpture, drawings, photographs and multiples.

GALERIE ALAIN BLONDEL

4 rue Aubry-le-Boucher, 75004 Paris ■ Tel: 01 42 78 66 67 ■ Fax: 01 42 78 47 90 ■ E-mail: galerie.blondeel@wanadoo.fr ■ Web: www.musexpo.com/galeries/blondeel ■ Tue-Fri 11:00-13:00/14:00-19:00, Sat 14:00-19:00 ■ Alain Blondel speaks English and German ■ Prices medium ■ Major credit cards

Paintings and sculptures, all realistic. Qualified expert.

GALERIE DE LA PLACE

17 Place des Vosges, 75004 Paris ■ Tel: 01 42 77 50 03 ■ Fax: 01 42 77 31 36 ■ Every day 14:00-19:00 ■ Daniel Lanson, Director ■ English spoken ■ Major credit cards

Contemporary figurative painting.

GALERIE DE MEDICIS

18 Place des Vosges, 75004 Paris ■ Tel: 01 40 29 92 11 ■ Fax: 01 40 29 91 52 ■ E-mail: medicis@galerie-modus.com ■ Web: www.galerie-modus.com ■ Everyday 10:00-19:30 ■ Véronique Botineau, Director ■ English and Spanish spoken ■ Prices medium to high ■ Professional discount ■ Major credit cards

Modern figurative paintings and sculptures.

GALERIE ANNE DE VILLEPOIX

11 rue des Tournelles, 75004 Paris ■ Tel: 01 42 78 32 24 ■ Fax: 01 42 78 32 16 ■ E-mail: villepoix@easynet.fr ■ Tue-Sat 11:00-19:00 ■ English spoken ■ Prices medium

Photographs, videos, sculptures, paintings of the XX century.

GALERIE DU CENTRE

5 rue Pierre-au-Lard, 75004 Paris ■ Tel: 01 42 77 37 92 ■ Fax: 01 42 77 26 31 ■ Web: www.galerie-du-centre.com ■ Tue-Sat 14:00-18:30 ■ Alain Matabasso speaks English and Spanish ■ Prices medium to high

Contemporary art: narrative, figurative.

GALERIE DU JOUR-AGNÈS B

44 rue Quincampoix, 75004 Paris ■ Tel: 01 44 54 55 90 ■ Fax: 01 44 54 55 99 ■ E-mail: jour@agnesb.fr ■ Web: www.agnesb.fr ■ Tue-Sat 10:30-19:00 ■ Tony Guererro ■ English spoken ■ Prices low to high ■ Major credit cards

Contemporary art. Gallery is noted for its excellent collection of photographs. Also some drawings and installations.

GALERIE AGATHE GAILLARD

3 rue du Pont Louis Philippe, 75004 Paris ■ Tel: 01 42 77 38 24 ■ Fax: 01 42 77 78 36 ■ Tue-Sat 13:00-19:00 ■ English spoken ■ Prices medium ■ Visa

Photographs after 1945.

GALERIE INSTANTS F. DESJOURS

17 quai aux Fleurs, 75004 Paris ■ Tel: 01 46 33 45 51 ■ Mon-Fri 9:00-13:00/15:00-19:00 ■ François Desjours speaks English ■ Prices medium to high ■ Major credit cards

Unusual moulds in plaster, resin and bronze, especially hands, children's and men's, and women's torsos.

GALERIE LAAGE - SALOMON

57 rue du Temple, 75004 Paris ■ Tel: 01 42 78 11 71 ■ Fax: 01 42 71 34 49 ■ E-mail: laagesalomon@compuserve.com ■ Tue-Fri 14:00-19:00, Sat 11:00-19:00 ■ Gabrielle Salomon and Delphine Perru speak English, German and Spanish ■ Prices medium

Contemporary sculptures and paintings.

GALERIE BAUDOIN LEBON

38 rue Sainte-Croix de la Bretonnerie, 74004 Paris ■ Tel: 01 42 72 09 10 ■ Fax: 01 42 72 02 20 ■ E-mail: Baudoin.lebon@wanadoo.fr ■ Tue-Sat 11:00-13:00/14:30-19:00 ■ English spoken ■ Prices medium to high

Contemporary art: paintings, sculptures, installations, collages. Specialists in Australian Aboriginal art and XIX and XX century photographs.

GALERIE MAEGHT

4 rue Saint-Merri, 75004 Paris ■ Tel: 01 42 78 43 44 ■ Fax: 01 42 78 27 61 ■ Tue-Sat 10:00-13:00/14:00-19:00 ■ English spoken ■ Prices medium to high ■ Professional discount

Contemporary paintings: Miro, Calder, Giacometti and young artists. There is also a bookshop of art editions in this magnificent XVII century private house in the centre of the Marais.

GALERIE NIKKI DIANA MARQUARDT
9 Place des Vosges, 75004 Paris ■ Tel: 01 42 78 21 00 ■ Fax: 01 42 78 86 73 ■ E-mail: marquarpfe@aol.com ■ Tue-Sat 11:00-18:00 ■ English spoken

Contemporary art: especially installations by Dan Flavin, Hiromix, Eric Weiss.

GALERIE GABRIELLE MAUBRIE
24 rue Sainte-Croix de la Bretonnerie, 75004 Paris ■ Tel: 01 42 78 03 97 ■ Fax: 01 42 74 54 02 ■ Tue-Sat 14:00-19:00 ■ English spoken ■ Prices medium

Avant-garde and contemporary art.

GALERIE NELSON
40 rue Quincampoix, 75004 Paris ■ Tel: 01 42 71 74 56 ■ Fax: 01 42 71 74 58 ■ E-mail: galerie.nelson@wanadoo.fr ■ Web: www.galerie-nelson.com ■ Tue-Sat 14:00-19:00 ■ Philip Nelson speaks English ■ Prices medium

Contemporary art: photographs, videos, paintings, drawings, sculptures, installations, multiples. Well-known artists: Thomas Ruff, Thomas Schutte and Rodney Graham. Young artists: Didier Courbot, Marie Jose Burki, Gert Verhoeven and Stephen Wilks. Their new annex, open by appointment, will show the work of unknown artists, in constantly changing shows.

GALERIE MAI OLLIVIER
50 rue Sainte-Croix de la Bretonnerie, 75004 Paris ■ Tel: 01 48 04 09 60 ■ Fax: 01 48 04 89 66 ■ Tue-Sat 11:00-13:00/14:30-19:00 ■ Mai Ollivier speaks English ■ Prices medium to high ■ 10-20% professional discount ■ Visa and Amex

Contemporary art and editions of artists' objects. Furniture, lighting and tapestries. 60% of contemporary African art.

GALERIE PAPILLON-FIAT
16 rue des Coutures Saint-Gervais, 75004 Paris ■ Tel: 01 40 29 98 80 ■ Fax: 01 40 29 07 19 ■ Tue-Fri 14:00-19:00, Sat 11:00-19:00 ■ Claude Papillon and Dominique Fiat speak English ■ Professional discount

A collection of contemporary paintings, sculpture, objects and installations.

GALERIE SAINT MERRI ART INUIT

9 rue Saint-Merri, 75004 Paris ■ Tel: 01 42 77 39 12 ■ Fax: 01 46 26 53 07 ■ E-mail: artinuit@artscom.com ■ Web: www.artscom.com/galeries/saintmerri ■ Tue-Thurs 14:30-19:00, Fri-Sat 11:00-19:00 ■ Martine Lena speaks English and Spanish ■ Prices medium to high ■ Professional Discount ■ Major credit cards

Specialist in Eskimo Art: Sculptures, engravings, books and documentation.

GALERIE VIDAL-SAINT PHALLE

10 rue du Trésor, 75004 Paris ■ Tel: 01 42 76 06 05 ■ Fax: 01 42 76 05 33 ■ Tue-Sat 14:00-19:00 ■ Bernard Vidal speaks English ■ Prices medium to high ■ Professional discount

Contemporary paintings and sculptures. Catalogues and framing.

GALERIE VIEILLE DU TEMPLE

23 rue Vieille du Temple, 75004 Paris ■ Tel: 01 40 29 97 52 ■ Fax: 01 42 71 39 75 ■ E-mail : galerievdutempl@infonie.fr ■ Tue-Sat 14:30-19:30 and by appointment ■ Marie-Hélène de la Forest Divonne speaks English ■ Prices medium ■ Professional discount ■ Major credit cards

Contemporary paintings, sculptures and photographs. Permanent exhibits of Abidine and George Ball, Pierre Collin, Philippe Helenon, Guy de Malherbe, Alexandre Hollan.

GALERIE PIERRE MARIE VITOUX

3 rue d'Ormesson, 75004 Paris ■ Tel: 01 48 04 81 00 ■ Fax: 01 48 04 56 99 ■ Web: www.od-arts.com/pierremarievitoux ■ Tue-Sat 14:00-19:00 ■ Directrice: Marie Vitoux speaks English and Spanish ■ Major credit cards

Contemporary drawings, engravings, paintings and sculptures.

GALERIE VIVENDI

28 Place des Vosges, 75004 Paris ■ Tel: 01 42 76 90 76 ■ Fax: 01 42 76 95 47 ■ E-mail: vivendi@galerie-modus.com ■ Web: www.galerie-modus.com ■ Everyday 10:30-20:00 ■ Mark Hachem ■ English spoken ■ Professional discount ■ Major credit cards

Contemporary paintings and sculptures. Art furniture.

JEAN-CLAUDE LEVET FINE ART GALLERY

51 rue Saint-Louis-en-l'Ile 75004 Paris ■ Tel: 01 43 54 36 47 ■ Fax: 01 40 51 77 92 ■ Every day 10:00-19:00 ■ Jean-Claude Levet speaks English ■ Prices medium ■ Professional discount ■ Diners, Amex

Late XIX century and early XX century Impressionist and Post-Impressionist paintings.

MEDIART

109 rue Quincampoix, 75004 Paris ■ Tel: 01 42 78 44 93 ■ Fax: 01 42 78 84 02 ■ E-mail: mediart@francenet.fr ■ Web: www.art.vianet.fr/galerie/mediart ■ Odile Schlemmer speaks English

Contemporary artists.

V

A L'IMAGERIE

9 rue Dante, 75005 Paris ■ Tel: 01 43 25 18 66 ■ Fax: 01 43 25 18 08 ■ E-mail: alimagerie@easynet.fr ■ Web: www.alimagerie.com ■ Mon-Sat 10:30-13:00/14:00-19:00 ■ Anne Martinière speaks English ■ 10% professional discount ■ Major credit cards

Original posters and lithographs before the 1960s. Cloth mounting and restoration.

ART ET COMMUNICATION

6 rue de Lanneau, 75005 Paris ■ Tel: 01 43 26 13 55 ■ Fax: 01 43 25 23 63 ■ Mon-Fri 14:00-19:00 or by appointment ■ Lise Cormery ■ English, Spanish and Japanese spoken ■ Professional discount ■ Major credit cards

Contemporary paintings, sculptures, engravings, art objects, table arts. The Grand Masters of the XIX and XX century.

GALERIE CHRISTINE COUDERC

6 rue de la Bucherie, 75005 Paris ■ Telfax: 01 43 29 44 41 ■ Tue-Sat 14:00-19:00 and by appointment ■ Christine Couderc speaks English ■ Prices medium ■ 20% professional discount

Paintings, both old and contemporary, art objects.

GALERIE PIERRE-MICHEL DUGAST

70 rue Gay-Lussac, 75005 Paris ■ Tel: 01 43 29 63 64 ■ Fax: 01 43 29 65 20 ■ Tue-Sat 11:00-12:30/15:30-19:00 ■ Prices medium ■ 10 to 20% professional discount

Paintings, sculptures and drawings by contemporary and little-known young artists.

GALERIE EMPREINTES

16 rue des Carmes, 75005 Paris ■ Telfax: 01 46 33 00 90 ■ Tue-Sat 15:00-19:00 ■ Ghyslaine Bargiarelli speaks English ■ Prices medium ■ 10 to 30% professional discount ■ Major credit cards

Contemporary figurative paintings and sculptures in bronze.

GALERIE R.G. MICHEL

17 quai Saint-Michel, 75005 Paris ■ Tel: 01 43 54 77 75 ■ Mon-Sat 9:30-19:00 ■ M. Michel ■ English and German spoken ■ Professional discount

XVI to XX century original estampes. Old and Modern drawings, original lithographs, decorative engravings, paintings and books. Periodic catalogue available by order.

GALERIE SAPHIR RIVE GAUCHE

84 bd Saint-Germain, 75005 Paris ■ Tel: 01 43 26 54 22 ■ Fax: 01 43 80 23 49 ■ Sun-Thurs 14:00-19:00 ■ Francine and Elie Szapiro speak English ■ Prices medium ■ 5 to 10% professional discount

Paintings, drawings and lithographs of the XIX and XX centuries. Old and new books and ancient Jewish art.

STUDIO DE L'IMAGE THÉÂTRE DE COLLECTION

14 rue des Carmes, 75005 Paris ■ Tel: 01 43 54 88 73 ■ Fax: 01 43 29 85 04 ■ Tue-Sat 15:00-20:00 ■ Philippe Grand speaks English ■ Prices medium to high ■ Professional discount ■ Major credit cards

Paintings, sculpture, photographs, and creation of events for artists.

VI

AITTOUARES GALLERY

2 rue des Beaux-Arts, 75006 Paris ■ Tel: 01 40 51 87 46 ■ Fax: 01 46 34 01 98 ■ E-mail: aittouares@wanadoo.fr ■ Web: www.aittaouares.com ■ Tue-Sat 10:00-13:00/14:00-19:00 ■ English spoken ■ Prices medium ■ Visa

Works on paper from late XIX century to 1960. Contemporary paintings, sculptures and ceramics.

ALERIC 1900-2000

8 rue Bonaparte, 75006 Paris ■ Tel: 01 43 25 84 20 ■ Fax: 01 46 34 74 52 ■ E-mail: dfleiss@orbital.fr ■ Web: www.orbital.fr/1900-2000 ■ Mon-Sat 10:00-12:30/14:00-19:00 ■ English, German, Spanish and Portuguese spoken ■ Prices medium to very high ■ Professional discount ■ Visa, Amex

Dada, Surrealist paintings, photographs, drawings and sculptures.

LUCIEN DURAND-LEGAILLARD

19 rue Mazarine, 75006 Paris ■ Tel: 01 43 26 25 35 ■ Fax: 01 43 25 05 56 ■ E-mail: gdl@hol.fr ■ Tue-Sat 10:00-12:30/14:30-19:00

Contemporary works of art.

GALERIE AKKA

22 rue de Seine, 75006 Paris ■ Tel: 01 43 54 66 75 ■ Fax: 01 43 25 01 32 ■ Tue-Sat 14:30-19:30 ■ Laurent Deschamps speaks English ■ Prices high ■ 15% professional discount ■ Major credit cards

Contemporary and modern art.

GALERIE ARNOUX

27 rue Guénégaud, 75006 Paris ■ Tel: 01 46 33 04 66 ■ Fax: 01 46 33 25 40 ■ E-mail: arnoux@parissimo.com ■ Web: www.parissi-mo.com/pages/arnoux.htm ■ Tue-Sat 11:00-13:00/14:00-19:00 ■ Jean-Pierre Arnoux speaks English and Spanish ■ Prices medium to high ■ Major credit cards

Abstract art of the 1950s by young painters and sculptors.

GALERIE BARÈS

32 rue de Seine, 75006 Paris ■ Tel: 01 55 42 93 95 ■ Fax: 01 55 42 94 36 ■ Mon-Sat 10:30-13:00/14:30-19:00 ■ Jean-Luc Barès ■ English, German, Italian and Spanish spoken ■ Prices medium ■ Professional discount ■ Major credit cards

XX century lithographs, engravings, and Modern illustrations.

GALERIE CLAUDE BERNARD

7-9 rue des Beaux-Arts, 75006 Paris ■ Tel: 01 43 26 97 07 ■ Fax: 01 46 33 04 25 ■ E-mail: galerie@claude-bernard.com ■ Tue-Sat 9:30-12:30/14:30-18:30 ■ English spoken ■ Professional discount

Old and contemporary paintings, sculptures.

GALERIE BERTHET-AITTOUARES

29 rue de Seine, 75006 Paris ■ Tel: 01 43 26 53 09 ■ Fax: 01 43 26 95 66 ■ E-mail: ,aittouares@claranet.fr ■ Web: www.galerie-ba.com ■ Tue-Sat 11:00-13:00/14:30-19:00 ■ Michel Aittouares speaks English ■ Prices medium to high ■ Professional discount possible

Paintings by contemporary artists. Drawings and water-colours by early XX century Masters.

♛ ARSÈNE BONAFOUS-MURAT

15 rue de l'Échaudé, 75006 Paris ■ Tel: 01 46 33 42 31 ■ Fax: 01 43 29 52 27 ■ E-mail: arsenebm@aol.com ■ Tue-Sat 13:00-19:00 ■ Arsène Bonafous-Murat, Hélène Bonafous-Murat, Catherine Costanzo ■ English and German spoken ■ Prices medium to high ■ 10% professional discount ■ Visa

XVI to XX century estampes and books relative to estampes. Monographs, catalogues-raisonnés and documentation. Periodic publication of catalogues of prices, themes or of general interest. Expertise and preparation of catalogues for auctions. Mr. and Mrs. Bonafous-Murat are qualified experts.

GALERIE BOURDON

79 bd Raspail 75006 Paris ■ Tel: 01 45 48 01 39 ■ Tue 14:00-19:00, Wed-Thurs 8:00-12:00/14:00-19:00, Fri 8:00-12:00 ■ Lucien Bourdon ■ Possible professional discount

Modern paintings on consignment.

GALERIE BREHERET

9 quai Malaquais, 75006 Paris ■ Telfax: 01 42 60 74 74 ■ Fax: 01 40 68 92 41 ■ Mon-Sat 10:30-19:00 ■ Michel Ducros and Gérard Poser speak English ■ Prices medium

Contemporary works, engravings, lithographs, watercolours, oils in small format.

GALERIE JEANNE BUCHER

53 rue de Seine, 75006 Paris ■ Tel: 01 44 41 69 65 ■ Fax: 01 44 41 69 68 ■ E-mail: Jeanne-bucher@easynet.fr ■ Web: www.od-arts/jeanne-bucher ■ Tue-Fri 9:00-18:30, Sat 10:00-12:30/14:30-18:00 ■ Jean-François Jaeger ■ English and Spanish spoken ■ Professional discount

Modern and contemporary art. Bissière, Tobey, Reichel, Szenes, Dubuffet, Vieira, Moser, Nallard. Books.

GALERIE CALLU MERITE

17 rue des Beaux-Arts, 75006 Paris ■ Tel: 01 46 33 04 18 ■ Fax: 01 40 51 82 21 ■ Tue-Fri 13:00-19:00, Sat 10:00-19:00 ■ François Callu-Merite ■ Prices medium ■ 5 to 10% professional discount ■ Major credit cards

Contemporary paintings and sculpture often of historical themes, Chaissac, Peyrissac, Lacasse, Bryen, Springer. Works of young artists (Art Actuel). Specialty: European abstract art of the 1950s.

GALERIE CANDILLIER

26 rue de Seine, 75006 Paris ■ Tel: 01 43 54 59 24 ■ Fax: 01 43 54 12 27 ■ Tue-Sat 10:00-13:00/14:30-18:00 ■ English spoken

Very nice prints, especially of Toulouse-Lautrec. Some paintings.

GALERIE COLETTE CREUZEVAULT

58 rue Mazarine, 75006 Paris ■ Tel: 01 43 26 67 85 ■ Fax: 01 43 25 25 70 ■ Tue-Sat 14:30-18:30 ■ Colette Creuzevault speaks English ■ Prices medium ■ 10 to 15% professional discount

Sculptures of the great masters, also high-quality paintings. Germaine Richier, César, Niki de Saint Phalle, exclusive representation of the young sculptor Sophido. Paintings by Matta, Lam, Kijno, Fassianos.

GALERIE F. SAGOT
20 rue de l'Abbé Grégoire, 75006 Paris ■ Telfax: 01 42 22 08 39 ■ Tue-Sat 11:00-19:00 and by appointment ■ Prices medium ■ 20% professional discount

Contemporary paintings.

GALERIE DEA
30 rue Bonaparte, 75006 Paris ■ Tel: 01 46 34 69 00 ■ Fax: 01 44 07 26 76 ■ Mon-Sat 10:00-19:00 (often closed 13:00-14:00) ■ English spoken ■ Prices medium ■ 15 to 20% professional discount

Contemporary paintings, furniture and articles of decoration. Beautiful and unusual works in glass and metal. Will take custom orders.

GALERIE MARIE DE HOLMSKY
80 rue Bonaparte, 75006 Paris ■ Tel: 01 43 29 08 90 ■ Fax: 01 45 00 59 97 ■ Tue-Sat 15:00-19:00 ■ English spoken ■ Prices medium ■ Professional discount ■ Major credit cards

Contemporary paintings, sculptures, artists' editions and expositions.

GALERIE DAMBIER-MASSET
5 rue des Beaux-Arts, 75006 Paris ■ Tel: 01 46 33 02 52 ■ Fax: 01 43 26 07 05 ■ Tue-Sat 10:00-13:00/14:30-19:00 ■ Prices medium

Contemporary paintings.

GALERIE ALAIN DE MONBRISON
2 rue des Beaux-Arts, 75006 Paris ■ Tel: 01 46 34 05 20 ■ Fax: 01 46 34 67 25 ■ Mon-Sat 10:00-12:30/14:30-18:30 ■ English, German and Spanish spoken ■ Prices medium ■ Amex, Visa

Tribal art of Africa, Oceania and America.

GALERIE DI MEO
9 rue des Beaux-Arts, 75006 Paris ■ Tel: 01 43 54 10 98 ■ Fax: 01 43 54 88 65 ■ Tue-Fri 10:00-13:00/14:30-19:00, Sat 10:00-19:00 ■ Donatello Di Meo speaks English, Spanish and Italian

Modern and contemporary paintings, by mostly young living artists.

GALERIE RAYMOND DREYFUS
3 rue des Beaux-Arts, 75006 Paris ■ Tel: 01 43 26 09 20 ■ Fax: 01 43 29 67 81 ■ Tue-Sat 10:30-12:45/14:30-18:45 ■ Raymond Dreyfus speaks English ■ Prices medium

Modern and contemporary paintings, lithographs, contemporary sculpture. Chu Teh Chun, Lanskoy, Mathieu, Schneider, Zao Wou-Ki.

GALERIE LUCIEN DURAND –LE GAILLARD
19 rue Mazarine, 75006 Paris ■ Telfax: 01 43 26 25 35 ■ Fax: o1 43 26 05 56 ■ Tue-Sat 11:00-13:00/14:30-19:00 ■ English spoken ■ Prices medium ■ Professional discount

Contemporary paintings, sculptures, photographs and installations.

GALERIE DE L'EMPEREUR
61 rue Bonaparte, 75006 Paris ■ Tel: 01 43 26 87 10 ■ English spoken

Realistic and "poetic" paintings, Brianchon, C. Caillard, Leguelt, N. Limouse.

GALERIE FLAK
8 rue des Beaux-Arts, 75006 Paris ■ Tel: 01 46 33 77 77 ■ Fax: 01 46 33 27 57 ■ Mon-Sat 11:00-13:00/14:30-19:30 ■ Edith Flak speaks English ■ Prices medium to high ■ Professional discount

Modern and contemporary paintings, sculptures, drawings, estampes, rare books.

GALERIE DU FLEUVE
6 rue de Seine, 75006 Paris ■ Tel: 01 43 26 08 96 ■ Fax: 01 43 28 28 91 ■ Tue-Sat 11:00-13:00/14:00-19:00 ■ Jacqueline Bellonte ■ English spoken ■ Prices medium ■ Professional discount ■ Amex

Modern and contemporary paintings and sculptures.

GALERIE 14
14 rue des Beaux-Arts, 75006 Paris ■ Tel: 01 56 24 00 34 ■ Fax: 01 56 24 00 48 ■ Tue-Sat 11:00-13:30/14:00-19:00 ■ Mme Bloch ■ English and Italian Spoken ■ Professional discount ■ Major credit cards

Essentially expositions of Louis Cane, painting, sculpture and furniture.

GALERIE FRAMOND
3 rue des Saints-Pères, 75006 Paris ■ Tel: 01 42 60 74 78 ■ Fax: 01 49 27 01 63 ■ Mon-Sat 10:00-12:30/14:30-19:00 ■ H.A. Gregor speaks English ■ Prices medium ■ 20% professional discount

Modern paintings.

GALERIE FURSTENBERG
8 rue Jacob, 75006 Paris ■ Tel: 01 43 25 89 58 ■ Fax: 01 43 25 95 83 ■ E-mail: furstenb@club-internet.fr ■ Tue-Sat 10:00-13:00/14:00-18:00 ■ English and German spoken ■ Professional discount ■ Visa and MC

Surrealism of the XX century and the works of young artists painting in a free figurative style. Well-known artists include Bellmer, Dali, De Chirico, Fichot, Fini, Kandinsky, Vogel.

GALERIE MARIE-JANE GAROCHE
33 rue de Seine, 75006 Paris ■ Tel: 01 43 26 89 62 ■ Fax: 01 46 33 69 44 ■ Tue-Sat 11:00-13:00/14:30-19:00 ■ English and Spanish spoken ■ Prices medium ■ Professional discount ■ major credit cards

Contemporary paintings.

GALERIE ARLETTE GIMARAY
13 rue de Seine, 75006 Paris ■ Tel: 01 46 34 71 80 ■ Fax: 01 46 34 04 57 ■ E-mail: arlettegimaray@wanadoo.fr ■ Tue-Sat 10:30-13:00/14:00-19:00 ■ Arlette Gimaray speaks English ■ Prices medium ■ Major credit cards

Contemporary paintings, sculptures and mixed techniques.

GALERIE GRILLON
44 rue de Seine, 75006 Paris ■ Tel: 01 46 33 03 44 ■ Fax: 01 46 33 93 81 ■ Tue-Sat 10:30-18:30 ■ English and Russian spoken ■ Prices low to high ■ Professional discount ■ Major credit cards

XIX and XX century original engravings and lithographs.

GALERIE GUISLAIN-ETATS D'ART
35 rue Guénégaud, 75006 Paris ■ Tel: 01 53 10 15 75 ■ Fax: 01 53 10 15 77 ■ Tue-Sat 10:30-13:00/14:00-19:30 ■ Frédéric Guislain ■ English spoken ■ Prices medium to high ■ Professional discount ■ Major credit cards

Contemporary art: paintings and sculptures of 1945 to 2000.

GALERIE LA HUNE BRENNER
14 rue de l'Abbaye, 75006 Paris ■ Tel: 01 43 25 54 06 ■ Fax: 01 40 46 84 81 ■ Tue-Fri 10:00-13:00/14:00-19:00, Sat 10:00-19:00 ■ Marc Brenner speaks English ■ Prices medium ■ Professional discount ■ Major credit cards

Contemporary art after 1950. lithographs, engravings, art books. Framing.

GALERIE JONAS
12 rue de Seine, 75006 Paris ■ Tel: 01 43 26 50 28 ■ Fax: 01 43 29 65 66 ■ Tue-Sat 9:30-12:30/14:30-18:30 ■ English spoken ■ Prices high ■ Professional discount

Paintings of the XIX century, Romantic and Barbizon Schools. Expert in XIX century paintings.

GALERIE ARNAUD LEFEBVRE
30 rue Mazarine, 75006 Paris ■ Tel: 01 43 26 50 67 ■ Fax: 01 44 07 05 19 ■ E-mail: ivar@wanadoo.fr ■ Mon-Sat 14:00-19:00 ■ English spoken

Contemporary paintings and sculpture.

GALERIE LEFOR-OPENO

29 rue Mazarine, 75006 Paris ■ Telfax: 01 46 33 87 24 ■ Web: www.od-arts.com/leforopeno ■ Tue-Sat 11:00-13:00/14:00-19:00 ■ Marie-Francine Adam-Openo ■ English spoken ■ Prices medium ■ 20 to 30% professional discount

Contemporary paintings and sculptures.

GALERIE CLAUDE LEMAND

16 rue Littré, 75006 Paris ■ Telfax: 01 45 49 26 95 ■ Wed-Sat 14:00-19:00 ■ Claude Lemand speaks English ■ Prices medium ■ 10 to 25% professional discount

Exclusive representation of contemporary international painters and sculptors. Unique pieces in bronze, estampes, illustrated books, works on paper.

GALERIE LOFT

3 bis rue des Beaux-Arts, 75006 Paris ■ Tel: 01 46 33 18 90 - Fax: 01 43 54 56 14 ■ E-mail: galofte@club-internet.fr ■ Tue-Sat 10:00-13:00/14:30-19:00 ■ Jean-François Roudillon ■ English and German spoken ■ Prices medium ■ Professional discount

Works by avant-garde young artists - figurative, narrative paintings. Chinoiserie.

GALERIE J. & H. LUHL

19 quai Malaquais, 75006 Paris ■ Tel: 01 42 60 76 97 ■ Fax: 01 42 60 20 19 ■ E-mail: galerieluhl@yahoo.fr ■ Web: www.antique-expo ■ Tue-Sat 14:00-19:00 ■ English, German, Dutch, Italian and Spanish spoken ■ Prices medium to high ■ Professional discount ■ Major credit cards

Japanese estampes, paintings and books.

GALERIE MENNOUR

60 rue Mazarine, 75006 Paris ■ Tel: 01 56 24 03 63 ■ Fax: 01 56 24 03 64 ■ Tue-Sat 14:00-19:00 ■ English spoken ■ Prices low to medium ■ Professional discount

Contemporary paintings, engravings, lithographs and photographs.

GALERIE MARION MEYER

15 rue Guénégaud, 75006 Paris ■ Tel: 01 46 33 04 38 ■ Fax: 01 40 46 91 41 ■ E-mail: mmeyer@club-internet,fr ■ Web: www.marion-meyer.com ■ Marion Meyer speaks English and German ■ Prices medium to high ■ Professional discount ■ Visa

Paintings, drawings, sculpture, photographs. Surrealists and Dadaists. Qualified expert on Man Ray.

♛ GALERIE MEYER-OCEANIC ART

17 rue des Beaux-Arts, 75006 Paris ■ Tel: 01 43 54 85 74 ■ Fax: 01 43 54 11 12 ■ E-mail: ajpmeyer@aol.com ■ Web: www.art-net.com/meyer.html ■ Mon-Sat 10:30-13:00/14:30-19:00 ■ Anthony J.P. Meyer ■ English, German and Italian spoken ■ Prices high to very high ■ Professional discount ■ Amex, Visa

Oceanic art. Tribal art from Melanesia, Polynesia, Micronesia and Australia.

GALERIE ERIC DE MONTBEL

34 rue de Seine, 75006 Paris ■ Tel: 01 43 29 34 31 ■ Fax: 01 43 29 36 32 ■ E-mail: galerie@eric-demonbel.com ■ Web: www. Eric-demonbel.com ■ Tue-Sat 11:00-13:00/14:30-19:00 ■ English spoken ■ Major credit cards

Modern art, abstract and figurative paintings and sculptures of little-known artists.

♛ GALERIE LELIA MORDOCH

40 rue de Seine, 2 rue de l'Échaudé, 75006 Paris ■ Tel: 01 46 33 29 30 ■ Fax: 01 46 33 94 52 ■ E-mail: lelia.mordoch.galerie@wanadoo.fr ■ Tue-Sat 13:00-19:00 ■ Lelia Mordoch and A. Passeron speak English and German ■ Prices medium

Works of living artists, leaning towards the abstract.

GALERIE MOSTINI

18 rue de Seine, 75006 Paris ■ Tel: 01 43 25 32 18 ■ Fax: 01 43 54 93 55 ■ Tue-Sat 11:00-13:00/14:00-19:00 ■ Elizabeth Mostini speaks English ■ Prices low to medium ■ 10% professional discount

Contemporary paintings and sculptures, art objects, ceramics, lighting.

GALERIE 1900-2000

8 rue Bonaparte, 75006 Paris ■ Tel: 01 43 25 84 20 ■ Fax: 01 46 34 74 52 ■ E-mail: dfleiss@orbital.fr ■ Web: www.orbital.fr/1900-2000 ■ Mon 14:00-19:00/Tue-Sat 10:00-12:30/14:00-19:00 ■ English spoken ■ Prices reasonable ■ 5 to 10% professional discount

Modern and contemporary paintings. Specialty: Surrealism and Dada.

GALERIE VIRGINIE PITCHAL

40 rue Jacob, 75006 Paris ■ Tel: 01 42 61 16 33 ■ Fax: 01 42 61 16 79 ■ E-mail: vpitchal@club-internet.fr ■ Tue-Sat 11:00-19:00 ■ English spoken ■ Professional discount ■ Major credit cards

Paintings and old drawings of the XVI to the XVIII century.

GALERIE PIXI

95 rue de Seine, 75006 Paris ■ Telfax: 01 43 25 10 12 ■ Tue-Sat 14:30-19:00, Sat 11:00-19:00 ■ Marie Victoire Poliakoff ■ English spoken ■ Prices medium ■ 10% professional discount ■ Visa

Contemporary art, paintings, sculptures, XX century lithographs, drawings of young artists.

GALERIE PROTÉE

38 rue de Seine, 75006 Paris ■ Tel: 01 43 25 21 95 ■ Fax: 01 40 46 04 02 ■ E-mail: galerie.protee@wanadoo.fr ■ Tue-Sat 10:00-12:30/14:00-19:00 ■ Laurence Izern and Jacques Pulvermacher speak English and Spanish ■ Prices medium to high ■ Professional discount ■ Major credit cards

Contemporary painting from the 1950s to the present: Bram Bogart, Gontard, Mathieu, Lindstrom, Cole Morgan, Eugène Leroy and more. Mme Izern is an expert to the Court of Appeals of Toulouse.

GALERIE PAUL PROUTÉ

74 rue de Seine, 75006 Paris ■ Tel: 01 43 26 89 80 ■ Fax: 01 43 25 83 41 ■ Tue-Sat 9:00-12:00, 14:00-19:00 ■ Sylvie Tocci Prouté and Annie Martinez Prouté speak English, German and Italian ■ Prices medium to high ■ 10% professional discount ■ Visa, MC

Drawings and prints of the XV to the XX century. Publication of three catalogues a year, two of which can be sent free-of-charge upon request.

GALERIE 53

53 rue de Seine, 75006 Paris ■ Fax: 01 56 24 23 00 ■ Tue-Sat 10:30-13:00/14:00-19:00 and by appointment ■ English spoken ■ Prices medium to high ■ 10% professional discount

XIX and XX century paintings and watercolours.

GALERIE F. SAGOT

20 rue de l'Abbé Grégoire, 75006 Paris ■ Telfax: 01 42 22 08 39 ■ Tue-Sat 14:00-20:00 ■ English and German spoken ■ Prices medium ■ Professional discount ■ Diners

Contemporary art, paintings, sculptures, travelling artists. Decorating advice.

GALERIE SAMAGRA - PARIS - MUNICH

52 rue Jacob, 75006 Paris ■ Tel: 01 42 86 13 04 ■ Fax: 01 44 74 03 31 ■ Mon 14:00-19:00, Tue-Sat 10:30-12:30/14:00-19:00 ■ English spoken ■ Prices medium to high ■ 5 to 25% professional discount

Contemporary abstract and expressionist paintings, sculptures. Humour and derision. Rental of paintings. Creation of artistic environments.

GALERIE SAMARCANDE
13 rue des Saints-Pères, 75006 Paris ■ Tel: 01 42 60 83 17 ■ Fax: 01 42 61 41 64 ■ E-mail: gal.samarcande@wanadoo.fr ■ Mon-Sat 10:00-13:00/14:00-19:00 ■ Joseph Uzan ■ English spoken ■ Prices medium ■ Professional discount ■ Amex, Visa

Antiquity: Rome, Greece, Egypt, Mesopotamia. Expert.

GALERIE SÉGUIER
10 rue Séguier, 75006 Paris ■ Tel: 01 46 33 26 93 ■ Fax: 01 40 51 73 09 ■ Web: www.calligraphie.com ■ Tue-Sat 15:00-19:00 ■ André Edouard ■ Prices reasonable

Contemporary paintings and sculptures.

GALERIE NATALIE SEROUSSI
34 rue de Seine, 75006 Paris ■ Tel: 01 46 34 05 84 ■ Fax: 01 46 33 03 37 ■ E-mail: galerieseroussi@wanadoo.fr ■ Mon-Sat 10:00-13:00/14:00-19:00 ■ Natalie Seroussi ■ English spoken

Mostly modern and contemporary paintings.

GALERIE SERRES
15 rue Bonaparte, 75006 Paris ■ Tel: 01 43 25 78 27 ■ Fax: 01 46 33 55 32 ■ Tue-Sat 10:30-19:00 ■ Jean-Philippe Mariaud de Serres speaks English ■ Prices high ■ 10% professional discount

Archaeological objects: Mesopotamian, Egyptian, Greek, Roman and Celtic. Qualified expert.

GALERIE DARTHEA SPEYER
6 rue Jacques-Callot, 75006 Paris ■ Tel: 01 43 54 78 41 ■ Fax: 01 43 29 62 39 ■ Tue-Fri 14:00-19:00/Sat 11:00-19:00 ■ English spoken

Contemporary paintings and sculptures.

GALERIE THIERRY SPIRA
19 rue Guénégaud, 75006 Paris ■ Tel: 01 46 33 18 19 ■ Fax: 01 46 33 20 21 ■ Tue-Sat 12:00-18:30 ■ English spoken ■ Visa

Abstract paintings of the 1950's and some contemporary works.

GALERIE STADLER
51 rue de Seine, 75006 ■ Tel: 01 43 26 91 10 ■ Fax: 01 46 34 73 97 ■ Tue-Sat 14:30-19:00 ■ English spoken ■ Prices very high ■ Professional discount

Contemporary paintings.

GALERIE LAURENT STROUK
25 rue Guénégaud, 75006 Paris ■ Tel: 01 55 42 16 55 ■ Fax: 01 55 42 14 56 ■ Tue-Sat 10:30-13:00/14:00-19:00 ■ English spoken

Contemporary paintings, especially the 1950s.

GALERIE R. TREGER
47 rue Mazarine, 75006 Paris ■ Tel: 01 46 33 81 60 ■ Fax: 01 46 33 81 60 ■ E-mail: Rtreger@easynet.fr ■ Web: www.od-arts.com/treger ■ Tue-Sat 14:00-19:30 ■ Antonio Saint Silvestre speaks English and Portuguese ■ Visa, Amex

International Outsider art.

GALERIE PATRICE TRIGANO
4 bis rue des Beaux-Arts, 75006 Paris ■ Tel: 01 46 34 15 01 ■ Fax: 01 46 34 64 02 ■ E-mail: artrigano@aol.com ■ Web: www.od-arts.com/patricetrigano ■ Tue-Sat 10:00-13:00/14:30-18:30 ■ Patrice Trigano ■ English spoken ■ Prices medium ■ Professional discount

Sculptures and paintings since 1940. Abstract art and realism.

GALERIE VENDÔME-V.R.G.
23 rue Jacob, 75006 Paris ■ Tel: 01 43 26 29 17 ■ Fax: 01 43 29 69 02 ■ Tue-Sat 11:30-13:00/14:30-19:30 ■ English spoken ■ Prices medium ■ Professional discount

Contemporary paintings, sculptures and glass objects by living artists.

GALERIE ALINE VIDAL
70 rue Bonaparte, 75006 Paris ■ Tel: 01 40 46 95 55 ■ Tue-Fri 13:00-18:00, Sat 14:00-19:00 ■ Aline Vidal speaks English ■ Prices medium

Contemporary art.

👑 GALERIE MICHEL VIDAL
3 rue des Beaux-Arts, 75006 Paris ■ Tel: 01 46 34 69 88 ■ Fax: 01 46 34 65 20 ■ E-mail: galrividal@club-internet.fr ■ Tue-Sat 14:30-18:00 ■ English spoken ■ Prices very high ■ Professional discount

Contemporary art: Man Ray, Duchamp, Piccabia. Research upon request.

GALERIE LUCIE WEILL-SELIGMANN,
ZALBER & DE NOBLET
6 rue Bonaparte, 75006 Paris ■ Tel: 01 43 54 71 95 ■ Fax: 01 40 51 82 88 ■ Tue-Sat 11:00-13:00/14:30-19:00 ■ Charles Zalber and Gonzague de Noblet speak English ■ Prices medium.

Drawings by modern and contemporary masters. Works on paper by artists of the XIX and XX centuries. Rugs of the Marie Cuttoli collection by Picasso, Arp, Miro, Klee, Léger, Laurens, Calder. The rugs cost up to 40,000 French Francs.

J. G. M. GALERIE
8bis rue Jacques-Callot, 75006 Paris ■ Tel: 01 43 26 12 05 ■ Fax: 01 46 33 44 83 ■ E-mail: jgm@easynet.fr ■ Tue-Fri 10:00-13:00/14:00-19:00, Sat 11:00-19:00 ■ Jean-Gabriel Mitterand ■ English, Spanish, German and Portuguese spoken ■ Prices varied ■ 10-20% professional discount

Contemporary sculptures and photographs. Consultant to companies for monumental sculpture: study, estimate, proposal and installation.

GALERIE KRIEF
103 rue de Sèvres, 75006 Paris ■ Tel: 01 45 27 27 05 ■ Fax: 01 43 25 53 27 ■ Tue-Sat 10:00-19:00 ■ Elizabeth Krief

Contemporary art.

MARCILHAC
8 rue Bonaparte, 75006 Paris ■ Tel: 01 43 26 47 36 ■ Fax: 01 43 54 96 87 ■ Mon-Sat 10:00-19:00 ■ English spoken ■ Prices high

XIX and early XX century paintings.

LAROCK-GRANOFF
13 quai de Conti ■ 75006 Paris ■ Tel: 01 43 54 41 92 ■ Fax: 01 46 33 77 90 ■ Mon-Fri 10:00-19:00 ■ Mary Larock ■ English spoken

Today's artists.

I.S. THOMAS
15 rue des Beaux-Arts, 75006 Paris ■ Telfax: 01 43 26 39 36 ■ E-mail: ythoms@investir.fr ■ Web: www.artnet.com/isthomas.html ■ Tue- Fri 14:00-19:00, Sat 11:00-19:00 ■ Yves Thomas ■ English spoken ■ Prices medium to high ■ Amex

Contemporary paintings and sculptures. Works on paper: gouaches, drawings and watercolours.

♛ VALLOIS
41 rue de Seine, 75006 Paris ■ Tel: 01 43 29 50 84 ■ Fax: 01 43 29 90 73 ■ E-mail: vallois@club-internet.fr ■ Web: www.vallois.com ■ Tue-Sat 10:00-13:00/14:00-19:00 ■ Sheryl Niedorf speaks English ■ Prices medium to high ■ Professional discount

Sculpture of the XX century. Catalogues available.

———————————— VII ————————————

ART 50
50 rue de Verneuil, 75007 Paris ■ Tel: 01 40 15 99 50 ■ Tue-Fri 14:00-19:00/Sat 11:00-13:00/14:30-19:00 ■ Claudine Legrand speaks English ■ Prices medium ■ Professional discount

Contemporary paintings and sculptures.

ANNICK DRIGUEZ
39 rue de Verneuil, 75007 Paris ■ Tel: 01 42 86 00 42 ■ Tue-Sat 15:00-19:00 ■ Annick Driguez speaks some English ■ Prices medium ■ Professional discount

XIX, XX century and contemporary sculptures and drawings by sculptors. A tendency toward the classic figurative.

EPOCA
60 rue de Verneuil, 75007 Paris ■ Tel: 01 45 48 48 66 ■ Fax: 01 45 44 85 82 ■ Mon-Fri 11:00-19:00/Sat 14:30-19:00 ■ English spoken ■ Prices medium to high ■ Professional discount

A remarkable collection: Indian art, paintings, sculptures, modern art, unusual objects and furniture. Creation of atmospheres. Sale and rental.

GALERIE AIR DE CHASSE
115 rue Saint-Dominique, 75007 Paris ■ Telfax: 01 42 60 25 98 ■ By appointment only Tue-Thu 14:00-19:00 ■ Eric Angot ■ English spoken ■ Prices medium to high ■ Professional discount

Animal Art of the XIX century: bronzes and paintings.

GALERIE HÉLÈNE APPEL
75 rue Saint-Dominique, 75007 Paris ■ Tel: 01 45 51 28 17 ■ Tue-Fri 11:00-18:00 ■ Hélène Appel speaks English ■ Prices medium ■ Professional discount

Original figurative paintings of living artists.

♛ GALERIE BELLIER
7 quai Voltaire, 75007 Paris ■ Tel: 01 42 60 74 72 ■ Fax: 01 40 20 93 52 ■ Tue-Sat 11:00-13:00/14:30-19:00 ■ Mr. Bellier speaks English ■ Prices high

Late XIX and XX century paintings.

♛ GALERIE BERÈS
25 quai Voltaire, 75007 Paris ■ Tel: 01 42 61 27 91 ■ Fax: 01 49 27 95 88 ■ E-mail: beres@easynet.fr ■ Mon-Sat 10:00-13:00/14:00-19:00 ■ English, German and Italian spoken ■ Major credit cards

XIX and XX century paintings, especially French.

BERGGRUEN
70 rue de l'Université, 75007 Paris ■ Tel: 01 42 22 02 12 ■ Fax: 01 42 22 57 43 ■ Mon-Fri 10:00-18:00 ■ Soizie Andouard speaks English

XX century paintings.

GALERIE DENIS BLOCH
52 rue de l'Université, 75007 Paris ■ Tel: 01 42 22 25 26 ■ Fax: 01 45 48 73 73 ■ By appointment only ■ Denis Bloch speaks English ■ Prices reasonable ■ Professional discount

Lithographs and engravings by XX century masters.

GALERIE SYLVIE BRULEY
27 rue de l'Université, 75007 Paris ■ Tel: 01 40 15 00 63 ■ Tue-Sat 14:30-19:00 ■ Sylvie Bruley speaks English ■ Prices low ■ 15% professional discount

Contemporary paintings and sculptures.

GALERIE CHISSEAUX RIVE GAUCHE
33 av de la Bourdonnais, 75007 Paris ■ Tel: 01 45 55 49 17 ■ Tue-Sat 13:30-19:00 ■ Frederique Foreau ■ English spoken ■ CB and Amex

Contemporary paintings, watercolours, period pastels.

GALERIE LINA DAVIDOV
210 bd Saint-Germain, 75007 Paris ■ Tel: 01 45 48 99 87 ■ Fax: 01 42 23 36 70 ■ Tue-Sat 11:00-12:30/14:00-19:00 ■ Lina Davidov speaks Spanish and English ■ Prices medium to high ■ Visa

Contemporary artists: J. Guinovart, R. Licata, C. Ginzburg, J. Tresaco, A. Mateu, A. de la Pisa, S. Sarduy, Angeles Ortiz, J. Pagola, C. Gallardo.

GALERIE DE HESDIN
46 rue du Bac, 75007 Paris ■ Tel: 01 45 48 13 29 ■ Fax: 01 45 48 19 28 ■ Tue-Fri 10:30-13:00/14:00-19:00, Sat 13:00-19:00 ■ English spoken ■ Prices reasonable ■ 10% professional discount

Contemporary paintings, drawings, pastels by young artists, known and unknown.

GALERIE MARTINE ET THIBAULT DE LA CHATRE
36 rue de Varenne, 75007 Paris ■ Tel: 01 45 48 82 99 ■ Fax: 01 45 49 05 84 ■ E-mail : webmaster@art.vianet.fr-n ■ Web : www.art.vianet.fr/actualite ■ Mon-Sat 11:00-19:00 ■ English spoken

Works by contemporary international artists: Claude Rutault, François Morellet, Raymond Hains, Gérard Deschamps, Glen Baxter, Peter Downsbrough, Raoul Marek, Olivier Mosset, Robert Barry, Sol Lewitt. Artists' books.

GALERIE DUPUTEL
20 rue de Beaune, 75007 Paris ■ Telfax: 01 42 97 47 92 ■ Mon-Fri 11:00-19:00 ■ David Duputel speaks English ■ Prices medium ■ Professional discount

XIX and XX century paintings, Barbizon School. Sculpture of the XIX century.

GALERIE DUVEAU-SAGE
42 rue de Verneuil, 75007 Paris ■ Tel: 01 42 61 83 56 ■ Tue-Sat 14:00-19:00

Paintings, sculptures, old drawings and objets d'art.

GALERIE ESCALE A PARIS-CHRISTIAN DESBOIS EDITIONS
14 av de la Bourdonnais, 75007 Paris ■ Tel: 01 45 55 85 53 ■ Fax: 01 45 56 06 16 ■ Tue-Sat 15:00-19:00 ■ Christian Desbois speaks English ■ Prices medium ■ Professional discount

Estampes, seriographs, lithographs, paintings, watercolours, pastels by artists of the cartoon genre. Specialist in "Bande Dessinée" (cartoons).

GALERIE JEAN FOURNIER
22 rue du Bac, 75007 Paris ■ Tel: 01 42 97 44 00 ■ Fax: 01 42 97 46 00 ■ Tue-Sat 10:00-12:30/14:00-19:00 ■ Jean Fournier ■ English spoken

Contemporary paintings of James Bishop, Stéphane Bordarier, Sam Francis, Simon Hantal, Joan Mitchell, Bernard Piffaretti, Jean-Paul Riopelle, Antonio Semeraro.

GALERIE DANIEL GERVIS
14 rue de Grenélle, 75007 Paris ■ Tel: 01 45 44 41 90 ■ Fax: 01 45 49 18 98 ■ By appointment ■ English spoken ■ Prices medium ■ Professional discount

Modern and contemporary paintings, sculpture, lithographs, engravings in limited editions.

GALERIE MICHEL GILLET
54 av de la Bourdonnais, 75007 Paris ■ Tel: 01 47 53 72 73 ■ Fax: 01 45 56 90 03 ■ E-mail: cca-michelgillet@wanadoo.fr ■ Mon-Fri 10:00-19:00, Sat 14:00-19:00 ■ Michel Gillet speaks English ■ Prices reasonable ■ 10% professional discount

Contemporary figurative painting works by young artists.

GALERIE SAMY KINGE
54 rue de Verneuil, 75007 Paris ■ Tel: 01 42 61 19 07 ■ Fax: 01 42 61 53 94 ■ E-mail: skinge@easynet.fr ■ Tue-Sat 14:30-19:00 ■ English, Italian and Arabic spoken ■ Prices medium ■ 15% professional discount

Modern post-1945 paintings, young contemporary artists. Surrealist and New Realist paintings. Expert in Surrealist paintings.

GALERIE LA POCHADE

16 rue de Lille, 75007 Paris ■ Tel: 01 42 86 04 80 ■ Fax: 01 43 29 75 11 ■ Tue-Sat 11:00-13:00/14:00-19:00 ■ Alain Digard and Philippe Fravelles speak English ■ Prices low to high ■ 10 to 30% professional discount depending on quantity

Modern and contemporary works on paper and paintings of known and little-known young artists. Specialists in works 1945 to 1980: Calder, Bertini, Gleizes, Fautrier.

♛ GALERIE LEEGENHOEK

23 quai Voltaire, 75007 Paris ■ Tel: 01 42 96 36 08 ■ Tue-Sat 14:30-18:30 ■ English spoken ■ Prices high

Old Master paintings. Superb.

GALERIE DES LYONS

9 rue de Beaune, 75007 Paris ■ Tel: 01 42 61 16 81 ■ Fax: 01 49 48 70 01 ■ Mon-Sat 11:00-12:30/14:30-19:00 ■ English spoken ■ Prices medium ■ 10% professional discount

XIX, XX century paintings.

GALERIE ILEANA BOUBOULIS

48 rue de Verneuil, 75007 ■ Telfax: 01 40 20 42 84 ■ E-mail: GalerieBouboulis@aol.com ■ Tue-Sat 11:00-19:00 ■ Ileana Bouboulis speaks English, Italian, Spanish and Greek ■ Prices medium to high ■ Professional discount ■ Major credit cards

Sculptures, paintings and drawings of the XX century.

GALERIE MAEGHT

42 rue du Bac, 75007 Paris ■ Tel: 01 45 48 45 15 ■ Fax: 01 42 22 22 83 ■ Tue-Sat 10:00-13:00/14:00-19:00 ■ English spoken ■ Prices medium to high ■ Professional discount

Lithographs and engravings of Miro, Calder, Giacometti, Matisse and young artists. Art editions.

GALERIE MERCIER-DUCHEMIN-CHANOIT

40 rue de l'Université, 75007 Paris ■ Tel: 01 42 86 00 40 ■ Fax: 01 42 86 03 02 ■ Mon-Sat 10:00-12:30/14:00-19:00 ■ English spoken ■ Prices medium ■ 10% professional discount

Antique and modern paintings, drawings and sculpture.

GALERIE MONEGIER DU SORBIER
14 rue de Beaune, 75007 Paris ■ Tel: 01 42 61 69 00 ■ Fax: 01 42 61 32 28 ■ Mon-Sat 10:30-12:30/15:00-19:00 ■ English spoken ■ Prices medium ■ 10% professional discount

Paintings of the second half of the XIX century to the early XX century, especially from Provence.

GALERIE ANTOINE VAN DE BEUQUE
15 Place Vauban, 75007 Paris ■ Tel: 01 44 18 30 04 ■ Fax: 01 44 18 30 05 ■ Mon-Fri 10:00-18:00 by appointment only

Principally a broker of high and very high-priced masters of the XIX and XX centuries. Offers expertise and will travel.

GALERIE RENN
14,16 rue de Verneuil, 75007 Paris ■ Tel: 01 42 61 25 71 ■ Tue-Sat 12:00-19:00 ■ Christian Longchamp ■ English, Italian and German spoken

Contemporary art exhibitions. Very nice gallery space.

KELLERMANN
55 rue de Varenne, 75007 Paris ■ Tel: 01 42 22 11 24 ■ By appointment only ■ Michel Kellermann speaks English ■ Prices reasonable

Modern and contemporary paintings and drawings. Specialist in Derain. Expert to the French Customs.

L'ART EN MOUVEMENT
17 rue Duvivier, 75007 Paris ■ Tel: 01 45 55 03 16 ■ Fax: 01 47 05 74 07 ■ E-mail: art-mouvement@wanadoo.fr ■ Web: www.art-en-mouvement.fr ■ Mon-Fri, Sun by appointment ■ Antoine Villeneau ■ English and Spanish spoken ■ Prices medium ■ 10 to 15% professional discount

Paintings, lithographs, sculptures, drawings, trompe l'oeil. Art services to corporations and associations.

ANNE LETTRÉE
204 bld Saint Germain, 75007 Paris ■ Tel: 01 45 44 24 05 ■ Fax: 01 42 84 37 78 ■ Mon-Sat 10:00-19:00 ■ English spoken

Contemporary paintings and sculptures, especially from the late 1950s to today. They also have original furniture designed by their artists.

LE CYGNE VERT
41 rue de Verneuil, 75007 Paris ■ Tel: 01 40 20 08 41 ■ Mon-Sat 11:00-19:00 ■ Julien Dufay speaks English ■ Prices medium ■ 20% professional discount

XIX, XX century sculptures and paintings.

ANDRÉ LEMAIRE

43 rue de Verneuil, 75007 Paris ■ Tel: 01 42 61 12 55 ■ Tue-Sat 15:00-19:00 ■ Catherine Hamelin speaks English ■ Prices reasonable ■ Professional discount

XIX century paintings and sculpture. Official Academy art.

DENISE RENÉ

196 bd Saint-Germain, 75007 Paris ■ Tel: 01 42 22 77 57 ■ Fax: 01 45 44 89 18 ■ Tue-Sat 10:00-13:00/14:00-19:00 ■ English spoken ■ Prices medium to high ■ Professional discount

Abstract art and art constructions.

GIANNA SISTU

29 rue de l'Université, 75007 Paris ■ Tel: 01 42 22 41 63 ■ Fax: 01 45 44 93 85 ■ E-mail: gsistu@club-internet.fr ■ Mon-Sat 10:00-19:00 ■ English spoken

Post-Impressionist, Modern and contemporary art.

VIII

ART ACTUEL

6 rue de Lisbonne, 75008 Paris ■ Tel: 01 45 22 01 66 ■ Fax: 01 45 22 64 19 ■ Mon-Fri 9:00-18:00 ■ Anne Kron ■ English spoken ■ Prices medium ■ Professional discount

Rental and sale of the works of contemporary artists, estampes, sculpture.

♛ ARTCURIAL

61 av Montaigne, 75008 Paris ■ Tel: 01 42 99 16 16 ■ Fax: 01 42 99 16 10 ■ Tue-Sat 10:00-19:15 ■ English spoken ■ Prices high ■ Major credit cards

Excellent quality modern and contemporary paintings, prints and sculptures by living artists. Jewellery, carpets and books.

ART FRANCE

36 av Matignon, 75008 Paris ■ Tel: 01 43 59 17 89 ■ Fax: 01 45 63 84 83 ■ Mon-Sat 10:30-18:30 ■ Carole Senille speaks English ■ 10 to 15% professional discount

Modern paintings, pastels, drawings, tapestries, sculpture, lithographs. Qualified expert with the Court of Appeals and the French Customs.

ARTS VIVANTS-GALERIE LANCRY

33 rue de Miromesnil, 75008 Paris ■ Tel: 01 42 66 16 48 ■ Fax: 01 42 66 16 30 ■ Mon-Fri 10:00-19:00 ■ Abraham Lancry speaks English ■ Prices medium ■ 25% professional discount on purchases over 20,000 FF

Figurative paintings by living painters. Sculptures and lithographs.

FABIEN BOULAKIA

10 av Matignon, 75008 Paris ■ Tel: 01 56 59 66 55 ■ Fax: 01 56 59 56 50 ■ Tue-Sat 10:00-18:00 ■ Prices high

Paintings and drawings.

CAILLEUX

136 rue du Faubourg-Saint-Honoré, 75008 Paris ■ Tel: 01 43 59 25 24 ■ Fax: 01 42 25 95 11 ■ Mon-Fri 9:00-12:30/14:00-18:00 ■ English spoken ■ Prices medium to high ■ 10% professional discount

High quality XVIII century French paintings and drawings.

GALERIE CAZEAU-BERAUDIÈRE

16 av Matignon, 75008 Paris ■ Tel: 01 45 63 09 00 ■ Fax: 01 45 63 09 90 ■ English spoken ■ Prices high

Paintings of the late XIX and early XX century.

GALERIE JEAN-LOUIS DANANT

36 av Matignon, 75008 Paris ■ Tel: 01 42 89 40 15 ■ Fax: 01 42 89 40 10 ■ E-mail: danant@cybercable.fr ■ English spoken ■ Prices high

Modern and contemporary paintings.

RICHARD DELH

34 av Hoche, 75008 Paris ■ Tel: 01 42 25 13 82 /01 42 25 13 83 ■ Fax: 01 42 56 38 84 ■ Tue-Sat 10:00-18:00 ■ Mr. Delh speaks a bit of English

Specialty is geometric constructions.

GALERIE ARIEL

140 bd Haussmann, 75008 Paris ■ Tel: 01 45 62 13 09 ■ Fax: 01 42 25 98 46 ■ Mon-Fri 10:00-12:30/14:30-18:30 ■ Joan Pollock ■ English spoken ■ Prices medium ■ Professional discount

Paintings of the Paris School, new figurative and abstract paintings, Cobra movement. Sculptures by Reinhoud and Subira-Puig.

♛ GALERIE JACQUES BAILLY

95 rue du Faubourg-Saint-Honoré, 75008 Paris ■ Tel: 01 40 06 06 60 ■ Fax: 01 40 06 96 86 ■ E-mail: galerie@jacques-bailly.com ■ Web: www.galerie-jacques-bailly.com ■ Mon-Sat 10:00-19:00 ■ English and German spoken ■ Professional discount

Post-Impressionist and School of Paris. Expert on the painter Jean Dufy. Preparation of a catalogue raissonné on Jean Dufy. Web: www.Jeandufy.com

♛ GALERIE HENRI BÉNÉZIT

20 rue de Miromesnil, 75008 Paris ■ Tel: 01 42 65 54 56 ■ Mon-Fri 11:00-18:00 ■ Jean-Pierre Bénézit speaks English ■ Prices medium to high ■ Professional discount

XIX, XX century paintings, drawings, watercolours and sculptures. Author of the remarkable "Dictionary E. Bénézit".

♛ GALERIE BERNHEIM-JEUNE

83 rue du Faubourg-Saint-Honoré, 75008 Paris ■ Tel: 01 42 66 65 03 ■ Tue-Sat 10:30-12:30/14:30-18:30 ■ English spoken ■ Prices high ■ Professional discount

Beautiful gallery with works of the Impressionists and present-day artists. Painting and sculpture.

GALERIE MICHELLE BOULET

14 rue La Boétie, 75008 Paris ■ Tel: 01 49 24 00 63 ■ Fax: 01 49 24 01 00 ■ Mon-Sat 11:00-19:00 ■ Michelle Boulet and Hulya Moray speak English ■ Prices medium to high ■ 15 to 35% professional discount

Paintings, drawings, lithographs, contemporary figurative sculptures, "trompe l'oeil" paintings, still life and fantasy paintings.

GALERIE BRAME & LORENCEAU

68 bd Malesherbes, 75008 Paris ■ Tel: 01 45 22 16 89 ■ Fax: 01 45 22 01 67 ■ Mon-Fri 9:00-12:30/14:30-19:00 ■ M. Lorenceau ■ English spoken ■ Prices high ■ Professional discount ■ Visa, Amex

Paintings, watercolours, drawings, sculpture 1820 to 1920.

GALERIE CAPLAIN-MATIGNON

29 av Matignon, 75008 Paris ■ Tel: 01 42 65 04 63 ■ Fax: 01 42 66 02 83 ■ Web: www.french-galleries.org ■ Mon-Fri 10:30-13:00/14:30-19:00 ■ Mrs. Christiane Vernin speaks English ■ Prices medium to high

Hyper-realistic contemporary paintings and sculptures.

GALERIE LOUIS CARRÉ

10 av de Messine, 75008 Paris ■ Tel: 01 45 62 57 07 ■ Fax: 01 42 25 63 89 ■ E-mail: Louiscarre@wanadoo.fr ■ Mon-Sat 10:00-12:30/ 14:00-18:30 ■ Patrick Bongers, President ■ English spoken ■ Prices medium to high

Modern and contemporary art. Authentication of the work of Jacques Villon.

GALERIE JEANNE CASTEL

3 rue du Cirque, 75008 Paris ■ Tel: 01 43 59 71 24 ■ Fax: 01 43 59 07 24 ■ Mon-Fri 10:00-13:00/14:00-19:00 ■ Livia Raffin speaks English ■ Prices medium to high

Modern and contemporary paintings and sculptures.

♛ GALERIE PHILIPPE CAZEAU & JACQUES DE LA BÉRAUDIÈRE

16 av Matignon, 75008 Paris ■ Tel: 01 45 63 09 00 ■ Fax: 01 45 63 09 90 ■ E-mail: cazeau.beraudiere@wanadoo.fr ■ Mon-Sat 10:00-19:00 ■ Philippe Cazeau, Jacques de la Béraudière ■ English, Spanish and Italian spoken ■ Prices high

Masters of Impressionism and Modern paintings and sculptures up to the 1970s.

GALERIE COLLE-GOBEAU

23 rue Jean-Mermoz, 75008 Paris ■ Tel: 01 42 89 49 64 ■ Mon-Fri 11:30-13:30/14:30-18:30

Modern and contemporary figurative painting, some XIX century paintings.

GALERIE JEAN COULON

32 av Matignon, 75008 Paris ■ Tel: 01 49 24 96 60 ■ Fax: 01 45 51 14 15 ■ Mon-Fri 10:30-12:30/14:30-18:30 ■ English spoken ■ Prices high

Paintings of the Grand Masters of the XIX and XX century.

GALERIE PHILIPPE HEIM

38 rue de Penthièvre, 75008 Paris ■ Tel: 01 45 61 16 36 ■ Fax: 01 45 63 09 78 ■ E-mail: ph.heim@worldonline.fr ■ Mon-Sat 9:30-13:00 ■ English spoken ■ Prices high

Drawings and paintings of the XIX and early XX century.

GALERIE DE LA PRÉSIDENCE

90 rue du Faubourg-Saint-Honoré, 75008 Paris ■ Tel: 01 42 65 49 60 ■ Fax: 01 49 24 94 27 ■ E-mail: galerie.presidence@wanadoo.fr ■ Mon-Sat 10:00-13:00/14:30-19:00 ■ English spoken ■ Prices of the market

Impressionist and post-Impressionist paintings.

GALERIE DELORME
21 rue de Miromesnil, 75008 Paris ■ Tel: 01 42 66 25 20 ■ Fax: 01 42 66 55 20 ■ E-mail: delorme@cybercable.fr ■ Mon-Fri 11:00-18:00 ■ Michel Delorme speaks English ■ Prices reasonable ■ Professional discount

French painters of the XX century.

GALERIE LES SINGULIERS
138 bd Haussmann, 75008 Paris ■ Tel: 01 42 89 58 38 ■ Tue-Fri 10:30-12:30/14:30-18:00, Sat 10:30-12:30 ■ English spoken ■ Professional discount

Paintings of the "New Realists", figurative paintings, narrative and avant-garde paintings.

GALERIE ERIC GALFARD
2 rue de Messine, 75008 Paris ■ Telfax: 01 45 62 45 60 ■ Tue-Sat 14:00-19:00 ■ English spoken ■ Prices low to medium ■ Professional discount

Contemporary paintings, engravings and sculptures.

👑 GALERIE MAURICE GARNIER
6 av Matignon, 75008 Paris ■ Tel: 01 42 25 61 65 ■ Fax: 01 45 61 12 33 ■ E-mail: galerie.Maurice.garnier@wanadoo.fr ■ Tue-Sat 10:00-13:00/14:30-18:00 ■ Maurice Garnier speaks English ■ Prices high

Works by Bernard Buffet exclusively.

GALERIE GRONDIN-THIBAULT
121 av des Champs Élysées, 75008 Paris ■ Tel: 01 43 29 44 63 ■ Fax: 01 43 29 42 00 ■ Mon-Sat by appointment ■ Eliane Grondin speaks English ■ Prices medium to high ■ Professional discount

European prints: Soutages, Zao Wou-Ki, André Masson, Olivier de Bré, Sonia De Iannay, Viera da Selva, Roberto Matta.

GALERIE FANNY GUILLON LAFFAILLE
4 av de Messine, 75008 Paris ■ Tel: 01 445 63 52 00 ■ Fax: 01 45 61 92 91 ■ E-mail: fanny@galerie-fgl.com ■ Web: www.galerie-fgl.com ■ Mon-Fri 10:00-12:30/14:30-18:00, Sat by appointment ■ Mme Fanny Guillon Laffaille speaks English ■ Prices medium to very high ■ 10% professional discount

Modern and contemporary paintings. Specialist in Raoul Dufy.

GALERIE HERAUD
24 av Matignon, 75008 Paris ■ Tel: 01 42 66 31 62 ■ Fax: 01 42 66 31 62 ■ Mon-Sat 10:00-19:00 ■ Prices responsible ■ Professional discount

Impressionist, Post-Impressionist and Modern paintings.

♕ GALERIE HOPKINS-THOMAS-CUSTOT
2 rue de Miromesnil, 75008 Paris ■ Tel: 01 42 65 51 05 ■ Fax: 01 42 66 90 28 ■ E-mail: hopkins@imaginet.fr ■ Mon-Fri 9:30-13:00/14:30-18:30 ■ Prices high ■ Professional discount ■ Amex
Impressionist and Modern paintings.

GALERIE JEAN-PIERRE JOUBERT
18 av Matignon, 75008 Paris ■ Tel: 01 42 65 00 79 ■ Fax: 01 47 42 63 81 ■ Tue-Fri 10:30-12:30/14:30-18:30 ■ English and Spanish spoken ■ Prices medium ■ Amex
Contemporary paintings and sculptures.

GALERIE LA CYMAISE
164 rue du Faubourg-Saint-Honoré, 75008 Paris ■ Tel: 01 42 89 50 20 ■ Fax: 01 45 63 99 78 ■ E-mail: PLS@club-internet.fr ■ Mon-Fri 09:30-12:30/14:30-18:30 ■ Amaury de Louvencourt speaks English ■ Visa
Paintings and sculptures of the XIX century. Animal art.

GALERIE LAMBERT ROULON
62 rue La Boétie, 75008 Paris ■ Tel: 01 45 63 51 52 ■ Fax: 01 42 89 59 24 ■ Mon-Sat 10:00-19:00 ■ M. Roulon ■ English spoken ■ Prices medium ■ Professional discount
Contemporary paintings.

GALERIE ALEXANDRE LEADOUZE
2 av Matignon, 75008 Paris ■ Tel: 01 42 89 26 83 ■ Fax: 01 42 89 27 03 ■ Tue-Sat 10:00-13:00/14:30-18:00 ■ Alexandre Leadouze ■ English spoken ■ Prices high ■ Professional discount ■ Major credit cards
Contemporary figurative paintings and sculptures.

LOUISE LEIRIS
47 rue de Monseau, 75008 Paris ■ Tel: 01 45 63 28 85 ■ Fax: 01 45 63 76 13 ■ Tue-Sat 10:00-19:00 ■ Quentin Laurens speaks English
Modern and contemporary works.

GALERIE LELONG
13-14 rue de Téhéran ■ Tel: 01 45 63 13 19 ■ Fax: 01 42 89 34 33 ■ E-mail: galerie.lelong@wanadoo.fr ■ Tue-Fri 10:30-18:00, Sat 14:00-18:30 ■ English spoken ■ Prices medium to very high ■ Professional discount ■ Visa
Modern and contemporary paintings and sculptures.

♛ GALERIE PIERRE LÉVY

28 av Matignon, 75008 Paris ■ Tel: 01 47 42 10 11 ■ Fax: 01 47 42 10 25 ■ E-mail: gallevy@aol.com ■ Web: www.artnet.com/levy.html ■ Mon-Sat 10:00-13:00/14:00-19:00 ■ Pierre Lévy, Sabine Teboul, Dominique Robin ■ English and Spanish spoken ■ Professional discount

Paintings by Impressionist and Modern Masters.

♛ GALERIE DANIEL MALINGUE

26 av Matignon, 75008 Paris ■ Tel: 01 42 66 60 33 ■ Fax: 01 42 66 03 80 ■ E-mail: galeriemalingue@compuserve.com ■ Mon 14:30-18:30, Tue-Sat 10:30-12:30/14:30-18:30 ■ English, German and Spanish spoken ■ Prices high to very high

Masters of Impressionism, Post-Impressionists and Modern painters.

GALERIE MARBEAU

4 rue de Miromesnil, 75008 Paris ■ Telfax: 01 42 66 22 86 ■ Tue-Fri 10:00-13:00/14:30-19:00, Sat 13:00-19:00 ■ English spoken ■ Prices high ■ Professional discount

Great names in Modern and contemporary painting and sculpture with a leaning towards the abstract.

♛ GALERIE MARTIN-CAILLE MATIGNON

75 rue du Faubourg-Saint-Honoré, 75008 Paris ■ Tel: 01 42 66 60 71 ■ Fax: 01 47 42 55 48 ■ Web:www.max-agostini.com ■ Mon-Fri 9:30-19:00, Sat 9 :30-13 :00/15 :00-19 :00 ■ English, Spanish, Italian, German and Greek spoken ■ Prices high ■ Major credit cards

Specializes in the great name painters of the XIX and XX centuries: especially the Impressionists. Certificates of authenticity gladly given.

♛ GALERIE MATIGNON

18 av Matignon, 75008 Paris ■ Tel: 01 42 66 28 16 ■ Fax: 01 42 66 48 74 ■ Mon-Fri 10:00-13:00/14:30-18:30 ■ English spoken ■ Prices high ■ Professional discount ■ Amex

Impressionist and Post-Impressionist painters, Picasso, Chagall, Buffet, Jansem. Sculpture of Bourdelle.

GALERIE MATIGNON 32

32 av Matignon, 75008 Paris ■ Tel: 01 40 07 06 37 ■ Fax: 01 40 07 06 38 ■ E-mail: a.henriquet@artfine-arts.com ■ Web: www.artfine-arts.com ■ Mon-Fri 14:00-19:00, mornings by appointment, Sat during Exhibitions ■ Alec Henriquet ■ English, Spanish and German spoken ■ Prices high

Post Impressionist 1880-1920: Pointilists, Schools of Port Aven and Rouen, the Nabis to the Fauves. Contemporary works by Mexican artists.

♕ GALERIE MATIGNON SAINT-HONORÉ
34 av Matignon, 75008 Paris ■ Tel: 01 43 59 35 31 ■ Fax: 01 45 61 20 39 ■ Mon-Fri 10:00-19:00, Sat 13:00-19:00 ■ English spoken ■ Prices medium to high ■ Professional discount

Paintings of the Paris School, Vlaminck, Utrillo, etc., XX century painters, Buffet, Kisling.

GALERIE M.B.
18 av Matignon, 75008 Paris ■ Tel: 01 42 65 22 23 ■ Fax: 01 42 65 27 16 ■ Mon-Sat 10:30-12:30/14:30-18:30 ■ Michèle Todt, Director ■ English, German, Spanish and Japanese spoken ■ Prices high ■ Visa

Impressionists and School of Paris paintings. Akagi and Rieti.

GALERIE EMMANUEL MOATTI
20 rue de l'Elysée, 75008 Paris ■ Tel: 01 44 51 67 67 ■ Fax: 01 44 51 67 68 ■ E-mail: emoatti@wanadoo.fr ■ Web: www.art-net.com/emoatti.html ■ Mon-Fri 10:00-13:00/14:15-19:00 ■ Emmanuel Moatti speaks English, German and Italian ■ Amex

Paintings and drawings of the XVI to the XIX century.

EMMANUEL MOATTI
84 rue du Faubourg-Saint-Honoré, 75008 Paris ■ Tel: 01 44 51 67 67 ■ Fax: 01 44 51 67 68 ■ E-mail: emoatti@wanadoo.fr ■ English spoken

Very good Old Master paintings and drawings of the XIX century.

GALERIE ENRICO NAVARRA
75 rue du Faubourg-Saint-Honoré, 75008 Paris and 16 av Matignon ■ Tel: 01 47 42 65 66 ■ Fax: 01 42 66 21 36 ■ Mon-Fri 10:30-19:00 ■ English spoken ■ Prices high

Specialty: Marc Chagall, Jean-Michel Bastia and others.

GALERIE NICHIDO
61 rue du Faubourg-Saint-Honoré, 75008 Paris ■ Tel: 01 42 66 62 86 ■ Fax: 01 42 66 91 97 ■ Tue-Sat 10:00-12:30/14:00-18:30 ■ Mme Tomomi Baumgarten ■ Japanese, English and Italian spoken ■ Prices medium to high ■ 10% professional discount ■ CB

Contemporary Japanese, French and American paintings, watercolours, lithographs. Sometimes sculptures. Artists include Blondel, Bottet, Brasilier, Fukumoto, Kakei, Kanamori, Lesieur, Christin, Menghini, Salzmann, Tave, Yamamoto.

♕ GALERIE ART MEL
63 rue du Faubourg-Saint-Honoré, 75008 Paris ■ Tel: 01 42 66 61 16 ■ Fax: 01 49 24 95 94 ■ Mon-Fri 9:30-12:00/14:00-17:45 ■ English and German spoken ■ Prices medium to high

The grand XX century painters, especially Utrillo and Valadon, Vlaminck, Fujita, Laurençin, Dufy, Kisling, Buffet, Van Dongen, Renoir, Picasso, Hamburg, Lorjou, Rouault, Léger, etc. Sculptures: Michel Tardy, Corzou.

PERREAU-SAUSSINE
72 rue du Faubourg-Saint-Honoré, 75008 Paris ■ Tel : 01 45 66 97 99 ■ English spoken ■ Tue-Sat 10:00-19:00 ■ Prices quite high

XIX and early XX century art.

GALERIE PILTZER
16 av Matignon, 75008 Paris ■ Tel: 01 43 59 90 07 ■ Fax: 01 43 59 90 08 ■ Mon-Sat 10:00-19:00 ■ Gerald Piltzer, Pick Keobandith ■ Prices medium to high ■ Amex

Modern and contemporary paintings and sculptures.

GALERIE ÉTIENNE SASSI
14 av Matignon, 75008 Paris ■ Tel: 01 42 25 64 77 ■ Fax: 01 42 25 59 29 ■ Mon-Fri 10:00-13:00/14:30-18:30 ■ English spoken ■ Prices medium ■ Professional discount

Impressionist, Post Impressionist paintings, sculptures and ceramics.

♛ GALERIE JOHN SAYEGH
178 rue du Faubourg-Saint-Honoré, 75008 Paris ■ Tel: 01 42 25 76 21 ■ Fax: 01 45 62 02 99 ■ Mon 14:30-19:00, Tue-Sat 10:30-19:00 ■ John Sayegh speaks English ■ Prices very high

Impressionist and Modern paintings and sculptures. Picasso, Laurençin, Zempicka, Modigliani, Kisling, Rodin, Maillol.

GALERIE TAMENAGA
18 av Matignon, 75008 Paris ■ Tel: 01 42 66 61 94 ■ Fax: 01 47 42 99 14 ■ E-mail: gal.tamenaga@wanadoo.fr ■ Mon-Sat 10:00-13:00/14:00-19:00 ■ Mr. Morita, Director ■ English, Japanese, Italian and German spoken ■ Prices very high ■ Professional discount ■ Major credit cards

Modern and contemporary paintings: Aizpiri, Bardone, Cottavoz, Guiramand, Gorriti, Haijima, Fusaro, Weisbuch.

♛ HABOLDT & CO.
70 rue du Faubourg-Saint-Honoré, 75008 Paris : Tel: 01 48 66 44 54 ■ E-mail: bobhaboldt@compuserve.com ■ Mon-Fri 9:30-18:30 ■ English spoken

Fine paintings and old drawings.

♕ DIDIER IMBERT FINE ART

25 rue Balzac, 75008 Paris ■ Tel: 01 53 75 83 83 ■ Fax: 01 53 75 83 84 ■ Mon-Fri 10:00-13:00/14:30-19:00 ■ Gail Brenner speaks English ■ Prices high

Paintings, drawings and sculptures by masters of the XIX and XX centuries. Representative of the estate of Henry Moore. Representative of the Colombian Artist Fernando Botero. Department of antique fans.

LES ORÉADES

52 rue de Moscou, 75008 Paris ■ Tel: 01 43 87 59 20 ■ Fax: 01 43 87 99 20 ■ Mon-Sat 11:00-19:00 and by appointment ■ Edmond Rosenfeld speaks English ■ Prices medium ■ Professional discount

Russian and French paintings of the XIX and XX centuries. Specialty: Russian paintings, watercolours and drawings. Organizes exhibitions of paintings with Russian provenance.

ODERMATT

71 rue du Faubourg-Saint-Honoré, 75008 Paris ■ Tel: 01 42 06 00 49 ■ Fax: 01 42 66 12 76 ■ Mon-Fri 10:00-19:00 ■ English spoken ■ Prices quite high

Modern and contemporary paintings.

♕ RENOU & POYET

164 rue du Faubourg-Saint-Honoré, 75008 Paris ■ Tel: 01 43 59 35 95 ■ Fax: 01 42 56 24 29 ■ E-mail: renou.poyet@wanadoo.fr ■ Mon-Fri 9:30-12:30/14:30-18:30 ■ Maurice Covo, President ■ English, Spanish and Italian spoken ■ Prices high ■ Professional discount

Impressionist, Post-Impressionist, Modern and contemporary paintings, gouaches, drawings, sculptures. Conservation, research, estimates, framing and restoration. Artists include: Adami, Alechinsky, Alsterlind, Ameztoy, Barye, Bonnard, Bourdelle, Chaissac, Chillida, Debré, Derain, Despiau, Garcia-Sevilla, Gilioli, Helion, Lanskoy, Quetglas, Renoir. Qualified expert.

♕ SCHNEERSON-LÉVY GALLERY

24 av Matignon, 75008 Paris ■ Tel: 01 42 65 11 11 ■ Fax: 01 42 65 11 77 ■ Web: www.schneerson-levygallery.com ■ Tue-Fri 10:00-13:00/14:00-19:00 ■ Mrs. Tessa Tavernetti, Director ■ English spoken ■ Prices high

Impressionist and Modern paintings, including Bonnard, Renoir, Monet and Manet.

UNIVERS DU BRONZE
27-29 rue de Penthièvre, 75008 Paris ■ Tel: 01 42 56 50 30 ■ Fax: 01 42 89 69 85 ■ E-mail: udbanttiq@club-internet.fr ■ Mon-Sat 10:30-12:30/14:00-19:00 ■ English spoken ■ Prices medium ■ 15% professional discount ■ Visa, Amex

XIX and XX century sculptures in bronze, terracotta and marble. Specialist in Barye, Mênes Fratin, Carpeaux, Sandoz, Pompon.

——————————— IX ———————————

NORBERT BOUTET
9 rue de la Grange Batelière, 75009 Paris ■ Tel: 01 44 79 03 71 ■ Fax: 01 48 00 00 76 ■ Mon-Fri 10:00-13:00/14:00-18:30 ■ English spoken ■ Prices medium ■ Professional discount

Paintings by XVIII and XIX century masters, primitive art, objects of curiosity.

GALERIE AITTOUARES
10 rue de la Grange Batelière, 75009 Paris ■ Tel: 01 45 23 41 13 ■ Fax: 01 42 47 03 90 ■ Mon-Fri 10:00-13:00/14:00-18:00 ■ Prices medium ■ Professional discount

Impressionist paintings and drawings. Abstract, Cubist and Surrealist art of the early XX century. Sculpture in bronze by César, Rodin, Daumier. Watercolours and works on paper. Drawings of Rodin and Carpeaux.

GALERIE CANESSO
8 rue Rossini, 75009 Paris ■ Tel: 01 40 22 61 71 ■ Fax: 01 40 22 61 81 ■ E-mail: mcanesso@canesso.com ■ Web: www.canesso.com ■ Mon-Fri by appointment ■ Maurizio Canesso speaks Italian and English

Marvellous Italian paintings of the Renaissance to the XVIII century.

——————————— X ———————————

ISABELLE BONGARD
91 Faubourg Saint-Denis, 75010 Paris ■ Tel: 01 43 14 08 18 ■ Fax: 01 43 14 25 55 ■ E-mail: i.bongard@magic.fr ■ By appointment ■ English, German and Italian spoken

Consultant in contemporary art. Advice on collecting, exhibiting and communications with individual collectors, companies and institutions.

ARTCODIS
151 rue Saint-Charles, 75015 Paris ■ Tel: 01 45 77 26 60 ■ Fax: 01 45 77 11 04 ■ Mon-Sat by appointment only ■ English spoken ■ Prices medium ■ 10 to 20% professional discount

Engravings, lithographs, seriographs, of well-known contemporary French and international artists in limited editions.

ESPACE D'ART YVONAMOR PALIX
13 rue Keller, 75011 Paris ■ Tel: 01 48 06 36 70 ■ Fax: 01 47 00 01 21 ■ E-mail: yapalix@aol.com ■ Sat 14:00-19:00 and by appointment ■ Yvonamor Palix, Maribel Nadal, Marco Serna ■ English, Spanish and Catalan spoken

Contemporary plastic arts: paintings, photographs, sculptures, objects, installations. Art editions.

GALERIE AKIE ARICHI
26 rue Keller, 75011 Paris ■ Tel: 01 40 21 64 57 ■ Fax: 01 42 74 26 60 ■ Tue-Sat 15:00-19:00 ■ Mrs. Arichi-Boulard speaks English ■ Prices medium ■ Possible professional discount ■ Major credit cards

Contemporary paintings, sculptures, engravings and lithographs.

DONGUY-APEGAC
57 rue de la Roquette, 75011 Paris ■ Fax: 01 40 21 83 84 ■ Tue-Sat 13:00-19:00 ■ Jacques Donguy ■ English spoken ■ Prices medium to high ■ Professional discount

Contemporary art, painting, objects, visual poetry, space for artistic activity, expositions, exhibitions of new visual technologies.

GALERIE CLAIRE BURRUS
16 rue de Lappe, 75011 Paris ■ Tel: 01 43 55 34 76 ■ Tue-Fri 14:00-19:00, Sat 11:00-19:00 ■ English spoken ■ Prices medium ■ Professional discount

Contemporary painting, sculptures, installations, videos.

GALERIE CLAUDE DORVAL
22 rue Keller, 75011 Paris ■ Tel: 01 48 06 35 67 ■ Fax: 0148 06 25 58 ■ Tue-Sat 14:00-19:00 ■ Claude Dorval speaks English ■ Prices medium ■ Professional discount

Contemporary paintings and sculptures. Abstract geometric works.

GALERIE LILIANE AND MICHEL DURAND-DESSERT
28 rue de Lappe, 75011 Paris ■ Tel: 01 48 06 92 23 ■ Fax: 01 48 06 92 24 ■ Tue-Fri 11:00-13:00/15:00-19:00, Sat 11:00-19:00 ■ Mr. Robin speaks English

Large collection of modern and contemporary painters.

GALERIE LA FERRONNERIE - BRIGITTE NEGRIER
40 rue de la Folie-Méricourt, 75011 Paris ■ Tel: 01 48 06 50 84 ■ Fax: 01 48 06 50 84 ■ E-mail: Brigitnegrier@magic.fr ■ Web: www.art.vianet.fr/actualite/galeries/ferronerie.html ■ Tue-Fri 14:00-19:00, Sat 13:00-19:00 ■ Brigitte Negrier speaks English, Portuguese and Spanish ■ Prices medium ■ Professional discount possible

Contemporary art: paintings, sculptures, photographs and prints of European, South American and Korean artists.

GALERIE ALAIN GUTHARC
47 rue de Lappe, 75011 Paris ■ Tel: 01 47 00 32 10 ■ Fax: 01 40 21 72 74 ■ Tue-Fri 14:00-19:00, Sat 11:00-13:00/14:00-19:00 ■ English and Spanish spoken ■ Prices medium

Contemporary paintings, sculpture, installations and photographs.

♛ GALERIE PATRICK SEGUIN
34 rue de Charonne and 8 rue de Tallandiers, 75011 Paris ■ Tel: 01 47 00 32 35 ■ Fax: 01 40 21 82 95 ■ E-mail: patrickseguin@free.fr ■ Web: www.patrickseguin.com ■ Mon-Fri 10:00-19:00, Sat 11:00-19:00 ■Armelle Durand ■ English spoken ■ Prices medium to high ■ Professional discount ■ Major credit cards

Contemporary art Modern design of the 1950s: Le Corbusier, Jeanneret, Jouve, Mouille, Noll, Perriand, Prouvé, Royère. Contemporary art: Ashkin, Grunfeld, Kern, Kneffel, Tremblay.

GALERIE LAVIGNES BASTILLE
27 rue de Charonne, 75011 Paris ■ Tel: 01 47 00 88 18 ■ Tue-Sat 11:00-19:00 ■ Jean-Pierre Lavignes speaks English ■ Prices medium ■ Professional discount

Contemporary paintings, drawings and sculpture.

GALERIE LE SOUS-SOL
9 rue de Charonne, Paris 75011 ■ Tel: 01 47 00 02 75 ■ Fax: 01 47 00 24 75 ■ E-mail: sous-so@club-internet.fr ■ Web: www.perso.club-internet.fr/sous-sol ■ Tue-Sat 14:30-19:00 ■ English spoken ■ Prices low to medium ■ Professional discount

Contemporary paintings, sculptures, photographs, videos.

GALERIE DE TUGNY LAMARRE

5 rue de Charonne, 75011 Paris ■ Tel: 01 48 05 84 16 ■ Fax: 01 40 21 82 95 ■ Tue-Sat 14:00-19:00 ■ Florence de Tugny speaks English ■ Prices medium ■ 10% professional discount

Contemporary paintings, sculptures, photographs. Contemporary furniture by artists.

K'ART

45 rue Amelot, 75011 Paris ■ Telfax: 01 42 72 83 40 ■ Mon-Sat 10:00-18:00 ■ Simone Kerven ■ English spoken ■ Prices medium

Contemporary works.

———————————— XIII ————————————

SERGE BENOIT

Cité Fleurie, Atelier # 25, 65 bd Arago, 75013 Paris ■ Tel: 01 43 31 80 74 ■ Tue-Sat 10:00-12:00/14:00-18:00 ■ The owner is a sculptor and painter ■ Prices medium ■ Professional discount

Contemporary paintings and sculpture in wood, stone or metal.

JENNIFER FLAY

70 rue Louise Weiss, 75013 Paris ■ Tel: 01 44 06 73 60 ■ Fax: 01 44 06 73 66 ■ Mon-Sat 10:00-19:00 ■ Prices low to medium

Contemporary works.

ALMINE RECH

24 rue Louise Weiss, 75013 Paris ■ Tel: 01 45 83 71 90 ■ Fax: 01 45 70 91 30 ■ Mon-Sat 10:00-19:00 ■ English spoken ■ Prices medium

Unusual contemporary works of art.

———————————— XIV ————————————

ORIGAMI

138 bd du Montparnasse, 75014 Paris ■ Tel: 01 43 20 49 14 ■ Fax: 01 43 35 41 14 ■ Mon-Fri 9:00-19:00 by appointment only ■ Françoise Echard speaks English ■ Prices medium ■ 10 to 20% professional discount

Contemporary paintings, tapestries and Origami sculptures.

STOPPENBACH & DELESTRE

36 rue Lafitte, 75009 Paris ■ Tel: 01 48 24 05 01 ■ Fax: 01 48 24 06 12 ■ E-mail: stopdel@easynet.fr ■ Web: www.artfrancais.com ■ English spoken ■ Prices high

XIX and early XX century paintings.

LA GALERIE D'ART
102 rue Cambronne, 75015 Paris ■ Tel: 01 42 73 19 99 ■ Tue-Sat 10:30-13:00/14:30-19:30 ■ Danielle Feinstein speaks English ■ Prices medium ■ 10% professional discount

Contemporary classic paintings, landscape, still lifes, flowers, watercolours, pastels. Also frames and framing.

GALERIE EFTE
1 rue Général Beuret, 75015 Paris ■ Tel: 01 43 28 99 19 ■ Fax: 01 48 28 79 69 ■ Wed-Sat 10:30-19:00 ■ Florence Touber ■ English spoken ■ Major credit cards

Contemporary paintings and sculpture.

MARIE-THERESE PEYRALADE
2 av Paul Déroulède, 75015 Paris ■ Tel: 01 47 34 69 94 ■ Fax: 01 43 68 34 34 ■ Thu-Mon 14:00-19:00 ■ English spoken ■ Prices medium ■ Professional discount

XIX and early XX century paintings.

ETERSO
37 rue Raynouard, 75016 Paris ■ Tel: 01 42 15 56 64 ■ Fax: 01 42 15 56 63 ■ Tue-Sat 10:00-18:00 ■ Jacques and Marc Lambert speak English ■ Prices medium

Impressionist to contemporary art.

GILLES DIDIER
38 rue Boileau, 75016 Paris ■ Tel: 01 40 71 04 41 ■ Fax: 01 47 43 09 68 ■ Every day by appointment ■ English spoken ■ Prices low to very high ■ Professional discount

Expert and dealer in antique and contemporary posters. Specialist in Cassandré, Lautrec and Cheret.

GALERIE NORBERT HANSE
38 av Victor-Hugo, 75016 Paris ■ Tel: 01 45 01 88 40 ■ Fax: 01 45 01 88 40 ■ Tue-Sat 10:30-12:30/15:30-19:00 ■ English spoken ■ Prices medium ■ Professional discount

Contemporary figurative paintings and sculpture, 1950s to the present.

GALERIE CLAUDINE LUSTMAN
11 rue Mérimée, 75116 Paris ■ Tel: 06 60 08 42 21 ■ Fax: 01 45 53 20 02 ■ E-mail: artes@club-internet.fr ■ By appointment ■ English and German spoken ■ Professional discount

Contemporary paintings and sculptures: Michèle Burles, Jean-Marc Scanreigh, Marguerite Noirel. Will advise on hanging collections.

──────────────── XVII ────────────────

GALERIE SERGE GARNIER
12 bd de Courcelles, 75017 Paris ■ Tel: 01 47 63 06 46 ■ Mon-Fri 13:00-19:00, Sat a.m. by appointment ■ English spoken ■ Prices medium ■ Professional discount

Contemporary and modern paintings.

GALERIE SAPHIR RIVE DROITE
69 av de Villiers, 75017 Paris ■ Tel: 01 44 40 26 84 ■ Fax: 01 43 80 23 49 ■ Sun-Thu 14:00-19:00 ■ English spoken ■ Prices medium ■ Professional discount

XIX and XX century paintings, drawings, lithographs, beautiful old books, old Jewish works of art.

GALERIE VARINE GINCOURT
110 bd de Courcelles, 75017 Paris ■ Tel: 01 42 27 20 16 ■ Tue-Sat 11:00-19:00, Mon 14:30-19:00 ■ English spoken ■ Prices medium ■ 5 to 10% professional discount

XX century figurative paintings, engravings, drawings, lithographs, watercolours, sculpture.

──────────────── XVIII ────────────────

GALERIE DU CHEVALIER ET DES COLLECTIONNEURS
42 rue Chevalier-de-la-Barre, 75018 Paris ■ Tel: 01 42 64 84 93 ■ Fax: 01 42 57 40 73 ■ Mon-Sun 10:30-18:30 ■ English spoken ■ Prices reasonable ■ Professional discount ■ Major credit cards

Classic and modern paintings.

GALERIE D'ART CHRISTINE DIEGONI
47 ter rue d'Orsel, 75018 Paris ■ Tel: 01 42 64 69 48 ■ Fax: 01 42 58 21 64 ■ Tue-Sat 14:00-19:00 and by appointment ■ Prices medium to high ■ Professional discount

Decorative arts of the XX century, ceramics, furniture, art objects, 1930s to 1970.

ANDRÉ ROUSSARD

13 rue du Mont-Cenis, 75018 Paris ■ Tel: 01 46 06 30 46 ■ Fax: 01 42 52 38 00 ■ Mon-Sun 11:00-20:00 ■ English spoken ■ Prices reasonable to high ■ 10 to 30% professional discount

XX century paintings, original and exclusive lithographs, estampes, books, catalogues and posters. Specialty: painters who worked in Montmartre. Restoration and framing.

TRANSPARENCE

42 rue Caulaincourt, 75018 Paris ■ Telfax: 01 42 23 74 45 ■ Tue-Sat 10:30-12:30/14:30-19:30 ■ Marie Savary speaks English ■ 20% professional discount

XIX, XX century paintings.

--------------------- XIX ---------------------

GALERIE LEONARDO

62 rue de Hautpoul, 75019 Paris ■ Tel: 01 42 40 13 11 ■ E-mail: Leonardo.sa@wanadoo.fr ■ Mon-Sat 14:00-19:00 ■ Leonardo de Sa speaks Spanish, English, Italian and Portuguese ■ Prices medium 5,000 to 30,000 FF ■ Professional discount

Contemporary art. Painters: Araguai, Bajalska, Guanse, Bruel, Hong Hyn Joo, Milet, Szegedi, Wybrands, Lunven. Sculpture by Moreira.

--------------------- XX ---------------------

ART FACTS

145 rue Pelleport, 75020 Paris ■ Tel: 01 43 58 62 04 ■ Fax: 01 43 58 62 83 ■ By appointment ■ English spoken ■ 10 to 20% professional discount

Post-war and contemporary prints, works on paper and illustrated books.

Special Categories of Art

--------------------- ANIMAL ART ---------------------

AU CHAT DORMANT

31 rue de Bourgogne, 75007 Paris ■ Tel: 01 45 50 38 06 ■ Tue-Sat 11:30-19:00 ■ Prices medium ■ 5 to 10% professional discount

Old and contemporary animal art, especially the cat. Paintings, bronzes and porcelain. Sculptures in wood, marionettes, screens, ink wells.

GALERIE AIR DE CHASSE

115 rue Saint-Dominique, 75007 Paris ■ Telfax: 01 42 60 25 98
■ By appointment only Tue-Thu 14:00-19:00 ■ Eric Angot ■ English spoken ■ Prices medium to high ■ Professional discount

Animal Art of the XIX century: bronzes and paintings.

GALERIE LA BILLEBAUDE

24 rue de Beaune, 75007 Paris ■ Tel: 01 42 97 40 87 ■ Tue-Sat 11:00-19:00 ■ Mr. Thierry Taruel, Fabienne le Calvez ■ English and Italian spoken ■ Professional discount

XIX century paintings and bronzes of animals and of the hunt. Restoration of paintings.

GALERIE LA CYMAISE

164 rue du Faubourg-Saint-Honoré, 75008 Paris ■ Tel: 01 42 89 50 20 ■ Fax: 01 45 63 99 78 ■ E-mail: PLS@club-internet.fr ■ Mon-Fri 09:30-12:30/14:30-18:30 ■ Amaury de Louvencourt speaks English ■ Visa

Paintings and sculpture of the XIX century. Animal art.

UNIVERS DU BRONZE

27-29 rue de Penthievre, 75008 Paris ■ Tel: 01 42 56 50 30 ■ Fax: 01 42 89 69 85 ■ E-mail: udbanttiq@club-internet.fr ■ Mon-Sat 10:30-12:30/14:00-19:00 ■ English spoken ■ Prices medium ■ 15% professional discount ■ Visa, Amex

XIX and XX century sculptures in bronze, terracotta and marble. Specialist in Barye, Mênes Fratin, Carpeaux, Sandoz, Pompon.

ANIMATION AND CARTOON ART

GALERIE CHRISTIAN DESBOIS

14 av de la Bourdonnais, 75007 Paris ■ Tel: 01 45 55 85 33 ■ Fax: 01 45 56 06 16 ■ E-mail: infos@desbois.com ■ Web: www.desbois.com ■ English spoken ■ Prices medium ■ 20% professional discount ■ Visa

Exclusively artists who design comic strips.

ARCHITECTURAL ART

GALERIE ARCHETYPE

17 rue des Francs-Bourgeois, 75004 Paris ■ Tel: 01 42 72 18 15 ■ Tue-Sat 11:00-19:00 ■ Elisabeth Pélegrin-Genel ■ Prices medium ■ Professional discount

Specialist in architectural drawings.

GALERIE ACTEON
8 rue de Beaune, 75007 Paris ■ Tel: 01 42 61 23 43 ■ Fax: 01 42 61 00 58 ■ Mon-Sat 15:00-19:00 or by appointment ■ English spoken ■ Professional discount

Automobile art, aviation, architectural, locomotion, everything that moves or flies, in drawings, paintings or models.

GALERIE VITESSE
48 rue de Berri, 75008 Paris ■ Tel: 01 42 25 48 13 ■ Fax: 01 48 25 06 04 ■ Mon-Sat 12:30-19:00 ■ Isabelle Nicolosi speaks English ■ Prices medium ■ 5% professional discount

Paintings, sculpture, lithographs on the themes of automobiles and aviation. Rentals for advertising and film productions.

CHRISTIAN AZAIS
48 rue Jean-Longuet, 92220 Bagneux ■ Tel: 01 47 74 89 58 ■ Fax: 01 40 90 97 09 ■ Mon-Sat 10:00-20:00 ■ English spoken ■ 20% professional discount

Paintings and art objects on the theme of automobiles. Antique arms, antique cars.

CINEMA ART

CINEDOC
45-53 Passage Jouffroy, 75009 Paris ■ Tel: 01 48 24 71 36 ■ Mon-Sat 10:00-19:00 ■ English spoken ■ Prices medium ■ Professional discount

A vast collection of 16,000 movie posters from the beginning of cinema to the present. Photos of the stars, books and reviews.

ART OF THE HUNT

TRF ANTIQUITÉS
16 rue de Beaune, 75007 Paris ■ Tel: 0142 61 11 33 ■ Fax: 01 42 61 11 51 ■ E-mail: trfantik@club-internet.fr ■ Web: www.artface.com ■ Mon-Sat 10:30-19:30 ■ Yves Cherest ■ English and Spanish spoken ■ Prices medium ■ Professional discount ■ MC and Visa

Cynegetic art - everything to do with the hunt: paintings, objets d'art and furniture.

ACHDJIAN GALLERY

10 rue de Miromesnil, 75008 Paris ■ Tel : 01 42 65 89 48 ■ Tue-Fri 10:00-18:00/Sat 10:00-16:00 ■ English spoken ■ Prices medium

Art of Turkmenistan.

GALERIE J. SOUSTIEL

146 bd Haussmann, 75008 Paris ■ Tel: 01 45 62 27 76 ■ Fax: 01 45 63 44 63 ■ By appointment ■ Laure Soustiel, Marie-Christine David ■ English and some Arabic spoken ■ Prices medium to high ■ Professional discount

Islamic art from North Africa, Egypt, Syria, Turkey, Iran and India. Ceramics, metalwork, miniatures and textiles. Expert.

OCEANIC ART

GALERIE MEYER-OCEANIC ART

17 rue des Beaux-Arts, 75006 Paris ■ Tel: 01 43 54 85 74 ■ Fax: 01 43 54 11 12 ■ E-mail: ajpmeyer@aol.com ■ Web: www.artnet.com/meyer.html ■ Mon-Sat 10:30-13:00/14:30-19:00 ■ Anthony J.P. Meyer ■ English, German and Italian spoken ■ Prices high to very high ■ Professional discount ■ Amex, Visa

Oceanic art. Tribal art from Melanesia, Polynesia, Micronesia and Australia.

PHOTO ART

GALERIE AGATHE GAILLARD

3 rue du Pont-Louis-Philippe, 75004 Paris ■ Tel: 01 42 77 38 24 ■ Fax: 01 42 77 78 36 ■ Tue-Sat 13:00-19:00 ■ Agathe Gaillard speaks English ■ Prices modest ■ Visa

Photo art after 1945.

GALERIE ZABRISKIE

37 rue Quincampoix, 75004 Paris ■ Tel: 01 42 72 35 47 ■ Fax: 01 40 27 99 66 ■ Tue-Sat 14:00-19:00 ■ Editha Carpenter speaks English

Photo gallery which also sells contemporary paintings and sculptures.

A L'IMAGE DU GRENIER SUR L'EAU
45 rue des Francs-Bourgeois, 75004 Paris ■ Tel: 01 42 71 02 31
■ Fax: 01 42 78 66 77 ■ E-mail: image.di-maria@wanadoo.fr ■
Web: www.image-di-maria.com ■ Mon-Sat 10:00-19:00, Sun
14:00-19:00 ■ Sylvain and Yves di Maria ■ English spoken ■
Prices medium ■ Professional discount ■ Major credit cards

Posters, estampes, postcards, books, photographs, old original documents of the XIX to XX centuries classified by theme and country of origin. Specialty: Art Nouveau and Art Deco.

A L'IMAGERIE
9 rue Dante, 75005 Paris ■ Tel: 01 43 25 18 66 ■ Fax: 01 43 25 18
08 ■ E-mail: alimagerie@easynet.fr ■ Web: www.alimagerie.com ■
Mon-Sat 10:30-13:00/14:00-19:00 ■ Anne Martinière speaks English ■ 10% professional discount ■ Major credit cards

Original posters and lithographs before the 1960s. Cloth mounting, restoration and old papers.

BRIGITTE BUSSIÈRE
43 rue de l'Arbre-Sec, 75001 Paris ■ Tel: 01 47 03 32 58 ■ Fax:
01 40 15 96 60 ■ Mon-Fri 9:30-12:30/14:30-18:30 by appointment ■ English spoken ■ Prices medium ■ Professional discount

Posters specializing in tourism and sports. High quality restoration of posters.

CINÉDOC
45-53 Passage Jouffroy, 75009 Paris ■ Tel: 01 48 24 71 36 ■
Mon-Sat 10:00-19:00 ■ English spoken ■ Prices medium ■ Professional discount

A vast collection of 16,000 movie posters from the beginning of cinema to the present. Photos of the stars, books and reviews.

GALERIE DOCUMENTS
53 rue de Seine, 75006 Paris ■ Tel: 01 43 54 50 68 ■ Fax: 01 43 29
10 25 ■ Tue-Sat 10:30-12:30/14:30-19:00 ■ Mireille Romand speaks
English ■ Prices medium ■ 10% professional discount ■ Visa, MC

Antique original posters, 1870 to 1950, and lithographs.

♛ LIBRAIRIE DE LATTRE

56 rue de l'Université, 75007 Paris ■ Tel: 01 45 44 75 30 ■ Fax: 01 45 44 83 53 ■ Mon-Fri 10:30-13:00/14:00-19:00 ■ Marché Vernaison, Marché aux Puces, ■ 99 rue des Rosiers, 93400 Saint-Ouen ■ Tel: 01 40 12 68 89 ■ Sat-Mon 9:30-18:00 ■ Dominique and Marie-Ange de Lattre speak English ■ Prices medium ■ 10% professional discount

Extraordinary collection of posters and books of the XIX and XX centuries. Theatre and film publicity, advertising, illustrations. Old books on the beaux-arts, travel, fashion, children's books.

POSTER TREASURES

38 rue Boileau, 75016 Paris ■ Tel: 01 40 71 04 41 ■ Fax: 01 47 43 09 68 ■ E-mail: posters@cybercable.fr ■ Web: www.poster-fair.com/pt/catalog.htm ■ G. Didier ■ By appointment only ■ English and Spanish spoken ■ Prices high ■ Professional discount

Original old posters by Cheret, Coppiello, Toulouse-Lautrec and others.

--- PRE-COLUMBIAN ART ---

GALERIE MERMOZ

6 rue du Cirque, 75008 Paris ■ Tel: 01 42 25 84 80 ■ Fax: 01 40 75 03 90 ■ Santo Micali ■ English and Spanish spoken ■ Prices medium to high

Pre-Columbian art from Mexico and Central America. Objects in jadeite, stone, serpentine and terracotta. From 1500 BC to 1500 AD.

GALERIE URUBAMBA

4 rue de la Bûcherie, 75005 Paris ■ Tel: 01 45 54 08 24 ■ Fax: 01 43 29 91 80 ■ E-mail: urubamba.galerie6@fnac.net ■ Tue-Sat 14:00-19:30 ■ Roberta Rivin, Directrice ■ English, Spanish and Portuguese spoken ■ Prices medium ■ Visa

Traditional objects, ancient and modern, from the native peoples of the Americas. Good collection of books in English and French on the subject. Catalogue of books and sale by correspondence.

--- PRINTS, DRAWINGS AND ENGRAVINGS ---

♛ GALERIE BARÈS

32 rue de Seine, 75006 Paris ■ Tel: 01 55 42 93 95 ■ Fax: 01 55 42 94 36 ■ Mon-Sat 10:30-13:00/14:30-19:00 ■ Jean-Luc Barès ■ English, German, Italian and Spanish spoken ■ Prices medium ■ Professional discount ■ Major credit cards

XX century lithographs, engravings, and Modern illustrations.

♛ ARSÈNE BONAFOUS-MURAT

15 rue de l'Échaudé, 75006 Paris ■ Tel: 01 46 33 42 31 ■ Fax: 01 43 29 52 27 ■ E-mail: arsenebm@aol.com ■ Tue-Sat 13:00-19:00 ■ Arsène Bonafous-Murat, Hélène Bonafous-Murat, Catherine Costanzo ■ English and German spoken ■ Prices medium to high ■ 10% professional discount ■ Visa

XVI to XX century estampes and books relative to estampes. Monographs, catalogues-raisonnés and documentation. Periodic publication of catalogues of prices, themes or of general interest. Expertise and preparation of catalogues for auctions. Mr. and Mrs. Bonafous-Murat are qualified experts.

GALERIE GRILLON

44 rue de Seine, 75006 Paris ■ Tel: 01 46 33 03 44 ■ Fax: 01 46 33 93 81 ■ Tue-Sat 10:30-18:30 ■ English and Russian spoken ■ Prices low to high ■ Professional discount ■ Major credit cards

XIX and XX century original engravings and lithographs.

GALERIE PAUL PROUTÉ

74 rue de Seine, 75006 Paris ■ Tel: 01 43 26 89 80 ■ Fax: 01 43 25 83 41 ■ Tue-Sat 9:30-12:00/14:00-19:00 ■ Sylvie Tocci Prouté and Annie Martinez Prouté speak English, German and Italian ■ Prices medium to high ■ 10% professional discount ■ Visa, MC

Drawings and prints of the XV to the XX century. Publication of three catalogues a year, two of which can be sent free-of-charge upon request.

JULIE MAILLARD

11 Passage Verdeau, 75009 Paris ■ Tel: 01 42 46 53 20 ■ Fax: 01 45 23 40 22 ■ Mon-Fri 13:00-19:00 ■ Some English spoken ■ Prices medium to high ■ Professional discount

Antique engravings from the late XV century to the late XIX century.

GALERIE R.G. MICHEL

17 quai Saint-Michel, 75005 Paris ■ Tel: 01 43 54 77 75 ■ Mon-Sat 9:30-19:00 ■ M. Michel ■ English and German spoken ■ Professional discount

XVI to XX century original estampes. Old and Modern drawings, original lithographs, decorative engravings, paintings and books. Periodic catalogue available by order.

TALABARDON & GAUTIER
134 rue du Faubourg-Saint-Honoré, 75008 Paris ■ Tel: 01 43 59 13
57 ■ Fax: 01 43 59 10 29 ■ Bertrand Gautier and Bertrand Talabardon ■ English spoken ■ Prices quite high ■ Professional discount
**Old Master and XIX century paintings, drawings and sculp-
tures.**

SPORTING ART

ART VIE
69 rue des Entrepreneurs, 75015 Paris ■ Tel: 01 45 79 60 60 ■
Mon-Sat 9:00-20:00 ■ Prices medium ■ 10 to 20% professional
discount
**Paintings, drawings, watercolours, engravings and art ob-
jects related to sports.**

GALERIE LA CYMAISE
164 rue du Faubourg-Saint-Honoré, 75008 Paris ■ Tel: 01 42 89
50 20 ■ Mon-Fri 9:30-12:30/14:30-18:30 ■ Amaury de Louvencourt speaks English ■ Prices high ■ 10% professional discount
**Sport paintings of the XIX and XX centuries. Hunting, shoot-
ing, racing, polo, coaching.**

TRIBAL ART

AFRICAN MUSE GALLERY
50 rue de l'Hôtel de Ville, 75004 Paris ■ Tel: 01 42 77 83 44 ■
Fax: 01 42 77 57 50 ■ E-mail: lucberthier.amg@libertysurf.fr ■
Tue-Sat 11:00-13:00/14:30-19:00 ■ Luc Berthier ■ English and
some German and Italian spoken ■ Prices medium to high ■ Professional discount ■ MC, Visa
Ancient tribal art from Africa and contemporary artists.

GALERIE O. KLEIMAN & L. STELLA
3 rue Jacques Callot, 75006 Paris ■ Tel: 01 43 25 35 25 ■ Fax:
01 43 25 31 34 ■ Tue-Sat 10:00-19:00
Primitive art.

GALERIE HÉLÈNE ET PHILIPPE LELOUP
9 quai Malaquais, 75006 Paris ■ Tel: 01 42 60 75 91 ■ Fax: 01
42 61 45 94 ■ Tue-Sat 11:00-12:30/14:00-19:00 ■ English spoken ■ Prices high
**Unique art objects of Black Africa and Indonesia. Some-
times pre-Columbian art and textiles.**

GALERIE MAJESTIC

27 rue Guénégaud, 75006 Paris ■ Tel: 01 43 54 78 56 ■ Mon-Sat 14:00-20:00 ■ Jean-Michel Huguenin ■ English spoken ■ Prices high ■ Professional discount

Popular and primitive art of the XIX century.

GALERIE ALAIN DE MONBRISON

2 rue des Beaux-Arts, 75006 Paris ■ Tel: 01 46 34 05 20 ■ Fax: 01 46 34 67 25 ■ Mon-Sat 10:00-12:30/14:30-18:30 ■ English, German and Spanish spoken ■ Prices medium ■ Amex, Visa

Tribal art of Africa, Oceania and America.

GALERIE NOIR ET BLANC

42 rue de Seine, 75006 Paris ■ Tel: 01 56 24 22 23 ■ Fax: 01 56 24 22 46 ■ Mon-Sat 10:00-13:00/14:30-19:30 ■ Jean-Louis Antignac ■ English and some Spanish spoken Prices medium ■ Most credit cards

Old, unusual and decorative objects of Black Africa in wood, wrought iron and bronze: sculptures, masks, doors and chairs.

GALERIE SAINT MERRI ART INUIT

9 rue Saint-Merri, 75004 Paris ■ Tel: 01 42 77 39 12 ■ Fax: 01 46 26 53 07 ■ E-mail: artinuit@artscom.com ■ Web: www.artscom.com/galeries/saintmerri ■ Tue-Thurs 14:30-19:00, Fri-Sat 11:00-19:00 ■ Martine Lena speaks English and Spanish ■ Prices medium to high ■ Professional Discount ■ Major credit cards

Specialist in Eskimo Art: Sculptures, engravings, books and documentation.

GALERIE MICHEL VIDAL

3 rue des Beaux-Arts, 75006 Paris ■ Telfax: 01 43 26 09 29 ■ Fax: 01 43 29 67 81 ■ Jean-Luc and Jacqueline André speak English ■ Prices medium ■ 20% professional discount

Primitive art of South Asia and Asiatic archaeological objects.

L'ASIE ANIMISTE

13 rue Mazarine, 75006 Paris ■ Tel: 01 43 54 28 31 ■ Fax: 02 54 72 78 14 ■ Tue-Sat 11:00-13:00/14:30-19:00 ■ Annick Cical ■ English and Spanish spoken ■ Prices medium ■ 20% professional discount ■ Visa

Tribal art and ethnic necklaces from the Himalayas and Indonesia.

MAZARINE 52
52 rue Mazarine, 75006 Paris ■ Tel: 01 46 33 86 99 ■ Fax: 01 46 28 39 11 ■ Mon-Fri 11:00-12:45/14:00-19:00, Sat 14:00-19:00 ■ Jean-Pierre Laprugne ■ German and English spoken ■ Prices medium ■ Professional discount

Traditional ethnographic objects of Africa and Oceania and Eskimo art.

NAST A PARIS
10 rue d'Alger, 75001 Paris ■ Tel: 01 47 03 34 74 ■ Fax: 01 42 61 23 87 ■ Tue-Sat 14:00-18:30 ■ Jean-Claude Reveillaud speaks English ■ Prices high ■ 15% professional discount

Black African art: modern and contemporary paintings and sculpture. Specialty: art of Zaire.

VALLUET
14 rue Guénégaud, 75006 Paris ■ Tel: 01 43 26 83 38 ■ Fax: 01 46 33 84 96 ■ E-mail: valluet@attglobal.net ■ Mon-Sat 10:30-13:00/14:00-19:30 ■ Christine Valluet, Yann Ferrandin ■ English spoken ■ Prices medium ■ Professional discount ■ Major credit cards

Tribal art of Africa, Oceania, Indonesia and North America.

ART REPRODUCTIONS

Reproductions d'art

GALERIE TROUBETSKOY
1 av Messine, 75008 Paris ■ Tel: 01 45 62 66 02 ■ Fax: 01 42 25 99 39 ■ Mon-Fri 9:30-13:00/14:00-19:00/Sat 10:30-18:30 ■ Arnaud Troubetskoy ■ English spoken ■ Prices depend on dimensions: Small: 1,500 Francs, Large 10,000 francs ■ Professional discount

Painted replicas on canvas, 17th century to the present. 18,000 different subjects. Stock of 100 subjects. Sizes up to 2.50 metres. On order, any paintings from any museum in the world.

────────────── OUTSIDE PARIS ──────────────

SEIGNEURET DIFFUSION
45 rue François de Troy 94360 Bry sur Marne ■ Tel: 01 48 81 48 73 ■ By appointment only ■ Prices medium to high.

Reproductions of paintings by the great masters.

ARTISANS

The artisans of the world are one of of mankind's most precious resources. The skills used for the creation and restoration of beautiful things will survive beyond the lifetime of any individual, no matter how famous or infamous he might have been.

Man's use of his hands in coordination with his imagination is nothing short of a miracle. Next time you look at a special piece of furniture, a beautifully bound book, a crystal goblet, a finely wrought iron gate, a stained glass window or a splendid serving dish, think of the millenia of creativity that went into them. From the time of the Crusades, France has been one of the world's leaders in fine craftsmanship.

In France the word "artisan" is an essential and proud part of the nation's patrimony. In spite of the brutal onslaughts of the industrial and electronic revolutions, France is, along with Italy, the true source of most of the beauty we live with and too often take for granted.

French artisans will always produce and protect the treasures of the civilized world. However, it is up to each one of us to give them our respect and support in every way possible.

The reader will note that many of the artisans are listed as "Compagnons du Devoir". This hard-earned title indicates that an artisan has sworn to uphold his honour and to fulfill his duty to the trade he practises. In order to be admitted to the "Compagnons du Devoir", upon completion of an apprenticeship, the artisan must then travel for three years and a day to various regions of France and work with the "Master Craftsmen" on their projects. When he has completed his training, he is required to produce a "chef-d'oeuvre" (a masterpiece). This is submitted for evaluation to a jury of "Compagnons". If the work is found worthy, he is honoured with the right to use the title, "Compagnon du Devoir".

Bronze Founders
Fondeurs et bronziers d'art

Founders cast in bronze, an alloy of copper and tin, to produce beautiful objects, from a necklace, a lamp, a table, a statue to a bell. They use either the lost wax or sand casting process to make their moulds. Their finished work requires the cooperation of three distinctly different craftsmen, the "turner", the "chiseller" and the "fitter". Until recently, they constituted three diffent trades, but now usually work together.

BLANCHET ET CIE
57 av Gambetta, 93170 Bagnolet ■ Tel: 01 49 93 06 41 ■ Fax: 01 48 97 17 37 ■ Mon-Fri 8:00-12:00/13:00-17:30, Fri closing 16:30 ■ English spoken ■ Mr. Landowski

Specialties: Art statuary using either the lost wax process or sand casting.
References: Dome of the Invalides, Prefecture of Bobigny, Doors of the French Ministry of Finance. They have been at it since 1872.

SOCIÉTÉ BRONZALUMAX FONDERIE THINOT
91 av de la République, 92230 Châtillon-sous-Bagneux ■ Tel: 01 42 53 42 65 ■ Mon-Fri 9:00-18:00 ■ Director: Mr. Thinot

Specialties: Casting massive silver objects and medals, (lost wax and sand casting), since 1947. References: The sculptors: Maillol, Germaine Richier, the Giacomettis, Belmondo and others.

FONDERIE CLEMENTI
17 rue du docteur Arnaudet, 92190 Meudon ■ Tel: 01 45 34 56 32 ■ Fax: 01 45 34 73 35 ■ Mon-Fri 7:30-12:30/13:30-17:00 ■ Mr. G. Clementi

Specialties: Statuary, in the lost wax process, on order from the artist, since 1963. References: Miro (Galerie Maeght), Musée Bourdelle, Nicky de Saint Phalle.

FONDERIE D'ART DUCROS
1 rue Baron, 75017 Paris ■ Tel: 01 42 29 22 39 ■ Mon-Fri 8:00-12:00/12:30-18:30 ■ Prices medium

Casting of sculpture in bronze, in limited numbered editions, using the lost wax process. Restoration and mounting of bronzes.

FLEURANT

Chemin du Halage, Z.I., 78270 Bonnières-sur-Seine ■ Tel: 01 30 98 90 11 ■ Mon-Fri 8:30-12:00/13:30-18:00 ■ Alain Brieu speaks English ■ Prices high

Bronze foundry. Lost wax casting. From the mould to final patinas. Original works of art and limited numbered editions. Realisations for artist-sculptors. They have a gallery of sculpture, paintings and engravings.

S.N. SOCRA S.A.R.L

ZAE De Saltgourde avenue du Château 24430 Marsac sur l'Isle –BP 237- 24052 Périgueux CTC Cédex 9 ■ Tel: 05 53 03 30 50 ■ Fax: 05 53 04 22 90 ■ Director : Patrick Palem ■ Jean Weiss

Specialty: Restoration of statuary in bronze or stone. Treatment of stone and restoration of mosaic pavements. References: The Bridge Alexander III in Paris, the mosaic pavement of Gangobie, the French Embassy in Denmark.

FONDERIE DE COUBERTIN

Domaine de Coubertin, Atelier St Jacques, 78470 St Rémy-les-Chevreuses ■ Tel: 01 30 85 69 62 ■ Fax: 01 30 85 69 30 ■ E-mail: info@fondation-coubertin.asso.fr ■ Web: www.usa.fondation-coubertin.asso.fr ■ Mon-Thu 8:00-12:30/13:30-18:00, Fri 8:00-12:30 ■ English spoken ■ Foundry: Mr. Dubos – Tel: 01 30 85 69 41 ■ Metalworks: Mr. Ambonati – Tel: 01 30 85 69 01 ■ Carpentry: Mr. Gimalac – Tel: 01 30 85 69 21

Specialties: Foundry, metalwork, carpentry. References: The balconies of the Château of Versailles, the Archangel of Mont Saint-Michel, the Equestrian Statue of the Esplanade of the Louvre. They have been working since 1973 in France, Japan, U.S.A., Austria and many Arab countries.

ETS BRONZE D'ART ET VITRIER

13 rue de Cotte, 75012 Paris ■ Tel: 01 43 44 17 55 ■ Fax: 01 43 44 17 23 ■ Mon-Fri 8:00-12:00/13:00-17:00 Mr. Lopez De Souza Antonio ■ English, Spanish and Portuguese spoken ■ Prices medium

Bronze worker, chiseller and finisher of bronze for decoration. Installations. Makes lighting and consoles in the old styles.

MME FRANCE MARIE LEHE

47 rue de Lyon, 75012 Paris ■ Tel: 01 43 43 40 49 - Fax: 01 43 43 14 18 ■ Mon-Fri 8:30-17:30 ■ Prices medium

Foundry for ornaments in bronze and brass. Sand casting and lost wax process.

MEILLEUR

32 rue des Amandiers, 75020 Paris , entrance: 15 rue Fernand Léger ■ Tel: 01 43 66 45 13 ■ Fax: 01 43 66 45 43 ■ E-mail: maison.meilleur@wanadoo.fr ■ Mon-Fri 8:30-12:00/13:00-18:00 , by appointment ■ English spoken

Specialties: Wrought ironwork, art bronze, all bronze and ironwork for architecture and decoration. Work experience: Bibliotheque Nationale in Paris, Palais de Fontainbleau, Palais de Compiegne, Conseil d'Etat and the Palais Royal (lanterns).

ATELIER METAFER

287 av du Président-Wilson, 93210 La Plaine-Saint-Denis ■ Tel: 01 48 20 49 06 ■ Fax: 01 48 20 05 87 ■ Mon-Fri 7:30-12:00/13:00-16:30 ■ Director: Marc Nouaille

Specialty: Restoration, ironwork, sculpture, metalwork. Custom work in all metals: wrought iron, stainless steel, bronze, aluminium. Work experience: The Presidential palaces in the Ivory Coast and Cameroun, the Royal Guard and Private Hospital in Riyadh, Saudi Arabia. The Marriot Hotel in Atlanta, Georgia. Sculpture casting: One of 100 meters in height for a hotel in Singapore, the Dolphins of Hong Kong Harbour, the Lalanne Dinosaurs in Santa Monica, CA.

ENTREPRISE TOULOUSE

10 rue Beautreillis, 75004 Paris ■ Tel: 01 48 87 82 85 ■ Fax 01 48 87 82 84 ■ Mon-Fri 8:00-12:00/14:00-18:00 ■ Contact: Jean-Claude Toulouse

Specialties: Chiselling of bronze, all metalwork, restoration of precious art objects. Work experience: Paul Getty Museum, Musée du Louvre, Château de Versailles, the treasures of many of Europe's cathedrals. All work is done in their own workshop.

Cabinet Makers, Marquetry Workers, Chair-makers
Ebénistes marqueteurs, menuisiers en sièges

The cabinet makers, marquetry workers and chair-makers of France can restore fine furniture and reproduce furniture of any period or style on order. They are some of the best in the world.

JEAN-LOUIS CHODORGE

16 place Saint-Pierre, 55000 Bar-le-Duc ■ Tel: 03 29 45 07 99 ■ Fax: 03 29 77 16 72 ■ Mon-Fri 8:00-17:00 ■ Contact: Jean-Louis Chodorge

Specialty: Restoration of antique marquetry. Master Artisan. Diploma of the École Boulle. Brochure upon request. New activity: fabrication of amphoras in terracotta – reproduction of ancient models.

♛ MICHEL GERMOND

78 quai de l'Hôtel-de-Ville, 75004 Paris ■ Tel: 01 42 78 04 78 ■ Fax: 01 42 78 22 74 ■ E-mail : jeannine.germond@wanadoo.fr ■ Web: www.grandsateliers.com ■ Mon-Fri 8:00-12:00/13:30-18:00 ■ English spoken ■ Director: Michel Germond

Specialties: Restoration of furniture, chairs, marquetry. Will repair small pieces of furniture on site.
Work experience: Furniture of the Bibliothèque Nationale, Furniture of the Queen's Chamber at Versailles, Château de Compiègne.

ENTREPRISE GROUX

73 bis route de Roissy 93290 Tremblay en France ■ Tel: 01 49 63 49 99 ■ Fax: 01 49 63 49 83 ■ E-mail: groux_sa@club-internet.fr ■ Martin Labouré and Mr. Gora ■ English spoken

Specialty: Restoration of works of art in wood or stone. Restoration of paintings and sculpture.
References: Church of Notre Dame de Poitiers, the Cathedral of Amiens, the Cathedral of Bordeaux, the west façade of the Cathedral Notre-Dame de Paris.

SERGE PRONIEWSKI

32 route du Château, 33460 Labarde ■ Tel: 05 57 88 90 46 ■ Fax: 05 57 88 36 29 ■ Mon-Sat 9:00-19:00 ■ English spoken ■ Contact: M. Proniewski

Specialty: Restoration of antique furniture, Boulle marquetry of the XVII and XVIII centuries. Restoration of gilded wood
Work experience: Works at the École Boulle, Counsel to the Atelier of the Musée du Louvre. Grand Prix régional des métiers d'art in 1986.

S.E.R.O.D. (SOCIÉTÉ D'EXPERTISE ET DE RESTAURATION D'OBJETS D'ART)

42 rue de Varenne, 75007 Paris ■ Tel: 01 45 44 54 78 ■ Fax: 01 45 49 05 38 ■ Mon-Fri 9:00-18:00 ■ English spoken ■ Director: Pierre Lévy.

Specialty: Restoration of furniture of the XVII and XVIII centuries, objects of the XIX century.
Work experience: Partridge House in England. Many years experience abroad.

PATRICK VASTEL

143 rue du Général-Leclerc, 50110 Tourlaville (Cherbourg) ■ Tel: 02 33 22 46 07 ■ Fax: 02 33 22 96 26 ■ E-mail: pvastel@aol.com ■ Mon-Fri 9:00-12:30/13:30-18:30, by appointment ■ Patrick Vastel speaks English

Specialty: Restoration of XVII and XVIII century marquetry. Work experience: The great dining room of the City Hall of Cherbourg. Clients come to this establishment from all over the world. École Boulle. Expert before the Court of Appeals, Caen.

Carpenters
Menuisiers

ART ET TECHNIQUES DU BOIS

11 rue Marcel Thil, 51100 Reims ■ Tel: 03 26 47 22 74 ■ Fax : 03 26 84 90 01 ■ Contact M. Loïc Lambert

Specialty: Staircases in wood for historic monuments, carpentry, parquet floors.
References: The steeple of the Church of St Jacques in Reims, the Place Ducal at Charleville-Mezières, the Church of Outines. Compagnon du Devoir.

AUBERT LABANSAT SA

57 Route de Coutances, 50190 Periers ■ Tel: 02 33 76 60 60 ■ Fax : 02 33 76 60 66 ■ Contact: M.Pierre.

Specialty: Historic conservation, carpentry, master carpentry, cabinet-making, half-timbering, old style parquets.
Work Experience: 20 churches, 3 abbeys, 3 cathedrals: Rouen, Le Havre, dozens of châteaux and private homes. Mont Saint-Michel, Parc of the Château de Versailles.

ENTREPRISE BLANCHON S.N

29 rue de Turcoing, Z.I. Romanet, 87000 Limoges ■ Tel: 05 55 30 16 70 ■ Fax: 05 55 30 46 38 ■ E-mail : blanchon.sn@wanadoo.fr ■ Mon-Fri 8:00-12:00/13:30-18:30 ■ Contact: Mr Ropital ■ English spoken

Specialty: Masonry, stonemasonry, carpentry, roofing, staff.
Work experience: Église de St-Michel-des-Lions (Limoges), Château de Sedières en Corrèze. Empress Place Building (National Museum of Singapore).

FONDATION DE COUBERTIN

Domaine de Coubertin, Ateliers St Jacques, 78470 St-Rémy-les-Chevreuses ■ Tel: 01 30 85 69 62 ■ Fax: 01 30 85 69 30 ■ Mon-Thu 8:00-12:30/13:30-18:00/Fri 8:00-12:30 ■ English spoken ■ Contact: M. Bonneau

Specialty: Foundry, metalwork, carpentry.
Work experience: The balconies of the Château de Versailles, the Archangel of Mont Saint-Michel, the Equestrian statue on the Esplanade of the Louvre.
Contracts completed in the U.S.A., Austria, Japan and the Middle East.

LES ATELIERS PERRAULT FRÈRES

30 rue Sébastien-Cady, 49290 St-Laurent-de-la-Plaine BP 2 ■ Tel: 02 41 22 37 22 ■ Fax: 02 41 22 37 37 ■ E-mail : contact@ateliersperrault.com ■ Web: www.ateliersperrault.com ■ Mon-Fri 8:00-12:00/13:30-17:30 ■ English spoken

Specialty: Traditional master carpentry, slate roofing, classical stonemasonry and carpentry: doors, windows, staircases, parquets, woodcarving.
Work experience: The Louvre, private houses on the Place des Vosges, Ile St-Louis, Chinon, Abbaye de Fontevrault, Cathedrale de Nantes. Cour des Comptes in Paris, Hôtel Lansay in Paris, Parliament of Britany. Private homes abroad.

ENTREPRISE MAMIAS

28-30 av Jean-Jaurès, 93220 Gagny ■ Tel: 01 43 02 43 88 ■ Fax: 01 43 02 94 42 ■ E-mail: mamias@mamias.fr ■ Web: www.mamias.fr ■ Mon-Fri 8:00-12:00/13:30-17:30 ■ English spoken ■ Director: M. Gueury

Specialty: Restoration of clocks, carillons and bells.
Work experience: The bells of Notre-Dame de Paris, the Cathedral at Chartres, the Basilica of the Sacré-Coeur in Montmartre, the Carillon in Washington, D.C.

Carpet, Textile, Tapestry and Embroidery Restorers
Restaurateurs en tapis, tapisseries, broderies et textiles anciens

Carpets, tapestries, embroideries and textiles require special care and maintenance. Light and dust as well as normal wear and tear cause deterioration. But remember, a skilled restorer can often work miracles.

The Artisan-specialist needed will depend on the type of restoration. The work can vary from a relatively simple but skilled operation like cleaning a Savonnerie carpet to the restoration of an important historical ensemble. Nine people worked on the Queen's chamber in Versailles for eleven years.

When a tapestry requires re-weaving, a small number of firms still possess the appropriate Jacquard handlooms and can carry out the most delicate restorations from original documents.

SOCIÉTÉ BOBIN
27 rue de la Vanne, 92120 Montrouge ■ Tel: 01 56 73 11 11 ■ Fax: 01 56 73 11 22 ■ Mon-Fri 8:00-18:00/Sat 8:30-12:30 ■ English spoken ■ Director: M.Bobin ■ Expert : M. Mourier

Specialty: Cleaning and restoration of carpets, tapestries and antique textiles.
Work experience: Musée du Louvre, Château de Versailles, Château de Fontainebleau. The company has ateliers in Nice.

♛ MAISON CHEVALIER
64 bd de la Mission-Marchand, 92400 Courbevoie ■ Tel: 01 47 88 41 41 ■ Fax: 01 47 88 64 52 ■ Mon-Fri 8:30-18:00 ■ English spoken ■ Directors: Dominique and Pierre Chevalier ■ Contact: Veronique Chevalier

Specialty: Restoration and cleaning of carpets and tapestries. Creators of a machine which allows cleaning without manipulation.
Work experience: Restoration and cleaning of tapestries for the Musée du Louvre (Gobelins XVII century). The Beauvais chairs in the Château de Versailles. Le Musée de Cluny. The company has ateliers in Bauge, Aubusson.

Gilders
Doreurs

Gilders are responsible for the beautiful gold leafing you see on the statues and domes of Paris. They do both outdoor and indoor work. Indoors, they will gild picture frames, mirrors, furniture and art objects.

There are three methods of gilding: Gold leaf gilding in which thin layers of gold are laid on wood, plaster or sculpted metal. This involves a series of 22 delicate operations: Gold or silver plating by means of electroplating; Mercury gilding, an alchemical formula which dates back to mediaeval times. While it is the most beautiful, the process is rare, costly and dangerous to use.

ATELIERS ROBERT GOHARD ET BEAUMONT
90 rue des Entrepreneurs, 75015 Paris ■ Tel: 01 45 78 89 68 ■ Fax: 01 45 79 78 09 ■ Web: www.gohard-ateliers.com ■ Mon-Thu: 8:00-18:00- Fri/8:00-17:00 ■ English spoken ■ Contact: M. Fabrice Gohard

Specialty: Restoration, gold leafing on wood, plaster or metal. Work experience: The Balustrades of the Queen's Chamber at Versailles, the Grilles of the Place Stanislas in Nancy, the Dome of the Invalides, the Flame of the Statue of Liberty in New York. Parliament of Rennes. The wedding room of the Palace of Versailles.

♛ MAISON MAHIEU
15 impasse des Primevères, 75011 Paris ■ Tel: 01 43 55 88 25 ■ Fax: 01 48 06 92 99 ■ Mon-Fri 8:00-12:00/13:00-16:45 ■ English spoken ■ Contact: Mlle Maurette

Specialty: Gold and silver plating on metal, bronze patinas. One of the last establishments permitted to practise mercury gilding. Work experience: Metropolitan Opera in New York, Getty Museum in Malibu, decorative hardware for the great apartments of Fontainebleau, the Trianon of Versailles, Château de Champs (Compiègne).

BRUNO GHEBI
102 av Bisch offsheim, 07710 Villars-sur-Var ■ Telfax: 04 93 05 77 80 ■ E-mail: bruno.ghebi@wanadoo.fr

Specialty: trompe l'oeil. Restorer of frecoes and all decorative painting on walls.

────────────── **LUTHIERS** ──────────────

A LA CORDE PINCÉE
20 rue de Verneuil, 75007 Paris ■ Tel: 01 42 60 29 36 ■ Claude Mercier Ythier ■ By appointment only

Buy, sell, rent and restore clavecins, epinettes, clavicordes.

ALLAIN CADINOT
Viaduc des Arts, 99 av Daumesnil, 75012 Paris ■ Tel: 01 43 41 43 43 ■ Fax: 01 43 41 72 36 ■ E-mail: cadinotflutes@wanadoo.fr ■ Web: www.cadinotflutes.com ■ Tue-Sat 9:30-13:00/14:00-19:00 ■ English spoken ■ Professional discount ■ Major credit cards

Internationally-known maker and restorer of transverse flutes. He is also the exclusive importer of transverse flutes made by the American firms, Haynes and Powell. A fine selection of contemporary music stands. Organizer of master classes and concerts.

ROGER LANNE
Viaduc des Arts, 103 av Daumesnil, 75012 Paris ■ Tel: 01 43 40 67 67 ■ Fax: 01 43 40 71 71 ■ Tue-Sat 9:00-12:00/13:30-18:30 ■ Roger Lanne ■ Some English and German spoken ■ Professional discount ■ Major credit cards

Creation and restoration of violins, cellos and bows. He is the luthier of the Paris Opera and an expert to U.F.E.

Masons and sculptors in stone
Maçons et Tailleurs de Pierre

ATELIER DE LA PIERRE
Route d'Augiargues 30250 Junas ■ Tel: 04 66 80 33 82 ■ Fax: 04 66 77 70 25 ■ Mon-Fri 8:00-17:00 ■ Contact: J. Mercier & M.Schildknecht

Specialty: All stonemasonry, hard or soft stone. Stone from Junas. Staircases on Saracen vaulting, bas-reliefs, engraving, stone carving.
Work experience: Restoration of the Conseil Général, Nîmes, Bell Tower of Caveirac, Hotel de Caderousse. Compagnon du Devoir. Many churches.

ATELIER JEAN-LOUP BOUVIER
9 rue du Ponant, BP212. 30133 Les Angles ■ Tel: 0 4 90 25 32 90 ■ Fax: 04 90 25 62 46 ■ E-mail : atelier.BOUVIER@wanadoo.fr ■ Mon-Fri 7:30-12:00/14:00-18:30 Sat 9:00-12:00

Specialty: Monumental sculpture.
References: The Louvre, The Senate, École Militaire, Assemblée Nationale, Notre-Dame of Paris, the Cathedral of Reims, the Cathedral of Troyes, the Cathedral of Albi.

ENTREPRISE BLANCHON
29 rue de Turcoing, Z.I. Romanet, 87000 Limoges ■ Tel: 05 55 30 16 70 ■ Fax: 05 55 30 46 38 ■ E-mail: blanchon.sn@wanadoo.fr ■ Mon-Fri 8:00-12:00/13:30-18:30 ■ Contact: M.Ropital

Specialty: Masonry, stonemasonry, carpentry, roofing, staff.
Work experience: Église de St-Michel-des-Lions (Limoges), Château de Sédières in Corrèze.

ENTREPRISE DEGAINE
19 rue de la Lancette, 75012 Paris ■ Tel: 01 44 67 87 10 ■ Fax: 01 43 07 08 75 ■ Mon-Fri 7:30-19:00 ■ Contact: M. Boudoul ■ English spoken

Specialty: Masonry, reinforced and pre-stressed concrete, stonemasonry.

Work experience: Mont-Saint-Michel, Palais de Fontainebleau, Musée d'Orsay, numerous private homes in the Marais, Église du Raincy (Seine-St-Denis), Palais des Ducs de Bourgogne (Dijon).

ENTREPRISE GROUX

73 bis route de Roissy 93290 Tremblay en France ■ Tel: 01 49 63 49 99 ■ Fax 01 49 63 49 83 ■ E-mail : groux_sa@club-internet.fr ■ Martin Labouré ■ M.Gora ■ English spoken

Specialty: Restoration of works of art in wood or stone. Restoration of paintings and sculpture.
References: Church of Notre Dame de Poitiers, the Cathedral of Amiens, the Cathedral of Bordeaux, th Cathedral Notre-Dame of Paris

ENTREPRISE PAVY

Z.I. Nord, 35 rue Thomas-Edison, 72650 La Chapelle Saint-Aubain ■ Tel: 02 43 47 03 03 ■ Fax: 02 43 47 03 09 ■ Mon Fri 8:00-12:30/13:30-19:00 ■ Director: Vincent Pavy

Specialty: Masonry, stonemasonry.
Work experience: Église du Vieux-Saint-Sauveur, Caen, Gallo-Roman Ramparts, Le Mans, Palais de Justice, Laval, Parliament of Britany, Saint-Benoit Church and the Church of the Visitation in Le Mans, Couvent des Uursulines in Château Gontier.

ENTREPRISE PRADEAU-MORIN

41 bd Soult, 75012 Paris ■ Tel: 01 43 15 10 10 ■ Fax: 01 43 15 10 15 ■ Charles Marceau ■ English spoken

Specialty: Masonry, stonemasonry.
Work experience: Renovation of the Louvre Museum (Paris), the National Assembly (Peristyle), Cathedrale de Beauvais, Les Invalides and the Musée d'Orsay (Paris).

SOCIÉTÉ ASO Atelier Sculpteur et Ornementation.

1 rue Emile Gabory 44330 Vallet ■ Tel: 02 40 36 25 45 ■ Fax: 02 40 36 29 60 ■ Mr. Guilbaud, Mr. Onbos

Specialty: Sculpture and restoration of stone and marble by laser and biomineralization.
Work experience: Notre-Dame-la-Grande in Poitiers, Institute of France in Paris and the wall of the Cathedral in Chartres.

S.N. SOCRA S.A.R.L

ZAE de Saltgourde Av.du château 24430 Marsac sur l'Isle –BP 237- 24052 Périgueux CTC Cédex 9 ■ Tel: 05 53 03 30 50 ■ Fax: 05 53 04 22 90 ■ Director M. Patrick Palem ■ Contact : Mr. Jean Weiss

Specialty: Restoration of statuary in bronze or stone. Treatment of stone and restoration of mosaic pavements.
Work experience: The Bridge of Alexander III in Paris, the pavement of Gangobie, the French Embassy in Denmark.

Ornamental Ironworkers
Ferronniers, métalliers, serruriers d'art

The "Ironworker" forges iron into decorative elements for use either indoors (banisters, fireplace accessories, lighting fixtures, furniture) or outdoors (portals, gates, balconies, handrails, garden furniture). Wrought iron work is often adorned with acanthus leaves and flowers. These effects are achieved by highly-skilled artisans known as "Chasers" or "Embossers" who cold-hammer the metal.

In contra-distinction, the "Metalworker" is a carpenter in metal. He specializes in roof frames and window and door casings. The two usually work together.

ATELIERS BATAILLARD
7 impasse Marie-Blanche 75018 Paris ■ Tel: 01 42 82 02 84 ■ Fax: 01 48 06 12 06 ■ Mon-Fri 9:00-13:00/14:00-18:00 ■ English spoken ■ Contact: M. Bataillard

Specialty: Stair railings, balconies, gates, grilles, lighting, furniture. Restoration of all metals: wrought iron, stainless steel, bronze, aluminium.
Work experience: Gates for the Presidential Palaces in Yamoussoukro (Ivory Coast) and Yaounde (Cameroun), the Baghdad Airport and the University of Riyadh. Design and installation of wrought iron staircases for private clients in the U.S.A.

FONDATION DE COUBERTIN
Domaine de Coubertin, Ateliers St Jacques, 78470 St-Rémy-les-Chevreuses ■ Tel: 01 30 85 69 62 ■ Fax: 01 30 85 69 30 ■ E-mail : info@fondation-coubertin.asso.fr ■ Web: www.usa.fondation-coubertin.asso.fr ■ Mon-Thurs 8:00-12:30/13:30-18:00, Fri 8:00-12:30 ■ English spoken ■ Contact: M. Bonneau

Specialty: Foundry, metalwork, carpentry.
Work experience: The balconies of the Château de Versailles, the Archangel of Mont Saint-Michel, the Equestrian statue on the Esplanade of the Louvre.
Contracts completed in the U.S.A., Austria, Japan and the Middle East.

♛ MEILLEUR
32 rue des Amandiers, 75020 Paris (entrance 15 rue Fernand Léger) ■ Tel: 01 43 66 45 13 ■ Fax: 01 43 66 45 43 ■ E-mail: maison.meilleur@wanadoo.fr ■ Mon-Fri 8:30-12:00/13:00-18:00 by appointment ■ Catherine Meilleur ■ English spoken ■ Prices high to very high ■ Professional discount

Custom work in bronze, brass and iron for interior and exterior decoration. Lighting: chandeliers, sconces, lanterns, lamps and adjustable reading lamps.
Decorative door and window hardware, special faucets.
Wrought iron balconies, stair railings, lighting. Restoration of the above for National Museums and private clients.
Work experience: Bibliothèque Nationale in Paris, Palais de Fontainebleu, Palais de Compiègne, Conseil d'Etat and the Palais Royal (lanterns).

LES METALLIERS CHAMPENOIS
11 rue de l'Etis, 51430 Bezannes ■ Tel: 03 26 36 21 33 - Fax: 03 26 36 22 15 ■ Web: www.lmc.com ■ Mon-Fri 8:00-12:00/14:00-18:00 ■ English spoken ■ Director: Jean Bourly

Specialty: Metalwork and ironwork.
Work experience: The Statue of Liberty in New York, the friezes on the balcony of the King's Chamber at Versailles, the Gates of the Place Stanislas in Nancy.

Plasterers and Stucco Workers
Staffers and Stucateurs

ENTREPRISE BLANCHON S.N
29 rue de Turcoing, Z.I. Romanet, 87000 Limoges ■ Tel: 05 55 30 16 70 ■ Fax: 05 55 30 46 38 ■ E-mail: blanchon.sn@wanadoo.fr ■ Mon-Fri 8:00-12:00/13:30-18:30 ■ Contact: M.Ropital ■ English spoken

Specialty: Masonry, stonemasonry, carpentry, roofing, staff.
Work experience: Église de St-Michel-des-Lions (Limoges), Château de Sédières in Corrèze. Empress Place Building (National Museum of Singapore).

LES NOUVEAUX ATELIERS MERINDOL
12bis route de Lyon, BP 607 84031 Avignon Cedex 3 ■ Tel: 04 90 82 11 14 ■ Fax: 04 90 85 59 77 ■ E-mail: merindol.nouveaux.ateliers@wanadoo.fr ■ Mon-Fri 8:00-12:00/14:00-17:00 ■ English spoken ■ Director: Pierre Mérindol

Specialty: Wood and stone carving. Work in plaster gypsum. Treatments consolidated with stone. Restoration.
Work experience: Statue of the Town of Lille, Place de la Concorde in Paris, Dome of the Invalides, portal of the Church of St-Trophime at Arles. Façader of the Garnier Opera House in Paris.

RENAUD PLATRE
Route de Bellevue, 16710 Saint Yriex ■ Tel: 05 45 95 55 15 ■
Fax: 05 45 92 60 10 ■ Mon-Fri 8:00-12:00/14:00-19:00■ Contact
M. Renaudeaux
Specialty: Plastering, staff, stucco.
**References: Casino de Dax, Château de Montchaude in
Charente, Musée Labanche in Brive, Theatre of Angoulème,
Goethe Institute of Bordeaux. Compagnon de Devoir.**

Restorers of Clocks and Bells
Restaurateurs d'horloges et carillons

ENTREPRISE MAMIAS
28-30 av Jean-Jaurès, 93220 Gagny ■ Tel: 01 43 02 43 88 ■ Fax: 01 43
02 94 42 ■ E-mail : mamias@mamias.fr ■ Web: www.mamias.fr ■ Mon-
Fri 8:00-12:00/13:30-17:30 ■ English spoken ■ Director: Mr. Gueury
Specialty: Restoration of clocks, carillons and bells.
**Work experience: The bells of Notre-Dame de Paris, the
Cathedral at Chartres, the Basilica of the Sacre-Coeur in
Montmartre, the Carillon in Washington, D.C.**

Restorer of Frescoes
Restauration des fresques

BRUNO GHEBI
102 av Bisch offsheim, 07710 Villars-sur-Var ■ Telfax: 04 93 05
77 80 ■ E-mail: bruno.ghebi@wanadoo.fr
**Specialty: trompe l'oeil. Restorer of frecoes and all decora-
tive painting on walls.**

Sculptors in Stone
Sculpteurs sur Pierre

LES NOUVEAU ATELIERS MERINDOL
12 bis route de Lyon, BP 607 84031 Avignon Cedex 3 ■ Tel: 04
90 82 11 14 ■ Fax: 04 90 85 59 77 ■ E-mail: merindol.nou-
veaux.ateliers@wanadoo.fr ■ Mon-Fri 8:00-12:00/14:00-17:00 ■
English spoken ■ Director: Pierre Mérindol

Specialty: Wood and stone carving. Work in plaster gypsum. Treatments consolidated with stone. Restoration.
Work experience: Statue of the Town of Lille, Place de la Concorde in Paris, Dome of the Invalides, portal of the Church of St-Trophime at Arles. Façade of the Garnier Opera House in Paris.

Stained Glass Window Makers
Vitraillistes

ATELIER AVICE – VITRAIL FRANCE
17 rue de Tascher, 72000 Le Mans ■ Tel: 02 43 81 18 60 ■ Fax: 02 43 82 15 58 ■ E-mail: vitrailfrance@a-t.fr ■ Mon-Fri 8:00-12:00/13:30-17:00/Fri closing 16:30 ■ English spoken ■ Director: Didier Alliou
Specialty: Restoration and creation of stained glass windows in all styles.
Work experience: Restoration of the stained glass windows in the Cathedrals of Chartres, Le Mans, Laval, the Pantheon in Paris and many other churches. Worked with France Vitrail International on the Basilica of Yamassoukro (Ivory Coast).

ATELIERS DUCHEMIN
14 av Georges-Lafenestre, 75014 Paris ■ Tel: 01 45 42 84 17 ■ Fax: 01 45 42 01 56 ■ E-mail: ateliers.duchemin@starnet.fr ■ Mon-Fri 9:00-12:00/14:00-17:30, Fri closing 17:00 ■ Director: Dominique Rousvoal-Duchemin
Specialty: Restoration of stained glass windows of all styles and creation.
Work experience: Chapel of Bang Pa In (Thailand), reconstitution of the stained glass in the Synagogue on the Rue Copernic in Paris. The Chapel of Ste Anne in Paris and many other churches. The Castel-Béranger in Paris. Grande Chancellerie de la Légion d'Honneur in Paris. The Brasserie Flo in Paris.

ATELIER 54
34 av du Charles de Gaulle, 54210 Saint Nicolas de Port ■ Tel: 03 83 45 26 02 ■ Fax: 03 83 46 94 94 ■ Mon-Fri 7:30-12:00/13:30-17:00 ■ Contact: Mr. Mengel
Specialty: Creation and restoration of stained glass.
References: Basilica of Saint Nicolas de Port, the Cathedral in Nancy, the Cathedrals in Madras, in Singapore and in Canada.

ATELIER FLEURY

4 rue Arzac, 31300 Toulouse ■ Tel: 05 61 59 26 42 ■ Fax: 05 61 59 34 47 ■ E-mail: j.d.fleury@wanadoo.fr ■ Mon-Fri 9:00-13:00/14:00-18:00 ■ contact : Mr. Fleury

Specialty: Restoration and creation of stained glass.
References: Church of Fleurance in Gers, the Cathedral of Saint Etienne in Toulouse, the Church of Beaugency in the Loiret.

ATELIER PAROT

Le Château, 21110 Aisery ■ Tel: 03 80 29 71 72 ■ Fax: 03 80 29 73 74 ■ E-mail: parot@ipac.fr

Specialty: Work for contemporary artists as well as creation and restoration of all types of stained glass.

ATELIER MIREILLE AND JACQUES JUTEAU

8 rue Alfred de Musset, 95120 Ermon ■ Tel: 01 34 15 70 97 ■ Fax: 01 34 14 45 76

Specialty: Creation and restoration of stained Glass.
References: The Cathedral of Chartres, Tours and Saint-Denis.

ATELIER DE SAINTE MARIE

12 Chemin de la Perche, 22800 Quintin ■ Tel: 02 96 74 92 28 ■ Fax: 02 96 74 84 15 ■ E-mail: messonnet@worldonline.fr ■ Contact: Michael Messonnet.

Restoration and creation of stained glass.
References: The Parliament in Brittany, The Abbey of Beauport, the Cathedral in Quimper, The Cathedral of Vannes, the Chapel Le Faouët Sainte-Barbe.

ATELIER JACQUES SIMON

44 rue Ponsardin, 51100 Reims ■ Tel: 03 26 47 23 15 ■ Fax: 03 26 40 90 32 ■ Web: www.atelier-simon.com ■ English spoken ■ Contact: Benoit et Stéphanie Marc

Restoration and creation of stained glass
References: All of Chagall's work abroad. The United Nations in New York, The Art Institute of Chicago.

BARTHE-BORDEREAU SARL

20 rue Florent Cornilleau, 49100 Angers ■ Tel: 02 41 34 82 30 ■ Fax: 02 41 60 03 69 ■ Mon-Fri 7:30-11:45/13:15-17:30 Fri 17:00 ■ Contact M. Rollo

Specialty: Restoration and creation of stained glass of all types.
References: Cathedrals in France, Martinique, Guadeloupe, Guyana.

MICHEL DURAND

4 rue Auguste Simon, 94700 Maisons Alfort ■ Tel: 01 43 76 64 06 ■ Fax: 01 49 77 81 62 ■ Mon-Fri 8:30-12:00/14:00-18:00 ■ Contact M. Deloffre

Specialty: Restoration and creation of stained glass.
References: Notre Dame du Havre, Cathedral of Beauvais, Château of Chambord, Church of Saint Louis des Invalides.

FRANCE VITRAIL INTERNATIONAL

20 rue Raspail, 92400 Courbevoie ■ Tel: 01 43 33 91 88 ■ Fax: 01 43 33 91 86 ■ Web: www.france-vitrail.fr ■ Mon-Fri 8:15-12:15/13:30-17:30, Fri closing 16:30 ■ English spoken ■ Contact M. Bonte

Specialty: Creation and restoration of all styles of stained glass. Work experience: 7,500 square metres of stained glass windows for the Basilica of Yamoussoukro, Ivory Coast. Hotel George V (Paris), Hotel Plaza Athenée (Paris). Thirty churches and cathedrals. Domes and windows in the Middle East and the Orient.

L'ATELIER DU VITRAIL

10 rue Fernand Malinvaud, BP 185, 87005 Limoges Cedex ■ Tel: 05 55 30 31 89 ■ Fax: 05 55 30 35 23 ■ Mon-Fri 8:00-12:00/14:00-18:00 ■ Contact Didier Bayle

Specialty: Restoration and creation of all types of stained glass
References: A great many cathedrals between the Loire and the Rhone.

LE VITRAIL

4 rue Brulard, 10000 Troyes ■ Tel: 03 25 73 38 87 ■ Fax: 03 25 73 38 88 ■ Mon-Fri 9:00-18:00 ■ Contact: Alain Vinum

Specialty: Restoration and creation of stained glass.
References: The Church of Antours in Beirut, the Basilica Saint Urban in Troyes, the Cathedral Saint Pierre and Saint Paul in Troyes, the Church of Saint Vit in Le Doux (contemporary creation).

LES ATELIERS GAUDIN

6 rue de la Grande-Chaumière, 75006 Paris ■ Tel: 01 43 26 65 62 ■ Fax: 01 43 54 96 55 ■ E-mail : vitraux@club-internet.fr ■ Mon-Thurs 8:00-13:15/13:15-16:45 Fri 15:45 ■ Contact: M. Blanc-Guérin

Specialty: Restoration and creation of stained glass windows of all styles. Work experience: Sainte-Chapelle de Paris, St-Etienne-du-Mont, Saint-Gervais Saint-Protais. Cathedral of Orleans.

JACQUES LOIRE
16 rue d'Ouarville, 28300 Chartres Leves ■ Tel: 02 37 21 20 71
■ Fax: 02 37 36 22 33 ■ E-mail : loire@galerie-du-vitrail ■ Web:
www.galerie-du-vitrail.com ■ Mon-Fri 8:00-12:00/13:30 ■ 17:30
■ English spoken ■ Director: Bruno and Hervé Loire
Specialty: Restoration and creation of stained glass windows in all styles. Work experience: Cathedral of Chartres, Église St-Eustache (Paris), Bon Samaritain. Restorations in Egypt, Ivory Coast, Persian Gulf States, United States.

M. JEAN MAURET
18160 Saint Hilaire en Lignières ■ Tel: 02 48 60 04 49 ■ Fax: 02 48 60 16 18
Stained glass creation and restoration.
References: Restoration: Cathedrals of Chartres, Bourges and Lyon. Creation: Prieuré of Villesalesmes (Vienne)

BRUNO DE PIREY
La Thuasnerie-Allouis, 18500 Mehun-sur-Yevre ■ Tel: 02 48 57 13 82
■ Fax: 02 48 57 38 37 ■ E-mail: depirey@wanadoo.fr ■ Mon-Fri 8:00-12:00/14:00-18:00 ■ English spoken ■ Director: Bruno de Pirey
Specialty: Restoration and creation of stained glass windows of all styles. Work experience: Chapelle du Val-de-Grâce, Paris. Cathedral St-Etienne, Hôtel des Echevins, Bourges.

VITRAUX D'ART WEINLING
823 route de Gray, 21850 St-Apollinaire ■ Tel: 03 80 71 60 39 ■
Fax: 03 80 72 23 41 ■ Mon-Fri 8:00-12:00/14:00-18:00 ■ English
and German spoken ■ Director: M. Jean-Albert Weinling
Specialty: Restoration and creation of stained glass windows in any style. A new technique: fusing of glass without lead. Work experience: Église de Rouvres en Plaines (Re-creation of XIV century window). Fontaines-en-Duesmois (Côte-d'Or). Restoration of the window "l'Arbre de Jessé", Chapelle des Oeuvres (Dijon) and many others.

Staircases
Escaliers

ART ET TECHNIQUES DU BOIS
31 rue Marcel Thil, 51100 Reims ■ Tel: 03 26 47 22 74 ■ Fax 03 26 84 90 01 ■ Contact M. Loïc Lambert
Specialty: Staircases in wood for historic monuments, carpentry, parquet floors.

References: The steeple of the Church of St Jacqes in Reims, the Place Ducal at Charleville-Mezières, the Church of Outines. Compagnon du Devoir.

LES CHARPENTIERS DE BOURGOGNE
4 rue Lavoisier, 21600 Longvic ■ Tel: 03 80 68 46 90 ■ Fax: 03 80 68 46 99 ■ Contact: M. Hubert Sauvain ■ English spoken

Specialty: Master carpentry, roofing, staircases.
Work experience: Église de St-Seine-l'Abbaye, Palais des Ducs at Dijon, Abbaye Saint-Germain of Auxerres, the Cathedral of Sens. Compagnon du Devoir.

ENTREPRISE LONGÉPÉ
82 rue Pierre Semard, 92320 Châtillon ■ Tel: 01 42 53 39 48 ■ Fax: 01 47 35 64 09 ■ Mon-Fri 7:30-18:00 ■ Contact: M. Fougère

Specialty: Staircases, handrails, railings, master carpentry.
Work experience: Private homes in the Marais, Paris, Les Halles de Mirecourt, La Cité Internationale des Arts, Paris. Compagnon du Devoir.

LES ATELIERS PERRAULT FRÈRES
30 rue Sebastien-Cady, 49290 St-Laurent-de-la-Plaine BP 2 ■ Tel: 02 41 22 37 22 ■ Fax: 02 41 22 37 37 ■ E-mail: contact@ateliersperrault.com ■ Web: www.ateliersperrault.com ■ Mon-Fri 8:00-12:00/13:30-17:30 ■ English spoken

Specialty: Traditional master carpentry, slate roofing, classical stonemasonery and carpentry: doors, windows, staircases, parquets, wood carving.
Work experience: The Louvre, private houses on the Place des Vosges, Ile St-Louis, Chinon, Abbaye de Fontevrault, Cathedral of Nantes, Cour des Comptes, Paris, Hôtel de Lansay, Paris, Parliament of Great Britain.

Wood Carvers
Sculpteurs sur bois

LES NOUVEAUX ATELIERS MERINDOL
12 bis route de Lyon, BP 607 84031 Avignon Cedex 3 ■ Tel: 04 90 82 11 14 ■ Fax: 04 90 85 59 77 ■ E-mail: merindol.nouveaux.ateliers@wanadoo.fr ■ Mon-Fri 7:00-12:00/14:00-17:00 ■ English spoken ■ Director: Pierre Mérindol

Specialty: Wood and stone carving. Work in plaster gypsum. Treatments consolidated with stone and restoration.
Work experience: Statue of the Town of Lille, Place de la Concorde in Paris, Dome of the Invalides, portal of the Church of St-Trophime at Arles. Façade of the Garnier Opera House in Paris.

LES ATELIERS PERRAULT FRÈRES
30 rue Sébastien-Cady, 49290 St-Laurent-de-la-Plaine BP 2 ■
Tel: 02 41 22 37 22 ■ Fax: 02 41 22 37 37 ■ E-mail : contact@ateliersperrault.com ■ Web: www.ateliersperrault.com ■
Mon-Fri 8:00-12:00/13:30-17:30 ■ English spoken

Specialty: Traditional master carpentry, slate roofing, classical stonemasonery and carpentry: doors, windows, staircases, parquets, woodcarving.
Work experience: The Louvre, private houses on the Place des Vosges, Ile St-Louis, Chinon, Abbaye de Fontevrault, Cathedrale de Nantes.

♛ Contract Craftsmen of Excellence

Here is a list of contract companies whose special skills and experience make them eminently eligible to restore historical sites, elegant homes and public buildings. Architects and decorators with major works to restore or furnish should give them careful consideration. They have the credits.

ART ET TECHNIQUE DU BOIS
31 rue Marcel-Thil, 51100 Reims ■ Tel: 03 26 47 22 74 ■ Fax: 03 26 84 90 01 ■ Mon-Fri 7:00-12:15/14:45-18:00 ■ Contact: Loïc Lambert

Specialty: Restoration of historic monuments. Staircases. Master carpentry (framing, panelling, wainscoting, parquet).
Work experience: The Bell Tower of the Église St Jacques in Reims, the Ducal Square in Charleville-Mezières, the Church of Outines. Compagnon du Devoir.

LE BATIMENT ASSOCIE
Zone Industrielle de Muizon, 51140 Jonchery sur Vesle ■ Tel: 03 26 02 90 02 ■ Fax: 03 26 02 94 09 ■ E-mail: info@batiment-associe.fr ■ Mon-Fri 7:30-12:00/13:30-18:00, Fri 12:00 ■ Contact: Pierre Possème

Specialty: Masonry, stonemasonry, master carpentry (bell towers).
Work experience: Marne Provincial Capitol building, Caisse d'Épargne, Reims, vaulted wine cellars, a dozen churches in the Marne. Compagnon du Devoir.

ENTREPRISE BLANCHON

29 rue de Turcoing, Z.I. Romanet, 87000 Limoges ■ Tel: 05 55 30 16 70 ■ Fax: 05 55 30 46 38 ■ E-mail : blanchon.sn@wanadoo.fr ■ Mon-Fri 8:00-12:00/13:30-18:30 ■ Contact: Mr. Ropital ■ English spoken

Specialty: Masonry, stonemasonry, carpentry, roofing, staff. Work experience: Église de St-Michel-des-Lions (Limoges), Château de Sédières in Corrèze. Empress Place Building (National Museum of Singapore).

BOURGEOIS ENTREPRISE

10-12 rue Stalingrad , 69120 Vaulx-en-Velin ■ Tel: 04 78 79 06 12 ■ Fax: 04 78 79 06 11 ■ Mon-Fri 8:00-12:00/13:30-17:30 ■ Director: Daniel Bordet ; PDG : Jean Archier

Specialty: Master carpentry, roofing, zinc covering, roof ornaments. Work experience: The Belfry of Amiens, Église de Villeneuve-l'Archevêque (Côte-d'Or), Hôtel de Ville (Lyon).

SOCIÉTÉ NOUVELLE CHANZY-PARDOUX

B.P 58 57155 Marly ■ Tel: 03 87 62 26 22 ■ Fax: 03 87 65 39 48 ■ Mon-Fri 8:00-12:00/14:00-18:00 ■ Contact: M. Collomb ■ English spoken

Specialty: Masonry, stonemasonry, master carpentry, roofing. Work experience: Restoration of the Cathedral at Strasbourg (35 years of work), Château de Lunéville (Meurthe-et-Moselle), the Regional Counsel of Metz, the Façades of the Arsenal of Metz. Château of Marderen.

LES CHARPENTIERS D'AUJOURD'HUI

16 rue Jules-Ferry, Z.I. Le Pontet, 69360 St-Symphorien-d'Ozon ■ Tel: 04 78 02 13 33 ■ Fax: 04 78 02 95 24 ■ Mon-Fri 7:00-18:00, Sat 8:00-12:00 ■ English spoken   ■ Contact: M. Fallone

Specialty: traditional master carpentry, reinforcement of structures. Work experience: Château de la Croix-Laval (Lyon region), National Conservatory of Music in Lyon. University Lyon II, the Chapel of Thizy (Lyon) Compagnon du Devoir.

LES CHARPENTIERS DE BOURGOGNE

4 rue Lavoisier, 21600 Longvic ■ Tel: 03 80 68 46 90 ■ Fax: 03 80 68 46 99 ■ Contact: M. Hubert Sauvain ■ English spoken

Specialty: Master carpentry, roofing, staircases. Work experience: Église de St-Seine-l'Abbaye, Palais des Ducs at Dijon, Abbaye of Saint-Germain in Auxerres, the Cathedral of Sens. Compagnon du Devoir.

LES CHARPENTIERS COUVREURS DU PERIGORD

19 rue des Pêcheurs, 24000 Périgueux ■ Tel: 05 53 09 40 57 ■ Fax: 05 53 54 09 33 ■ Mon-Fri 8:00-18:00 ■ Contact: Mr. Houdusse

Specialty: Master carpentery, classical stonemasonery and slate roofing.
Work experience: Église de la Mazière-Basse (Corrèze), Château de Beauregard-de-Terrasson (Dordogne), Église d'Ordiap (Pyrénées), Cathedral of Sarlat (Dordogne), Château de Lanquais (Dordogne).

AUX CHARPENTIERS DE FRANCE

av de la Plesse, Chemin Départemental 59, 91 Villebon-sur-Yvette ■ Tel: 01 69 34 32 60 ■ Fax: 01 69 34 70 39 ■ Mon-Fri 7:00-12:00/13:30-16:30 ■ Contact: M. Delaunay

Specialty: Master carpentry in traditional and modern styles.
Work experience: The Campaniles of the Musée d'Orsay, the Salle des Fêtes of the Elysées Palace in Paris, maintenance of the Paris Opera House.
Compagnon du Devoir.

ENTREPRISE SOCIÉTÉ NOUVELLE DELESTRE

24 allée François-1er, 41000 Blois ■ Tel: 02 54 43 95 63 ■ Fax: 02 54 42 39 16 ■ Contact: M. Quivogne

Specialty: Master carpentry, roofing, plumbing, zinc covering, roof ornaments.
Work experience: Restoration of the Châteaux of Blois, Chambord, Valençay, Chaumont-sur-Loire, Cathedrals of Blois and Tours.

ENTREPRISE FOURQUET

Le Péage, Pérouges, 01800 Meximieux ■ Tel: 04 74 61 03 22 ■ Fax: 04 74 34 70 23 ■ E-mail : jl.fouquet@worldonline.fr ■ Mon-Sat 8:00-12:00/13:30-18:00 ■ Contact: J.-L. Fourquet

Specialty: Roofing, zinc covering, metallic roofing. Work experience: Abbaye d'Ambronay, Bell Tower of Argentière, lead roofing of the Château d'Eau, Montpellier. Compagnon du Devoir.

GENTIL SARL

217 Maison Dieu 21220 Fixin ■ Tel : 03 20 52 64 70 ■ Fax : 03 80 52 96 25 ■ E-mail: sarl-gentil@wanadoo.fr ■ Mon-Fri 7:30-19:00 ■ M.Maurice gentil

All types of roofing. Zinc, slate, etc.
References: Banque de France in Lyon (tuiles vernissées) ; lycée Diderot in Langres (zinc naturel) ; Francoeur in Paris (zinc) ; centre social et bibliothèques in Lormes (zinc)

ENTREPRISE INDELEC
61 Chemin des Postes, 59500 Douai ■ Tel: 03 27 94 49 44 Fax:
03 27 94 49 45 ■ Mon-Fri 8:00-12:00/14:00-18:00 ■ English
spoken

**Specialty: Roof ornaments in hand worked copper, weather
vanes, lightning rods.**
**Work experience: Cathedrale d'Amiens, Cathedrale de Lille,
Châteaux of Chambord, Cheverny, Blois, Valençay. Supplier
of lightning rods for the USA.**

ENTREPRISE LANCTUIT
12 rue du Point-du-Jour, B.P. 805-27027 Vernon Cedex ■ Tel: 02
32 64 52 52 ■ Fax: 02 32 51 81 44 ■ Mon-Fri 8:00-12:00/13:30-
18:00 ■ Contact: Charles Teresa ■ In Paris: 114bis rue Michel
Ange 75016 Paris ■ Tel: 01 46 51 52 40

**Specialty: Masonry, stonemasonry, stone carving, master
carpentry, roofing, heating, plumbing. All trades required for
the restoration of historic monuments.**
**Work experience: Cour de Cassation, Ile-de-la-Cité, Paris,
Château de Gaillon, Abbaye du Bec-Hellouin (Normandy).**

ETABLISSEMENT PIERRE LARROCHE
21 rue Ausone, 33000 Bordeaux ■ Tel: 05 56 44 76 81 ■ Fax: 05
56 48 04 16 ■ Mon-Fri 8:00-12:30/14:00-18:00 ■ Contact: Pierre
Larroche

**Specialty: Stonemasonry, cleaning, renovation of old build-
ings.**
**Work experience: Château Larivet du Haut-Brion (Leognan),
Église Notre-Dame de la Merci (Haillan), Château de la Mis-
sion (Pessac).**

ENTREPRISE MAHE
24 bd Henri-Arnauld, 49000 Angers ■ Tel: 02 41 87 60 52 ■ Fax:
02 41 87 60 14 ■ Mon-Fri 7:00-19:00 ■ Director: Gilles Roulland

Specialty: Slate roofing and zinc covering.
**Work experience: Renovation of slate rooves: in XVIII centu-
ry structure in Maryland and the Anglican Church in Cen-
treville, Mairie de Salanches, Château in Pornic, Catholic
University of Angers.**

ENTREPRISE PAVY
Z.I. Nord, 35 rue Thomas-Edison, 72650 La Chapelle-St-Aubin ■
Tel: 02 43 47 03 03 ■ Fax: 02 43 47 03 09 ■ Mon Fri 8:00-
12:30/13:30-19:00 ■ Director: Vincent Pavy

Specialty: Masonry, stonemasonry.
**Work experience: Église du Vieux-Saint-Sauveur, Caen, Gal-
lo-Roman Ramparts, Le Mans, Palais de Justice, Laval.**

ENTREPRISE PLÉE

Les Grands-Champs, Chanceaux-sur-Choisille, 37001 Tours ■ Tel: 02 47 41 00 75 ■ Fax: 02 47 51 20 63 ■ Mon-Fri 8:00-12:00/13:30-18:00 ■ Contact: Mr. Dominique Plée ■ English spoken

Specialty: Treatment and reinforcement of structures with armatures.
Work experience: Château de Blois, Château d'Azay-le-Rideau, Galerie Vivienne, Paris.

ENTREPRISE PRADEAU-MORIN

41 bd Soult, 75012 Paris ■ Tel: 01 43 43 32 54 ■ Fax: 01 43 40 37 47 ■ Mon-Fri 8:30-12:30/13:00-17:30 ■ Contact: Charles Marceau ■ English spoken

Specialty: Masonry, stonemasonry.
Work experience: Renovation of the Louvre Museum (Paris), the National Assembly (Peristyle), Cathedrale de Beauvais, Les Invalides and the Musée d'Orsay (Paris).

AUX QUATRE COURONNES

B.P. 9, Charentilly, 37390 La Touche ■ Telfax: 01 47 56 79 70 ■ Mon-Fri 8:00-18:00 ■ Contact: Mr. Campistron

Specialty: Restoration of stone constructions.
Work experience: Châteaux de Villandry and Tours, Domaine de Fontenailles.
Compagnon du Devoir.

RENAUD PLATRE

Route de Bellevue, 16710 Saint-Yriex ■ Tel: 01 45 95 55 15 ■ Fax: 01 45 92 60 10 ■ Mon-Fri 8:00-12:00/14:00-19:00 ■ Director: Guy Renaudeaux

Specialty: Plaster, staff, stucco.
Work Experience: Casino de Dax, Château de Monchaude (Charente), Musée Labanche (Brive-en-Corrèze). Compagnon du Devoir.

ENTREPRISE SORT ET CHASLES

51 bld de la Liberté 92320 Châtillon ■ Tel: 01 55 58 18 18 ■ Fax: 01 55 58 18 19 ■ E-mail : sorechale-idf@wanadoo.fr ■ Web: www.sorale.com ■ Mon-Fri 8:00-12:00/14:00-17:30 ■ Paris Tel: 01 55 58 18 10

Specialty: Plaster, staff, Italian stucco.
Work experience: Casino of Gibraltar, Restoration of the ceilings of the Musée d'Orsay, Pyramid of the Louvre, the ship "Le Souverain des Mers" (St-Nazaire). Compagnon du Devoir.

THOMANN HANRY

56 rue Molitor, 75016 Paris ■ Tel: 01 46 51 23 26 ■ Fax: 01 47 43 11 03 ■ E-mail: thomannhanry75@aol.com ■ Mon-Fri 8:30-18:00 ■ English spoken

Specialty: Cleaning of façades by a special copyright process called "gommage". This technique is without sand, water, dust, abrasives, chemicals or scaffolding.

♔ The Great Ateliers of France
Les Grands Ateliers de France

45 rue Boissy d'Anglas, 75008 Paris ■ Tel: 01 42 68 14 18 ■ Fax: 01 42 68 13 49 ■ E-mail: infor@grandsateliers.com ■ Web Site: www.grandsateliers.com ■ www.craftsmen.com

This select organization of Artisans represents some of the very best that France, and indeed the world, has to offer. Dedicated to the highest standards of craftsmanship and a strict moral code, they provide a last bastion of defense against the destruction of the artisan system. They are self-policing in that each member, representing the various specialties, must be re-evaluated every year and then re-elected into the group of "LES GRANDS ATELIERS".
If the quality of their work falls below the high standards required by the group, or if they have lapsed into questionable dealings, then they will be dropped.
Call for appointments.

SERGE AMORUSO
39 rue du Roi-de-Sicile, 75004 Paris ■ Tel: 01 48 04 97 97 ■ Fax: 01 42 76 90 33
Bags, belts and cases.

GILBERT AVE
14 rue Commines, 75003 Paris ■ Tel: 01 42 72 72 29
Clock and barometer hands.

PIERRE-FRANCOIS BATTISTI
6 rue Louis-Nicolas-Clérambault, 75020 Paris ■ Telfax: 01 43 58 77 07 ■ By appointment ■ Pierre-François Battisti speaks English ■ Prices high ■ Professional discount
Creation of decorative panels in all styles and of all epochs, particularly XVIII century through Art Deco to contemporary. Decorative painting for boiseries, faux finishes, patinas. Trompe l'Oeil.

ART ET CREATIONS
Jean-Jacques Bedetti and Christian Bedetti
9 rue des Cordiers, 35400 St Malo ■ Tel: 02 99 40 16 48 ■ Fax:
02 99 40 18 85

Embossing, gilding and inlay work.

ANNE BLAIN-YARDIM
8 rue des Brefords, 91720 Maisse ■ Telfax: 64 99 30 67 ■ By appointment ■ English spoken ■ Prices medium

Soft ground etching on marquetry and silver.

RENATO BOARETTO MASCARADE
74 bld Malesherbes, 75008 Paris ■ Telfax: 01 42 25 09 28

Creation of musical automates. Entirely designed and made by Boaretto. Unique pieces, limited series and custom-made works.

PIERRE BONNEFILLE
5 rue Bréguet, 75011 Paris ■ Tel: 01 43 55 06 84 ■ Fax: 01 43 55 04 92

Decorative painting based on materials, textures and colours.
References: the walls of the Café Marly, the Bernardaud Salon de Thé on the rue Royale in Paris. The Christian Lacroix boutiques in Paris, Milan and Moscow. Pierre Bonnefille also designs furniture in single copies and limited editions.

CHRISTIAN BONNET
60 rue Lepeletier de St-Fargeau, 89100 Sens ■ Tel: 03 86 95 22 70 ■ Fax: 03 86 65 40 88

Restorer of antique tortoise-shell objects.

FRANCE BONNIMOND-DUMONT
16 rue Saint-Charles, 75015 Paris ■ Tel: 01 43 33 01 79 ■ Fax: 01 47 89 86 67 ■ By appointment ■ Anne Bonnimond-Dumont speaks English ■ Professional discount

Restoration of paintings, painted murals and frescoes of all periods. A scientific analysis can be prepared after examination, upon request. One of the best. Museum quality work.

ALAIN BOUCHARDON
10 avenue Foch, 60300 Senlis ■ Tel: 03 44 53 10 15 ■ Fax: 01 44 53 39 73 ■ Mon-Fri 8:00-12:00/13:30-17:00 and by appointment ■ Prices medium

Restoration of paintings on canvas and on wood: especially large canvases. Re-mounting, re-constitution of wood elements, transposition. Welcomes visitors.

REMY BRAZET

22 rue des Belles-Feuilles, 75116 Paris ■ Tel: 01 47 27 20 89 ■
Fax: 01 47 55 68 90 ■ Mon-Fri 8:30-18:00 ■ Remy Brazet speaks
English ■ Prices high

Traditional upholstery of walls and antique chairs. Fabrication of draperies, slipcovers, bedspreads and sheers. Supplier to the National Museums.

ALAIN CARTIER

68 rue Henri Barbusse, 60320 Bethisy Saint-Pierre ■ Telfax: 03
44 39 86 51

Upholstery, wallcoverings and draperies.

LISON DE CAUNES

20 rue Mayet, 75006 Paris ■ Tel: 01 40 56 02 10 ■ Fax: 01 42 19
53 70

Straw marquetry. Creation and restoration.

PHILIPPE CECILE

20 rue Geoffroy l'Angevin, 75004 Paris ■ Telfax: 01 44 54 00 61

Restoration of embroideries, rugs and tapestries.

GUY CHANEL

17 avenue des Marronniers, 91600 Savigny-Orge ■ Tel: 01 69 96
05 89 ■ Fax: 01 69 96 12 79 ■ E-mail: guy.chanel@wanadoo.fr ■
Web: http://perso.wanadoo.fr/g-chanelsellier/

Custom-made saddles.

PIERRE CORTHAY

1 rue Volney, 75002 Paris ■ Tel: 01 42 61 08 89 ■ Fax: 01 42 61
04 00

Shoe and bootmaker. Men, women and for riders of horses.

PATRICK DESSERME

17 rue du Pont-aux-choux, 75003 Paris ■ Tel: 01 42 72 02 66 ■
Fax: 01 42 72 50 91

Glass shaper, reconstruction. Glass covers, street lamps, basins.

SIMON-PIERRE ETIENNE

55 rue Popincourt, 75011 Paris ■ Tel: 01 47 00 77 81 ■ Fax: 01
48 05 14 25 ■ Mon-Fri 8:00-12:00/13:30-18:00 ■ Simon Etienne
speaks English

Restoration of antique furniture, marquetry, and art objects of the XVII and XVIII centuries.

ATELIER D'ART MARTINE FLÉ

25 avenue Jean-claude Delubac 94420 Le Plessis-Trévise ■ Tel: 01 45 94 65 66 ■ Fax: 01 45 76 74 53 ■ Mme Michèle Henon.

Cordovan leathers, decorative lacquers.

MICHEL GERMOND

78 quai de l'Hôtel-de-Ville, 75004 Paris ■ Tel: 01 42 78 04 78 ■ Fax: 01 42 78 22 74 ■ E-mail: jeannine.germond@wanadoo.fr ■ Mon-Fri 8:00-12:00/13:30-18:00■ Prices high

Restoration of XVII, XVIII and XIX century furniture in marquetry and chairs. Expert counsel in the purchase of items of collection. Expert before the Court of Appeals, Paris. Co-founder of the Grands Ateliers de France. Administrator of the Society for the Encouragement of the Artistic Professions. (S.E.M.A)

ATELIERS GUSTAVE GERNEZ

5bis Place Léon Blum, 75011 Paris ■ Tel: 01 44 93 86 30 ■ Fax: 01 44 93 86 31 ■ Guy Delteil

Printer and engraver.

ATELIER GRAVELINE

rue de la Gare, 63290 Ris ■ Tel: 04 73 94 68 54 ■ Fax: 04 73 94 69 25 ■ Pascal and Isabelle Graveline

Fine cutlery, replicas of antique knives.

GROUX

65 Avenue de Saumur, 86170 Blaislay-Etables ■ Tel: 05 49 45 42 47 ■ Fax: 05 49 54 42 47 ■ Thomas Vieweger and Aude Vieweger de Cordoue

Restoration of sculpture.

MAISON JOBBÉ DUVAL

3 rue de Bertrand, 35000 Rennes ■ Tel: 02 99 38 72 10 ■ Fax: 02 99 36 18 37 ■ M. Olivier Jobbé Duval

Gilded woods. Maison founded in 1843. Olivier Jobbé Duval represents the fifth generation.
References: Rennes Cathedral, the Brittany Parliament in Rennes.

ATELIER KERAMOS

24 rue Violet, 75015 Paris ■ Telfax: 01 47 50 88 70 ■ E-mail: keramos@wanadoo.fr ■ Jean-Claude Guillemot and Jacqueline Guillemot

Restorers of faience and china.

JEAN-PIERRE LEHMANS - GALERIE 20

20 rue Mirabeau, 75016 Paris ■ Tel: 01 45 20 95 79 ■ Fax: 01 42 30 85 39 ■ E-mail: galerie20@easynet.fr

Art restorer. Specialist in pastels and engravings.

MAISON GEORGES LE MANACH
31 rue du Quatre-septembre, 75002 Paris ■ Tel: 01 47 42 52 94 ■ Fax: 01 47 42 02 04 ■ Anne Biosse Duplan and Olivier Biosse Duplan

Maker of fabrics, prints and upholstery for decoration.

ATELIER XAVIER LINARD
La Garenne – 18 Petite rue, 89140 Pont-sur-Yonne ■ Tel: 03 86 66 35 95 ■ Fax: 03 86 66 33 59 ■ Xavier Linard

Fine cabinetry and shelving.

ATELER LUMONT
12 rue Cacheux, 92400 Courbevoie ■ Tel: 01 47 89 56 90 ■ Jean-Jacques Coron

Restorer of china, faience and terracotta.

NICOLAS MARISCHAEL
4 rue de Saintonge, 75003 Paris ■ Tel: 01 42 78 07 63 ■ Fax: 01 42 78 53 67 ■ E-mail: orfevre@club-internet.fr

Gold and silversmith.

MS ISABELLE DE MARSEUL-MONTERAN
14 rue des Joueries, 78100 St Germain en Laye ■ Tel: 01 30 61 00 72 ■ Fax: 01 30 61 41 14

Decorative lacquering.
References : Château de Versailles, Museum of Decorative Arts in Paris. Works for cabinetmakers and the great antique dealers.

METHODE ET PLATRE
Mr Louis-Marie ARNAUDEAU
22 voie d'Issy 92240 Malakoff ■ Tel: 01 46 48 60 66 ■ Fax: 01 46 48 60 70

Stucco, staff, moulds.

FABRICE MICHA
2 rue de la Grande Trouée, Les Corbiers, 77640 Jouarre ■ Tel: 01 60 22 08 92 ■ Fax: 01 60 22 89 49

Wood carver. Creation and restoration.

FRANCIS MIGEON
5 avenue de la Trémoille, 94100 St-Maur ■ Tel: 01 42 83 85 88 ■ Fax: 01 42 83 58 48

Sculptor in ivory. Creation and restoration.
References: participation in the restoration of the pipe organs in the Chapel of the Château de Versailles.

ATELIER VON NAGEL

20 rue Bouvier, 75011 Paris ■ Tel: 01 44 93 20 93 ■ Fax: 01 44 93 20 94 ■ E-mail: vonnagel@dial.olcane.com ■ Reinhard Von **Nagel** **Creator** and restorer of clavichords.

SABLAGE BASTILLE OUSTRY

36 Bld de la Bastille, 75012 Paris ■ Tel: 01 43 43 47 35 ■ Fax: 01 43 43 24 54

Sand-blasted glass frosting and engraving. Unique pieces, made on special order.

PHILIPPE PRUTNER

22 rue de l'Echiquier, 75010 Paris ■ Tel: 01 48 24 02 15 ■ Fax: 01 48 24 12 96

Creation and restoration of mechanical movements. Clocks particularly.

ETIENNE RAYSSAC

8 rue Faidherbe, 75011 Paris ■ Tel: 01 40 09 05 59 ■ Fax: 01 40 09 10 54

Sculpture in wood, clay and lost-wax casting for bronze. Works for thr Historic Monuments Commission. Gates on the Place Vendôme , Gothic windows at the Château de Blois-Orcan in Brittany, Parliament of Brittany in Rennes.

PIERRE REVERDY

5 rue de l'Egalité, 26100 Romans ■ Tel: 04 75 05 10 15 ■ Fax: 04 75 02 28 40 ■ Web: www.reverdy.com

Plain Damascus steel hunting knives.

MAISON RIOT
Mme Jeanne PRIVAT

24 rue de la Folie-Méricourt, 75011 Paris ■ Tel. 01 47 00 34 47 ■ Fax: 01 47 00 85 35 ■ Mon-Fri 8:30-12:00/13:30-18:00 ■ Jeanne Privat speaks English ■ Prices medium

Metal plating with gold and silver. Restoration of all metal objects, silver, bronze and pewter. Specialty: silver. Restoration and re-gilding of furniture bronzes, chandeliers, clocks.

MARBRERIE ROUGER

21 Rue Alexis Lepère, 93100 Montreuil ■ Tel: 01 49 88 12 61 ■ Fax: 01 48 59 27 24 ■ Mon-Fri 8:00-12:00/13:00-17:30 ■ Jean-Yves Rouger speaks English ■ Prices medium ■ Professional discount

Marble workshop. Restoration of marble and sculptures in marble and other stone. Pedestals for bronzes. Custom bathrooms.

ALAIN DE SAINT EXUPERY

Château du Fraysse, 24120 Terrasson ■ Tel: 05 53 50 00 05

Restoration and conservation of antique locks and keys.

JEAN-LUC SEIGNEUR
5 Allée Charlotte, 93360 Neuilly Plaissance ■ Tel: 01 43 00 58 03
■ Fax: 01 43 00 58 07

Engraver on metal: gilding and embossing metals.

CHRISTIAN THIROT
22 rue Victor Hugo, 93250 Villemomble ■ Tel: 01 48 54 57 69 ■
Fax: 01 48 54 57 69

Restoration of scientific instruments and "eglomized" glasses.

BERNARD VEILLAULT
17 rue du Bois Cerdon, 94460 Valenton ■ Tel: 01 43 86 47 47 ■
Fax: 01 43 86 48 15

Art metalwork. Specialist in wrought iron staircases.
Works in NY, LA, a balcony for the Louis Jouvet Theatre in Paris.

XYLOS
5 Cité de la Roquette, 75011 Paris ■ Tel: 01 43 57 88 13 ■ Fax:
01 40 21 78 51 ■ Francis Ballu, Rémi Colmet Daâge and Martin
Spreng

Furniture-maker and restorers. Creation of decorative elements.
Cabinet makers: customed-designed furniture.

Artisans by Arrondisement
Antique Furniture Restoration
Ebénistes

IV

👑 **MICHEL GERMOND**
78 quai de l'Hôtel-de-Ville, 75004 Paris ■ Tel: 01 42 78 04 78 ■
Fax: 01 42 78 22 74 ■ By appointment ■ E-mail: jeannine.germond@wanadoo.fr ■ Web: www.grandsateliers.com ■ Michel
Collet speaks English ■ Prices high

Restoration of furniture and chairs of the XVII, XVIII, XIX centuries. Specialist in marquetry. Expert advice on the confirmation of authenticity and the valuation of high quality antique furniture.
Member of Les Grands Ateliers. Expert to the Court of Appeals, Paris. World-renowned expert.

♔ ATELIER A. BRUGIER

74 rue de Sèvres, 75007 Paris ■ Tel: 01 47 34 83 27 ■ Fax: 01 40 56 91 40 ■ Mon-Fri 8:00-17:30 By appointment ■ Nicole Judet-Brugier speaks English ■ Prices high to very high ■ 10 to 15% professional discount

Restoration of lacquer: Chinese, Japanese, Art Deco. Painted furniture. Stock of lacquered panels and screens of the XVII and XVIII centuries. Table bases.

JEAN-PAUL JOUAN

10 rue Perronet, 75007 Paris ■ Telfax: 01 45 48 64 20 ■ Tue-Sat 9:00-12:00/14:00-19:00 ■ Barbara Jouan speaks English ■ Prices medium ■ Professional discount

Restoration of antique furniture and art objects. Especially XVIII century.

REINOLD FILS

233 rue du Faubourg-Saint-Honoré, 75008 Paris ■ Tel: 01 47 63 47 19 ■ Fax: 01 53 81 07 55 ■ E-mail: reinold@libertysurf.fr ■ Mon-Fri 8:00-12:00/13:00-18:30/Sat 13:00-18:30 ■ English spoken ■ Prices medium to high ■ Professional discount

Restoration of XVIII century European marquetry furniture and chairs.

INTARSIO

94 av Philippe-Auguste, 750011 Paris ■ Telfax: 01 43 48 50 37 ■ Mon-Sat 9:00-18:00 by appointment ■ Claude-Sara Tomor and Sbero Beritognolo speak English

Restoration of XVII and XVIII century furniture, especially Boulle marquetry. Specialists in making wall panels and tables of Scagliola.

DIDIER MAULET

38 rue Traversière, 75012 Paris ■ Tel: 01 43 44 44 08 ■ Mon-Sat 9:00-19:00 ■ English spoken ■ Prices medium ■ Professional discount

Restoration of XVIII century marquetry furniture.

FABRY

4 rue Gramme, 75015 Paris ■ Tel: 01 42 50 94 64 ■ Mon-Fri 8:30-12:00/13:00-17:30 ■ Jean-François Fabry speaks English ■ Prices medium

Restoration of XVIII and XIX century furniture and chairs.

♔ ROLAND INGERT

32 rue Mathurin-Régnier, 75015 Paris ■ Tel: 01 47 83 57 49 ■ Mon-Fri 8:00-12:00/14:00-18:00

Restoration of lacquer furniture and art objects: Chinese and Japanese, 1925 lacquer. Restoration for museums and châteaux.

─────────────── XVII ───────────────

DIDIER GILLERY

2 rue Gervex, 75017 Paris ■ Tel: 01 43 80 98 17

Restoration of XVII, XVIII and XIX century furniture, chairs and objects. Marquetry in mahogany and lacquering.

♔ GEORGES LECLERQ

8 rue Ruhmkorff, 75017 Paris ■ Telfax: 01 40 55 06 23 ■ Mon-Fri 9:00-12:00/14:00-18:00 ■ Laurent Leclercq speaks English

Restoration of antique furniture. Specialist in Boulle marquetry. Re-caning of chairs and upholstery. Works for the Mobilier National and Historic Monuments.

─────────────── XX ───────────────

JACQUES POISSON

17 Cité Aubry, 75020 Paris ■ Tel: 01 43 71 73 09 ■ Fax: 01 40 24 26 20 ■ Web: www.franceantiq.fr ■ Mon-Fri 8:30-18:00 ■ Prices high ■ 10% professional discount

Restoration of Boulle marquetry. Qualified expert.

─────────────── OUTSIDE PARIS ───────────────

♔ PATRICK VASTEL

143 rue du Général Leclerc, 50110 Tourlaville, Cherbourg ■ Tel: 02 33 22 46 07 ■ Fax: 02 33 22 96 26 ■ E-mail: pvastel@aol.com ■ Mon-Fri 9:00-12:00/13.30-18:30/Sat by appointment ■ Patrick Vastel speaks English

Restoration of XVII and XVIII century furniture. Specialist in marquetry and creator. Expert to the Cour d'Appel of Caen.

Caning - Repair and Restoration
Cannage

CANNAGE ET PAILLAGE
58 rue de Charonne, 75011 Paris ■ Tel: 01 48 05 29 40 ■ Mon
14:00-18:00 Tue-Thu 9:00-18:00 Fri 9:00-12:00 ■ Prices medium
All types of repairs for cane furniture in the old manner. Up-holstery, decoration.

GEORGES LECLERQ
8 rue Ruhmkorff, 75017 Paris ■ Telfax: 01 40 55 06 23 ■ Mon-Fri
9:00-12:00/14:00-18:00 ■ Laurent Leclercq speaks English
Re-caning and upholstery of chairs. Restoration of antique furniture.

Clock Repair and Restoration
Horlogerie

──────────────── III ────────────────

ART DU TEMPS
1 Cité Dupetit-Thouars, 75003 Paris ■ Tel: 01 48 04 87 27 ■ Mon
14:00-18:00 Tue-Fri 9:00-12:00/14:00-18:00/Sat by appointment
■ Alexandre Matula speaks English ■ Prices low ■ 30% profes-sional discount
Repair and restoration of antique watches, pendulum clocks and carillons. Manufacturer of parts for antique movements.

CENTRE TECHNIQUE REPARATION HORLOGERE
150 rue du Temple, 75003 Paris ■ Tel: 01 42 72 03 33 ■ Fax: 01 42
72 01 90 ■ Mon-Fri 9:00-17:00 ■ English spoken ■ Prices high
Repair of antique watches and restoration of pendulum clocks. Repair of chronometers of the Ministry of the Army.

MICHEL ROBILLARD
7 bd des Filles du Calvaire, 75003 Paris ■ Tel: 01 48 87 52 38 ■
Tue-Sat 9:30-12:15/14:15-18:45 ■ Prices medium
Specialist in the repair of antique pendulum clocks. Sale and repair of clocks and watches.

DANIEL GENDRON
281 rue Saint-Jacques, 75005 Paris ■ Telfax: 01 46 33 35 01 ■ Tue-Fri 15:00-19:00/Sat 10:00-13:00 ■ Daniel Gendron speaks English ■ Prices very high

Restoration of antique pendulum clocks and antique watches. Master Artisan.

GENDROT
12 bd Saint-Germain, 75005 Paris ■ Telfax: 01 43 54 18 84 ■ Tue-Fri 14:30-19:00 ■ Prices medium to high ■ Professional discount

Restoration of antique pendulum clocks from the XVI to the end of the XIX centuries.

—————————— IX ——————————

GUY KOBRINE
14 rue Cadet, 75009 Paris ■ Tel: 01 45 23 18 84 ■ Mon-Fri 9:00-13:30/15:00-18:45 ■ Some English spoken ■ Prices based on free estimates

Qualified expert in the repair and restoration of the famous-name wrist watches and XIX century pocket watches.

—————————— XIII ——————————

PHILIPPE BAILLE
68 bd Blanqui, 75013 Paris ■ Tel: 01 43 36 09 42 ■ Tue-Sat 10:30-12:30/14:00-19:00 ■ English Spoken ■ Prices high

Restoration of antique and modern clocks, watches and music boxes.

—————————— XIV ——————————

LUCIEN COULON
44 rue des Plantes, 75014 Paris ■ Tel: 01 45 42 95 53 ■ Tue-Sat 10:00-13:00/15:30-19:30 ■ Prices medium ■ 20% professional discount

Forty years experience in the repair of antique and modern pendulum clocks and watches. All types of movements.

LE TEMPS RETROUVÉ HORLOGERIE ANCIENNE
123 rue de Rome, 75017 Paris ■ Tel: 01 42 27 76 28 ■ Tue-Fri 11:00-19:00/Sat 10:00-14:00 ■ Prices medium ■ 15% professional discount

Restoration and repair of all antique clock and watch movements.
Purchase and sale.

BERNARD PIN
7 rue Pierre-Bonnard, 75020 Paris ■ Tel: 01 43 56 82 34 ■ Fax: 01 43 67 86 92 ■ E-mail: bernardpin@aol.com ■ Mon-Sat by appointment ■ Bernard Pin speaks English

Restoration of antique clocks, music boxes, singing birds and musical pendulum clocks. Restorations for the national museums.

DANIEL MORNAS
"ATELIER P. MONNETTE"
8 rue des Chantiers, 78000 Versailles ■ Tel: 01 39 50 50 33 ■ Fax 01 39 53 78 58 ■ Tue-Sat 10:00-18:00 ■ Prices medium

Restoration of antique pendulum clocks.

Fans-Antique Restoration and Custom Fabrication
Éventails-restauration d'ánciens et fabrication sur mesure

♛ ATELIER HOGUET
2 bd de Strasbourg, 75010 Paris ■ Tel: 01 42 08 19 89 ■ Fax : 01 42 08 30 91 ■ E-mail : eventail@cyberbrain.com ■ Mon-Wed 14:00-18:00

Restoration and custom fabrication of fans in all designs, since 1872. The Musée de l'Eventail is open to the public on Mondays, Tuedays and Wednesdays between 14:00 and 18:00. The collection is extraordinary and displays fans from the XVII century to the present.

Gilders on Wood
Doreurs sur bois

VII

JOHNY BORG - CADRES LAPOLI
45 rue Vaneau, 75007 Paris ■ Tel: 01 42 22 57 96 ■ Fax: 01 42 84 07 51 ■ Tue-Sat 14:30-18:30 ■ Prices medium to high ■ Professional discount

Restoration of gilded wood (bois doré) furniture and objects. Custom frames in French, Italian and Dutch styles. Reproduction of classical stone masonry frames.

XI

ATELIER DE LA FEUILLE D'OR
173 rue du Faubourg-Saint-Antoine, 75011 Paris ■ Telfax: 01 40 02 02 65 ■ Mon-Fri 8:30-18:00/Sat by appointment ■ Marie Dubost speaks English ■ Prices high

Restoration of XVII, XVIII and XIX century objects in gilded or painted wood. Restoration of painted antique furniture. Custom framing. Gilding and lacquering.

XIII

👑 **ATELIERS JEAN ALOT**
101 rue de Patay, 75013 Paris ■ Tel: 01 45 82 80 32 ■ Fax: 01 44 24 51 90 ■ E-mail: infos@grandsateliers.com ■ Web: www.grandsateliers.com ■ Mon-Fri 8:00-18:00/Sat 8:00-12:00 ■ Prices medium ■ Professional discount

Gilding on wood, wood sculpture, restoration of all objects and furniture in gilded wood. Specialist in French furniture of the XVII and XVIII centuries. Custom framing. Master Artisan. Expert to the Tribunals.

XVI

THELLIER
105 rue Lauriston, 75116 Paris ■ Telfax: 01 47 04 32 83 ■ Tue-Sat 10:00-12:30/14:30-19:00 ■ Philippe-Louis Mexler speaks English ■ Prices medium ■ Professional discount

Gilding and restoration of wood furniture and objects. Restoration of lacquer and patinas. Custom framing and restoration of paintings.

ATELIER DU BOIS DORÉ

80 av des Ternes, 75017 Paris ■ Tel: 01 45 74 67 58 ■ Fax: 01 45 74 72 49 ■ Mon 14:30-19:00 Tue-Sat 9:00-12:30/14:30-19:00 ■ English spoken ■ Prices medium to high ■ Professional discount

Restoration of gilded wood furniture, objects and frames. Antique reproductions of gilded wood furniture in limited editions.

JEAN-PAUL MARCHAIS

52 avenue de Saint-Ouen 75018 Paris ■ Telfax: 01 46 27 53 02 ■ Mon-Fri 10:00-13:30/15:00-19:00/Sat 11:00-14:00 ■ Laurent Marchais speaks English ■ Prices medium ■ 10% professional discount

Restoration of all gilded wood and plaster with fine gold leafing. Supplier to the Mobilier National.

ATELIERS JACQUES GOUJON

5 Villa Guelma, 75018 Paris ■ Tel: 01 42 64 95 83 ■ Fax: 01 42 23 95 50 ■ E-mail: atelierjacquesgoujon@cybercable.fr ■ Mon-Fri 9:00-19:00 ■ Jacques Goujon speaks English ■ Prices high ■ 10% professional discount

Restoration of antique gilded wood. Custom reproductions. All types of gold leafing. Restoration of antique lacquer. Wood sculpture and restoration of sculptured wood furniture.

YOURI DMITRENKO

26 rue des Montiboeufs, 75020 Paris ■ Telfax: 01 40 30 40 83 ■ Mon-Fri 9:00-18:30, Sat by appointment ■ Youri Dmitrenko speaks English

Restoration of gilded wood furniture, chairs, frames, mirrors, boiseries (wood panelling). Workshop specializes in the restoration of XVIII century French and German furniture and art objects.

ROBERT DUVIVIER

30 rue de Sablonville, 92200 Neuilly-sur-Seine ■ Tel: 01 47 22 25 90 ■ Fax: 01 46 43 01 49 ■ Tue-Sat 9:00-13:00/14:00-19:00 ■ English spoken ■ 10% professional discount

Restoration of all types of gilded wood. Custom framing. Restoration of engravings and paintings. Master Artisan.

ATELIER DE DORURE - ANTOINE PALOMARES
1635 rue Louis-Blériot, 78530 Buc ■ Tel: 01 39 56 01 24 ■ Mon-
Sat 10:00-19:00 ■ Spanish spoken

**Restoration of art objects with fine gold leafing on wood
and metal. Artisan of the fifth generation.**

Glass Artists
Artistes sur verre

———————————— **III** ————————————

👑 P. DESSERME
17 rue du Pont-aux-Choux, 75003 Paris ■ Tel: 01 42 72 02 66 ■
Fax: 01 42 72 50 91 ■ Mon-Fri 8:00-12:00/13:30-17:30 Fri 16:30
■ Some English spoken ■ Prices medium to high

**Reputed to be one of the best glass artists in Paris. Glass-
es, mirrors, furniture, lanterns, glass covers for clocks and
much more. Custom work.**

———————————— **IV** ————————————

GALERIE LE SUD/LES MAITRES VERRIERS
23 rue des Archives, 75004 Paris ■ Tel: 01 42 78 42 37 ■ Tue-
Sat 10:30-19:30 ■ Sébastien Aschero speaks English ■ Prices
medium to high ■ 10% professional discount

**Blown glass by the Masters (Maîtres Verriers). Novaro, Pieri-
ni, Guillot, Fievet, Deutler, Marion, Monod, Guittet, Durand-
Gasselin, Schamschula, Luzoro, Lepage, Baquère, Deniel,
Pertshire and others. Decorative objects in Murano glass.**

———————————— **XI** ————————————

BERNARD PICTET
47 rue Oberkampf, 75011 Paris ■ Tel: 01 48 06 19 25 ■ Fax: 01
43 55 31 45 ■ Mon-Fri 9:00-13:00/14:00-18:00 ■ English spoken
■ Prices very high ■ Professional discount

Fine-quality engraving and decoration on glass.

ART DU VITRAIL
16 passage de la Folie-Régnault, 75011 Paris ■ Tel: 01 43 73 85 44 ■ Mon-Fri 9:00-18:00 By appointment ■ Contact: Joëlle Koumskoff ■ English spoken ■ Prices medium
Restoration and creation of stained glass windows of all styles.

──────────────── **OUTSIDE PARIS** ────────────────

JEAN-PIERRE BAQUÈRE
5 rue Bouin, 92700 Colombes ■ Tel: 01 47 86 09 49 ■ Fax: 01 47 85 83 47 ■ Mon-Sat 9:30-17:00 and by appointment ■ Jean-Pierre Baquère and Isabelle Emmerique speak English and Spanish ■ Prices low ■ Professional discount
Blown glass creations decorated in gold leaf, platinum and palladium. Series of 50 made in a year. Hand made perfume bottles. Restoration of glass.

TECHNIQUE TRANSPARENTE
70 rue Jean-Bleuzen, 92170 Vanves ■ Tel: 01 46 38 76 76 ■ Fax: 01 46 38 74 00 ■ E-mail: tech.trans@worldonline.fr ■ Mon-Fri 8:00-18:00 ■ Prices high
Architectural and structural applications of glass. Engraving and decoration.

Icons
Icônes

──────────────── **XIII** ────────────────

ATELIER SAINT LUC
36 bd Arago, 75013 Paris ■ Tel: 01 43 31 10 22 ■ E-mail: atelier.saint-luc@wanadoo.fr ■ Mon-Fri by appointment ■ Didier Gulmann speaks English, Spanish and Greek spoken
Painting of icons in the traditional manner with a double layer of 24 ct gold leafing. On order.

──────────────── **XX** ────────────────

MR. FREDERIC COCAULT
5 rue Ernest-Lefèvre, 75020 Paris ■ Tel: 01 40 31 54 23 ■ Tue-Sat 10:00-19:00 ■ Lydia Manic speaks English ■ Prices medium to high
Restoration of icons, antique gilding and conservation of polychrome on wood.

MME ISABELLE CLEMENT
Bat B, 33 rue Fernand-Combette, 93100 Montreuil ■ Tel: 01 48 70 87 97 ■ Mon-Sat by appointment ■ Prices medium

Restoration of Greek, Russian and Byzantine icons.

Decorative Ironwork
Ferronnerie d'art

ATELIERS BATAILLARD
7 impasse Marie-Blanche, 75018 Paris ■ Tel: 01 42 23 04 33 ■ Fax: 01 42 54 96 80 ■ Mon-Fri 9:00-13:00/14:00-18:30 and Sat by appointment ■ Mr. Bataillard ■ English spoken ■ Prices high ■ 10 to 20% professional discount

Beautiful custom creations in wrought iron: staircases, furniture, chandeliers, lamps, door hardware, sconces, grilles, gates, fences, grille-work for stair railings. Traditional and contemporary styles.

MEILLEUR
32 rue des Amandiers, 75020 Paris Entrance 15 rue Fernand Léger ■ Tel: 01 43 66 45 13 ■ Fax: 01 43 66 45 43 ■ E-mail: maison.meilleur@wanadoo.fr ■ Mon-Fri 8:30-12:00/13:00-18:00 and by appointment ■ English spoken

Custom wrought iron work. Railings, balconies, tables, lighting. Top quality.

PATRICK MILLOT
39 bd Saint-Simon 93700 Drancy ■ Tel: 01 41 60 00 22 ■ Fax: 01 41 60 01 72 ■ Mon-Fri 8:00-12:00/13:00-17:00 by appointment ■ Prices high ■ Professional discount

Decorative wrought iron work. All custom. Specialty: curved stair railings. Balconies, furniture, lighting. Custom work in brass, such as display cases for shops, brass framework for fireplaces. Metal construction. Work in stainless steel and metal locks.

Lacquerers
Laqueurs

VII

ATELIER A. BRUGIER
74 rue de Sèvres, 75007 Paris ■ Tel: 01 47 34 83 27 ■ Fax: 01 40 56 91 40 ■ Mon-Fri 8:00-17:30 and by appointment ■ Nicole Judet-Brugier speaks English ■ Prices medium to high ■ Professional discount

Specialists in the restoration of lacquer and painted furniture. Will custom make from old or contemporary designs. Beautiful collection of antique lacquered panels and screens.

XV

ROLAND INGERT
32 rue Mathurin-Régnier, 75015 Paris ■ Tel: 01 47 83 57 49 ■ Mon-Fri 8:00-12:00/14:00-18:00

**Restoration of lacquer furniture and art objects: Chinese and Japanese, 1925 lacquer.
Restoration for museums and châteaux.**

OUTSIDE PARIS

CLAUDE DAMEX
ZAE La Pépinière 1, rue des Quarante Arpents 78220 Viroflay ■ Tel: 01 30 24 77 87 ■ Fax: 01 30 24 79 37 ■ By appointment ■ Mme Dalex speaks English

Fine lacquer work. Creation and restoration.

ALM DECOR
Formerly ATELIERS SAIN & TAMBUTE & BERNARD ROGER
10 rue Andre Joineau, 93310 Le Pré-Saint-Gervais ■ Tel: 01 48 91 98 64 ■ Mon-Fri 8:30-12:30/13:30-17:30

Decorative lacquer. Restoration of furniture and objects. Creation of decorative finishes on panels, screens, furniture and objects.

LES LAQUES CLAUDE - CLAUDE CORNEVIN
22 rue du Gue, 92500 Rueil-Malmaison ■ Tel: 01 30 53 53 79 ■
Tue-Sat 10:00-12:00/15:00-19:00 ■ Pierre Cornevin speaks English ■ Prices medium

Restoration of XVIII and XIX century furniture and objects in Chinese lacquer. Creation of low tables, objects, screens, fans and other.

SERGE TIRARD
4 rue Charles de Gaulle, 78860 Saint-Nom La-Bretèche ■ Tel: 01 34 62 10 14 ■ Fax: 01 30 56 73 93 ■ Mon-Fri 9:00:12:00/14:00-18:00 ■ English spoken ■ Prices medium ■ Professional discount

Fine restoration of European and Oriental lacquer furniture and objects.

Leather - Creation and Restoration
Objets en cuir – Création et restauration

——————————— VI ———————————

ANDRÉ MINOS
6 rue Gît-le-Coeur, 75006 Paris ■ Telfax: 01 43 54 61 78 ■ Mon-Sat 9:30-13:00/Afternoons by appointment ■ Prices medium

Restoration of leather objects, old books. Bookbinding.

ATELIER MAZARINE
42 rue Mazarine, 75006 Paris ■ Tel: 01 43 25 18 52 ■ Mon-Fri 9:00-13:00/14:00-19:00 and by appointment ■ English spoken ■ Prices medium ■ 10% professional discount

Bookbinding in leather and toile. Restoration of leather. Custom-made leather articles: photo albums, calendars, address books, cases, boxes.

——————————— XI ———————————

LEWIS ET FILS DOREURS
18 rue du Moulin-Joly, 75011 Paris ■ Tel: 01 43 57 45 28 ■ Fax: 01 47 00 42 33 ■ Mon-Fri 8:00-12:00/13:00-17:00 Fri 16:00 ■ Marie Santillana speaks English ■ Prices medium

Leather desk sets and accessories in limited editions. Custom leatherwork, chasing and gilding.

ATELIER PHILIPPE MARTIAL

8 rue du Général Guilhem, 75011 Paris ■ Tel: 01 47 00 71 72 ■ Fax: 01 43 55 41 56 ■ E-mail : philippe.martial3@wanadoo.fr ■ Mon-Fri 8:30-13:00/14:00-17:30 ■ Prices medium ■ Professional discount

Superb leather work. Creation of diverse objects in wood covered in leather, with or without chasing and gilding. Jewellery cases, boxes in all shapes and sizes, liqueur cases, small cabinets, desk sets, frames, briefcases, decorative objects. Classical book binding. Restoration of leather. Works for Hermès and other great Houses.

XVII

LEMERLE FRÈRES

62 rue Legendre, 75017 Paris ■ Tel: 01 46 22 28 56 ■ Fax: 01 48 88 01 83 ■ Mon-Fri 7:30-12:00/13:30-18:30 ■ Xavier Lemerle speaks English ■ Prices high ■ Professional discount

Restoration of old leathers of Cordova, leather chairs, desks and all decorative leather. Traditional restoration, hand dyeing of leathers and gold leafing.

Lithography & Engraving
Lithographie & gravure

ATELIER POINT & MARGE PARIS EDITIONS

45 rue Marx Dormoy, 75018 Paris ■ Telfax: 01 42 09 44 09 ■ Mon-Fri by appointment only ■ Jorge de Sousa Noronha speaks Spanish, Portuguese and English

Art lithographer. Expert in contemporary lithography and estampes. Works directly with artists. He writes technical books about print making and publishes regular articles in French revues.

IMPRESSION

35 av Général-Pierre-Billotte, 94000 Creteil ■ Tel: 01 43 77 96 16 ■ By appointment ■ Michel Roger and Martin Nisser ■ Swedish spoken

Engraving of prints for artists.

Metal - Decorative finishers
Décorateurs sur metaux

LES MAITRES ARGENTEURS
19 rue du Pinacle, 93170 Bagnolet ■ Tel: 01 43 60 90 67 ■ Fax: 01 43 60 65 33 ■ Mon-Fri 8:00-12:00, 13:00-17:00, Fri 8:00-12:00 ■ Frédéric Lebat speaks English

Gold and silver plating, patinas for decorative hardware and statuary. Nickel plating and statuary bronze finishes.

♕ **MAISON MAHIEU**
15 impasse des Primevères, 75011 Paris ■ Tel: 01 43 55 88 25 ■ Fax: 01 48 06 92 99 ■ Mon-Fri 8:00-12:00/13:00-17:00 ■ Edith Maurette speaks English ■ Prices high

Mercury gilding, gold plating by electro-plating, all finishes: silver, bronze, antique patinas. Restoration of bronze objects. The best. Top-quality workmanship.

TEXIER
2 rue de la Roquette, 75011 Paris ■ Tel: 01 47 00 70 59 ■ Fax: 01 43 38 14 25 ■ Mon-Fri 8:00-12:00/13:00-18:00 ■ Prices low to medium ■ 15% professional discount

Gilding on metal: electro-plating, silver plating, patinas. Work on historic monuments.

Miniatures
Miniatures

MME MICHELE BOURDESSOL
18 rue de l'Abreuvoir, 75018 Paris ■ Tel: 01 42 54 98 35 ■ Web: www.antiquaires-contact.com/bourdessol ■ By Appointment ■ English spoken

Painter of miniatures on ivory and other noble materials. Portraits. Restoration. International clientel.

Mosaics
Mosaïque

––––––––––––– XIV –––––––––––––

CESARE BIZI
8 rue du Commandant Mouchotte, 75014 Paris ■ Tel: 01 43 21
28 81 ■ By appointment ■ Prices high ■ Professional discount
Mosaic artist. Creation and installation. Restoration of antique mosaics.

Decorative Painting
and Trompe l'Oeil
Peinture décorative et trompe-l'oeil

––––––––––––– VII –––––––––––––

MARIE YUKIKO POUQUET
104 rue du Bac, 75007 Paris ■ Cell: 06 09 86 46 05 ■ Fax: 01 45
49 19 63 ■ E-mail: makikotte@yahoo.fr ■ English and Japanese
spoken
Faux-finishes and trompe l'oéil, false marble, patinas, stucco, painted furniture, decoration.

––––––––––––– IX –––––––––––––

👑 **ATELIER QUENTIER**
15 rue Henry-Monnier, 75009 Paris ■ Tel: 01 48 78 64 35 ■ Fax:
01 48 78 22 79 ■ Mon-Fri 8:00-19:00 ■ Prices high ■ Professional discount
**Decorative painting and lacquering. Restoration of painted
and lacquered furniture and objects. All styles of decorative
painting. Member of the Grands Ateliers.**

XIV

CÉRAMIQUE DELABRUYERE SANGALLI
15 rue Bardinet, 75014 Paris ■ Tel: 01 45 45 36 66 ■ Mon-Fri by appointment ■ Lisyane Sangalli speaks English ■ Prices medium ■ Professional discount

Decorative painting on tiles. Bathrooms, kitchens, entrance halls, restaurants, shops, terraces, tabletops. Lamps and porcelain vases. Will also work to clients' designs.

👑 MERIGUET-CARRÈRE
84 rue de l'Abbée Groult, 75015 Paris ■ Tel: 01 48 28 48 81 ■ Fax: 01 45 32 57 84 ■ Mon-Fri 8:00-12:00/14:00-18:00 ■ English spoken ■ Prices high

Decorative painting, trompe l'oeil, gilding and faux finishes. Restoration of painted objects. Top-quality.

VALLIÈRE
6 villa de la gare , 92170 Vanves ■ Tel: 01 46 38 38 38 ■ Fax: 01 46 38 33 56 ■ Mon-Fri 8:00-12:00/13:30-19:00 ■ Carole Brion speaks English ■ Prices medium ■ 5 to 10% professional discount

Decorative painting, ceiling clouds and trompe l'oeil for residential and commercial clients. Restoration of façades.

Restoration of Bronze
Restauration de bronze

BRONZE DECORATION ETIENNE ET DORÉ
4 passage Josset, 75011 Paris ■ Tel: 01 43 55 33 42 ■ Fax: 01 43 55 13 17 ■ Mon-Fri 9:00-12:00/13:30-18:30 ■ Prices medium to high ■ Professional discount

Repair and restoration of all objects in bronze. Reproduction of bronzes of all periods. Restoration of chandeliers and replacement of missing crystal.

ATELIER COUSTE
3 passage Rauch, 75001 ■ Tel: 01 43 79 71 01 ■ Mon-Tue-Fri 8:00-12:00/13:30-17:00 ■ Mme Couste speaks English ■ Prices medium to high ■ Professional discount

Restoration of all art bronze: clocks, furniture bronzes, chandeliers, candelabra.

GILBON ET COROLLER
4 rue de Cotte, 75012 Paris ■ Tel: 01 43 43 94 55 ■ Fax: 01 43 43 96 87 ■ Mon-Fri 9:00-12:30/14:00-18:00 ■ English spoken ■ Prices high ■ Professional discount

Restoration of all-metal objects of all periods: crystal chandeliers, electrification, statues (all sizes), clocks, all metal furniture, patinas, chiselling, mounting.
Custom creations for National Museums and major corporations.

FERNANDO MOREIRA
172 rue de Charonne, Bât 2 B 75011 Paris ■ Tel: 01 43 72 91 72 ■ Fax: 01 43 79 11 48 ■ Mon-Fri 8:00-17:00, Sat by appointment ■ Fernando Moreira speaks English ■ 10 to 20% professional discount

Restoration and repair of XVIII century art bronze and furniture bronzes. Bronze gilding, antique patinas, chiselling and mounting. Restoration of ivory.

MAISON SCHMITT
41 rue du Faubourg-du-Temple, 75010 Paris ■ Tel: 01 42 08 05 43 ■ Fax: 01 42 08 49 92 ■ Mon-Fri 8:00-12:30/13:30-18:00 ■ English spoken ■ Professional discount

Restoration of XVIII and XIX century bronze. Custom-reproduction of bronze objects and furniture bronzes. Mercury gilding and silver plating.

TOULOUSE
10 rue Beautreillis, 75004 Paris ■ Tel: 01 48 87 82 85 ■ Fax : 01 48 87 82 84 ■ Mon-Fri 8:00-12:00/14:00-18:00/Fri closing 15:00 ■ Prices high

Restoration of art objects in bronze: clocks, sconces, andirons, crystal chandeliers, furniture bronzes. Restorer of historic monuments.

Restoration of Paintings
Restauration de tableaux
The Great Ateliers of France

——————————— IV ———————————

ATELIER MURIEL & JEAN-FRANÇOIS GUIGUE
4 place Edmond-Michelet, 75004 Paris ■ Tel: 01 42 72 88 74 ■
E-mail: guigue-locco@cybercable.fr ■ Mon-Fri 10:00-
19:00/Weekends by appointment ■ Prices medium ■ 10 to 20%
professional discount

Restoration of paintings, XVI to XX century, and older.

——————————— VI ———————————

ATELIER BERNARD DEPRETZ
30 rue Jacob, 75006 Paris ■ Tel: 01 43 26 60 14 ■ Mon-Fri 10:00-
12:00/14:00-19:00 ■ Prices medium ■ 20% professional discount

**Restoration of old and contemporary paintings. Re-mount-
ing, transposition, lightening of varnish.**

——————————— VII ———————————

MME MONIQUE DUCHATEAU
4 rue Casimir-Périer, 75007 Paris ■ Tel: 01 45 55 08 40/60 96 00
93 ■ Fax: 01 45 51 56 99 ■ By appointment ■ Some English spoken ■ Prices reasonable ■ Professional discount

**Restoration of works on paper: drawings, watercolours,
gouaches, pastels, Japanese estampes, parchment.**

——————————— IX ———————————

MME BRIGITTE MALAVOY
5 rue de Provence 75009 Paris ■ Tel: 01 42 46 15 25 ■ Fax: 01
40 22 61 90 ■ Mon-Fri by appointment ■ English and Italian spoken ■ Prices high

**Restoration of paintings on wood, canvas or copper from
the XVI to the XX century. Works for the French Museums.
Has established a school.**

ATELIER DU TEMPS PASSÉ
Viaduc des Arts, 5 avenue Daumesnil 75012 Paris ■ Tel: 01 43 46 86 27 ■ Mon-Sat 10:00-18:00 By appointment ■ English and Spanish spoken ■ Prices medium ■ 10 to 20% professional discount

Restoration of paintings, especially easel paintings, all art objects in polychrome and frames.
Work experience includes National Museums and French Embassies all over Europe as well as private collectors worldwide.

JEAN-JACQUES COQUERY
45 rue Amelot, 75011 Paris ■ Tel: 01 43 57 52 72 ■ Mon-Fri 10:00-13:00/14:00-18:30 ■ English spoken ■ Prices high

Restoration of easel paintings on canvas from the XVI century to the present. Oils and acrylics.
Work experience for the Monuments Historiques.

MME NATHALIE PINCAS
11 rue Schelcher, 75014 Paris ■ Tel: 01 43 27 52 27 ■ Fax: 01 43 21 70 90 ■ By appointment ■ English spoken ■ Prices medium

Restoration of old and Modern paintings.
Work experience includes National Museums.

ATELIER WROBEL
63 rue Daguèrre, 75014 Paris ■ Tel: 01 43 22 23 93 ■ By appointment ■ English spoken ■ Prices medium

Restoration of old, Modern and contemporary paintings.
Member of the International Council of Museums.

XVII

YVES CRINEL
47 rue Ampère, 75017 Paris ■ Tel: 01 43 80 67 08 ■ Mon-Sat 9:00-18:00 ■ By appointment ■ Italian spoken

Restoration of paintings.

ATELIER ANNE ALABASTRI
4 rue Hermann-Lachapelle, 75018 Paris ■ Telfax: 01 42 55 55 60 ■ Mon 9:00-12:00/Tue-Fri 9:30-12:30/14:00-19:00/Sat 10:00-

13:00/14:00-16:00 By appointment ■ English and Italian spoken
■ 5% professional discount

Restoration of paintings. Re-mounting using traditional and modern methods, treatment, cleaning, re-touching, chemical analyses and examination by ultra-violet, infra-red and X-ray.

XX

MME MICHELLE BOUCARD
75 rue d'Avron, 75020 Paris ■ Tel: 01 43 56 04 66 ■ Mon-Sat
9:00-18:00 ■ Prices medium ■ 10% professional discount

**Restoration of paintings. Cleaning and re-mounting.
Work experience includes the Historic Monuments.**

NEUILLY

L'ATELIER DU TEMPS
10 rue Bailly, 92200 Neuilly-sur-Seine ■ Telfax: 01 47 45 04 81 ■
Cell: 06 81 96 04 91 ■ By appointment ■ Jean-Claude Blaquière
speaks English ■ Prices medium

Restoration of XVII and XVIII century paintings. Oils on canvas, panels, murals, frescoes. Advice on conservation and restoration. Maintenance of collections. Treatment and cleaning of old panels, re-fixing, re-mounting, re-touching and lightening of varnish.

LE PORT MARLY

L'ATELIER - ANNA PONIATOWSKI
6 rue Jean Jaurès 78 560 Le Port Marly ■ Telfax: 01 39 58 57 95
■ Mon-Sat 10:00-19:00 by appointment ■ English spoken

Restoration of paintings of all periods.

CROISSY-SUR-SEINE

ATELIER DE RESTAURATION DE TABLEAUX
47 av de Verdun, 78290 Croissy-sur-Seine ■ Tel: 01 39 76 95 50
■ Fax: 01 39 76 49 61 ■ Mme. De Cornulier Lucinière ■ English
spoken ■ Prices medium

Restoration of old and Modern paintings. Works for Museums, associations, dealers and private clients.

ROLAND GENOVESIO
5 rue Jean-Baptiste Clément 93400 Saint-Ouen ■ Tel: 01 40 10
84 51 ■ Web: www.studio-genovesio.fr

Restoration of paintings. Reproductions. Work for Museums, Historic Monuments, dealers and individual clients. Decoration of Textiles.

Restoration of Parasols and Umbrellas
Restauration de parasols et parapluies

PEPS
223 rue Saint-Martin, 75003 Paris ■ Telfax: 01 42 78 11 67 ■
Mon 9:00-19:00/Tue-Fri 13:30-18:30 ■ Jocelyne Marcourt
speaks English

Restoration of all parasols and umbrellas, old and recent. Custom recovering of umbrellas, large and small. Sale of selected models.

Restoration of Porcelain, Faience and Ceramics
Restauration de porcelaine, faïence et céramique

——————————— VIII ———————————

MME MONIQUE LEROY
58 rue de Londres, 75008 Paris ■ Tel: 01 43 87 17 88 ■ Tue-Fri
by appointment ■ Mme Leroy speaks English

A master at her craft. Madame Leroy restores porcelain for the top antique dealers, Christie's and Sotheby's, the Louvre and the Center of Archaeological Restoration of Florence. Works also in terracotta and other materials. Expert to the Cour d'Appel, Paris.

X

JEAN-PIERRE ROYER

20 rue de Chabrol, 75010 Paris ■ Tel: 01 47 70 46 74 ■ Mon-Fri 9:00-12:00 ■ Eric Royer speaks English

Restoration of art objects in porcelain, faience, terracotta, crystal, pâte de verre (Gallé, Daum). Repair of glass and ceramic. Restoration of antique bronzes, chiselling, mounting, re-mounting and restoration of crystal chandeliers. Electrification.

XI

MME SOPHIE MUGUET

173 rue du Faubourg Saint-Antoine, 75011 Paris ■ Telfax: 01 43 42 39 46 ■ E-mail : atel-rest-ceram@easynet.fr ■ Mon-Fri 10:00-18:00 ■ Prices medium

Restoration of broken or incomplete ceramic. Research into materials and colours. Invisible repairs. Firm estimates.

XVII

ATELIER SOUCHET

18 rue Biot, 75017 Paris ■ Tel: 01 45 22 53 47 ■ Tue-Fri 11:00-17:30 ■ Fabien Souchet speaks English ■ Prices medium to high

Restoration of faience, porcelain, enamel, terracotta, old dolls.

XVIII

YVES MEROVIL

19 rue Marc Seguin, 75018 Paris ■ Tel: 01 46 07 01 55 ■ Mon-Fri 8:30-17:30 ■ English spoken

Repair and restoration of porcelain, terracotta, ceramics. Gilding of objects in wood. High quality work.

ATELIER LUMONT
12 rue Cacheux, 92400 Courbevoie ■ Tel: 01 47 89 56 90 ■ By appointment
Restoration of faience, porcelain, bisquit, terracotta, ivory, collages, plaster. Master Artisan.

Restoration of Posters
Restauration d'affiches

BRIGITTE BUSSIÈRE
43 rue de l'Arbre-Sec, 75001 Paris ■ Tel: 01 47 03 32 58 ■ Fax: 01 40 15 96 60 ■ Mon-Fri 9:30-12:30/14:30-18:30 by appointment ■ English spoken ■ Prices medium ■ Professional discount
High quality and complete restoration of posters. Bleaching and linen backing. Expertise and evaluation. Sale of posters specializing in tourism and sports.

PATRICE DASSONVILLE
14 rue Daru, 75008 Paris ■ Tel: 01 42 67 53 64 ■ Fax: 01 42 89 03 22 ■ Every day 8:30-23:00 by appointment ■ English spoken ■ Prices medium ■ Professional discount
Excellent restoration of old and contemporary posters. Linen backing. Works mainly for the museums.

L'ATELIER
106 av Marguerite-Renaudin, 92140 Clamart ■ Telfax: 01 46 48 95 91 ■ Mon-Fri 9:00-12:30/14:00-19:30 ■ English, Italian and Spanish spoken ■ Prices medium ■ Professional discount
Restoration of all types of posters. Very high quality. Works for museums, cinemas, collectors and dealers. Expertise and estimations.

Restoration of Silver and Cutlery
Restauration d'orfèvrerie et coutellerie

ATELIER RIOT
24 rue de la Folie-Méricourt, 75011 Paris ■ Tel. 01 47 00 34 47

■ Web: www.grandsateliers.com ■ Mon-Fri 8:30-12:00/13:30-18:00 ■ Jeanne Privat speaks English ■ Prices medium

Restoration of all metal objects, silver, bronze and pewter. Specialty: silver. Restoration and re-gilding of furniture bronzes, chandeliers, clocks.

CHASTEL COUTELIER ORFÈVRE

190 bd Haussman, Paris 75008 ■ Telfax: 01 45 63 20 59 ■ Mon-Fri 10:00-18:00 ■ English and Spanish spoken

Repair of cutlery, replacement of knife blades. Restoration and repair of objects in silver and pewter. Sale of cutlery, pocket and hunting knives, good selection of table knives and professional cooking knives.

MAURICE CHEVALIER

26 rue des Gravilliers, 75003 Paris ■ Tel: 01 42 74 18 11 ■ Mon-Fri 8:00-12:00/13:00-17:00 ■ Prices medium

Repair of objects in silver.

LES MAÎTRES ARGENTEURS

19 rue du Pinacle, 93170 Bagnolet ■ Tel: 01 43 60 90 67 ■ Fax: 01 43 60 65 33 ■ Thu-Fri 8:00-17:00 ■ Frédéric Lebat speaks English ■ Prices medium ■ Professional discount

Restoration and repair of all objects in gold, silver, pewter and bronze. Gilding and silver plating.

COUTELLERIE DE PASSY

17 rue de l'Annonciation, Paris 75016 ■ Telfax: 01 42 24 77 46 ■ Tue-Sat 10:30-18:30 ■ English spoken ■ 5% professional discount

Repair and replating of silver since 1922.

EPPE FRÈRES

5 rue Chapon, 75003 Paris ■ Tel: 01 48 87 78 65 ■ Mon-Fri 8:00-12:00/13:30-18:00 ■ Guy Eppe speaks English ■ Prices medium

Gilding and silver plating of all metals, silverware and jewellery. Antique patinas, silver plating of cutlery. Nickle plating.

MADELEINE NOE
2 passage Saint-Sebastien, 75011 Paris ■ Tel: 01 43 55 62 07 ■
Mon-Fri 8:30-12:00/13:00-18:00
Restoration and re-plating of silver. Small production of silver trays and goblets.

LES ORFÈVRES DE SEVIGNÉ
2 passage Saint-Sebastien, Paris 75011 ■ Telfax: 01 47 00 15 32
■ Mon-Fri 8:30-12:00/13:00-18:30 ■ Prices medium ■ Professional discount
Restoration of special silver objects, as well as bronze. Repair and re-silvering of cutlery.

Wood Carvers - Restoration and Fabrication
Sculpteurs sur bois

III

JEAN RENOUVEL
3 rue Elzévire 75003 Paris ■ Tel: 01 42 72 15 28 ■ Mon-Fri 8:00-12:00/14:00-18:00 ■ Prices medium
Wood carving: boiseries (wood panelling), chairs and consoles. Fabrication and restoration.

XI

VINCENT MOUCHEZ
106 rue de Montreuil, 75011 Paris ■ Telfax: 01 43 73 22 47 ■
Mon-Fri 9:00-18:00
Carving of ornaments in wood. Wood panelling, wainscoting, copies of antique furniture and chairs. Creation and restoration.

PARIS SUBURBS

♕ BREDY
63 rue Albert Dhalenne 93407 Saint-Ouen ■ Tel: 01 43 75 47 87 ■
Fax: 01 40 12 60 05 ■ Mon-Fri 7:30-12:00/13:30-17:30/Fri closing
17:00 ■ Jean-Pierre Fancelli speaks English ■ Prices high

One of the best in France. Fine wood carving of panelling, fire-places, doors and gates, parquets, windows, lanterns and chandeliers in wood, frames. Sculpture of wood ornaments and statuary, chairs and armchairs. Restoration and creation. Work experience: the National Museums and Châteaux of France, the Palaces of Versailles, Fontainebleau and Compiègne, Notre-Dame de Paris. The Corcoran Gallery, Washington D.C.

Viaduc des Arts

9 to 129 Avenue Daumesnil, 75012 Paris.

Just around the corner from the Place de la Bastille, near the Gare de Lyon, the City of Paris has renovated an old viaduct, utilizing the spaces under the arches for beautiful workshops and showrooms for 46 special artisans and creators. You will find everything from gilders to luthiers, to specialists in making copper pots and original furniture. Well worth the trip.

CREANOG# 9 ■ Tel: 01 55 78 82 80 ■ Fax: 01 55 78 82 81 ■ E-mail: creanog@ubiquando.com ■ Web: www.creanog.ubi-quando.com ■ Mon-Fri 8:00-20:00 ■ Laurent Noges ■ English, German and Spanish spoken

Embossing, marking, hot stamping and inlaying on paper, for artists' prints, invitations, business cards and haute couture packaging.

LORENOVE #11 ■ Tel: 01 40 01 90 01 ■ Fax: 01 40 01 94 95 ■ Toll free: 0800 220 220 ■ Mon-Sat 10:00-19:00

Made-to-measure windows and doors. Design and installation of period windows and contemporary styles. Double-glazed leaded windows. Their references include the windows of the Viaduc, chateaux all over France, apartment and office buildings, ski chalets and private homes. Eight showrooms around the country.

RIPAMONTI #13 ■ Tel: 01 43 40 80 80 ■ Fax: 01 43 40 80 01 ■ Mon-Fri 8:00-19:00 ■ Franco Ripamonti ■ Italian and some English spoken

Stone is their specialty: sculpture, fireplaces and hearths, tables, fountains, Saracen arched staircases, statuary, flooring, sun-dials and mosaics. They also work in marble and marble with inlaid terracotta. Restoration of marble and stone for historic buildings. Excellent references.

MAISON FEY #15 ■ Tel: 01 43 41 22 22 ■ Fax: 01 43 41 11 12
■ Mon-Sat 8:30-18:00 ■ Michael Fey ■ Dominique Fey speaks
English ■ Professional discount ■ Major credit cards

Specialists in "faux" leather book spines for walls and partitions. Everything in extraordinary gilded leathers: furniture, boxes, desktops and blotters, filing cabinets; polychromed Cordova leather for upholstery of walls. Clients include French Embassies, deluxe hotels and movie stars like John Malkovich.

LE BONHEUR DES DAMES #17 ■ Tel: 01 43 42 06 27 ■ Fax: 01
43 42 06 44 ■ E-mail: bonheurdesdames@wanadoo.fr ■ Web:
www.pro.wanadoo.fr(bonheurdesdames) ■ Mon 14:00-19:00,
Tue-Sat 10:30-19:00 ■ Mme Cécile Vessière ■ English and some
German spoken ■ Visa

Creation of works in embroidery. Supplies of all materials for embroiderers including kits. Cushions, pictures, Christmas stockings and a collection of miniature Persian carpets. Framing service.

MALHIA KENT #121 ■ Tel: 01 53 44 76 76 ■ Fax: 01 53 44 76
77 ■ E-mail: malhia@wanadoo.fr ■ Mon-Sat 8:00-20:00 ■ Christian Pays ■ English and most other languages spoken ■ Professional discount ■ Major credit cards

Hand-woven fabrics for the world's top couturiers: Chanel, Dior, Givenchy, Kenzo, Fendi, Donna Karen, Versace, Valentino, Geoffrey Beene, Bill Blass, etc. Sometimes you can snap up remnants. Extraordinary and well worth a visit.

MÉTIER COSTUMIER #19 ■ Tel: 01 43 40 38 38 ■ Fax: 01 43 40
70 39 ■ Mon-Fri 9:00-12:30/13:30-18:00, Fri close 17:00 ■
Stéphane Rollot ■ English spoken ■ Mainly to professionals

Pascale Métier comes from several generations of costume makers. The company has collected costumes from all over Europe and they also create and make costumes, faithful to the period, for theatrical, opera and film companies all over the world.

ATELIER N'O #21 ■ Tel: 01 43 46 26 26 ■ Fax: 01 43 46 31 45
■ Tue-Sat 11:30-19:00, Sun 14:00-19:00 ■ Thierry Durot, Evelyne Viladrich ■ English spoken ■ Professional discount ■ Visa

Creation of "treasures of nature" for table and general decoration: stone, sand, shells, plants, flowers, wood. You can buy them ready-made, have them made to your taste, or buy the elements and make them yourself. Unusual photo albums made from re-cycled paper. These are sold finished but you can order the colours you want. Personalized company gifts.

SEMA #23 ■ Tel: 01 55 78 85 85 ■ Fax: 01 55 78 86 15 ■ Tue-Fri 10:00-19:00

Information and exhibitions with the aim of developing arts and fine crafts.

AISTHESIS #25 ■ Tel: 01 53 33 00 45 ■ Fax: 01 53 33 00 15 ■ E-mail: jérômecordie@hotmail.com ■ Web: www.aisthesis.com ■ Tue-Sat 9:00-13:00/14:00-18:00 ■ Jérôme Cordie speaks English ■ Major credit cards

Creation and restoration of fine furniture and art objects. Specialist in galuchat, wood marquetry and precious materials such as mother-of-pearl, tortoise-shell, bone, horn. Regular exhibitions by artists working in wood or galuchat. Works for museums, antique dealers, decorators and private individuals.

HOULÈS # 27 ■ Tel: 01 43 46 25 50 ■ Fax: 01 43 46 25 53 ■ Tue-Sat 10-12:15/13:15-18:30 ■ Danièle Garnier ■ Some English spoken ■ Professional discount ■ Major credit cards

Superb trimmings, decorative accessories, fabrics and sheers, drapery hardware.

V.I.A. # 29-37 ■ Tel: 01 46 28 11 11 ■ Fax: 01 46 28 13 13 ■ E-mail: via.asso@holl.fr ■ Web: www.via.org

Promotional space for exhibitions and events dealing with French furniture and decorative objects.

LE VIADUC CAFÉ #41-43 ■ Tel: 01 44 74 70 70 ■ Fax: 01 44 74 70 71

HOME INTRA DESIGN #47 ■ Tel: 01 44 75 34 34 ■ Fax: 01 44 75 34 42 ■ Mon-Sat 9:00-12:00/14:00-18:00 ■ Mme Odile Audouard and Patrick Audouard d'Avirez ■ English spoken ■ Professional discount

Upholsterers of fine furniture, restoration of chairs and sofas. Custom trimmings and superb choice of fabrics.

CÉCILE ET JEANNE # 49 ■ Tel: 01 43 41 24 24 ■ Fax: 01 43 41 60 60 ■ E-mail: cecjeanne@aol.com ■ Mon-Fri 9:30-19:00, Sat 12:00-19:00, Sun 14:00-19:00

Creators of unusual contemporary jewellery.

ATELIER MICHEL PINTADO #51 ■ Tel: 01 46 28 80 80 ■ Fax: 01 46 28 88 11 ■ Mon-Fri 10:00-13:00/14:30-20:00 ■ Some English spoken

Sculptured wood furniture to order. Unique signed models in precious woods. Original hand-crafted lighting, consoles, commodes, low tables, frames. Miniature furniture and furnishings.

IMAGINNE #53 ■ Tel: 01 43 41 84 84 ■ Fax: 01 43 41 86 87 ■ Mon-Fri 14:00-19:00 and by appointment ■ Jean-Claude Schlemer ■ Some English spoken ■ Professional discount ■ Major credit cards

Contemporary one-off furniture in natural stone, marble, granite and corian.

SEMAEST # 55-57 ■ Tel: 01 43 45 98 98 ■ Fax: 01 43 47 03 28 ■ Mon-Fri 9:00-13:00/14:00-18:00, Fri close 17:00 ■ Sylvie Froissart ■ #55 Tel: 01 43 45 45 35 ■ #57 Tel: 01 40 01 99 09

Exhibitions of artisans and creators.

VERTICAL #63 ■ Tel: 01 43 40 26 26 ■ Fax: 01 43 40 34 34 ■ E-mail: courrier@atelier-vertical.com ■ Web: www.atelier-vertical.com ■ Mon 15:00-20:00, Tue-Fri 10:00-13:00/14:30-20:00, Sat 11:00-13:30/15:00-20:00

Vegetal sculpture, contemporary floral furnishings and decorations. Interesting and quite beautiful.

YAMAKADO #65 ■ Tel: 01 43 40 79 79 ■ Fax: 01 43 40 79 80 ■ E-mail: yamakado@hol.fr ■ Web: www.yamakado.com ■ Mon-Sat 10:00-19:00, Sun 15:00-19:00 ■ Hirouyuki and Agnes Yamakado ■ Japanese and English spoken

Creation and manufacture of contemporary furniture and home furnishings.

ESPACE CYRILLE VARET # 67 ■ Tel: 01 44 75 88 88 ■ Fax: 01 44 75 88 89 ■ E-mail: courrier@cyrillevaret.com ■ Web: www.cyrillevaret.com ■ Mon-Sun 10:00-19:00 ■ Cyrille Varet speaks English ■ Amex, Visa

Unusual contemporary steel furniture: chairs, tables, low tables, bar stools, lighting and decorative accessories.

GALERIE CLAUDE SAMUEL #69 ■ Tel: 01 53 17 01 11 ■ Fax: 01 53 17 07 08 ■ E-mail: claudesamuel@compuserve.com ■ Web: www.claude-samuel.com ■ Mon 14:00-19:00, Tue-Fri 10:00-13:00/14:00-19:00, Sat 11:00-19:00 ■ Claude and Elizabeth Samuel speak German, English and some Italian

Contemporary paintings, sculpture, photography, installations and collages.

ATELIERS ROBIN TOURENNE #71 ■ Tel: 01 43 07 59 25 ■ Fax: 01 43 46 18 50 ■ Mon-Fri 9:00-13:00/14:00-18:00, Sat 14:00-18:00 ■ Robin Tourenne

Conservation and restoration of old and contemporary paper of all formats: antique posters, maps, engravings, wallpapers and colour panels. Cloth backing and framing.

BAGUÈS #73 ■ Tel: 01 43 41 53 53 ■ Fax: 01 43 41 54 55 ■ E-mail: baguesparis@minitel.net ■ Mon-Fri 9:00-18:00, Sat 10:00-18:00 ■ Jean-Jacques Corre ■ English spoken ■ Professional Discount ■ Major credit cards

Fine collection of bronze and wrought iron lighting: 8,000 models have been created since 1840. Period lighting in bronze and crystal, chandeliers, lamps, sconces. Restoration services.

AU PÈRE TRANQUILLE #75-77 ■ Tel: 01 43 43 64 58 ■ Fax: 01 43 43 35 21

Café-restaurant.

LE CADRE D'OR #79 ■ Tel: 01 43 45 71 71 ■ Fax: 01 43 45 75 10 ■ Mon-Sat 10:00-19:00 ■ Jacques-Henri Varichon ■ English and some German spoken ■ Major credit cards

Specialist in fine framing and mounting of contemporary art objects. Unique designs and special patinas. A line of comfortable armchair-hammocks. Works for museums.

ATELIER GUIGUE & LOCCA #81 ■ Telfax: 01 43 44 99 55 ■ Mon-Fri 9:30-19:00, Sat by appointment ■ Jean-François Guigue and Muriel Locca ■ Some English, German and Italian spoken ■ Professional discount ■ Diners

Creation and restoration of painted furniture, decorative panels and objects. Trompe l'oeil, antique patinas and finishes. Creation and manufacture of hi-fi speaker units. They give classes.

MARIE LAVANDE #83 ■ Tel: 01 44 67 78 78 ■ Fax: 01 44 67 01 78 ■ Mon-Fri 9:30-12:30, Sat 14:30-18:30 ■ Joëlle Serres is the creator associated with the designer Angélique

Specialists in the restoration of embroidery and lace and cleaning and ironing of delicate antique linen, baptismal robes, wedding veils, folkloric headdresses. Creation of superb hand-embroidered household linen. Classes in embroidery and lacemaking. Extraordinary.

PASCAL MAINGOURD #85 ■ Tel: 01 43 41 46 46 ■ Fax: 01 43 41 72 73 ■ Mon-Fri 8:30-12:30/13:30-18:30, Sat 14:30-18:30 ■ English spoken ■ Visa

Furniture and wall upholstery, custom curtains, draperies, blinds, decorative objects. Custom sofas to measure. Exclusive line of Gustavian furniture. Excellent choice of fabrics.

ARDUSTYL #87 ■ Tel: 01 44 75 96 96 ■ Fax: 01 44 75 99 55 ■ Mon-Fri 9:00-12:00/13:00-18:00, Sat 10:00-12:00/13:00-18:00 ■ Bernard Dupré

Wood gilding, copies of antique frames and picture framing. Restoration of gilded wood objects, furniture, frames, consoles, barometers, musical instruments, mirrors and statues. Creation of contemporary gilded objects.

MEDIACRYPTAGE #89 ■ Tel: 01 43 45 03 03 ■ Fax: 01 43 45 49 00 ■ E-mail: cryptage@imaginet.fr ■ Mon-Fri 9:00-19:00 ■ Gilles Decome and Patrice Le Goux ■ English and German spoken

Retouching and mounting of photographs, portraits and illustrations. Colourization of black and white photos.

👑 **ATELIER LE TALLEC** #93-95 ■ Tel: 01 43 40 61 55 ■ Fax: 01 43 07 71 81 ■ Mon-Fri 8:00-18:00 ■ Director: Mme Laurence de la Grange ■ English spoken ■ Professional discount ■ Major credit cards

Custom designed hand-painted porcelain. These fine craftsmen create the Tiffany & Co. private stock of 20 exclusive hand-painted china designs, as well as their own custom work. It takes 20 years for an artisan to master the repertoire of Le Tallec designs. Some stock available.

AUTOMATES ET POUPÉES #97 ■ Telfax: 01 43 42 22 33 ■ Tue-Sat 10:30-18:30 ■ Sylviane Dugas and Camille Guillebert ■ A bit of English ■ Major credit cards

Restoration of mechanical toys, antique dolls, teddy bears and music boxes. They also create dolls' clothes from antique fabrics.

ALLAIN CADINOT #99 ■ Tel: 01 43 41 43 43 ■ Fax: 01 43 41 72 36 ■ E-mail: cadinotflutes@wanadoo.fr ■ Web: www.cadinot-flutes.com ■ Tue-Sat 10:00-13:00/14:00-19:00 ■ English spoken ■ Professional discount ■ Major credit cards

Internationally-known maker and restorer of transverse flutes. He is also the exclusive importer of transverse flutes made by the American firms, Haynes and Powell. A fine selection of contemporary music stands.

FIREWORKS #101 ■ Tel: 01 46 28 30 42 ■ Fax: 01 46 28 18 10 ■ Mon-Sat 10:00-19:00 ■ Scott Slagermann ■ English spoken

Design and creation of contemporary blown glass sculpture, furniture, and decorative objects. Beautiful.

ROGER LANNE #103 ■ Tel: 01 43 40 67 67 ■ Fax: 01 43 40 71 71 ■ Tue-Sat 9:00-12:00/13:30-18:30 ■ Roger Lanne ■ Some English and German spoken ■ Professional Discount ■ Major credit cards

Creation and restoration of violins, cellos and bows. He is the luthier of the Paris Opera and an expert to U.F.E.

ASTIER DE VILLATTE #107 ■ Tel: 01 43 45 72 72 ■ Fax: 01 43 45 77 30 ■ Mon-Fri 8:30-18:00 ■ Professional discount ■ Major credit cards

A workshop for the creation of objects, dishes, vases, goblets, and garden pots in ceramic and enamelled terracotta. Glassware and cutlery. Special editions of furniture in natural woods with antique patinas.

PROLOGUE ENSEMBLIER #109 ■ Tel: 01 53 33 03 03 ■ Fax: 01 53 33 03 04 ■ Mon-Sat 10:30-18:30 ■ Marc Jitiaux ■ English spoken ■ Professional discount ■ Amex, Visa

Contemporary designs in furniture, arts of the table with lots of Limoges, and decorative objects, made by a group of artists, painters, sculptors.

♔ **ATELIERS DU CUIVRE ET DE L'ARGENT** #111 ■ Tel: 01 43 40 20 20 ■ Fax: 01 43 40 60 60 ■ Mon-Sat 10:00-18:00 ■ Professional discount ■ Major credit cards

This is a real museum of copper and silver with a remarkable collection of hundreds of unique pieces. The workshop creates and restores beautiful silver, from candlesticks to cutlery or large platters. The copper pots and cooking utensils are remarkable. They will even make you a copper bathtub if you want it.

LES TERRES CUITES DES RAIRIES # 113 ■ Tel: 01 53 02 49 00 ■ Fax: 01 53 02 49 01 ■ E-mail: terres.cuites.des.rairies@wanadoo.fr ■ Web: www.rairies.com ■ Mon-Fri 10:00-12:30/14:00-19:00, Sat 10:00-12:30/14:00-18:00 ■ Artist-designer: Michel Fedi ■ Italian, Spanish and some English spoken ■ Professional discount ■ Major credit cards

Manufacturer of natural and enamelled terracotta and decorative ceramic for tiles, wall panels, bottle racks, barbecues and decoration. They restore historic buildings and work to plan for complete installations. Great.

SILICE – GILLES CHABRIER #115 ■ Tel: 01 43 43 36 00 ■ Fax: 01 43 43 38 00 ■ Mon 14:00-18:00, Tue-Fri 10:00-18:30, Sat 14:00-19:00 ■ Manager: Cilvy Bouche ■ Some English spoken

Gilles Chabrier is a very talented glass sculptor. His work includes an extraordinary collection of head sculptures in glass, tables, lighting, small decorative objects and even a chimney piece.

ATELIER LEBEAU #117 ■ Tel: 01 43 45 96 05 ■ Fax: 01 43 45 96 66 ■ Mon-Thu 9:00-18:00, Fri 9:00-17:00, Sat by appointment ■ Joseph Hegybiro ■ Hungarian, Italian and some English spoken ■ Professional discount

Design, fabrication and restoration of sculptured and gilded wood frames. Framing. Restoration of all objects in sculptured gilded wood and polychrome. Works for the major Paris museums, painters, galleries and private individuals.

L'ACADEMIE DU VIADUC DES ARTS #119 ■ Tel: 01 43 40 75 75 ■ Fax: 01 43 40 74 74

Classes in painting, sculpture, drawing, engraving and perspective, for the public, of all ages, given by Francoise Frugier and eight professors of the great art schools.

MATIÈRES #123 ■ Tel: 01 44 74 01 05 ■ Fax: 01 44 74 01 15 ■ Cell: 06 60 64 01 05 ■ Mon-Fri 9:00-19:00, Sat 11:00-19:00, Sun 14:00-19:00 ■ Gérard Houdin, Alain Aparicio ■ English and Italian spoken ■ Prices medium to high ■ Major credit cards

This family of craftsmen has three specialties: trompe l'oeil painting for walls, floors and ceilings. Michèle Houdin works worldwide. Alain Aparicio works in decorative iron, copper, brass and silver, making everything from furniture, portals, staircases and jewellery to table-settings and pens. The atelier makes original and unique decorative objects to order.

ARTEFACT #125 ■ Tel: 01 44 74 95 95 ■ Fax: 01 44 74 94 94 ■ E-mail: artefacts@wanadoo.fr ■ Mon-Fri 9:00-18:00 ■ Rod Marawi ■ English spoken

Designs, makes and restores architectural models and relief plans. Reproduction in miniature of historic buildings, in plexiglass, resin and wood.

JEAN-CHARLES BROSSEAU #129 ■ Tel: 01 53 33 82 00 ■ Fax: 01 53 33 82 02 ■ Mon-Fri 10:00-13:00/14:30-20:00 ■ Some English spoken

Creator of fetching and comfortable hats, and a well-known perfume line.

ART FOUNDRIES
Fonderies d'Art

III

MEGAFONTE FRANCE
147 rue du Temple, 75003 Paris ■ Tel: 01 42 71 79 00 ■ Fax: 01 42 71 79 01 ■ Mon-Thurs 9:30-18:00/Fri 9:00-15:00 ■ Evelyne Sitbon speaks English ■ Prices medium ■ Professional discount

Casting of all metals, gold, silver, bronze, brass and pewter. Delivered rough or finished as ordered. Work in precious metals for the jewellers of Paris and non-precious metals for haute-couture accessories.

IV

ENTREPRISE TOULOUSE
10 rue Beautreillis, 75004 Paris ■ Tel: 01 48 87 82 85 ■ Mon-Fri 8:00-12:00/14:00-18:00

Chiseling of bronze and work in all metals. Restoration of precious art objects. Work experience: Paul Getty Museum, the Louvre, Chateau de Versailles, the treasures of the cathedrals.

XII

MME FRANCE MARIE LEHE
47 rue de Lyon, 75012 Paris ■ Tel: 01 43 43 40 49 - Fax: 01 43 43 14 18 ■ Mon-Fri 8:30-17:30 ■ Prices medium

Foundry for ornaments in bronze and brass. Sand casting and lost wax process.

XVII

FONDERIE D'ART DUCROS
1 rue Baron, 75017 Paris ■ Tel: 01 42 29 22 39 ■ Mon-Fri 8:00-12:00/12:30-18:30 ■ Prices medium

Casting of sculpture in bronze, in limited numbered editions, using the lost wax process. Restoration and mounting of bronzes.

MEILLEUR

32 rue des Amandiers, 75020 Paris ■ Tel: 01 43 66 45 13 ■ Fax: 01 43 66 45 43 ■ Mon-Fri 8:30-12:00/14:00-18:00 and by appointment ■ Catherine Meilleur and Claude Delorme speak English ■ Prices high to very high ■ Professional discount

Founders of bronze and wrought iron in decoration and architecture. Work experience: Bibliotheque Nationale in Paris, Palais de Fontainebleau, Palais de Compiègne, the lanterns of the Conseil d'Etat and the Palais Royal.

—————————— PARIS SUBURBS ——————————

BLANCHET LANDOWSKI

57 av Gambetta, 93170 Bagnolet ■ Tel: 01 43 61 16 41 ■ Fax: 01 48 97 17 37 ■ Mon-Fri 8:00-12:00/13:00-17:30, Fri closing 16:30 ■ English spoken ■ Prices high

This foundry specializes in statuary using both sand casting and the lost wax process. They do the final chiseling as well as the finishing. Their work experience includes the restoration of major historic bronze statues in France as well as casting for well known contemporary sculptors. Also the Dome of Les Invalides, Prefecture de Bobigny, doors at the Louvre.

FLEURANT

Chemin du Halage, Z.I., 78270 Bonnières-sur-Seine ■ Tel: 01 30 98 90 11 ■ Mon-Fri 8:30-12:00/13:30-18:00 ■ Alain Brieu speaks English ■ Prices high

Bronze foundry. Casting, sand and lost wax, to final patinas. Original works of art and limited numbered editions. Realisations for artist-sculptors.

FONDERIE CLEMENTI

29 rue du Lieutenant-Batany, 92190 Meudon ■ Tel: 01 45 34 56 32 ■ Fax: 01 45 34 73 35 ■ Mon-Fri 7:30-12:30/13:30-17:00 ■ English spoken ■ Prices high

Specialty in statuary, using the lost wax process. Clients include: Miró (Galerie Maeght), Artcurial, Musée Bourdelle.

ARTISANS' SUPPLIES
Fournitures pour artisans

ADAM MONTPARNASSE
11 bd Edgar-Quinet, 75014 Paris ■ Tel: 01 43 20 68 53 ■ Fax: 01 43 21 23 72 ■ Mon 9:30-12:30/13:30-19:00, Tue-Sat 9:30-19:00 ■ English spoken ■ Prices medium ■ 15% professional discount for students ■ Major credit cards

Products for the artist and the restorer. Mouldings and hand-turned elements for furniture restoration. Technical books.

ART ET CONSERVATION
75 rue Rateau, Zone Urba Parc, Bat B1 93120 Courneuve ■ Tel: 01 43 11 26 10 ■ Fax: 01 43 11 26 19 ■ E-mail: artetco@aol.com ■ Mon-Thu 09:00-12:30/13:30-17:30, Fri 9:00-12:30/13:30-16:00 ■ Written English (fax or e-mail) ■ Prices medium

Unsized polyester fabrics. Gold, or gold substitute, for retouching. Hot spatula and other products and materials used for restoration and conservation of works of art. Catalogue in French language available upon request.

👑 BERTHELOT
184 rue du Faubourg-Saint-Honoré, 75008 Paris ■ Tel: 01 45 63 34 07 ■ Fax: 01 45 63 00 99 ■ E-mail: Berthelot.beaux-arts@wanadoo.fr ■ Mon-Fri 9:30-19:00, Sat 12:30-4:30 ■ English spoken ■ Professional discount ■ Visa and MC

Artisan's supplies, paints, papers, glues, tools as well as framing, gilding and restorations.

👑 BHV - BAZAAR DE L'HOTEL DE VILLE
52 rue de Rivoli, 75004 Paris ■ Tel: 01 42 74 90 00 ■ Fax: 01 42 74 96 79 ■ Mon-Sat 9:30-19:00, Wed evening until 22:00 ■ Prices reasonable

A very large department store with a basement wonderland of everything imaginable for the artisan, handyman, gardener, etc. If it exists, you'll find it here. Don't hesitate to explore the upper floors for more treasures for the woodworker, the framer, and other decorative accessories.
Maybe the best of its kind in the world.

👑 CHARBONNEL
13 quai de Montebello, 75005 Paris ■ Tel: 01 43 54 23 46 ■ Fax: 01 43 29 94 12 ■ For export: 5 rue René Panhard, 72018 LeMans ■ Tel: 02 43 83 83 00 ■ Fax: 02 43 83 85 29 ■ Intl: 02 43 83 83 15

Very good quality and a wide range of paints and artists' and artisans' supplies.

DECORS BURACH

11 rue Faidherbe, 75011 Paris ■ Telfax: 01 43 72 12 18 ■ Mon-Fri 8:30-12:00/13:30-18:30, Sat 8:30-12:00 ■ Prices medium

All wood materials for ebenistes and carpenters. Mouldings and hand-turned articles in wood for furniture restoration.

DUGAY

92 rue des Rosiers, 93400 Saint-Ouen (In the Marché aux Puces) ■ Tel: 01 40 11 87 30 ■ Fax: 01 40 12 26 32 ■ Thu-Mon 9:00-18:00 ■ Prices reasonable ■ Professional discount

Nearly 2,000 different products for artisans, ebenistes, gilders, painters of trompe l'oeil and restorers of furniture and marble.

L'ECLAT DE VERRE

2 bis rue Mercoeur, 75011 Paris ■ Tel: 01 43 79 23 88 ■ Fax: 01 43 79 23 34 ■ Mon 14 :00-18:30, Sat 9:30-18 :30 ■ Prices medium ■ 15 % professional discount

Everything for the framer: 500 different models of mouldings (baguettes). Papers for mattes and backing. Art papers. They will cut and assemble frames on the spot. Everything supplied for painting on porcelain.

ETS JULLIEN

42 rue Saint-Jacques, 75005 Paris ■ Tel: 01 43 54 52 56 ■ Fax: 01 43 26 16 77 ■ Mon-Fri 8:30-12:00/13:30-18:00, Fri 8:30-17:00 ■ Discount after 10 dozen

Best selection of leather for book-binding.

LE BONHEUR DES DAMES

18 av Daumesnil, 75012 Paris ■ Tel: 01 43 42 06 27 ■ Fax : 01 43 42 06 44 ■ E-mail: bonheurdesdames@wanadoo.fr ■ Web: www.pro.wanadoo.fr(bonheurdesdames) ■ Mon 14:00-19:00, Tue-Sat 10:30-19:00 ■ English spoken ■ Major credit cards

Creation of works in embroidery. Supplies of all materials for embroiderers including kits. Cushions, pictures, Christmas stockings and a collection of miniature Persian carpets. Framing service. Sale by correspondence.

OUVRAGE LA BOÉTIE

29 rue La Boétie, 75008 Paris ■ Tel: 01 42 65 22 84 ■ Fax: 01 40 17 07 36 ■ Mon-Sat 10:00-18:00 ■ Mr. Rividi ■ English, Spanish, Hebrew and Turkish spoken

Manufacturer of all kinds of cottons for upholstery for traditional and contemporary styles of chairs. Table linens. T-shirts embroidered by hand.

♔ RELMA

6 rue Danton, 75006 Paris ■ Tel: 01 43 25 40 52 ■ Fax: 01 43 26 52 94 ■ 3 rue des Poitevins, 75006 Paris ■ Mon-Fri 8:30-12:00/14:00-18:00 ■ English spoken ■ Prices medium ■ Professional discount

Best selection of papers, canvases, leathers, for book binding, leather-working, packaging, framing.

♔ ROUGIER ET PLÉ

13 bd des Filles-du-Calvaire ■ Tel: 01 44 54 81 00 ■ Fax: 01 42 76 03 90 ■ Mon-Sat 9:30-19:00 ■ Web: http://www.rougeretple.fr ■ English spoken ■ Prices reasonable

Everything for the artisan and the artist: the professional and the amateur. Special attention is focussed on simplified products for the amateur. Graphic arts, beaux-arts, restoration, hobbies and crafts. A very large section is devoted to children's crafts.

SENNELIER COULEURS DU QUAI VOLTAIRE

3 quai Voltaire, 75007 Paris ■ Tel: 01 42 60 72 15 ■ Fax: 01 42 61 00 69 ■ E-mail: sennelie@club-internet.fr ■ Web: www.arts-vianet.fr/annonce/magasin.sennelier ■ Tue-Sat 9:00-12:30/14:00-18:30, Mon 14:00-18:30 ■ English, Spanish, Portuguese spoken ■ 10% discount for students in Paris schools ■ Prices medium to high ■ Major credit cards
Also at: 4 bis rue de la Grande Chaumière, 75006 Paris ■ Tel: 01 42 60 29 38

Full selection of artists' materials: paints, pastels, aquarelles, crayons, art papers from all over the world. Canvases for the artist, the graphic artist and designer. A delightful atmosphere.

TEXLIBRIS

34 rue du Sentier, 75002 Paris ■ Tel: 01 42 33 86 97 ■ Fax: 01 42 36 36 67 ■ Web: http://www.texlibris.fr ■ Mon-Fri 9:00-13:00/14:00-17:00 ■ English spoken ■ Prices medium ■ Professional discount

Manufacturer of cloth in over 300 colours and weaves, marbled papers (hand and machine-made), flocked paper, PVC paper, wood-grain printed papers for book binding, stationery, box manufacturing, framing. Acid-free adhesive tape.

ARTISTS' SUPPLIES
Fournitures pour artistes

ADAM MONTPARNASSE
11 bd Edgar-Quinet, 75014 Paris ■ Tel: 01 43 20 68 53 ■ Fax: 01
43 21 23 72 ■ Mon 9:30-12:30/13:30-19:00, Tue-Sat 9:30-19:00
■ English spoken ■ Prices medium ■ 15% discount for students
■ Visa and MC
**Products for the artist and the restorer. Mouldings and hand
turned elements for furniture restoration. Technical books.**

ADAM MONTMARTRE
96 rue Damrémont, 75018 Paris ■ Tel: 01 46 06 60 38 ■ Fax: 01
42 59 06 83 ■ Mon 9:30-12:30/13:30-19:00, Tue-Sat 9:30-19:00
■ English spoken ■ Professional discount ■ 15% discount for students ■ Visa and MC accepted
**All products for the graphic and beaux-arts. Frames and
framing. Models and moulds. Delivery service.**

ARTECH PHOENIX
65-67 rue Moulin des Près, 75013 Paris ■ Tel: 01 45 88 39 39 ■
Fax: 01 45 88 39 00 ■ English spoken ■ Professional discount ■
Major credit cards
**All supplies for the artist, oils, watercolours, papers, canvas,
stretchers.**

♕ **ARTES
BEAUX-ARTS**
26 rue Vavin, 75006 Paris ■ Tel: 01 40 26 47 16 ■ Fax: 01 43 54
61 69 ■ Mon-Sat 10:00-19:00 ■ English spoken ■ Prices medium
**Complete line of supplies for the artist. Best known brands
of colours in oils, aquarelles, acrylics, gouaches, vinyls, pigments. Brushes, easels, canvas and stretchers. Paints for
silk screening and porcelain. Supplies for calligraphy. Papers. Framing supplies. Canvas stretched on order. Porcelain firing. Fixing of silk screens. Art books.**

ARTISTE PEINTRE
54 bd Edgar-Quinet, 75014 Paris ■ Tel: 01 43 22 31 71 ■ Fax: 01
43 22 41 79 ■ Mon-Sat 9:30-19:00 ■ English spoken ■ Prices
low to medium ■ 10% professional discount

Manufacturers of canvas. All artists supplies, wholesale and retail. Brushes, all colours in oils, aquarelles, pastels, gouaches, acrylics.

♔ CHARBONNEL

13 quai de Montebello, 75005 Paris ■ Tel: 01 43 54 23 46 ■ Fax: 01 43 29 94 12 ■ Web: www.lefranc.bourgeois.com ■ For export: COLART Intl. 5 rue René Panhard, 72028 LeMans ■ Tel: 02 43 83 83 00 ■ Fax: 02 43 83 83 29 ■ Intl: 02 43 83 83 15 ■ Visa and MC

Very good quality and a wide range of paints and supplies for artists, engravers and artisans.

CLETON

41 rue Saint Sabin, 75005 Paris ■ Tel : 01 47 00 10 41 ■ Professional discount ■ Major credit cards

Pigments, varnishes, fine colours, abrasives and adhesives, gilding supplies and sculpture tools and supplies.

♔ DUGAY

92 rue des Rosiers, 93400 Saint-Ouen ■ (In the Marché aux Puces) ■ Tel: 01 40 11 87 30 ■ Fax: 01 40 12 26 32 ■ Thurs-Mon 9:00-18:00 ■ Prices reasonable ■ Professional discount

Nearly 2,000 products for artists, artisans, gilders, restorers of furniture and marble, painters of trompe l'oeil. Worth the trip.

LA PALETTE DU FAUBOURG

16 rue du Faubourg-du-Temple, 75011 Paris ■ Tel : 01 48 05 51 85 ■ Open every day and all day ■ Professional discount ■ Visa and MC

Supplies for the graphic and beaux-arts, paper, canvases, stretchers. Everything for the professional and schools.

PAPETERIE DU PONT LEGENDRE

57 rue Legendre, 75017 Paris ■ Tel: 01 47 63 69 90 ■ Fax: 01 47 63 92 40 ■ Mon-Fri 9:30-18:00 ■ English spoken ■ Prices medium ■ Professional discount

Products for the beaux-arts and graphic artist.

PARIS AMERICAN ART

4 rue Bonaparte, 75006 Paris ■ Tel: 01 43 26 79 85 ■ Fax: 01 43 54 33 80 ■ Tue-Sat 10:00-13:00/14:00-18:30 ■ Jo Diamond speaks English ■ Prices medium to high ■ Professional discount

All material for artists: oils, pastels, aquarelles, crayons, brushes, papers, classic canvases, easels, books.

♕ LA REGLE D'OR

47 rue St. Jacques, 70014 Paris ■ Tel: 01 45 65 21 06 ■ Fax: 01 45 81 67 76 ■ Tue-Fri 9:30-12:30/14:00-19:00, Sat 11:00-18:45 ■ Emmanuel Delivet speaks English ■ Prices low ■ Professional discounts ■ Major credit cards

All products for the beaux-arts. Brushes (fine and extra fine). Oils, aquarelles, gouaches, acrylics, pastels, pigments, canvases, stretchers. 76 different choices of prepared or raw canvases. All supplies for restorers. Supplier to the National Museums.

♕ SENNELIER COULEURS DU QUAI VOLTAIRE

3 quai Voltaire, 75007 Paris ■ Tel: 01 42 60 72 15 ■ Fax: 01 42 61 00 69 ■ E-mail: sennelie@club-internet.fr ■ Web: www.arts-vianet.fr/annonce/magasin.sennelier ■ Tue-Sat 9:00-12:30/14:00-18:30, Mon 14:00-18:30 ■ English, Spanish, Portuguese spoken ■ 10% discount for students in Paris schools ■ Prices medium to high ■ Major credit cards
Also at: 4bis rue de la Grande Chaumière, 75006 Paris ■ Tel: 01 42 60 29 38

Full selection of artists' materials: paints, pastels, aquarelles, crayons, art papers from all over the world. Canvases for the artist, the graphic artist and designer. A delightful atmosphere.

──────── **OUTSIDE PARIS** ────────

LA THÉIÈRE DE BOIS

5 bis rue Exelmans, 78000 Versailles ■ Tel: 01 39 53 72 85 ■ Fax: 01 39 51 52 81 ■ Tue-Sat 9:30-18:00 ■ English spoken ■ Prices medium ■ Professional discount ■ Major credit cards

Full line of supplies for artists. Framing services and a training studio in framing. Art papers photo albums. Products for the porcelain artist

BATHROOMS
Salles de bains

BATH BAZAAR
  BATH BAZAAR MADELEINE
  23 bd de la Madeleine, 75001 Paris ■ Tel: 01 40 20 08 50
  BATH BAZAAR VICTOIRES
  2 rue d'Aboukir, 75002 Paris ■ Tel: 01 55 34 37 17
  BATH BAZAAR MONTPARNASSE
  6 av du Maine, 75015 Paris ■ Tel: 01 45 48 89 00
  Mon-Sat 10:00-19:00 ■ English spoken ■ Professional discount ■ Major credit cards

A very large selection of bath accessories, varying in quality and price.

─────────────── III ───────────────

👑 **JACOB DELAFON**
Showroom : Hôtel du Grand Veneur ■ 60 rue de Turenne, 75003 Paris ■ Tel: 01 40 27 04 50 ■ Fax: 01 48 04 91 50 ■ Mon-Fri 9:30-18:30, Sat 10:00-17:30 ■ English spoken ■ Prices medium to high

Everything for bathroom installations. Top quality and beautiful showroom.

─────────────── IV ───────────────

A L'ÉPI D'OR
17 rue des Bernardins, 75005 Paris ■ Tel: 01 46 33 08 47 ■ Tue-Fri 10:00-18:00 ■ Prices medium to high ■ Professional discounts

Antique-style bathrooms and bathroom fittings. Creations and re-editions. Wash-basins, faucets and bathroom accessories.

─────────────── VI ───────────────

BAIN ROSE
11 rue d'Assas, 75006 Paris ■ Tel: 01 42 22 55 85 ■ Fax: 42 22 35 94 ■ Tue-Sat 10:30-13:00/14:00-18:30 ■ English spoken ■ Prices high ■ 10 % professional discount ■ Visa

Bathrooms of 1900 to 1930. Antique and reproduction basins, furniture, faience for the bath in Art Nouveau/Art Deco styles.

BEAUTÉ DIVINE

40 rue Saint-Sulpice, 75006 Paris ■ Tel: 01 43 26 25 31 ■ Mon 14:00-19:00, Tue-Sat 10:00-13:00/14:00-19:00 ■ Mme Claire ■ English spoken ■ Prices medium ■ Professional discount ■ Major credit cards

Wonderful bathroom accessories, old and contemporary. Lighting, lampshades, pillows and decorative objects. Beautiful things.

VIII

CRISTAL ET BRONZE

19 av de Friedland, 75008 Paris ■ Tel: 01 45 61 92 20 ■ Fax: 01 42 25 96 11 ■ E-mail: cristal-et-bronze@wanadoo.fr ■ Mon-Fri 9:30-18:30 ■ Valerie Bataillard ■ English, German and Spanish spoken ■ Prices medium to high ■ Professional discount

Faucets and deluxe accessories for the bathroom. Hand-carved crystal objects: lamps, vases, carafes, glasses and more. Supplier of faucets to the Hotels George V, The Crillon, The Ritz and The Plaza Athenée.

PORCHER

16 Place de la Madeleine, 75008 Paris ■ Tel: 01 42 65 28 07 ■ Fax: 01 99 38 28 28 ■ Mon-Sat 10:00-18:30 ■ English spoken ■ Major credit cards

High quality bathroom fittings and accessories.

XI

CASCADE

26 bd Richard-Lenoir, 75011 Paris ■ Tel: 01 48 06 14 79 ■ Fax: 01 43 38 34 79 ■ E-mail: cascade-bains@free.fr ■ Mon-Sat 9:00-19:00 ■ English spoken ■ Prices high ■ 25% professional discount

Creators of their own high-quality line of bathrooms and accessories, including hydro-massage showers, furniture, decorative hardware in crystal and bronze.

GODIN BATH

6 bd Richard Lenor, 75011 Paris ■ Tel: 01 48 07 88 35 ■ Fax: 01 43 55 17 31 ■ Mon-Sat 10:00-12:30/14:00-19:00 ■ Major credit cards

Good selection for the bathroom and will work on plans.

♕ SERDANELLI

270 rue Lecourbe, 75015 Paris ■ Tel: 01 40 60 13 13 ■ Fax: 01 40 60 98 75 ■ Mon-Fri 9:30-13:00-14:00-18:30 ■ English spoken ■ Prices high ■ Professional discount

Large selection of knobs and levers in semi-precious stones and bronze. Marine finishes. Lots of faucets. They do a lot of yacht installations.

AUX SALLES DE BAINS "RETRO"

29-31 rue des Dames, 75017 Paris ■ Telfax: 01 43 87 88 00 ■ Web: www.perso.wanadoo.fr/sbr ■ Mon-Sat 11:00-19:00 by appointment ■ Vera Beboutoff speaks English ■ Prices low to high ■ 10% professional discount ■ Showroom: Trocadéro 27: rue Benjamin Franklin 75016 Paris ■ Tel: 01 47 27 14 50

Fully-restored antique bathtubs, basins, faucets, bathroom lighting and accessories. Custom-made faucets and copies of antique faucets.

♕ J. DELEPINE

104 bd de Clichy, 75018 Paris ■ Tel: 01 46 06 89 70 ■ Fax: 01 42 23 63 82 ■ Web: www.sogesec.net/j-delepine ■ English spoken ■ Prices medium to very high ■ Professional discount ■ Major credit cards

Extraordinary complete bathroom installations. From the simple to the remarkably luxurious. Cascade faucets, shower enclosures and bathtubs and accessories in faux finishes. Excellent choice of faucets. Mirrors and cabinets.

♕ MEILLEUR

32 rue des Amandiers, 75020 Paris ■ Tel: 01 43 66 45 13 ■ Fax: 01 43 66 45 43 ■ Mon-Fri 8:30-12:00/13:00-18:00 by appointment ■ Catherine Meilleur speaks English ■ Prices high to very high ■ Professional discount

Beautiful selection of faucets in exclusive designs. All types of lighting and small tables. Third generation bronze craftsmen.

GME

12 Addresses on the edge of Paris in all directions.

1.7km from the Porte d'Orleans, 47 avenue Aristide Briand 94117 Arceuil Cedex ■ Tel: 01 49 85 15 19 ■ Porte de la Villette, 70 bld Félix Faure 93300 Aubervilliers ■ Tel: 01 48 39 96 50 ■ Paris La Défense, 15 rue Paul Lescop 92000 Nanterre ■ Tel: 01 47 25 25 30 ■ We suggest you call this number to secure the address of your most convenient outlet ■ Fax: 01 49 85 95 08 ■ Mon to Sat 7:30-18:30 ■ Professional discount ■ Major credit cards

A vast collection of everything for the bath from the most inexpensive to the mid-high range. Tubs, basins, shower enclosures, toilets, bidets, accessories. Tiles, plumbing supplies and accessories. Cabinets of all sizes and angles, mirrors.

BILLIARDS

Billards

---
v

BILLARDS SOULIGNAC
8 rue Bertholet, 75005 Paris ■ Tel: 01 43 31 49 75/Atelier: 01 39 56 25 45 ■ Tue-Fri 10:00-13:00/14:15-19:00, Wed 10:00-13:00/15:00-19:00, Sat l0:00-12:00/14:00-18:00 ■ English and German spoken ■ Prices low ■ Major credit cards

Fabrication of billiard tables and games, all in wood. Restoration and sale of old billiard tables. Skilled furniture-maker who can produce beautiful billiard tables. They also restore furniture and rent on occasion. Oddly enough: they also sell children's books.

DÉCOR D'AUTREFOIS
2 rue Le Chatelier, 75017 Paris ■ Telfax: 01 47 66 46 03 ■ Fax: 01 40 53 80 47 ■ Mon-Fri 10:00-13:00, Afternoons by appointment ■ Some English spoken ■ Prices medium ■ 15% professional discount

Billiard tables and accessories.

BOOKS
Librairies

When you travel in France, especially in Paris, you will find that most French people consider themselves intellectually and culturally superior to almost everyone else on earth. Their system of education, plus the French notion of logical thought bequeathed by Descartes, gives them a sense of security about all this, even though, when they travel, the French soon discover that other great cultures do exist.

But the French do give a great deal of respect to their writers. There has hardly ever been a poet or novelist who does not have a Paris street named for him or a statue erected in his honor. In France, when you have written even one single book, you are revered for life. This is in sharp contrast to America where people ask, "what has he, or she, done lately?"

Books in France are not sold in the same way as they are in America. With few exceptions, Paris bookshops are small, cozy and often dusty and crowded. However, as in London, things are changing with the arrival of super-stores and on-line book-sellers.

English language books are sold in just a few places. If a neighbourhood Parisian bookshop carries current English language books, they will be tucked off in a corner somewhere and are usually the recent best sellers. However, thanks to the fact that Paris has always had a considerable number of American and British expatriates in their midst, there are plenty of second-hand bookshops with marvellous collections.

This section of ALL PARIS begins with antique and rare books and then follows on with the specialty subjects. The authors have tried to select the best shops that carry books dealing with things of interest to the designer, the architect and the discriminating homemaker.

Booksellers
Antique and Rare

III

LIBRAIRIE MUSÉE CARNAVALET
23 rue Sévigné, 75003 Paris ■ Tel: 01 42 74 08 00 ■ Fax: 01 47 74 04 08 ■ Tue-Sun 10:00-17:30 ■ English and Spanish spoken■ Prices medium ■ 5% Professional discount ■ Major credit cards

Books on Paris and a good collection of maps of Paris.

VI

BENELLI
244 rue Saint-Jacques, 75005 Paris ■ Tel: 01 46 33 73 51 ■ Fax: 01 40 51 01 39 ■ Mon-Fri 11:30-18:30, Sat by appointment ■ A little English spoken ■ Prices medium ■ 10% professional discount ■ Major credit cards

Antique books from XV to XIX century. Expert to the Court of Appeals, Paris.

CHRISTIAN GALANTARIS
15 rue des Saints-Pères, 75006 Paris ■ Tel: 01 47 03 49 65 ■ Fax: 01 42 60 42 09 ■ Mon-Fri 10:30-12:00/14:30-18:30 ■ Christian Galantaris speaks English ■ Prices medium to high ■ Professional discount

Antique collectible books. Expert to the Court of Appeals of Paris. Organization of public sales of books internationally.

LIBRAIRIE MICHEL BOUVIER
14 rue Visconti, 75006 Paris ■ Tel: 01 46 34 64 53 ■ Fax: 01 40 46 91 40 ■ By appointment ■ Michel Bouvier speaks English ■ Prices medium

Antique, rare and precious books. Old documents. Qualified expert.

LIBRAIRIE CLAUDE BUFFET
7 rue Saint-Sulpice, 75006 Paris ■ Tel: 01 43 26 61 79 ■ Fax: 01 46 33 51 24 ■ Tue-Sat 10:30-12:30/14:30-18:30 ■ Blanche Buffet speaks English ■ Prices medium ■ Professional discount

French literature from the XIX and XX centuries. Original editions and rare works no longer in print. They will research works on request.

LIBRAIRIE DE L'ABBAYE – PINAULT
27 rue Bonaparte, 75006 Paris ■ Tel: 01 43 54 89 99 ■ Fax: 01 43 29 81 69 ■ Tue-Sat 10:00-12:30/14:00-19:00 and by appointment ■ Régine Bernard speaks English ■ Prices medium to high ■ Professional discount ■ Visa and Amex

Antique books on bibliophilism. Antique books of the XVI to the XVIII centuries. Autographs and manuscripts, autographed musical scores, small-format books, autographed manuscripts. Stock: 5,000 volumes, 30,000 autographs. Jacques-Henri Pinault is an expert to the Court of Appeals, Paris.

LIBRAIRIE LÉONCE LAGET

88 rue Bonaparte, 75006 Paris ■ Tel: 01 43 29 90 04 ■ Fax: 01 43 26 89 68 ■ E-mail: liblaget@wanadoo.fr ■ Web: www.franceantiq.fr/slam/laget ■ Véronique Delvaux, PDG, speaks English ■ Tue-Fri 9:00-13:00/14:00-18:30, Sat 10:00-17:00 ■ Major credit cards

A lovely atmosphere. And a fine collection of rare books, especially on architecture, the fine arts and collectibles.

FERNAND MARTINEZ

97 rue de Seine, 75006 Paris ■ Tel: 01 46 33 08 12 ■ Mon-Sat 10:00-18:30 ■ Prices medium ■ 10% professional discount

Antique prints, engravings and original lithographs on France and other countries. Old maps, some old books and framed engravings.

NEUF MUSES

41 quai des Grands Augustins, 75006 Paris ■ Tel: 01 43 26 38 71 ■ Fax: 01 43 26 06 11 ■ Mon-Fri 14:00-18:30, Mornings and Sat by appointment ■ Alain Nicolas speaks English ■ Prices medium ■ Professional discount ■ Major credit cards

Antique books, autographs and manuscripts. Qualified expert to the Court of Appeals, Paris.

LE PONT TRAVERSÉ

62 rue de Vaugirard, 75006 Paris ■ Tel: 01 45 48 06 48 ■ Tue-Fri 12:00-19:00, Sat 15:00-19:00 ■ Some English and Spanish spoken■ Prices medium ■ Professional discount

Rare books of poetry, literature, beaux-arts. Original and out-of-print editions.

LIBRAIRIE THOMAS SCHELER

19 rue de Tournon, 75006 Paris ■ Tel: 01 43 26 97 68 ■ Fax: 01 40 46 91 46 ■ E-mail: basane@aol.com ■ Mon-Sat 10:00-13:00/14:30-19:00 ■ Bernard Clavreuil ■ English and Spanish spoken ■ Visa

Rare books of the XV to the XIX century particularly on science, medicine,voyages, French literature. A catalogue published three times a year.

LIBRAIRIE VALETTE

11 rue de Vaugirard, 75006 Paris ■ Tel: 01 43 26 45 64 ■ Fax: 01 46 33 62 98 ■ Pierre Dreyfus ■ English spoken

Rare books and manuscripts in French literature from the XVI to the XX century. Bindings.

L'OR DU TEMPS

25 rue de l'Echaudé, 75006 Paris ■ Tel: 01 43 25 66 66 ■ Fax: 01 44 07 08 70 ■ Web: www.galaxiedion.com ■ Mon-Sat 13:00-19:30 ■ Pierre Rojanski ■ English spoken ■ 10% professional discount ■ Visa

Books of old literature and specialized books on Surrealism and Dadaism. Catalogues available.

─────────── VII ───────────

LIBRAIRIE ELBE

213 bd Saint-Germain, 75007 Paris ■ Tel: 01 45 48 77 97 ■ Fax: 01 45 48 73 67 ■ Tue-Sat 10:00-13:00/14:00-18:30 ■ J.L. Bonvallet Speaks English ■ Prices medium ■ Major credit cards

Old and rare books especially on the subjects of the hunt, horses and racing. Also posters, postcards and Paris city views.

LIBRAIRIE DE LATTRE

56 rue de l'Université, 75007 Paris ■ Tel: 01 45 44 75 30 ■ Fax: 01 45 44 83 53 ■ Mon-Fri 10:30-13:00/14:00-19:00 ■ Marché Vernaison, Marché aux Puces, 99 rue des Rosiers, 93400 Saint-Ouen ■ Tel: 01 40 12 68 89 ■ Sat-Mon 9:30-18:00 ■ Dominique and Marie-Ange de Lattre speaks English, Spanish and German ■ Prices medium ■ 10% professional discount ■ Major credit cards

Extraordinary collection of posters and books of the XIX and XX centuries. Theatre and film publicity, advertising, illustrations. Old books on the beaux-arts, travel, fashion, children's books.

─────────── VIII ───────────

LIBRAIRIE BERÈS

14 av de Friedland, 75008 Paris ■ Tel: 01 45 61 00 99 ■ Fax: 01 43 59 79 13 ■ Mon-Sat 9:00-12:30/14:00-18:00 ■ Pierre Berès ■ English, German, Dutch and Italian spoken ■ Prices high

Rare books.

♛ LIBRAIRIE AUGUSTE BLAIZOT

164 rue du Faubourg-Saint-Honoré ■ 75008 Paris ■ Tel: 01 43 59 36 58 ■ Fax: 01 42 25 90 27 ■ E-mail: blaizot@wanadoo.fr ■ Web: www.franceantiq.fr/slam/blaizot ■ Tue-Sat 9:30-12:30/14:00-18:30 ■ Claude Blaizot ■ English spoken ■ Prices medium to high ■ 10% professional discount ■ Visa

Antique and modern books, original editions, illustrated books. Specialty: rare and precious editions of French literature. Beautiful bindings, classical and very special contemporary.

JADIS ET NAGUÈRE

166 rue du Faubourg-Saint-Honoré, 75008 Paris ■ Tel: 01 43 59 40 52 ■ Fax: 01 45 62 93 54 ■ Mon-Fri 11:00-19:00, Sat 14:00-19:00 ■ English spoken ■ Professional discount

Books of the XVI to XX centuries, beautifully bound. Bibliophilism. Watercolours, Art Nouveau and Art Deco drawings and engravings.

LIBRAIRIE LARDANCHET

100 rue du Faubourg-Saint-Honoré, 75008 Paris ■ Tel: 42 66 68 32 ■ Fax: 01 49 24 07 87 ■ E-mail: lardan@club-internet.fr ■ Web: www.franceantiq.fr/lardanchet ■ Mon-Sat 9:30-19:00 ■ English spoken ■ Prices high ■ Visa and Amex

Antique and Modern books, documents on the beaux-arts. Superbly bound.

LIBRAIRIE HENRI PICARD ET FILS

126 rue du Faubourg-Saint-Honoré, 75008 Paris ■ Tel: 01 43 59 28 11 ■ Fax: 01 43 59 04 02 ■ E-mail: hpicard@worldnet.fr ■ Mon-Sat 10:00-20:00 ■Some English spoken ■ Prices medium ■ 10% professional discount ■ Major credit cards

Founded in 1860. High quality antique and modern books, engravings and prints. Books of bibliophilism. Children's books.

JEAN CHRÉTIEN

178 rue du Faubourg-Saint-Honoré, 75008 Paris ■ Tel: 01 45 63 52 66 ■ Fax: 01 45 63 65 87

Literature, biography of the XVII to the XIX century. Beautifully bound books. M. Jean Chrétien is an expert to the Court of Appeals in Paris.

───────────── IX ─────────────

♔ LIBRAIRIE CHAMONAL

5 rue Drouot, 75009 Paris ■ Tel 01 47 70 84 87 ■ Fax: 01 42 46 35 47 ■ E-mail: chamonal@club-internet.fr ■ Mon-Fri 9:00-18:30, Sat 9:00-12:00 call first on Sat ■ English and Italian spoken ■ Prices low to high ■ Professional discount ■ Visa, Amex

Rare and precious books from the XV to the late XIX centuries, mainly in French. Specializing in marine, voyages, medicine, science, gastronomy. Beautiful bindings.

AU VIEUX DOCUMENT

6 bis rue de Chateaudun, 75009 Paris ■ Tel: 01 48 78 77 84 ■ Fax: 01 48 78 18 84 ■ Mon-Fri 10:30-12:00/14:00-18:00 ■ Foucauld Bachelier speaks English ■ Prices medium ■ 10% professional discount ■ Major credit cards

Antique and modern books: literature, beaux-arts, travel, leisure, sports, gastronomy. Framing for old engravings and prints.

LES FLEURS DU MAL

24 rue Chaligny, 75012 Paris ■ Tel: 01 43 40 63 34 ■ Mon-Sat 14:30-20:00 ■ Prices low ■ Professional discount

Antique and second-hand books.

LES FLEURS DU MAL

7 rue Auguste-Bartholdi, 75015 Paris ■ Telfax: 01 40 59 88 46 ■ E-mail: pagesvolantes@easynet.fr ■ Tue-Sat 12:00-19:00 ■ Prices medium ■ Professional discount for bookshops ■ Major credit cards

Antique and modern books. Specialty: Research on out-of-print books and specialized subjects. Beautiful old illustrated children's books.

LIVRES DE A TO Z

3 rue des Moines, 75017 Paris ■ Telfax: 01 42 29 49 19 ■ Mon-Sat 10:30-13:00/14:00-19:00 ■ E-mail: livresaz@club-internet.fr ■ English spoken ■ Prices medium ■ 10 to 20% professional discount ■ Major credit cards

Books of the XIX and XX centuries: Literature, beaux-arts, history. Research service offered free.

Architecture,
Fine Arts & Decoration

LIBRAIRIE DE L'AMEUBLEMENT ET DE LA DECORATION

23 rue Joubert, 75009 Paris ■ Tel: 01 42 82 09 21 ■ Fax: 01 40 16 43 65 ■ Mon-Fri 12:00-19:00 ■ Danielle Tétard ■ Prices medium ■ Professional discount ■ Visa and MC

Excellent collection of contemporary books on woods, furniture styles, interior architecture and design, antiques, art objects and collectibles. Sale by correspondence and free catalogue available on request. If they don`t have it they will know where to find it. Extremely helpful.

♔ LIBRAIRIE DES ANTIQUAIRES
Le Louvre des Antiquaires (street level) ■ 2 place du Palais-Royal, 75001 Paris ■ Tel: 01 42 61 56 79 ■ Tue-Sat 11:00-19:00 ■ Prices medium ■ 5% professional discount ■ Major credit cards

Books on antiques, collectibles, decoration, XVIII and XIX century furniture, art objects, Art Deco. Most in French, a few in English.

ARCHIVES LIBRAIRIE
52 rue Mazarine, 75006 Paris ■ Tel: 01 43 54 12 64 ■ Fax: 01 40 46 84 22 ■ Tue-Sat 14:00-19:00 ■ English spoken ■ Prices medium to high ■ Professional discount ■ Major credit cards

XX century books, all documentation and samples of architecture, decorative arts, beaux-arts. 2 or 3 catalogues available every year.

GALERIE ARENTHON
3 quai Malaquais, 75006 Paris ■ Tel: 01 43 26 86 06 ■ Fax: 01 43 26 62 08 ■ E-mail: arenthon@easynet.fr ■ Mon-Fri 8:30-12:30/15:00-19:00, Sat closed 18:00 ■ English and Italian spoken ■ Prices medium ■ Major credit cards

XX century illustrated books, reference books on artists, documentation on engravings and a good poster collection.

JEAN-LOUIS BARBERY
2 rue des Grands Degrès, 75005 Paris ■ Tel: 01 43 25 33 76 ■ Tue-Sat 13:00-19:00 and by appointment ■ Annick Barbery speaks English ■ Prices medium ■ l0% professional discount ■ Traveller cheques.

XIX and XX century books and prints. Books on the beaux-arts: painters, engravers, architecture, fabrics, etc. Original editions. Antique and modern prints: Architecture, views, artists engravings. Japanese prints.

LIBRAIRIE DU CAMÉE
70 rue Saint-André des Arts, 75006 Paris ■ Tel: 01 43 26 21 70 ■ Fax: 01 43 29 38 88 ■ Mon-Sat 11:00-17:45 ■ Prices medium

Old and contemporary books on trades, artisanat, decoration, architecture, decorative arts, beaux-arts.

♔ LIBRAIRIE DU COMPAGNONNAGE
2 rue de Brosse, 75004 Paris ■ Tel: 01 48 87 88 14 ■ Fax: 01 48 04 85 49 ■ Mon-Fri 11:00-18:30, Sat 14:00-18:00 ■ English spoken ■ Prices medium ■ Major credit cards

Works on the specialized building trades, restoration and decoration. "How to" books on every discipline including artisanat and architecture. Sale by correspondence. Catalogue upon request.

LIBRAIRIE DU COMPAGNONNAGE (MUSEUM)
10 rue Mabillon, 75006 Paris ■ Tel: 01 43 26 25 03 ■ Mon-Fri 14:00-18:00 (closed from 07/14 to 09/15)

This museum representing the building trades, stonemasons, master carpenters, roofers, plumbers, zinc workers, ebenistes and metalworkers displays the qualifying models "Les chefs-d'Oeuvre" of apprentices who then become members of the Guilds (Compagnons). Some books on these trades are available in French. Discs and cassettes on the songs of the Compagnon.

LIBRAIRIE DU CYGNE
17 rue Bonaparte, 75006 Paris ■ Tel: 01 43 26 32 45 ■ Fax: 01 43 26 92 68 ■ Mon-Fri 10:00-12:00/14:30-19:00 and by appointment ■ Prices medium ■ 10% professional discount

Old books on decorative arts, books of fabric samples, drawings and decorative panels.

👑 LIBRAIRIE BOUTIQUE RMN
10 rue de l'Abbaye, 75006 Paris ■ Tel: 01 43 29 21 45 ■ Fax: 01 43 29 66 53 ■ Mon 10:30-13:00/14:30-18:30, Tue-Fri 10:00-18:30, Sat 10:30-18:30 ■ English spoken ■ Publishers and journalists discounts ■ Major credit cards

Outlet for all the exhibition books: works produced by the National Museums.
Catalogue available and sale by correspondence. Youths' section, multi-media and a gift shop.

F.M.R.
FRANCO MARIA RICCI
12 rue des Beaux-Arts, 75006 Paris ■ Tel: 01 46 33 96 31 ■ Fax: 01 43 25 79 06 ■ e-mail: fmr.ba.yd@wanadoo.fr ■ Tue-Sat 10:00-13:00/14:30-19:00 ■ English spoken ■ Prices medium ■ 10% professional discount ■ Major credit cards

Contemporary books on architecture, art, design and decoration.

👑 BIBLIOTHEQUE FORNEY
1 rue Figuier, 75004 Paris ■ Tel: 01 42 78 14 60 ■ Tue-Fri 13:30-20:30, Sat 10:00-20:00 ■ English spoken

The beautiful old Hotel de Sens. Extensive collection of works on architecture, applied arts. decorative arts, interior decoration, gardens and landscaping. Fabulous collection of antique books. Favorite research hangout for the dedicated professional and students of art, decoration, design and architecture. Books for reference and not for sale but they do have copy service. Worth a visit.

LIBRAIRIE LECOINTRE DROUET

9 rue de Tournon, 75006 Paris ■ Tel: 01 43 26 02 92 ■ Fax: 01 46 33 11 40 ■ Tue-Sat 10:00-19:00, Sat closing 18:00 ■ English spoken ■ Prices medium ■ Professional discount ■ Visa

Books dating from the beginning of the XIX century to just prior to the second world war, specializing in architecture and decorative and applied arts. In all languages.

♛ LIBRAIRIE LÉONCE LAGET

88 rue Bonaparte, 75006 Paris ■ Tel: 01 43 29 90 04 ■ Fax: 01 43 26 89 68 ■ E-mail: liblaget@wanadoo.fr ■ Web: www.franceantiq.fr/slam/laget ■ Véronique Delvaux, PDG, speaks English ■ Tue-Fri 9:00-13:00/14:00-18:30, Sat 10:00-17:00 ■ Major credit cards

Excellent collection of rare old and contemporary editions on the history of art, ancient and modern, from the beginning to now: architecture, painting, sculpture, costumes, ceramics, beaux-arts and applied arts.

LIBRAIRIE MAEGHT

42 rue du Bac, 75007 Paris ■ Tel: 01 45 48 45 15 ■ Fax: 01 42 22 22 83 ■ E-mail: galerie.maeght@noos.fr ■ Tue-Sat 9:30-19:00 ■ Prices from a few francs for a postcard to a Braque lithograph for FF100,000.00 ■ English spoken ■ 10 to 30% professional discount ■ Major credit cards

Beautiful books on art, large collection of catalogues of exhibitions of Foundation Maeght. Art editions, lithographs, modern and contemporary artists' posters, Braque, Chagall, Miro, Calder, Giacometti, Léger and others. Monographs and engravings.

♛ LIBRAIRIE DU MUSÉE DES ARTS DECORATIFS

105-107 rue de Rivoli, 75001 Paris ■ Tel: 01 42 96 21 31 ■ Fax: 01 42 96 23 75 ■ Mon-Sun 10:00-19:00, Wed 10:00-21:00 ■ Major credit cards ■ English spoken .

A treasure house for the period 1900 to 1930 and all other periods covering architecture, design, furniture, plastic arts, beauxarts, fabric designs, decorative hardware, table arts, gardens - all possible areas of decoration. Sale by correspondence.
NOTE: Just next door you will find the Bibliothèque (Library) of the Musée des Arts Decoratifs. It is the repository of just about everything in the vast history of French decoration. You are perfectly welcome to use the facility for research as long as you provide ID. Unfortunately it is undergoing extensive renovations but will open shortly.

LIBRAIRIE F. DE NOBELE

35 rue Bonaparte, 75006 Paris ■ Tel: 01 43 26 08 62 ■ Fax: 01 40 46 85 96 ■ Mon-Fri 9:00-12:00/14:00-19:00 ■ English spoken ■ Prices low to very high ■ Professional discount ■ Major credit cards

Antique and modern books on the arts: architecture, painting, applied arts, furniture, decoration.

OUTREMER

Librairie Maritime ■ 17 rue Jacob, 75006 Paris ■ Tel: 01 46 33 47 48 ■ Fax: 01 43 29 96 77 ■ E-mail: outremer@librairie-outremer.com ■ Web: Http://www.librairie-outremer.com ■ Mon-Sat 10:00-19:00 ■ Prices medium to high ■ Professional discount ■ Major credit cards.

Books dealing mainly with the former French colonies, especially the islands of the Caribbean and Pacific.

LIBRAIRIE LE PETIT PRINCE

121 bd Saint-Michel, 75005 Paris ■ Tel: 01 43 54 45 60 ■ Fax: 01 40 51 07 51 ■ E-mail: lepetiprice@easynet.fr ■ Mon-Sat 9:30-19:00 ■ Sylvie Moussaian ■ English and Russian spoken ■ Professional discount ■ Visa

Books for collectors: XVII to XIX century books on the beaux-arts and related subjects and literature. Some contemporary books on the fine and applied arts.

GALERIE DE LA SORBONNE

52 rue des Écoles, 75005 Paris ■ Tel: 01 43 25 52 10 ■ Mon-Sat 10:30-19:30 ■ 1 square Paul Painlevé 75005 Paris ■ Tel: 01 46 33 83 69 ■ Prices medium ■ Professional discount

Extensive collection of second-hand books on architecture of all schools, particularly XX century. Famous architects from Haussmann to the great masters of today. They also have other sections dealing with the humanities, literature, poetry, theatre, music and dance.

LIBRAIRIE VISIONS

184 bd Saint-Germain, 75006 Paris ■ Telfax: 01 45 48 77 91 ■ Web: www.apertolibro.com ■ Tue-Sat 10:30-19:00 ■ English and German spoken ■ Professional discount ■ Major credit cards

Excellent collection of art books at reasonable prices. Books on painting, sculpture, drawing, decorative arts, photography.

XXè SIÈCLE ET SES SOURCES

4 rue Aubry-le-Boucher, 75004 Paris ■ Tel: 01 42 78 15 49 ■ Fax: 01 42 78 47 90 ■ Mon 14:30-18:30, Tue-Fri 10:30-12:30/14:30-18:30, Sat 14:30-18:30 ■ Yves Toutut ■ Prices medium ■ 10% professional discount on old books ■ Major credit cards

Antique and recent reference books and documentation on art, architecture and decoration between 1870 and the present day.

LIBRAIRIE ARTCURIAL
61, avenue Montaigne 75008 Paris ■ Tel: 01 42 99 16 16 ■ Fax: 01 42 99 16 10 ■ Web: www.artcurial.com ■ Tue-Sat 10:30-19:00 ■ English spoken ■ Prices high

Rare books as well as contemporary publications: books on artists and their works. Books on decoration, the graphic arts, design, sculpture, photography and civilization.

Animation & Comics

L'AGE D'OR
59 and 61 rue Raymond-Losserand, 75014 ■ Tel: 01 42 79 89 89 ■ Tue-Sat 15:30-19:30

Old comic strips and old works for children, albums, documents and illustrated books 1920-1960. Jean-Louis Duriez is President of the Chambre Européenne Syndicale des Antiquaires Reunis et Experts en Bandes Dessinées et Papiers Anciens, la "C.E.S.A.R."

ALBUM
6 rue Dante, 75005 Paris ■ Tel: 01 43 54 67 09 ■ Web: www.album.fr ■ Tue-Sat 10:00-20:00 ■ English spoken ■ Prices medium ■ Professional discount ■ major credit cards

American comic books and English language comic strips from the sixties to the present, movie magazines and books on cinema.

AUX LIVRES D'ALESIA
13 rue Daval, 75011 Paris ■ Telfax: 01 47 00 98 77 ■ Mon-Sat 14:30-19:00 ■ Prices medium ■ Professional discount
Interesting collection of 1920 to the present, American and French comic strips, children's books and books on scouting.

LIBRAIRIE ROLAND BURET
6 passage Verdeau, 75009 Paris ■ Tel: 01 47 70 62 99 ■ Fax: 01 42 46 00 75 ■ Tue-Fri 12:15-18:45 ■ Roland Buret ■ English spoken ■ Prices high ■ Visa

Cartoon art: old comic strips and original cartoon cells. Albums, old newspapers with original comic strips.

FANTASMAK
17 rue de Belzunce, 75010 Paris ■ Tel: 01 48 78 72 44 ■ Tue-Sat 15:30-19:00

1950's and 1960's comic strips. Old detective and mystery novels. Cinema posters.

LIBRAIRIE NATION

4 bd de Charonne, 75020 Paris ■ Tel: 01 43 73 01 04 ■ Fax: 01 43 70 42 93 ■ E-mail: lib_nat@club-internet.fr ■ Web: www.bd-net.com ■ Mon-Sat 10:00-19:00 ■ Gilles and Marc speak English ■ They have a frequent-buyer card ■ Visa

Substantial collection of French cartoons and comic strips. Original cells and drawings, quite often signed by the author. They also bind comic strips and have them autographed at no extra charge. Occasionally have on offer cartoons from other countries.

ODYSSÉE

160 av Parmentier, 75010 Paris ■ Tel: 01 42 40 10 68 ■ Mon-Fri 11:00-19:30, Sat 14:30-19:30 ■ Prices low ■ English spoken

Second-hand books, rare and out-of-print. Specialties: comic strips, detective and mystery novels, science fiction, fantastic stories; psychoanalysis, psychology, pedagogy; contemporary literature. Cinema.

AUX FILMS DU TEMPS

8 rue Saint-Martin, 75004 Paris ■ Tel: 01 42 71 93 48 ■ Fax: 01 42 71 94 84 ■ Mon 14:00-19:30, Tue-Sat 11:30-19:30 ■ English spoken ■ Prices medium ■ 5% professional discount ■ Major credit cards

Old and recent books in English and French on all aspects of the cinema, photos and posters. Sale by correspondence.

Arms & Military

ARMES ET COLLECTIONS

19 av de la République, 75011 Paris ■ Tel: 01 47 00 68 72 ■ Fax: 01 40 21 97 55 ■ Mon 12:00-19:00, Tue-Sat 10:00-19:00 ■ English spoken ■ Prices medium ■ Professional discount ■ Major credit cards

Vast collection of books, of which 75% are in English, on arms, uniforms, conflicts, military and utilitarian vehicles. Video-cassettes on planes, wars, elite forces.

Contemporary

F.M.R. FRANCO MARIA RICCI
12 rue des Beaux-Arts, 75006 Paris ■ Tel: 01 46 33 96 31 ■ Fax:
01 43 25 79 06 ■ E-mail: fmr.ba.yd@wanadoo.fr ■ Tue-Sat
10:00-13:00/14:30-19:00 ■ English spoken ■ Prices in all ranges
■ Major credit cards
**Special art editions, broad collection of works in French,
English and Spanish on architecture, artists and painting.**

FLAMMARION
19 rue Racine, 75006 Paris ■ Tel: 01 43 29 12 52 ■ Fax: 01 43
26 47 81 ■ Mon-Fri 9:30-13:00/14:15-18:30 ■ Prices medium ■
Professional discount
**The retail outlet for this large publisher, distributor. They also op-
erate the bookshops in several of the Paris Museums, including
the Musée des Arts Decoratifs (Museum of the Decorative Arts)
on the rue de Rivoli. Their publications include every aspect of
architecture and design as well as a broad range of other subjects. There are only a few works in English.**

FNAC FORUM
1 rue Pierre-Lescot, 75001 Paris ■ Parking Forum des Halles,
Sud, Porte Berger ■ Tel: 01 40 41 40 00 ■ Fax: 01 40 41 40 86 ■
Web: www.fnac.com ■ Mon-Sat 10:00-19:30 ■ English spoken ■
Prices medium ■ Major credit cards
**A supermarket of bookstores. Run on the same principles as
an American chain, there is, in this location, a good collection
of works on the beaux-arts as well as a vast general offering
in all other subject areas. FNAC have several locations.**

GALLIMARD
15 bd Raspail, 75007 Paris ■ Tel: 01 45 48 24 84 ■ Fax: 01 42
84 16 97 ■ E-mail: lib.gallimard@wanadoo.fr ■ Mon-Sat 10:00-
19:00 ■ English spoken ■ Prices medium ■ Professional discount ■ Major credit cards
**Fine selection of works on the beaux-arts and decoration in
the French language. Mme Berthaume is the specialist.**

GIBERT-JEUNE
5 place Saint-Michel, 75005 Paris ■ Tel: 01 56 81 22 22 ■ Fax:
01 56 81 21 51 ■ E-mail: info@gibertjeune.fr ■ Web: www.gib-
ertjeune.fr ■ Mon-Sat 9:00-19:30 ■ English spoken ■ Prices
medium ■ Professional discount
**This well-known Latin Quarter institution for students of all
ages has a special section devoted to decoration and the
beaux-arts. Well worth exploring as you will find works in
English and a splendid collection in French.**

LIBRAIRIE DU DICTIONNAIRE

98 bd du Montparnasse, 75014 Paris ■ Tel: 01 43 22 12 93 ■ Fax: 01 43 22 01 77 ■ E-mail: lamaison@artinternet.fr ■ Web: www.imdd.com ■ Mon-Sat 9:15-18:30 ■ Michel Feutry ■ English spoken ■ 5% professional discount ■ Major credit cards

A vast collection of dictionaries of all specialties in all languages. A catalogue of 5,000 titles available. They ship all over the world. They have a CD-ROM available and sell on-line.

LIBRAIRIES FLAMMARION 4 – LA MAISON RUSTIQUE

26 rue Jacob, 75006 Paris ■ Tel: 01 42 34 96 60 ■ Fax: 01 42 34 96 62 ■ Mon-Sat 10:00-19:00 ■ Olivier Pochard ■ English and Persian spoken ■ 5% professional discount ■ Major credit cards

Special books on decoration, gardens, botany, floral art, cookbooks, books on wine, etc. A play space for kids available. Free catalogues and shipping to all parts of the world.

LIBRAIRIE LA HUNE

170 bd Saint-Germain, 75006 Paris ■ Tel: 01 45 48 35 85 ■ Fax: 01 45 44 49 87 ■ Mon-Sat 10:00-23:45 ■ English spoken ■ Prices medium ■ Professional discount ■ Major credit cards

Ask for Mr. Pajaud. He runs the section on architecture, decorative arts, graphics and interior design with works in many languages, including English.

Gastronomy & Oenology

LIBRAIRIE GOURMANDE

4 rue Dante, 75005 Paris ■ Tel: 01 43 54 37 27 ■ Fax: 01 43 54 31 16 ■ Web: www.librairie-gourmande.fr ■ 7 days a week 10:00-19:00 ■ English spoken ■ Prices medium ■ Professional discount ■ Major credit cards (except Amex and Diners)

From the XVI century to today, books on food and wine. Some in English.

LIBRAIRIE REMI FLACHARD

9 rue du Bac, 75007 Paris ■ Telfax: 01 42 86 86 87 ■ Mon-Fri 10:30-12:30/14:30-18:30 ■ Prices high ■ Professional discount

Antique and recent works on gastronomy and oenology from the XV century to the present.

LA LIBRAIRIE DES GOURMETS
98 rue Monge, 75005 Paris ■ Tel: 01 43 31 16 42 ■ Fax: 01 43 31 60 32 ■ Mon-Sat 10:30-19:00 ■ Web: www.librairie-des-gourmets.com ■ English spoken ■ Prices average ■ 5% discount to holders of Carte de Fidélité ■ Major credit cards

Recent works and re-editions of books from 200 B.C. to the present. From Apicius to the great chefs of today.

History

BOUTIQUE DE L'HISTOIRE
24 rue des Écoles, 75005 Paris ■ Tel: 01 46 34 03 36 ■ Fax: 01 43 26 83 96 ■ E-mail: bhistoire@compuserve.com ■ Web: www.bhistoire.com ■ Mon 14:00-19:00, Tue-Sat 9:00-19:00 ■ Pierre and Michelle Borella speak English ■ Prices medium ■ Professional discount ■ Major credit cards

New and second-hand books on history from all parts of the world. Will sell by correspondence.

♛ **LIBRAIRIE HISTORIQUE CLAVREUIL**
37 rue Saint-André-des-Arts, 75006 Paris ■ Tel: 01 43 26 71 17 ■ Fax: 01 43 54 95 37 ■ Tue-Fri 10:00-13:00/14:00-19:00, Mon and Sat 10:00-13:00/14:00-18:00 ■ English spoken ■ Prices average ■ Professional discount ■ Major credit cards

This splendid old bookshop specializes in the history of France from the VI century to the end of the XIX century. Books in all languages date from the XV century. They will undertake heraldic research. They have a good selection of works on the beaux-arts. They also specialize in the military arts, relating to the French revolution and the Napoleonic wars.

Orientalism

LIBRAIRIE ORIENTALISTE PAUL GEUTHNER
12 rue Vavin, 75006 Paris ■ Tel: 01 46 34 71 30 ■ Fax: 01 43 29 75 64 ■ E-mail: Geuthner@geuthner.com ■ Web: www.geuthner.com ■ English spoken ■ Mon 14:00-18:30 Tue-Fri 9:00-12:30/14:00-18:30 ■ Professional discount ■ Major credit cards

Antique books on archaeology, linguistics, history of religions, ethnology of the Mediterranean, Caucasion Central Asia, India, Tibet, the Far East, Black Africa, the Americas and the Hebraic and Islamic worlds.

Sciences

BERNARD MAILLE
3 rue Dante, 75005 Paris ■ Tel: 01 43 25 51 73 ■ Mon-Fri 14:00-18:00 ■ Bernard Maille speaks English ■ 10% professional discount to bookstores ■ Visa

Antique books on the exact sciences (mathematics, physics, chemistry), natural science, medicine. Catalogues published in all these categories.

FABRICE BAYARRE
21 rue de Tournon, 75006 Paris ■ Tel: 01 43 54 91 99 ■ Fax: 01 43 54 58 78 ■ Fabrice Bayarre speaks English ■ Prices medium ■ 10% professional discount

Antique books on the sciences and medicine.

L'INTERSIGNE LIVRES ANCIENS
66 rue du Cherche-Midi, 75006 Paris ■ Tel: 01 45 44 24 54 ■ Fax: 01 45 44 50 55 ■ E-mail: tersign@cybercable.fr ■ Web: www.slam-livre.fr/tersign ■ Mon-Fri 14:00-18:30 and by appointment ■ Alain and Nevine Marchiset speak English ■ Prices medium ■ 10% professional discount ■ Visa and master cards

Antique books, documents concerning the sciences, medicine, philosophy, Freemasonry, occult sciences, curiosities. Orders by correspondence. Five new illustrated catalogues per year upon request.

Sports

LIBRAIRIE DES ALPES
6 rue de Seine, 75006 Paris ■ Tel: 01 43 26 90 11 ■ Fax: 01 44 07 03 66 ■ Tue-Fri 10:30-12:30/14:30-19:00, Sat 10:00-17:00 ■ English spoken ■ Prices medium

Old and recent books, engravings and posters on alpinism and speleology. First editions of works by Jules Verne.

"LE SPORTSMAN"
7 bis rue Henri-Duchêne, 75015 Paris ■ Telfax: 01 45 79 38 93 ■ Friday 11:00-20:00 and by appointment ■ Prices high

Antique documentation on sports: Books, reviews, photos, programmes, posters, etc.

Voyages

LIBRAIRIE DUDRAGNE
86 rue de Maubeuge, 75010 Paris ■ Tel: 01 48 78 50 95 ■ Fax: 01 40 05 98 04 ■ Mon-Fri 9:00-13:00/14:00-18:00, Sat by appointment ■ Patrick Dudragne speaks English ■ Prices medium ■ 5 to 10% professional discount

XVI to XIX century books and engravings on voyages to all parts of the world. Maps and atlases of this period. Decorative prints.

LIBRAIRIE LEPERT ET SCHELER
42 rue Jacob, 75006 Paris ■ Tel: 01 42 61 42 70 ■ Fax: 01 42 61 46 03 ■ E-mail: lepert@club-internet.fr ■ Wed-Sat 15:00-18:00 and by appointment ■ Lucie Scheler speaks English ■ Prices medium ■ Professional discount ■ Major credit cards

Antique and rare editions specializing in voyages to all parts of the world.

LA TROISIEME VEILLE
40 rue Milton, 75009 Paris ■ Tel: 01 40 16 13 87 ■ Tue-Sat 10:00-13:30/15:00-19:30 ■ Michel Sarlin speaks English ■ Prices medium ■ 10% professional discount

Antique and modern books especially on voyages.

English language books

ABBEY BOOKSHOP- LIBRAIRIE CANADIENNE
29 rue de la Parcheminerie, 75005 Paris ■ Tel: 01 46 33 16 24 ■ Fax: 01 46 33 03 33 ■ E-mail: abparis@compuserve.com ■ Web: www.ourworld.compuserve.com/homepages/abaparis ■ Mon-Sat 11:00-20:00 ■ Brian Spence ■ English German and Italian spoken ■ Prices medium ■ Major credit cards

Books from all parts of Canada, the United States, and Great Britain : English, American; new and out-of-print. Bibliographic research and sale by correspondence. Orders taken for all Canadian, Quebecois, and Anglo-American works. Second-hand books. Objets du Canada.

♛ BRENTANO'S

37 av de l'Opéra, 75002 Paris ■ Tel: 01 42 61 52 50 ■ Fax: 01 42 61 07 61 ■ E-mail: brentanos@brentanos.fr ■ Web: www.brentanos.fr ■ Mon-Sat 10:00-19:30 ■ English spoken ■ Prices medium ■ Professional discount ■ Major credit cards (except Diners, minimum of 300FF for Amex).

Excellent English/French language bookshop with all the latest. Good selection of current books on the beaux-arts, antiques, decoration, history, current affairs, current biography. Most of the books on antiques, furniture and decoration are in French. The latest American magazines and a special department for English language videos and audio cassettes. A touch of Fifth Avenue in Paris.

♛ GALIGNANI

224 rue de Rivoli, 75001 Paris ■ Tel: 01 42 60 76 07 ■ Fax: 01 42 86 09 31 ■ E-mail: galignani@gofornet.com ■ Web: www;aligastore.fr ■ Mon-Sat 10:00-19:00 ■ English spoken ■ Prices medium ■ Professional discount ■ Major credit cards

Anglo-American-French bookstore with an excellent and broad collection on all subjects. The latest works of fiction and non-fiction. Their beaux-arts section is international with many works in English. Sale by correspondence to all countries.

♛ SAN FRANCISCO BOOK COMPANY

17 rue Monsieur le-Prince, 75006 Paris ■ Tel: 01 43 29 15 70 ■ Fax: 01 43 29 52 48 ■ E-mail: sfbooks@easynet.fr ■ Mon-Sat 11:00-21:00, Sun 14:00-21:00 ■ L.P. Wood (also ask for Phil) ■ English spoken ■ 10% professional discount ■ Visa and MC for orders over 1,000 French Francs or for internet orders.

Marvellous dynamic selection of second-hand books, especially English and American literature, books on music, jazz, history. A great browsing section of paper-back books.

♛ W. H. SMITH

248 rue de Rivoli, 75001 Paris ■ Tel: 01 44 77 88 99 ■ Fax: 01 42 96 83 71 ■ E-mail: whsmith.france@wanadoo.fr ■ Mon-Sat 9:00-19:30 ■ Everyone speaks English ■ Prices medium ■ Professional discount ■ Major credit cards

35,000 titles in English as well as a good selection of English and American magazines. Well-organized stacks include books on interior design, architecture, furniture, antiques.

SHAKESPEARE & CO.
37 rue de la Bûcherie, 75005 Paris ■ Tel: 01 43 26 96 50 ■ Open
7 days a week from noon to midnight ■ English spoken

**This famous old landmark dates back to the traditions of Sylvia
Beech, publisher of James Joyce and good friend of the expatri-
ate writers of the 1920s and 1930s. They have selections in the
fields of design, architecture, furniture, etc. The shop holds the
best collection of Hemingway, Joyce, Fitzgerald and others of the
period. One thing is certain, the choice is highly volatile, changing every week with new acquisitions in English and French.**

TEA AND TATTERED PAGES
24 rue Mayet, 75006 Paris ■ Tel: 01 40 65 94 35 ■ English spoken ■ Prices reasonable

**15,000 second-hand English books. American tea room with
American and a few English gifts such as quilts and teapots.
It is a charming place.**

Bookbinding and Restoration
Reliure et restauration

AMELINE
320 rue Saint-Honoré, 75001 Paris ■ Tel: 01 42 60 50 65 ■ Mon-
Fri 10:00-18:00 ■ Prices medium to high

**Deluxe contemporary bindings. Leathers and papers, hand
dyed and airbrushed. Full bindings and half bindings. Classes in binding on Mondays and Wednesdays.**

JEAN-BERNARD ALIX
52 rue Saint-André-des-Arts, 75006 Paris ■ Telfax: 01 43 54 28
17 ■ Mon-Fr 10:00-18:00 ■ English spoken ■ Prices high ■ Professional discount for libraries

**High quality classic and contemporary bindings for original
editions.**

ANNE DE BROVES
11 rue Géricault, 75016 Paris ■ Telfax: 01 42 24 84 58 ■ Mon-Fri
9:30-12:30/14:30-17:30 ■ English spoken

**Binding for the bibliophile. Restoration of old, rare books
and boxes of the XIX century.**

BUISSON

4 rue d'Aligre, 75012 Paris ■ Tel: 01 43 07 19 25 ■ Mon-Fri 9:00-12:00/14:00-19:00 ■ Prices medium

Restoration of old books, XVI to XX century. Specialists in restorations after flood or fire. For libraries and collectors. Some binding. Master artisan.

ANICK BUTRÉ

18 rue Violet, 75015 Paris ■ Tel: 01 42 24 89 08 ■ Fax: 01 45 79 50 64 ■ E-mail: aaab@cybercable.fr ■ Web: www.aaab.fr.st ■ Mon-Sat 9:00-12:00/14:00-18:00 ■ English spoken

Beautiful bookbinding. Especially original creations for artists.

ALAIN DEVAUCHELLE

98 rue du Faubourg-Poissonnière, 75010 Paris ■ Tel: 01 48 78 67 12 ■ Mon-Fri by appointment

Superb quality classic bookbinding using old-style techniques. Restoration of antique books.

DUPIN DE ST CYR

30 bis av du Château Bertin, 78400 Chatou ■ Tel: 01 39 55 85 90 (atelier) / 01 34 80 95 30 ■ Fax: 01 30 53 15 52 ■ E-mail: agirec@lemel.fr ■ Mon-Fri by appointment ■ English, Portuguese and Spanish spoken

Binding of art books a specialty. Extensive work for libraries. Adult courses in bookbinding.

JEAN DE GONET

8 rue Edouard-Lecroy, 75011 Paris ■ Telfax: 01 43 38 06 57 ■ Mon-Fri 9:00-13:00/14:00-18:00, Fri closing 17:00 ■ Jean de Gonet speaks English ■ Prices medium to high

Very contemporary binding using RIM technique (reticulated injected mould). This creates a more supple spine so that the book will remain open without damage while photocopying or during reference. It also affords long-lasting protection. Ideal method for protection of old works in museums, libraries, etc.

MME CLAUDE HONNELAÎTRE

14 rue du Cardinal-Lemoine, 75005 Paris ■ Telfax: 01 43 54 89 88 ■ Mon-Fri 9:00-13:00/14:30-18:00, Sat PM by appointment ■ Prices reasonable to high

Excellent quality contemporary binding, using classic techniques. Bindings follow book themes and are intricately worked, exquisitely embossed.

JEHANNE LAEDERICH

22 bd Edgar-Quinet, Bat. B, 75014 Paris ■ Tel: 01 43 20 92 32 ■ Mon-Fri 9:00-12:00/14:00-18:00, Sat by appointment ■ English spoken ■ Prices medium

Classic and contemporary bindings, restoration of antique bindings, parchment bindings (monastery technique). Gives classes. Holder of the Gold Medal of Master Artisan.

ALAIN LOBSTEIN

9 rue Félix-Faure, 75015 Paris ■ Telfax: 01 45 57 46 20 ■ Mon-Fri 9:00-12:00/14:00-19:00

Classical and original styles of book binding. Courses in gilding, engraving and binding.

RELIEURE SUR COUR
BRIGITTE BLANC

46 rue Monsieur-le-Prince, 75006 Paris ■ Tel: 01 44 07 28 71 ■ Mon-Thu 14:30-19:00, Tue-Wed, Fri-Sat 10:00-13:00/14:30-19:00 ■ English spoken ■ Prices medium

All kinds of binding, classic and contemporary, but especially finely-worked contemporary. Special-occasion books, such as birthdays, weddings, anniversaries, retirements, visitors' books, bound memorabilia of all kinds.

FLORENT ROUSSEAU

34 rue Ballu, 75009 Paris ■ Telfax: 01 45 26 70 58 ■ Mon-Fri 9:30-12:00/14:00-18:00 ■ Professional discount for minimum of 10 books

Classical and contemporary bookbinding, embossing and gold leafing. Restoration. Art papers. Japanese binding.

JACKY VIGNON

2 rue Gonnet, 75011 Paris ■ Telfax: 01 44 64 78 28 ■ Mon-Sat 9:00-12:30/14:00-18:30 ■ English and some Spanish spoken ■ Professional discount for minimum of 10 books

Restoration of all books. Bookbinding for libraries. Contemporary decorated bookbindings. Courses in gilding.

SOLANGE DE VERBIZIER

75 rue Buffon, 75005 Paris ■ Tel: 01 43 37 53 68 ■ Mon-Sat 9:00-13:00/14:00-18:00

Books bound in leather and fabric. Restoration of books. Courses in bookbinding.

Gold Leafing on Books
Dorure sur reliure

LA FEUILLE D'OR
7 rue de La Tour d'Auvergne, 75009 Paris ■ Telfax: 01 42 82 17 36 ■ Mon-Fri 8:30-12:30/14:00-18:30 ■ M. Vatonne ■ Pascale Thérond speaks English ■ Prices medium ■ Professional discount on quantities

Specializes in gold leafing by hand on leather-bound books. Restoration of gold leafing on old books. Gold leafing of designs on modern and contemporary bindings. Titles. Unique models and in small series. Gold leafing on leather for furnishing and leather-covered objects. Very high quality work.

PATRICK PROUTEAU
24bis av René Coty, 75014 Paris ■ Tel: 0143 27 53 32 ■ By appointment

Hot gilding, titling in gold by hand or machine.

EUGÈNE DE VERBIZIER
75 rue Buffon, 75005 Paris ■ Tel: 01 43 31 25 26 ■ Mon-Fri 10:00-12:30/14:00-18:00

"Dorure soignée and demi-soignée". Which means roughly: "painstaking" and "less-painstaking". Courses in gilding.

CARPETS AND TAPESTRIES

Tapis et tapisseries

II

CASA LOPEZ
34 Galerie Vivienne, 75002 Paris ■ Tel: 01 42 60 46 85 ■ Fax: 01 49 27 99 17 ■ Mon-Sat 10:30-18:30 ■ Director: Bernard Magniant ■ English spoken ■ Prices medium ■ Professional discount ■ Major credit cards

Interesting decorative carpets and rugs. Original creations of Bernard Magniant.

JULES FLIPO
49bis rue Sainte-Anne, 75002 Paris ■ Tel: 01 47 03 44 77 ■ Fax: 01 47 03 47 57 ■ Some English spoken ■ M.Barthélémy ■ Prices medium to high ■ Professional discount

A specialist in the creation of original carpets and rugs for over 100 years. Original creations of Manuel Canovas and Patrick Frey. Large choice of carpets in all fibres for residential and contract use. Custom and stock. Professionals only.

♛ TOULEMONDE-BOCHART
10 rue du Mail, 75002 Paris ■ Tel: 01 40 26 68 83 ■ Fax: 01 40 26 67 19 ■ Web: www.toutlemondebochart.fr ■ Mon-Sat 9:30-18:00 ■ English, Spanish and German spoken ■ Prices medium to high ■ Professional discount ■ Major credit cards.
They are also at: 29 bd Raspail, 75007 Paris ■ Tel: 01 45 48 05 71 ■ 1 rue Violet, 75015 Paris ■ Tel: 01 45 75 97 88 ■ These shops close for lunch

Tapestries and carpets in original designs by Andrée Putman, Jean-Jacques Baume, Christian Duc, Didier Gomez, Hilton Macconico, Pascal Morgue, Hélène Yardley. Some of these are on permanent exhibit at the Cooper-Hewitt Museum in New York and regularly shown at the Musée des Arts Decoratifs in Paris.

III

ARTIS FLORA
75 rue Vieille-du-Temple, 75003 Paris ■ Tel: 01 48 87 76 18 ■ Fax: 01 48 87 98 60 ■ Web: www.artis-flora.com ■ Mon-Sat 10:00-19:00 ■ Jean-François Gravier speaks English ■ 20% professional discount ■ Major credit cards

Reproductions of antique tapestries, hand woven, as well as machine woven, and printed giving an antique patina. Decorative cushions and table throws.

ANATOLIE KILIM

52 rue Dauphine, 75006 Paris ■ Tel: 01 44 07 29 52 ■ Fax: 01 43 54 17 93 ■ E-mail: anatoliekilim@abayland.com ■ Web: www.abay-land.com/boutique/anatoliekilim ■ Sun, Mon, Tue, Thu, Fri, Sat 9:30-19:30 ■ Mr. Enbiya speaks English and Arabic ■ Prices medium ■ 20% professional discount ■ Major credit cards

Kilims woven by hand. Restoration of kilims and carpets. Cleaning, pickup and delivery.

TAPIS BOUZNAH

55 bd Raspail, 75006 Paris ■ Telfax: 01 42 22 52 26 ■ Mon-Sat 10:00-19:00 and by appointment, Sun 10:00-14:00 ■ Mr. Bouznah speaks English ■ Prices medium ■ 10 to 20% professional discount ■ Major credit cards

Antique and contemporary carpets from Iran, the Caucasus and Turkey. Cleaning and repair services.

GALERIE DIURNE

45 rue Jacob, 75006 Paris ■ Tel: 01 42 60 94 11 ■ Fax: 01 43 44 07 49 ■ Tue-Sat 11:00-13:00/14:30-19:00 ■ English spoken ■ Professional discount ■ Visa

Remarkable custom creations by Marcel Zelmanovitch, made in Katmandu, in all sizes.

👑 ROBERT FOUR

8, rue des Saints-Pères 75007 Paris ■Tel: 01 40 20 44 96 ■ Fax: 01 40 20 44 97 ■ E-mail: rfour@club-internet.fr ■ Mon 14:00-19:00/Tue-Sat 10:00-19:00 ■ Mme Monique Claude-Lanier ■ English spoken

**Contemporary tapestries of artists: Sonia Delaunay, Magritte, Klée, Picasso, Douanier Rousseau, Folon, Miotte, Lurçat, Toffoli, made in Aubusson.
Restoration and Anbusson.**

VII

GALERIE AFSARI

67 av de Suffren, 75007 Paris ■ Tel: 01 45 66 45 48 ■ Fax: 0145 67 30 76 ■ Tue-Sun 11:00-19:00 ■ Siyamak Afsari speaks English ■ Prices medium

Antique Oriental and European carpets, kilims and tapestries.

BAYAT GHP
7 rue de Verneuil, 75007 Paris ■ Tel: 01 42 86 80 94 ■ Fax: 01 42 86 90 33 ■ Web: www.artfase.com/bayat ■ Mon-Sat 11:00-19:30 ■ Louei Bayat speaks English ■ Professional discount ■ Major credit cards

XVI to XIX century carpets: Large sizes, Indian, Persian and French Savonnerie and Aubusson tapestries. Restoration. Expert.

♛ **GALERIE CHEVALIER**
17 quai Voltaire, 75007 Paris ■ Tel: 01 42 60 72 68 ■ Fax: 01 42 86 99 06 ■ E-mail: chevalier@francenet.fr ■ Web: www.galerie-chevalier.com ■ Mon 14:00-19:00, Tue-Fri 10:00-13:00/14:00-19:00, Sat 11:00-19:00 ■ English spoken ■ Visa and Amex

The best of antique carpets and tapestries, European and Oriental. Restoration and cleaning. The Chevalier brothers are extraordinarily knowledgable. Qualified experts. Restoration.

LAURENT TAPIS
101 av de la Bourdonnnais, 75007 Paris ■ Tel: 01 45 50 40 21 ■ Tue-Sat 10:30-19:30 ■ Mr. Laurent speaks English and Spanish ■ Prices medium ■ Professional discount ■ Major credit cards

Antique and contemporary Oriental carpets. Repair and washing.

TAI PING CARPETS
30 rue des Saints-Pères, 75007 Paris ■ Tel: 01 42 22 96 54 ■ Fax: 01 45 44 28 92 ■ Mon-Fri 9:30-13:00/14:00-18:30, Sat 14:00-19:00 ■ English spoken ■ Prices high ■ Professional discount ■ Major credit cards

Carpets and rugs by contemporary creators as well as custom-made carpets to your design, including Savonnerie types.

———————————— VIII ————————————

ARTCURIAL
61 avenue Montaigne, 75008 Paris ■ Tel: 01 42 99 16 16 ■ Fax: 01 42 99 16 10 ■ Web: www.artcurial.com ■ Tue-Sat 10:30-19:00 ■ English spoken ■ Prices high

Numbered editions of designs of the great contemporary artists woven into carpets.

👑 GALERIE FRANCK SABET-CENTRE FRANCAIS DES TAPIS D'ORIENT
217 rue du Faubourg-Saint-Honoré, 75008 Paris ■ Tel: 01 45 61 12 95 ■ Fax: 01 53 76 05 16 ■ Mon-Sat 10:00-19:00 ■ English spoken ■ Prices high ■ Professional discount ■ Major credit cards

Specialty: Antique Oriental carpets, and modern kilims in silk. Collection Sabet Persepolis. Beautiful collection.

HADJER ET FILS
102 rue du Faubourg-Saint-Honoré, 75008 Paris ■ Tel: 01 42 66 61 13 ■ Fax: 01 42 66 66 03 ■ E-mail: hadjer@hadjer.fr ■ Mon-Sat 10:30-19:00 ■ Reynold Hadjer speaks English ■ Amex

Antique European and Oriental carpets and tapestries. Restoration, expertise.

HENIDE TAPIS
25 rue La Boétie, 75008 Paris ■ Tel: 01 42 65 62 30 ■ Fax: 01 42 65 75 48 ■ Web: www.tapis-henide.com or www.letapis.com ■ Mon-Fri 9:30-12:00/14:00-18:30 ■ Mr. de Leon speaks English ■ Prices medium to high ■ Professional discount

Antique Oriental and European carpets, antique tapestries, tapestries of contemporary artists. Atelier of restoration. Qualified expert.

ROBERT MIKAELOFF
23 rue La Boétie, 75008 Paris ■ Tel: 01 42 65 24 55 ■ Fax: 01 49 24 05 16 ■ Mon-Sat 9:00-12:00/14:00-19:00 ■ Robert Michaeloff speaks English, German and Persian ■ Prices very high ■ Major credit cards

Beautiful Persian carpets and rare European carpets. Tapestries and rare objects.

PRESTIGE DE PERSE
122 bd Haussmann, 75008 Paris ■ Tel: 01 45 22 05 48 ■ Fax: 01 43 87 53 32 ■ E-mail: prestigef.ahi@hotmail.com ■ Mon-Fri 10:30-18:30 ■ Farhad and Farideh Ahi speak English ■ Prices medium ■ 5 to 10% professional discount ■ Major credit cards

Antique Oriental carpets. Antique French carpets (Aubusson and Savonnerie). French and Flemish tapestries. Antique embroidery and fabrics.

—————————————— IX ——————————————

TAPIS AMSTERDAM
96 rue d'Amsterdam, 75009 Paris ■ Tel: 01 45 26 72 94 ■ Fax: 01 48 74 40 99 ■ Mon-Sat 9:30-19:00 ■ Jean-Pierre and Nicole-France Bénichou speak English ■ Prices medium ■ 25% professional discount ■ Major credit cards

Oriental carpets, antique and modern, reproductions, cleaning. Restoration.

NISSIM

32 rue du Faubourg-Saint-Antoine, 75012 Paris ■ Tel: 01 43 43 78 00 ■ Fax: 01 43 43 82 12 ■ Mon-Sat 10:00-19:30 ■ Guy and Philippe Nissim speak English ■ Prices medium ■ 5 to 20% professional discount ■ Major credit cards

Traditional Oriental carpets and tapestries.

--- XV ---

AUX TRESORS DE LA PERSE

1 av Paul Déroulède, 75015 Paris ■ Tel: 01 45 67 38 28 ■ Thu-Sun 10:00-19:00 ■ Morteza Kafi speaks English ■ Prices low ■ 20% professional discount

Oriental carpets, especially Persian, some from Pakistan, Turkey, China.

--- XVI ---

GALERIE CARDO

61 av Kléber, 75116 Paris ■ Tel: 01 47 27 08 45 ■ Fax: 01 47 27 88 21 ■ Mon-Sat 10:00-19:00 ■ Masoud and Yahya Moghadaszadeh speak English ■ Prices medium ■ Professional discount on quantities ■ Major credit cards

Antique and recent Persian carpets in wool and silk. Kilims, Persian and Chinese art objects.

MOMTAZ TAPIS

17 rue de la Tour, 75116 Paris ■ Tel: 01 42 15 09 09 ■ Fax: 01 42 15 06 43 ■ Mon 14:00-19:00, Tue-Sat 10:00-19:00 ■ Patrick and Philippe Momtaz speak English ■ Prices high ■ 15% professional discount ■ Major credit cards

Specialists in Oriental carpets in silk and in large dimensions. Restoration and estimates.

TAPIS POINCARÉ

88 av Raymond-Poincaré, 75116 Paris ■ Tel: 01 45 00 67 26 ■ Fax: 01 45 00 23 41 ■ Mon-Sat 10:00-19:00 ■ Albert Bellaiche speaks English ■ Prices medium ■ 20% professional discount ■ Major credit cards

Oriental carpets of all origins, recent, old and antique. Non-slip liners. Cleaning and restoration of carpets and tapestries.

MONA
40 bd Gouvion-Saint-Cyr, 75017 Paris ■ Tel: 01 45 72 28 55 ■
Mon-Sat 10:00-12:00/14:00-19:00 ■ Mahmood Masghati speaks
English ■ Prices medium
Oriental carpets, objects, furniture and old miniatures.

LANGTON & GRIFF
23 rue du Général-Leclerc, 78000 Versailles ■ Tel: 01 30 21 66
25 ■ Web: www.tapislangton.com ■ Tue-Sat 10:30-12:30/14:00-
19:00 ■ Paula and Nicolas Sargenton speak English ■ Prices
medium ■ 30 to 40% professional discount
**Oriental carpets, tapestries and kilims, antique and contem-
porary. Restoration and cleaning.**

Carpet, Textile
and Tapestry Restoration

AU JARDIN D'ISPAHAN
9 rue de Bassano, 75116 Paris ■ Tel: 01 47 20 38 95 ■ Fax: 01
47 23 67 60 ■ Mon-Fri 9:00-18:00, Fri closing 17:00 ■ English
spoken ■ Professional discount
High quality restoration of carpets and tapestries.

DELARUE-TURCAT
94 rue du Bac, 75007 Paris ■ Tel: 01 45 48 56 74 ■ Fax: 01 45
48 02 42 ■ Tue-Fri 10:15-12:30/14:15-19:00, Sat 10:30-
12:30/14:30-19:00 ■ English spoken ■ Prices medium to high ■
Professional discount
Restoration and cleaning of antique tapestries and carpets.

👑 **HENRIETTE GUICHARD**
8 rue des Pyramides, 75001 Paris ■ Tel: 01 42 60 40 40 ■ Mon-
Sat 11:00-18:30 ■ English spoken ■ Prices medium to high ■
Professional discount
**Restoration of tapestries and Aubusson carpets of all peri-
ods. Reproduction and custom designs of canvases for
needlepoint, as well as all supplies. Will make screens and
cushions.**

♛ MAISON CHEVALIER

64 bd de la Mission-Marchand, 92400 Courbevoie ■ Tel: 01 47 88 41 41 ■ Fax: 01 47 88 64 52 ■ Mon-Fri 8:30-18:00 ■ English spoken ■ Directors: Dominique and Pierre Chevalier ■ Contact: Veronique Chevalier

Specialty: Restoration and cleaning of carpets and tapestries. Creators of a machine which allows cleaning without manipulation.
Work experience: Restoration and cleaning of tapestries for the Musée du Louvre (Gobelins XVII century). The Beauvais chairs in the Château de Versailles. Le Musée de Cluny. The company has ateliers in Bauge, Aubusson.

Tapestry and Embroidery, Custom Work and Materials

♛ MAISON SHOKKOS

27 rue d'Assas, 75006 Paris ■ Tel: 01 42 22 26 02 ■ Mon 14:00-19:00, Tues-Fri 10:30-12:00/14:00-19:00 ■ Prices medium to high ■ Professional discount

Restoration of old tapestries. Custom-reproductions of antique and contemporary designs. Canvases prepared for all types of needlepoint. All materials available.

TAPISSERIES DE LA BUCHERIE

2 rue du Haut-Pavé, 75005 Paris ■ Telfax: 01 40 46 87 69 ■ E-mail: needlepoint@bucherie.com ■ Web: www.bucherie.com ■ Mon-Fri 10:00-19:00, Sat 14:00-19:00 ■ Dominique Siegler speaks English ■ Prices medium to high ■ Professional discount ■ Major credit cards

Needlepoint classes in English and French.
1,000 documents from the Middle Ages to Loire tapestries to the present. Top quality custom work with hand dyed wools. Pillows, screens, panels, chairs. Estimates provided. Everything for needlepoint, custom made or "do-it-yourself". All types of kits and materials.

VOISINE

12 rue de l'Église, 92200 Neuilly ■ Tel: 01 46 37 54 60 ■ Fax: 01 46 24 23 28 ■ Web: www.voisine.fr ■ Mon-Sat 10:00-13:00/14:30-19:00 ■ English spoken ■ Prices medium ■ Professional discount ■ Major credit cards

All kits for embroidery and tapestry.

CHAIRS
Sièges

V

DANIEL PIERRE
22 rue des Boulangers, 75005 Paris ■ Telfax: 01 43 54 15 11 ■
Mon-Fri 8:30-12:30/13:30-18:00 ■ Prices medium to high ■ Professional discount

Specialist in the restoration of antique chairs. Works for the best antique dealers and collectors.

VI

ETAT DE SIÈGE
1 quai de Conti, 75006 Paris ■ Tel: 01 43 29 31 60 ■ Fax: 01 43 29 84 97 ■ 21 avde Friedland, 75008 Paris ■ Tel: 01 42 56 64 75 ■ Fax: 01 45 61 29 47 ■ E-mail: etatdesiege@free.fr ■ Web: www.etatdesiege.com ■ Mon 14:00-19:00/Tue-Sat 11:00-19:00 ■ English and Italian spoken ■ Prices high ■ 10% professional discount ■ Major credit cards

Specialist in chairs, from Louis XIII to today.

VIII

ETAT DE SIÈGE
21 av Friedland, 75008 Paris ■ Tel: 01 42 56 64 75 ■ Fax: 01 45 61 29 47 ■ Mon 14:30-19:00, Tue-Sat 10:30-19:00 ■ Mr. Dominique Choay ■ English spoken ■ Prices medium to high ■ Amex, Visa

Contemporary chairs and reproductions of antique styles. Choice of finish and fabrics.

IX

L'ART DU SIEGE
CLAUDE BERNARD HUBERT
21 rue Joubert, 75009 Paris ■ Tel: 01 48 74 25 08 ■ Fax: 01 48 74 76 90 ■ Web: www.antique-expo.com/artdusiege or www.art-face.com/artdusiege ■ Mon-Fri 9:00-13:00/15:00-17:00 ■ Prices high to very high ■ Professional discount

Fabrication of chairs in all classic styles. Restoration and upholstery.

LA CHAISERIE DU FAUBOURG

26 rue de Charonne, 75011 Paris ■ Telfax: 01 43 57 67 51 ■ Mon-Sat 9:00-12:30/14:00-19:00 ■ Prices medium to high ■ Professional discount

Fabrication of chairs, sofas, beds, in classic styles. Repair and restoration. Caning.

STRAURE

95 rue du Faubourg-Saint-Antoine, 75011 Paris ■ Tel: 01 43 47 20 50 ■ Mon-Fri 8:00-12:00/13:15-17:00 ■ Prices medium ■ 5 to 10% professional discount

Specialist in restoration and fabrication of chairs. Very high-quality.

TAPISSERIE MENDÈS

41 rue Basfroi, 75011 Paris ■ Tel: 01 40 09 08 41 ■ Mon-Sat 8:00-12:00/13:00-19:00 ■ Prices medium

Restoration and custom fabrication of sofas and chairs. Full upholstery service.

CHEZ L'ARTISAN

71 rue de Charenton, 75012 Paris ■ Telfax: 01 43 43 48 20 ■ Tue-Sat 9:00-13:00/14:00-18:00 ■ Prices low ■ 25% professional discount

Fabrication of chairs, armchairs and sofas in all styles. Upholstery. Wall upholstery and restoration of furniture

PHILIPPE SIRAUD

59 av d'Iena, 75016 Paris ■ Tel: 01 45 00 33 08 ■ Fax: 01 45 00 29 42 ■ E-mail: philippe.siraud@wanadoo.fr ■ Web: www.philippe-siraud.fr ■ Mon-Fri 9:00-18:00, Sat by appointment ■ English and Russian spoken ■ Prices medium ■ Professional discount

Chairs, tables in wood and aluminium. Works for hotels, boutiques and individuals.

(SEE ALSO UPHOLSTERERS)

DECORATIVE ARTS
OF THE TWENTIETH CENTURY

I

♔ GALERIE DU PASSAGE
20-22 Galerie Véro-Dodat, 10 rue Croix-des-Petits-Champs, 75001 Paris ■ Tel: 01 42 36 01 13 ■ Fax: 01 40 41 98 86 ■ E-mail: gpassage@club-internet.fr ■ Tue-Sat 11:00-19:00 ■ Pierre Passebon ■ English spoken ■ Prices medium to high ■ Professional discount

XX century decorative arts. From entire rooms and curiosities to unusual pieces such as the pair of wedding chests of the late Duke and Duchess of Windsor. An eclectic mix of furniture, decorative objects and, sometimes, wonderful Giacometti lamps. Furniture by Jean-Michel Frank, Alexandre Noll, Jean Royère, Christian Bérard.

GALERIE LELOUCH
10 Galerie Vero-Dodat, 10 rue Croix-des-Petits-Champs, 75001 Paris ■ Tel: 01 40 13 94 03 ■ Cell: 06 90 07 68 ■ E-mail: lelouch@wanadoo.fr ■ Tue-Sat 12:00-19:00 ■ Jean-Marc Lelouch ■ English spoken ■ Prices medium to high ■ Professional discount

A choice of furniture and decorations for the entire house from pure Le Corbusier to Neoclassicism.

GALERIE ERIC PHILIPPE
25 Galerie Véro Dodat, 10 rue Croix-des-Petits-Champs, 75001 Paris ■ Tel: 01 42 33 28 26 ■ Fax: 01 42 21 17 93 ■ E-mail: ericphil@worldnet.fr ■ Web www.ericphilippe.com ■ Tue-Sat 14:00-19:00 ■ Eric Philippe speaks English ■ Prices medium ■ Professional discount

Decorative arts of 1910 to 1950.

II

CHEZ MAMAN
4 rue Tiquetonne, 75002 Paris ■ Telfax: 01 40 28 46 09 ■ E-mail : spaceage@libertysurf.fr ■ Mon-Sat 12:00-20:00 ■ Marie Sohlen and Eva Juge ■ English and Swedish spoken ■ Prices medium ■ Professional discount

Scandinavian, Italian, American and some French furniture, lighting and accessories of the 1950s, 1960s and 1970s.

LA CORBEILLE

5 Passage du Grand Cerf, 75002 Paris ■ Tel: 01 53 40 78 77 ■ Fax: 01 40 26 29 01 ■ E-mail: corbeill@cybercable.fr ■ Mon-Sat 13:00-19:00 ■ Fabien and Christine Bonillo ■ English spoken ■ Prices medium ■ Professional discount ■ MC, Visa

Designer furniture of the 1950s and contemporary paintings.

──────────────── III ────────────────

GALERIE À REBOURS

97 rue Vielle du Temple, 75003 Paris ■ Tel: 01 42 72 53 12 ■ Mon-Sat 14:00-19:00 ■ Patrick Favardin ■ English spoken ■ Professional discount

French furniture and ceramics of the 1950s. Patrick Favardin has written several books on the subject, including "Les Années 50".

GALERIE FIFTEASE

7 rue du Perche, 75003 Paris ■ Telfax: 01 40 27 04 40 ■ E-mail: infor@fiftease.com ■ Web: www.fiftease.com ■ Tue-Sat 14:30-19:30 ■ Guillaume Roullin & Alexandre Ulliac ■ English spoken ■ Prices medium ■ Professional discount

Specialists in French and European furniture and decorative arts of the 1950s.

──────────────── IV ────────────────

GALERIE NEOTU

25 rue du Renard, 75004 Paris ■ Tel: 01 42 78 96 97 ■ Fax: 01 42 78 26 27 ■ E-mail: neotuparis@aol.com ■ Web: www.neotu.com ■ Mon-Sat 12:30-19:00 ■ Pierre Staudenmeyer ■ English spoken ■ Prices medium to high ■ Professional discount ■ Major credit cards

Furniture of post-war design and craft editions of contemporary furniture.

LA COMPAGNIE DES LUCIOLES

2 place du Marché Sainte-Catherine, 75004 Paris ■ Tel: 01 42 72 65 10 ■ Fax: 01 49 45 03 05 ■ Cell: 06 60 15 03 88 ■ Thu-Mon 14:00-20:00 ■ Alain Bechade ■ Some English spoken ■ Prices medium ■ Professional discount

Furniture and decorative objects, mainly French, 1905 to 1950.

DOWN TOWN
33 rue de Seine, 75006 Paris ■ Tel: 01 46 33 82 41 ■ Fax: 01 43 29 10 75 ■ E-mail: information@galerie-downtown.com ■ Web: www.ga-lerie-downtown.com ■ Tue-Sat 10:30-19:00 ■ François Laffanour ■ English spoken ■ Professional discount ■ Major credit cards

Furniture and lighting by XX century architects: Prouvé, Per-riand, Mouille, Royère, Le Corbusier, Eames, Nelson and Noguchi.

👑 GALERIE 54
54 rue Mazarine, 75006 Paris ■ Tel: 01 43 26 89 96 ■ Fax: 01 43 29 36 29 ■ E-mail: galerie54@club-internet.fr ■ Tue-Sat 14:30-19:00 ■ Eric Touchaleaume and Jean-Pierre Bouchard ■ English spoken ■ Professional discount

Furniture of the architect creators of the XX century, includ-ing Prouvé, Le Corbusier, Mouille, Jouve, Noll and Perriand.

👑 LA GALERIE MODERNE
52 rue Mazarine, 75006 Paris ■ Tel: 01 46 33 13 59 ■ E-mail: pb@lagaleriemoderne.com ■ Web: www.lagaleriemoderne.com ■ Tue-Sat 14:00-19:00 ■ Pierre Boogaerts ■ English spoken ■ Professional discount ■ Major credit cards

Rental and sale of classic design furniture of the 1950s to 1970: Nelson, Eames, Saarinen, Jacobsen, Colombo, Paulin.

LA GALERIE SCANDINAVE
31 rue du Tournon, 75006 Paris ■ Tel: 01 43 26 25 32 ■ Fax: 01 53 10 22 61 ■ E-mail: info@lagaleriescandinave.com ■ Web: www.la-galeriescandinave.com ■ Tue-Sat 11:00-20:00 ■ Philippe Menager, Nicolas Hug, André Lecompte ■ English spoken ■ Prices medium to high ■ Professional discount ■ Major credit cards

Furniture, lighting, glass, ceramics and decorative objects of the 1950s to 1970 by the Scandinavian designers Hans Wegner, Finn Juhl, Poul Kjaerholm and Borge Mogenson. Original pieces no re-editions.

SCHMOCK BROC
15 rue Racine, 75006 Paris ■ Telfax: 01 46 33 79 98 ■ Cell: 06 07 69 88 95 ■ E-mail: najka@club-internet.fr ■ Mon-Fri 13:00-20:00, Sat 10:30-19:30 ■ Anne-Marie Otte, owner and Nadine Clément ■ English spoken ■ Prices medium to high ■ Profes-sional discount ■ Amex and Visa

Purchase, sale and rental of furniture, lighting and decorative objects of the designers of the 1950s, 1960s and 1970s. Very large choice of lighting.

♛ OLIVIER WATELET
11 rue Bonaparte, 75006 Paris ■ Tel: 01 43 26 07 87 ■ Fax: 01 43 25 99 33 ■ E-mail: watelet@club-internet.fr ■ Tue-Sat 10:30-13:00/14:30-19:00 ■ Matthieu de Prémont, Director/Decorator/Author ■ English spoken ■ Prices high ■ 10% professional discount ■ Visa and MC

Decorative arts of the 1930s, 1940s and 1950s and specially the greats of the 1940s: Jacques Quinet, Arbus, Poillerat, Royère.

— VII —

GALERIE JEAN-FRANÇOIS DUBOIS
15 rue de Lille, 75007 Paris ■ Tel: 01 42 60 40 17 ■ Fax: 01 42 96 04 24 ■ Mon-Sat 14:00-19:00 ■ Jean-François Dubois speaks English ■ Prices medium to high ■ Professional discount ■ Amex, Visa

Decorative arts of the XX century: everything.

— XI —

BO PLASTIC
31 rue de Charonne, 75011 Paris ■ Tel: 01 53 36 73 16 ■ Fax: 01 53 36 01 49 ■ E-mail: boplas@club-internet.fr ■ Mon-Sat 11:00-20:00 ■ Valentina speaks English ■ Prices medium ■ Professional discount

Furniture of the XX century created by architect designers of the 1960s and 1970s and some pieces from the 1950s, as well as a few contemporary items.

DREAM ON GALERIE
70 bd Beaumarchais, 75011 Paris ■ Tel: 01 43 38 50 25 ■ Fax: 01 43 38 71 41 ■ E-mail: dreamongalerie@free.fr ■ Mon-Sat 13:00-20:00/Sun by appointment ■ Stephane Rault ■ English spoken ■ Prices medium

Specialist in designer furniture of the XX century.

GALERIE PATRICK SEGUIN

5 rue des Tallandiers, 75011 Paris ■ Tel: 01 47 00 32 35 ■ Fax: 01 40 21 82 95 ■ E-mail: patrickseguin@free.fr ■ Web: www.patrick-seguin.com ■ Mon-Fri 10:00-19:00, Sat 11:00-19:00 ■ Armelle Durand ■ English spoken ■ Prices medium to high ■ Professional discount ■ Major credit cards

Modern design: Le Corbusier, Jeanneret, Jouve, Mouille, Noll, Perriand, Prouvé, Royère. Contemporary art: Ashkin, Grunfeld, Kern, Kneffel, Tremblay.

GALERIE SOFT

27 rue de Charonne, 75011 Paris ■ Telfax: 01 43 14 22 50 ■ Mon-Sat 11:00-13:00/14:00-19:00 ■ Eric Gros de Beler ■ English spoken ■ Prices medium to high ■ Professional discount

Furniture, lighting, objects of art, hi-fi of the years 1960 to 1970.

XIII

GALERIE KREO

1 rue Zadkine, 75013 Paris ■ Tel: 01 53 60 18 42 ■ Fax: 01 53 60 17 58 ■ E-mail: kreogal@club-internet.fr ■ Web: www.kreo.com ■ Tue-Fri 14:00-19:00, Sat 11:00-19:00 ■ Didier Krzentowski ■ English spoken ■ Prices medium ■ Professional discount

Wonderful large gallery with original pieces by designers of the 1950s to 1980. The gallery represents today's ourstanding designers: Jasper Morrison (for the Tate Gallery), Mark Newson, Ron Arad, Martin Szekely, the Radi Designers, Erwan and Ronan Bouroullec, Pierre Charpin. All numbered unique pieces.

XVIII

GALERIE CHRISTINE DIEGONI

47ter rue d'Orsel, 75018 Paris ■ Tel: 01 42 64 69 48 ■ Fax: 01 42 58 21 64 ■ Tue-Sat 14:00-19:00 ■ Christine Diegoni ■ Prices medium to high ■ Professional discount

Applied arts of the XX century. Lighting and furniture by George Nelson, Jean Prouvé, Gino Sarfatti and especially Florence Knoll.

PAGES 50-70
15 rue Yvonne Le Tac, 75018 Paris ■ Tel: 01 42 52 48 59 ■ Fax: 01 42 26 16 51 ■ E-mail: olivierlive@aol.com ■ Tue-Sat 14:00-19:00 ■ Olivier Verlet ■ Some English spoken ■ Prices medium ■ Professional discount

Design and ceramics of the 1950s and 1960s.

---------------------------------- XX ----------------------------------

XXO
147 bd Davout, 75020 Paris ■ Tel: 01 40 30 95 75 ■ Fax: 01 40 30 95 94 ■ E-mail: info@xxo.com ■ Web: www.xxo.com ■ Mon-Fri 9:30-12:30, Sat 14:30-18:00, Sun by appointment ■ English, Spanish and Italian spoken ■ Professional discount ■ Major credit cards

Specialists in the rental, sale, purchase and expertise of designers' furniture of the 1960s through the 1970s. Orientation towards vintage plastic design.

---------------------------- MARCHÉ AUX PUCES ----------------------------

LEMONNIER LAROCHE
Marché Paul Bert, 100-110 rue des Rosiers, Allée 7, Stand 420, 93400 Saint-Ouen ■ Cell: 06 80 46 69 73 ■ Fax: 01 39 53 04 37 ■ Sat-Sun 10:00-18:00 ■ E-mail: clemo60@club-internet.fr ■ Web: www.clemmonier.com ■ Christophe Lemmonier and Anne Laroche ■ English spoken ■ Prices medium ■ Professional discount

Furniture and lighting of the designers of the 1960s: Eames Saarinen and Knoll.

LUDLOW
Marché Malassis, 142 rue des Rosiers, 93400 Saint-Ouen ■ Cell: 06 16 49 03 05 ■ E-mail: calime5548@aol.com ■ Web: www.ludlowgallery.com ■ Fri 10:00-13:00, Sat-Sun 10:30-18:00 ■ Marine Garnier ■ English spoken ■ Prices medium ■ Professional discount

Specialist in the American designers of the 1950s: McCobb, Robsjohn Gibbings, Eames, Kagan and others.

NICOLAS DENIS & MATTHIAS JOUSSE
Marché Paul Bert, 110 rue des Rosiers, Allee 4, Stand 180, 93400 Saint-Ouen ■ E-mail: Matthias@cybercable.fr ■ Fri 07:00-12:00,Sat-Mon 10:00-18:00

Furniture of the artists and designers of the 1970s , Paulin, Mourge, Talon, Colombo, Panton.

VINGTIÈME SIÈCLE
Marché Paul Bert, 100-110 rue de Rosiers, Allée 6, Stand 93, 93400 Saint-Ouen ■ Telfax: 01 49 45 11 09 ■ Thu-Mon 09:00-18:00 ■ Bruno Ract-Madoux ■ English spoken ■ Professional discount ■ Major credit cards

Furniture of the 1950s to today: Morgue, Paulin, Eames, Bertoia, Florence Knoll, Sotsass.

OLIVIER WATELET
59 rue des Rosiers, opp. Marché Paul Bert, 93400 Saint-Ouen ■ Tel: 01 40 12 76 58 ■ Fri-Mon 8:0-18:00 ■ Olivier Watelet ■ English and Italian spoken ■ Prices medium ■ Professional discount

XX century decorative arts: 1930s, 1940s, 1950s.

FABRICS

Tissus

♕ **CSTA - CHAMBRE SYNDICALE DES TEXTILES D'AMEUBLEMENT**
15 rue de la Banque, 75002 Paris ■ Tel: 01 42 86 04 05 ■ Fax: 01 42 86 05 25 ■ Mon-Fri 10:00-18:30 except during August.

This showroom, located near the Bourse, is a convenient exhibition space open to professionals only. It offers a one-stop view of the latest fabrics of the CSTA members. Samples can be provided, however, the fabrics are purchased directly from the individual editors. The following Editors are members of CSTA.

BOUSSAC FADINI
27 rue du Mail, 75002 Paris ■ Tel: 01 42 21 83 00 ■ Fax: 01 42 21 83 70 ■ Web: www.boussac-fadini.fr ■ Mon-Fri 9:00-18:00 ■ English spoken

Huge collection of furnishing fabrics. Prints, solids, jacquards.

BRUNSCHWIG & FILS
8 rue du Mail, 75002 Paris ■ Tel: 01 44 55 02 50 ■ Fax: 01 44 55 02 55 and 31 rue des Petits Champs, 75001 Paris ■ Tel: 01 42 96 93 18 ■ Fax: 01 42 86 94 38 ■ Mon-Fri 9:00-18:00 ■ English spoken ■ Professional discount ■ Major credit cards

Large and beautiful collection of fabrics and trimmings.

♕ **CHARLES BURGER**
39 rue des Petits-Champs, 75001 Paris ■ Tel: 01 42 97 46 19 ■ Fax: 01 42 97 46 06 ■ Mon-Fri 9:00-17:30 ■ Catherine speaks English

Specialty: printed fabrics from XVIII century documents using 200-year-old cylinders. Silks, velvets. Remarkable selection of Toiles de Jouy, 39 inches wide.

MANUEL CANOVAS
6 rue de l'Abbaye, 75006 Paris ■ Tel: 01 43 29 91 36 ■ Fax: 01 45 04 04 83 ■ Mon-Fri 9:30-18:30 ■ English spoken ■ Public showroom: 5 place de Furstemberg, 75006 Paris ■ Tel: 01 45 03 72 00 ■ Fax: 01 45 04 04 83 ■ Mon-Sat 9:30-18:30

Jacquards, prints from old documents and contemporary, stripes, solids, ottomans. 2,500 references.

CASAL-AMELIE PREVOT-DRIOT-GRADI
40 rue des Saints-Pères, 75007 Paris ■ Tel: 01 44 39 07 07 ■ Fax: 01 40 49 09 54 ■ Mon-Fri 9:30-13:00/14:00-18:00 ■ Daphné Sandoz speaks English

Contemporary fabrics: jacquards, structured designs, silks, ottomans, toiles. Specialty: coordinates.

COLFAX & FOWLER AND JANE CHURCHILL
7 place de Furstemberg, 75006 Paris ■ Tel: 01 40 51 95 30 ■ Fax: 01 40 51 87 65 ■ Mon- Sat 9:30-18:30 ■ English spoken ■ Open to the public

A new showroom for these beautiful lines of fabrics.

COTONNIERE D'ALSACE/LES EDITIONS PAULE MARROT
98 rue de Rennes, 75006 Paris ■ Tel : 01 44 39 74 84 ■ Fax : 01 44 39 74 85 ■ E-mail: cotonniere@rmcnet.fr ■ Tue-Sat 10:00-12:00/14:00-19:00 ■ Major credit cards

Specialty: cottons, prints, Toiles de Jouy, contemporary designs.

CREATION BAUMANN
48 rue de Grenelle, 75007 Paris ■ Tel: 01 45 49 08 22 ■ Fax: 01 45 49 31 22 ■ Web: www.creationbaumann.com ■ Mon-Fri 9:00-12:30/14:00-18:00 ■ English spoken

Large collection of sheers. Flame-resistant fabrics. Prints, jacquards, blinds, interior automatic blinds, self-adhesive fabrics for walls.

DECORTEX
3 rue Chabanais, 75002 Paris ■ Tel: 01 42 86 81 39 ■ Fax: 01 42 86 81 27 ■ English spoken

A large collection of furnishing fabris.

DESTOMBES
35 rue du Sentier, 75002 Paris ■ Tel: 01 42 33 61 05 ■ Fax: 01 42 33 04 09 ■ Mon-Fri 9:00-12:30/13:30-17:30 ■ English spoken

Tapestries, velvets, silk blends, jacquards.

FARDIS
6 bis rue de l'Abbaye, 75006 Paris ■ Tel: 01 43 25 73 44 ■ Fax: 01 43 54 22 78 ■ Mon 14:00-18:00 Tue-Sat 9:30-18:30 ■ English spoken

Prints, jacquards, satins, silk blends, cottons, wallpaper.

LA FILANDIERE-CHRISTIAN LANZANI
64 avenue Ledru-Rollin, 75012 Paris ■ Tel: 01 44 75 75 07 ■ Fax: 01 44 75 75 09 ■ Mon-Fri 8:30-18:00 ■ English spoken

Specialty: tapestries for upholstery and wall panels, hand- and machine-woven. Wide width jacquards, velvets, damasks, silk weaves.

CHRISTIAN FISCHBACHER
13 rue du Mail, 750002 Paris ■ Tel: 01 42 96 25 25 ■ Fax: 01 42 96 25 26 ■ Web: www.fischbacher.ch ■ Mon-Fri 9:00-12:30/13:30-18:00 Fri 17:00 ■ English spoken

Sheers, solids, chintz, moires, upholstery fabrics in classical and contemporary designs.

GALERIE ROBERT FOUR
8 rue des Saints-Pères, 75007 Paris ■ Tel: 01 40 20 44 96 ■ Fax: 01 40 20 44 97 ■ Web: www.franceantiq.fr/sna/rfour ■ Mon 14:00-19:00, Tue-Sat 10:00-19:00 ■ English spoken

Tapestries, carpets, restoration. Manufactured by Aubusson.

LES IMPRESSIONS EDITIONS
8 rue Hérold 75001 Paris ■ Telfax: 01 42 21 32 44 ■ Mon-Fri 10:00-18:00/Fri 17:00 ■ English spoken

Specialty: solids in a wide variety of weaves.

JAB
155 bd Haussmann, 75008 Paris ■ Tel: 01 53 89 00 00 ■ Fax: 01 53 89 00 05 ■ Mon-Fri 9:00-17:30 ■ English spoken

Prints, solids, silk blends, jacquards, sheers.

JERO
13, rue du Mail 75002 Paris ■ Tel: 01 40 20 45 60 ■ Fax: 01 40 20 45 61 ■ E-mail for France: cial.France.jero.fr@wanadoo.fr ■ E-mail for export: cial.export.jero.fr@wanadoo.fr ■ Mon-Fri 9:00-12:00/13:00-17:15 ■ Elisabeth Gottlieb speaks English

Furnishing fabrics, sofas, accessories.

👑 **LELIÈVRE**
13 rue du Mail, 75002 Paris ■ Tel: 01 43 16 88 00 ■ Fax: 01 43 16 88 03 ■ E-mail: comfra@lelievre.tm.fr ■ Web: www.lelievre.tm.fr ■ Mon-Fri 9:00-18:00, Fri closing 17:00 ■ Patrick Lelièvre ■ English, German and Spanish spoken ■ Prices low to very high ■ Professional discount

Catering to the professional only, Lelièvre has, in every sense, the most complete line of French furnishing fabrics, from the classics to the contemporary. They have added Tassinari and Chatel and Chotard to their line of superb silks, velvets, damasks, jacquards. They also have some good wide width fabrics.

👑 **GEORGES LE MANACH**
31 rue du Quatre-Septembre, 75002 Paris ■ Tel: 01 47 42 52 94 ■ Fax: 01 47 42 02 04 ■ E-mail: lemanach@wanadoo.fr ■ Web: www.grandsateliers.fr ■ Mon-Fri 9:00-12:00/14:00-17:45 ■ Anne Biosse Duplan ■ English, Spanish, German and Dutch spoken ■ Prices medium to very high ■ Professional discount

Manufacturers of silk fabrics since 1829. They have 4,000 designs, of which 300 are currently available. The others can be made-to-order. There are approximately 100 prints available from XVIII and XIX century documents. They have supplied fabrics for the Getty Museum, the Chateau of Fontainebleau and the palace of The Grand Duke of Luxembourg.

LUCIANO MARCATO
23 rue du Mail, 75002 Paris ■ Tel: 01 42 21 17 18 ■ Fax: 01 42 21 04 14 ■ Mon-Fri 9:00-18:00 ■ Danielle Boulogne ■ English, Italian and Spanish spoken ■ Professional discount

High-end fabrics for draperies and upholstery. Carpets.

METAPHORES
Showroom: 6 rue du Mail, 75002 Paris ■ Telfax: 01 47 03 34 49 ■ Mon-Fri 9:30-13:00/14:00-18:00 Fri: 17:00 also at: 7 place de Furstemberg, 75006 Paris ■ Telfax: 01 46 33 03 20 ■ Office: 21 rue Cambon, 75001 Paris Tel: 01 44 55 37 00 ■ Fax: 01 44 55 37 09 ■ Mon-Sat 10:30-13:00/13:30-19:00 ■ English spoken

Fine selection of furnishing fabrics. The best choice of taffetas.

OSBORNE & LITTLE
4 rue des Petits Pères, 75002 Paris ■ Tel: 01 42 86 91 00 ■ Fax: 01 42 86 90 92 ■ E-mail: paris@osborneandlittle.fr ■ Mon-Thu 9:00-18:00, Fri 9:00-17:00 ■ Mme Mayer, Commercial Director ■ English, Italian and Spanish spoken ■ Prices high ■ Trade only

Furnishing fabrics and wallpapers. Clients include top Paris hotels.

J. PANSU
42 rue du Faubourg-Poissonnière, 75010 Paris ■ Tel: 01 42 46 72 45 ■ Fax: 01 42 46 66 85 ■ Mon-Fri 8:30-12:30/14:00-18:00 ■ English spoken

Prints, solids, wide-width blends, velvets. Antique and reproduction tapestries by appointment.

♚ EDMOND PETIT
23 rue du Mail, 75002 Paris ■ Tel: 01 40 13 83 44 ■ Fax: 01 40 13 83 43 ■ Mon-Fri 9:30-18:00 ■ Elvira Welter ■ English and Portuguese spoken ■ Professional prices

Classical French styles: damasks, silks, velvets, jacquards, tapestry, taffetas cherilles. Trimmings. Flame resistent fabrics. Theatre curtains. Fabrics to custom order.

♕ L. RUBELLI
Showrooms for public and professionals: 6 bis rue de l'Abbaye, 75006 Paris ■ Tel: 01 43 54 27 77 ■ Mon: 9:30-13:00/14:00-18:00 Tue-Thu 9:30-17:00 Sat 9:30-13:00/14:00-18:00
11-13 rue de l'Abbaye, 75006 Paris ■ Tel: 01 43 54 27 77 ■ Fax: 01 43 54 97 32 ■ Mon 9:00-13:00/14:00-18:00 Tue-Thu 9:00-18:00 Fri 9:00-17:00 Sat 9:30-13:00/14:00-18:00 ■ English spoken

Complete line of furnishing fabrics: prints, jacquards, silks, damasks, velvets. Tops in designs and colours and magnificent quality.

SAHCO HESSLEIN
17 rue du Mail, 75002 Paris ■ Tel: 01 42 60 04 46 ■ Fax: 01 47 03 47 17 ■ Mon-Thu 9:30-17:45, Fri 9:30-17:00 ■ English and German spoken

Contemporary designs: solids, jacquards, prints, sheers. Drapery hardware.

SANDERSON
19 rue du Mail 75002 Paris ■ Tel: 01 40 41 17 70 ■ Fax: 01 40 41 17 71 ■ Mon-Fri 8:30-13:00/14:00-17:30 Fri 16:30 ■ Mr. Riou speaks English

Furnishing fabrics and a selection of paints.

SAT CREATIONS
25-27 rue du Mail, 75002 Paris ■ Tel: 01 45 08 07 60 ■ Fax: 01 42 36 51 48 ■ E-mail: satcreat@club-internet.fr ■ Mon-Fri 8:45-12:00/13:30-17:30 ■ Marion Salmona speaks English and Spanish ■ Professional discount

Furnishing fabrics: satins, velvets, jacquards, silks, taffetas, moires, Toiles de Jouy. Specialist: wide width solids, and the best selection of wide width Toiles de Jouy.

SOULEIADO
78 rue de Seine, 75006 Paris ■ Tel: 01 43 54 15 13 ■ Fax: 01 43 54 84 45 ■ Mon-Sat 10:00-19:00 ■ English spoken ■ Major credit cards ■ 39 rue Proudhon,13150 Tarascon ■ Tel: 04 90 91 08 80 ■ Fax: 04 90 91 01 08

Specialty: printed country cottons. Table linens.

TACO EDITIONS
3 rue de Furstemberg, 75006 Paris ■ Tel: 01 40 46 94 82 ■ Fax: 01 46 33 51 05 ■ Mon-Sat 10:00-18:30 ■ English spoken

Prints, jacquards, solids. Flame resistent fabrics.

VERASETA

18 rue des Petits-Champs, 75002 Paris ■ Tel: 01 42 97 52 62 ■ Fax: 01 40 20 95 27 ■ E-mail: veraseta@gofornet.com ■ Mon-Fri 8:30-12:15/13:45-18:00, Fri closing 17:00 ■ Pierre Lorton speaks English

Specialty: Natural silks in taffetas, failles, satins, damasks. Excellent quality.

VEREL DE BELVAL/LE CRIN

4 rue de Furstemberg, 75006 Paris ■ Telfax: 01 43 26 17 89 ■ 6 rue du Mail, 75002 Paris ■ Telfax : 01 47 03 34 49 ■ 21 rue Cambon, 75001 Paris ■ Tel : 01 42 96 99 47 ■ Fax: 01 42 96 99 46 ■ Mon-Sat 10:00-13:00/14:00-18:30 ■ English spoken

Specialty: natural silks, brocades, velvets, taffetas, cotton jacquards. Great collection

VOGHI

21 rue Bonaparte, 75006 Paris ■ Tel: 01 43 54 85 44 ■ Fax: 01 40 51 83 59 ■ Mon-Sat 10:00-18:30 ■ English spoken

Printed Kashmirs. Special collection.

ZIMMER ET ROHDE

2 rue du Bouloi, 75001 Paris ■ Tel: 01 42 33 15 15 ■ Fax: 01 42 33 68 15 ■ website: zr-group.com ■ Mon-Fri 9:00-18:00 ■ English Spoken

Classical and contemporary fabrics.

Independent of the CSTA

BISSON BRUNEEL

109 bd Beaumarchais, 75003 Paris ■ Tel: 01 40 29 95 81 ■ Fax: 01 40 29 05 28 ■ Mon-Fri 10:00-13:00/14:00-19:00, Sat 14:00-19:00 ■ English spoken

Contemporary designs, jacquards, plaid throws, sheers.

♕ BRAQUÉNIÉ & CIE

111 bd Beaumarchais, 75003 Paris ■ Tel: 01 48 04 30 03 ■ Fax: 01 48 04 30 39 ■ Mon-Fri 9:00-18:00 ■ English spoken

Superb-quality fabrics. Large collection based on old documents. Carpets in jacquard designs, rugs, Aubusson tapestries, needlepoint. All can be custom made. Now part of the Groupe Pierre Frey.

CHELSEA TEXTILES
13-15 rue du Mail, 75002 Paris ■ Tel: 01 40 26 50 11 ■ Fax: 01 40 26 66 43 ■ Web: www.chelsea-textiles.co.uk ■ Mon-Fri 10:00-18:00 ■ Xavier Boyaval ■ English spoken ■ Professional discount

Fabrics, embroidered fabrics, cushions, needlepoint and carpets.

COLONY
28, rue Jacob, 75006 Paris ■ Tel: 01 43 29 61 70 ■ Fax: 01 43 54 73 79 ■ E-mail: tissuscolony@aol.com ■ Mon-Fri : 9 :30-18 :30 Sat : 11 :00-18 :30 ■ English spoken

Furnishing fabrics, jacquards, damasks based on ancient documents.

COMOGLIO
22 rue Jacob, 75006 Paris ■ Tel: 01 43 54 65 86 ■ Fax: 01 40 51 70 56 ■ Mon 15 :00-18 :30 Tue-Sat 10:00-18:30 ■ English spoken ■ Visa, Amex

Fabrics from Comoglio and Braquénié. The entire collection is 2m50 (97.5 inches) wide.

DESCHEMAKER
22 rue du Mail, 75002 Paris ■ Tel: 01 40 13 14 03 ■ Fax: 01 42 33 73 11 ■ Mon-Fri 9:00-18:00 / Fri 17:00 ■ English spoken

Velvets, jacquards and prints. Beautiful line of contemporary sofas and armchairs.

♛ **PIERRE FREY**
2 rue de Furstemberg, 75006 Paris ■ Tel: 01 46 33 73 00 ■ Fax: 01 42 96 85 38 ■ 111 bd Beaumarchais, 75003 Paris ■ Tel: 01 48 04 30 03 ■ Mon-Sat 10:00- 12:00/14:00-18:30 ■ English spoken ■ Showroom for professionals only: 47 rue des Petit-Champs, 75001 Paris ■ Tel: 01 44 77 36 00 ■ Fax: 01 42 96 85 38

Prints, jacquards, toiles, damasks. Collections of Pierre Frey, Braquénié, Comoglio, Lauer, Jim Thompson, Dedar Telar, Andrew Martin.

LE BOUCHER S.A - JAC DEY
4 rue de l'Avenir, 76960 Notre Dame de Bondeville ■ Tel: 02 35 74 50 50 ■ Fax: 01 35 76 38 15 ■ E-mail: leboucher@leboucher.fr ■ Website: www.leboucher.fr ■ Mon-Fri 8:30-12:30/ 13:30-17:30

Specialty: prints. Flame resistant fabrics.

MARITAC-TEXUNION

31 bd Bourdon, 75004 Paris ■ Tel: 01 48 87 72 13 ■ Fax: 01 48 87 23 83 ■ Mon-Fri 9:00-11:45/14:00-17:30

Prints, cottons, satins, cotton toiles, linen and cotton weaves.

MARVIC FRANCE

5 rue du Mail, 75002 Paris ■ Tel: 01 44 50 56 50 ■ Fax: 01 44 50 56 54 ■ E-mail: catmart@club-internet.fr ■ Mon-Fri 9:00-13:00/14:00-18:00 ■ Catherine Martin ■ English, Italian, German and Japanese spoken ■ Prices medium to high ■ 30 to 50% professional discount

A large collection of decorating fabrics including toiles de Jouy, moires jacquards, chenilles, silks.

NOBILIS

38, rue Bonaparte 75006 Paris ■ Tel: 01 43 29 12 61 ■ Mon-Sat: 10:30-18:30 ■ Web: www.nobilis.fr ■ English spoken ■ Prices medium to high

Large selection of prints, stripes, damasks, silks.

♛ PRELLE & CO.

5 place des Victoires, 75001 Paris ■ Tel: 01 42 36 67 21 ■ Mon-Fri 9:00-12:30/14:00-18:00 ■ English spoken ■ Prices very high

Highest quality silks and other fabrics. Superb custom reproductions of antique fabrics and silks. Museum quality. Founded in 1752.

SIMRANE

23-25 rue Bonaparte, 75006 Paris ■ Tel: 01 43 54 90 73/01 46 33 98 71 ■ Fax: 01 46 33 15 86 ■ Mon-Sat 9:30-19:00 ■ English spoken ■ Professional discount ■ Major credit cards

Fabrics and decorative accessories.

TISSUS L'ABEILLE

234 rue du Faubourg Saint-Antoine, 75012 Paris ■ Tel: 01 44 93 14 14 ■ Fax: 01 44 93 14 16 ■ Mon-Fri 9:00-12:30/14:00-18:00 ■ Guy and Catherine Balzarotti speak English

Satins, prints, chintz, damasks, velvets.

WINTER FRANCE

1 rue du Mail, 75002 Paris ■ Tel: 01 42 61 04 04 ■ Fax: 01 42 61 88 22 ■ Mon-Fri 9:30-12:30/13:00-18:00 ■ Liliane Hernot ■ Professional discount ■ CB

Specialty: wide-width fabrics for upholstery, draperies and wall-coverings. They also sell Italian fabrics, cashmeres, linens and plaids.

Fabric Specialties

AUVER A SOIE S.A.
ETABLISSEMENT L. BOUCHER
102 rue Reaumur, 75002 Paris ■ Tel: 01 42 33 52 92 ■ Fax: 01 42 33 14 44 ■ Mon-Fri 8:30-17:00 ■ Jean-Marie Boucher speaks English ■ Professional discount ■ Major credit cards.

Manufacturer of silk threads for all uses: embroidery, tapestry, sewing, weaving. Other threads: metallic, chenille, rayon and natural silk.

GRIFFINE
37 rue du Capitaine-Guynemer, 92090 Paris La Defense ■ Tel: 01 47 88 51 30 ■ Fax: 01 47 88 87 81 ■ Mon-Fri 8:00-18:00 ■ Jean Aran and Marie-Anne Morer speak English ■ Prices medium ■ 5% professional discount

Coated fabrics.

ILE DE FRANCE
66 rue du Chalons, 59202 Tourcoing ■ Tel: 03 20 25 99 40 ■ Fax: 03 20 26 47 62 ■ English and German spoken

Custom fabrics of all types for Editors and the contract market: minimum of 150 yards.

LA SOIE DISANT
36 rue de Verneuil, 75007 Paris ■ Tel 01 42 61 23 44 ■ Tue-Sat 10:30-18:30 ■ English spoken

Furnishing fabrics, specialists in silks. Wide range of beautiful colours. Some embroidered fabrics and designs of the top editors.

SIMONNOT ET GODARD
33 rue Vivienne, 75002 Paris ■ Tel: 01 42 33 94 60 ■ Fax: 01 40 39 06 95 ■ Mon-Fri 9:00-12:00/13:30-17:30 ■ Benjamin and Francois Simonnot speak English ■ Prices high

High-quality cotton in regular and wide-widths. Wools, silks.

👑 **TOILES DE MAYENNE**
9 rue de Mezières, 75007 Paris ■ Tel: 01 45 48 70 77 ■ Fax: 01 45 49 28 91 ■ 112 avenue Achille Péretti, 92200 Neuilly-sur-Seine ■ Tel: 01 47 22 94 48 ■ Factory: Fontaine-Daniel, 53101 Mayenne ■ Tel: 02 43 00 34 80 ■ Fax: 02 43 00 35 75 ■ Web: www.toiles-de-mayenne.com ■ Tue-Sat 10:00-13:30/14:30-18:30 ■ English spoken ■ Prices low to medium ■ Professional discount

Large selection of furnishing fabrics, especially cotton toiles in solids and prints. Wide widths. Mail or fax orders for custom draperies and sheers, bedspreads, cushions.

Fabric: Antique

LES INDIENNES-TISSUS ANCIENS
10 rue Saint-Paul, 75004 Paris ■ Tel: 01 42 72 35 34 ■ Fax: 01 42 72 78 85 ■ Mon-Sat 14:30-19:00, Sun & mornings by appointment ■ English spoken ■ Prices high ■ 12 to 20% professional discount

Antique fabrics: XVI, XVII, XVIII centuries. Kashmir shawls: XVIII, XIX centuries. Objects of art. Mme Virginie David organizes antique textile auctions at the Drouot auction rooms. Museum quality. Qualified expert.

Fabric: Embroidered

PHILIPPE CECILE
7 rue Geoffroy l'Angevin, 75004 Paris ■ Telfax: 01 44 54 00 61 ■ Mon-Fri 9:00-12:00/14:00-17:00, Fri close at 16:00, Sat by appointment ■ Prices medium to high

Master craftsman. Embroidery and ornamentation of furnishing fabrics. Creation, restoration and replicas.

JEAN-FRANÇOIS LESAGE
207 rue Saint-Honoré, 75001 Paris ■ Tel: 01 44 50 01 01 ■ Fax: 01 44 50 12 10 ■ Mon-Fri 14:30-18:30 ■ E-mail: jflesage@infonie.fr ■ Web: www.jeanfrancoislesage.com ■ Manager, Stephanie Decloux ■ English and Italian spoken ■ Prices high ■ Professional discount ■ Major credit cards

Hand-embroidered furnishing fabrics of the highest quality. Cushions, curtains, chairs, bed-spreads and fabrics by the yard.

Fabric: Hand Painted and Printed

MARYVONNE DE FOLLIN
21 rue Ernest-Deloison, 92200 Neuilly ■ Tel: 01 47 22 38 51 ■ By appointment ■ English spoken ■ Prices medium to high

Paintings on silk for decorative wall panels, screens, ceilings, upholstery, cushions, ottomans. Gorgeous colours and totally unique. Beautiful shawls.

▟ GEORGES KRIVOSHEY
46 rue Albert-Thomas, 75010 Paris ■ Tel: 01 40 40 04 35 ■ Fax: 01 42 45 88 30 ■ Mon-Fri 10:00-13:00/14:00-19:00 ■ Isabelle Versini speaks English

Atelier for printing on textiles. Reproductions of all motifs: antique and contemporary designs adapted for all projects. Printing on velvet, silk, leather.
Specialty: Artisanal work of quality in the highest tradition. Reproduction of motifs of the Renaissance, XVII, XVIII centuries using techniques of those periods.

Trimmings
Passementerie

Trimmings go back to the time of Adam and Eve. When men and women began to adorn themselves, they started a trend which has never slackened. In the annals of art history, we find trimmings on the fringes of the Venus of Lespugue (15,000 BC) on display in the Museum of Man in Paris. All ancient cultures show visual records of the use of tassels, feathers, pompons, cords, braids and fringes. From China through India, Egypt, the South Pacific and Ancient America, we find strings of beads, feather ornaments, decorative shells and elaborately painted masks. Today, Haute Couture and Haute Décoration would not be what they are without the "trimmings". They are an essential part of decoration for walls, draperies, chairs, cushions, carpets, etc.

▟ DECLERCQ PASSEMENTIERS
15 rue Etienne-Marcel, 75001 Paris ■ Tel: 01 44 76 90 70 ■ Fax: 01 42 33 13 75 ■ Web: www.declerqpassementiers.fr ■ Mon-Fri 8:30-18:00 ■ English spoken

Trimmings, braids, cords, tassels. Distributor of the products of Passementerie Nouvelle.

▟ HOULÈS (TRIMMINGS)
18 rue Saint-Nicolas, 75012 Paris ■ Tel: 01 43 44 65 19/01 64 24 55 00 ■ Fax: 01 64 24 71 76 ■ Web: www.houles.com ■ Mon-Fri 8:30-17:30 ■ Gilles Drapanaski and Virginie Wittmer speak English ■ Prices high ■ Professional discount

Superb collection and choice of trimmings, braids, tassels, tie-backs, cords, all woven accessories. Drapery hardware and upholstery tools.

♕ PASSEMENTERIE DU MARAIS
6 bd des Filles-du-Calvaire, 75011 Paris ■ Tel: 01 47 00 56 82 ■ Tue-Sat 9:30-12:45/14:00-18:15 ■ English spoken ■ Prices low to high ■ 5 to 10% professional discount

Special selection of braids and fringes for lampshades.

♕ LA PASSEMENTERIE NOUVELLE (CLAUDE DECLERC)
15 rue Etienne-Marcel, 75001 Paris ■ Tel: 01 42 36 30 01 ■ Fax: 01 42 33 13 75 ■ Mon-Fri 9:00-18:00 ■ Prices high ■ Professional discount

Excellent collection of everything in trimmings.

♕ LES PASSEMENTERIES DE L'ILE-DE-FRANCE
11 rue Trousseau, 75011 Paris ■ Tel: 01 48 05 44 33 ■ Fax: 48 05 04 36/30 35 75 39 ■ Mon-Fri 9:00-17:30/Fri closing 17:00 ■ English spoken

Outstanding and complete collection of trimmings.

♕ REYMONDON (PASSEMENTERIE)
13 rue Richard-Lenoir, 75011 Paris ■ Tel: 01 43 56 21 30 ■ Fax: 01 43 56 89 78 ■ Mon-Fri 8:30-12:30/13:30-17:00/Fri closing 16:00 ■ Prices high ■ Professional discount

One of the best suppliers of trimmings in France. Beautiful.

FIREPLACES
& ACCESSORIES
Cheminées et accessoires

♚ A.B.J. CHEMINÉES
Marché aux Puces, Marché Dauphine, Stand 105 and Workshop: 4 rue Lécuyer ■ Tel: 01 40 12 27 17 ■ Fax: 01 40 12 87 44 ■ E-mail: contact@abj-cheminee.com ■ Web: www.abj-cheminee.com ■ Mon-Sun 9:30-18:00 ■ Mr. David Bouskila ■ Some English spoken ■ Wide price range ■ Professional discount ■ Major credit cards

Antique fireplaces of every period and every style in stone, marble, wood. Excellent selection in marble.

CAMUS
Marché aux Puces ■ 88 rue des Rosiers, workshop: 5 rue Eugène-Lumeau, 93400 Saint-Ouen ■ Tel: 01 40 10 88 59 ■ Fax: 01 40 11 82 17 ■ Web: www.rogercamus.com ■ Mon-Sun 10:00-18:00 ■ English spoken ■ Prices medium ■ 5 to 10% professional discount

XVIII and XIX century wood, marble and stone fireplaces. Restoration and installation.

♚ GALERIE MARC DELIGNY
40 rue Mazarine, 75006 Paris ■ Tel: 01 56 24 82 11 ■ Fax: 01 56 24 84 68 ■ Mon-Sat 11:00-19:00 ■ Marc Deligny, sculptor ■ Prices medium to high

Wonderful statuary and fountains made by Marc Deligny. Extraordinary collection of antique objects of decoration and architectural elements in stone, marble and terracotta. He will make to order perfect replicas in the tradition of the period, whether it be the XVII, XVIII century or later. Marc Deligny follows in the footsteps of his father. Restoration of historic monuments, such as the Louvre.

DIGIART
Marché aux Puces ■ Marché Vernaison, 105 rue des Rosiers, Allée 1/3, Stand 14 ■ Tel: 01 40 11 61 34/01 40 12 68 95 ■ Fax: 01 40 12 12 60 ■ Sat-Mon and by appointment ■ Gilles Zoi speaks English ■ Prices medium ■ 10 to 20% discount ■ Major credit cards

Marble fireplaces and consoles. Lighting, clocks, mirrors and other decorative objects.

GODIN CHEMINÉES

6 bd Richard Lenoir, 75011 Paris ■ Tel: 01 48 07 88 35 ■ Fax: 01 43 55 17 31 ■ Mon-Sat 10:00-12:30/14:00-19:00 ■ Professional discount ■ Major credit cards

In business since 1840, they offer some very old free-standing wood-burning fireplaces. They also have one of the largest collections of classical fireplaces of all periods and all styles. They also manufacture fireplaces in all styles to produce heating as well as provide beauty. Their designers will work directly with the client and the client's own designer.

♛ LES JARDINS DU ROI SOLEIL

32 bd de la Bastille, 75012 Paris and 41 rue Saint-Honoré, 78000 Versailles ■ Tel: 01 43 44 44 31 ■ Fax: 01 43 44 44 52 ■ Web: www.jardinsroisoleil.com ■ Mon-Fri 9:30-12:00/14:00-18:30 ■ M. Jean Jiquel and Caroline Fried ■ English and Spanish spoken

Fireplace accessories of antique and contemporary designs. Fireplace plaques a specialty. They also sell the Orange Tree Tubs designed for the Sun King at Versailles. These are the best in the world.

JEAN LAPIERRE

58 rue Vieille-du-Temple, 75003 Paris ■ Tel: 01 42 74 07 70 ■ Fax: 01 42 74 37 60 ■ Web: www.cheminees-lapierre.com ■ Tue-Sat 11:00-19:00 ■ Michel David speaks English ■ Prices medium ■ Professional discount

Antique fireplaces in stone and wood from all periods, as well as replicas. Stone, flagstone, terracotta tiles, oak doors, stone framework for doors and windows, old oak Versailles parquet and various architectural elements.

L.V.S. ANTIQUITÉS

10 rue de Beaune, 75007 Paris ■ Tel: 01 42 96 90 90 ■ Fax: 01 42 96 90 92 ■ E-mail: LVSantiqites@wanadoo.fr ■ Web: www.art-face.com/LVS_antiquites ■ Mon-Sat 10:00-13:00/14:00-19:00 ■ Stèphane and Virginie Baquet ■ English spoken ■ Professional discount ■ Major credit cards

Antique fireplace accessories, fireplaces, furniture, art objects, paintings and drawings of the XVII, XVIII and XIX century.

♛ ANDRÉE MACÉ

266 rue du Faubourg-Saint-Honoré, 75008 Paris ■ Tel: 01 42 27 43 03 ■ Fax: 01 44 40 09 63 ■ E-mail: andree.mace@wanadoo.fr ■ Mon-Sat 9:00-12:30/14:00-18:30 ■ Dominique de Grivel ■ English and Spanish spoken ■ Prices medium to high ■ 10% professional discount ■ Amex

Extraordinary collection of fireplaces in stone, marble and wood. Statues, fountains, columns from the XV to the XVIII century, mostly French. Architectural elements of the XIX century. Garden ornaments and much more. Also expert installation of fireplaces. Their collection is splendid.

PIERRE MADEL
22 rue Jacob, 75006 Paris ■ Tel: 01 43 26 90 89 ■ Fax: 01 40 46 07 09 ■ Tue-Fri 15:00-19:00, Sat 11:00-12:30/15:00-19:00 ■ English spoken ■ Prices medium ■ 10% professional discount ■ Visa, MC, Amex

Very nice antique iron and bronze accessories for the fireplace.

JEAN MAGNAN CHEMINÉES
241 rue de la Croix-Nivert, 75015 Paris ■ Tel: 01 48 42 35 32 ■ Fax: 01 45 32 42 04 ■ Tue-Sat 14:00-19:00/or 9:00/22:00 by appointment ■ Prices medium ■ Professional discount ■ Major credit cards

Manufacturer of contemporary fireplaces and accessories, barbecues, grilles, bread and pizza ovens.

LA MAISON DU FER FORGÉ
42 bd Raspail, 75007 Paris ■ Telfax: 01 45 48 51 69 ■ Tue-Sat 10:00-19:00 ■ English spoken ■ 10 to 15% professional discount ■ Most credit cards

Fireplaces, especially copies of antique fireplaces. Beautiful cast iron accessories.

PROVINCES DE FRANCE
59 rue de Maubeuge, 75009 Paris ■ Tel: 01 42 80 28 62 ■ Web: www.loiseletdiffusion.com ■ Mon-Sat 10:00-12:30/14:00-19:00 ■ English spoken ■ Prices medium to high ■ Professional discount

Special collection of 200 models of cast iron backplates for fireplaces. These are quite special.

FRAMES AND FRAMING
Cadres et Encadreurs

Frames

IV

ATELIER P. LONZA & M. BERGER
2 rue Castex, 75004 Paris ■ Tel: 01 42 78 82 12 ■ Mon-Fri 9:30-13:00/14:00-18:00

Frames, pedestals and mountings.

VI

👑 **G. BAC**
35-37 rue Bonaparte, 75006 Paris ■ Tel: 01 43 26 82 67 ■ Fax: 01 46 34 51 58 ■ E-mail: gbac@cybercable.fr ■ Mon-Fri 9:00-12:00/14:00-19:00 ■ Georges Gross ■ English, German and Italian spoken ■ Professional discount ■ Major credit cards

Gilded wood frames from France, Spain, Holland and Italy. French mirrors and consoles. Some of the XVI century and mainly XVII and XVIII century. Wonderful collection.

👑 **REYNAL HERVOUËT**
40 rue de l'Université, 75006 Paris ■ Tel: 01 42 61 24 18 ■ Fax: 01 42 61 25 19 ■ Tue-Sat 11:00-12:30/14:00-19:00

Exceptional antique frames, chairs and gilded furniture. Mainly XVIII century.

VIII

👑 **CADRES LEBRUN**
155 rue du Faubourg-Saint-Honoré, 75008 Paris ■ Tel: 01 45 61 14 66 ■ Fax: 01 45 61 97 49 ■ Mon-Fri 14:30-19:00 ■ Annick Lebrun and Virginie Fouquin Lebrun ■ English spoken ■ Prices high ■ 10% professional discount

Some of the best antique gilded frames in Paris. Frames from the XV to the XIX centuries. Mirrors, consoles, barometers. They will make presentations in your home. Restoration, sculpture and gilding. Their clients include many of the great collectors of the world.

MAISON EDOUARD GROSVALLET
126 bd Haussmann 75008 Paris ■ Telfax 01 45 22 19 68 ■ Mon-Fri 10:00-12:00/14:30-18:00 ■ English and Spanish spoken

Antique mirrors, consoles and frames of all styles.

Framing

**MICHEL SELIM
ALTUGLAS**
10 rue du Mail, 75002 Paris ■ Tel: 01 42 36 38 74 ■ Fax 01 42 36 44 49 ■ Mon-Fri 9:00-12:30/13:30-17:30 ■ Prices medium to high ■ Professional discount

Custom-made items in plexiglass for the presentation of art objects. Table frames, columns, boxes.

V

APARTELIER
47 rue Censier, 75005 Paris ■ Tel: 01 43 36 14 74 ■ Wed-Sat 15:00-20:00, Sun by appointment ■ Jacques Maréchal speaks English ■ Prices medium

Framing, restoration: paintings, engravings, art objects.

ATELIER CHRISTIAN DE BEAUMONT
11 rue Frédéric-Sauton, 75005 Paris ■ Tel: 01 43 29 88 75 ■ Fax: 01 40 51 88 06 ■ Tue-Sat 11:00-13:00/15:00-19:00 ■ English spoken ■ Prices high ■ 15% professional discount

Creation and fabrication of frames, stands and accessories for presentation of decorative objects. Creation of furniture and accessories in unique editions.

UNE IMAGE EN PLUS
19 rue Saint-Séverin, 75005 Paris ■ Tel: 01 43 25 83 85 ■ Fax 01 43 25 51 35 ■ Mon-Sat 10:00-24:00 ■ English spoken ■ Prices medium ■ Major credit cards

Framing of art posters, postcards, film posters, concert posters and photos of stars.

VI

ART DE L'ENCADREMENT
9 rue de l'Odéon, 75006 Paris ■ Telfax: 01 40 51 70 61 ■ Web: www.encadrements.com ■ Mon-Fri 9:00-12:00/13:00-17:00 ■ Prices medium ■ Professional discount on quantity

Framing of paintings, drawings, engravings. Old-style and modern frames.

JEAN ESTEVE

3 rue Jacques-Callot, 75006 Paris ■ Telfax: 01 43 54 19 10 ■ E-mail: esteve.jeanmax@easynet.fr ■ Tue-Sat 9:30-12:30/14:30-18:30 ■ Prices medium ■ 20 to 50 % professional discount ■ Major credit cards

Framing. Restoration of frames, paintings, engravings, pastels.

HAVARD PÈRE ET FILS

123 bd du Montparnasse, 75006 Paris ■ Tel: 01 43 22 34 87 ■ Fax: 01 43 20 42 87 ■ Web: www.havard.fr ■ Mon-Fri 9:00:12:30/14:00-18:30 Sat 9:00-12:00 ■ English spoken ■ Professional discount ■ Major credit cards

Custom frames. Gilding. Restoration of paintings.

ATELIER GUILLAUME MARTEL

2 rue du Regard 75006 Paris ■ Telfax: 01 45 49 02 07 ■ Tue-Sat 9:00-11:45/14:30-19:00 ■ English spoken

Custom framing in unusual and original designs. Classical style frames. Leafing in gold, copper, silver, platinum and aluminium.

THE PARIS AMERICAN ART CO.

4 rue Bonaparte, 75006 Paris ■ Tel: 01 43 26 09 93 ■ Fax: 01 43 54 33 80 ■ Tue-Sat 10:00-13:00/13:45-18:30 ■ English spoken ■ Prices medium to high ■ Professional discount

Gilded frames in classic styles. Restoration. Modern frames. Antique frames, mirrors, frames for miniatures, engravings, drawings and paintings. Framing.

VII

OISEAUX BLEUS

23 rue Augereau, 75007 Paris ■ Telfax: 01 47 05 94 58 ■ Tue-Sat 10:00-12:30/14:30-19:00 ■ Monique Lazou speaks English ■ Prices medium ■ Professional discount

Framing of drawings, engravings, water-colours, paintings. Presentation of objects. Old-style hand washing for drawings and engravings. Restoration.

BERTHELOT
184 rue du Faubourg-Saint-Honoré, 75008 Paris ■ Telfax: 01 45 63 34 07 ■ Mon-Fri 9:15-18:30, Sat 9:30-12:30/14:30-18:00 ■ English spoken ■ Prices medium ■ 10% professional discount

Frames and framing in classical-styles. Reproduction of antique-style frames. Gold leafing of frames and all objects in wood. Limited editions and reproductions of classic sculpture in bronze.

PHILIPPE MULER
24 rue de la Ville-l'Evêque, 75008 Paris ■ Tel: 01 42 65 43 38 ■ Fax: 01 42 65 08 13 ■ E-mail: p.muller@wanadoo.fr ■ Tue-Fri 14:00-19:00, Sat 10:00-13:00 ■ Philippe Muler speaks English ■ Prices very high ■ 10% professional discount

Specialty: Mounting of all types of artwork. Antique frames, non-reflective glass, anti-ultra-violet glass, plexiglass. Chemical free mattes and backings. High quality. Restoration of frames and old mountings.

RAPID CADRE
7 rue du Commandant-Rivière, 75008 Paris ■ Tel: 01 42 56 06 08 ■ Fax: 01 42 56 80 58 ■ Web: www.rapid-cadre.com ■ Mon-Fri 9:30-18:30 ■ Marie-France Paul-Reynaud speaks English ■ Prices medium ■ 10 to 20% professional discount

Framing of posters, paintings, engravings. Old-style hand colour washing. Rapid service.

X

P.M. ROUSSEAU
Previously Ets Pieton ■ 105 rue La Fayette, 75010 Paris ■ Tel: 01 48 74 21 23 ■ Fax: 01 45 26 25 29 ■ Mon-Fri 8:00-19:00 ■ Pierre-Marie Rousseau speaks a bit of English ■ Prices medium ■ 5 to 10% professional discount

Fabrication of classical style frames in gilded wood. Expertise and restoration of antique frames.

BENEDETTI ESTÈVE
80 rue de Charonne, 75011 Paris ■ Tel: 01 43 71 21 35 ■ Tue-Fri 9:00-12:00/14:00-19:00, Sat 9:00-12:00/15:00-18:00 ■ Italian spoken ■ Professional discount

Framing in all styles; of paintings, lithographs, drawings. Restoration of frames, gold and silver leafing.

MAISON ZWOLINSKI

33 rue Amelot, 75011 Paris ■ Tel: 01 43 55 63 80 ■ Fax: 01 43 55 52 20 ■ Mon-Sat 10:00-18:00 ■ Laurent and Karine Zwolinski speak English ■ Prices low ■ Professional discount ■ Major credit cards

Framing, mirrors for boutiques. Restoration of paintings, objets d'art. Also a small gallery of paintings.

―――――――――――――― XII ――――――――――――――

👑 ATELIER LEBEAU

117 avenue Daumesnil 75012 Paris ■ Tel: 01 43 45 96 05 ■ Mon-Thu 9:00-18:00, Fri 9:00-17:00, Sat by appointment ■ Joseph Hegybiro ■ Hungarian, Italian and some English spoken

Design, fabrication and restoration of sculptured and gilded wood frames. Framing. Works for the major regional and foreign museums, painters, galleries and private individuals. Objects in gilded wood.

CLAUDE GALATRY

43 rue de la Gare de Reuilly, 75012 Paris ■ Tel: 01 43 07 24 92 ■ Mon-Sat 9:00-12:00/14:00-18:00 ■ Prices medium ■ 20% professional discount

Framing and fabrication of frames, especially for miniatures, round and oval.

―――――――――――――― XIII ――――――――――――――

👑 ALOT

101 rue de Patay, 75013 Paris ■ Tel: 01 45 82 80 32 ■ Fax: 01 44 24 51 90 ■ Mon-Fri 8:00-18:00, Sat 8:00-12:00 ■ Prices medium ■ Professional discount

Framing. All types of gilding on wood. Wood carving. Restoration of all objects and furniture in gilded wood. Specialist in French gilded furniture of the XVII and XVIII centuries. Qualified expert.

―――――――――――――― XV ――――――――――――――

BADIA-ENCADREMENT

55 rue Blomet, 75015 Paris ■ Tel: 01 42 73 00 82 ■ Tue-Sat 9:30-12:30/14:00-19:00 ■ Prices low ■ Spanish spoken ■ Professional discount. ■ Major credit cards

Gilding and framing in all styles, restoration of paper, paintings. Fabrication of mounts for art objects.

MARIE-LAURE DE LAPEROUSE

24 rue Violet, 75015 Paris ■ Tel: 01 45 75 00 08 ■ Tue-Sat 10:00-13:00/14:00-19:00 ■ English spoken ■ Prices medium ■ Professional discount ■ Major credit cards

Framing and restoration of frames. Frames for paintings, mounting of collectibles, fans, stamps, pipes, butterflies. Restoration of paintings and paper.

XVI

GALERIE COROT

8 rue Corot, 75016 Paris ■ Tel: 01 42 88 46 80 ■ Tue 10:00-12:30/15:00-19:00, Wed-Sat 10:00-19:00 ■ Prices medium ■ 20% professional discount

Classical and modern framing. Restoration of paintings, old engravings, charcoal drawings and pastels.

LA MAISON DU CADRE

96 rue de la Tour, 75116 Paris ■ Tel: 01 45 04 75 73 ■ Fax: 01 45 04 75 79 ■ Mon-Sat 9:30-19:00 ■ Hinda Zerbib speaks English ■ Prices medium to high ■ 10% professional discount

Antique frames. Gilding. Fabrication of frames in all styles and all types of framing. Restoration of antique frames. Restoration of paintings, pastels, engravings. High quality work and materials.

J.L. VERDIÉ

21 rue du Bois-le-Vent, 75016 Paris ■ Telfax: 01 45 25 02 74 ■ Web: www.auteuil.com or www.passy.com ■ Tue-Sat 10:00-12:30/14:00-19:00 ■ Jean-Louis Verdié speaks English ■ Major credit cards

Traditional framing in classical styles. Old-style hand-colour washing. Gilding, restoration of gilded wood.

MIREILLE MATHIEU

50 rue de l'Assomption, 75016 Paris ■ Tel: 01 42 88 50 51 ■ Tue-Sat 10:00-13:00/14:30-19:00 ■ Mireille Mathieu speaks English ■ Prices medium to high ■ Professional discount

Studio and boutique of framing. Restoration of engravings, frames, gilding.

JEAN-MICHEL RAPP

40 rue Poussin, 75016 Paris ■ Tel: 01 46 51 13 45 ■ Fax: 01 46 51 32 37 ■ E-mail: jmrapp@club-internet.fr ■ Web: www.en-cadreur.net ■ Tue-Sat 10:30-13:00/14:00-19:00 ■ English spoken ■ Professional discount ■ Major credit cards

Framing in antique and modern styles. Restoration of paintings. Cleaning of engravings and framing of fans. Master Artisan.

THELLIER

64 rue de Longchamp, 75116 Paris ■ Tel: 01 47 04 32 83 ■ Fax: 01 47 27 66 02 ■ Tue-Sat 10:00-12:30/14:30-19:00 ■ English spoken ■ Prices medium ■ Professional discount

All kinds of gilding and framing, restoration. Excellent quality.

───────── XVII ─────────

♔ ATELIER DU BOIS DORÉ

80 av des Ternes, 75017 Paris ■ Tel: 01 45 74 67 58 ■ Fax: 01 44 74 72 49 ■ Mon-Sat 9:00-12:30/14:00-19:00 ■ English spoken

Choice of 1,500 antique frames. 300 moulding styles for reproductions of antique frames. Framing. Restoration of gilded wood. Creation, in very limited editions, of furniture and objects in gilded wood.

BERENGÈRE POLACK

27 rue de Chazelles, 75017 Paris ■ Telfax: 01 46 22 70 93 ■ Tue-Fri 10:00-19:00, Sat 11:00-19:00 ■ English spoken ■ Prices medium ■ Professional discount ■ Visa

Framing, bookbinding, art objects.

TOP CADRES

33 rue Lemercier, 75017 Paris ■ Tel 01 40 08 03 70/01 40 08 05 48 ■ Mon-Sat 9:00-17:45 ■ Mr. and Mrs. Le Fur ■ English, Spanish and Arabic spoken ■ Professional discount ■ Visa

Framing of canvases and works under glass. Large choice of antique style and comtemporary frames. Their clients include antique and art dealers, top hotels and well-known artists.

LA BAGUETTE DE BOIS
44 rue Lepic, 75018 Paris ■ Tel: 01 46 06 36 80 ■ Fax: 01 42 54 54 92 ■ Tue-Sat 9:30-19:00 ■ Prices medium ■ 10% profession-al discount

An excellent framing establishment. They take special pains to make sure you choose the right frame for the subject. Wonderful selection of antique-style frames. Framing in all styles from classical through modern.

PEINTRES SANS FRONTIÈRES
2 av Moderne, 75019 Paris ■ Tel: 01 42 38 05 82 ■ Fax: 01 42 00 42 25 ■ Mon-Fri 9:30-13:30/14:30-18:30 ■ Pierre Estrada speaks English ■ Prices low ■ Professional discount

Framing of all kinds. They are wholesalers.

ESPACE 20
22 villa Riberolle, 75020 Paris ■ Tel: 01 43 79 78 14 ■ Fax: 01 43 48 13 08 ■ Mon-Sat 9:00-12:00/14:00-17:00 ■ Prices medium ■ 20% professional discount

Framing of paintings and drawings. Specialty: photograph-ic framing.

GALERIE 20
ÉTIENNE LEROY-PIERRE LEROY
288 rue des Pyrenées, 75020 Paris ■ Tel: 01 43 66 83 88 ■ Tue-Wed-Fri-Sat 10:00-12:30, Thu and Sun 11:00-13:30 ■ Prices medium ■ 20% professional discount

Framing, restoration. Custom glass cases (vitrines) for ob-jects. Specialty: old paintings. Also photo re-touching.

L'ATELIER D'ENCADREMENT
Carreau de Neuilly, 108 av Charles de Gaulle, 92200 Neuilly ■ Tel: 01 47 38 14 94 ■ Fax: 01 47 38 63 99 ■ Mon-Sat 9:00-19:00 ■ Patrick Bertrand ■ English spoken ■ 10% discount for artists

The authors swear by this establishment. Pleasant, efficient and economical. They offer classical and contemporary framing. Restoration of paintings and frames. They will also deliver and hang your pictures for you. Cleaning of engrav-ings. Mirrors, bathroom shelves, showcases, tables and smoked glass items.

♛ ROBERT DUVIVIER

30 rue de Sablonville, 92200 Neuilly ■ Tel: 01 47 22 25 90 ■ Fax: 01 46 43 01 49 ■ Tue-Sat 9:00-13:00/14:00-19:00 ■ Miss Duvivier speaks a little English ■ Prices medium to high ■ 10% professional discount ■ CB

Reproduction frames of all styles, Louis XIV to contemporary. Restoration of paintings and silding all sculptured wood items. Excellent-quality work.

FURNITURE

Children's Furniture
Meubles d'enfant

———————————— VII ————————————

CÂLIN CÂLINE
200 bd Saint-Germain, 75007 Paris ■ Tel: 01 42 22 22 96 ■ Fax: 01 60 16 46 94 ■ E-mail:calincaline.ifrance.com ■ Mme Danielle Jorrand ■ English spoken ■ Prices medium ■ Mayor credit cards
Everything for children's rooms. Cots, beds, chairs, chests of drawers, lamps and a beautiful line of linens.

LA BELLE ÉTOILE
11 rue Rousselet, 75007 Paris ■ Tel: 01 45 66 05 75 ■ Mon-Fri 10:00-18:30, Tue-Wed 14:00-18:30 ■ English spoken ■ Prices medium ■ Mayor credit cards
Baby linens, furniture and clothing. Line of textiles for babies' rooms.

———————————— NEUILLY ————————————

LE PETIT ATELIER
25 rue de Chartres, 92200 Neuilly ■ Tel: 01 46 43 03 54 ■ By appointment ■ Céline Valentine ■ English spoken ■ Prices medium
Custom painted furniture for children's rooms. Paintings, frames, and decorative objects. Small chairs from FF300 ($ 45.00) and toy boxes from FF200 ($ 30.00).

Contemporary Furniture
Meubles contemporains

———————————— III ————————————

ALICE ALIANCA
15 rue Elzévir, 75003 Paris ■ Tel: 01 42 71 20 65 ■ Fax: 01 42 71 62 07 ■ Mon-Sat 10:00-19:00 ■ English and Spanish spoken ■ Professional discount ■ Amex, Visa
Beautiful designs of furniture and accessories by contemporary artists. Lighting, linen, table arts. Wood objects from Togo by Danielle Bordet. Very nice cabinet knobs in glass by Laurent Benn.

BAKER FURNITURE
Hôtel du Grand Veneur, 60 rue de Turenne, 75004 Paris ■ Tel: 01 44 54 50 70 ■ Fax 01 48 04 91 50 ■ Mon-Sat 9:30-18:30 ■ Christine Stevens ■ English spoken ■ Major credit cards
Classic furniture in English style. High-quality American company.

YVES HALARD
27 quai de La Tournelle, 75005 Paris ■ Tel: 01 44 07 14 00 ■ Fax: 01 44 07 10 30 ■ Mon-Sat 10:00-18:30 ■ Michelle Halard ■ English spoken ■ Professional discount ■ Amex, Visa
Beautiful line of sofas, armchairs, lamps and decorative objetcs. Sofas made to measure.

GALERIE DEA
30 rue Bonaparte, 75006 Paris ■ Tel: 01 46 34 69 00 ■ Fax: 01 44 07 26 76 ■ Mon-Sat 10:00-19:00 ■ David Rucli ■ English spoken ■ Prices medium to very high ■ Professional discount ■ Amex, Visa, MC
Artist's own designs of metal furniture. Metal and glass objetcs and jewellery. All made to order.

NOBILIS
29 rue Bonaparte, 75006 Paris ■ Tel: 01 43 29 12 71 ■ Fax: 01 43 29 77 57 ■ English spoken ■ Prices medium ■ Professional discount
Their own exclusive line of contemporary furniture, lamps and fabrics.

VII

LIGNE ROSET
189 bd Saint-Germain, 75007 Paris ■ Tel: 01 45 48 54 13 ■ Fax: 01 45 44 01 20 ■ Web: www.ligne-roset.tm.fr ■ Mon 14:00-19:00/Tue-Sat 10:00-19:00 ■ English spoken ■ Prices medium to high ■ Major credit cards ■ 15 avenue Matignon 75008 Paris ■ Tel 01 42 25 94 19 ■ Fax 01 45 63 59 62 ■ 25 rue du Faubourg Saint-Antoine 75011 ■ Tel 01 40 01 00 05 ■ Fax 01 40 01 00 07 ■ 99 avenue du Maine 75014 ■ Tel 01 43 21 65 70 ■ Fax 01 43 27 99 10
Large choice of contemporary furniture, chairs, carpets and accessories. Lots of outlets.

POLTRONA FRAU

242bis bd Saint-German, 75007 Paris ■ Tel: 01 42 22 74 49 ■ Fax: 01 45 49 42 04 ■ Tue-Sat 11:00-13:00/14:00-19:00 ■ Marie-Magdeleine Liberge ■ English spoken ■ Prices medium to hish ■ Professional discount ■ Major credit cards

Italian high quality contemporary furniture specially chairs, armchairs and sofas. These are usually in leather, some fabrics.

TECNO

242 bd Saint-German, 75007 Paris ■ Tel: 01 42 22 18 27 ■ Fax: 01 45 44 15 91 ■ Mon-Fri 10:00-13:00/14:00-18:00 and by appointment

High quality contemporary furniture and lighting.

──────────── VIII ────────────

BESSON RIVE DROITE

46 av Marceau, 75008 Paris ■ Tel: 01 47 20 75 35 ■ Fax: 01 47 20 15 62 ■ Mon-Fri 10:00-18:00 ■ English spoken ■ Major credit cards

Small line of contemporary furniture and sofas, wallpapers, fabrics, rugs. Also at 39 rue Bonaparte, 75006 Paris.

PROTIS

153 rue du Faubourg-Saint-Honoré, 75008 Paris ■ Tel: 01 45 62 22 40 ■ Fax: 01 45 62 57 71 ■ Web: www.protis.fr ■ Mon-Fri 9:15-19:00, Sat 10:00-13:00/14:30-18:30 ■ Georges Assouline speaks English ■ Prices medium ■ 15% professional discount

Contemporary furniture: sofas, bookcases, tables, chairs, desks, for the office and the home.

GUY STÈPHANE

225 rue du Faubourg-Saint-Honoré, 75008 Paris ■ Tel: 01 46 22 21 52 ■ Mon 15:00-19:00, Tue-Sat 10:00-19:00 ■ Prices medium ■ Professional discount

Contemporary furniture, sofas, chairs, mirrors, lighting, decorative objects.

──────────── IX ────────────

MAPLE EUROPE LTD

5 rue Boudreau, 75009 Paris ■ Tel : 01 53 43 86 00 ■ Fax : 01 53 43 86 01 ■ Web: maple@mapleparis.com ■ Philip Parnell ■ English spoken ■ Major credit cards

English furniture, objects and art.

LE BIHAN
4 rue du Faubourg-Saint-Antoine, Paris 75011 ■ Tel: 01 43 43 06 75
■ Fax: 01 43 42 10 37 ■ E-mail abadie@club-internet.fr ■ Web:
www.lebihan_Paris.com ■ Mon 14:00-19:00, Tue-Sat 10:00-19:00,
Thu closes 21:00 ■ O. Abadie, Director ■ English, German and Italian spoken ■ Prices high ■ Professional discount ■ Major credit cards
High quality contemporary furniture.

XII

BAGUÈS
Viaduc des Arts, 73 avenue Daumesnil 75012 Paris ■ Tel: 01 43
41 53 53 ■ Fax: 01 43 41 54 55 ■ E-mail: baguesparis@minitel.net
■ Mon-Fri 9:00-18:00, Sat 10:00-18:00 ■ Jean-Jacques Corre ■
English spoken ■ Professional Discount ■ Major credit cards
**Fine collection of bronze and wrought iron lighting: 8,000
models have been created since 1840. Period lighting in
bronze and crystal, chandeliers, lamps, sconces. Restoration services. High-quality contemporary furniture, lighting,
mirrors and decorative objects.**

THOMAS DE LUSSAC
20 rue Raffet, Paris 75016 ■ Tel: 01 42 30 52 91 ■ Fax: 01 42 25
61 25 ■ Thomas de Lussac ■ English and Spanish spoken ■ Professional discount
**Furniture, lamps and sofas. Hard-painted porcelain. Sells to
Bergdorf and Aspreys.**

MARINA DE BOURBON
112 bd de Courcelles, 75017 Paris ■ Tel: 01 47 63 42 01 ■ Fax:
01 40 53 96 50 ■ Mon-Sat 10:30-19:30 ■ English spoken ■
Prices medium to high ■ Visa, Amex
**Nice mixture of contemporary and antique furniture, lighting
and decorative objects.**

Rattan Furniture
Meubles en rotin

DÉCOUVERTE
245 rue du Faubourg-Saint-Antoine, 75011 Paris ■ Tel: 01 43 72 85
61 ■ Fax: 01 43 72 24 86 ■ Mon-Sat 10:30-13:00/14:00-19:30 ■
English spoken ■ Prices medium ■ 10 to 15% professional discount
Contemporary rattan furniture, for home and office.

ROTIN D'AUJOURD'HUI
65 av Gambetta, 75020 Paris ■ Tel: 01 46 36 90 32 ■ Fax: 01 44 62 09 11 ■ Web www.lerotindaujourdhui.com ■ Tue-Sat 9:30-12:00/14:00-19:00 ■ English spoken ■ Prices medium ■ Major credit cards

Custom fabrication and repair of rattan furniture, objects and gifts.

Custom Contemporary Furniture
Meubles contemporains sur mesure

———————————— V ————————————

ATELIER CHRISTIAN DE BEAUMONT
11 rue Frédéric Sauton, 75005 Paris ■ Tel: 01 43 29 88 75 ■ Fax: 01 40 51 88 06 ■ Tue-Sat 11:00-13:00/15:00-19:00 ■ English spoken ■ Prices high ■ 15% professional discount

Creation and fabrication of furniture and lighting, frames, accessories for presentation of decorative collectibles.

———————————— VI ————————————

LES MIGRATEURS
54 rue Jacob, 75006 Paris ■ Tel. 01 42 86 81 50 ■ Fax: 01 42 86 81 67 ■ E-mail: les.migrateurs@wanadoo.fr ■ Web: www.lesmigrateurs.com ■ Mon 14:00-19:00, Tue-Sat 10:00-19:00 ■ Henry Personnaz ■ English, Spanish and Italian spoken ■ Professional discount ■ Major credit cards

Contemporary furniture, sofas, lighting and objects. Custom creations to order.

———————————— VII ————————————

COHERENCE
31 bd Raspail, 75007 Paris ■ Tel: 01 42 22 15 83 ■ Fax: 01 45 48 54 17 ■ Mon-Sat 10:00-19:00 ■ Sylvie Legrand ■ English spoken ■ Prices high ■ 10% professional discount ■ Major credit cards

Custom sofas and armchairs. Low tables, lighting and accessories.

♕ **MARIE-CHRISTINE DE LA ROCHEFOUCAULD**
16 rue de l'Université, 75007 Paris ■ Tel: 01 42 86 02 40/01 42 61 22 22 ■ Fax: 01 42 60 21 17 ■ E-mail: mc@de-la-rochefoucauld.fr ■ Web: www.de-la-rochefoucauld.fr ■ Mon-Sat 10:30-13:15/14:00-19:00 ■ English spoken ■ Prices medium to high ■ Professional discount ■ major credit cards

Original creations of Marie-Christine de la Rochefoucald: Table bases made of stacks of antique books, painted cabinets, armchairs upholstered in tapestry, small sofas, lighting, cushions, tablecloths bordered in velvet. Special editions of aged fabrics.

♔ SANTANGELO
209-211 bd Saint-Germain, 75007 Paris ■ Tel: 01 45 48 09 61 ■ Fax: 01 40 49 06 41 ■ Tue-Sat 10:00-12:30/15:00-19:00 ■ Mme Santangelo ■ Italian and some English and Spanish spoken ■ Prices high ■ Professional discount

Superb tables and panels created to order in marble and semi-precious stones and mosaic. All custom creations.

———————————— IX ————————————

♔ RICHARD PEDUZZI
41 rue de la Tour d'Auvergne 75009 Paris ■ Tel: 01 49 70 00 01 ■ Fax: 01 42 81 06 75 ■ E-mail: rpeduzzi@ensad.fr ■ By appointment ■ Italian and English spoken ■ Prices high ■ Professional discount

Artist's own designs of furniture made to order in beautiful forms, in cherry and other fruit woods. Tables, chairs, benches, desks, chests of drawers. All unique models by this world-renowned set designer.

Display Cabinets
Vitrines

VITRINES VENDÔME
81 rue des Archives, 75003 Paris ■ Tel: 01 42 72 58 38 ■ Fax: 01 42 72 65 59 ■ E-mail: vendom@mail.com ■ Mon-Fri 9:00-12:00/13:00-18:00 ■ English spoken ■ Prices high

High-quality display cabinets for the home, stores, hotels, museums, galleries. All dimensions. Installation.

Plexiglass

MICHEL SELIM
10 rue du Mail, 75002 Paris ■ Tel: 01 42 36 38 74 ■ Fax: 01 42 36 44 49 ■ Mon- Fri 9-12:30/13:30-17:30 ■ Prices medium to high ■ Professional discount

Custom creation of furniture and objects in plexi-glass.

Custom Reproduction Furniture
Reproduction de meubles sur mesure

---------------------------------- XI ----------------------------------

♕ ASTELLE
59 rue du Faubourg-Saint-Antoine, 75011 Paris ■ Tel: 01 43 43 09 39 ■ Fax: 01 43 43 44 62 ■ Tue-Sat 9:00-12:30/14:30-18:30 ■ Pierre Vasseur speaks some English ■ Prices medium to high ■ Professional discount

Fine creation and re-creation of chairs, armchairs, sofas and tables. Made-to-measure bookshelves and wood panelling. Excellent wood sculptor and craftsman.

ATELIERS DE BRIMBOIS-BOISERIES ET DECORATIONS
5 cité Beauharnais, 75011 Paris ■ Tel: 01 43 71 76 30 ■ Fax: 01 43 71 74 84 ■ Web: www.boiseries-deco.fr ■ Mon-Fri 8:00-11:45/13:30-18:00 ■ English spoken ■ Prices high

Reproduction classical style furniture and contemporary creation, specializing in marquetry.

DEGROOTE ET MUSSY
12 passage de Taillandiers, 75011 Paris ■ Tel: 01 48 05 13 91 ■ Web: www.m2paris.com ■ Mon-Fri 8:30-19:00 ■ Christian Mussy speaks English ■ Prices medium to high ■ Professional discount

Custom furniture in all classical styles and contemporary.

NOUVEAUX MEUBLES D'ART
179 rue du Faubourg-Saint-Antoine, 75011 Paris ■ Tel: 01 43 07 24 75 ■ Fax: 01 43 07 42 47 ■ Web: http://perso-club.internet.fr/diver01 ■ Mon-Sat 8:00-12:00/14:00-18:00 ■ Jean-Paul Bart speaks English ■ Prices medium to high ■ Professional discount ■ Major credit cards

Top-quality custom reproductions of antique furniture.

BERNARD RIMOLDI
3 passage Rauch, 75011 Paris ■ Tel: 01 43 79 78 59 ■ Mon-Fri 8:00-12:00/14:00-18:00, Sat 8:00-12:00 ■ Prices medium ■ Professional discount

All classical styles of furniture custom made to order.

---------------------------------- XII ----------------------------------

JEAN-LUC FAUCHEUX
19 rue Claude-Tillier, 75012 Paris ■ Tel: 01 43 48 86 91 ■ Mon-Fri 8:00-18:00 ■ Prices medium

Copies of all antique furniture styles to measure.

ERIC LAURENT-LASSON
159 rue Saint-Charles, 75015 Paris ■ Tel: 01 45 54 65 22 ■ Fax: 01 44 25 18 65 ■ Mon-Fri 8:00-17:00 ■ Diane Laurent-Lasson and Jean-Michel Reginster speak English ■ Prices medium ■ 20% professional discount

Restoration of furniture and gilding. Work experience: Maison de Victor Hugo, museums, public buildings.

------------ **XVI** ------------

JEAN-MARC DESLOUBIÈRES
27 rue de Longchamp, 75116 Paris ■ Tel: 01 45 53 24 91 ■ Fax: 01 47 27 07 03 ■ Mon-Fri 10:30-19:00 ■ English and Spanish spoken

Reproductions of XVII, XVIII, XIX century, 1930's. Buy and sell.

------------ **SAINT-OUEN** ------------

BENOIT MARCU
7 rue Madeleine, 93400 Saint-Ouen ■ Tel: 01 40 11 15 23 ■ Mon-Sat 8:30-12:30/13:30-17:30 ■ Prices medium ■ Professional discount

Creation of copies of antique furniture of the XVII and XVIII centuries. Also creation of contemporary furniture.

------------ **OUTSIDE PARIS** ------------

👑 **PATRICK VASTEL**
143 rue du Général-Leclerc, 50110 Tourlaville, Cherbourg ■ Tel: 02 33 22 46 07 - Fax: 02 33 22 96 26 ■ E-mail: pvastel@aol.com ■ Mon-Fri 9:00-12:00/13:30-18:30 and by appointment ■ English spoken ■ Prices medium ■ Professional discount

Custom re-creation of period furniture. Expert to the Cour d'Appel of Caen. One of the best.

ETS PIERRE COUNOT BLANDIN
B.P.1, 88350 Liffol-le-Grand ■ Tel: 03 29 06 62 40 ■ Fax: 03 29 06 78 04 ■ E-mail: count@aol.com ■ Web: www.plab.org/counot ■ Mon-Fri by appointment ■ Jean-Pierre Duhoux and Philippe Counot speak English ■ Prices high ■ Professional discount

High quality reproduction of antique furniture and chairs, including Art Deco.

GARDENS
Jardins

Garden, Terrace and Landscape Designers
Paysagistes et aménagement de jardins et terrasses

IV

L'ART DU COTÉ DES JARDINS
14 rue des Jardins Saint-Paul, 75004 Paris ■ Tel: 01 48 87 21 41 ■ Fax: 01 48 87 19 75 ■ E-mail: artcotejardins@wanadoo.fr ■ Web: www.art-cote-jardins.fr ■ Mon-Fri 9:30-13:00/14:00-17:30 ■ Michel Girard ■ English spoken ■ Professional discount

Landscapers. Full terrace installation and planting. Excellent choice of furniture, treillis and pots. Everything made to measure.

LES JARDINS DU TROUBADOUR
10 rue des Lions Saint-Paul, 75004 Paris ■ Tel: 01 42 77 81 85 ■ Fax: 01 42 77 35 95 ■ By appointment ■ Marie-Thérèse Le Ménestrel speaks a little English ■ Prices medium

Design, planting and maintenance of city gardens, balconies, terraces and interior gardens. Specialist on plants for shade.

VI

♕ CHRISTIAN TORTU
6 Carrefour de l'Odéon, 75006 Paris ■ Tel: 01 43 26 02 56 ■ Fax: 01 43 29 71 99 ■ E-mail: christian.tortu@wanadoo.fr ■ Mon-Sat 10:00-20:00 ■ Italian and English spoken ■ Major credit cards

Top floral designer. From bouquets to complete floral interiors. His theme is simplicity, natural to rustic.

♕ DANIEL GUITTAT
68 bd de la Tour Maubourg, 75007 Paris ■ Tel : 01 45 51 32 42
■ Fax: 01 60 07 20 95 ■ E-mail : daniel.guittat@wanadoo.fr ■
Web : www.daniel-guittat.fr ■ Mon-Sat 8:30-20:30, Sun 11:00-
13:00 ■ Some English spoken ■ Major credit cards

Floral design for all occasions, from birth to death. Every occasion, happy and sad. One of the best.

♕ LACHAUME
10 rue Royale, 75008 Paris ■ Tel: 01 42 60 59 74 ■ Fax: 01 42
97 44 55 ■ Mon-Fri 8:00-19:00, Sat 8:00-18:00 ■ English spoken
■ Amex, Visa

Master florist. Quite marvellous.

LES JARDINS DE MATISSE
4 av Percier, 75008 Paris ■ Tel: 01 56 59 90 54 ■ Fax: 01 40 76 01
10 ■ E-mail: lesjardinsdematisse@wanadoo.fr ■ Web: www.jardins-
dematisse.com ■ Mon-Fri 8:30-20:00, Sat 9:00-19:00 ■ Jean-Marc is
in charge ■ English and Spanish spoken ■ Major credit cards

Floral design and creation for private and public spaces. Mainly interior design but some exterior work for small spaces.

DOMINIQUE BOYER
5 place Pinel, 75013 Paris ■ Tel: 01 45 84 56 99 ■ Fax: 01 45 86
73 00 ■ Mon-Fri by 9:30-18:30 by appointment ■ German spoken ■ Prices medium ■ Professional discount

Adviser on gardens, landscapes and environments: public and private spaces.

PARIS VERT
7 rue des Patures, 75016 Paris ■ Tel: 01 42 88 43 12 ■ Fax: 01
42 88 90 50 ■ Mon-Fri-Sat by appointment ■ Xavier Tabard ■
Prices medium

Creation and maintenance of green spaces: balconies, ter-races and gardens. Supplier of green plants for offices and maintenance.

♕ CLAUDE QUINQUAUD
15 rue Chaillot, 75016 Paris ■ Tel: 47 20 24 25 Fax: 01 47 20 53 76 ■ Mon-Fri 9:00-20:30 ■ English, Portuguese and Vietnamese spoken ■ Major credit cards

One of the great creators of floral design for every occasion. His work is outstanding and a visit to his showroom a pleasure.

─────────────── XVIII ───────────────

BERTRAND PAULET
49 rue des Poissonniers, 75018 Paris ■ Tel: 01 42 64 42 67 ■ Fax: 01 42 64 04 96 ■ Mon-Fri 9:00-18:00 by appointment ■ English spoken ■ Prices medium

Landscape designer: Conception and installation of gardens and terraces.

─────────────── EDGE OF PARIS ───────────────

HERMÈS
182 av Charles-de-Gaulle, 92200 Neuilly-sur-Seine ■ Tel: 01 46 24 50 12 ■ Fax: 01 46 24 66 41 ■ Web: www.hermesjardinerie.com ■ Mon-Sat 9:00-19:30 ■ Prices medium to high ■ Professional discount ■ Major credit cards

Landscaping of gardens, terraces and patios. Complete installations with green and flowering plants. Large choice of plants, pots and accessories.

JARDECO
33 av André Morizet, 92100 Boulogne ■ Tel: 01 46 03 22 23 ■ Fax: 01 49 46 50 32 ■ Web: www.jardeco.fr ■ Mon-Fri 9:15-12:30/13:30-18:00

Complete installation of gardens, terraces and balconies. Automatic sprinkling systems. Large choice of treillis in every shape and size.

Garden Accessories and Supplies
Accessoires et fournitures de jardin

─────────────── I ───────────────

AU BON CULTIVATEUR
12 quai de la Mégisserie, 75001 Paris ■ Tel: 01 42 33 93 29 ■ Tue-Sun 9:00-18:30 ■ Yves Peteremann ■ Prices medium ■ Major credit cards

Trees, plants, shrubs, vines, aquariums, fish.

AU BON JARDINIER

12 quai de la Mégisserie, 75001 Paris ■ Tel: 01 42 36 41 23 ■ Fax: 01 40 26 21 60 ■ Tue-Sat 8:00-19:00, Sun in season ■ Didier Bru ■ Some English spoken ■ Visa

Vegetable seeds, plants and herbs. Specialty: climbing plants and flowers and marvellous cacti. Fresh vegetables and salads. Good selection of terracotta pots.

CLAUSE JARDIN

2 bis quai de la Mégisserie, 75001 Paris ■ Tel: 01 42 33 41 42 ■ Fax: 01 40 39 96 91 ■ Tue-Sun 9:30-18:30 ■ Mme Plume Gallas ■ English spoken ■ Prices medium ■ Visa

Indoor and outdoor green plants. Terrace planting and maintenance. Bulbs, seeds, pottery.

DELBARD

16 quai de la Mégisserie, 75054 Paris 75001 ■ Tel: 01 44 88 20 ■ Fax: 01 44 88 80 16 ■ Web: www.delbard.fr ■ Open every day 10:00-18:30 ■ Nicole Guettman, Nicole Auclair; David Frendo, landscape gardener ■ English and Spanish spoken ■ Prices medium ■ Visa

Indoor and outdoor plants. Design and planting of large and small gardens and terraces. They have 15 garden centres in Paris, the suburbs and the major cities of France. Excellent catalogue available.

IL GIARDINO

20 quai de la Mégisserie, 75001 Paris ■ Tel: 01 42 33 89 52 ■ Fax: 01 42 33 09 89 ■ E-mail: ilgiardino@wanadoo.fr ■ Web: www.ilgiardino-paris.com ■ Open every day 9:30-19:00 ■ Christophe Chabry ■ English spoken ■ Amex and Visa

Excellent selection of seeds, including Unwins. Planting and maintenance of gardens and terraces. Installation of automatic watering systems.

JARDINERIE DU QUAI

2ter quai de Mégisserie, 75001 Paris ■ Tel: 01 42 36 55 94 ■ Open every day from 9:00-18:00 ■ Alex Bandeira ■ Spanish and English spoken ■ Prices medium ■ Major credit cards

Everything for gardens and terraces: plants, fertilizer, tools, pots, accessories.

LA TERRACE SUR LES QUAIS

10 quai de la Mégisserie, 75001 Paris ■ Tel: 01 45 08 09 10 ■ Fax: 01 45 08 50 25 ■ Mon 10:00-18:00, Tue-Sat 9:30-19:00 ■ Some English and Spanish spoken ■ Prices medium ■ Major credit cards

Interesting pots, picture frames and accessories. Teak furniture, garden tools and watering cans.

♕ LE CEDRE ROUGE

22 av Victoria, 75001 Paris ■ Tel: 01 42 33 71 05 ■ Fax: 01 40 26 46 78 ■ Mon 12:45-19:00,Tue-Fri 10:45-19:00, Sat 10:00-19:00, Sun 11:00-18:00 ■ Damien Kammerer, Murielle Galian ■ English, German, Italian and Spanish spoken ■ Amex, Visa Landscape gardener: Christophe Borias - 1 bd Emile Augier, 75016 Paris ■ Tel: 01 45 24 62 62 ■ Fax: 01 45 24 62 00 ■ Other shops ■ 25 rue Duphot, 75008 Paris ■ Tel: 01 42 61 81 81 ■ Fax: 01 42 61 81 82 ■ 116 rue du Bac, 75007 Paris ■ Tel: 01 42 84 84 00 ■ Fax: 01 42 84 84 01

Lovely decorative objects for interior gardens and terraces; planting; furniture; lighting from all over the world; tableware. Beautiful tables and pots of volcanic stone in 36 colours; *lave émaillée* tile for interior and exterior. Aquatic plants and a great collection of scented candles. This is the largest of their shops.

LE JARDIN DE VICTORIA

24 av Victoria, 75001 Paris ■ Tel: 01 42 33 84 07 ■ Fax: 01 45 08 89 80 ■ Tue-Sat 9:30-19:00 ■ Laurence Fournier ■ English and some Spanish spoken ■ Visa

Plants, seeds and fertilizer. Decorative pottery, accessories and tools. Creation and maintenance of terraces, gardens and balconies. Installation of automatic irrigation.

LE PRINCE JARDINIER

121 Arcade Vallois, Jardin du Palais-Royal, 75001 Paris ■ Tel : 01 42 60 37 13 ■ Fax : 01 42 60 76 75 ■ E-mail : lpj-paris@wanadoo.fr ■ Mon-Sat 10:00-19:00 ■ Prince Louis-Albert de Broglie ■ English spoken ■ Prices medium to high ■ Visa, MC

The gardener Prince sells beautiful garden accessories, tools, pots. Delightful and worth a visit.

♕ PARIS-HOLLANDE

1, rue des Lavandières Sainte-Opportune, 75001 Paris ■ Tel : 01 42 36 82 68 ■ Fax : 01 45 08 14 37 ■ Tue-Sat ■ 9:30-18:30 ■ Mr. Roland Baurens speaks a little of every language

He is the big seed specialist. Seeds from everywhere in the world and he will find whatever you need. A great treat.

TRUFFAUT

85 quai de la Gare, 75013 Paris ■ Tel: 01 53 60 84 50 ■ Fax: 01 53 60 84 51 ■ Everyday 10:00-20:00 ■ Pierre Peckmez ■ English spoken ■ Prices medium ■ Visa, MC

Garden supplies and accessories; large choice of seeds and books on gardening; watering systems; aquariums, fish, hamsters. Garden furniture, barbecues and lots of pots.

VILMORIN

4 quai de la Mégisserie, 75001 Paris ■ Tel: 01 42 33 61 62 ■ Fax: 01 40 26 18 28 ■ Autumn : Mon-Sat 9:30-18:30 ■ Spring Mon-Sun 9:30-19:30 ■ Pascal Drouin ■ Visa

In business since 1747! An extraordinary place devoted to seeds and potted plants. Good selection of pots and accessories. Terrace planting and garden maintenance. Great choice of Bonsai.

Garden Fountains - Manufacture & Installation
Fontaines de jardin - Fabrication et installation

--------------------- IX ---------------------

PROVINCES DE FRANCE

59 rue de Maubeuge, 75009 Paris ■ Tel: 01 48 78 34 22 ■ Fax 01 42 80 28 62 ■ E-mail : info@loiselet.com ■ Web: www.loiselet.com ■ Mon-Sat 10:00-12:30/13:30-19:00 ■ Laurent Gaudy and Maximilien Lebras ■ English spoken ■ Professional discount ■ Major credit cards

Excellent selection of cast-iron garden fountains in classic designs. A large choice of rustic cast-iron bistro tables and table bases. Wrought iron garden furniture, tables, consoles, lanterns. Fireplace accessories. The largest choice in France of cast iron fire-backs. Will custom make-to-measure wrought iron stair railings, balconies and security guards for windows.

--------------------- MARCHÉ AUX PUCES ---------------------

MARC MAISON

Marché Paul Bert, Allée 6, Stand 83, 96 rue des Rosiers, 93400 Saint-Ouen ■ Tel : 0140 12 52 28 ■ Fax: 01 40 12 26 47 ■ E-mail: marcmaison@easynet.fr ■ Web: www.marcmaison.com ■ Sat-Mon 9:00-18:00 ■ Marc Maison ■ English spoken Prices medium to high ■ Professional discount

Fountains in stone, marble and cast iron. XIX century decorative objects for the garden: urns, vases and sculpture.

FRIGEBRICE
139 av d'Argenteuil, 92600 Asnières-sur-Seine ■ Tel: 01 47 93 62 56 ■ Fax: 01 40 86 14 81 ■ Web: www.frigebrice.fr ■ Mon-Fri 8:00-12:00/13:00-17:00/Fri closing 16:00 ■ Stèphane Rose speaks English ■ Prices medium ■ Professional discount

Manufacturer of fountains, cold water and hot. Mobile wash-basins. Maintenance and repair of fountains of all brands.

Garden Furniture
Meubles de jardin

JARDINS DE PLAISANCE
72 bd de la Tour-Maubourg, 75007 Paris ■ Tel: 01 45 55 98 52 ■ Fax: 01 45 50 38 32 ■ E-mail: daniel.guittat@wanadoo.fr ■ Web: www.daniel-guittat.fr ■ Tue-Sat 9:30-19:30 ■ Daniel Guittat ■ English, Spanish and Italian spoken ■ Prices medium to high ■ Professional discount ■ Major credit cards

Garden furniture in teak and wrought iron in contemporary and classical styles. Fountains; wonderful cast iron and lead Medici and Chambord vases in antique styles; pottery and wooden parasols.

MAISON DU WEEK-END
26 rue Vavin, 75006 Paris ■ Tel: 01 43 54 15 52 ■ Fax: 01 40 51 72 07 ■ E-mail: la-maison-du.we@faxvia.net ■ Tue-Sat 11:00-19:30 ■ Marianne Moreaud ■ English and Italian spoken ■ Prices medium to high ■ Professional discount ■ Amex, Visa

Very good choice of garden furniture in moulded aluminium and treated chestnut (*lamellé collé*). Both can stay outside in all weather. Large selection of everything for the table and general decorative accessories for the house.

PASSWORLD FRANCE
11 bd de la Tour Maubourg, 75007 Paris ■ Tel: 01 45 55 45 65 ■ Fax 01 45 55 20 56 ■ Mon-Fri 9:00-19:00 ■ Pascal Boucard speaks English ■ Prices medium to high ■ Professional discount

Garden furniture and exterior decorations.

ROYAL ARROW FRANCE
206 bd Saint-Germain, 75007 Paris ■ Tel: 01 45 49 49 89 ■ Fax: 01 60 07 20 95 ■ Web: www.royal-arrow.com ■ Mon-Sat 10:00-19:00 ■ English spoken ■ Prices medium to high ■ Professional discount ■ Major credit cards

Beautiful garden furniture in teak.

TECTONA
3 av de Breteuil, 75007 Paris ■ Tel: 01 47 35 70 70 ■ Fax: 01 47 35 37 66 ■ Web: www.tectona.fr ■ Spring: Mon-Sat 10:00-19:00 Autumn: Tues-Sat 10:30-18:30 ■ Geneviève Murith ■ English and German spoken ■ Prices medium to high ■ Professional discount ■ MC, Visa

Specialists in high quality garden furniture in teak. Very good choice. Parasols in wood: round, rectangular and square. Folding furniture in metal and teak.

Garden Ornaments and Statuary
Ornements et statuaire de jardin

♔ **GALERIE MARC DELIGNY**
40 rue Mazarine, 75006 Paris ■ Tel: 01 56 24 82 11 ■ Fax: 01 56 24 84 68 ■ Mon-Sat 11:00-19:00 ■ Marc Deligny, sculptor ■ Prices medium to high

Wonderful statuary and fountains made by Marc Deligny. Extraordinary collection of antique objects of decoration and architectural elements in stone, marble and terracotta. He will make to order perfect replicas in the tradition of the period, whether it be the XVII, XVIII century or later. Marc Deligny follows in the footsteps of his father. Restoration of historic monuments, such as the Louvre.

♔ **LES JARDINS DU ROI SOLEIL**
32 bd de la Bastille, 75012 Paris ■ Tel: 01 43 44 44 31 ■ Fax: 01 43 44 44 52 ■ E-mail: jrs@jardinsroisoleil.com ■ Web: www.jardinsroisoleil.com ■ Mon-Fri 10:00-12:00/14:00-16:00 ■ Jean Jiquel and Caroline Fried ■ English and Spanish spoken ■ Prices medium ■ Professional discount

Orange Tree Tubs designed for Louis XVI at Versailles. Superb craftsmanship. Perhaps the best on the market. They also have fireplace accessories.

♔ **ANDRÉE MACÉ**
266 rue du Faubourg-Saint-Honoré, 75008 Paris ■ Tel: 01 42 27 43 03 ■ Fax: 01 44 40 09 63 ■ E-mail: andree.mace@wanadoo.fr ■ Mon-Sat 9:00-12:30/14:00-18:30 ■ Dominique de Grivel ■ English and Spanish spoken ■ Prices medium to high ■ 10% professional discount ■ Amex

XV to XVIII century French garden ornaments and architectural elements. Also a selection of antique fireplaces of all periods. Superb choice.

See also **Architectural Elements.**

Greenhouses and Pavilions
Serres et jardins d'hiver

SERRES ET FERRONERIES D'ANTIN
Rte de Vendome 41360 Savigny sur Braye ■ Tel: 01 45 69 37 23 ■ Fax: 01 45 95 18 54 ■ E-mail: sarl.hager@wanadoo.fr ■ Web: www.galerie-artisanale.com/serresdantan ■ Mon-Fri 8:00-12:00/13:30-18:00 ■ Roger Hager ■ English spoken

They build beautiful conservatories and greenhouses in wrought iron and glass. Clients include The Elysée Palace and museums.

Lattice and Trellis
Treillage

ART DECO TREILLAGE
11 rue Émile Sehet, 95157 Taverny Cedex ■ Tel: 01 30 40 02 08 ■ Fax: 01 30 40 01 64 ■ Mon-Fri 9:00-12:00/13:30-18:00 ■ Gérard Augustin ■ English spoken ■ Prices medium ■ Professional discount

Manufacturer of decorative treillis to order, as well as everything else in wood required for terraces.

LEMAIRE TRICOTEL
16 av Paul Langevin, 95222 Herblay Cedex ■ Tel: 01 30 26 33 44 ■ Fax: 01 30 26 33 55 ■ Web: www.clotures-lemaire.fr ■ Mon-Fri 8:00-12:00/13:30-18:00 ■ Bruno Payelle ■ English spoken ■ Prices medium to high ■ Professional discount ■ Visa

Decorative trellis, pergolas of their own stock designs and custom made to measure. Lots of planters.

TRÉILLAGES MARTIN
58 av Général-de-Gaulle, 94170 Le Perreux sur Marne ■ Tel: 01 43 24 05 57 ■ Fax: 01 48 71 33 94 ■ Mon-Fri 7:30-12:00/13:00-18:00 ■ Mr. Philippe Martin ■ Prices medium

Manufacturers of decorative trellis. Broad choice. Installation.

GENEALOGISTS
Généalogistes

I

ANCÊTRES ITALIENS
3 rue Turbigo, 75001 Paris ■ Tel: 01 46 64 27 22

For those who need a genealogist to trace Italian heritage, this centre is equipped to suggest qualified experts in Italy. They are also specialists in tracing families of Protestant or Jewish origin in Europe.

CENTRE D'ENTRAIDE GÉNÉALOGIQUE DE FRANCE
3 rue Turbigo, 75001 Paris ■ Tel: 01 40 41 99 09 ■ Fax: 01 40 41 99 63 ■ Mon 10:00-18:00, Wed 14:00-18:00, Fri 14:00-18:00, Sat 10:00-12:30 ■ President: Mr. Hubert Cottin ■ English, German and Spanish spoken

Non-profit society of 1,000 members, French and International, who are interested in researching their family roots. The society counsels on ways and means of research and its library is well stocked with French documentation and international publications. The members have a moral obligation to help each other with their time and knowledge. Their quarterly review is *La France Généalogique.* Minimal membership fee.

ETUDE GÉNÉALOGIQUE DU LOUVRE
320 rue Saint-Honoré, 75001 Paris ■ Tel: 01 42 86 05 06 ■ Fax: 01 42 86 05 56 ■ Mon-Fri by appointment ■ Director: Mr. Denis Beaupeux

Specialists in genealogical research for succession.

V

COUTOT-ROEHRIG
21 bd Saint-Germain, 75005 Paris ■ Tel: 01 44 41 80 80 ■ Fax: 01 43 29 16 17 ■ Web: www.coutot-roehrig.com ■ Mon-Fri by appointment ■ Director: Mr. Jean-Claude Roehrig ■ English and Spanish spoken

World-wide research for inheritance.

CHAMBRE SYNDICALE DES GÉNÉALOGISTES ET HERALDISTES DE FRANCE

74 rue Saint-Pères, 75007 Paris ■ Tel: 01 45 44 76 50 ■ Fax: 01 45 44 43 32 ■ Mon-Fri by appointment ■ Founder and President: Mr. Yves du Passage ■ English spoken

Genealogical research into French ancestry. Preparation of detailed documentation and family trees.

ANNE-SOPHIE CHEVALIER

82 rue de Charenton 75012 Paris ■ Telfax: 01 43 43 53 23 ■ Mon-Sat by appointment ■ Some English spoken

Genealogical research and history. Preparation of family trees. World-wide research.

MAÎTRE GENEVIÈVE DE MORANT

85 bd Pasteur, B.P. 211, 75015 Paris ■ Telfax: 01 43 21 55 33 ■ Mon-Fri by appointment ■ English and Italian spoken

Genealogy: research and genealogical tableaux prepared. Judicial services: all procedures for name changes, adjunction to surnames, rights of and to nobility. Specialist in French nobility and French ancestry. Mme de Morant is an attorney.

XVI

ETUDE GÉNÉALOGIQUE MAILLARD

7 rue Alboni, 75016 Paris ■ Tel: 01 42 24 97 64 ■ Fax: 01 45 25 77 60 ■ Web: www.etude-maillard.com ■ Mon-Fri 9:00-13:00/14:00-18:00 ■ PDG: Mr. Gérard Foreau, DG: Mr. Bruno Duval ■ Most languages spoken

Research for inheritance.

CABINET GÉNÉALOGIQUE MYRIAM PROVENCE

29, rue Tandou, 75019 Paris ■ Tel: 01 42 40 58 26 ■ Fax: 01 42 45 46 35

Covering all France and French territories: Specialist in historical and family research: Research into ancestors, descendants, family histories, history of homes, villages or enterprises. Research into bibliographies, transcription of family texts and drawing of family trees and heraldry.

CERCLE D'ETUDES GÉNÉALOGIQUES ET HERALDIQUES DE L'ILE DE FRANCE

46 route de Croissy, 78110 Le Vésinet ■ Tel: 01 39 76 11 52 ■ Mon-Sat by appointment ■ Director: Philippe Jost ■ Some English and Spanish spoken

Group of 600 genealogists engaged in all types of genealogical research into French ancestry. The Cercle is computerising birth and baptismal certificates for the regions of the Yvelines and the Val d'Oise from before the Revolution. They publish a quarterly bulletin of general interest called *Stemma*.

MME FRANCOISE RAMIREZ DE ARELLANO

11 Quai Paul Doumer, 92400 Courbevoie ■ Tel: 01 43 34 83 85 ■ By appointment

Genealogical research into Franco-Spanish ancestry.

HARDWARE

Door, Window and Cabinet Hardware
Serrurerie decorative

French Decorative Hardware has a tradition going back to Roman times. The most beautiful designs of levers, knobs, surface locks, cremones and espagnolettes began in the Middle Ages, continued on through the XVIII, XIX and into the XX century. Sometimes called the jewellery of a gracious home, there are exquisite originals which still adorn the great homes and chateaux of Europe. Skilled designers, chisellers and gilders have drastically declined in numbers, but there are still enough of them to meet the demands of the most discriminating clients. One important word of advice: When you order French decorative hardware, you will need someone to specify the door details to make certain the hardware will fit and function perfectly and be adaptable to any domestic locks. Remember: European standards can be different from similar American products and you want to be sure everything goes smoothly. The highest quality and the most beautiful French hardware is always made to order and the manufacturer is capable of dealing with any problems. Communication is the key.

ARDIMPEX
Quai de la Ferronnerie, 08330 Vrigne-aux-Bois ■ Tel: 03 24 52 22 22 ■ Fax: 03 24 52 73 62 ■ Mon-Fri 8:00-12:00/13:30-17:30 ■ Export Director, Mr. Oger ■ English and Italian spoken ■ Professionals only

Basic hardware for mass building: hardware for shutters, doors and windows in steel or cast iron.

"AUX BRONZES DE STYLE"
74 rue du Faubourg-Saint-Antoine, 75012 Paris ■ Tel: 01 43 43 36 36 ■ Fax: 01 43 43 46 50 ■ Mon-Fri 9:00-19:00/Sat 10:00-19:30 ■ English spoken ■ Prices medium to high ■ Professional discount

Bronze cabinet hardware. Middle range.

BRASS
34 bd de la Bastille, 75012 Paris ■ Tel: 01 44 67 90 61 ■ Fax: 01 44 67 90 69 ■ Mon-Fri 8:30-12:30/13:30-17:00 ■ Jean-Yves Rosier ■ Prices medium ■ Professional discount ■ Major credit cards

Large choice of brass hardware for doors, windows and furniture, as well as letterboxes and curtain rods. Catalogues available.

♛ BRICARD
1 rue de la Perle, 75003 Paris ■ Tel: 01 42 77 71 68 ■ Fax: 01 42 77 61 06 ■ Mon-Thu 10:00-13:00/14:00- 18:00, Fri 10:00-16:00 ■ English spoken ■ Prices medium to high ■ Professional discount

Some of the most beautiful hardware in the world. All styles, all finishes. One of the oldest, largest and greatest collections. Visit their museum.

BRONZES DE FRANCE
6 rue Royal, 75008 Paris ■ Tel: 01 44 75 09 09 ■ Fax 02 33 62 23 32 ■ Mon-Thu by appointment, Fri 9:00-16:00 ■ English spoken ■ Prices medium to high

Large selection of hardware for windows, doors and cabinets. Second level.

♛ FONTAINE
190 rue de Rivoli, 75001 Paris ■ Tel: 01 42 61 51 53 ■ Fax: 01 42 61 04 13 ■ Mon-Fri by appointment ■ Geneviève Berton speaks English ■ Prices medium ■ Professional discount

Company founded in 1740. Small museum collection of decorative hardware. Specialists in mortise locks and magnetic card-operated locks. Stock of antique hardware available for sale. In many cases one-of-a-kind. Special collection of everything from doorknockers to espagnolettes. All finishes available over solid brass.

♛ REMY GARNIER
30bis bd de la Bastille, 75012 Paris ■ Tel: 01 43 43 84 85 ■ Fax: 01 43 46 13 76 ■ Mon-Fri 9:00-12:30/13:30-18:00 ■ English spoken ■ Prices medium to high ■ Professional discount

Remy Garnier founded the company in 1834. One of the finest collections of decorative hardware of all periods. Everything for doors and windows. Reliable for large projects. Restoration of old hardware and anything else in bronze. In-house finishing.

LA QUINCAILLERIE

4 bd Saint-Germain, 75005 Paris ■ Tel: 01 46 33 66 71 ■ Fax: 01 43 29 80 58 ■ Mon-Fri 10:00-13:00/14:00-19:00, Sat 10:00-13:00/14:00-18:00 ■ English spoken ■ Prices high ■ Professional discount

Distributor of contemporary hardware, designed by architects and designers, for windows, doors and furniture. Will custom make any design. Bathroom accessories across the street.

LEJEUNE FRÈRES

209 rue du Faubourg-Saint-Antoine, 75011 Paris ■ Tel: 01 43 72 27 37 ■ Fax: 01 43 72 99 26 ■ Mon-Fri 9:00-12:00/14:00-18:00, Sat closing 17:00 ■ Some English spoken ■ Prices medium ■ Professional discount

200 years of experience making decorative hardware for furniture, knobs, levers, keys and keyholes in many finishes. Lower-cost line.

♛ MEILLEUR

32 rue des Amandiers, 75020 Paris ■ Tel: 01 43 66 45 13 ■ Fax: 01 43 66 45 43 ■ Mon-Fri 8:30-12:00/13:00-18:00 by appointment ■ Catherine Meilleur and Claude Delorme speak English ■ Prices high to very high ■ Professional discount

Highest-quality custom-made decorative hardware for windows and doors in bronze with a large choice of finishes. Beautiful selection of faucets in exclusive designs. All types of lighting and small tables. Third generation bronze craftsmen.

MEUNIER ET FILS – BRONZES DE STYLE

77 rue de Charonne, 75011 Paris ■ Tel: 01 43 71 22 62 ■ Fax: 01 43 71 79 40 ■ Mon-Fri 9:00-19:00, Sat 10:00-19:30 ■ English spoken ■ Prices medium to high ■ 20% professional discount

Specialist bronzes for furniture and cabinets. Some door hardware. Middle range.

RENNOTTE

161 Faubourg-Saint-Antoine, 75011 Paris ■ Tel: 01 43 43 39 58 ■ Fax: 01 43 41 50 27 ■ Mon-Fri 9:00-12:30/14:00-18:30 ■ Some English spoken ■ Prices medium to high ■ Professional discount

Large collection of cabinet and furniture hardware. Catalogue upon request.

SCHMIDT
15-17 passage de la Main-d`Or, 75011 Paris ■ Tel: 01 48 06 57 19 ■ Fax: 01 48 06 62 22 ■ Mon-Fri 8:30-18.00 ■ Fernande Schmidt speaks English and Spanish ■ Prices medium to high ■ Professional discount

Founded in 1928. Large selection of door, window and furniture hardware. Wide choice of finials for staircases as well as lighting and showcases. Decorative work in brass for shops, offices and homes. Two price levels. Catalogue upon request.

RAYMOND SCHMITT
41 rue du Faubourg-du-Temple, 75010 Paris ■ Tel: 42 08 05 43 ■ Fax: 01 42 08 49 92 ■ Mon-Fri 8:30-12:30/13:30-18:30 ■ English spoken ■ Prices medium ■ Professional discount

Specialist in custom decorative hardware for furniture. Finishes in gold or silver. Restoration and reproduction of bronzes from models. No catalogue. Only custom work.

SERDANELI
270 rue Lecourbe, 75015 Paris ■ Tel: 01 40 60 13 13 ■ Fax: 01 40 60 98 75 ■ Mon-Fri 9:30-13:00-14:00-18:30 ■ English spoken ■ Prices high ■ Professional discount

Large selection of knobs and levers in semi-precious stones and bronze. Marine finishes. Lots of faucets. They do a lot of yacht installations.

SÉRIE RARE
6 rue de l'Odeon, 75006 Paris ■ Tel: 01 55 42 92 10 ■ Fax: 01 55 42 92 52 ■ E-mail: serierare@wanadoo.fr ■ Mon-Fri 12:00-19:00 ■ Marie-Luce Podva speaks English and German ■ Prices medium ■ Professional discount ■ Major credit cards

Small and original collection of door and furniture hardware in contemporary designs, objects, lamps and jewellery. Matching drapery hardware. Catalogue upon request.

TOUT PARIS
111 East 80th Street, New York, NY 10021 ■ Tel: (212)288-9730 ■ Fax: (212)249-9501 ■ E-mail: Toutparis@aol.com ■ By appointment only ■ French and English spoken

America's leading supplier of the highest quality French decorative hardware. All styles, all finishes and thousands of models to choose from. Catalogue available as well as internet ordering service.

Drapery Hardware
Tringles à rideaux

BLOME
13 rue du Mail, 75002 Paris ■ Tel: 01 40 15 64 82 ■ Fax: 01 15 64 92 ■ Mon-Fri 9:00-12:30/13:30-17:00, Fri closes 16:00 ■ Mme Evelyn Durand ■ English spoken ■ Professional discount ■ Trade only

Remarkable collection of curtain and drapery rods in lots of imaginative styles.

👑 HOULÈS
18 rue Saint-Nicolas 75012 Paris ■ Tel: 01 43 44 65 19 ■ Fax: 01 64 24 71 76 ■ Mon-Fri 8:30-17:30 ■ English spoken ■ Prices medium to high ■ Professional discount ■ Major credit cards
27 Viaduc des Arts ■ Tel: 01 43 46 25 50 ■ Fax: 01 43 46 25 53 ■ Tue-Sat 10-12:15/13:15-18:30 ■ Daniele Garnier ■ Some English spoken ■ Professional discount ■ Major credit cards

Large choice of high-quality decorative drapery hardware. They are known for their most extraordinary collections of trimmings. Houlès is now world wide with showrooms in London and the major design centres of the U.S.

👑 MARIN ET TULLET
7 rue de Monceau, 75008 Paris ■ Tel: 01 42 25 09 10 ■ Fax: 01 42 25 81 04 ■ Mon-Fri 8:00-18:00 ■ Michel Bourdon speaks English ■ Prices high ■ Professional discount

They have the reputation for having the best selection of drapery hardware. Large selection of curtain rods in wood, brass and wrought iron in classical and contemporary styles. Decorative hardware for furniture and trimmings.

OBJET INSOLITE
109 bd Beaumarchais, 75003 Paris ■ Tel: 01 42 71 30 94 ■ Fax: 01 42 71 27 85 ■ E-mail: lampes@objetsinsolite.com ■ Mon-Fri 10:00-18:30 ■ English spoken ■ Prices medium ■ Major credit cards

Patinated bronze curtain rods and accessories.

SITRA
95 rue du Faubourg-Saint-Antoine, 75011 Paris ■ Tel: 01 43 43 88 88 ■ Fax: 01 43 41 80 82 ■ Mon-Fri 8:30-18:00 ■ Prices medium to high ■ Professional discount

Drapery rods in brass, wood and iron in every shape and style. Large selection of interior and exterior blinds, shades and awnings.

General Hardware
Quincaillerie

♛ BHV - BAZAR DE L'HOTEL DE VILLE
52 rue de Rivoli, 75004 Paris ■ Tel: 01 42 74 90 00 ■ Fax: 01 42 74 96 79 ■ Mon-Sat 9:30-19:00, Wed until 22:00 ■ Prices reasonable

There are thousands of good hardware stores in and around Paris, but for convenience, economy and a special treat we suggest a visit to BHV. There, you will find a vast hardware supermarket of every hardware item you can imagine. Begin in the basement and work your way up from general hardware and garden supplies, through architectural elements, a complete wood-working shop, decorative hardware and drapery hardware. Don't miss it.

HOME FURNISHINGS AND ACCESSORIES

ALCHIMIE LOINTAINE
40 rue de Verneuil, 75007 Paris ■ Tel: 01 42 61 33 60 ■ Fax: 01 42 61 33 60 ■ E-mail: alchimie@esther.net ■ Mon 14:00-20:00 Tue-Sat 11:00-20:00 Often open on Sunday ■ Jean-René and Esther Gossart, Pascal ■ English and Spanish spoken ■ 10% professional discount ■ Major credit cards excepted Amex.

Objects and furniture from Indonesia and Morocco.

MICHÈLE ARAGON
Telfax 01 43 25 87 69 ■ Mon 14:00-18:00, Tue-Sat 10:30-13:00/14:00-19:00 ■ Michèle Aragon ■ English, Spanish and Italian spoken ■ Visa, MC

Everything for the house: beds, lamps, linens and furniture. Mostly XIX century.

BHV - BAZAR DE L'HOTEL DE VILLE
52 rue de Rivoli, 75004 Paris ■ Tel: 01 42 74 90 00 ■ Fax: 01 42 74 96 79 ■ Mon-Sat 9:30-19:00, Wed until 22:00 ■ Prices reasonable

Marvellous hardware store with everything else for the home.

BIGGIE BEST
9-11 rue des Lavandières-Saint-Opportune, 75001 Paris ■ Tel: 01 40 41 03 13 ■ Fax: 01 40 41 03 23 ■ Mon 14:00-19:00,Tue-Sat 10:30-19:00 ■ Jean Cavalade ■ English spoken ■ 10% professional discount ■ Major credit cards

Fabrics, papers and paints, furniture, draperies, bedcovers cushions, lamps, accessories.

DEMEURE EN VILLE
23 rue Jacob, 75006 Paris ■ Telfax: 01 56 24 96 04 ■ Mon 14:00-19:00, Tue-Sat 10:30-19:00 ■ Philippe Pasi ■ English spoken ■ Major credit cards

Contemporary furniture in wood and wrought iron. 1930-1940 lamps. Decorative objects in glass and galuchat. Custom work.

ELIZABETH BUSSON EDITIONS
20 place de la Madeleine, 75008 Paris ■ Tel: 01 42 65 26 06 ■ Fax: 01 47 42 30 06 ■ Mon-Sat 10:00-18:00 ■ Elizabeth Busson speaks English ■ Prices medium ■ 10% Professional discount

XVIII century French furniture from Provence, painted furniture, mirrors, pier glasses, faience, Toiles de Jouy, chairs, lamps, old screens, decorative country.

CASA DESIGN
16 avenue Victoria, 75001 Paris ■ Tel: 01 42 36 36 68 ■ Fax: 01 42 36 06 80 ■ Mon-Sat 10-19:00 ■ Jacqueline Arquié and Frederique Serfati speak some English ■ Major credit cards

Italian contemporary furniture, generously sized sofas, lighting and accessories. High quality.

CASOAR
15 rue Boissy d'Anglas, 75008 Paris ■ Tel: 01 47 42 69 51 ■ Fax 01 40 07 04 17 ■ Mon-Sat 10:30-13:30/14:30-19:00 ■ Isabelle & Charles Casoar ■ English spoken

Very good selection of silver frames and decorative accessories.

COMPAGNIE FRANÇAIS DE L'ORIENT ET DE LA CHINE
163 bd Saint-German, 75006 Paris ■ Tel. 01 45 48 00 18 ■ Tue-Sat 10:30-13:30/14:00-19:00 ■ English, Italian and Spanish spoken ■ Prices medium ■ Major credit cards

Great selection of Oriental furniture, textiles and accessories at their 7 shops.

PIERRE FREY
22 rue Royale, 75008 Paris ■ Telfax: 01 49 26 04 77 ■ Mon-Sat 10:00-19:00 ■ Mme Véronique de Catheu ■ English spoken ■ Major credit cards

A large selection of home furnishings including furniture, glassware, cushions, tableware, table linens, throws, bedspreads, frames, lampshades, lamps. Charming atmosphere.

GALERIE MAISON & JARDIN
120 rue du Faubourg-Saint-Honoré, 75008 Paris ■ Tel: 01 45 61 93 30 ■ Fax: 01 45 63 56 16 ■ Mon-Fri 10:00-18:30 ■ Philippe Sermadiras ■ English spoken ■ Prices high

Antique furniture and decorative objects. Sofas and armchairs. Antique and contemporary lamps. Prints and engravings. Will consult on decoration.

LA CHAISE LONGUE
30 rue Croix des Petits Champs, 75001 Paris ■ Tel: 01 42 96 32 14 ■ 3 rue Princesse, 75006 Paris ■ Tel: 01 43 29 62 39 ■ 20 rue des Francs Bourgeois, 75003 Paris ■ Tel: 01 48 04 36 37 ■ 2 rue de Sèze, 75008 Paris ■ Tel 01 44 94 01 61 ■ Web: www.chaiselongue.com ■ Every day 11:00-19:00 ■ Prices medium ■ All credit cards

A selection of interesting home furnishings from tableware to lamps.

LA MAISON DU WEEK-END
26 rue Vavin, 75006 Paris ■ Tel: 01 43 54 15 52 ■ Fax 01 40 51 72 07 ■ Tue-Sat 11:00-19:00 ■ Marianne Moreaud ■ English and Italian spoken ■ Prices medium ■ Amex, Visa

Great selection of everything for the home: inside and out.

LA SAMARITAINE
77 rue de Rivoli, 75001 Paris ■ Tel: 01 40 41 20 20 ■ Fax 01 40 41 28 28 ■ Mon-Sat 9:30-19:00, Thu evening to 22:00 ■ Open Sunday in Dec ■ Major credit cards

Everything for the house in the main store.

LE BON MARCHÉ
24 rue de Sevrès, 75007 Paris ■ Tel: 01 44 39 80 00 ■ Mon-Sat 9:30-19:00 ■ Major credit cards

Excellent store with a section devoted to individual antique dealers.

♛ LE CEDRE ROUGE
22 av Victoria, 75001 Paris ■ Tel: 01 42 33 71 05 ■ Fax: 01 40 26 46 78 ■ Mon 12:45-19:00, Tue-Fri 10:45-19:00, Sat 10:00-19:00, Sun 11:00-18:00 ■ Damien Kammerer ■ English and Italian spoken ■ Amex, Visa

Lighting from all over the world. Beautiful tables of volcanic stone in 36 colours, large pots of lava, terracotta and enamel. Interior and exterior tiles, aquatic plants and a superb collection of scented candles. Decoration of interior gardens and terrace planting, garden and terrace furniture. They also have stores in the 7th, 8th and 16th arrondisements. This is their main store with the largest stock. They are friendly, knowledgeable and charming and located around the corner from the Chatelet theatre.

LIGNE ROSET
189 bd Saint-Germain, 75007 Paris ■ Tel: 01 45 48 54 13 ■ Fax: 01 45 44 01 20 ■ Web www.ligne-roset.tm.fr ■ Mon 14:00-19:00/Tue-Sat 10:00-19:00 ■ English spoken ■ Prices medium to high ■ Major credit cards ■ 15 avenue Matignon 75008 Paris ■ Tel 01 42 25 94 19 ■ Fax 01 45 63 59 62 ■ 25 rue du Faubourg Saint-Antoine 75011 ■ Tel 01 40 01 00 05 ■ Fax 01 40 01 00 07 ■ 99 avenue du Maine 75014 ■ Tel 01 43 21 65 70 ■ Fax 01 43 27 99 10

Large choice of contemporary furniture, chairs, carpets and accessories. Lots of outlets.

MODÉNATURE
3 rue Jacob, 75006 Paris ■ Tel: 01 29 62 54 ■ Fax 01 43 29 62 74 ■ Web: www.modenature.com ■ Tue-Sat 10:30-19:00 ■ English spoken ■ Amex, Visa

Great selection of furniture, lighting and accessories.

REFLETS DU TEMPS

12 rue de Verneuil, 75007 Paris ■ Tel: 01 42 92 02 04 ■ Fax: 01 42 92 02 05 ■ Tue-Sat 10:30-12:30/14:30-19:30 ■ Mme Traineau ■ English spoken ■ Visa

Reproductions of antique furniture. Chairs.

ROCHE BOBOIS

193 &197 bd Saint-Germain, 75007 Paris ■ Tel: 01 42 22 11 12/01 45 48 46 21 ■ Fax 01 42 84 12 37 ■ Mon 14:00-19:00, Tue-Sat 10:00-19:00

Complete line of home furnishings. Lots of outlets. Call for other addresses.

SIMRANE

23 rue Bonaparte, 75006 Paris ■ Tel: 01 43 54 90 73 ■ Fax: 01 46 33 15 86 ■ Mon-Sat 10:00-19:00 ■ Sophie du Tertre ■ English spoken ■ 10% professional discount ■ Major credit cards

Decorations for the home. Table linens, bed-spreads, draperies, throws, cushions, 80 colours of silk by the metre, accessories for the pocket, bedroom or bath, shelf fixtures and some ceramics.

TEXTURES

55 rue des Saints-Pères, 75006 Paris ■ Tel: 01 45 48 90 88 ■ Fax 01 42 84 05 95 ■ Mon 14:30-18:30, Tue-Sat 10:00-18:30 ■ English, German and Spanish spoken ■ Major credit cards

Designers Guild line of fabrics, wallpapers, sofas and accessories. Will make blinds, curtains, bedspreads.

TORVINOKA

4 rue Cardinale, 75006 Paris ■ Tel: 01 43 25 09 13 ■ Fax: 01 40 51 89 46 ■ Tue-Fri 10:00-19:00, Mon 14:00-19:00 English spoken ■ 10% professional discount to architects ■ Visa

Contemporary European furniture, and objects for the home. Designs by Alvar Aalto of Finland.

TOUCHES DE PROVENCE

6 rue Cardinale, 75006 Paris ■ Telfax: 01 40 46 01 79 ■ Web: www.touchedeprovence.com ■ Tue-Sat 10:30-13:00/15:00-19:30 Wed 15:00-19:30 ■ Mme. Esther Abel ■ English, Italian and Spanish spoken ■ Prices reasonable ■ 10% professional discount ■ Major credit cards

XVIII and XIX century furniture and painted provincial furniture. Antique porcelain. Contemporary decorative objects.

KITCHENS AND ACCESSORIES
Cuisines et Accessoires de cuisine

FRANCIS BATT
180 av Victor Hugo, 75116 Paris ■ Tel: 01 47 27 13 28 ■ Fax: 01 47 55 63 70 ■ E-mail: francis.batt@wanadoo.fr ■ Mon-Sat 10:00-19:00 ■ Miss Batt and Francis Batt ■ 22 rue des Huissiers, 92200 Neuilly ■ Tel: 01 47 22 98 20 ■ Fax: 01 47 22 22 14 ■ Mon-Sat 10:00-13:30/14:30-19:00, both open some Sundays in Dec. ■ Mrs. Kok ■ English and Spanish spoken ■ Major credit cards
Excellent choice of kitchen utensils, tableware and accessories.

CHARLES BIGANT
11bis rue du Commandant Pilot, 92200 Neuilly ■ Tel: 01 46 24 24 12 ■ Fax: 01 46 37 06 92 ■ E-mail: cuisinecharlesbigant@compuserve.com ■ Mon-Sat 9:00-12:30/14:00-19:00 ■ Véronique Clerempuy ■ English, German and some Spanish spoken ■ Prices medium to high ■ Professional discount
Custom cabinetry for kitchens, as well as for bathrooms and dressing rooms. Can furnish appliances, but no plumbing.

BINOVA-ESPACE SAINT-HONORÉ
161 rue du Faubourg-Saint-Honoré, 75008 Paris ■ Tel: 01 42 89 16 38 ■ Fax: 01 45 63 44 69 ■ Mon-Sat 10:30-19:00 ■ Jean-Charles Crausaz ■ English spoken ■ 10% professional discount
Furniture and appliances for complete kitchen installations. From conception through installation.

BOFFI STUDIO PARIS
234 bd Saint-Germain, 75007 Paris ■ Tel: 01 42 84 11 02 ■ Fax: 01 45 49 25 52 ■ E-mail: boffiparis@wanadoo.fr ■ Web: www.boffi-paris.com ■ Mon 14:00-19:00, Tue-Sat 10:00-13:00/14:00-19:00 Philippe Gilman ■ English, Spanish and Italian spoken
Specialist in contemporary high-quality kitchens. Interesting contemporary designs and colours. From concept to installation.

BULTHAUP
9 rue Villersexel, 75007 Paris ■ Tel: 01 45 49 10 05 ■ Fax: 01 45 49 10 52 ■ Mon-Sat 10:00-13:00/14:00-19:00 ■ Marc Vougny ■ Some English spoken ■ Major credit cards
Efficient and elegant contemporary kitchens with all functional elements and accessories. Will work from your plans.

BULTHAUP ETOILE - CUISINE

6 av Carnot, 75017 Paris ■ Tel: 01 43 80 28 16 ■ Fax: 01 43 80 34 48 ■ Web: www.etoilecuisine.tm.fr ■ Tue-Sat 10:00-13:00/14:00-19:00 ■ Jean-Charles Crausaz ■ English spoken ■ 10% professional discount

Kitchen furniture and appliances of excellent quality. From concept to installation.

♚ CHRISTIANS OF FRANCE

193 bd Saint-Germain, 75007 Paris ■ Tel: 01 45 48 57 57 ■ Fax: 01 45 48 57 56 ■ Mon-Sat 10:00-13:00/14:00-19:00 ■ Patrick Babu ■ English spoken ■ Prices high ■ Professional discount ■ Major credit cards

Very high-quality craftsmanship for kitchens and bathrooms. Will help with the planning and will install. They are also in London and New York.

CUISINES BOFFI

157 rue du Faubourg-Saint-Honoré, 75008 Paris ■ Tel: 01 42 89 41 17 ■ Fax: 01 40 75 04 12 ■ E-mail: boffimarket@boffi.it ■ Web: www.boffi.it ■ Mon-Sat 10:00-13:00/14:00-19:00 ■ English and Italian spoken ■ Professional discount

Concept, design, installation and renovation of kitchens and bathrooms. Beautiful quality.

♚ DEHILLERIN

18 rue Coquillière, 75001 Paris ■ Tel: 01 42 36 53 13 ■ Fax: 01 42 36 54 80 ■ Web: www.e-dehillerin.com ■ Mon 8:00-12:30/14:00-18:00, Tue-Sat 8:00-18:00 ■ English spoken ■ Prices medium to high ■ MC over 150FF

Very high-quality kitchen utensils of professional level. Superb collection of copper pots and pans.

GODIN CUISINES

6 bd Richard Lenoir, 75011 Paris ■ Tel: 01 48 07 88 35 ■ Fax: 01 43 55 17 31 ■ Mon-Sat 10:00-12:30/14:00-19:00 ■ Professional discount ■ Major credit cards

Very good-quality kitchen installations, cabinets, countertops, floors. Complete installations to client's designs.

ITALIA CUCINE

202 bd Saint-Germain, 75007 Paris ■ Mon 13:30-18:30, Tue-Fri 9:30-12:30/13:30-18:30, Sat 9:30-12:00/14:00-18:30 ■ Prices medium to high ■ Professional discount ■ Major credit cards

Sleek contemporary Italian kitchens.

JONIEL

33 bd Raspail, 75007 Paris ■ Tel: 01 45 44 59 92 ■ Fax: 01 45 48 76 03 ■ Mon-Sat 10:00-12:00/14:00-19:00 ■ Michel Marié ■ Prices medium to high ■ Major credit cards

Beautiful and efficient kitchens custom designed for every purpose.

👑 LA CORNUE

18 rue Mabillon, 75006 Paris ■ Tel: 01 46 33 84 74 ■ Fax: 01 40 46 93 85 ■ E-mail: 101501.2534@compuserve.com ■ Mon-Sat 10:00-13:00/14:00-18:30 ■ Brigitte Baranes ■ English spoken ■ Prices high ■ 10% professional discount ■ Major credit cards

Remarkable French stoves made to order in any size. Exceptional work by skilled artisans. It can take three months to make them. Good accessories.

LE COMPTOIR DE LA CUISINE

43 av de Friedland, 75008 Paris ■ Tel: 01 53 75 10 00 ■ Fax: 01 53 75 10 05 ■ E-mail: comptoirdelacuisine@wanadoo.fr ■ Web: www.venetacucine.com ■ Mon-Sat 10:00-19:30 ■ Eric Calossi ■ English spoken ■ Prices medium to high ■ Professional discount ■ Visa

Specialist of "beautiful kitchens". Work-tops in stainless steel, granite, glass, wood and more. Planning and installations.

7e DIMENSION

160 rue de Grenelle, 75007 Paris ■ Tel: 01 45 50 38 38 ■ Fax: 01 45 50 39 13 ■ Mon-Sat 9:00-13:00/14:00-19:00 ■ English and Italian spoken ■ Professional discount ■ Major credit cards

Italian designed and manufactured kitchens. Good quality, innovative clean designs and good choice of colours. Complete planning and installation.

👑 A. SIMON

36 rue Etienne-Marcel and 48 rue Montmartre, 75002 Paris ■ Tel: 01 42 33 71 65 ■ Fax: 01 42 33 68 25 ■ E-mail: simon.sa@wanadoo.fr ■ Tue-Sat 8:30-18:30 ■ English spoken ■ Prices medium to high ■ Professional discount

For the amateur and the professional, everything for cooking and serving food and wine. Marvellous quality.

👑 ZEPTER

240bis bd Saint-Germain, 75007 Paris ■ Tel: 01 42 22 43 37 ■ Fax: 01 42 22 44 93 ■ Mon-Sat 10:00-19:00 ■ Michel Vigouroux ■ English, Italian, German, Greek and Spanish spoken ■ Prices medium to high ■ Professional discount ■ Major credit cards

Cooking utensils, table arts and cutlery. Superb designs, by this Swiss company, made in Northern Italy. Don't miss.

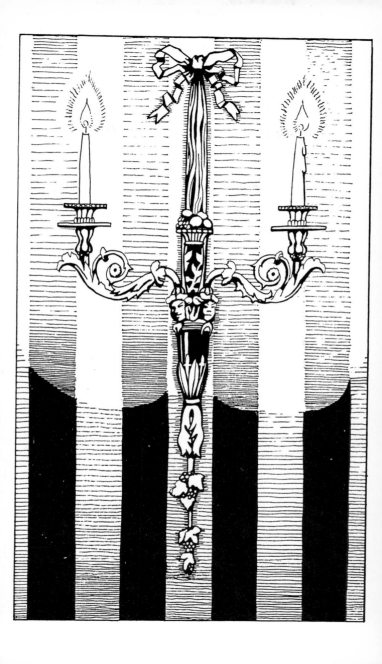

LIGHTING
Luminaires

III

DELISLE
4 rue du Parc-Royal, 75003 Paris ■ Tel: 01 42 72 21 34 ■ Fax: 01 42 72 04 79 ■ E-mail: jmd@delisle.fr ■ Web: www.delisle.f ■ Mon-Fri 9:00-12:00/14:00-18:00 and by appointment ■ Jean-Michel Delisle ■ English and Italian spoken ■ Prices high ■ Professional discount

Superb quality lighting of all kinds. The highest-quality reproductions of classical designs from the Renaissance to contemporary in bronze and wrought iron. Chandeliers, ceiling lamps, suspension lamps, indoor and outdoor lanterns, sconces, table and desk lamps, standing lamps, outdoor lighting. Collection of 4,000 models to choose from as well as designs to order. Some beautiful small tables. Clients include the world's finest museums, private homes and hotels. Restoration service. Member of the Comité Colbert.

IV

ARLUMIÈRE
8 av Victoria, 75004 Paris ■ Tel: 01 42 71 23 42 ■ Fax: 01 42 71 87 50 ■ Mon 14:00-19:00, Tue-Sat 10:00-19:00 ■ Prices medium to high ■ 10 to 20% professional discount ■ Major credit cards

Representatives of 80 international suppliers of lighting. Specialty: all types of halogen lamps, standing, desk and wall lamps. Large choice of Murano glass. Custom design of original models.

V

LUMIÈRE DE L'OEIL
4 rue Flatters, 75005 Paris ■ Telfax: 01 47 07 63 47 ■ E-mail: lumiara@aol.com ■ Web: http://members.aol.com/lumiara/homepage.html ■ Tue-Fri 14:00-19:00, Sat 11:00-17:00 ■ Mr. Ara ■ English and German spoken ■ Prices medium ■ Foreign checks accepted

Restoration of antique lighting 1850-1925, oil lamps, gas lamps, into working condition. Electrification and wiring to halogen. Beaded fringes made to measure. Specialist in lighting work for historic monuments, museums, theatre and cinema. Hundreds of lamps for sale.

SCHMOCK BROC

15 rue Racine, 75006 Paris ■ Telfax: 01 46 33 79 98 ■ Cell: 06 07 69 88 95 ■ Mon-Fri 13:00-20:00, Sat 10:30-19:30 ■ Anne Marie Otte and Nadine Clément ■ English spoken ■ Prices medium to high ■ Professional discount ■ Amex and Visa

Large choice of lighting by designers of the 1950s, 1960s and 1970s. Furniture and decorative objects.

CONIL

1 rue de Varenne, 75007 Paris ■ Tel: 01 45 49 19 85 ■ Fax: 01 45 49 19 92 ■ Mon-Sat 11:00-13:00/15:00-19:30 ■ Mme Monique Conil ■ Prices medium to high ■ Professional discount ■ Amex, Visa

Lamps in leather and ostrich. 4 models made by hand: Ios, Minds, Sirnos, Paros.

MONTAGNIER

24 rue de Grenelle, 75007 Paris ■ Tel: 01 45 48 16 41 ■ Fax: 01 42 84 01 10 ■ Mon-Fri 9:00-12:30/14:30-18:30 ■ Some English spoken ■ Prices high ■ Professional discount

High quality ceiling and suspension lamps, crystal chandeliers, interior lanterns, sconces, exterior lighting. Styles: Louis XIV, Louis XV, Louis XVI, Empire, Art Deco. Restoration and repair. Custom work.

VOLT ET WATT ASSOCIES

29 bd Raspail, 75007 Paris ■ Tel: 01 45 48 29 62 ■ Fax: 01 45 44 55 67 ■ Mon-Sat 10:00-19:00 ■ Bruno-Jean Herbin and Erick Boronat speak English and Spanish ■ Professional discount ■ Visa, MC

Contemporary lighting by young French creators. Classics of the XX century.

♔ BAGUÈS

Viaduc des Arts, 73 av Daumesnil 75012 Paris ■ Tel: 01 43 41
53 35 ■ Fax: 01 43 41 54 55 ■ E-mail: baguesparis@minitel.net
■ Mon-Fri 9:00-18:00, Sat 10:00-18:00 ■ Jean-Jacques Corré ■
English spoken ■ Professional discount ■ Major credit cards

**Fine collection of bronze and wrought iron lighting: 8,000
models have been created since 1840. Period lighting in
bronze and crystal, chandeliers, lamps, sconces. Restoration services. For the last century, one of the best known
creators of superb quality lighting in all styles as well as occasional furniture. Decorative objects.**

DOME

182 bd Haussmann, 75008 Paris ■ Tel: 01 45 62 74 47 ■ Fax: 01
45 62 83 72 ■ 10:00-13:00/14:00-18:00 Mon-Fri from October to
March and Tue-Sat from April to September ■ Claudie Perrot
speaks English ■ Prices high ■ 15% professional discount ■ Visa

Good contemporary and custom lighting.

VERONESE

184 bd Haussmann, 75008 Paris ■ Tel: 01 45 62 67 67 ■ Fax: 01
42 25 79 66 ■ Mon-Fri 9:00-12:30/14:00-18:30, Sat 10:00-
12:30/14:00-18:30 ■ English spoken ■ Prices high ■ 10% professional discount

**Special creations, working with architects and decorators,
of high quality crystal chandeliers.**

ART ET STYLE

Atelier: 172 rue de Charonne, 75011 Paris ■ Tel: 01 40 09 09 00
■ Fax: 01 40 09 77 55 ■ Mon-Fri 9:00-12:00/14:00-18:00 ■ Eng-
lish spoken ■ Prices high
Showroom : ARTISAN BRONZIER, 9 rue Saint-Sébastien 75011
Paris ■ Tel: 01 47 00 37 37 ■ Mon-Sat 9:00-12:00/14:00-18:00 ■
English spoken ■ Prices high ■ Web: www.tisserant.fr

**Bronze lighting in all styles, sconces, table lamps, ceiling
lamps, lanterns, crystal chandeliers. Occasional tables, consoles. Restoration and repair.**

BRINGAS ET FILS

8 rue Froment, 75011 Paris ■ Tel: 01 47 00 74 74 ■ Mon-Fri 9:00-
12:30/14:00-18:30 ■ Didier-Jacques Bringas speaks English ■
Prices medium to high ■ Professional discount

**Custom made crystal chandeliers, bronze wall sconces,
lamps, objects and occasional furniture. Restoration.**

LES LUMINAIRES LUCIEN GAU

2 rue de la Roquette, 75011 Paris ■ Tel: 01 48 05 22 11 ■ Fax: 01 48 05 09 33 ■ Web: www.luminaires-gau.fr ■ Pascal Gau speaks English ■ Prices medium ■ Professional discount

Major collection of period style halogen lighting fixtures. Classic styles of all types of lighting: Louis XIII to Louis XVI, Empire, rustic, Art Nouveau, Art Deco, the 1950s. Contemporary lighting. Low voltage spotlight systems and lighting for pictures.

JACQUES CHARPENTIER

41 rue de Lappe, 75011 Paris ■ Tel: 01 43 55 62 33 ■ Fax: 01 48 07 22 94 ■ Mon-Fri 9:30-18:00 ■ Thierry Charpentier speaks English, Hervé Charpentier speaks German ■ Prices medium ■ Professional discount

First Empire, Modern, contemporary and English wall lamps, table lamps, desk lamps and standing lamps. Custom work.

FOURCOUX-PRINCE

24 passage Gustave-Lepeu, 75011 Paris ■ Tel: 01 43 71 09 78 ■ Fax: 01 43 71 88 16 ■ Mon-Fri 9:00-12:00/13:45-18:00 ■ Christine Prince speaks English ■ Prices medium to high

Reproductions of chandeliers, wall, table and desk lamps in the styles of Louis XIV, Louis XV, Louis XVI, First Empire and contemporary. High quality.

K.S. LUMINAIRE DECORATIF

92 av Phillippe-Auguste, 75011 Paris ■ Tel: 01 43 71 22 15 ■ Fax: 01 43 71 88 13 ■ Tue-Sat 10:00-12:00/14:00-19:00 ■ English spoken ■ Prices medium ■ 15% professional discount

Specialist in importation of lighting in Murano glass. Custom lampshades.

LUSTRA DECORS

22 rue de la Roquette, 75011 Paris ■ Tel: 01 43 55 84 16 ■ Fax: 01 48 06 90 25 ■ Mon-Fri 8:30-12:00/13:30-18:00 ■ Mr. Marchat speaks English ■ Prices medium ■ Professional discount

Major contract contemporary lighting specialists. Bracket lamps, free standing, desk and floor lamps. Halogen floor lamps. They work from drawings and blue prints. Work experience includes the White House in Washington, D.C., the Beverly Wilshire Hotel and the U.S. Ambassadors' residences in London, Paris and Brussels.

RAYNAUD

172 rue de Charonne, 75011 Paris ■ Tel: 01 43 79 59 37 ■ Fax: 01 43 79 75 02 ■ Web : www.raynaud-paris.com ■ Mon-Fri 9:00-12:00/13:00-17:30 ■ Gisèle Renouard speaks English ■ Prices medium ■ Professional discount

Over 600 models of traditional styles, from Louis XIV to contemporary, rustic and English. Chandeliers, sconces, ceiling and suspension lamps, indoor lanterns, wall lamps, table and desk lamps, standing lamps, halogen standing lamps, luminous sculptures. Restoration, repair and work off plans.

––––––––––––––––––––––––– XIV –––––––––––––––––––––––––

ATELIER JEAN PERZEL

3 rue de la Cité-Universitaire, 75014 Paris ■ Tel: 01 45 88 77 24 ■ Fax: 01 45 65 32 82 ■ Web: www.jean-perzel.com ■ Mon-Fri 9:00-12:00/13:00-18:00 Sat 10:00-12:00/14:00-19:00 ■ Prices medium to high ■ Professional discount

The 1930s specialist. Excellent original, signed and copyrighted designs since 1931. Ceiling lamps, suspension, wall, table and desk lamps. Restoration and repairs.

MAX LE VERRIER

30 rue Deparcieux, 75014 Paris ■ Tel: 01 43 22 62 95 ■ Mon-Fri 9:00-12:00/14:00-17:30 ■ Prices medium to high

The company was founded in 1919 by Max Le Verrier, a bronze sculptor, designer and worker in decorative casting. In addition to the bronze sculptures - animals, figures and decorative objects for desks - their specialty is also small objects and luminous sculptures in the 1930s style in decorative cast iron and signed by well-known artists. Specialty: art deco lamps.

––––––––––––––––––––––––– XV –––––––––––––––––––––––––

MAUFACTOR

76 rue de l'Amiral-Roussin, 75015 Paris ■ Tel: 01 42 50 99 72 ■ Fax: 01 42 50 96 80 ■ Mon-Fri 9:00-17:00 ■ English spoken ■ Prices medium to high

High quality contemporary lamps: table, desk, standing. Wall lamps, lighting for pictures. Made-to-order designs. Production in large quantity possible for offices and hotels.

BERTHE ARDAINE
75 rue Boissière, 75116 Paris ■ Tel: 01 45 00 94 49 ■ Fax: 01 45 00 52 77 ■ Mon-Sat 8:30-18:00 ■ Prices medium

Contemporary lighting and montage of lamps. Choice of lampshades: paper, silk, card and fabrics, all made to measure.

BARBIER
28 rue Copernic, 75116 Paris ■ Tel: 01 47 27 44 77 ■ Fax: 01 47 27 62 84 ■ Mon-Fri 10:00-13:00/14:00-19:00 ■ Gérard Barbier ■ English spoken ■ Prices medium ■ Visa

Very good contemporary lighting. Lighting for the exterior and for paintings. Decorative bulbs and restoration.

GALERIE SAN MARCO
3 rue Benjamin Franklin, 75116 Paris ■ Tel: 01 42 15 22 00 ■ Fax: 01 42 15 20 47 ■ Web: www.galerie-sanmarco.com ■ Mon-Sat 10:00-19:00 ■ Prices medium ■ 20% professional discount

The largest choice in France of Venetian glass: Chandeliers, sconces, standing lamps, candelabra, mirrors, consoles, sculptures, glasses, flacons, decorative objects, vases, table lamps. All exclusively in Murano glass.

JEAN DURST
49 rue Pierre-Demours, 75017 Paris ■ Tel: 01 47 63 54 58 ■ Fax: 01 47 63 39 50 ■ Tue-Sat 10:00-13:00/14:30-19:00 ■ Jean Durst speaks English ■ Prices medium to high ■ 10% professional discount

Lighting in bronze and crystal. Antique lighting and copies of old styles. Mounting of lamps, custom lampshades and restoration of all types of antique lighting.

POTENTIEL
10 bis rue Muller, 75018 Paris ■ Tel: 01 42 23 14 04 ■ Fax: 01 42 54 02 63 ■ E-mail: info@potentiel.fr ■ Web: www.potentiel.fr ■ Mon-Fri 9:30-20:00 ■ Gilles Beaumont speaks English ■ 30% professional discount

Contemporary lighting: suspension and wall lamps, halogen standing lamps, projectors. Special wall lamps for bathrooms. Original custom designs.

♛ CHARLES

Showroom: 18-20 rue Soleillet, 75020 Paris ■ Tel: 01 43 49 51 50 ■ Fax: 01 43 49 61 08 ■ Web: www.charles.fr ■ Mon-Fri 9:00-12:00/14:00-18:00 ■ Gallery: 34 rue Bonaparte, 75006 Paris ■ Tel: 01 43 25 60 04 ■ Chrystiane Charles speaks English ■ Professional discount

Remarkable selection of a broad range of unusual and original designs in styles ranging from Louis XIV to today. Every work hand-crafted by designers and artisans who have been at their trade for four generations. Everything from chandeliers to lanterns, classic sconces, standing and halogen floor lamps to sculptured decorative table lamps. Custom designs for fashion pace-setters. Restoration and repair.

♛ MEILLEUR

32 rue des Amandiers, 75020 Paris (entrance 15 rue Fernand Léger) ■ Tel: 01 43 66 45 13 ■ Fax: 01 43 66 45 43 ■ E-mail : maison.meilleur@wanadoo.fr ■ Mon-Fri 8:30-12 :00/13 :00-18:00 by appointment ■ English spoken ■ Prices high ■ Professional discount

One of the very best custom creators of classic and contemporary style lighting. Chandeliers, lamps, lanterns and beautifully chiselled bronze sconces. Their own creations of standing, articulated floor lamps, with articulated shades. These are the world's best. Beautiful tables in bronze and gold leafed steel. Custom designs and creation of unique models. Restoration. These are the *bronziers* who worked with Henri Samuel to bring together the XVIII and XX centuries. There are also some beautiful tables and lamps created for Givenchy.

OUTSIDE PARIS

AMBIANCE LUMIÈRE

65 quai Auguste-Blanqui, 94141 Alfortville ■ Tel: 01 43 68 45 22 ■ Fax: 01 43 75 75 01 ■ Web: www.lumiere.com ■ Mon-Fri 10:00-12:30/13:30-17:30 ■ English spoken ■ Prices medium to high ■ Professional discount

Festive lighting products. Fairy lights for decorating shop windows. Illumination of monuments. Decorative lighting for casinos and discothèques. Will work closely with architects and designers on major projects.

Antique Lighting
Luminaires anciens

♛ **GALERIE DES LAMPES**
9 rue de Beaune, 75007 Paris ■ Tel: 01 40 20 14 14 ■ Mon-Sat
10:30-13:00/14:00-19:00 ■ Mme Newman ■ English, German,
Italian and Spanish spoken ■ Prices medium to high ■ Professional discount

Beautiful selection of antique lamps.

♛ **MARTINE KLOTZ**
DECORS LUMINEUX
9 rue de Belloy, 75116 Paris ■ Tel: 01 47 27 92 64 ■ Fax: 01 47
27 27 90 ■ Mon-Fri 8:30-12:30/13:30-17:30 ■ Martine Klotz
speaks English ■ 10% professional discount

Specialist in restoration and improvement of antique lighting and crystal chandeliers by disguising wiring with trompe-l'oeil. Lighting for pictures. Specialist in indirect lighting. Consultation services.

♛ **KIN LIOU**
81 rue du Bac, 75007 Paris ■ Tel: 01 45 48 80 85 ■ Fax: 01 42
84 32 78 ■ Tue-Sat 10:30-19:00, Mon 14:00-19:00 ■ English
spoken ■ Prices medium ■ Professional discount ■ Amex, Visa

Unusual XIX century lamps made of bronze candlesticks representing men and women from all over the world, with an Orientalist influence; specially created lampshades.

♛ **A. COLIN MAILLARD**
11 rue de Miromesnil, 75008 Paris ■ Telfax: 01 42 65 43 62 ■
Mon 14:00-18:30, Tue-Fri 10:30-12:30/14:00-18:30, Sat 14:00-
18:30 ■ Pierre-Jacques Chauveau ■ English spoken ■ Prices
medium to high ■ Professional discount

Antique lamps; lampshades made to order.

♛ Lampshades
Abat-jour

III

GEORGES FICHET
26 rue Saint-Gilles, 75003 Paris ■ Tel: 01 42 72 32 65 ■ Thu-Sat 10:00-12:00/14:00-18:00 ■ Some English spoken ■ Prices medium ■ *Atelier:* 26, avenue de Verdun, 78170 La Celle Saint-Cloud ■ Tel : 01 39 18 14 46 ■ Wed-Sat 10:00-12:00/14:00-19:00

Made-to-measure lampshades. Restoration of all types of lighting. They sell antique lamps which they have restored.

DANIEL SCHMIDT
37 bd Beaumarchais, 75003 Paris ■ Tel: 01 42 72 67 45 ■ Fax: 01 42 72 16 33 ■ Tue-Fri 9:00-13:00/14:30-18:30, Sat 9:00-13:00 ■ Daniel Schmidt speaks English ■ Prices medium ■ 20% professional discount

All styles of lampshades to measure. Very careful finish and quick delivery. Creation of original models and good selection of bases.

IV

PAUL-ÉMILE
10 rue de Jarente, 75004 Paris ■ Tel: 01 48 87 21 21 ■ Mon-Fri 10:00-12:30/14:00-18:00 ■ English spoken ■ Prices medium ■ 10% professional discount

Lampshades made to measure. Simple and complex mounts. Repair of antique lamps.

VI

ISABELLE ROUTIER
9 rue de Savoie, 75006 Paris ■ Tel: 01 46 33 36 58 ■ Fax: 01 44 07 18 66 ■ Mon-Fri by appointment ■ Isabelle Routier speaks English ■ Prices medium to high ■ Professional discount

All styles of lampshades made by hand. Mounting of lamps. Custom-creations of lamps and lampshades.

VII

ANTICA
38 rue de Verneuil, 75007 Paris ■ Tel: 01 42 61 28 86 ■ Mon 13:30-18:30 Tue-Fri 10:00-18:30 Sat 10:00-13:00 ■ Arlette Clérin speaks English ■ Prices high ■ 10% professional discount ■ Ma-

jor credit cards

Custom lampshades in all shapes and in all materials, including hand-sewn silk in classic old styles. Beautiful.

MJMS

3 rue Saint-Dominique, 75007 Paris ■ Tel: 01 45 44 03 37 ■ Fax: 01 45 48 29 91 ■ Mon-Fri afternoons by appointment ■ Marie-Joseph Maze-Sencier speaks English ■ Prices medium ■ Professional discount

All kinds of hand-made lampshades, classical and contemporary. Will also make from your fabric.

X

ANNICK CARUSO

10 rue de Lancry, 75010 Paris ■ Tel: 01 42 41 10 93 ■ Mon-Fri 9:00-17:30, Fri 16:00 ■ English spoken ■ Prices low ■ Professional discount ■ Major credit cards

Lampshades to measure. Classical and contemporary styles, hand-painted. Objects mounted as lamps. Oriental vases available as bases.

XI

PASSEMENTERIE DU MARAIS

6 bd des Filles-du-Calvaire, 75011 Paris ■ Tel: 01 47 00 56 82 ■ Tue-Sat 9:30-12:45/14:00-18:15 ■ English spoken ■ Prices low to high ■ 5 to 10% professional discount

Exclusively supplies for making lampshades: from frames ("carcasses"), to all types of fabrics, braids, fringes, everything. They will mount and electrify your bases using silk covered wiring. They will also advise on "how-to".

XII

PLAS DUCLEROIR ABAT-JOUR

8 rue Dagorno, 75012 Paris ■ Tel: 01 43 07 84 97 ■ Fax: 01 43 45 50 65 ■ 61 rue de Picpus 75012 ■ Tel: 01 43 43 42 98 ■ Web: www.abatjourplas.com ■ Mon-Fri 9:30-12:30/13:30-18:30, Saturdays Oct-April ■ Gilles Plas speaks English ■ Prices medium ■ Professional discount

Fabrication of all types of lampshades: classical to contemporary, stretched fabric, pagoda shapes, skirts. Fully-lined. Hand and machine-made. Residential and contract work in quantity for hotels and offices. Lamps in unbreakable resin for the hotel market.

RUYS
63 rue de l'Ouest, 75014 Paris ■ Tel: 01 43 22 93 81 ■ Tue-Sat
10:30-12:30/15:00-19:00 ■ Prices high ■ Professional discount

Lampshades made to measure. Repair of lamps and halogens of all types.

ALEXANDRE
74 rue Fondary, 75015 Paris ■ Tel: 01 45 75 21 26 ■ Tue-Sat
10:00-19:00 ■ Prices medium to high ■ Professional discount ■
Major credit cards

Alexandre has created over 1000 original and unique creations of lampshades in the last 15 years. They will work from your ideas or their own. Contemporary and especially classical styles.

ABAT-JOUR DOMINIQUE KERGUENNE
27 rue Franklin, 75016 Paris ■ Tel: 01 47 27 17 21 ■ Fax: 01 47
27 66 07 ■ Tue-Sat 10:00-18:30 ■ Visa, Amex

Lamp shades made to measure. Lamp bases, mounting of lamps.

SEMAINE
20 rue Nicolo, 75016 Paris ■ Tel: 01 45 20 06 69 ■ Fax: 01 42 24
79 77 ■ Tue-Sat 10:30-19:00 ■ Some English spoken ■ Prices
low to medium ■ Professional discount ■ Major credit cards (excepted Amex)

Marie-France Petit specializes in pleated lampshades. She also carries some toiles in stripes and checks for a more country look.

CARVAY
3 av de Villiers, 75017 Paris ■ Tel: 01 47 63 56 32 ■ Mon-Sat
9:30-13:00/14:00-19:00 ■ Prices medium

Lamp shades made to order. Mounting of lamps.

IMPROMPTU

8 rue Gustave-Flaubert, 75017 Paris ■ Tel: 01 42 27 62 99 ■ Fax: 01 42 27 62 22 ■ Tue-Sat 10:00-12:30/14:00-19:00 ■ Dominique Henriot speaks English ■ 15% professional discount ■ Major credit cards

Custom lampshades of all types: paper, fabric, hand pleating. Restoration and electrical mounting of old lamps.

Parts and Accessories for Lighting
Accessoires de luminaires

GIRARD SUDRON

47 rue des Tournelles, 75003 Paris ■ Tel: 01 44 59 22 20 ■ Fax: 01 42 74 7072 ■ E-mail: e.carre@girardsudron.com ■ Mon-Fri 8:30-17:30, Fri closing 16:00 ■ Elizabeth Carré speaks English ■ Prices medium ■ Professional discount

5,000 different components for lighting fixtures, as well as light bulbs, lighting glassware, candle bulbs, halogen lamps. 100 years of expertise.

JANVIER

17 rue Pastourelle, 75003 Paris ■ Tel: 01 42 72 14 11 ■ Fax: 01 42 72 54 19 ■ Mon-Fri 8:00-12:30/13:30-17:30 ■ English spoken ■ Prices medium ■ Professional discount

Accessories for lighting in decorative bronze and wrought iron. Over 100,000 stampings for lighting, chandeliers and furniture. Figures, animals, bookends, etc. Furniture hardware in unfinished bronze. Custom work.

SWAROVSKI

15 bd Poissonnière, 75002 Paris ■ Tel: 01 44 76 15 15 ■ Fax: 01 44 76 15 00 ■ Web: www.swarovski.com ■ Mon-Thu 9:00-12:30/13:30-18:00, Fri 9:00-12:00 ■ English spoken ■ Prices medium to high

The world's leader in the production of cut crystal elements for chandeliers and lighting. Classic and contemporary. For lighting manufacturers only.

LIBRARY SHELVES AND CLOSETS

Bibliothèques et rangements

---------------------------- VII ----------------------------

DRESSING
224 bd Saint-Germain, 75007 Paris ■ Tel: 01 42 22 00 04 ■ Mon 14:00-19:00, Tue-Sat 10:00-13:00/14:00-19:00

Great custom closets.

---------------------------- VIII ----------------------------

CESAM
169 bd Haussmann, 75008 Paris ■ Tel: 01 45 61 04 16 ■ Fax: 01 45 63 46 07 ■ Tue-Fri 10:00-19:00, Sat 10:00-12:00/14:00-18:00 ■ English and Spanish spoken ■ Prices high ■ Professional discount

Bookshelves and closets, custom and stock. Very high-quality.

---------------------------- XII ----------------------------

LA MAISON DU PLACARD
57-59 rue de Lyon, 75012 Paris ■ Tel: 01 40 02 01 10 ■ Fax: 01 40 02 09 50 ■ Mon-Sat 9:30-12:30/14:00-19:00 ■ Mr Pedro Cepel ■ Spanish and Portuguese spoken

Custom closets. Large choice.

---------------------------- XIV ----------------------------

PRISM ALL
211 bd Raspail, 75014 Paris ■ Tel: 01 43 20 37 53 ■ Fax: 01 43 22 75 42 ■ Mon-Sat 9:00-18:00 ■ Prices medium ■ 20 to 30% professional discount

Modular shelves for libraries and glass display cabinets.

---------------------------- SURESNES ----------------------------

NEVES
99 rue des Bas-Rogers, 92150 Suresnes ■ Tel: 01 46 97 80 80 ■ Fax: 01 46 97 80 70 ■ Web: www.neves-fabrication.com ■ Mon-Fri 8:00-12:00/13:00-17:30 ■ Anne Laurent speaks English ■ Professional discount

Manufacturer of modular units for closets, dressing rooms, room dividers, library shelving and offices.

INPLACARDS

Rue Andre-Citroen, 78140 Velizy-Villacoublay ■ Tel: 01 34 65 35 70 ■ Fax: 01 34 65 95 68 ■ Wed-Fri 11:00-20:00, Sat-Sun 10:00-20:00 ■ English spoken ■ Prices high ■ Professional discount

Sliding and pivoting doors, room dividers, closets and dressing rooms. Made-to-measure.

LINEN - HOUSEHOLD AND TABLE
Linge de maison et de table

IV

MERIDIEM
9 quai de Bourbon, 75004 Paris ■ Tel: 01 46 33 21 27 ■ Fax: 01 44 07 25 92 ■ Tue-Fri 13:00-19:00, Sat 10:30-19:00 ■ Ann Halvorsen speaks English ■ Prices medium ■ 20% professional discount

Custom-made household linens for table, bath and bedroom. Linen and blends of cotton and linen in natural colours.

VI

MANUEL CANOVAS
5 rue de Furstemberg, 75006 Paris ■ Tel: 01 43 26 89 31 ■ Fax: 01 40 46 07 70 ■ Mon 11:00-18:30, Tue-Sat 10:00-18:30 ■ English spoken ■ Prices high

Household linens. Sheets and duvet/comforter covers. Tablecloths, napkins, table sets, household perfumes, dishes.

VII

DESCAMPS
115 rue Saint-Dominique, 75007 Paris ■ Tel: 01 45 51 58 64 ■ Fax: 01 45 50 26 71 ■ 44 rue de Passy, 75016 Paris ■ Tel: 01 42 88 10 01 ■ Fax: 01 45 20 50 29 ■ Mon-Sat 10:00-19:00 ■ English spoken ■ Prices medium ■ 10% professional discount ■ Web: www.descamps.com

Wide range of good-quality household linen. Descamps has outlets in almost every arrondissement in Paris.

VIII

AGNÈS COMAR
7 av George V, 75008 Paris ■ Tel: 01 49 52 01 89 ■ Fax: 01 49 52 01 67 ■ Fax: 01 49 52 01 67 ■ Mon 13:00-19:00, Tue-Sat 11:00-13:00/14:00-19:00, Wed 10:00-13:00/14:00-19:00 ■ Dominique Dubel ■ English spoken ■ Prices medium to high ■ Professional discount ■ Major credit cards

Contemporary designs of high-quality household and table linen. Decorative objects and interior decoration.

♕ FRETTE

49 rue du Faubourg-Saint-Honoré, 75008 ■ Tel 01 42 66 47 70 ■ Fax: 01 42 66 98 98 ■ Mon-Sat 10:00-19:00 ■ English spoken ■ Prices medium to high ■ 10% professional discount ■ Major credit cards

Excellent quality and wide range of table and household linens.

♕ PORTHAULT

18 av Montaigne, 75008 Paris ■ Tel: 01 47 20 75 25 ■ Fax: 01 40 70 09 26 ■ English spoken ■ Prices medium to very high ■ 10% professional discount ■ Major credit cards

Beautiful linens for the table and the household. Fine linen for children and a good choice of gift items.

LA MAISON REVE

29 rue Marbeuf, 75008 Paris ■ Tel: 01 43 59 02 46 ■ Fax: 01 45 61 22 29 ■ Mon-Sat 10:00-19:00 ■ English spoken ■ Major credit cards

Attractive collection of table and household linens. Household gifts.

--- XV ---

BRODWAY FRANCE

71 rue Fondary, 75015 Paris ■ Tel: 01 45 77 18 53 ■ Fax: 01 45 77 26 83 ■ Mon-Fri 9:30-18:00 ■ English spoken ■ Prices medium ■ Professional discount

Embroidery by machine of household linens and furnishing fabrics for sofas and draperies. Will work on small quantity orders.

--- XVI ---

CHATELAINE

170 av Victor-Hugo, 75116 Paris ■ Tel: 01 47 27 44 07 ■ Fax: 01 47 27 19 85 ■ Tue-Fri 9:30-18:30, Sat 9:30-12:30/14:30-18:30 ■ Prices high ■ Visa, Amex

All household linens. Layettes and childrens' clothes 0 to 12 years. Custom household linens, made to measure at no extra charge. Alterations free of charge.

♛ PENELOPE

19 av Victor-Hugo, At the back of the Courtyard, 75116 Paris ■ Tel: 01 45 00 90 90 ■ Fax: 01 40 67 16 82 ■ Mon-Fri 9:30-18:30 ■ English and Spanish spoken ■ Visa

A gathering of remarkable women who handcraft some of the most beautifully embroidered linen in the world. Large choice of household and table linen, layettes, embroidered towels, tablecloths, sheets embroidered to match their mohair blankets, gadgets and table sets. Specialty: Custom-made tablecloths and napkins in exclusive designs. Superb quality. Designs to match your antique china, crystal or any idea you may have. Penelope is a non-profit organization of skilled women.

♛ MARIE LAVANDE

Viaduc des Arts, 83 av Daumesnil ■ Tel: 01 44 67 78 78 ■ Fax: 01 44 67 01 78 ■ Mon-Fri 9:30-12:30, Sat 14:30-18:30 ■ Joëlle Serres is the creator associated with the designer Angelique

Specialists in the restoration of embroidery and lace and cleaning and ironing of delicate antique linen, baptismal robes, wedding veils, folkloric headdresses. Creation of superb hand-embroidered household linen. Classes in embroidery and lacemaking. Extraordinary.

♛ NOEL

1 av Pierre-1er-de-Serbie, 75116 Paris ■ Tel: 01 40 70 14 63 ■ Fax: 01 40 70 05 25 ■ Web: www.noelparis.com ■ Mon-Sat 10:00-19:00 ■ English spoken ■ Professional discount ■ Major credit cards

Hand and machine embroidered table and household linen of the highest quality. Custom orders to the client's design or the designs of Noel. 1,300 designs in their archives to choose from. Beautiful nightwear.

--------- OUTSIDE PARIS ---------

SIRETEX

17 rue Montgolfier, 93110 Rosny sous Bois ■ Tel: 01 49 35 11 11 ■ Fax: 01 49 35 10 11 ■ Mon-Fri 8:00-12:00/13:00-18:00 ■ English spoken ■ Professional discount

Manufacturers of household linen. Towelling 420 gms/m?, 550 gms/m? and 620 gms/m?. Towels in all sizes, robes/dressing gowns. Bed linen in all dimensions. Tablecloths in American percale.

Antique Linen

SOPHIE DUPONT
49 rue Ramey, 75018 Paris ■ Tel: 01 42 54 69 30 ■ Mon-Sat
14:00-19:00 ■ Sophie Dupont speaks English ■ Prices medium
■ Professional discounts

**XVIII and XIX century furniture and decorative objects. Lots
of antique linen.**

FUCHSIA DENTELLES
2 rue de l'Ave-Maria, 75004 Paris ■ Telfax: 48 04 75 61 ■ E-mail
elise.rodolphe@wanadoo.fr ■ Every day 11:30-19:00 ■ English
spoken ■ 15 to 20 % professional discount ■ Major credit cards

**Antique table and household linen as well as lace, col-
lectibles and 1900s fashion. Wedding dresses and baptismal
clothes.**

SOURIS VERTE
Village Saint-Paul, 23 rue Saint-Paul, 75004 Paris (Courtyard) ■
Tel: 01 42 74 79 76 ■ Thurs-Mon 11:00-19:00 ■ English spoken
■ Prices medium ■ 20% professional discount ■ Major credit
cards

**Lace, buttons and braids. Old tablecloths and napkins. Dec-
orative household objects. Trimmings and some glassware.**

MARCHÉ AUX PUCES

Marché Serpette
MONIQUE LARDE
Allée 1, Stand 28 ■ Tel: 01 40 10 02 21

Antique household linen, lace and antique clothes.

Marché Vernaison
L'ARLEQUIN
Allée 7, Stands 128-128 bis ■ Tel: 01 40 11 16 38

Old linen, lace, decorative objects and fashion.

FRANCINE DENTELLES
Allée 7, Stands 121-123 and 140bis ■ Tel : 01 40 10 93 96

**Wonderful collection of old linen, lace, fabrics, objects and
1900s fashions.**

IRMA
Allée 9, Stand 200 ■ Tel: 40 10 08 57
Old linen, buttons, lace and glassware.

Care of Antique Linen

♛ MARIE LAVANDE
Viaduc des Arts, 83 av Daumesnil ■ Tel: 01 44 67 78 78 ■ Fax:
01 44 67 01 78 ■ Mon-Fri 9:30-12:30, Sat 14:30-18:30 ■ Joëlle
Serres is the creator associated with the designer Angelique
Specialists in the restoration of embroidery and lace and cleaning and ironing of delicate antique linen, baptismal robes, wedding veils, folkloric headdresses. Creation of superb hand-embroidered household linen. Classes in embroidery and lacemaking. Extraordinary.

MIRRORS
Miroirs

---------------------- VI ----------------------

THE PARIS AMERICAN ART CO.
2 rue Bonaparte, 75006 Paris ■ Tel: 01 43 26 09 93 ■ Fax: 01 43
54 33 80 ■ Tue-Sat 10:00-13:00/13:45-18:30 ■ English spoken ■
Prices medium to high ■ Professional discount

**Mirrors in gilded antique frames. Gilded frames in classical
styles. Restoration. Mirrors in modern frames. Antique
frames, frames for miniatures, engravings, drawings and
paintings.**

♔ **GALERIE NAVARRO - MIROIRS ANCIENS**
15 rue Saint-Sulpice, 75006 Paris ■ Telfax: 01 46 33 61 51 ■ Tue-
Sat 15:00-19:00 ■ Mme Colette Navarro ■ Spanish and Italian spoken ■ Prices high ■ Professional discount ■ Major credit cards

**XVII, XVIII and XIX century mirrors in sculptured gilded wood and
decorative objects. Barometers, putti and decorative freizes.**

---------------------- VIII ----------------------

MAISON GROSVALLET
126 bd Haussmann, 75008 Paris ■ Telfax 01 45 22 19 68 ■ Mon-
Fri 9:30-12:00/14:30-18:00 ■ English and Spanish spoken

Antique mirrors, consoles and frames of all styles.

♔ **CADRES LEBRUN**
155 rue du Faubourg-Saint-Honoré, 75008 Paris ■ Tel: 01 45 61
14 66 ■ Fax: 01 45 61 00 65 ■ Mon-Fri 14:30-19:00 ■ English
spoken ■ Prices high ■ 10% professional discount

**Antique mirrors from the XV to the XIX centuries. Antique
gilded frames from the XV to the XIX centuries.**

---------------------- XI ----------------------

MARTINE ZWOLINSKI
33 rue Amelot, 75011 Paris ■ Tel: 01 43 55 63 80 ■ Fax: 01 43
55 52 20 ■ Mon-Fri 9:00-12:00/14:00-18:00, Sat 9:30-12:30 ■
Laurent and Karine Zwolinski speak English ■ Prices low ■ Professional discount

Framed mirrors for boutiques. Framing services.

♛ ATELIER DU BOIS DORÉ

80 av des Ternes, 75017 Paris ■ Tel: 01 45 74 67 58 ■ Fax: 01 44 74 72 49 ■ E-mail: aboisdore@hotmail.com ■ Web: www.aboisdore.com ■ Mon-Sat 9:00-13:00/14:30-19:00 ■ English spoken ■ Prices medium to high ■ Professional discount ■ Visa, MC

Antique mirrors and framing for mirrors. Choice of 1,500 antique frames. 300 moulding styles for reproductions of antique frames. Framing. Restoration of gilded wood.

―――――――― MARCHÉ AUX PUCES ――――――――

LA GALERIE DES GLACES

87 rue des Rosiers, 93400 Saint-Ouen ■ Tel: 01 40 11 17 52 ■ Fax: 01 45 22 52 99 ■ Fri 9:00-12:00, Sat 8:30-18:30, Sun-Mon 10:00-18:30 ■ English spoken ■ Prices reasonable ■ 20% professional discount

All styles of antique mirrors in gilded wood and gilded plaster. Gilded bronze decorative objects.

LES MIROIRS DE FRANCE

109 rue des Rosiers, 93400 Saint-Ouen ■ Tel: 01 40 10 25 29 ■ Sat-Sun 10:00-17:00, Mon 13:30-16:00 ■ Prices low ■ Professional discount

Mirrors in gilded wood of the XVIII and XIX centuries.

♛ MARIE-EVE ROSENTHAL

Marché Serpette, Allee 4, Stand 13 ■ 110 rue des Rosiers, 93400 Saint-Ouen ■ Tel: 01 40 12 04 85 ■ Fax: 01 39 69 46 21 ■ Prices medium ■ Professional discount

One of the best selections of antique gilded wood mirrors in Paris. All periods, all styles, all sizes.

(SEE ALSO: ANTIQUE DEALERS)

PACKING AND SHIPPING
Emballage et Transport

NOUVELLE ATLANTIC
62 rue Mirabeau, 94200 Ivry-sur-Seine ■ Tel: 01 46 72 74 36 ■
Fax: 01 46 70 71 45 ■ Mon-Fri 8:00-12:00/13:00-18:00 ■ Umberto Siani and Agnès Delest speak English ■ Prices medium

Specialists in packing fine art and antiques. Regular weekly groupings to all international destinations. Customs agents. Can also provide complete containers 20' and 40'. Correspondents in all the major ports of the world. Documents prepared in English.

CAMARD
Marché aux Puces ■ 140 rue des Rosiers, 93400 Saint-Ouen ■
Tel: 01 40 12 84 45 ■ Fri-Mon 9:00-19:00 ■ Prices medium

Packing and shipping service direct from the Flea Market to all parts of the world.

ANDRÉ CHENUE ET FILS
5 bd Ney, 75018 Paris ■ Tel: 01 53 26 68 00 ■ Fax: 01 40 37 22 28 ■ Mon-Fri 8:30-12:15/13:30-17:15 ■ English spoken ■ Prices average

Experts in the packing and shipping of fine works of art and antiques. They work extensively with the Museums of Paris.

DESBORDES
14 rue de la Vega, 75012 Paris ■ Tel: 01 44 73 84 96/01 44 73 84 84 ■ Fax: 01 43 42 51 48 ■ Mon-Fri 8:00-12:00/14:00-18:00 ■ Annnick Farina speaks English ■ Prices medium

Packing and shipping of antiques and works of art to all destinations.

ALAN FRANKLIN TRANSPORT
2 rue Étienne Dolet, 93400 Saint-Ouen ■ Tel: 01 40 11 50 00 ■ Fax: 01 40 11 48 21 ■ Web: www.alanfranklintransport.co.uk ■ Every day 7:00-19:00 ■ Christophe Leprince et Isabelle Gatrigues speak English ■ Prices medium

Transport throughout Europe of antiques, paintings, sculpture and works of art by road. Air freight shipments worldwide and sea freight consignments via the U.K.

HEDLEY'S HUMPERS LIMITED
Marché Paul Bert 102 rue des Rosiers 93400 Saint-Ouen ■ Tel: 01 40 10 94 00 ■ Fax: 01 40 10 05 64 ■ E-mail: andy@hedleyshumpers.com ■ Fri-Mon 9:00-19:00 ■ English spoken

Service of expert packing and shipping of fine art and antiques, directly from the Flea Market and elsewhere to all parts of the world by air, sea and road. Weekly containers.

INTERNATIONAL ART TRANSPORT (I.A.T)
54 av Lenine, 94250 Gentilly ■ Tel: 01 41 17 41 17 ■ Fax: 01 49 85 91 31 ■ Mon-Fri 9:00-12:30/13:30-17:30 ■ English spoken. ■ Prices medium

Packing and shipping of antiques and works of art. Export documents arranged.

EMBALLAGES LENORMAND
53-55 rue de Verdun, BP 24, 93161 Noisy-le-Grand Cedex ■ Tel: 01 43 03 38 73 ■ Fax: 01 43 04 33 99 ■ Mon-Fri 8:00-12:00/13:00-17:00 ■ Prices medium ■ 10% professional discount

Specialists in packing of furniture and art objects. International movers and shippers.

UPS - UNITED PARCEL SERVICE
87 av de l'Aérodrome, BP 39, 94310 Orly ■ Tel: 01 48 92 50 00 ■ Fax: 01 48 92 50 52 ■ Mon-Fri 8:00-19:00 ■ English spoken

The best-known American small package express, door-to-door, air shipping service to America and 100 other countries. Very reliable and very fast.

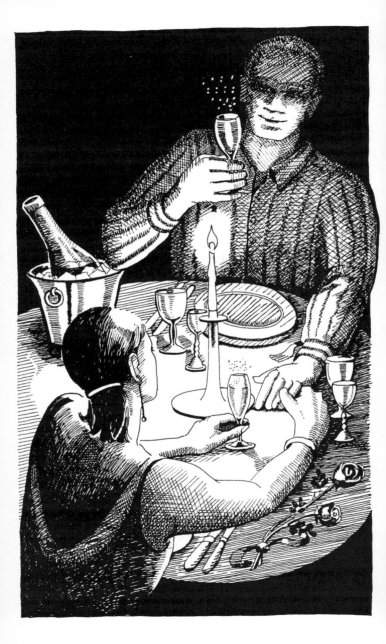

TABLE ARTS
Arts de la table

Tableware, once the exclusive province of royalty and the upper classes has, since the middle of the XVIII century, become a symbol of prosperity. The origins of tableware can be traced back to the earliest history of man. Table utensils and food vessels are amply illustrated in ancient Chinese, Egyptian, Persian, Greek and Pre-Colombian civilizations.

France is the world's leader in tableware exports. The United States is the biggest and best customer.

Paris, the ever-manageable city, has a concentration of tableware suppliers in two areas. On the rue Royale and in the Galerie Royale are the top names with their beautiful showrooms. On the rue de Paradis, in the heart of one of the older neighborhoods of Paris, you can visit the showrooms of the manufacturers and, even if they only sell to professionals, a non-professional can make choices, obtain prices and be directed to the showroom where purchases can be made. Some of the merchants offer discounts which others in higher rent areas cannot do. Make certain you ask for your "detaxe", or tax refund, if you are carrying anything home with you. If your purchases are shipped you will also avoid the hefty sales tax.

Crystal and Glass
Cristal et verre

The history of French glass-making can be traced back to the XII century. The use of glass goes back at least a thousand years before that. The French province of Lorraine produces the beautiful glass and crystal as it exists today. They were so good at their craft, that these Lorrainers attracted the attention of the Kings of France, and it was the Cristalleries Saint-Louis which first discovered the technique of making flawless crystal such as that now made by the artisans of Baccarat, Daum and Lalique.

You can also find good quality factory-made product from Verreries Cristalleries d'Arques. Their production is enormous and they are the international leader in their field.

For hand-blown glass, the principal source is the Verrerie de Biot. If you find yourself in the hills above Cannes on a pleasure trip, the Biot glassworks are worth a visit. Not quite the same as the island of Murano in Venice, but very interesting.

CRYSTAL

─────────── II ───────────

♛ DAUM
4 rue de la Paix, Paris 75002 ■ Tel. 01 42 61 25 25 ■ Fax: 01 40 20 96 71 ■ Mon 11:00-19:00 Tue-Sat 10:00-19:00 ■ Caroline de Valroger ■ English and German spoken ■ Major credit cards
The superb Daum crystal, some good porcelain and glass art.

─────────── VII ───────────

DAUM
167 bd Saint-Germain, 75006 Paris ■ Telfax: 01 42 22 16 12 ■ Mon 11:00-13:00/14:00-19:00 Tue-Sat 10:00-13:00/14:00-19:00 ■ English spoken ■ Major credit cards
Magnificent Daum crystal. Some porcelain, glass furniture and objects.

─────────── VIII ───────────

♛ BACCARAT
11 place de la Madeleine, 75008 Paris ■ Tel: 01 42 65 36 26 ■ Fax: 01 42 65 06 64 ■ Mon-Sat 10:00-19:00 ■ English and Japanese spoken ■ Prices medium to very high ■ Professional discount ■ Major credit cards
Superb crystal and glass. Crystal furniture and objects. A trip to the Baccarat Museum on the rue de Paradis is a treat.

👑 BOUTIQUE CRISTAL SAINT-LOUIS

13 rue Royale, Paris 75008 ■ Tel. 01 40 17 01 74 ■ Fax: 01 40 17 03 87 ■ Mon-Sat 10:00-18:30 ■ Sylvie Vigulé ■ English and German spoken ■ Prices medium to very high ■ Professional discount ■ Major credit cards

A wonderland of handmade French crystal glasses, decanters, flasks, trays, crystal works of sculpture. The showroom also carries some porcelain and silver from their sister company, Puiforcat.

👑 LALIQUE

11 rue Royale, Paris 75008 ■ Tel: 01 53 05 12 12 ■ Fax: 01 42 65 59 06 ■ Web: www.lalique.com ■ Mon-Wed 10:00-18:00 Tue-Thu-Fri 9:30-18:00 Sat 9:30-19:30 ■ Dominique Ferret ■ English and Japanese spoken ■ Prices high ■ Major credit cards

Fabulous examples of the fine art of blown and handcut crystal. Glasses, goblets, decanters, flasks, everything in the art of crystal, including tables and decorative objects. In addition they have a collection of fine French porcelain.

— X —

👑 BACCARAT

30 bis rue de Paradis, 75010 Paris ■ Tel: 01 47 70 64 30 ■ Fax: 01 48 24 29 01 ■ Mon-Fri 10:00-18:30/Sat 10:00-18:00 ■ English spoken ■ Prices high to very high ■ All credit cards

In the same splendid building where the marvellous Baccarat Crystal Museum displays 2,000 works of crystal art, blown and hand cut since 1764, there is a retail shop where you can buy crystal services, decorative pieces, vases, chandeliers. A choice of 1,500 references.

ART GLASS

— IV —

👑 GALERIE LE SUD/LES MAITRES VERRIERS

23 rue des Archives, 75004 Paris ■ Tel: 01 42 78 42 37 ■ Tue-Sat 10:30-19:00 ■ Sébastien Aschero speaks English ■ Prices medium to high ■ 10% professional discount

Blown glass by the Masters (Maîtres Verriers) Novaro, Pierini, Guillot, Fievet, Dreutler, Marion, Monod, Guittet, Durand-Gasselin, Schamschula, Luzoro, Lepage, Baquère, Deniel, Perthshire and others. Decorative objects in Murano glass.

VERRE ET ROUGE

19 rue de Miromesnil, Paris 75008 ■ Telfax: 01 42 65 75 65 ■ Mon-Fri 10:00-19:00, Sat during December ■ Christiane Follias speaks English ■ Prices medium ■ 10 to 20% professional discount

Engraving on blown glass. Personalized engraving of monograms, names, text, logos of companies, crests. Large choice of paper weights, flacons, flasks, vases and lamps by the great contemporary Masters.

VERREGLASS

32 rue de Charonne, 75011 Paris ■ Telfax: 01 48 05 78 43 ■ Tue-Sat 12:30-19:00 ■ Claudius Breig speaks English ■ Prices low to medium ■ Professional discount

1920-1960 glass. Some lighting and wrought iron.

Porcelain and Earthenware
Porcelaine et faience

Chinese porcelain arrived in France through Italy in the early part of the XVI century. Venice had become, thanks to Marco Polo, the most important trading centre with the Far East and Chinese porcelain was an important import item.

The secrets for producing porcelain were eventually discovered almost simultaneously by craftsmen in France and Germany in the XVII century. At this time, Louis Poterat, of Rouen, developed a formula and technique and began producing the first fine French porcelain. Now there are approximately 30 porcelain manufacturers in France. All have their outlets in Paris and most are active in the export market.

Earthenware was already an established art before the secrets of porcelain were discovered, but it was not until the XVI century that the Italian technique of "Majolica" was developed (scenery painted on white opaque enamel). French earthenware is produced mainly in the northern part of France and in the Loiret. Much earthenware produced by artists with handpainted scenery is made in Provence. Moustiers is an important center.

--------------------------------- I ---------------------------------

♕ GALLERY DU MANUFACTURE DE SÈVRES
4 place André-Malraux, 75001 Paris ■ Tel: 01 47 03 40 20 ■ Fax: 01 42 61 40 54 ■ Mme Solange Blon ■ English and Spanish spoken ■ Prices high to very high ■ Major credit cards

Superb Sèvres porcelain. Re-editions of XVIII and XIX century tableware and contemporary creations. Biscuit sculpture.

You can also visit the Sèvres Museum * Every day except Tuesday 10:00-17:00 * Tel: 01 41 14 04 20 for guided tour. Louis XV is responsible for setting up the Manufacture and it was moved to its current site in 1870, where it has continued to flourish making services for the courts of Europe and for the rich and famous. There are also regular exhibitions of works by contemporary artists.

--------------------------------- IV ---------------------------------

♕ QUIMPER FAIENCE
84 rue Saint-Martin, Paris 75004 ■ Telfax: 01 42 71 93 03 ■ website: www.hb-henriot.com ■ Mon-Sat 11:00-19:00 ■ English spoken ■ Visa and MC accepted

Wonderful collection of faience from Quimper.

--------------------------------- VII ---------------------------------

♕ DRAGESCO CRAMOISAN
13 rue de Beaune, 75007 Paris ■ Tel: 01 42 61 18 20 ■ Fax: 01 42 85 40 37 ■ Mon-Sat 10:30-13:00/13:30-19:00 ■ Bernard Dragesco and Didier Cramiosan speak English ■ Prices high to very high ■ 10 % professional discount ■ Major credit cards

XVI to XIX century porcelain and glass. Suppliers to the great museums of the world: Louvre, Versailles, Sèvres, British Museum, Getty, Chicago Museum.

LE GRAND TOURNE
Headquarters: 40390 Saint-Martin-de-Seignaux ■ Tel: 01 59 56 10 28 ■ Fax: 01 59 56 17 21 ■ Showroom: 184 rue de l'Université, 75007 Paris ■ Tel: 01 45 51 36 26 ■ Mon-Fri 8:00-12:00/14:00-18:00 ■ Bernard de Sisteron speaks English ■ Prices very high ■ 20% professional discount

Manufacturer of handpainted Limoges fine porcelain. Handprinted fabrics in exclusive designs. Appointed to the Royal European Courts.

👑 BERNARDAUD

11 rue Royale, Paris 75008 ■ Tel. 01 47 42 82 66 ■ Fax: 01 49 24 06 35 ■ Mon-Fri 9:30-18:30, Sat 10:00-19:00 ■ Anne Jensen ■ English, Japanese and Spanish spoken ■ Prices medium to very high ■ professional discount ■ Major credit cards

Superb designs in porcelain. Porcelain vases and boxes. Also a vast line from Saint Louis, Cristofle, Arcuit , Baccarat, and silver place settings.

👑 ERCUIS & RAYNAUD

Gallery Royale, 9 rue Royale and 8bis rue Boissy d'Anglas, 75008 Paris ■ Tel: 01 40 17 01 00 ■ Fax: 01 40 17 01 07 ■ Mon-Sat 9:30-18:30 ■ Anne Beneton ■ English spoken ■ Major credit cards

Excellent silver and porcelain.

👑 ROBERT HAVILAND & C. PARLON

3 rue du Faubourg Saint-Honore, 75008 Paris ■ Tel: 01 42 66 38 20 ■ Fax: 01 42 66 23 60 ■ Mon-Sat 10:30-13:30/14:30-18:30 ■ Sabine de Zan-Nouthors ■ English spoken ■ Prices medium to high ■ Professional discount

Porcelain of Limoges.

👑 TRÉSORS DU PASSÉ

131 rue du Faubourg-Saint-Honoré, 75008 Paris ■ Tel: 01 42 25 05 39 ■ Tue-Sat 14:30-19:30/Mornings by appointment ■ Prices high ■ Professional discount

XVIII century French porcelain and faience. Chinese porcelain, Famille Verte and Famille Rose and East India Company porcelain of the XVII & XVIII centuries.

VILLEROY ET BOCH

21 rue Royale, Paris 75008 ■ Tel. 01 42 65 81 84 ■ Fax: 01 49 24 96 18 ■ website: www.villeroy-boch.com ■ Mon-Sat 10:00-18:15 ■ English spoken ■ Prices medium to high ■ Major credit cards BP 45 95142 Garges-les-Gonesse Cedex ■ Tel: 01 34 45 21 21 ■ Fax: 01 39 93 49 21 ■ Contact : M. Nicolas-Luc Villeroy

Porcelain and fine bone china. Crystal and silver. Gifts.

——————— **X** ———————

PORCELAINE DE SOLOGNE

32 rue de Paradis, 75010 Paris ■ Tel: 01 45 23 15 86 ■ Fax: 01 42 46 05 12 ■ Mon-Thu 9:00-12:30/14:00-17:30 Fri 9:00-12:30 ■ English spoken ■ Prices medium

Manufacturer of Limoges porcelain. Professionals only.

SOLAFRANCE
34 rue de Paradis, 75010 Paris ■ Tel: 01 47 70 92 96 ■ Fax: 01 45 23 14 44 ■ Mon-Fri 9:00-12:00/13:00-17:00 ■ English and Portuguese spoken

For professionals only. Representation of several manufacturers of porcelain, crystal and silver. Some of their own editions of porcelain and glassware lines.
Non-professionals can make their choice and be directed to a retail outlet.

──────────── OUTSIDE PARIS ────────────

CÉRAMIQUE DE VINCENNES
Atelier, 21 rue du Midi, 94300 Vincennes ■ Tel: 01 43 98 31 55 ■ Fax: 01 43 98 37 64 ■ Thierry Cheyrou and Dominique Paramythiotis speak English ■ Prices medium to high ■ 20% professional discount

Manufacturers of high-quality porcelain, faience and silver sold under their trade mark Palais Royal Paris. The knives have porcelain handles. They will custom produce special series.

──────────── CUSTOM CREATIONS ────────────

MME ANNIE FRANCE DANG
10 rue Montgallet, 75012 Paris ■ Tel: 01 43 07 92 71 ■ Mon-Fri 9:00-12:00/14:00-18:30 by appointment ■ Prices medium to very high ■ 6% professional discount

Creation of special decoration on porcelain and glass. Decors in fine gold engraving. Custom reproductions.

Ceramics
Céramiques

──────────── V ────────────

ARTISANAT RÉALITÉ
6 rue Le Goff, 75005 Paris ■ Tel: 01 43 54 59 59 ■ Fax: 01 46 34 81 15 ■ Tue-Sat 11:00-19:30 ■ Raymond Sauvaire speaks English ■ Prices high ■ Master card and Visa

Contemporary ceramic art, jewellery.

VI

FANCE FRANCK
47 rue Bonaparte, 75006 Paris ■ Telfax: 01 43 26 15 99 ■ e-mail: morimura@fresurf.fr ■ By appointment only ■ English spoken ■ 10 to 20% professional discount

Unique works in porcelain, stoneware, terracotta. Panels and pottery.

♔ LEFÈBVRE ET FILS
24 rue du Bac, 75006 Paris ■ Tel: 01 42 61 18 40 ■ Fax: 01 42 86 91 58 ■ E-mail: antkle@club-internet.fr ■ Mon-Sat 10:00-12:30/14:00-19:00 ■ Georges and Louis Lefèbvre speak English ■ Prices medium to high ■ Professional discount

Extraordinary antique European ceramics of the XVI to the XIX centuries. Expert to the Cour d'Appel, Paris.

LA MAISON IVRE
38 rue Jacob, 75006 Paris ■ Tel: 0142 60 01 85 ■ website: www.fourmis.com/maison.ivre ■ Tue-Sat 10:30-19:00 ■ Jacques Nobecourt speaks English ■ Prices medium ■ Major credit cards

Large selection of pottery handmade by French artisans. Varnished clay pots, art ceramics, stoneware. Everything for the table, Provence style, including table linen.

MME ULRIKE WEISS – CÉRAMIQUES
12 passage des Taillandiers, 75011 Paris ■ Tel: 01 47 00 24 47 ■ Fax: 01 47 00 24 47 ■ By appointment ■ Ulrike Weiss speaks English ■ Prices medium

Ceramic products for the table and for decoration. Unique and humorous in character. Development of ceramic designs for industrial production. Porcelain and stoneware.

Silversmiths
Orfèvres

The use of silver for eating utensils owes its origins to the natives of North and South America. Silver had been used at least 5,000 years before Christ for ornamental purposes and was considered by the Egyptians to be more precious than gold.

The Conquistadores, after they had pillaged the Inca and Aztec civilizations of most of their gold, turned their attention to silver and loaded their galleons with tons of it.

Charles V of Spain caused the first vulgarization of the precious metal and created the first silversmithy, producing plates and table utensils which were then traded to the other royal households of Europe.

Much of the older silver plate and utensils created by the artisans of the time has not survived. The metal would often be melted down to finance wars or other indulgences.

----------------------------------- I -----------------------------------

♔ BUCCELLATI
4 place Vendome, 75001 Paris ■ Tel: 01 42 60 12 12 ■ Fax: 01 49 27 98 04 ■ Mon-Sat 10:00-19:00 ■ Gianmaria Buccellati ■ Most languages spoken ■ Prices high to very high ■ Major credit cards

Silversmith. Superb silver.

♔ GEORG JENSEN
239 rue Saint-Honoré, 75001 Paris ■ Tel: 01 42 60 07 89 ■ Mon-Sat 10:00-12:30/13:30-18:30 ■ English spoken ■ Prices high

Superb collection of cutlery and objects in contemporary designs of silver, plated silver and stainless steel.

----------------------------------- III -----------------------------------

ESCHWEGE
42 rue Meslay, 75003 Paris ■ Tel: 01 42 78 51 94 ■- Fax: 01 42 78 47 63 ■ Mon-Fri 8:30-12:30/13:30-17:30 ■ English spoken ■ Prices medium ■ Professional discount

Custom fabrication, restoration and repair of silver, pewter and objects in other metals. Classic silver and plated silver place-settings and objects.

ÉTAINS DU MARAIS
26 rue des Gravilliers, 75003 Paris ■ Tel: 01 42 78 73 70 ■ Fax: 01 42 78 11 16 ■ Mon-Fri 9:00-12:00/13:00-17:30 ■ Stéphane Dodin speaks English ■ Prices medium ■ Professional discount

Silver, pewter, silver plate, stainless steel. Custom fabrication, repair, restoration, re-silvering.

👑 MARISCHAEL

4 rue de Saintonge, 75003 Paris ■ Tel: 01 42 78 07 63 ■ Mon-Sat 8:00-12:00/14:00-18:00 ■ English spoken ■ Prices high ■ Professional discount

Everything for the table in solid and plated silver. XVIII and XIX century silver. Custom creations in contemporary designs. Restoration of fine silver.

👑 VOGLUX

3 rue de Saintonge, 75003 Paris ■ Tel: 01 42 72 67 51 ■ Fax: 01 42 72 32 60 ■ E-mail: voglux@wanadoo.fr ■ Mon-Fri 9:00-17:30 ■ Some English spoken ■ Prices medium

Manufacturer of silver tableware, cups and plates for baptisms, champagne buckets and gifts. Re-silvering of cutlery.

VIII

👑 CHRISTOFLE

9 rue Royale, 75008 Paris ■ Tel: 01 49 33 43 00 ■ Fax: 01 49 33 43 22 ■ Web: www.cristofle.com ■ Mon-Sat 9:45-18:30 ■ Veronique Buisine ■ English, Spanish, Italian, German and Japanese spoken ■ Prices medium to high ■ Major credit cards
Other CHRISTOFLE outlets:
24 rue de la Paix, 75002 Paris ■ Tel: 01 42 65 62 43 ■ 95 rue de Passy, 75016 Paris ■ Tel: 01 46 47 51 27 ■ 1 rue Marboeuf 75008 Paris ■ Tel: 01 45 48 16 17

A name known the world over and well deserved. Their huge selection includes both solid and plated silver.

👑 ODIOT ORFÈVRE

7 place de la Madeleine, 75008 ■ Tel: 01 42 65 00 95 ■ Fax: 01 42 66 49 12 ■ Mon- Sat 10:00-19:00 ■ English spoken ■ Prices high ■ 25% professional discount ■ Major credit cards

Creation of silver for the table. Enormous collection in solid silver, antique and contemporary. Collectors' items.

👑 PUIFORCAT ORFÈVRE

2 av Matignon, 75008 Paris ■ Tel. 01 45 63 10 10 ■ Fax. 01 42 56 27 15 ■ Mon-Sat 9:30-18:30 ■ English spoken ■ Prices medium to high 22 rue François-Ier, Paris 75008 ■ Tel. 01 47 20 74 27 ■ Fax: 01 47 20 01 62 ■ Tue-Sat 9:30-18:30 ■ Major credit cards

One of the largest collections of solid and plated silver. They also carry Limoges porcelain, some crystal and a collection of table linens.

ATELIER BLETTON
1 passage Saint-Sébastien, 75011 Paris ■ Tel: 01 47 00 85 98 ■ fax : 01 47 00 85 42 ■ Mon-Fri 9:00-12:00/14:00-18:00 ■ English spoken ■ Prices low ■ Professional discount

Fabrication and restoration of silver. Re-plating.

SAINT-HILAIRE
11 chemin de la Montagne, 94510 La Queue-en-Brie ■ Tel: 01 49 62 23 62 ■ Fax: 01 49 62 23 69 ■ Web: www.ercuis.com/ ■ Mon-Fri 9:00-18:00 ■ Isabelle Rigail and Isabelle Ferrer speak English ■ Paris store: Gallery Royale, 8bis Boissy D'Anglas, 75008 Paris ■ Tel: 01 42 66 59 21 ■ Fax: 01 40 17 01 07 ■ Mon-Sat 9:30-18:30 ■ Francoise Barrotin ■ English spoken ■ Prices medium to high ■ Professional discount possible

Manufacturers of excellent-quality silver-plated tableware.

♛ PIERRE MEURGEY
20 bd des Filles-du-Calvaire, 75011 Paris ■ Tel: 01 48 05 82 65 ■ Fax: 01 48 05 71 05 ■ Mon- 14:00-18:00 Tue-Fri 9:30-18:00 Sat 9:00-13:00■ English spoken

Custom creations in plated silver. Pierre Meurgey holds the record in the "Guinness Book of Records" for making the world's largest fork - 86 inches.

MAISON MOSSLER
22 bd des Filles-du-Calvaire, 75011 Paris ■ Tel: 01 48 05 50 28 ■ Fax: 01 40 21 94 31 ■ Tue-Sat 10:00-19:00 ■ English spoken ■ Prices medium to high ■ Professional discount ■ Major credit cards

Manufacturer of silver, solid and plated, for all uses. Restoration, repair, re-silvering. Also carries good selection of porcelain and antiques. Bridal registry.

ORFÈVRERIE DU MARAIS
1 rue Robert et Sonia Delaunay, 75011 Paris ■ Tel: 01 43 71 25 04 ■ Fax: 01 43 71 20 48 ■ Mon-Fri 8:30-18:30 ■ François Cadoret speaks English ■ Prices low■ Professional discount

Fabrication of silver tableware. Restoration and repair.

SCHWARTZ ORFÈVRE
24 rue de la Folie-Méricourt, 75011 Paris ■ Tel: 01 47 00 76 02 ■ Mon-Fri 9:00-19:00 ■ Jacques Schwartz speaks English ■ Prices medium

Fabrication of silver articles used for religious purposes: chalices, patons and ciboria. Repairs of all silver.

👑 **ATELIERS DU CUIVRE ET DE L'ARGENT**
Viaduc des Arts, 111 av Daumesnil, 75012 Paris ■ Tel: 01 43 40
20 20 ■ Fax: 01 43 40 60 60 ■ Mon-Sat 10:00-18:00 ■ Professional discount ■ Major credit cards

**This is a real museum of copper and silver with a remarka-
ble collection of hundreds of unique pieces. The workshop
creates and restores beautiful silver from candlesticks to
cutlery or large platters. The copper pots and cooking utensils are remarkable. They will even make you a copper bathtub if you want it.**

AUGER
13 av d'Eylau, 75116 Paris ■ Tel: 01 45 53 34 25 ■ Fax: 01 54 70
98 07 ■ Mon-Fri 8:30-17:30 ■ Janine Mandeville speaks English
■ Prices medium ■ 10% professional discount

**Antique silver and jewellery. Silversmiths since 1690. Cus-
tom fabrication of everything in silver. Repair of cutlery.**

THIERRY LEFÈVRE-GRAVE
24 rue Durantin, 75018 Paris ■ Telfax: 01 42 23 65 60 ■ website:
http://perso-libertysurf.fr/lefevre-grave ■ By appointment ■ Thierry Lefèvre-Grave speaks English ■ Prices medium to high ■ Professional discount

Creation of art objects in silver: jewellery, furniture, statuary.

Recognizing Silver

**Prior to the French Revolution, hallmarks "poinçons" on
French crafted silver were complex, but provided a
virtual identity card of its origin. The hallmark gave a
precise geographic origin, the date of fabrication, the
name of the Master and the establishment where it was
created. Pieces pre-dating 1790 should always show 4**

hallmarks. After the revolution, in 1797, the system was simplified. XIX century silver should show three hallmarks, the losange of the master, the pompon of guarantee and the title of the company.

For the amateur silver hunter, there are two methods recommended, using the hand and the nose. First, pick up the piece and judge its heft. A little practice and you can become pretty good at it. Compare it with a piece you already have and know well. Then memorize how it feels. For the really skilled amateur there is a sworn-by technique. Silver does give off a distinctive odor and once you have committed this smell to your memory you will never forget it. Try it for yourself. Take a linen handkerchief, or even the bottom of a cotton shirt, and rub it on the silver. It will give off its distinctive and familiar smell. Also, you can rub the silver vigorously with the palm of your hand, a little saliva might help as well. Then put your nose to it. If the distinctive odor is not present, BEWARE!

Antique silver

IV

ARGENTERIE DE TURENNE
19, rue de Turenne, 75004 Paris ■ Tel: 01 42 72 04 00 ■ Fax: 01 42 72 08 24 ■ E-mail: adturenne@worldonline.fr ■ Tue-Sat 10:30-19:00 ■ Catherine Perroud ■ English and Italian spoken ■ 10% Professional discount
All table arts in solid and plated silver. Bridal registry.

VII

A LA MINE D'ARGENT
108 rue du Bac, 75007 Paris ■ Tel: 01 45 48 70 68 ■ Fax: 01 45 49 06 55 ■ Mon-Fri 10:00-19:00/Sat 11:00-18:00 ■ Daniel Chifman and Simona Kletzkine speak English ■ Prices medium ■ 10% professional discount
Antique solid silver. Plated contemporary silver, porcelain and crystal. Repair of knives and re-silvering.

♛ KUGEL

279 rue Saint-Honoré, 75008 Paris ■ Tel: 01 42 60 19 45 ■ Fax: 01 42 61 06 72 ■ E-mail: kugel@francenet.fr ■ English spoken ■ Prices high ■ Professional discount

One of the great collections of silver, XV to XIX century. Their collection of art objects and antiques is unusual as well as beautiful.

OLIVIER

63 Passage Jouffroy, 75009 Paris ■ Tel: 01 45 23 26 23 ■ E-mail: olivier.orfevrerie@wanadoo.fr ■ Mon-Fri 10 :0013 :00/14 :00-19 :00 ■ Olivier Pomez ■ English and Spanish spoken ■ Prices medium to high ■ Professional discount

XVIII and XIX century silver, mainly French. Some early XX century.

Pewter

FLOR'

35 rue de Paradis, 75010 Paris ■ Tel: 01 48 24 47 28 ■ Mon-Fri 10:00-18:00 ■ English spoken ■ Prices medium ■ Professional discount

Specialists in pewter. This outlet represents the production of: Les Étains de la Fontaine; Les Étains de l'Abbaye et Anjou; Les Étains à la Rose; Les Étains du Prince (paintings on pewter tablets); Les Étains du Grand Duc; Les Étains à La Licorne; La Maison de l'Etain; Signature Royale; Etains d'Autrefois; Art Métal. All these manufacturers are from the region of Angers and Lyon. One of the best collections in Paris. Boxes of Limoges.

LA LICORNE

14 rue Manin 75019 Paris ■ Tel: 01 42 08 42 47 ■ Fax: 01 42 08 23 ■ Mon-Fri 8:30-18:30 ■ English spoken ■ Prices medium to high ■ Major credit cards

Pewter in all shapes and sizes, tea services, soup tureens.

Tableware

--- I ---

DEHILLERIN
18 rue Coquillière, 75001 Paris ■ Tel: 01 42 36 53 13 8 ■ Fax: 01 42 36 54 80 ■ website: www.e-dehillerin.com ■ Mon 8:00-12:30/14:00-18:00/Tues-Sat 8:00-18:00 ■ English Spoken ■ Prices medium to high ■ All Credit cards

High-quality professional kitchen utensils. Marvellous selection of copper serving dishes, pots and pans.

MURIEL GRATEAU BOUTIQUE
130-133 Galerie de Valois, Jardins du Palais-Royal, 75001 Paris ■ Tel: 01 40 20 90 30 ■ Fax: 01 42 96 12 32 ■ Mon-Sat 11:00-12:30/13:00-19:00 ■ English spoken ■ Prices medium to high ■ Professional discount ■ Major credit cards

XIX century French faience, Murano glass, embroidered and plain table linens in a choice of 66 colors.

LA VIE DE CHÂTEAU
17 rue de Valois, 75001 Paris ■ Tel. 01 49 27 09 82 ■ Mon-Sat 13:00-19:00 ■ Prices high ■ Professional discount

Antique table services.

--- II ---

A. SIMON
36 rue Etienne-Marcel and 48 rue Montmartre, 75002 Paris ■ Tel: 01 42 33 71 65 ■ Fax: 42 33 68 25 ■ Mon-Sat 8:30-18:30 ■ English spoken ■ Prices medium to high ■ Professional discount

One of the highlights of Paris for the cook, professional or amateur. A vast selection of high-quality cookware, utensils and ceramics, porcelain, crystal and glass. Treasures you never even thought of. Feast your eyes on their copper.

--- IV ---

SÉRIE RARE
6 rue de l'Odéon, 75006 Paris ■ Tel: 01 55 42 92 10 ■ Fax: 01 55 42 92 52 ■ E-mail: serierare@wanadoo.fr ■ Mon-Fri 12:00-19:00 ■ Manager: Marie-Luce Podva ■ English and German spoken ■ Prices medium ■ Professional discount ■ Major credit cards

Original collection of knife-rests, trivets, candelabra and frames in decorative bronze. Lamps and an unusual line of doorknobs and levers in various bronze finishes.

TAIR MERCIER
7 bd Saint-Germain, 75005 Paris ■ Tel: 01 43 54 19 97 ■ Fax: 01 43 25 57 22 ■ E-mail: tiarmere@club-internet.fr ■ Tue-Fri 11:00-19:00/Sat 14:00-19:00 ■ Judith Tair Mercier speaks English ■ Prices medium ■ Master cards and Visa

Designs of contemporary table arts products.

LA TUILE A LOUP
35 rue Daubenton, 75005 Paris ■ Tel: 01 47 07 28 90 ■ Fax: 01 43 36 40 95 ■ E-mail: tuilealoup@aol.com ■ website : www.latuilealoup.com ■ Mon 13:00-19:00 (excepted on summer) Tue-Sat 10:30-19:30 ■ Marie-France Joblin speaks English ■ Prices medium ■ 5% professional discount ■ Visa, MC, Amex

Table arts, traditional French artisan objects, ceramics, cutlery, pottery, glass. Table linens and a fine library of recipe books in French.

LA CASA PASCAL
15 rue d'Assas, 75006 Paris ■ Tel: 01 42 22 96 78 ■ Fax: 01 45 49 43 83 ■ Mon 14:00-19:00/Tue-Sat 10:00-19:00 ■ Prices low ■ 10% professional discount ■ Major credit cards

White Limoges porcelain, some with decorative finish. Glassware, cutlery, lamp bases, decorative perfume boxes.

DAULIAC SUBRA ANTIQUITÉS
67 rue du Cherche-Midi, 75006 Paris ■ Tel: 01 42 22 14 16 ■ Mon 14:00-19 :30 Tue-Sat 11:00-19:30 ■ Prices medium ■ 20% professional discount ■ Major credit cards

1920-1940 table arts, bathroom accessories, lighting, silver, small furniture. Qualified expert.

PORTOBELLO
56 rue Notre-Dame-des-Champs, 75006 Paris ■ Tel: 01 43 25 74 47 ■ Tue-Sat 11:00-13:00/14:00-19:00 ■ Catherine Remoissenet speaks English ■ Prices low

Antique linen and table arts, decorative objects, mirrors, lamps, engravings and paintings.

SOULEIADO
78 rue de Seine, 75006 Paris ■ Tel: 01 43 54 15 13 ■ Fax: 01 43 54 84 45 ■ Mon-Sat 10:00-19:00 ■ English Spoken ■ Prices medium ■ Professional discount

Beautiful provincial-style fabrics, tablecloths, table sets and porcelain.

TORVINOKA
4 rue Cardinale, 75006 Paris ■ Tel: 01 43 25 09 13 ■ Fax: 01 40 51 89 46 ■ Mon 14:30-19:30/Tue-Sat 10:00-19:30 ■ Françoise Schryne speaks English ■ Prices medium ■ 10% professional discount on furniture

Contemporary table arts, objects, glasses, dishes, table settings, tole. Animal figures in porcelain and glass. Exclusive furniture line designed by Alvar Aalto of Finland.

VII

AUX ARMES DE FRANCE
4 rue de Babylone, 75007 Paris ■ Tel: 01 45 48 05 06 ■ Tue-Sat 10:30-18:30 ■ Prices medium

Silver, porcelain de Saxe, jewellery, plated silver, crystal. Repairs of knives and silver.

♔ DÎNERS EN VILLE
27 rue de Varenne, 75007 Paris ■ Tel: 01 42 22 78 33 ■ Fax: 01 45 44 87 25 ■ web: www.dinersenville.com ■ Mon 14:00-19:00/Tue-Sat 11:00-19:00 ■ English, Italian and Spanish spoken ■ Prices medium to very high ■ 10% professional discount ■ All credit cards except Amex

Large selection of porcelain, faience, antique and contemporary silver, crystal and table linens.

LAURE JAPY ET CIE
34-36 rue du Bac, 75007 Paris ■ Tel: 01 42 86 96 97 ■ Fax: 01 42 86 96 97 ■ Tue-Sat 10:30-19:00 ■ English spoken ■ Prices medium ■ Major credit cards

Everything for the table. Linen, crystal, porcelain, silver, lighting, candles.

♔ SIÈCLE
24 rue du Bac, 75007 Paris ■ Tel: 01 47 03 48 03 ■ Fax: 01 47 03 48 01 ■ E-mail: siecleparis@wanadoo.fr ■ web: www.chateauxcountry.com ■ Tue 11:30-19:00 Wed-Sat 10:30-19:00 ■ English and German spoken ■ Prices low to high ■ 10 to 20% professional discount

Beautiful and original creations for the table, especially the table linen and cutlery collections. Linen, silk, silver, crystal, rare wood, shagreen, mother-of-pearl. Marriage lists.

BRODERIES DE FRANCE
37 bis rue de Ponthieu, 75008 Paris ■ Tel: 01 43 59 60 73 ■ Mon-Sat 9:00-21:00 ■ Prices medium ■ 15% professional discount

Hand-embroidered linen, crystal, silver-plated table settings and trays, Limoges porcelain.

CARTIER
51 rue François-Ier, Paris 75008 ■ Tel: 01 53 93 95 50 ■ Mon-Fri 9:00-19:00 ■ English spoken ■ Prices high

An attractive table arts department with a selection of well-known names in English bone china, French porcelain, crystal and silver. Marriage lists.

CHRISTIAN DIOR
30-32 av Montaigne, 75008 Paris ■ Tel: 01 40 73 53 40 ■ Fax: 01 47 20 00 60 ■ Mon-Sat 10:00-19:00 ■ English spoken Also 16 rue de l'Abbaye 75006 Paris ■ Tel: 01 56 24 90 53 ■ Fax: 01 54 24 95 34

Special exclusive lines of tableware, objects for the home and gifts. Beautiful dinner services like the new deco design bone china "Rayures 55" and the classic 1972 ecological line of platters. Exclusive services in hand-made porcelain with special themes, the "Harlequin" crystal line, trays in plexi and fabric, faience with "Jardin ... la Francaise" theme. Frames in plated silver, wood and marquetry. Marriage lists.

HERMÈS
24 rue du Faubourg-Saint-Honoré, 75008 Paris ■ Tel: 01 40 17 47 17 ■ Fax: 01 40 17 47 18 ■ Mon-Sat 10:00-13:00/14:30-18:30/Tue-Fri 10:00-18:30 ■ All languages spoken ■ Prices high

Exclusive lines of Limoges porcelain, Saint-Louis crystal and table settings. Marriage lists.

MEDIONI CHAMPS-ELYSEES
112 rue La Boetie, 75008 Paris ■ Tel: 01 42 25 93 39 ■ Fax: 01 45 62 29 04 ■ Mon-Sat 10:15-19:00 ■ Henri Medioni speaks English ■ Prices high to very high ■ 15 to 20% professional discount

Wide selection of high-quality table arts. Porcelain, crystal, silver, pâte de verre.

AURELIA PARADIS
21 bis rue de Paradis, 75010 Paris ■ Tel: 01 42 47 07 00 ■ Fax: 01 48 00 92 85 ■ web: www.aurelia-paradis.com ■ Mon-Fri 9:30-18:45 ■ English spoken ■ Prices medium to high ■ Professional discount ■ Major credit cards

Large selection of the great manufacturers of crystal, porcelain, lighting, objects, gifts. Marriage lists.

CRISTALLERIE PARADIS

17 rue de Paradis, 75010 Paris ■ Tel: 01 48 24 72 15 ■ Fax: 01 44 79 01 08 ■ web: www.limoges-shop.com ■ Mon-Sat 10:00-19:00 ■ English spoken ■ Prices low to high ■ 15% professional discount

Limoges porcelain, crystal of Baccarat and Saint-Louis, silverware, gifts. Their own editions of Limoges boxes. Marriage lists.

EDITIONS PARADIS

29 rue de Paradis, 75010 Paris ■ Tel: 01 45 23 05 34 ■ Fax: 01 45 23 23 73 ■ Mon-Sat 10:00-19:00 ■ English, German and Spanish spoken ■ Prices medium to high ■ Professional discount

An extensive collection of the top brands of crystal, porcelain, lighting, objects, gifts. Marriage lists.

FLOR'

35 rue de Paradis, 75010 Paris ■ Tel: 01 48 24 47 28 ■ Mon-Fri 10:00-18:00 ■ English spoken ■ Professional discount

Pewter and boxes from Limoges.

FONCEGRIVE PARIS

36 rue du Paradis, 75010 Paris ■ Tel: 01 42 47 18 25 ■ Fax: 01 42 47 08 03 ■ Tue-Sat 10:00-18:00 ■ English spoken ■ Prices medium to high ■ Professional discount possible

Porcelain of Herend, Royal Doulton, Minton, Fabergé, Sarah Anderson and Royal Albert. Murano glass of Nason. Department of gift items. Marriage lists.

LIMOGES-UNIC

58 rue de Paradis, 75010 Paris ■ Tel: 01 47 70 61 49 ■ Fax: 01 45 23 18 56 ■ E-mail: limogesunicmadronet@wanadoo.fr ■ Mon 10:00-13:00/14:00-18:30/Tue-Sat 10:00-18:30 ■ Mlle Kassam and Anne Lecomte speak English ■ Prices medium to high ■ 10% professional discount and Maison Madronet 34 rue de Paradis ■ Tel: 01 47 70 34 59 ■ Mon-Sat 10:00-13:00/14:00-18:30

Large collection of porcelain, crystal, silverware and gifts.

LUMICRISTAL
22 bis rue de Paradis, 75010 Paris ■ Tel: 01 47 70 27 97 ■ Fax: 01 45 23 23 73 ■ Mon-Sat 9:30-19:00 ■ English spoken ■ Prices medium to high ■ Professional discount

Top brands of porcelain and crystal, Puiforcat silver.

LA TISANIÈRE
21 rue de Paradis, 75010 Paris ■ Telfax: 01 47 70 22 80 ■ Mon-Sat 10:00-18:30 ■ English spoken ■ Prices low to medium ■ Professional discount

5,000 different models of white Limoges porcelain, oven-proof and decorative. Re-editions, in collaboration with the Musee Conde, of XVIII century Porcelaine de Chantilly: "La Brindille", "L'Oeillet" and "Kakiemon". Glasses.

— XII —

♛ CONSTANCE MAUPIN
11 rue du Docteur-Goujon, 75012 Paris ■ Tel: 01 43 07 01 28 ■ Tue-Sat 10:00-13:00/14:30-19:30 ■ Constance Maupin speaks some English ■ Prices medium ■ Professional discount

Specialist in antique table arts and everything remotely concerned with the decor of the dining room: dishes, glassware, decorative objects, paintings, linen and small furniture. Custom and coordinated linen, faience and porcelain.

— XVII —

L'ORFÈVRIER
87 av des Ternes, 75017 Paris ■ Tel: 01 45 74 15 86 ■ Fax: 01 45 74 07 04 ■ E-mail: lorfevrier@wanadoo.fr ■ Mon 14:00-19:30/ Tue-Sat 10:00-19:30 ■ English spoken ■ Prices medium ■ Professional discount

Manufacturer of silver-plated table arts: trays, platters, cutlery, goblets, chafing dishes, lamps, everything. Porcelain and crystal.

LA TABLE EN FÊTE
73 place Docteur Felix-Lobligeois, 75017 Paris ■ Tel: 01 46 27 75 49 ■ Tue-Sat 10:00-12:00/14:00-19:00 ■ Some English spoken ■ Prices medium ■ Professional discount

Old and antique table settings. Dishes, glasses, solid and plated silver cutlery and objects.

Candles
Bougies

CIR
22 rue Saint-Sulpice, 75007 Paris ■ Tel : 01 43 26 46 50 ■ Fax : 01 43 54 61 77 ■ Mon-Tue 10:00-12:30/13:30-18:50, Wed-Sat 10:00-18:50 ■ Solange Breiss ■ Some English spoken ■ Prices medium to high ■ Professional discount ■ Major credit cards

Large choice of candles for the table and for decoration. Lots of colours and extra-large sizes; small animal forms for gifts. One of the best.

DIPTYQUE
34 bd Saint-Germain, 75005 Paris ■ Tel: 01 43 26 45 27 ■ Fax: 01 43 54 27 01 ■ E-mail: diptyque@diptyque.tm.fr ■ Mon-Sat 10:00-19:00 ■ English and Italian spoken ■ Prices medium ■ Amex, Visa

A choice of 48 types of scented candles; room sprays and burning essences. Ten different eaux de toilette and eight assorted soaps. Delightful place. They also have hand-woven wool throws from Wales.

POINT A LA LIGNE
67 av Victor-Hugo, 75016 Paris ■ Tel: 01 45 00 87 01 ■ Fax: 01 45 00 84 95 ■ Mon-Sat 10:00-19:00 ■ English spoken ■ Prices high ■ Professional discount

Perfumed candles for decoration. All classical candles for table arts. Two new collections each year. Very large choice

VEILLEUSES FRANÇAISES
17 rue de l'Yser, 94400 Vitry-Sur-Seine ■ Telfax: 01 46 80 86 83 ■ Mon-Thu 8:00-12:00/13:00-16:30, Fri 8:00-11:00 ■ Michel Cardosi, Yannick Guillossou ■ English spoken ■ Prices medium ■ 10% professional discount for orders of over 5,000 pieces

Oil lamps and their accessories. Decorative candles of unusual design for household and religious purposes (Shabath, Buddhist and Yoga meditation).

UPHOLSTERERS
Tapissiers

"Tapissiers" in France occupy a very special place in the decorating hierarchy. They are, first of all, artisans in the true sense of the word, having learned a difficult and demanding trade. Their skills, apart from upholstery, include just about everything to do with decorating and they can provide valuable advice and assistance in finding artisans in other trades to work on a project. They have a profound knowledge of fabrics and can be invaluable in helping choose fabrics for all purposes, be it furniture, curtains or walls.

ATELIER GARNERO
101 rue de la Croix-Nivert, 75015 Paris ■ Telfax: 01 45 31 40 56 ■ Mon-Fri 9:00-12:30/14:00-18:30, Sat 9:00-12:00 ■ Italian spoken ■ Prices medium ■ Professional discount

Upholstery of chairs, sofas and walls. Window treatments. Complete service

♛ REMY BRAZET
22 rue des Belles-Feuilles, 75116 Paris ■ Tel: 01 47 27 20 89 ■ Fax: 01 47 55 68 90 ■ Web: www.grandsateliers.fr ■ Mon-Fri 8:30-18:00 ■ Remy Brazet speaks English ■ Prices high ■ Professional discount

Wall upholstery. Specialist in upholstery of antique chairs. All types of window treatments.
Work experience: National Museums, Château de Fontainebleau, Château de Malmaison, Château de Pau. Member of the Grands Ateliers.

PHILIPPE & CORNELIA CONZADE
99 rue Jouffroy d'Abbans, 75017 Paris Tel: 01 47 63 57 45 ■ Fax: 01 40 54 92 81 ■ Mon-Fri 9:00-19:00 ■ Cornelia Conzade speaks English ■ Prices medium ■ 10 to 15% professional discount

Upholstery in the traditional manner. Window treatments and wall upholstery.

CREATIONS MOURRA
102 rue de Charonne, 75011 Paris ■ Tel: 01 43 71 03 07 ■ Fax: 01 43 71 34 28 ■ Mon-Fri 8:30-19:00 ■ English spoken ■ Prices medium ■ Professional discount

All kinds of upholstery and decoration. Window treatments.

⚜ DANIEL DELAPLACE
13 av Parmentier and 39 Cité Industrielle, 75011 Paris ■ Tel: 01 43 79 68 97/01 48 05 47 33 ■ Fax: 01 43 79 67 03/01 48 05 05 41 ■ Web: www.delaplace.fr ■ Mon-Fri 8:00-12:00/13:00-17:00 ■ Prices high ■ Professional discount

One of the very best. Creation of armchairs and sofas, made in the traditional manner. Upholstery of walls and furniture. All window treatments. Works in the palaces, museums, embassies and finer homes of the world.

⚜ HIRAM DECORATION
34 rue Perronet, 92200 Neuilly ■ Telfax: 01 47 45 06 78 ■ Cell: 06 11 49 47 16 ■ By appointment ■ Philippe Poirier ■ English spoken ■ 25% discount on elements of decoration

Excellent wall upholsterer who provides general services of traditional furniture upholstery, curtain making and decoration advice.

LES ATELIERS DES ORIGINES
2 place du Thorigny, 75003 Paris ■ Tel: 01 44 54 98 98 ■ Fax: 01 44 54 98 99 ■ Mon-Fri 9:00-18:00 ■ Mme Claire Orengo ■ English spoken ■ Professional discount

General upholstery: walls, furniture, cushions, bedspreads, curtains. They sell cushions and lampshades.

PASCAL MAINGOURD
22bis av Rapp, 75007 Paris ■ Tel: 01 47 05 86 83 ■ Fax: 01 47 53 77 92 ■ E-mail: pascalemaingourd@wanadoo.fr ■ Veronique Maingourd ■ English spoken ■ Professional discount ■ Visa

Their atelier has a full upholstery service for furniture, wall upholstery, curtains, blinds, decorative objects. Excellent choice of fabrics and a collection of Gustavian furniture.

⚜ ROBERT SEIGNEUR
6 rue des Quatre-Vents, 75006 Paris ■ Tel: 01 43 26 92 41 ■ Fax: 01 45 44 87 74 ■ E-mail: seigneur@tapissier.fr ■ Web : www.tapissier.fr ■ Mon-Fri 8:00-18:00 ■ Robert Seigneur speaks English ■ Prices medium to high ■ Professional discount

Fine upholstery of armchairs, sofas, chairs, walls. Curtains. Works for major international decorators and will travel.

TAPISSERIE DELOISON
15 rue Ernest Deloison, 92200 Neuilly ■ Tel: 01 46 24 61 23 ■ Fax; 01 46 24 61 23 ■ Tue-Fri 9:30-12:30/14:00-18:30, Sat 9:00-12:30 ■ Estelle Bossé ■ English, Spanish and Italian spoken

Re-upholstery of all types of seating. Curtains, blinds, flimsies, cushions, bedspreads and bedheads, and lampshades. Large choice of fabrics of the important editors.

TAPISSERIE ET DECORATION TRADITIONNELLES

64 rue de Longchamp, 75016 Paris ■ Tel: 01 47 04 09 66 ■ Fax: 01 47 04 09 67 ■ E-mail: 75016TDT@aol.com ■ Mon-Fri 8:30-17:00 and by appointment ■ Christian-Henri Werdmüller ■ English spoken ■ Professional discount ■ Credit cards

Upholstery of walls, sun ceilings, sofas and chairs. Works for the top antique dealers, the Mobilier Nationale and private individuals.

TAPISSERIE 27

27 quai des Grands-Augustins, 75006 Paris ■ Telfax: 01 43 26 17 85 ■ Mon-Sat 10:00-18:30 ■ Professional discount

Specialists in the upholstery of XVIII and XIX century chairs.

TEODOR

14 rue de Pontoise, 75005 Paris ■ Tel: 01 46 33 00 08 ■ Fax: 01 40 46 09 92 ■ E-mail: teodor@dial.oleane.com ■ Mon-Fri 9:00-13:00/14:00-19:00, Sat 10:00-18:00 ■ Prices medium ■ Professional discount

All types of upholstery.

♛ PHILIPPE WYTERS

51 rue Saint-Louis-en-l'Ile, 75004 Paris ■ Tel: 01 43 54 35 12 ■ Mon-Fri 9:00-18:00 and by appointment ■ Prices medium ■ Professional discount

Specialists in the upholstery of antique and reproduction chairs. Restoration.

───────────── BOULOGNE ─────────────

ENTREPRISE GUILLON-ARIENTI

13 rue d'Aguesseau, 92100 Boulogne-Billancourt ■ Tel: 01 46 05 78 81 ■ Tue-Sat 10:30-12:30/15:30-20:30 ■ Onar Metin speaks English

Wall upholstery and window treatments. Upholstery of chairs and sofas. Window and bed treatments.

IDEA DECORATION

131ter rue du Château, 92100 Boulogne-Billancourt ■ Tel: 01 46 05 98 10 ■ Fax: 01 41 10 81 16 ■ Tue-Sat 10:00-12:00/14:00-19:00 ■ Jean-Pierre Laurent speaks English ■ Prices medium ■ 10% professional discount

Traditional upholstery of walls and chairs. Window treatments. Dropped ceilings of PVC with a lacquer look.

WALLPAPERS
Papiers peints

BESSON
32 rue Bonaparte, 75006 Paris ■ Tel: 01 40 51 89 64 ■ Tue-Sat
9:30-18:30 ■ 46 av Marceau, 75008 Paris ■ Tel: 01 47 20 75 35
■ English spoken ■ Prices medium
**Designs from Frey, Canovas, Etamine. They specialize in co-
ordinates of wallpapers and fabrics. Very good.**

MANUEL CANOVAS
6 rue de l'Abbaye, 75006 Paris ■ Tel: 01 43 29 91 36 ■ Fax: 01
45 04 04 83 ■ Mon-Fri 9:00-18:30 ■ English spoken ■ Prices
medium to high
Beautiful selection of their own wallpapers and fabrics.

ETAMINE
3 rue Jacob, 75006 Paris ■ Tel: 01 43 25 70 65 ■ Fax: 01 43 25
92 76 ■ Mon-Sat 9:30-13:00/14:00-18:30 ■ Marilyne Rioult and
Chrystelle Thouan speak English ■ Prices medium ■ Professional discount
**Excellent selection of wallpapers to coordinate with their
fabrics.**

FARDIS
6 bis rue de l'Abbaye, 75006 Paris ■ Tel: 01 43 25 73 44 ■ Fax:
01 43 54 22 78 ■ Tue-Sat 9:00-18:00 ■ English spoken ■ Prices
medium ■ Professional discount
Their own interesting designs of wallpaper and fabrics.

PIERRE FREY
2 rue de Furstemberg, 75006 Paris ■ Tel: 01 46 33 73 00 ■ Fax:
01 42 96 85 38 ■ Mon-Sat 10:00-12:00/14:00-18:30 ■ English
spoken ■ Prices medium to high
Superb collection of wallpapers, coordinated with fabrics.

NOBILIS
29 rue Bonaparte, 75006 Paris ■ Tel: 01 43 29 21 50 ■ Fax: 01
43 29 77 57 ■ Mon-Sat 9:30-18:30 ■ English spoken ■ Prices
medium to high ■ Professional discount
A very good selection of wallpapers and coordinates.

CAROLLE THIBAUT-POMERANTZ
Paris ■ Tel: 01 45 04 54 68 ■ Fax: 01 45 04 11 53 ■ By appointment ■ New York City ■ Tel: (212)759-6048 ■ Fax: (212)308-3486 ■ By appointment ■ English and French spoken ■ 10% professional discount ■ Amex

Extraordinary collection of antique hand-painted wallpaper panels, decorative arts, objects and furniture of the late XIX and early XX century.

ZUBER
5 bd des Filles du Calvaire, 75003 Paris ■ Tel : 01 42 77 23 52 ■ Fax : 01 42 77 17 98 ■ Mon-Fri 9:00-18:00 ■ English spoken ■ Prices high ■ Professional discount ■ Major credit cards

Wonderful choice of scenic wallpapers. They have showrooms in New York and London.

Restoration of Wallpapers

MERIGUET-CARRÈRE
84 rue de l'Abbaye-Groult, 75015 Paris ■ Tel: 01 48 28 48 81 ■ Fax: 01 45 32 57 84 ■ Mon-Fri 8:00-12:00/14:00-18:00 ■ English spoken ■ Prices high ■ Professional discount

Restoration of antique wallpapers, trompe l'oeil and gilding. His work experience includes the historic monuments of France including the Palace of Versailles.

WINE CELLAR EQUIPMENT
Equipement de Cave

AU CHÊNE LIÈGE
74 bd Montparnasse, 75014 Paris ■ Tel: 01 43 22 02 15 ■ Fax: 01 42 79 81 23 ■ Tue-Sat 9:30-12:30/13:45-18:30 ■ Prices medium ■ Professional discount

A large assortment of articles for serving wine. Accessories for the bar, decanters, glasses. The cork specialists.

EUROCAVE
25 avenue Charles-de-Gaulle, 75016 Paris ■ Tel: 01 45 00 52 55 ■ Fax 01 45 00 45 83 ■ Mon-Fri 9:00-19:00/Sat 9:00-12:00/14:00-18:00 ■ English spoken ■ Prices medium ■ Professional discount

Large stock and made to order temperature controlled armoires for wine. Sizes from 50 to 2,800 bottles. Catalogue in English available upon request.

LA CAVE BACCHUS
106 av Philippe-Auguste, 75011 Paris ■ Tel: 01 43 72 00 55 ■ Fax: 01 43 72 91 71 ■ Mon-Fri 9:00-12:00/14:00-18:00 ■ English spoken ■ Prices medium to high ■ 15% professional discount

Custom and stock armoires for wine storage. Wide selection of special wine dispensing equipment for restaurants and hotels. An exciting new refrigerated wine barrel. They also build and equip complete wine cellars for restaurants, hotels and private individuals.

LESCENE-DURA
63 rue de la Verrerie, 75004 Paris ■ Tel: 01 42 72 08 74 ■ Fax: 01 42 76 09 69 ■ Tue-Sat 9:30-19:00 ■ Prices reasonable ■ 10% professional discount

Articles for the wine cellar and the bar. Accessories for wine tasting. Special armoires for wine storage.

L'ESPRIT & LE VIN
81 av des Ternes, 75017 Paris ■ Tel: 01 45 74 80 99 ■ Fax: 01 45 72 03 32 ■ Mon 14:00-19:00, Tue-Sat 10:00-13:00/14:00-19:00 ■ Diane de Saint-Alban ■ English and Spanish spoken ■ Major credit cards

Extraordinary choice of everything for serving and tasting wine: decanters, glasses, corkscrews and much more.

LE LOUVRE DES ANTIQUAIRES

2 Place du Palais Royal, 75002 Paris ■ Tue-Sun 11:00-19:00:

HÉLÈNE D'HELMERSEN

17-19 Allée Desmalter ■ Tel: 01 42 97 43 33 ■ Fax: 01 49 28 98 89 ■ E-mail: helmerse@club-internet.fr ■ English spoken ■ Possible professional discount ■ Visa, Amex

Superb collection of liqueur caddies and boxes of the XIX century.

GALERIE HÉRITAGES

8 Allée Weisweiller ■ Tel: 01 42 97 55 12

Wine cellar objects.

LAURENT OÏFFER

8 Allée Jacob ■ Tel: 01 40 20 90 95 ■ Fax: 01 40 20 90 97 ■ E-mail: loiffer@aol.com ■ English and Spanish spoken ■ Professional discount ■ Major credit cards

Antique corkscrews and other collectibles.

M.J. SENEMAUD

8 Allée Majorelle ■ Tel: 01 42 60 19 09

Collectibles for the wine cellar.

THE MARKETS OF PARIS

Les Marchés de Paris

A trip to Paris without visiting the street markets would be missing an incredible experience. These exciting markets, including the The Flea Market (Marché aux Puces), The Village Suisse, The Village Saint Paul, contain an enormous amount of the good, the bad and the wonderful.

Exploring these markets can be the greatest challenge the canny shopper can ever face in his or her life. Thousands, yes, thousands of dealers of all types, shapes and sizes, offer everything from museum quality antiques, art and collectibles to the purest junk.

The best known of these markets is The Marché aux Puces at Saint-Ouen on the outskirts of the city. Named after the sand flea, which very likely infested the area when market gardeners tilled the soil and supplied vegetables to the city people of Paris, The Marché aux Puces is comprised of several different markets, each offering a different quality of merchandise and certainly different atmospheres.

Visitors should make an exploratory visit and then decide where they might wish to concentrate their attention. It is amazing how quickly one can become oriented to what might seem at first to be a confused, sprawling mass. Be patient, look at everything, bargain carefully and buy wisely. Then you will never be disappointed.

We have selected those markets and individual merchants whose wares may best suit the needs of the professional or the individual looking for something special. We have not listed them all since it takes a very short time to suffer from serious overload.

The markets of Paris are always a delight. For the skilled treasure hunter, there is no better reward than a surprise discovery. You will be astonished at how many of the market people speak English.

Le Village Suisse

78 av de Suffren and 54 av de La Motte-Picquet, 75015 Paris ■ Tel: 01 47 34 13 82 ■ Fax: 01 44 49 02 20 ■ Contact: Mr. Michel d'Istria

The Village Suisse was 100 years old in the year 2000. It first came to being in the great Paris Exposition in 1900, the year the Eiffel Tower was completed. After going through several reincarnations, it has become a centrally located facility which now houses 150 dealers and has become one of the better-quality antique and art markets of Paris. The atmosphere is very pleasant and rarely crowded. The market is open Thursday, Friday, Saturday, Sunday and Monday from 11:00 to 19:00. Remember, lunch is considered sacred so most merchants will close from 12:30 to 13:30, or longer.

─── PLACE DE GENÈVE ───

1. **GALERIE DE VILLIERS**
   Tel: 01 45 66 06 52
   Art Books, deluxe editions, estampes, framing.

2. **ADAM**
   Tel: 01 45 67 23 99
   French, English and Italian furniture of the XVIII century.

3. **J. HAYE "BROC-EN-TOUT"**
   Tel: 01 45 67 49 85 ■ Fax: 01 45 67 78 84
   Furniture, curiosities, art objects, especially chairs.

5/6. **LE GRENIER DE GRAND-MÈRE**
   Tel: 01 47 83 32 84 - Fax: 01 46 47 71 65
   Restoration specialists in furniture of Boulle and Napoleon III.

9. **SPINELLA**
   Tel: 01 45 66 56 62
   XIX century bibelots and glass.

11. **CONTE ANTIQUITÉS**
   Tel: 01 47 83 41 83 ■ Fax: 01 42 60 14 72
   XVIII & XIX century furniture, paintings and art objects.

12. **LE COIN RÊVÉ**
Tel: 01 47 34 07 29
XVIII century furniture and bibelots.

13. **CORINNE ANTIQUITÉS**
Tel: 01 43 06 47 03
XVIII and XIX century furniture, lighting and bibelots.

———————— PLACE DE LAUSANNE ————————

14. **MARTINE SUTTON-GRENEE**
Tel: 01 45 67 46 29
XVIII and XIX century decorative objects.

16/17/18. **J. HAYE "BROC EN TOUT"**
Tel: 01 45 67 49 85 ■ Fax: 01 45 67 78 84
Antique fireplace accessories, furniture of the XVIII and XIX Century.

19. **MARCHAND D'OUBLI**
Tel: 01 43 06 84 41
XVII and XVIII century paintings, gilded wood sculptures

20/21. **LA GRANDE ROUE**
Tel: 01 45 66 42 38 ■ Fax: 01 48 85 31 36 - Jacques Perquis
XVIII to XX century furniture, lighting, paintings, art objects.

23. **SIGRID**
Tel: 01 45 67 41 43 - Sigrid Julicher
Antiques from the XVII to the XIX century.

24. **DENISE CHARLES**
Tel: 01 53 69 01 00
XVII and XVIII century tapestries, furniture and objects.

———————— PLACE DE BERNE ————————

28. **CATHERINE HIRSCH**
Tel: 01 45 66 00 99 ■ Fax: 01 40 68 76 97
Furniture and art objects of the XVIII and XIX centuries.

29/30. **LACAZE, RENÉ-JULIEN**
Tel: 01 45 66 78 36
Antiques and decorations.

32. **CHRISTIANE DANIEL**
Tel: 01 45 67 59 55
Antiques, ceramics, faiences, art objects.

33. YVES PLASSARD
Tel: 01 45 66 05 55
Furniture and gilded mirrors. Restoration of antique gilding.

34/35. MARCHAND D'OUBLI
Tel: 01 43 06 84 41
XVII and XVIII century paintings, furniture and bibelots. Fruitwood furniture sculptures and painted wood sculptures.

36/37. ANTONIN RISPAL
Tel: 01 47 83 72 34
Art Nouveau and Art Deco.

38. LA FILLE DU PIRATE
Tel: 01 47 34 06 76
Antique arms, antique scientific instruments, marine items.

39. GÉRALDINE
Tel: 01 40 56 02 23
Antique furniture of the haute epoque, furniture, faience, bibelots.

———————————— PLACE DE LUCERNE ————————————

44/45/52. MICHEL D'ISTRIA
Tel: 01 43 06 47 87 ■ Fax: 01 44 49 02 20
Antique furniture and objects. Qualified expert.

49/51. ROXANE
Tel: 01 45 66 51 56 ■ Roxane Sabatrier
XVIII and XIX century paintings, curiosities.

50. CATHERINE HIRSCH
Tel: 01 45 66 00 09 ■ Fax: 01 40 68 76 97
XVIII and XIX century furniture and bibelots. Expert.

54/55. MME SYBILLE DE VOLDÈRE
Tel: 01 45 66 54 53
Flemish paintings XVII and XVIII century. Venetian paintings.

56. ANCELLE
Tel: 01 43 06 21 99
Antique frames.

57. AXELLE BOZON
Tel. 01 45 67 44 44 ■ Fax: 01 44 18 95 44
XIX century antique drawings, engravings, paintings, bibelots.

58. **GALERIE OLIVIA II**
Tel: 01 43 06 85 39 ■ Telfax: 01 40 65 95 92 ■ Cell: 06 60 44 26 01
Antique silver and art de la table.

ALLÉE DE FRIBOURG
---

42. **J. HAYE "BROC EN TOUT"**
Tel: 01 45 67 49 85 ■ Fax: 01 45 67 78 84
XVIII and XIX century furniture chairs and reproductions.

44/45. **MICHEL D'ISTRIA**
Tel: 01 43 06 47 87 ■ Fax: 01 44 49 02 20
Antique furniture and objects. Qualified expert.

46. **JEANINE KUGEL**
Tel: 01 47 34 62 74
International expert on Viennese bronzes.

47. **LE HUSSARD BLEU**
Tel: 01 47 34 81 24
A wonderful collection of lead soldiers and toys.

48. **AUX VIEUX FRIBOURG**
Tel: 01 47 34 91 97
XVIII century furniture and art objects.

GRANDE ALLÉE
---

13. **CORINNE ANTIQUITÉS**
Tel: 01 43 06 47 03
Furniture, lighting and bibelots of the XVIII and XIX century.

14/26. **MARTINE SUTTON GRENÉE**
Tel: 01 45 67 46 29
XVIII and XIX century furniture and bibelots.

28/50. **CATHERINE HIRSCH**
Tel: 01 45 68 00 09 ■ Fax: 01 40 58 76 97
Antiques and art objects. XVIII and XIX century.

40/41. **REGIS AERNOUTS**
Tel: 01 47 34 85 10
Antiques, decorative objects.

48. **AUX VIEUX FRIBOURG**
Tel: 01 47 34 91 97
XVIII and XIX century furniture.

49. **ROXANE**
Tel: 01 45 66 51 56
Antiques, curiosities and paintings.

58. **GALERIE OLIVIA II**
Tel: 01 43 06 85 30 ■ Telfax: 01 40 65 95 82 ■ Cell: 06 60 44 26 01
Antique silver and table arts.

59. **GALERIE JABERT**
Tel: 01 43 06 45 55 ■ Fax: 01 45 67 68 94
Antique tapestries, carpets, restorations and expertise.

70. **PHILIPPE MICHEL**
Tel: 01 45 67 90 74
XVIII, XIX century antiques, bibelots and some Art Deco.

71/72. **MICHEL CAFLER**
Tel: 01 45 67 89 67 ■ Fax: 01 44 49 91 82 ■ Cell: 06 08 78 06 58
Art Deco and XVIII and XIX century antiques and bibelots.

79. **LE KÉPI ROUGE**
Tel: 01 45 67 59 83 ■ Christian Blondeau
Historical collectibles, arms, military art and lead soldiers.

88. **ERIC SAGET**
Tel: 01 43 06 07 22
Antiques and decoration.

89/90. **A. & J. BESREST**
Tel: 01 45 67 59 61
XVIII and XIX century antiques; especially bibliotheques.

91. **LA VIEILLE EUROPE**
Tel: 01 43 06 61 87
Antique sculpture and decorative items.

92. **MÉLODIE DU TEMPS**
Tel: 01 42 73 23 08
Antique dealer who specializes in small furniture for collectors.

93/94. **A. GIOE**
Tel: 01 43 06 25 01
Upholstered and cherry wood furniture.

95. **EN QUATRE-VINGT-QUINZE**
Tel: 01 43 06 31 76 ■ J. Daveau
Furniture, clocks, of the XVIII and XIX century. Carpets, tapestries and ivories.

59/60. JABERT
Tel: 01 43 06 45 55 ■ Fax: 01 45 67 68 94
Antique tapestries, European and Asian carpets. Restoration.

61/62/63. BOUTIQUE ÉCOSSAISE
Tel: 01 45 65 63 08 ■ Fax: 01 40 11 73 53
English and northern European antiques.

64. LUC JOLLIVET
Tel: 01 45 67 88 95
Antique furniture and lanterns.

65. GHISLAINE CHAPLIER
Tel: 01 45 67 30 55
Interesting and exciting collectibles.

66. ART PRIMITIFS
Tel: 01 47 83 93 03 ■ Fax: 01 47 83 26 10
Primitive art.

67. CATHERINE BELLAICHE
Tel: 01 42 73 30 05 ■ Fax: 01 40 56 90 64
Oriental and contemporary carpets, decorative objects.

68/68. JEAN LOUIS KARSENTY
Tel: 01 445 67 72 08 ■ Cell: 06 07 91 33 73 ■ Car: 01 49 93 45 79
Antiques of the XVII and XVIII century, interior decoration.

70. PHILIPPE MICHEL
Tel: 01 45 67 89 67 ■ Fax: 01 49 26 01 41
XVIII and XIX century paintings, furniture, art objects.

───── **GRAND PLACE** ─────

75. CATHERINE BELLAICHE
Tel: 01 42 73 30 05 ■ Fax: 01 40 56 90 64
Antique and contemporary carpets, restoration and decorations.

76/76bis. GALERIE MAXINE FUSTIER
Tel: 01 47 34 13 82
Superb XVIII and XIX century furniture and art objects. Specialist in Directoire and Consulat.

77. **LA CHEMINÉE**
Tel: 01 45 66 88 71 ■ Mme Fraignoz
Fire dogs, fireplace accessories.

96. **EN QUATRE-VINGT-QUINZE**
Tel: 01 43 06 31 76
XVIII and XIX century furniture, clocks, carpets, tapestries.

──────────── AVENUE DE CHAMPAUBERT ────────────

110. **L'INTEMPORELLE**
Tel: 01 40 56 91 97
Art Deco furniture of the 1930s.

113. **PIERRE SAVINEL**
Tel: 01 45 66 09 76 ■ Cell: 06 09 61 96 87
Antique furniture and objects from the XVII to XIX century.

148. **L'ÉCHOPPE MARINE**
Tel: 01 43 06 88 96 ■ Fax: 01 43 06 54 50
Marine and scientific collectibles, ancient objects.

155/156. **AUX ARMES D'ANTAN - MARYSE RASO**
Tel: 01 47 83 71 42 ■ Fax: 01 47 34 40 99
Antique arms, military souvenirs, catalogue available.

158. **ANNE & PENELOPE**
Tel: 01 47 34 94 54
Furniture, art objects of China, ivories and carved stone.

──────────── PLACE DE LUGANO ────────────

79/80/81. **LE KÉPI ROUGE**
Tel: 01 45 67 59 83 ■ Christian Blondieau
Historical souvenirs, lead soldiers, antique arms, paintings.

82. **L'HEURE DE ROBERT**
Tel: 01 45 66 74 53
Antique jewellery and jewellery repair.

83. **MICHEL WEGIEL**
Tel: 01 45 66 96 28
Antiquities, art objects. Decorative items.

84. **JEAN-CLAUDE WILLEMIN**
Tel: 01 45 67 10 12 ■ Tel: 02 37 64 90 13 ■ Fax: 02 37 64 90 87
Furniture and objects from the XVII to the XIX century.

85. **GÉRARD SANTOLLINI - LES ARTS DE L'ATLAS**
Fax: 01 43 06 91 94
XVIII and XIX century furniture, objects. Art of the Atlas Mountains.

86. **MAISON HAN - MARTINE NATHAN**
Tel: 01 47 34 24 60 ■ Fax: 01 42 02 17 90
Chinese archaeology, bronzes and terracottas.

87/98/99. **GALERIE SAADA**
Tel: 01 45 67 59 14
Furniture and art objects of the XVIII century and First Empire.

100/101. **GALERIE OLIVIA 1**
Tel: 01 43 06 85 30 ■ Telfax: 01 40 65 95 82 ■ Cell: 06 60 44 26 01
Table arts, antique silver.

─────────────── **RUE ALASSEUR** ───────────────

103. **MAISON HAYE**
Tel: 01 45 67 49 85
Articles for XVIII and XIX century fireplaces, chairs, furniture. Also reproductions.

105. **A. & J. BESREST**
Tel: 01 45 67 59 61
XVIII, XIX century furniture especially bibliotheques.

108/109. **SUR LES AILES DU TEMPS**
Tel: 01 47 83 50 19
XVIII and XIX century antiques, decorative items.

─────────────── **AVENUE PAUL DÉROULÈDE** ───────────────

114/114bis. **PHILIPPE MINARET**
Tel: 01 45 66 02 59 ■ Cell: 06 09 61 96 87
XVIII and XIX century furniture, paintings and art objects.

149. **MÉMOIRES**
Tel: 01 45 66 09 72 ■ Christine Deboes
Regional furniture in natural woods: XVIII to XIX century.

155/156. **AUX ARMES D'ANTAN**
Tel: 01 47 83 71 42 ■ Fax: 01 47 34 40 99 - Maryse Raso
Antique arms, military souvenirs. Qualified expert.

─────────────── **ALLÉE DU VALAIS** ───────────────

120. **ENTRE TEMPS**
Tel: 01 45 67 68 07
XVIII and XIX century antiques, art objects.

121. LES ATELIERS SAINT-GERVAIS
Tel: 01 45 67 29 39
Restoration of old master paintings.

122. CARIATIDES SOVERINI
Tel: 01 47 83 74 70
XVIII and XIX century French and English furniture.

124. PIERRE VIGUIE
Tel: 01 40 56 38 37
Mahogany furniture, Directoire, Empire. Restorations.

125. GILLES BODARD
Tel: 01 43 06 44 18 ■ Fax: 01 43 06 36 19
Antiques and jewellery.

128/132. MONIQUE DE CHAMARD
Tel: 01 47 34 47 38
Paintings of the XIX and XX century.

130. JEAN-PIERRE PALLEAU
Tel: 45 66 02 33
XVII and XVIII century French furniture and art objects. Specialty: French regional furniture.

134/135. LE 7e JOUR
Tel: 01 45 66 09 06
Furniture and objects from the early XIX century.

139. MARYSA
Tel: 01 47 34 75 32
Caves for liqueurs, cave for cigars and boxes.

143. MONIQUE DESPRAIRIES
Tel: 01 43 06 36 81
Small natural wood XIX century furniture, mirrors, chairs.

──────── ALLÉE DU GRAND SAINT-BERNARD ────────

111/114. PHILIPPE MINARET
Tel: 01 45 66 02 59 ■ Cell: 06 09 61 96 87
XVIII and XIX century furniture, paintings and objects of art.

113. PIERRE SAVINEL
Tel: 01 45 66 09 76
Furniture for stereos. Installation of stereos.

144. ANTIQUITÉS HERBERT
Tel: 01 47 34 83 61
XVIII and XIX century French furniture.

145/146. JEAN-CHRISTIAN DAVEAU
Tel: 01 47 83 69 31 ■ Fax: 01 40 56 09 25
Art Deco furniture, paintings and sculpture.

———— SOUS-SOL COUR ANGLAIS ————
(Entry on Grand Place)

1/2. HANRI KUSZELEWIC
Tel: 01 45 66 91 24
XVIII and XIX century English and French furniture.

3/16/18. BRITISH IMPORT ANTIQUITIES
Tel: 01 45 67 87 61
XIX century English and European mahogany furniture.

4. LIBRAIRIE AH! LES BEAUX LIVRES
Fax: 01 44 49 91 66
They buy and sell old and new books.

5. LUCETTE VINCENT
Tel: 01 43 06 48 84
Necklaces and bracelets in semi-precious stones.

8. M. & MME HOFFER - LES NOUVELLE HYBRIDES
Tel: 01 40 65 96 17
XVIII and XIX century furniture, bibelots and paintings.

11. ROIG LAMBERT
Tel: 01 43 06 44 63
Antique lamps, shades.

12. JACINTHE - GALERIE D'ART
Tel: 01 42 73 34 43
Antiques, decoration.

13. JEAN LEVY LECLERE
Tel: 01 47 83 64 11
Antiques, art objects, curiosities.

22. 7 FOIS 7
Tel: 01 43 06 83 96
XIX century paintings, art objects and decoration.

The Flea Market
Le Marché aux Puces

The Marché aux Puces is easily reached by Metro to the Porte de Clignancourt, by taxi or by private car directly to the rue des Rosiers. There is ample parking space available in the Marché Malassis, on the roof of the Marché Serpette, the garages on the rue Marie-Curie, rue Docteur-Bauer and rue Eugène-Bertoux.

All the main markets, Biron, Vernaison, Malassis, Dauphine, Serpette and Paul Bert, are entered from the rue des Rosiers, the main street.

There are plenty of restaurants and cafés to rest your tired feet and have a meal. We recommend the Restaurant Biron. The food is good, the host and all the family are charming and give excellent service. However, there are lots of good places to eat.

Unless you have a particular dealer in mind and have targeted on a specific purchase, plan to spend at least half a day browsing. A full day is even better. Remember, tastes and market demands are constantly changing, so if you are looking for some popular item, prepare to pay a market price. Otherwise, you are in for some pleasant surprises. Bargaining is the order of the day. Be patient. Impulse buyers often regret at leisure. Try to establish something of a personal relationship with the dealer. They love to know something about you and your problems. Take them into your confidence. When you do, you will find them more sympathetic and negotiations will go more smoothly. Finally, be sure to ask for a certificate of guarantee, if you are being sold an antique, or a note on the *provenance* if it is an old painting.

Most merchants are open on Saturday and Sunday from 9:30 to about 18:30. A few are open on Friday and Monday by appointment. It is best to call to avoid disappointment.

The Marché Aux Puces is enormous and the authors have tried to select the best and the brightest. Please keep in mind that the turnover of offerings is quite rapid. Don't expect to return a month later and find the "heart's desire" you passed by the first time around.

For those of you who cannot bear to be away from the computer, there is a Webite: www.lespuces.fr. This might be useful for follow-up after a visit, however, there is no substitute for looking, touching, feeling and tasting.

One thing is certain: one visit is never enough.

MARCHÉ ANTICA

99 rue des Rosiers, 93400 Saint-Ouen

A well laid out small market with a few good dealers. It is certainly worth a visit.

BOUTIQUE C
XVIII and early XIX century small furniture, chairs and armchairs in mahogany and walnut. XVIII and XIX century paintings and porcelain.

FRANCK ANTIQUITÉS - Boutique H
Tel: 0140 11 82 60 ■ Fax: 01 42 39 14 97
XIX century Japanese and Chinese furniture, curiosities and decorative objects.

FRANCK ANTIQUITÉS - Boutique I
Tel: 01 40 11 82 60
English furniture and decorative items. XIX century English silver, paintings and boxes.

BOUTIQUE G
Tel: 0140 11 82 60
Oriental carpets, kilims and tapestries.

MILAD ANTIQUITÉS – Boutique F
Tel: 01 40 11 52 83
Antiques and architectural elements from India.

POT, Michel - GOLD HORN - Boutique J
Tel: 01 40 10 09 84
XVI to XX century books, drawings, engravings and paintings, some furniture.

85 rue des Rosiers and 118 av Michelet, 93400 St-Ouen
Open every Saturday, Sunday and Monday 9:30-6:30

The Marché Biron is one of the most interesting markets in the Puces. Allée 1 has a mixture of almost all of the classic French furniture styles intermingled with dealers in lighting, Art Nouveau furniture, a few unusual garden ornaments, antique posters, some fine art, glassware and silver. Allée 2 is devoted to excellent offerings of furniture and objects from Normandy and Brittany plus a few things from Provence. Most of it is XVIII and XIX century with some from the early to the mid XX century. You will find a few art and graphics dealers; all-in-all, quite good quality. When you finish exploring Allée 1 flop down and rest your feet. Have a tall cold Perrier Menthe or something stronger at the Restaurant Biron at the very top.

ALLÉE 1

ABECASSIS, Paul ■ Stand 125 ■ Tel: 01 40 12 82 38 ■ Fax: 01 40 10 13 08 ■ English spoken ■ Professional discount
Furniture and portraits of the XIX century.

AMBRE ■ Stand 68 ■ Tel: 01 40 12 17 01 ■ Fax: 01 40 26 43 27
Alain Couet speaks English
XVIII and XIX century furniture, objects, decorative elements.

A L'OPALINE ■ Stand 106 ■ Tel: 01 41 59 69
Objects of the XVIII century and small furniture.

ANTIQUITIES GILBERT ■ Stand 47 ■ Tel: 01 40 10 23 32 ■ Fax: 01 40 12 19 56 ■ Gilbert Cohen speaks Spanish and Arabic ■ Professional discount ■ Visa, Amex
Furniture and bronzes of the XVIII century.

LES AUTHENTIQUES ■ Stand 130 ■ Tel: 01 40 12 12 50
Antique jewellery.

AVNER ANTIQUITÉS ■ Stand 46 ■ Tel: 01 40 11 19 23 ■ Avner Tzala speaks English ■ Amex
XIX century furniture and bronzes.

BAKERDJIAN, Eric ■ Stand 18 ■ Tel: 01 40 11 20 89/01 48 78 93 39
Antique tapestries and Oriental carpets. Restoration and cleaning.

BARBANEL, Claude ■ Stand 88 ■ Tel: 01 40 12 33 35
XIX century furniture and objects. XVIII and XIX century glass.

BERMAN FRÈRES ■ Stand 9 ■ Tel: 01 40 10 12 95 ■ Maurice Berman speaks English ■ Professional discount ■ Amex, Visa
Lighting, objets d'art, bronzes and Napoleon III furniture.

BERRO, Pascal ■ Stand 72 ■ Tel: 01 40 12 14 18 - Fax: 01 48 78 43 82
Art Nouveau, Art Deco 1900-1930. Glass objects by Daum, Gallé, Walter, Rousseau, Muller. Bronzes, ceramics, furniture.

BITOUN, Jacques ■ Stand 8 ■ Tel: 01 40 11 96 54
Antique porcelain. XVIII and XIX century Meissen and other German XVIII century porcelain.

BOLAND, Elisabeth ■ Stand 98 ■ Tel: 01 40 11 38 22
Art Nouveau and Art Deco. Lalique glass and perfume bottles.

BROPHY, Suzanne ■ Stand 135bis
Diverse and interesting furniture, objects. Great garden benches.

BRUDASZ, Judith ■ Stand 86 bis ■ Cell: 06 1037 3255 ■ Fax: 01 40 10 13 08 ■ English spoken ■ Professional discount
1940s jewellery, accessories from Hermès, Chanel. Art Nouveau and Art Deco.

BRUYNEEL, Frédérique ■ Stand 22 ■ Tel: 01 40 12 93 27 ■ Fax: 01 40 10 13 08 ■ English and Italian spoken ■ Minimum 10% professional discount
Furniture and objets d'art of the XVIII and XIX century in marquetry, gilded wood, chandeliers, lamps. Carpets, bronzes, photos. Repairs.

CARPENTIER, Henri ■ Stand 33 ■ Tel: 01 40 12 21 73 ■ English spoken ■ Professional discount
XIX century furniture and objets d'art.

CHOSES ET AUTRES CHOSES ■ Stand 15 ■ Tel: 01 40 11 94 08 ■ Fax: 04 78 32 32 26 ■ English and Italian spoken ■ Professional discount ■ Major credit cards
Art Deco, Art Nouveau, chandeliers, glass, ceramics and wrought iron.

CLERC, Philippe ■ Stand 121bis ■ Tel: 01 40 11 59 69
Neoclassical (1780-1830) mahogany furniture, art objects, drawings and engravings.

DANIÈLE, B. Giromini ■ Stand 122 ■ Tel: 01 40 12 83 59 ■ Fax: 01 45 26 48 84 English spoken ■ Professional discount
XVII, XVIII and XIX century furniture, paintings and decorative objects.

DATURA ■ Stand 44 ■ Tel: 01 40 12 70 35 ■ Cell: 06 89 42 69 90 ■ Nicole Mostini ■ English spoken ■ Professional discount ■ Major credit cards
Decorative arts of the XX century; furniture, paintings, bronzes and objets d'art.

DAVID'S ■ Stand 21 ■ Tel: 01 40 12 40 04 ■ Fax: 01 45 76 88 06 ■ David Sasson speaks English ■ Professional discount
XIX century furniture and decorative objects.

DESNOUES, Jacques ■ Stand ■ Tel: 01 40 10 26 70
XIX century furniture and objects. XVIII century reproduction marquetry, bronze objects. Porcelain mounted on bronze.

DOUCHIN, Jacques ■ Stand 134 ■ Tel: 01 40 11 35 89 ■ English and German spoken ■ Professional discount ■ MC
English and French furniture of the XVIII and XIX century. Garden furniture.

DUCHEMIN, Thérèse ■ Stand 24 ■ Cell: 06 81 14 89 84 ■ English spoken
Natural wood and marquetry furniture and objets d'art

DEHOUX-DUINAT, Marie ■ Stand 129 ■ Cell: 06 12 98 90 76 ■ Fax: 01 40 10 13 08 ■ English and Spanish spoken ■ Professional discount ■ Major credit cards
Art Nouveau and Art Deco. Articles of the 1950s to 1970s.

GALERIE M. DUPRÉ, ■ Stand 91 ■ Tel: 01 40 11 54 67 ■ Visa, Amex
Paintings of the XIX century. Frames and framing.

EDOUARD, Jacqueline - Stand 29 ■ Tel: 01 40 10 23 00
Rare watches, silver, exceptional art objects.

ELCABAS, Gabriel ■ Stand 127 ■ Tel: 01 42 54 10 66 ■ Fax: 01 42 64 28 62 ■ Cell: 06 13 24 54 54 ■ Professional discount ■ Major credit cards
Furniture, lighting, decorative objects of Art Deco 1910 to 1940.

ELISABETH - Stand 66 ■ Tel: 01 40 11 12 00 ■ Fax: 01 47 47 02 82
Art Nouveau and Art Deco glass and furniture. Glass by Gallé, Daum, Schneider, Sabino, Murano, Lalique, with certificates. Miniatures, boxes in gold and silver. Russian objects and collectibles.

EMBERGER, Henri ■ Stand 25 ■ Tel: 01 40 10 99 26 ■ Fax: 01 30 34 47 47 ■ English spoken
Toys, games and decorative objects.

EMMANUEL ET TAL ■ Stand 127 ■ Tel: 01 40 10 99 00 ■ E-mail: jackline1@aol.com ■ Web: www.antique-expo.com/opivia ■ Emmanuel Redon ■ English spoken ■ Professional discount ■ Major credit cards
Old silver, silver and bronze centerpieces, candelabra and decorative accessories.

EVELYNE ANTIQUITÉS ■ Stand 13 ■ Tel: 01 40 10 09 99 ■ Fax: 01 40 36 48 98 ■ Jacob Chiche ■ English spoken ■ Amex and CB
Napoleon III art objects, furniture, porcelain.

FISCHER ■ Stand 75ter ■ Tel: 01 40 12 40 46 ■ Fax: 01 46 21 09 09 ■ English spoken ■ Professional discount ■ Major credit cards
XIX and XX century paintings.

FITOUSSI, Lucien ■ Stand 77 ■ Tel: 01 40 10 05 70 English and Arabic spoken ■ Amex, Visa
XIX century objets d'art.

GAIGNON, Claude ■ Stand 7
Mixture of furniture and objects.

GALERIE R.B. ■ Stand 39 ■ Tel: 01 40 12 96 75 ■ Roseline Brown speaks English
Napoleon III, Art Deco.

GITTON, Thierry ■ Stand 101 ■ Tel: 01 40 11 52 46 ■ Fax: 01 45 74 19 70
Charles X and Napoleon III Opalines and furniture. Italian water- colours.

HEIMROTH, Alain ■ Stand 51 ■ Tel: 01 40 11 02 37 ■ Fax: 01 46 22 18 85
Furniture and objects of character of all periods.

HOFFMANN, Roland ■ Stand 75 ■ Tel: 01 40 12 87 29
Furniture, art objects, wood panelling (boiseries).

ISABELLE ■ Stand 112 ■ Tel: 01 40 10 12 90 ■ Fax: 01 40 10 13 08
XIX century furniture and unique objects.

JAM ■ Stand 1 ■ Tel: 01 40 10 84 09
Posters and paintings.

JACKIE ■ Stand 61 ■ Tel: 40 12 36 66 ■ Fax: 01 40 12 04 62 ■
English and Spanish spoken ■ Professional discount ■ Amex, Visa
French provincial furniture.

KAPE, Simone, **ESCAPADE** ■ Stand 90 ■ Tel: 01 40 11 14 59 ■
Fax: 01 40 10 13 08 ■ English and German spoken ■ Professional discount ■ Visa, Euro-card.
Furniture, chairs and objets d'art of the period of Napoleon III.

KNUTH ■ Stand 26 ■ Tel: 01 40 12 24 57 ■ Spanish spoken
XVIII and XIX century furniture and objects.

KOLSKY, Gisele ■ Stand 53
Specialty: tables.

KRIVONOS, Michel ■ Stand 41 ■ Tel: 01 40 11 38 97 ■ Fax: 01 40 10 13 08 ■ Cell: 06 62 54 38 97 ■ Professional discount
Table arts, furniture and chairs.

LALUQUE, Claude ■ Stand 92 ■ Tel: 01 40 12 85 51 ■ Fax: 01 40 10 13 08
Art Nouveau glass, Gallé, Daum, bronzes and objects. Qualified expert.

LAMBREQUIN ANTIQUITÉS ■ Tel: 01 40 12 07 71/(16) 86 96 51 24
Antique furniture, paintings, drawings and decorative objects.

LARGEAULT, Nicole - Stand 107 ■ Tel: 40 12 83 54 ■ Fax: 01 56 26 61 63 ■ English and Spanish spoken ■ Professional discount ■ Major credit cards
Art Nouveau and Art Deco.

LAFAYETTE ANTIQUES ■ Stand 86 ■ Cell: 06 09 66 14 70 ■ Fax: 04 **72** 41 94 34 ■ Anne Sophie and Jacques Polette. English and Italian spoken ■ Professional discount ■ Major credit cards
XVIII and XIX century furniture, lighting and decorative objects. Restoration.

LEPOT, Françoise ■ Stand 65 ■ Tel: 01 40 11 29 69
Old engravings.

LEVANNIER, Alice et Luc ■ Stand 50 ■ Cell: 06 09 02 41 34 ■ Fax:
01 47 34 91 00 ■ E-mail: alicelev@clubinternet ■ English spoken
**Dolls, porcelain, bronzes engravings and some furniture of
the XVII, XVIII and XIX century.**

LE MANOIR ■ Stand 187 ■ Tel: 01 46 11 05 46 ■ English spoken
■ Professional discount
XIX century mahogany and rustic furniture.

LOEFFLER BROC-ART ■ Stand 113 ■ Tel: 01 40 12 31 10 ■
English and German spoken ■ Professional discount
Art of the extreme Orient; Japan and China.

LUCCA, Lucien ■ Stand 139 ■ Tel: 01 40 12 01 65 ■ Fax: 01 64
93 10 30 ■ M. and Mme Lucca speak English ■ Professional discount
XVIII and XIX century rustic furniture.

MAGIC GLASS ■ Stand 31■ Tel: 01 40 10 01 09 ■ Michel Fasa
■ English spoken ■ Professional discount ■ Major credit cards
Art Nouveau.

MARC, Marcel ■ Stand 54 ■ Tel: 01 40 10 24 80
Antiques, lighting, repair of chandeliers.

MARX, Jean-Claude ■ Stand 64 ■ Tel: 01 40 12 36 66 ■ Fax: 01
40 12 04 62
**Provincial furniture in fruit woods, lighting and decorative
objects.**

MARZET, Claude-Annie ■ Stand 97 ■ Tel: 01 40 11 95 49
**Art Nouveau glass: Rousseau, Walter, Decorchemont. Gallé,
and Daum. Ceramics.**

MASLIAH, Guy ■ Stand 111 ■ Tel: 01 40 12 61 56/01 47 47 48 37
**XVIII and XIX century antiques from Japan and China: furni-
ture, bronzes, ceramics. Some French antiques.**

MEKIESS, Claude ■ Stand 36 ■ Tel: 01 40 11 26 12 ■ Professional discount
XIX century items.

MEKIESS, David ■ Stand 20 ■ Tel: 01 40 12 95 93 ■ Fax: 01 42
51 47 73 ■ E-mail: mekiess@club-internet.fr ■ English spoken
Furniture and objets d'art of the XIX century.

MILLANT, Catherine ■ Stand 219, 221 ■ Tel: 01 40 11 87 83 ■ Fax: 01 42 56 28 05 ■ English spoken
Antiques for decoration.

MOREL-ZYSSET ■ Stand 79 ■ Tel: 01 40 10 11 50 ■ German, English and Japanese spoken
Art Nouveau, Gallé, Daum, Icart. Also bronzes.

MORIN, Michel ■ Stand 16-18 ■ Tel: 01 40 11 19 10 ■ Fax: 01 44 53 04 27 ■ English, German, Italian spoken ■ Professional discount ■ Major credit cards
Objects of charm for decoration. Popular Art.

NACHTIGAL, Olivier ■ Stand 87 ■ Tel: 01 40 11 28 91
Art Nouveau and Art Deco.

NATLYNE ■ Stand 49 ■ Tel: 01 40 11 04 64 ■ Fax: 01 40 10 13 08 ■ M. Picard speaks English ■ Professional discount
Regional XVIII century French furniture .

ODIN, Elizabeth ■ Stand 66 ■ Tel: 01 40 11 12 00 ■ English spoken
Art Deco and Art Nouveau glass and Chinese art.

ORSO ■ Stand 96 ■ Tel: 01 60 80 43 00
XIX century marquetry furniture.

PORTEFAIX, Huguette ■ Stand 121 ■ Tel: 01 40 10 13 40
Art Nouveau and Art Deco.

RAFFY, Guy ■ Stand 83 ■ Tel: 01 47 70 36 51
Old books, maps, engravings.

RENAUD, Geoffroy ■ Stand 102 ■ Tel: 01 40 12 26 54 ■ Fax: 01 45 53 12 50 ■ E-mail: anne.deconincki@universal.fr ■ English spoken ■ 10% professional discount ■ Amex, Visa
Arts of the XX century, Art Deco. Design service.

MAILLIARD, Yvette ■ Stand 48 ■ Tel: 01 40 11 26 72 ■ Fax: 01 40 10 13 08
XIX century lighting, lamps, porcelain, tole, bronze, bronze sconces, mirrors.

RUIZ, Dominique ■ Stand 85 ■ Tel: 01 40 11 32 75 ■ Fax: 01 48 91 29 75 ■ English spoken ■ Professional discount ■ Amex, Visa
Art Deco, Art Nouveau.

SABATIER Nadine ■ Stand 135
XVIII and XIX century furniture, bronzes, fine porcelain and decorative objects.

SAINT PIERRE, Catherine - Stand 123 ■ Tel: 01 40 10 29 80
XIX century furniture and objects of curiosity. XVII to XIX century antique French and other fabrics. Antique trimmings.

SAMY ANTIQUITÉS ■ Stand 52 ■ Tel: 01 40 11 56 78
Napoleon III furniture, crystal, chandeliers and art objects, clocks, sculpture.

SAY, Alexia ■ Stand 100 ■ Tel: 01 40 12 11 07 ■ Fax: 01 40 10 13 08 ■ English spoken ■ Professional discount ■ Major credit cards
Art Nouveau, Art Deco glass; Daum, Gallé, Lalique. Coffee offered.

PAUL MILGEN SCHAFFLER ■ Stand 75bis ■ Tel: 01 40 12 89 56 ■ Fax: 01 40 10 13 08 ■ English and German spoken
Diverse objects.

SCHWETZ, Charles ■ Stand 5 ■ Tel: 01 40 11 98 94
Meissen porcelain, paintings, pastels. European and Oriental porcelain, small furniture and table arts.

SPITZER, Annie ■ Stand 114 ■ Cell: 06 14 08 33 37 ■ English spoken
Art Deco, Pâtes de Verre, Daum, Gallé. Small furniture, gueridons.

SZLOS, Daniel et Fils ■ Stand 55 ■ Tel: 01 40 10 82 60 ■ Fax: 01 42 54 16 47 ■ English spoken ■ 10 to 20% professional discount
Furniture and objects of the period of Napoleon III.

TEBOUL, Alain ■ Stand 38 ■ Tel: 01 40 18 68 49 ■ Fax: 01 40 10 18 08 ■ English and Spanish spoken ■ 20% professional discount ■ Major credit cards
Objets d'art and furnishings of the XIX century.

THEVENIN, Aurelia et Laurence ■ Stand 103 ■ Tel: 01 40 12 59 44 ■ Cell: 06 09 96 89 24 ■ English and Italian spoken ■ 15% professional discount ■ Visa
Art Nouveau and Art Deco.

TOBOGAN ANTIQUES ■ Stand 32 ■ Tel: 01 40 10 03 90 ■ Fax: 01 40 12 33 90 ■ Philippe Zoi ■ English, Italian and German spoken ■ Professional discount ■ Visa, Amex
French furniture, sculpture, paintings and objets d'art of the XIX century. Restoration.

TOUPENET, Raymond ■ Stand 6 ■ Tel: 01 40 12 71 77 ■ Fax: 01 47 86 22 00 ■ English spoken ■ Professional discount
Glass, furniture and objets d'art from the period 1900 to 1940.

TOURNIGAND, Valerie ■ Stand 94-95 ■ Tel: 01 40 12 20 17 ■ Fax: 01 40 10 13 08 ■ English spoken
Lighting and decorative objects.

TOURNIGAND, Yvette ■ Stand 34 ■ Tel: 01 40 11 05 55
Lighting.

TRADITION ■ Stand 56 ■ Tel: 01 40 12 66 91
**XVIII century furniture and XIX century paintings.
Qualified expert.**

VERSAILLES ANTIQUES ■Stand 27 ■ 01 49 45 13 43 ■ Fax: 01 49 45 13 29 ■ English and German spoken ■ 20% professional discount ■ Major credit cards
Furniture and objets d'art of the XIX century. Specialist in Sevres.

LES VERRES DE NOS GRANDS-MÈRES ■ Stands 2 and 3 ■ Tel: 01 40 12 72 19 ■ Fax: 01 40 12 65 13
Glass and crystal. Assortment of antique and contemporary glasses, odd lots and complete sets, decanters.

AU VIEUX MOULIN ■ Stand 12 ■ Tel: 01 40 11 11 82
XIX century French and English furniture, objects, chandeliers, pier glasses, office furniture.

WAJCMAN, Robert ■ Stand 132 ■ Tel: 01 40 11 18 63/01 42 54 12 84
XIX century furniture in mahogany and walnut. XVIII and XIX century faience, copper and brass.

ALLÉE 2

Allée 2 is rich in French country furniture and art objects. There are fine examples of armoires from Normandy and Brittany and interesting furniture from old shops, offices, bakeries, pharmacies, architects' offices, libraries and old cafés. There are a few good offerings of good classic Louis XV and Louis XVI furniture as well as lots of good collectibles.

ANGELOU, Dominique ■ Stand 141 ■ Tel: 01 40 12 66 29 ■ Fax: 01 46 07 57 85 ■ English and Spanish spoken ■ Professional discount
XVII and XVIII century furniture and decorative objects.

ATHIAS, Monique ■ Stand 140 ■ Tel: 01 40 12 93 85
Quite a nice collection of Posters.

AU FIL DES TEMPS ■ Stand 161 ■ Telfax: 01 40 11 78 77 ■ Marc and Mme Fèvre speak English ■ Possible professional discount ■ Major credit cards
XVIII to early XIX (1833) century furniture. Also drawings, paintings, lithographs and engravings. Certificates of expertise furnished. Will undertake restoration by confirmed artisans if necessary. Qualified expert.

BLANC, Gérard ■ Stand 160 ■ Tel: 01 40 12 43 75
Old store furniture and curiosities.

BOURIQUET, Jacques ■ Stand 165 ■ Tel: 01 40 10 23 56 ■ English spoken ■ Professional discount
XVIII and XIX century furniture in natural fruit woods, objects of curiosity and paintings.

BOUTELOUP, Huguette ■ Stand 169 ■ Tel: 01 34 87 12 20 ■ English spoken ■ Professional discount
XVIII and XIX century furniture.

BOUTET, Gérard ■ Stand 160bis ■ Tel: 01 40 10 82 50 ■ Professional discount
XVIII and XIX century desks and furniture.

BOYER, Brigitte ■ Stand 176 ■ Tel: 01 40 12 26 49 ■ Fax: 01 47 63 11 86 ■ Amex
Rustic furniture, Murano glass and objets de kitsch.

BRIS, Nicole ■ Stand 175 ■ Tel: 01 40 11 32 80 ■ English spoken ■ Professional discount
Rustic furniture and paintings.

CLAVERIE, Elisabeth ■ Stand 179 ■ Tel: 01 42 59 51 57
Oriental Art.

DANIÈLE B. ■ Stand 146 ■ Tel: 01 40 12 83 59
XVIII and XIX century furniture and decorative objects.

DELAGE, Jean-François ■ Stand 194 bis ■ Tel: 01 40 11 26 09
XVIII and XIX century furniture.

DESCHAMPS, Philippe ■ Stand 144 ■ Tel: 01 40 11 68 93 - Fax: 42 52 78 87 ■ English spoken ■ Professional discount
Regional and Ile de France furniture in natural woods. Objects and accessories for decoration from the XVII, XVIII and XIX century.

DESPRAIRIES, Monique ■ Stand 143 ■ Tel: 01 40 10 94 68 ■ English and Italian spoken ■ Professional discount
XVIII and XIX century regional rustic furniture.

DE RIDDER, Thierry ■ Stand 201 ■ Tel: 01 40 11 28 38
French rustic furniture of the XVIII and XIX centuries.

DOREL-LE SALON DE MUSIQUE ■ Stand 174 ■ Tel: 01 40 12 57 70 ■ Fax: 01 40 53 89 49 ■ English, Spanish and Italian spoken ■ Professional discount for export ■ Amex
Antique musical instruments, lecterns, music stands. Mirrors.

DOUKANE ■ Stand 205 ■ Tel: 01 40 11 59 69 ■ English spoken ■ 30% professional discount ■ Amex
Furniture and mirrors of the XVIII and XIX century.

ENTRE-TEMPS ■ Stand 167/168 ■ Tel: 01 40 10 25 94 ■ Fax: 01 46 37 27 03 ■ E-mail: cdautais@aol.com ■ Catherine Dautais speaks English ■ Professional discount ■ Major credit cards
XVIII and XIX century furniture and decorative objects.

FERRAND, Jean Luc et B. ■ Stands 147/148/153 ■ Tel: 01 49 45 00 97 ■ Fax: 01 41 31 17 38 ■ Cell: 06 08 78 43 37 ■ E-mail: Jean.Luc.F@wanadoo.fr ■ English spoken ■ Professional discount ■ Major credit cards
XVIII century French regional furniture in natural and painted wood.

FRYDE, Aline ■ Stand 145 ■ Tel: 01 40 11 50 39 ■ English spoken ■ Professional discount
Regional furniture of Provence and Lyon, of the XVIII century. Old paintings.

GANTOV, Ernesto ■ Stand 183 ■ Tel: 01 40 12 59 75 ■ Spanish, English and Italian spoken ■ 10% professional discount
Furniture: Directoire, fruit woods and mirrors.

KUSZELEWIC, Henri ■ Stand 177 ■ Tel: 01 40 12 20 63 ■ English spoken ■ Professional discount for export
Library shelves and commodes.

LAMREQUIN ANTIQUITÉS ■ Stand 183bis ■ Tel: 01 40 12 07 71 ■ Italian and Spanish spoken
Antique furniture, paintings, drawings and decorative objects.

LEFÈVRE-BARAT ■ Stand 148bis ■ Tel: 01 40 12 53 82 ■ Blandine Lefèvre speaks English
Small furniture and objets de charme.

LE LAVANDIN ■ Stand 172 ■ Tel: 01 40 10 83 89 ■ Jeanne Godec speaks English
XIX century furniture.

LE MANOIR ■ Stand 187 ■ Tel: 01 46 11 05 46 ■ English spoken ■ Professional discount
XIX century mahogany and rustic furniture.

MARTINEAU-CHERIGUENE, Hélène ■ Stand 171 ■ Tel: 01 34 86 35 16 ■ Professional discount
Old office and shop furniture, bookcases, worktables, filing cabinets.

MATHIVET, Fabien ■ Stand 97 ■ Cell: 06 07 50 38 13 ■ English and Spanish spoken ■ 5% Professional discount
XX century decorative works of art.

MINET, Annie, Mérenda, Luc ■ Stand 62 ■ Tel: 01 30 88 54 55 ■ Fax: 01 30 88 54 04 ■ English and Italian spoken
Furniture and objects from Japan and China. Statuary from Africa and Southeast Asia.

MUSSON, Michel ■ Stand 196 ■ Cell: 06 80 02 14 52 ■ English spoken
Office and marine furniture.

PRÉFÉRENCES ■ Stand 202 ■ Tel: 01 40 11 63 67 ■ Cell: 06 03 51 18 22 ■ Virginie Mazurkiewicz speaks English ■ 20 to 30% professional discount
XVIII and XIX century furniture, jewellery and canes.

RENAUDIE ■ Stand 180 ■ Cell: 06 03 79 97 35 ■ Fax: 01 30 34 47 47 ■ Mme Claude Renaudie speaks English ■ Professional discount
Antique furniture from offices and shops and objects of voyage and curiosity.

REVON, Dominique ■ Stand 203 ■ Tel: 01 40 11 99 49 ■ Fax: 01 40 10 13 08 ■ Dominique Revon speaks English ■ 5 to 10% professional discount
Furniture of the XVII, XVIII and XIX century. Regional furniture and paintings from all periods

ROZETTE ■ Stand 207 ■ Tel: 01 40 10 07 30 ■ English spoken ■ 30% professional discount ■ Amex
French furniture from the end of the XIX century to the beginning of the XX century.

TABLES DU PASSÉ ■ Stand 142 ■ Tel: 01 40 10 00 57 ■ Fax: 01 42 56 38 63 ■ Jean-René d'Ambrosis speaks English ■ Professional discount ■ Visa, Amex
XVIII and XIX century furniture, lamps, objets d'art.

THIEBAUT, Bertrand ■ Stand 173 ■ Tel: 01 40 12 48 85
Antique scientific instruments, marine objects, curiosities.

TREY, Anatol ■ Stand 166 ■ Tel: 01 40 10 01 57 ■ Fax: 01 42 08 35 48 ■ English and Russian spoken
XVIII and XIX century furniture and decorative elements. Expert.

TREY, Boris ■ Stand 163 ■ Tel: 01 40 10 01 57 ■ English, German, Russian, Italian spoken
XIX century painted regional furniture, paintings and objets of curiosity.

UNIL ■ Stand 170 ■ Tel: 01 40 17 59 69 Vincent Brugerie speaks English ■ 20 to 25% professional discount
XIX century furniture.

MARCHÉ CAMBO

This small covered market houses several first class dealers in a pleasant atmosphere. Drop in on your way to the Marché Biron. Hours are: Fri 10:00-12:00, Sat-Sun 10:00-18:00.

ANTIQUITÉS CAMILLE ■ Stand 12 ■ Tel: 01 44 45 91 71 ■ Fax: 01 49 45 91 71 ■ English spoken ■ Professional discount
XVIII and XIX century French furniture.

BADIN, M. J. ■ Stand 14 ■ Telfax: 01 40 86 86 79 ■ English and Spanish spoken ■ Professional discount
Objects of charm and curiosity, XVII, XVIII and XIX century textiles. Faience and silver.

BARTH, Walfredo ■ Stand 20 ■ Tel: 01 49 45 06 56 ■ English, Spanish and Portuguese spoken ■ Professional discount ■ Major credit cards
Ceramics, Art Nouveau and Art deco drawings of the XIX and XX century.

BOUR, Claudine ■ Tel: 01 49 48 04 97 ■ English spoken ■ Professional discount
Furniture and objects of decoration. Antique linens and lace.

BRUGIÈRE, Hubert ■ Stand 32 ■ Tel: 01 40 10 99 45 ■ Fax: 01 56 24 90 33 ■ English spoken ■ Professional discount
Antique arms.

LA BOUTIQUE ■ Tel: 01 40 12 26 21 ■ Fax: 01 40 10 99 16 ■ English, Italian, German and Spanish spoken ■ Professional discount ■ Major credit cards
Objects and furniture of the XIX century. Fountains and objects in marble.

LA CAMPHRIÈRE ■ Tel: 06 09 49 28 41 ■ M. Ratineaud ■ English spoken Professional discount
Rustic furniture of the XVIII and XIX century, bibelots and some paintings.

CHONINGBAUM, Hervé ■ Tel: 01 40 11 44 14 ■ English spoken ■ Major credit cards
Furniture and objects of charm.

DIBA ■ Tel: 06 71 34 06 73 ■ English and Persian spoken ■ Professional discount ■ Major credit cards
Furniture and objects of the XVIII and XIX century

TONELLI, Corinne ■ Tel: 01 40 12 36 53 ■ English spoken
Natural wood furniture and objects of decoration.

FRANZINI, Thierry ■ Stand 1 ■ Tel: 01 40 12 24 84 ■ English spoken
Furniture of the XVIII and XIX century, objets d'art, grandfather clocks candelabra and faience.

GALERIE THÉORÈME ■ Tel: 01 40 12 32 97 ■ Fax: 01 40 15 93 23 ■ Vincent l'Herrou speaks English ■ Professional discount ■ Major credit cards
Furniture and objets d'art of the XVIII century.

GARANJOUD, Patrick ■ Stand 7 ■ Tel: 01 40 11 26 69 ■ Fax: 01 40 11 26 69 ■ English and Italian spoken ■ Professional discount
Furniture, objects and paintings of the XVII, XVIII and XIX century as well as some from the XX century

GREGORIAN, Gérard ■ Tel: 01 60 11 62 79 ■ Isabelle de Valicourt speaks English and Spanish ■ Professional discount
XVI, XVII and XVIII century regional furniture. Expert.

LA MAISON DU ROY ■ Tel: 01 42 99 47 14 ■ Fax: 01 42 61 14 99 ■ Pascal Lemoine speaks English ■ Professional discount
XVIII century furniture and decoration. Paintings.

PETIT, William ■ Tel: 01 45 47 57 05 33 ■ E-mail: w.petit@club-internet.fr ■ English spoken
Musical instruments.

ROBAIN, Guillaume ■ Tel: 01 40 11 14 50 ■ Fax: 01 47 31 13 98 ■ English spoken ■ Professional discount
Furniture and objets d'art.

––––––––––– **MARCHÉ DAUPHINE** –––––––––––

140 rue des Rosiers, 93400 Saint-Ouen ■ Cell: 06 09 48 84 51 ■ Fax: 01 40 10 07 94 ■ Sat 9:00-18:30 ■ Sun 10:00-18:30

A handsome new building, all under glass: it houses 300 stands, from whom the authors have chosen dealers with antiques, art and decorative objects of interest.
This market also displays an overwhelming amount of "brocante" (second-hand) merchandise, but it is well worth the browsing. You never know?

BAS, Deljam G. ■ Stand 34 ■ Telfax: 01 40 10 26 69 ■ E-mail: Dauphine@antika.com ■ English and Persian spoken ■ Professional discount ■ Major credit cards
Carpets, tapestries, embroideries, textiles. Also cleaning and restorations.

A.B.J. CHEMINÉES ■ Stand 105 and 4 rue Lécuyer ■ Tel: 01 40 12 27 17 ■ Fax: 01 40 12 87 44 ■ E-mail: contact@abj-cheminee,com ■ Mr. Dave Bouskila ■ Major credit cards
A selection of antique fireplaces and a few mirrors.

ABSINTHE ■ Stand 228 ■ Cell: 06 82 24 36 35 ■ Mr. Bernardino speaks English, Spanish, Portuguese ■ 20% professional discount
Arts of the table, bibelots, objets d'art and small furniture.

AGESILAS, Corinne ■ Stand 82/83 ■ Tel: 01 40 10 13 64 ■ English spoken ■ Professional discount ■ Amex
Majolica, jugs, Furniture of the XVIII and XIX century.

AMBIANCE ■ Stand 108 ■ Tel: 01 40 10 98 55 ■ Fax: 01 40 12 04 62 ■ Alexis speaks English ■ Professional discount ■ Amex
Nice provincial furniture.

ANNICK TILLY ■ Stand 191/192 ■ Tel: 01 34 50 65 69 ■ Cell: 06 62 12 80 77 ■ English spoken
Publicity posters, chromos, reviews, old papers and children's curiosities.

ANTHAR DE SCHUYTER – LIBRAIRIE ANCIENNE ■ Stand 218 ■ Tel: 01 40 11 17 25 ■ English spoken ■ Professional discount
Old and rare books, original engravings, manuscripts, the paintings of the artist Claude Remusat.

ANTIK DECORS ■ Stand 66 ■ Cell: 06 14 30 30 59 ■ Fax: 01 45 86 55 20 ■ Frank Monsonego speaks English ■ 20 to 30% professional discount ■ Major credit cards
XVII, XVIII and XIX century furniture and paintings.

ANTIQUITÉS DEVOT ■ Stand 138 ■ Telfax: 01 40 11 46 22 ■ Web: www.antiqu itiesdevot.com.fr ■ Professional discount ■ Visa and Eurocard
XVIII and XIX century antiques.

ART-CC ■ Stand 207/212 ■ Telfax: 01 49 48 03 30 ■ Anne Legall ■ English spoken ■ Professional discount ■ Visa
Paintings, watercolours, drawings, lithographs, sculpture and posters. Illustrated books on the beaux arts.

ART-CO ■ Stand 52 ■ Tel: 01 30 34 26 10 ■ Fax: 01 34 70 00 52 ■ E-mail: artco@antiquities-france.com ■ Web: www.antiquities-france.com ■ Philippe Morateur ■ English spoken ■ Professional discount ■ Visa, Amex
Art Deco, decorative objects, paintings of all periods. Also furniture restoration.

ARTCOL ANTIQUITÉS ■ Stand 80 ■ Tel: 01 46 55 17 61 ■ Cell: 06 81 96 67 45 ■ English spoken ■ Professional discount ■ Amex
XVIII and XIX century furniture and objects.

ART ET CUIRS ■ Stand 35/36 ■ Tel: 01 40 11 52 21 ■ English spoken
Furniture and objets d'art of the XVIII and XIX century.

ARIA ■ Stand 51 ■ Tel: 01 40 10 91 78/01 47 22 54 36 ■ English spoken ■ 20% professional discount ■ Major credit cards
XVIII and XIX century paintings, objects for decoration, porcelain, faience and sculpture.

ATTANASIO ■ Stand 124 ■ Tel: 01 49 45 03 80 ■ Fax: 01 48 72 93 32 English spoken
Paintings of the XVII, XVIII and XIX century. Modern paintings up until 1940.

AU BONHEUR DU JOUR ■ Stand 11 ■ Tel: 01 40 11 64 30 ■ English spoken ■ 10 to 15% professional discount
Collectible photographs of the XIX and XX centuries.

AU PETIT LOUVRE ■ Stand 84 ■ Cell: 06 10 01 88 82 ■ Farhad Semsari ■ Professional discount ■ Major credit cards
Tapestries, Aubusson and all sorts of carpets. Cleaning and restoration.

AU SOURIRE D'ARIANE ■ Stand 135 to 139 ■ Tel: 01 40 12 23 84 ■ Cell: 06 14 46 14 43 ■ Fax: 01 40 12 23 84 ■ Jean-Pierre Timsit, Mlle Khattari ■ English, Spanish, Italian and Arabic spoken ■ 15% professional discount ■ Major credit cards
XVII, XVIII and XIX century paintings. Modern paintings and objets de vitrine from the far east.

AXANA ■ Stand 45 ■ Tel: 01 40 12 87 77 ■ Mme Moryoussef ■ A little English ■ Professional discount ■ Visa.
Art Nouveau, Art Deco.

BAILLY ■ Stand 217 ■ Cell: 06 60 42 48 67 ■ E-mail: librairiebailly@wanadoo.fr ■ Italian and English spoken ■ Professional discount
Engravings and rare books. Religious items.

BALLESTEROS ■ Stand 188 ■ Tel: 01 49 45 92 62 ■ English and Spanish spoken ■ Professional discount ■ Major credit cards
XIX century and Modern paintings.

BAUER ■ Stand 130 ■ Tel: 01 46 07 67 47 ■ English and Spanish spoken
Old rare books and documents.

BEAUVAL ANTIQUITÉS ■ Stand 68 ■ Tel: 01 40 11 70 81 ■ Meneval Sixti ■ English spoken
Old paintings and small furniture.

BLONDEL COTTREAU ■ Stand 4/5 ■ Tel: 01 40 11 72 71 ■ Major credit cards
Rustic decorations.

BOUCAUD DIODORE ■ Stand 122 ■ Tel: 01 43 42 90 82 ■ Cell: 06 03 96 28 20 ■ Professional discount
Furniture and objets d'art of the XVIII and XIX century.

BOUKORTT ■ Stand 200 ■ Tel: 01 49 45 19 96 ■ Italian spoken ■ Visa, MC
Paintings of the XIX and XX century. Bibelots, jewellery, crystal of Baccarat, Daum.

BOULLOCHE, Laurent ■ Stand 18 ■ Cell: 06 11 27 23 45 ■ Fax: 01 42 19 93 72 ■ Charles Boulloche
Old repainted furniture.

BOUTAL, David ■ Stand 239 ■ Cell: 06 62 19 66 04 ■ E-mail: marjo@wanadoo.fr ■ English spoken
Porcelain and faience, Quimper, Limoges. Tôle, enamels, jugs and bibelots.

BOUTIQUE LYDIA ■ Stand 101 ■ Tel 01 40 11 49 51 ■ Fax: 01 44 92 01 11 ■ Lydia Chapellier ■ Professional discount ■ Major credit cards
Antique dresses, hats, fantasy jewellery, accessories: all from 1900 to 1970. Some old furs, handbags and accessories from Hermès, Dior and Chanel.

BRIS, Patrick ■ Stand 154 ■ Telfax: 01 47 81 55 52 ■ E-mail: brispat@club-internet.fr ■ English spoken ■ Professional discount ■ Major credit cards
XIX century furniture.

BROCANT'HEURE ■ Stand 233 ■ Tel: 01 40 12 27 02 ■ Fax: 01 40 12 27 02 ■ Romain Rea ■ English spoken ■ Visa, MC
Second-hand watches and bracelets, collectible lighters.

BRUNEAU, Philippe ■ Stand 219 ■ No telephone
Second-hand objects. Some XIX century furniture.

BUFFETEAU, Bertrand ■ Stand 19 Cell: 06 62 04 86 47 ■ English and Spanish spoken
Objects for decoration and utility.

BUZARE, Hélène ■ Stand 133 ■ Tel: 01 49 45 03 63 ■ Fax: 01 45 45 52 05 ■ English spoken ■ Professional discount ■ Major credit cards
XVIII and XIX century furniture, objects, paintings, porcelain and lamps.

CENTAURE ■ Stand 112/113 ■ Tel: 01 40 12 83 93 ■ Fax: 01 40 12 38 93 ■ English spoken ■ professional discount ■ Visa, Amex
Bronzes: very interesting.

CARMEILLE-BAGEAUX ■ Stand 265 ■ Tel: 01 43 49 02 23 ■ Fax: 01 43 49 28 41 Stephane Carmeille ■ Italian spoken
Furniture, objects and paintings from the XIX century to 1925

CHARLES, Jean-Claude ■ Stand 64bis ■ Cell: 06 14 03 06 96 ■ Professional discount
Furniture, lighting and curtains from the XIX century to the 1950s.

DESCHUWER, Jean-Marie ■ Stand 37 ■ English and German spoken ■ Professional discount ■ Major credit cards
Paintings and furniture from the XIX century. Antique pianos.

DAUPHINE 57 ■ Stand 57 ■ Tel: 01 40 12 61 44 ■ Fax: 01 34 48 97 90 ■ Web: www.chez.com/dauphine57/ ■ Mr. Dudek ■ English and Spanish spoken ■ Major credit cards
Furniture and paintings of the XVIII and XIX centuries. Cut crystal and Porcelain de Sèvres.

JOËLE DECOOL ■ Stand 147 ■ Tel: 01 40 11 48 64 ■ Fax: 01 46 47 82 09 ■ English and Spanish spoken ■ Prices high ■ Professional discount
Biedermeier furniture from northern Europe, Denmark, Sweden and Russia.

DIAMANTINA ■ Stand 98 ■ Tel: 01 40 12 71 79 ■ Fax: 01 42 78 76 69 ■ English spoken ■ Professional discount ■ Major credit cards
Antique and second-hand jewellery and some paintings.

EISENBERG, Henri (OPUS 31) ■ Stand 31 ■ Tel: 01 40 11 65 67 ■ English, Hebrew, Arabic and German spoken ■ Major credit cards
Paintings and drawings of Henri Eisenberg, portraits and restoration of paintings.

EMMANUEL, Boo ■ Stand 30 ■ Cell: 06 14 53 80 43 ■ Fax: 01 42 62 09 49 ■ English and Spanish spoken ■ 10% professional discount ■ CB
Paintings and Orientalist objects.

EXOTIC KALAGAS ■ Stands 224/225/230/231 ■ Tel: 01 40 12 86 28 ■ Fax: 01 40 35 42 43 ■ Edith Bodart speaks English, Portuguese, Spanish and Italian ■ Major credit cards
Furniture and architectural pieces. Jade from the Far East.

FEUGÈRE, Stand 91 ■ Tel: 01 40 12 93 50 ■ Fax: 01 40 10 07 84 ■ English spoken ■ Professional discount ■ Amex
Impressionist paintings. Paintings of the Barbizon School, Furniture of the XVIII and XIX century.

FIDALGO ■ Stand 205 ■ Tel: 01 40 10 03 62 ■ English, Spanish and Portuguese spoken ■ Professional discount ■ Major credit cards
Silver and antique jewellery.

FISCHER, Danielle ■ Stand 109 ■ Tel: 01 40 10 01 55 ■ Fax: 01 43 20 02 07 ■ English and Spanish spoken ■ Professional discount
Bibelots and objets de vitrine.

FLAJSZER, Céline ■ Stand 73 ■ Tel: 01 40 11 36 49 ■ Cell: 06 09 65 17 11 ■ English and German spoken ■ Professional discount ■ Major credit cards
Objects, bibelots, glass, antique jewellery, paintings and ceramics.

FRANCE-ASIE TRADING ■ Stand 22 ■ Tel: 01 40 12 85 50 ■ Fax: 01 40 12 69 78 ■ Professional discount
Natural wood furniture from Asia.

FRENKIEL, Eric ■ Stand 141 ■ Telfax: 01 40 12 77 83 ■ English and Italian spoken ■ Professional discount ■ Major credit cards
Rustic furniture from the XV and XVI centuries.

GALERIE ESMERALDA ■ Stand 126 ■ Tel: 01 40 11 54 37 ■ Dominique Boutard ■ English spoken ■ Professional discount ■ Major credit cards
He calls himself a "Generalist" Take your chances.

GALERIE MUZE ■ Stand 202 ■ Tel: 01 43 32 55 25 ■ Fax: 01 43 32 04 01 ■ E-mail: muze@antikita.com ■ Web: www.antikita.com ■ Mr. Zehmour ■ Visa, Amex
Judaica, Popular Jewish art, paintings, objects books, documents.

GALERIE OREA-VALSYRA ■ Stand 87 ■ Tel: 01 49 45 98 35 ■ Fax: 01 69 52 25 62 ■ Cell: 06 10 35 62 73 ■ English spoken ■ Professional discount ■ Major credit cards
Enamels from 1875 to 1930. Art Deco furniture.

GERMANO, Monique ■ Stand 240 ■ Tel: 01 40 12 95 29 ■ English and German spoken ■ 20 to 30% professional discount ■ Major credit cards
Objects in tôle and enamel. Antique faience, collectible writing objects, small antique office furniture.

GIRAUD, Dominique ■ Stand 183/184 ■ Tel: 01 49 45 94 61 ■ Fax: 01 40 41 02 97 ■ English spoken ■ Professional discount ■ Visa
Furniture, mirrors of the 1930s and 1940s, chairs and sofas of 1930 to 1940.

GOAS, Annick ■ Stand 220 ■ Tel: 01 40 10 11 95 ■ English and Spanish spoken ■ Major credit cards
Tribal art, ethnic jewellery from Indonesia and the Himalayan countries.

JALLIER, Alain ■ Stands 39/138/140 ■ Tel: 01 40 11 38 07/01 34 66 23 21 ■ English spoken ■ Visa, Amex
XVII, XVIII and XIX century furniture, paintings and objets d'art.

JAMIN, Laurent ■ Stand 14 ■ Tel: 01 40 11 46 28 ■ English spoken ■ Professional discount ■ All except Amex
XVIII, XIX and XX century furniture, bibelots, paintings and clocks.

JANE DE LIVRON ■ Stand 270 ■ Tel: 01 42 60 17 79 ■ Shop: 01 40 11 26 88 ■ English and Spanish spoken
Boxes, display objects, silver and plated wares. Collectible antiques.

KASHANI, S. Afsari ■ Stand 7/8 ■ Cell: 06 80 57 06 53 ■ English spoken ■ Major credit cards
Carpets and tapestries.

KLEIN, Michel **"HAUTE EPOQUE"** ■ Stand 131 ■ Tel: 01 40 11 58 51 ■ Fax: 01 42 72 18 14 ■ English and Spanish spoken ■ Professional discount ■ Amex
Furniture, objets d'art, decoration of the Haute Epoque, the Middle Ages, the Renaissance and the XVII century. Certificate of authenticity for each purchase. Expert.

L'ADJOLATE ■ Stand 114 ■ Telfax: 01 40 10 10 86 ■ Cell: 06 09 48 27 86 ■ Laurence Vauclair ■ Professional discount ■ Major credit cards
Majolica, porcelain, Meissen, jugs.

LALEY, Nadia Chanaz ■ Stand 110/111 ■ Tel: 01 40 20 99 25 ■ Fax: 01 43 86 17 56 ■ English, Italian and Arabic spoken ■ Professional discount ■ Major credit cards
French and Italian objects and furniture of the XVII and XVIII century.

LA SOURCE DU SAVOIR ■ Stand 216 ■ Tel: 01 43 55 95 32 ■ English spoken
Old books and phonograph records.

LAZAROVICI, Bernard ■ Stand 43 ■ Tel: 01 40 10 00 45 ■ English spoken ■ Professional discount ■ Major credit cards
Old engravings, estampes, original lithographs of the period 1863 to 1934, especially of the caricaturist SEM.

LEFÈVRE, Valérie ■ Stand 238 ■ Cell: 06 12 56 77 72 ■ English spoken
Faience, objets d'art of the period of Napoleon III.

LEROUX, Thierry ■ Stand 201 ■ Tel: 01 40 11 02 13 ■ English spoken ■ Major credit cards
Publicity posters from bistros, toys, lighting, linens.

LIBRAIRIE GALERIE ORIENTALE ■ Stand 189 ■ Cell: 06 03 82 87 78 ■ Arabic and Berber spoken ■ 20% professional discount ■ Major credit cards
Books and prints of North Africa and the Middle East.

LIBRAIRIE LUC MONOD ■ Stand 195 ■ Tel 01 46 33 57 57 ■ Fax: 01 46 33 19 84 ■ German, English, Russian and Italian spoken
Illustrated books of the 1920s, books on artists, photographs and books on photography.

LES COLLECTIONEURS ■ Stand 100 ■ Tel: 01 40 12 85 63 ■ English spoken ■ Professional discount ■ Major credit cards
Antique watches.

LE COURBARIL ■ Stand 156 ■ Tel 01 40 10 05 51 ■ English spoken ■ Major credit cards
Antiques, paintings and objets d'art.

LEDA DÉCORS ■ Stands 60-61 ■ Tel: 01 40 12 74 88 ■ Fax: 01 40 12 23 33 ■ English, German and Italian spoken ■ 20 to 35% professional discount ■ Visa, Amex
XVIII and XIX century furniture, tapestries and chairs. Gilded mirrors, decorative objects, tole, lighting.

LE PRÊTRE, Gérard ■ Stand 187 ■ Cell: 06 85 95 98 59 ■ Fax: 01 40 09 80 69 ■ English and Italian spoken ■ Professional discount
Bistro furniture, objects from the Black Forest and hunting memorabilia.

LE PRINCE ■ Stand 76 ■ Tel: 01 40 10 02 71 ■ Fax: 01 47 46 12 54 ■ English and Persian spoken ■ Professional discount ■ Major credit cards
Carpets and tapestries.

L'IRE DE L'ÊTRE ■ Stand 208/213 ■ Telfax: 01 40 10 02 38 ■ Jacques Desse ■ English spoken ■ Professional discount ■ Major credit cards
Old and rare books, illustrated books and engravings.

LONGUEVILLE, Daniel ■ Stand 79 ■ Cell: 06 60 74 82 12 ■ Tel: 01 39 62 09 96 ■ English spoken ■ Professional discount
XVIII and XIX century furniture, objects and paintings. Also mirrors, chandeliers. Restoration of furniture.

LUC B ■ Stand 149/150 ■ Tel 01 40 12 89 80 ■ Luc Bouveret ■ English spoken ■ 15 to 20% professional discount ■ Visa
XVIII and XIX century furniture.

MAE ■ Stand 44 ■ Tel 01 49 45 06 04 ■ Fax: 01 39 18 02 98 ■ English spoken ■ Visa, MC
XIX century paintings, sculpture, furniture and objets d'art.

MAJ ANTIQUITÉS ■ Stand 32 ■ Tel: 01 40 12 62 14 ■ English spoken ■ Professional discount ■ Major credit cards
Faience and bibelots.

MARLIN, Marie-Thérèse ■ Stand 248 ■ Tel: 01 40 27 48 39 ■ English spoken
French faience of the XIX century and early XX century. Art Deco ceramics, Quimper.

MARTIN, Michel ■ Stand 184 ■ Tel: 04 40 11 54 61 ■ Fax: 04 67 43 94 55 ■ English and Italian spoken ■ Professional discount
Marine objects and scientific instruments.

MARTINEL, Marie-José ■ Stand 15 ■ Tel: 01 40 11 46 28 ■ English spoken ■ Professional discount ■ Major credit cards.
XIX and XX century furniture, bibelots and paintings.

MAUDUY, David ■ Stand 206 ■ Tel: 01 42 55 35 89 ■ English, Spanish and Italian spoken ■ 30% professional discount
A mixed bag of furniture, paintings and objects from various periods.

MÉLANCOLIE ■ Stand 123 ■ Tel: 01 45 54 12 82 ■ Cell: 06 13 52 22 55 ■ English spoken ■ Professional discount
XVIII and XIX century furniture and objets d'art.

MORIN ■ Stand 194 ■ Cell: 06 82 33 39 40 ■ Emmanuelle Morin ■ English spoken
Old and rare books, many illustrated.

NICOLEVY ■ Stand 159 ■ Tel: 01 43 71 42 30 ■ Mr. Teddy Sitbon ■ English and Arabic spoken ■ Professional discount ■ Amex
Paintings from the late XIX century to early XX century from North Africa and former French colonies.

OUAISS DAUPHINE ■ Stand 104 ■ Tel: 01 40 11 18 38 ■ E-mail: houaiss@teaser.fr ■ English and Spanish spoken ■ Professional discount ■ Major credit cards
Prestigious watches for the collector.

PAGEZY ■ Stand 264 ■ Cell: 06 81 76 11 13 ■ English spoken ■ Amex
XVIII and XIX century furniture and objets d'art.

PARSA ■ Stand 120/121 ■ Cell: 06 07 73 14 09 ■ Tel: 01 48 55 87 09 ■ English spoken ■ 10 to 20% professional discount
Specialist in sofas and club-chairs of 1880 to 1950.

PEARCE, John ■ Stand 267 ■ Tel: 01 40 12 74 87 ■ English spoken ■ Professional discount ■ Major credit cards
Marine furniture, suitcases, sports articles, navigable model sail boats.

PRESENTS PASSÉS ■ Stand 23 ■ Tel: 01 40 12 87 36 ■ Fax: 01 40 24 22 76 ■ Isabelle Malevy ■ English spoken ■ Amex
Antique tools, popular art.

PRESTIGE ■ Stand 56 ■ Tel: 01 40 11 14 64 ■ Fax: 01 43 87 53 32 ■ Cell: 06 11 68 68 11 ■ English and Spanish spoken ■ Professional discount ■ Major credit cards
Tapestries and antique textiles, embroideries, curtains and trimmings.

RAPHAELE, Arnoux ■ Stand 73 ■ Cell: 06 13 57 58 55 ■ English spoken
XIX century wood and leather furniture.

RASPAIL, Richard ■ Stand 68/79 ■ Tel: 01 40 12 78 49 ■ English spoken ■ Amex
Decorative objects and furniture of different periods.

REDIER, Hélène ■ Stand 85 ■ Tel: 01 40 11 17 72 ■ Major credit cards
French and Russian silver and antique jewellery.

RICCI, Jean ■ Stand 16 ■ Tel: 01 40 12 32 10 ■ Cell: 06 07 45 17 06
Old collectible watches.

RODELET ■ Stand 197 ■ Tel: 01 40 11 27 00 ■ Fax: 01 44 91 99 15 ■ English spoken
Autographs, ancient documents, parchments and objects of curiosity.

ROY ANTIQUITÉS ■ Stand 38 ■ Cell: 06 11 64 80 23 ■ Tel: 05 49 44 90 64 ■ Fax: 05 49 47 31 71 ■ English spoken
Furniture, paintings, objets d'art of the XVII, XVIII and XIX century.

SAINSÈRE, Jacqueline ■ Stand 203/204 ■ Tel: 01 40 12 42 36 ■ English spoken ■ Professional discount ■ Amex
Decorative objects, faience, porcelain, inkwells, curiosities, paintings, books, painted furniture of the XVIII, XIX and early XX century.

SARFATI, Marie-Paule ■ Stand 39 ■ Tel: 01 40 11 28 07/01 40 11 26 48 ■ English spoken ■ 20% professional discount ■ Major credit cards
XVIII century to 1930 furniture.

SCHWARTZ, Denyse ■ Stand 24/25 ■ Tel: 01 49 45 14 36 ■ Major credit cards
Antique linens and collectible clothes from the 1940s to the 1950s.

SFEZ ■ Stand 175 ■ Tel: 01 49 45 16 03
Gilding on wood and porcelain.

SHANAZ ■ Stand 12 ■ Tel: 01 40 1139 70 ■ Charlotte Chavanne ■ English spoken ■ Professional discount ■ All bank cards
XVIII century armoires and tables. All kinds of furniture restorations.

SOLEIL NOIR ■ Stand 58/59 ■ Tel: 01 40 12 74 09 ■ Rodolphe Perret ■ English spoken ■ Professional discount ■ Amex
Arts and archaeology of Egypt and Asia: Han, Tang, Ming. XVIII and XIX century Chinese and Japanese furniture, Indian and Thai sculpture from the XI to the XVI century.

SOPHIA ■ Stand 28/29 ■ Cell: 06 09 69 42 98 ■ Tel: 01 40 12 55 84 ■ English spoken ■ Professional discount ■ Major credit cards
XVIII and XIX century paintings, decorations and furniture.

SOURICE, Benilde ■ Stand 42 ■ Tel: 01 40 12 88 00 ■ Fax: 01 46 82 66 74 ■ Professional discount ■ Major credit cards
Mirrors, boxes, furniture, paintings, faiences and bronzes.

TCHINE TCHINE ■ Stand 235/236 ■ Tel: 01 40 10 15 41 ■ Patrick Guay ■ English and Spanish spoken ■ Professional discount ■ All except Amex
Fabrics and dishes of all periods.

TURLAN, Philippe ■ Stand 86 ■ Tel: 01 40 12 28 92 ■ Fax: 01 45 89 50 21
Second-hand furniture and objects.

ULUG, UMUT ■ Stand 223/229 ■ Tel 01 40 11 92 21 ■ Fax: 01 69 24 52 88 ■ English spoken ■ 30% professional discount ■ Major credit cards
Kilims from Turkey, the Caucasus and Iran. Fabrics, artisanal furniture.

URDA ■ Stand 266 ■ Cell: 06 80 03 28 03 ■ Web: www.curiosite1/saint_ouen/urda.htm ■ English spoken ■ Professional discount ■ Amex
Art Deco furniture, paintings and drawings.

VENS ■ Stand 130/140 ■ Tel: 01 40 11 32 97 ■ English and Spanish spoken ■ Professional discount for export
Antiques from various periods, furniture, bronzes, paintings and clocks.

VISION ■ Stand 69 ■ Tel: 01 40 11 19 95 ■ Fax: 01 40 11 39 95 ■ M. Bonnefille ■ English spoken ■ Professional discount
Furniture and objects from China.

ZEITUN, Guy ■ Stand 89 ■ Cell: 06 08 74 30 78 ■ Tel: 01 49 48 03 32 ■ E-mail: ludovicz@yahoo.fr ■ Italian, English and Spanish spoken ■ Professional discount ■ Major credit cards
Old paintings, including some from the Impressionist period and Old Masters from the XVIII and XIX centuries. Some from the early XX century, Impressionists and the Barbizon School.

ZOMOURI ■ Stand 3 ■ Cell: 06 80 35 70 87 ■ Professional discount
Carpets and tapestries.

────────── MARCHÉ MALASSIS ──────────

142 rue des Rosiers ■ Tel: 0140 12 06 87 ■ Fax: 01 40 12 10 69

A handsome modern building with its own parking facility in the basement. Fully equipped with escalators, coffee bars and excellent lighting, the market displays a broad mix of the better stuff and the amusing. A few of the merchants with well-defined specialties deserve a visit. It is not of the quality level of some of the other markets.

ANT 17 ■ Stand 170 ■ Tel: 01 40 11 47 27 ■ English spoken ■ 15 to 20% professional discount
Antique furniture and paintings.

ANTIC HIER ■ Stand 231 ■ Cell: 06 61 81 24 38 ■ Elizabeth Benathau speaks English ■ 10% professional discount
Jewellery and objets de vitrine.

CHARAFZADAH ■ Cell: 06 13 61 43 79 ■ M. Soltani
Carpets, tapestries and objets d'art.

EN PASSANT PAR LÀ ■ Stand 175 ■ Cell: 06 10 80 05 18 ■ Mme Chatry ■ A bit of English and German ■ 10% professional discount for export
Small furniture, objects, bibelots, paintings, engravings, drawings of the XIX and XX centuries. Framing and replating.

GALERIE MAXIMILIEN ■ Stand 100 ■ Tel: 01 40 12 02 82 ■ M. Movenaud ■ English spoken ■ Visa, Amex
Paintings and furniture of the XVIII and XIX century, glass and chairs.

GHISLAIN ANTIQUE ■ Cell: 06 09 09 41 13 ■ Fax: 01 42 50 14 68 ■ English spoken ■ 15% professional discount
Tapestries of the XVII to the XIX century. Furniture in natural wood. Objects of decoration and club-chairs.

HETEAU, Pierre ■ Stand 56 to 58 ■ Tel: 01 40 87 05 79
Second-hand furniture.

L'ACANTHE ■ Stand 147/148 ■ Cell: 06 09 62 39 25 ■ Frédéric Juven ■ English and Italian spoken ■ Professional discount
Furniture in the provincial style, some of it painted, some patinated. Decorative objects.

LA BOUTIQUE ■ Stand 183 ■ Tel: 01 40 11 24 13 ■ English and Portuguese spoken ■ Professional discount ■ Major credit cards
Furniture for decoration and marble statuary.

LIBRAIRIE BOULOUIZ-FEREZ ■ Stand 235 ■ Tel: 01 40 11 49 21 ■ Fax: 01 40 35 66 17 ■ M. Boulouiz speaks English ■ Professional discount
Books old and new as well as documents dealing with the beaux-arts and travel. Books on the Middle East, Egypt.

L'HOMME DE PLUME ■ Stand 211 and 213 ■ Tel: 01 40 11 49 33 ■ Fax: 01 42 04 12 73 ■ Françoise Leray speaks English ■ 20% professional discount for export ■ Major credit cards
PENS, PENS, PENS.

LUDLOW ■ Stand 206 ■ Cell: 06 84 68 55 07 ■ Marine Garnier ■ English and Spanish spoken ■ Professional discount
Furniture from the 1950s to the 1970s.

MERCIER, Patrice ■ Stand 229 ■ Cell: 06 60 02 07 35 ■ Fax: 01 45 48 13 47 ■ English spoken ■ 20% professional discount
French furniture of the XVIII and early XIX century and objets d'art.

MEYER, Laurence ■ Stand 213 ■ Cell: 06 60 05 61 82 ■ English spoken
Antiques and second-hand. Some furniture, paintings and objects of the XVIII and XIX century

NOURT ■ Stand 138 to 141 ■ Tel: 01 40 11 85 66 ■ Cell: 06 11 71 48 40 ■ Gérard Nourt speaks English ■ Major credit cards
Carpets, tapestries and embroideries of the XVII, XVIII and XIX century

PEDEZERT ■ Stand 48 ■ Tel: 01 40 12 84 01 ■ Maryse Pedezert speaks English ■ Professional discount ■ Major credit cards
Furniture, lighting and paintings of the XIX century. Decoration.

RAFFIER, Colette ■ Stand 168 ■ Tel: 01 49 45 18 87 ■ 10 to 20% professional discount
XVIII and XIX century furniture and objets d'art.

RONDEURS DES JOURS ■ Stands 59 and 60 ■ Tel: 01 40 11 48 98 ■ Jean Dreyfus speaks English ■ Professional discount ■ Visa, Amex
Palissyware, majolica, ceramics from Provence and curiosities.

——————— MARCHÉ PAUL BERT ———————

104 rue des Rosiers and 18 rue Paul-Bert, 93400 Saint-Ouen

The Marché Paul Bert is one of the largest and the most typical of the Paris Flea Markets. With over 200 shops covering every imaginable specialty, it has become a favourite shopping mall for professionals from all over the world. The dealers of the Paul Bert are good negotiators, but the quality of their wares certainly deserves hard bargaining from both buyers and sellers. Much of the market is outdoors so summertime browsing becomes a real pleasure.

ANDRÉ, Jean-Jacques ■ Stand 147 ■ Tel: 01 40 11 26 10 ■ English and Spanish spoken ■ Professional discount
Objects of character, silver, curiosities of all periods.

STÉ AUVERNOISE DECORATION ■ Stands 58ter/101/163/176 ■ Tel: 01 60 80 34 45 ■ Fax: 01 60 80 41 97 ■ English spoken
Decoration, wrought iron mirrors, lighting and painted furniture.

BACHELIER ANTIQUITÉS ■ Stand 17 ■ Tel: 01 40 11 89 98 ■ Fax: 01 40 11 72 08 ■ E-mail: Bachelier.antiquites@wamadoo.fr ■ www.Bachelier.antiquites.com ■ English spoken ■ Professional discount ■ Amex,Visa
Kitchen objects, wine objects, potteries from the southwest, Provence, Alsace, Savoie, wicker-work and baskets. Old shop furniture and rustic furniture.

BARGHEERA ■ Stand 127 ■ Tel: 01 40 11 37 69 ■ E.Guillon, Manager ■ English spoken ■ Professional discount ■ CB accepted
Art and decoration of the XX century.

BELAYCH, Christian ■ Stand 129 ■ Tel: 01 40 11 68 99/01 45 00 44 96 ■ Fax: 01 45 00 70 27 ■ English spoken ■ Professional discount
XVIII and XIX century furniture and some paintings.

BERTRAN, Michel ■ Stand 132 ■ Tel: 02 35 98 24 06 ■ Fax: 02 35 88 75 20 ■ English spoken
Impressionist paintings, furniture, bibelots and curiosities.

BLOENAU, Wolfgang ■ Stand 257 ■ Allée 5 ■ Tel: 01 40 11 91 14 ■ English, German, Italian and Spanish spoken
Engravings of the XVII, XVIII and XIX century. Small furniture of the XVIII and XIX century. Instant photographs on request.

CARPENTIER ■ Stand 11, 19 ■ Tel: 06 09 69 22 96 ■ Fax: 01 45 22 53 16 ■ E-mail: antiqu@club-internet.fr ■ English spoken
Decorative objects and lighting.

CHEZ DANY ■ Stand 105 ■ Tel: 01 40 11 13 60 ■ English spoken ■ Professional discount
Lighting, chandeliers and bibelots of the XIX century.

DAGOMMER, Chantal ■ Stand 71 ■ Tel: 01 40 11 09 29 ■ English spoken ■ 15% professional discount
Antique textiles, costumes and collectible dolls.

DEBOSCKER, Olivier ■ Stand 204bis, Allée 5 ■ Tel: 01 43 26 76 24 ■ Fax: 01 53 36 71 85 ■ English spoken
Decorative objects.

DECO-BISTRO ■ Stand 87, Allée 6 ■ Tel: 03 85 32 10 52 ■ Fax: 03 85 51 36 21 ■ Jean-Luc Perrier ■ English spoken
Bistro furniture. Restorations.

DELIGNY, Sophie ■ Stand 406, Allée 7 ■ Cell: 06 08 98 10 72 ■ Fax: 05 45 29 08 97 ■ English spoken
Fireplaces, fountains, elements of decoration, ornaments in stone, marble and terracotta.

DES TEMPS EN TEMPS ■ Stand 119 ■ Tel: 01 40 11 00 51 ■ Fax: 01 49 53 95 92 ■ Pierre Guerraz ■ English and Spanish spoken ■ Professional discount ■ Credit cards accepted
Curiosities, paintings, faience, small furniture.

FOUCHARD ■ Stand 232, Allée 6 ■ Tel: 01 40 12 76 69 ■ English spoken
Wrought iron beds, lamps of the XIX century.

GAIGNON, Christophe ■ Stand 169, Allée 3 ■ Tel: 01 39 97 77 03 ■ Fax: 01 39 97 58 02 ■ English spoken ■ Professional discount ■ Major credit cards
XVIII, XIX and XX century country furniture of good quality. Lighting.

GALERIE DREVET ■ Stand 214, Allée 5 ■ Tel: 01 40 11 91 14 ■ Fax: 01 42 54 74 69
Chandeliers, beds, small furniture of the XVIII and XIX century.

GIL D'ART ■ Stand 43, Allée 1 ■ Cell: 06 12 21 11 27 ■ English spoken ■ 20% professional discount
Art Deco of 1930 to the 1950s.

GRIZOT, Cyril & Marie ■ Stand 216, Allée 5 ■ Tel: 01 40 10 82 13 ■ Fax: 01 46 40 15 03 ■ English spoken
Furniture and decorative objects from the 1930s to the 1970s.

JACQUELIN, Marie-Noëlle ■ Stand 198, Allée 5 ■ Tel: 01 40 19 88 31 ■ English and Spanish spoken
Objects, curiosities and collectibles.

JALLOT, **Perle** and **BERNARD**, Jane ■ Stand 32 ■ Tel: 01 49 45 14 85 ■ English and Spanish spoken
Antique textiles. Wood sculpture and gilding.

KERDRAIN, Emmanuelle and **Lionel** ■ Stand 115 ■ Tel: 01 39 50 64 22 ■ Fax: 01 30 21 59 51 ■ English spoken ■ Professional discount ■ MC
Furniture and objects of the XVIII century. Clocks and objects of decoration.

KRAMER, Nicole ■ Stand 202, Allée 5 ■ Tel: 01 40 12 73 16 ■ English and Spanish spoken ■ Professional discount ■ Major credit cards
Objets de vitrine, boxes, miniatures, historic collectibles and antique eyeglasses.

LABERGÈRE, Remy ■ Stand 242, Allée 6 ■ Cell: 06 84 20 11 37 ■ Professional discount
Furniture and objects from the end of the XVIII century and beginning of the XIX. Toiles de Jouy, papers.

LENTZ ■ Stand 237, Allée 5 ■ Cell: 06 07 35 99 19 ■ English spoken
Antiquities and XX century decorative objects.

MAISON MARC ■ Stand 83, Allée 6 ■ Cell: 06 60 62 61 80 ■ Fax: 01 40 12 26 47 ■ E-mail: marcmaison@easynet.fr ■ www.marcmaison.com ■ English spoken
Garden antiques and architectural antique elements.

MAUMY, Nicole ■ Stand 99 ■ Tel: 01 40 11 15 17
Objects of curiosity, silver and glass.

MATTERN, Charles ■ Stand 404 ■ Allée 7 ■ Telfax: 01 43 66 45 14 ■ English and German spoken ■ Professional discount ■ Major credit cards
Terracotta jars and ornaments. Decorative objects.

"PAPILLON" ■ Stand 172 ■ Tel: 01 40 11 17 22 ■ English and Italian spoken ■ Professional discount
Antique dolls, doll houses, doll clothes, old teddy bears and other stuffed animals. Old cinema photographs, some autographed.

PERACHES, Michel ■ Stand 21 ■ Tel: 01 40 12 30 05 ■ Professional discount ■ Major credit cards
Antiquities, curiosities and decoration.

PFENNIGER, Marie-Claude ■ Stand 15 ■ Tel: 01 40 12 36 90 ■ English spoken
Decorative objects, bamboo furniture, bathroom furniture, lighting, fireplace accessories.

RENAUD, Geoffrey ■ Stand 108 ■ Tel: 01 40 12 26 54 ■ Fax: 01 45 53 12 50 ■ E-mail: anne.deconnincki@universal.fr ■ English spoken ■Professional discount ■ Amex, Visa
Decorative arts of the XX century, art deco. Design service.

REYNAUD, Martine ■ Stand 247 ■ Tel: 01 40 12 28 40
Furniture and French pop-art objects, wrought iron and curiosities.

SCHWEIZER, Lisette et Henri ■ Stand 217 ■ Tel: 01 40 12 47 34 ■ German and Italian spoken ■ Professional discount
Lighting and furniture of 1900 to 1950s, objects for decoration.

TEISSIER, Renaud ■ Stand 286 ■ Tel: 01 30 95 74 05 ■ English spoken ■ 20% professional discount
Military antiques and collectibles, bibelots, post cards, antique instruments.

THÈMES ■ Stand 402/416 ■ Telfax: 01 40 11 33 01 ■ Andre Hayat ■ English spoken ■ Major credit cards
Art Deco furniture 1930 to 1940.

USANDIVARAS, Norma ■ Stand 325 ■ Cell: 06 12 99 98 71 ■ Fax: 01 40 12 67 13 ■ Spanish spoken ■ Professional discount
XVIII century furniture and objects.

VALLI ■ Stand 149, Allée 3 ■ Tel: 01 49 48 04 65 ■ English spoken
Industrial furniture and art. Curiosities.

VALLI, Luc ■ Stand 236, Allée 6 ■ Cell: 06 07 59 59 44 ■ English spoken
Furniture and decorations.

———————— **MARCHÉ SERPETTE** ————————

110 rue des Rosiers, 93400 Saint-Ouen ■ Tel: 01 40 11 54 14

The Marché Serpette is not only one of the most fascinating markets in the Puces, but the most accessible by car. There is a rooftop parking lot and the market is just down a winding staircase.
The Marché Serpette is a marvellous place to explore at any time and especially in bad weather. The antiques, art and collectibles are excellent: some of the best you will find anywhere.

MATHIEU-MALOT ■ Stand 7 ■ Cell: 06 60 43 25 95 ■ Fax: 01 42 08 51 58 ■ English spoken ■ Professional discount
Arts of the XX century, 1930-1950. Furniture, paintings and bibelots.

GARRY ■ Stand 10 ■ Tel: 01 40 10 02 87 ■ Russian, English, German and Italian spoken ■ 15 to 20% professional discount ■ Major credit cards
Russian art, icons, signed jewellery, collectibles, canes. Qualified expert.

LASKI, Stanislas ■ Stand 12 ■ Tel: 01 40 12 08 88 ■ Fax: 01 42 03 29 87 ■ English spoken ■ Professional discount
XVIII and XIX century furniture, bibelots, objects of charm and decoration.

GLB CREATION ■ Stand 22 ■ Tel: 01 40 12 91 60 ■ Fax: 01 37 22 39 40 ■ E-mail: glb.creation@wanadoo.fr ■ Gilles Billaud speaks English ■ Professional discount
Decoration. Furniture and art objects.

GAMMES ■ Stands 27/29bis/30 ■ Tel: 01 40 11 63 60 ■ Fax: 01 44 91 91 61 ■ Philippe Druz ■ English spoken ■ Professional discount ■ Visa, Amex
XVII, XVIII and XIX century furniture and decorative objects.

ARTÉMISE ET CUNÉGONDE ■ Stand 28 ■ Tel: 01 40 10 02 21 ■ Telfax: 01 46 26 20 78 ■ Monique Larde ■ English spoken ■ Visa
Antique lace, embroidery and household linens. Period clothing of the XIX and XX century.

DERIOT, Gilles and **VALENTIN-SMITH, Michel** ■ Stand 37 ■ Tel: 01 40 12 75 62 ■ Fax: 01 42 27 92 80 ■ Professional discount
Generalists; a bit of everything.

GABORIAUD, Marc et Gisèle ■ Stand 40 ■ Tel: 01 40 11 26 92 ■ Fax: 01 42 55 86 66 ■ E-mail: gisg@club-internet.fr ■ English spoken ■ Professional discount ■ Amex
Silver and decorative objects. Expert.

ALLÉE 2

COLLIGNON, Jacques ■ Stand 1 ■ Tel: 01 40 11 80 91 ■ English spoken ■ Professional discount ■ Major credit cards
Antique paintings; particularly Impressionist, Fauves, Cubist, Symbolist, Surrealists.

ISLE OF VIEW ■ Stand 6 ■ Tel: 06 12 06 40 67 ■ Fri, Sat, Sun, Mon 10:00-18:00 ■ Georges Guillaume Cassan speaks good English ■ Prices modest to high ■ Professional discount
XX century decorative objects and furniture.

WEITZ, Dominique ■ Stand 14 ■ Tel: 01 42 46 35 95 ■ Fax: 01 43 78 95 04 ■ English spoken ■ 20% professional discount ■ MC and Amex
Drawings, watercolours and figurative paintings from the early XIX century to 1940.

ALLÉE 3

COUGOULE-DEVERGNE, Sophie ■ Stand 1 ■ Tel: 01 40 12 66 65 ■ Fax: 01 40 12 10 62 ■ E-mail: nantic@aol.com ■ English and Italian spoken ■ Professional discount ■ Visa
Italian furniture and lighting.

FOREST, Jacques ■ Stand 7 ■ Tel: 01 40 11 96 38 ■ Fax: 01 45 01 58 33 ■ English spoken ■ Professional discount ■ Major credit cards
Furniture, paintings and objects of charm.

FOREST, Olwen ■ Stand 7 ■ Tel: 01 40 11 96 38 ■ Fax: 01 45 01 58 33 ■ English spoken ■ Professional discount ■ Major credit cards
Costume and designer jewellery from the 1920s to 1960s. Hollywood jewellery worn by the stars. Art Deco crystal, plated silver, bathing beauties. Very special.

VOYAGES ■ Stand 10 ■ Tel: 01 49 45 09 56 ■ Fax: 01 53 10 01 09 ■ E-mail: voyages@wanadoo.fr ■ Web: www.elisiodasneves@wanadoo.fr ■ English and Portuguese spoken ■ Professional discount ■ Amex, Visa
Everything in the way of travelling gear, Vuitton, Hermès, Goyard.

BONNET, Marc ■ Stand 12 ■ Cell: 06 08 61 22 81 ■ Tel: 01 40 11 34 60 ■ Amex
Arts of the XIX and XX century, furniture, paintings and objects.

LE MONDE DU VOYAGE ■ Stand 15 ■ Tel: 01 40 12 64 03 ■ Fax: 01 49 41 93 19 ■ E-mail: hzizul@club-internet.fr ■ Mme Helen Zisul ■ English spoken Professional discount ■ Major credit cards
Antique vintage luggage. Excellent collection of Louis Vuitton and Hermès. Pocketbooks by Hermès and Chanel jewellery. Restoration miracles. Excellent selections.

QUITARD ■ Stand 18 ■ Tel: 01 40 10 00 24 ■ Fax: 01 34 87 63 22 ■ Prices high ■ Professional discount ■ Major credit cards
XVII and XVIII century antiques and objects.

ART ET DESIGN ATIQUITÉS ■ Stand 19 ■ Tel: 01 45 67 22 74 ■ Fax: 01 45 67 22 74 ■ Ralph Konnemann speaks English, German, Russian and Chinese ■ Professional discount
Art Deco furniture. Design and restoration.

ALLÉE 4

ROSENTHAL, Philippe ■ Stand 3 ■ Tel: 01 40 11 54 14
Leather easy chairs and club-chairs.

ART DECO LUMINAIRES ■ Stand 10 ■ Telfax: 01 40 12 28 08 ■ Radovan Haltuf speaks English and Spanish ■ Professional discount ■ Amex
Signed Art Deco pieces, Lalique, Sabino, Muller, Schneider, Degue. Also lamps, appliques and lanterns. Some small furniture from the period 1900 to 1940. Restoration.

♛ **ROSENTHAL, Marie-Eve** ■ Stands 11-13 ■ Tel: 01 40 12 04 85 ■ Fax: 01 39 69 45 77 ■ English spoken ■ Professional discount ■ Major credit cards
The best collection of XVIII century gilded wood mirrors, XIX century gold leafed fireplace mirrors. XVIII and XIX century pier glasses. Art Nouveau mirrors 1925. Most of the mirrors have their original gold leafing.

ARGARACE ■ Stand 12 ■ Telfax: 01 48 29 87 01 ■ Christophe Perreaut ■ English and Spanish spoken ■ Professional discount ■ MC
Furniture and paintings, objects and curiosities of the XVI to the XX century.

PERLOFF, Evelyne ■ Stand 14 ■ Tel: 01 45 39 81 97
Medals, antique collectibles and objects of curiosity.

L'INSOLITE ■ Stand 17 ■ Tel: 01 49 45 16 18 ■ Catherine Dupont-Midy ■ English spoken ■ Professional discount
Antique toys, objects of charm "insolites".

ALLÉE 5

ALNOT, Colette ■ Stand 19 ■ Tel: 01 49 48 03 59 ■ Fax: 01 40 41 93 83 ■ English and Italian spoken ■ 20% professional discount
Decoration and paintings as well as antiques of the XVIII, XIX and XX century.

ROCHMANN, Joël ■ Stand 25 ■ Tel: 01 40 11 97 15 ■ Cell: 06 81 15 49 60 ■ English and German spoken
Arts of the XX century 1930 to 1960. Furniture, paintings, drawings, lighting, decoration.

ALLÉE 6

TOUSSAINT, Francis ■ Stands 8-10 ■ Tel: 01 40 12 79 45 ■ Fax: 01 53 10 01 09 ■ E-mail: francistoussaint@wanadoo.fr ■ English spoken ■ 10% professional discount ■ Major credit cards
Art of the table XIX and XX century. Porcelain, crystal, silver and copper.

NEVIS-GOLESSIAN ■ Stand 9 ■ Tel: 01 49 45 96 30 ■ Fax: 01 45 94 13 81 ■ English and Persian spoken ■ Professional discount
Objets d'art and paintings of the XIX and XX century.

CHOLLET, Xavier ■ Stand 11 ■ Tel: 01 40 12 22 14 ■ English spoken ■ Professional discount ■ Major credit cards
XIX century furniture, lighting, curiosities and decorative objects.

JAGER, Jean-Marc ■ Stand 12 ■ Tel: 01 49 45 07 05
XX century paintings, sculptures and objects of curiosity.

MORGE, Jean-Jacques ■ Stand 13 ■ Tel: 01 40 12 36 00 ■ Fax: 01 64 28 77 67 ■ E-mail: morge.jj@infonic.fr ■ English spoken ■ Professional discount ■ Major credit cards
Couches, club-chairs, canapes in leather. Usually a good selection.

MOREUX, Laurent ■ Stand 23 ■ Cell: 06 08 34 36 83 ■ Fax: 01 47 57 16 39 ■ English spoken ■ Professional discount
Decorative arts of the XIX and early XX century. Furniture, lighting and ceramics.

——————————— **MARCHÉ JULES-VALLÈS** ———————————

7-9 rue Jules-Vallès, 93400 Saint-Ouen ■ Fax: 01 47 47 56 40 ■ Thu 7-12:00/Fri 7:00-12:00/Sat-Sun 7:00-18:00/Mon 7:00-18:00

Patrick Parent is President of the Council. Prices are, of course, negotiable and range from low to high. The market has second-hand goods as well as some authentic antiques. There are collectibles, military

memorabilia, old household linens, watches and clocks, toys, paintings. All of this resides in a covered gallery with 100 shops dealing in everything from old books to feathered masks, prints, glassware and curiosities. It offers low prices in a picturesque setting.

―――――――――― MARCHÉ DES ROSIERS ――――――――――

This market is in a small, self-contained, building which houses a concentration of dealers in Art Nouveau and Art Deco. It is just off the rue des Rosiers at 3 rue Paul-Bert.

PAUL GENER ■ Stand 14 ■ Tel: 01 40 12 43 62
Art Nouveau and Art Deco glass. Some furniture.

MICHEL GIRAUD GALERIE ■ Stand 7 ■ Tel: 01 40 11 21 15 ■ Fax: 01 46 41 00 65
Specialist in Art Nouveau and Art Deco, 1900 to 1930. What they don't have, they'll find for you. They are experts in 1900s cameo glass.

BERNARD LIAGRE ■ Stand 6 ■ Tel: 01 40 10 18 91
Art Nouveau and Art Deco glass, ceramics, bronzes, lighting and furniture.

CHRISTIAN SERRES ■ Stand 8 ■ Tel: 01 40 12 97 65
Art Nouveau and Art Deco glass and lighting.

―――――――――――― MARCHÉ L'USINE ――――――――――――

18 rue des Bons-Enfants ■ Tel: 01 40 12 42 14 (Guardian)

A remarkable collection of architectural elements for interior and exterior. 10,000 square feet on two levels. A choice for professionals. The best time to go is early Thursday or Friday.

SOCIÉTÉ ANTIQUITÉ FRANCO-ANGLAISE ■ Stand 18 ■ Tel: 01 40 12 20 38 ■ Fax: 01 38 94 50 55 ■ M. Quentin and M. Vignerons ■ English spoken ■ Professional discount
A large space devoted to the sale of English furniture of various styles and periods. Reproductions.

99 rue des Rosiers and 136 av Michelet, 93400 Saint-Ouen

The Marché Vernaison is one of the best and is certainly the oldest market in Saint-Ouen. It is also one of the largest. From the 300 merchants in the Vernaison, the authors have carefully selected those they consider the best and most reliable. In choosing, we have kept in mind the needs of the decorator, the architect and the sophisticated individual.

AGATHE ■ Stand 174, Allée 8 ■ Tel: 01 40 10 18 19 ■ German, English and Polish spoken ■ Professional discount
Second-hand jewellery and bibelots.

ART ET CRISTAL ■ Stand 7, Allée 1 ■ Tel: 01 49 45 94 23 ■ Fax: 01 30 90 63 92 ■ English spoken ■ 30% professional discount ■ Visa and CB
Quite beautiful chandeliers. Lighting in bronze and crystal and coloured glass fruit.

AU GRENIER DE LUCIE ■ Stand 77, Allée 4, Stand 139 ■ Tel: 01 40 12 94 42 ■ Fax: 01 39 95 97 08 ■ Mr and Mme Dufour speak English ■ Professional discount ■ Major credit cards
Fantasy jewellery of the 1950s. Watches of the XVIII, XIX and the XX century. Porcelain boxes.

BERTRAND ■ Stand 16, Allée 1 ■ Tel: 01 59 42 99 13 ■ Fax: 01 40 12 25 43 ■ English and German spoken ■ 15% professional discount ■ Major credit cards
Antique silver.

BOULANGIER, Jean-Pierre ■ Stand 110, Allée 6 ■ Cell: 06 81 70 47 35 ■ Fax: 01 40 21 94 13 ■ J. P. Boulangier speaks English ■ Professional discount
Collectibles, frames, boxes mainly of the period of Napoleon III and the 1920s.

BOULEVARD DES ECRITURES ■ Stand 128, Allée 7 ■ Cell: 06 60 88 40 52 ■ Tel: 01 46 26 78 23 ■ Fax: 01 46 26 78 23 ■ Veronique François speaks English ■ Professional discount
Writing instruments, pens, inkwells, old papers and publicity objects. Old school objects, notebooks, cards, tablets.

👑 **CATAN** ■ Allée 9, Stand 227 ■ Tel: 01 40 10 19 41 ■ Tel: 01 39 39 64 59 55 ■ Fax: 01 39 89 21 28 ■ Cell: 06 60 43 09 85 ■ E-mail: Alaincatan@aol.com
Remarkable extra-large tables made of a combination of old wood elements and new. XVIII century rustic natural wood furniture, bridal armoires, tables, commodes, buffets. Some of the best work we have ever seen.

CHAPPUY ■ Allée 5, Stand 88 ■ Tel: 01 40 10 91 10 ■ Fax: 01 47 85 78 68 ■ E-mail: chappuyfr@aol.com ■ Mme Françoise Chappuy speaks English and Italian ■ 10% professional discount
Collectible keyrings (publicity) of the 1960s.

👑 **DE LATTRE**, Marie-Ange et Dominique ■ Allée 1, Stand 47 ■ Tel: 01 40 12 68 89 ■ Fax: 01 45 44 83 53 ■ E-mail: jberthiaux@multimania.com ■ Very good English, Spanish and German spoken ■ 10% professional discount ■ Major credit cards
XIX and XX century posters and books. One of the best poster collections in Paris. Prints and advertising posters. They also offer the possibility of linen backing for posters. Browsing their bookshelves for early editions is a distinct pleasure and the prices are very fair.

DUPUY, Martine ■ Allée 4, Stand 81 ■ Tel: 01 40 12 07 57 ■ English and Spanish spoken ■ Possible professional discount
Collectible postcards, small objets d'art, small paintings and old paper.

FRANCINE DENTELLES ■ Allée 7 Stands 121 to 123, 140bis ■ Tel: 01 40 10 93 96
Wonderful collection of old linen, lace, fabrics, objects and 1900s fashions.

FRANÇOISE ■ Allée 1 Stand 4 and Stand 33 ■ Tel: 01 40 12 56 65 ■ Telfax: 01 42 62 33 93 ■ English spoken ■ Professional discount ■ Major credit cards
Excellent and wide range of XIX century silver, objects.

GALERIE DES FIGURATIFS ■ Stand 85, Allée 5 ■ Tel: 01 48 79 57 58 ■ Web: www.rape-bopp.tm.fr ■ Eric Geneste speaks English ■ Professional discount ■ Major credit cards
Archaeological artifacts, especially Egyptian, curiosities and wrought iron.

LHOMOND ■ Stand 11and Stand 23, Allée 1 ■ Tel: 01 45 23 13 80 ■ 01 45 23 13 84 ■ Chantal l'Homond speaks English ■ Visa, Amex
Fabrics and original Aubusson tapestries.

HORDE ■ Stand 111, Allée 6 ■ Tel: 01 69 09 51 60 ■ Michel Horde ■ Professional discount ■ Amex
Antique furniture and bibelots.

LE PASSÉ D'AUJOURD'HUI ■ Stand 148, Allée 7 ■ Cell: 06 80 13 14 04 ■ Fax: 01 42 62 29 36 ■ Chantal Steenhaut ■ English spoken
Old posters. Very nice ones.

LIBERTY'S ■ Stand 105, Allée 3/5 ■ Tel: 01 48 82 23 23 ■ Fax: 01 48 82 49 54 ■ E-mail: liberty@libertys.com ■ Web: www.libertys.com/ ■ Pierre Beroux ■ French, German, Italian and Japanese spoken ■ Professional discount ■ Major credit cards
Grandfather clocks and other clocks. Boxes and papers. Enamels of Longwy, Quimper, Gien, Baccarat, Clichy and some majolica. Art Deco jewellery.

MAUREL, Paul ■ Stand 41, Allée 1 ■ Fax: 42 36 50 07 ■ Paul Maurel speaks English and Spanish
Old books of the 1900s, old children's books, Art nouveau and Art deco posters 1900 to 1950. Advertising engravings of Paris. Very nice.

SALAT, Patrice ■ Stand 108 ■ Tel: 01 40 10 99 15/01 43 87 89 90 ■ Italian, English and Spanish spoken ■ Professional discount ■ MC, Visa
Old drawings and watercolours.

SETRUK, Guy-Laurent ■ Stand 152, Allée 7 ■ Tel: 01 40 12 38 09 ■ Fax: 01 47 09 19 38
Antique furniture and objects.

G. SCHERPEREEL ■ Stand 130, Allée 7 ■ Tel: 01 47 88 01 62 ■ English spoken
Collectible toys.

SCHULER, Françoise and Didier ■ Stand 33, Allée 1 ■ Tel: 01 40 12 56 65 ■ Fax: 01 42 62 23 93 ■ E-mail fdschuler@minitel.net ■ English, Spanish and Japanese spoken ■ 20% possible discount ■ Major credit cards
Antique textiles before 1930, costumes, linen, silks, draperies and fans.

LES TROUVAILLES DE THEA ET JEAN-MARC ■ Stand 233, Allée 9 ■ Tel: 01 40 11 87 60 ■ English and German spoken ■ Major credit cards
Old toys, dolls and doll furniture, paintings bibelots and collectible lighting.

VAN GOOL, Johannes ■ Stand 165, Allée 8 ■ Tel: 01 45 85 70 54 ■ English, German, Dutch and Russian spoken ■ 15% professional discount
Clocks and lighting.

───────────── RUE ANSELME ─────────────

YANE ET LE BATON MAGIQUE ■ 73 rue Anselme ■ Tel: 01 40 11 55 48 by appointment
Contemporary works of art: paintings, drawings, sculpture.

───────────── RUE JULES-VALLÈS ─────────────

An outdoor market where a diligent search could turn up some interesting finds. Worth the effort.

LA DÉCORATION ANGLAISE ■ 36 rue Jules-Vallès ■ Tel: 01 40 11 54 44
Lamps in pate-de-verre, "black men" statues, English objects of curiosity, English style furniture in pine, carved wooden animals, signs and advertising posters.

GALERIE CHRISTINE ■ 16 rue Jules-Vallès ■ Tel: 01 40 12 22 79/01 48 93 69 19
XVIII and XIX century furniture, engravings, paintings, bronzes, chandeliers, mirrors, art objects, dolls.

MARC MAISON ■ 15 rue Jules-Vallès ■ Tel: 01 40 12 52 28 ■ Fax: 01 40 12 26 47 ■ E-mail: marcmaison@easynet.fr ■ Web: www.marcmaison.com ■ English spoken ■ Prices medium to high ■ Professional discount
A large selection of architectural elements for the exterior and interior: all in stock. Fountains, grilles and gates in wrought iron, flooring, paneling, doors, gates, marble, lead statuary, fireplaces and elements for the garden. Also restorations.

LA REMISE ■ 19 rue du Plaisir ■ Tel: 01 40 11 42 81
Regional furniture.

───────────── RUE LÉCUYER ─────────────

This street is the Flea Market as it used to be. Lots of second-hand stuff, but several very good dealers who deserve a second look. You might find a surprise or two.

A.B.J. CHEMINÉES ■ 4 rue Lécuyer ■ Tel: 01 40 11 44 78 ■ Fax: 01 40 12 87 44
Antique fireplaces: stone, marble, wood. Sometimes a few gilded antique mirrors.

LIBRAIRIE DE L'AVENUE - H. Veyrier ■ 31 rue Lécuyer ■ Tel: 01 40 11 95 85/01 46 33 20 18
Rare books. This second hand bookstore has an excellent collection. Take a look at their collection of antique engravings.

J.L.V. ANTIQUITÉS ■ 18ter rue Lécuyer ■ Tel: 01 40 12 30 84 ■ Fax: 01 40 11 59 17
XVII, XVIII and XIX century paintings, furniture and decorative objects.

─────────── MARCHÉ LÉCUYER ───────────

8 rue Lécuyer ■ Tel: 01 40 11 46 51
Several merchants who are very well known to the decorating trade. Rustic and period furniture. Stained glass, engraved glass, gilded wood, old and contemporary paintings, decorative objects. New merchandise arrives on Thursday and Friday mornings.

─────────── RUE PAUL-BERT ───────────

The genuine Flea Market atmosphere. This street runs off the rue des Rosiers and leads to the Marché Paul Bert. The merchants rate a visit.

ART INTER ■ 1 rue Paul-Bert ■ Tel: 01 40 11 11 80
Decorative objects of the XIX century to Art Nouveau. Lamp bases, chandeliers, objects in crystal and earthenware.

SEMA - Roger Adjinsoff et Fils ■ 13 rue Paul-Bert ■ Tel: 01 40 11 25 69
Architectural elements, fireplaces in stone, wood and marble, wood panelling, wrought iron gates and grilles, parquet, fountains, garden statues. Also at 55 rue des Rosiers.

─────────── RUE DES POISSONNIERS ───────────

ALDO FRÈRES ■ 39 rue des Poissonniers ■ Tel: 01 40 12 66 55
Antique architectural elements: fireplaces in marble and stone, wrought iron grilles and gates, wood panelling, doors, decorative elements for interior and exterior.

This is the main street of the Marché aux Puces. There are several high-quality dealers in antiques, mirrors and collectibles. Here is our choice.

A, ANTIQUITIES ■ 84 rue des Rosiers ■ Tel: 01 40 10 00 70 ■ Web: http://www.astrolabs.com
XIX century furniture and objects of decoration.

ABOUCAYA ■ 116 rue des Rosiers ■ Tel: 01 40 12 79 91
XIX century furniture, paintings and photographs.

AIDJOLATE ANTIQUITIES ■ 140 rue des Rosiers ■ Tel: 01 40 10 10 86 ■ Cell: 06 09 48 27 86
Porcelain and barbotines.

ART DU SIÈGE ■ 78 rue des Rosiers ■ Tel: 01 40 12 44 27 ■ Cell: 06 09 16 24 67 ■ Fax: 01 40 11 76 90
Traditional fabrication and restoration of chairs, sofas and antique furniture.

ATELIER MARCEAU ■ 4 Passage Marceau ■ Tel: 01 40 11 08 17
Frames and mirrors.

AUCLERT, Christian ■ 73 rue des Rosiers ■ Telfax: 01 40 11 09 22/01 40 12 60 52
Antique four-poster beds, chairs, marquetry furniture. Restoration.

MAISON BEYS ■ 118 rue des Rosiers ■ Tel: 01 40 12 69 99/01 40 12 79 90
Delightful clutter, but take a good look. It could be worth your while. Large and interesting collection of XVII to XIX century furniture, fireplaces in marble and wood, clocks of the XVIII and XIX centuries, XVIII and XIX century paintings, faience, arms, glass and decorative objects.

BDV DÉCORATION ■ 154 rue des Rosiers ■ Tel: 01 40 11 42 04
Art Deco furniture and decorative objects.

LEON BENAIM ■ 97 rue des Rosiers ■ Tel: 01 40 11 02 25
XVIII and XIX century furniture and decorative objects.

BOUTIQUE 75 ■ 122 rue des Rosiers ■ Tel: 01 40 12 56 70
Garden ornaments.

BOUTIQUE ÉCOSSAISE ■ 97 rue des Rosiers ■ Tel: 01 40 12 23 43
English and northern European antiques.

👑 **ETS CAMUS** ■ 88 rue des Rosiers and 5 rue Eugène-Lumeau ■ Tel: 01 40 10 88 59/01 43 44 14 02 ■ Fax: 01 40 11 82 17
Antique fireplaces in marble and wood, sculptures for the garden, statues, fountains. Architectural elements. Usually excellent quality.

CHINARD ANTIQUITIES ■ 123 rue des Rosiers ■ Tel: 01 40 12 07 13
A sometimes fascinating mix of decorative items.

COHEN, Eliane ■ 99 rue des Rosiers (Corner of the Marché Vernaison) ■ Tel: 01 40 11 05 73
XIX century to 1900-1930 bronzes, lighting and small furniture.

ROGER CUPERTY ■ 152 rue des Rosiers ■ Telfax: 01 49 48 01 83 ■ Cell: 06 60 05 35 299 ■ Some English spoken ■ Prices modest ■ Professional discount ■ Visa
Wide selection of mirrors of the XIX century. Mirrors in the styles of the XVII and XVIII century as well.

DECO LIGHT ART DECO ■ 107 rue des Rosiers ■ Tel: 01 42 62 77 08 ■ Cell: 06 09 62 03 96 ■ Fax: 01 44 92 47 43
Art Deco lighting, furniture, armchairs, cocktail bars, dining room suites. Some of it very nice.

DIGIART ■ 105 rue des Rosiers ■ Tel: 01 40 12 68 95
Fireplaces, lighting sconces and mirrors. We rate it as good.

DISCOPHILE ■ 125 rue des Rosiers ■ Tel: 01 40 12 07 28
Old collectible phonograph records.

👑 **DUGAY** ■ 92 rue des Rosiers ■ Tel: 01 40 11 87 30 ■ Fax: 01 40 12 26 32
Supplies for restoration and maintenance of furniture and all art objects. One of the largest and best stocks in Paris.

ELCABAS ■ 99 rue des Rosiers ■ Tel: 01 40 11 05 75 ■ Fax: 01 42 64 28 62
Art Deco objects and lighting.

FINKEL ■ 121 rue des Rosiers ■ Tel: 01 40 11 77 82
Furniture, objets d'art, porcelain and lighting of the period of Napoleon III.

FRANCIS ■ 117 rue des Rosiers ■ Tel: 01 4 0 12 96 90
Decorative objects of the XIX century.

♛ **GALERIE EMMANUEL ZELKO** ■ 89 rue des Rosiers ■ Tel: 01 40 12 24 58/01 40 11 21 01 ■ Fax: 34 67 03 45
Amazing collection of XIX century furniture, mirrors, lighting, clocks and decorative objects. Great fireplace accessories. Suppliers to many of the palaces of the Orient. The Zelkos are charming, knowledgeable and dependable. One of the best in Paris.

GLUSTIN SARL ■ 140 rue des Rosiers ■ Tel: 0140 10 24 22 ■ Fax: 01 40 11 73 53 ■ Cell: 06 09 82 79 18 ■ E-mail: glustin@wanadoo.fr ■ Sat,Sun, Mon 10:00-18:00 Serge Glustin speaks English ■ Prices quite high ■ Major credit cards
Large dining tables and a large series of chairs of the late XIX and early XX century. Consoles, buffets and mirrors as well.

IVANOVIC ■ 152 bis rue des Rosiers ■ Tel: 01 40 50 04 75
Old clocks and small furniture.

KROUGLY, E. ■ 41 rue des Rosiers ■ Tel: 01 40 11 35 78
Decorative hardware for furniture in bronze and iron. Old locks, "sabots", casters, and lots more. You will be pleasantly surprised by their collection.

MARTINE MATHOUET
91 rue des Rosiers, 93400 Saint-Ouen ■ Telfax: 01 49 45 16 13 ■ E-mail: mem.antiques@wanadoo.fr ■ Sat-Mon 10:00-18:00 ■ English spoken ■ Prices high ■ Major credit cards
Art Deco, 1930-1940, lighting, furniture, decorative objects and crystal by Daum and Baccarat.

JEAN MICHEL ■ 101 rue des Rosiers ■ Tel: 01 40 11 41 44
Carpets.

KALFON ■ 120 rue des Rosiers ■ Tel: 01 4 0 11 95 11
Decorative objects.

CHARLES KAPLON ■ 113 rue des Rosiers ■ Tel: 01 40 11 69 19
Mirrors, lighting, clocks and furniture of the XIX century.

LES GALERIES DES GLACES ■ 87 rue des Rosiers, 93400 Saint-Ouen ■ Tel : 01 40 11 17 52 ■ E-mail: galerieglaces@yahoo.com ■ Priscilla Cuperty speaks some English ■ Prices medium ■ Professional discount ■ Major credit cards
Large selection of period mirrors: Louis XV, Louis XVI, Louis Philippe. Some pretty good gilding.

LES MIROIRS DE FRANCE ■ 109 rue des Rosiers, 93400 Saint-Ouen ■ Tel : 01 49 48 07 78 ■ www.lesmiroirsdefrance.com ■ Sat, Sun, Mon 10 :00-18 :00 ■ English spoken ■ Prices medium
Mirrors; most of them gilded.

MAISON PELLIER ■ 140 rue des Rosiers ■ Tel: 01 40 11 62 26
Antique country furniture.

PIERRE MAITRE ■ 103 bis rue des Rosiers ■ Tel: 01 40 10 22 45
Furniture, chairs and decorative objects.

MINGEI ■ 119 rue des Rosiers ■ Tel: 01 40 11 72 20 ■ Cell: 06 07 47 05 10
Art of Japan. Objects in lacquer and an interesting collection of parasols.

MODERNISM ■ 115 rue des Rosiers ■ Tel: 01 40 12 55 22 ■ Fax: 01 40 11 02 99
Decorative objects.

MURIEL ■ 133 rue des Rosiers ■ Tel: 01 40 12 75 17
Decorative objects, collectibles.

LES PERLES D'ANTAN
142 rue des Rosiers, RDC # 301 ■ Cell: 06 08 00 4333 ■ Sat, Sun, Mon 10:00-13:00 ■ Flora Barlan speaks English ■ Professional discount
Antique trimmings of the years 1900 to 1930. Braids, tassels as well as trimmings for clothes.

PRESTIGE ANTIQUITIES ■ 109 rue des Rosiers ■ Tel: 01 40 30 06 20 ■ Cell: 06 12 80 96 29
Mirrors and pier glasses.

RAPHAEL ■ 105 rue des Rosiers ■ Tel: 01 40 11 49 92 ■ Cell: 06 09 13 82 74 ■ Fax: 01 40 12 41 25
Old and modern paintings, some of the Barbizon School.

SERNA DE PARIS ■ 154 rue des Rosiers ■ Tel: 01 40 10 04 14
Lighting.

MAURICE STROK ■ 152 rue des Rosiers ■ Tel: 01 47 07 98 83
Antique fireplaces.

TEMPS JADIS ■ 127 rue des Rosiers ■ Tel: 01 40 12 85 99
Paintings and lots of objects of what they call curious.

VERGNES ET BARLAN ■ 119 rue des Rosiers, 93400 Saint-Ouen ■ Tel: 01 49 45 02 74 ■ Fri, Sat, Sun. Mon 10 :00-18 :00 ■ Some English spoken ■ Prices medium
Trimmings for couture and furnishings.

VIEILLES PIERRES DU MELLOIS ■ 132 rue des Rosiers ■ Tel: 01 40 12 54 79 ■ Fax: 01 43 57 92 41
Antique architectural elements.

OLIVIER WATELET ■ 59 59 rue des Rosiers ■ Tel: 01 40 1275 58
Furniture and lighting of the 1940s.

Le Village Saint-Paul

This charming and very accessible market is located in the Marais (the Fourth Arrondissement), one of the oldest and certainly one of the most historically interesting quarters of Paris. It is situated on the rue Saint-Paul with easy access by Metro or by car from the Quai des Celestins through to the rue de Rivoli.

ANTIQUITÉS ERIC DUBOIS ■ 9 rue Saint-Paul ■ Tel: 01 42 74 05 29 ■ Open every day 11:00-19:30
African art.

ANTIQUITÉS JAPONAISES ■ 17 rue Saint-Paul ■ Telfax: 01 42 77 98 02 ■ Thurs-Mon 12:00-19:00
Japanese antiques.

ARISTOTE ■ 23/25 rue Saint-Paul (court) ■ Tel: 01 42 77 92 94 ■ Daily 13:00-19:00
Art objects, lamps and vases of the XIX and XX century.

AU RENDEZVOUS DES DAMES CURIEUSES ■ 15 rue Saint-Paul ■ Tel: 01 4 2 72 51 41 ■Thu-Mon 12:00-19:00
A curious mix of objects, clothing, linens, brocante.

HÉLÈNE DALLOZ BOURGUIGNON ■ 14 rue des Jardins ■ Tel: 01 42 71 83 25
Restoration and conservation of paintings, old and contemporary.

COUP DE COEUR ■ 1 rue Charlemagne ■ Tel: 01 48 87 50 31 ■ Daily 12:00-19:00
Furniture and objets d'art of the XIX century.

AU DEBOTTE ■ 7 rue Charlemagne (court) ■ Tel: 01 48 04 85 20 ■ Daily 13:00-19:00
XVIII century furniture and decoration.

FUCHSIA ■ 2 rue Saint-Paul ■ Tel: 01 48 04 75 61 ■ Every day 12:00-19:00
Antique lace, styles of 1900 to 1930. Old bed linens, table linens, table arts, antique fans, old fabrics and braids, doll's accessories.

GALERIE CLAUDE ET LIMA ■ 15/17 rue Saint-Paul ■ Tel: 01 42 77 98 02 ■ Thu-Mon 11:00-19:00
Japanese antiques.

GALERIE TAO ■ 5 rue du Pont Louis-Philippe ■ Tel: 01 40 29 95 45
Arts of Asia.

GRISE ■ 19 rue Saint-Paul ■ Tel: 01 42 72 46 25 ■ Daily 12:00-19:00
Furniture and objects 1900 to the present.

HISTOIRES DE TABLES ■ 9 rue Saint-Paul (courtyard) ■ Tel: 01 48 56 23 59 ■ Daily 12:00-19:00
Arts of the table 1800 to 1950.

LA LICORNE ■ 25 rue Saint-Paul ■ Tel: 01 42 72 46 02 ■ Thu-Mon 11:00-19:00
XVIII century furniture, wood sculpture and old musical instruments.

LIBRAIRIE F. MAGNIN ■ 25 rue Charles V ■ Tel: 01 42 72 67 00 ■ Daily 14:00-19:00
Collectible postcards: some books as well.

MANDARINE ■ 17 rue Saint-Paul ■ Tel: 01 42 71 51 45 ■ Thu-Mon 11:00-19:00
Antiques and restorations.

LA MANDRAGORE ■ 9 rue Saint-Paul ■ Tel: 01 40 27 96 00 ■ Daily 12:00-19:00
Paintings and art objects of the XIX and XX century.

MAYERLING ANTIQUITÉS ■ 13 rue Saint-Paul (court) ■ Tel: 01 44 59 83 22
Antique furniture and art objects.

METROPOLIS ■ 5bis rue Saint-Paul ■ Tel: 01 42 77 58 71 ■ Daily 12:00-19:00
Furniture and objects of the 1930 and 1940s.

LA SOURIS VERTE ■ 23 rue Saint-Paul (court) ■ Tel: 01 42 74 79 76 ■ Thu-Mon 11:00-19:00
Antique linens, trimmings and old buttons.

L'OTTOCENTO ■ 2 rue Ave Maria (court) ■ Tel: 01 42 71 81 90 ■ German and Italian spoken
Restoration of furniture.

LES SAGITTAIRES ■ 17 rue Saint-Paul ■ Tel: 01 40 29 06 08 ■ Daily 12:00-19:00
Furniture and suspended lamps of the XIX century.

AU PASSE-PARTOUT ■ 21 rue Saint-Paul ■ Tel: 01 42 72 94 94 ■ Daily 13:00-19:00
Unique collectibles.

LE PORTIQUE ■ 21 rue Saint-Paul (court) ■ Tel: 01 42 76 04 73 ■ Daily 12:00-19:00
Furniture, books and pâtes de verre.

L'ÉVENTAIL ■ 25 rue Saint-Paul ■ tel: 01 44 61 05 50 ■ Daily 11:00-19:00 ■ Closed Tue and Wed
Antiques, jewellery, brocante, some paintings and objets de charme.

AU PUCERON CHINEUR ■ 23 rue Saint-Paul ■ Tel: 01 4 2 72 88 20 ■ Daily 12:00-19:00
Silver and second-hand items.

SYLVAIN CALVIER ■ 13 rue Saint-Paul ■ Tel: 01 48 87 69 27 ■ E-mail: **sylvaincalvier@desphotographies.com** ■ Web: **www.desphotographies.com**
Photographic art of the XIX and XX century.

VALÉRIE DELAGE ■ 23/25 rue Saint-Paul (court) ■ Tel: 01 42 77 01 68 ■ Every day 13:00-19:00
Excellent restorer of fine furniture.

CLAUDE WAGNER ■ 17 rue Saint-Paul (court) ■ Daily 12:00-19:00
Antique dolls, doll houses and restoration of dolls.

LA VILLE DE

R.S. Antoine

P. S. Paul

P. au Iour

H. de Ville

P. de Greve

Pont nostre
Dame

Les Halles

R. S. Honoré

R. Coquilliere

Ceste ville est un autre monde
Dedans un monde florissant
En peuples et en biens puissant
Qui de toutes choses abonde

J. Nicasse